A Companion to C

BLACKWELL COMPANIONS TO AMERICAN HISTORY

This series provides essential and authoritative overviews of the scholarship that has shaped our present understanding of the American past. Edited by eminent historians, each volume tackles one of the major periods or themes of American history, with individual topics authored by key scholars who have spent considerable time in research on the questions and controversies that have sparked debate in their field of interest. The volumes are accessible for the non-specialist, while also engaging scholars seeking a reference to the historiography or future concerns.

BLACKWELL COMPANIONS TO HISTORY

BLACKWELL COMPANIONS TO BRITISH HISTORY

BLACKWELL COMPANIONS TO EUROPEAN HISTORY

BLACKWELL COMPANIONS TO WORLD HISTORY

A COMPANION TO COLONIAL AMERICA

Edited by

Daniel Vickers

Blackwell
Publishing

© 2003, 2006 by Blackwell Publishing Ltd

BLACKWELL PUBLISHING
350 Main Street, Malden, MA 02148-5020, USA
9600 Garsington Road, Oxford OX4 2DQ, UK
550 Swanston Street, Carlton, Victoria 3053, Australia

The right of Daniel Vickers to be identified as the Author of the Editorial Material in this Work has been asserted in accordance with the UK Copyright, Designs, and Patents Act 1988.

First published 2003 by Blackwell Publishers Ltd
First published in paperback 2006 by Blackwell Publishing Ltd

1   2006

Library of Congress Cataloging-in-Publication Data

A companion to Colonial America / edited by Daniel Vickers
        p. cm. – (Blackwell companions to American history)
    Includes bibliographical references and index.
    ISBN 0-631-21011-3
      1. United States–History–Colonial period, ca. 1600–1775.   2. United States–
    Social conditions–To 1865.   I. Vickers, Daniel.   II. Series
    E187 .C75 2003
    973.2–dc21

                                                                2002008981

ISBN-13: 978-0-631-21011-5 (hardback)
ISBN-13: 978-1-4051-4985-3 (paperback)
ISBN-10: 1-4051-4985-X (paperback)

A catalogue record for this title is available from the British Library.

Set in 10 on 12 pt Galliard
by Ace Filmsetting Ltd, Frome, Somerset

The publisher's policy is to use permanent paper from mills that operate a sustainable forestry policy, and which has been manufactured from pulp processed using acid-free and elementary chlorine-free practices. Furthermore, the publisher ensures that the text paper and cover board used have met acceptable environmental accreditation standards.

For further information on
Blackwell Publishing, visit our website:
www.blackwellpublishing.com

Contents

About the Contributors

David G. Anderson is an archaeologist at the Southeast Archeological Center of the National Park Service in Tallahassee, Florida. He is the author of *The Savannah River Chiefdoms: Political Change in the Late Prehistoric Southeast* (1994), and co-editor (with Kenneth E. Sassaman and Robert C. Mainfort, Jr.) of *The Paleoindian and Early Archaic Southeast* (1996), *The Archaeology of the Mid-Holocene Southeast* (1996), and *The Woodland Southeast* (2002).

Holly Brewer is Associate Professor of Early American History at North Carolina State University. She is the author of *By Birth or Consent: Children, Law, and Revolution in England and America, 1550–1820* (2002).

John Brooke is Professor of History at Ohio State University. He has been awarded fellowships by the NEH, the Guggenheim Foundation, and the ACLS. His first two books, *The Refiner's Fire* (1994) and *The Heart of the Commonwealth* (1989), won the Bancroft Prize and the Merle Curti Prize respectively.

Cary Carson is Vice President for Research at the Colonial Williamsburg Foundation, Williamsburg, Virginia. He works alongside colleagues from most of the disciplines that contribute to consumer revolution studies — economic and social historians, architectural historians, archaeologists, anthropologists, and curators.

Edward Countryman is University Distinguished Professor in the Clements Department of History at the Southern Methodist University. He is the author of *A People in Revolution* (1981; Bancroft Prize, 1982), *Americans, A Collision of Histories* (1996), *Shane* (with Evonne von Heussen-Countryman, 1999), and *The American Revolution* (revised edition, 2002).

Robert Ferry is Associate Professor of History at the University of Colorado at Boulder. He is the author of *The Colonial Elite of Early Caracas: Formation and Crisis, 1567–1767* (1989).

Sylvia Frey is Professor of History at Tulane University and Director of the Deep South Regional Humanities Center. She has been NEH Distinguished Professor at the University of Richmond, Pitt Professor of American History at the University of Cambridge, and is an Honorary Fellow of Newnham College, University of Cambridge. Her major publications include *Water from the Rock: Black Resistance in a Revolutionary Age* (1991) and *Come Shouting to Zion: African American Protestantism in the American South and British Caribbean to 1830* (with Betty Wood, 1998).

Allan Greer is Professor of History at the University of Toronto. He is the author of *Peasant, Lord, and Merchant: Rural Society in Three Quebec Parishes, 1740–1840* (1985), *The Patriots and the People: The Rebellion of 1837 in Rural Lower Canada* (1993), and *The People of New France* (1997).

Richard R. Johnson is Professor of History at the University of Washington. He is the author of *Adjustment to Empire: The New England Colonies, 1675–1715* (1981) and *John Nelson, Merchant Adventurer: A Life Between Empires* (1991).

Carol Karlsen is Associate Professor of History and Women's Studies at the University of Michigan. She is the author of *The Devil in the Shape of a Woman: Witchcraft in Colonial New England* (1987; 1998) and co-editor of *The Journal of Esther Edwards Burr, 1754–1757* (1984). Her *The Salem Witchcraft Outbreak of 1692: A History in Documents* is forthcoming.

Ned Landsman is Professor of History at the State University of New York at Stony Brook. He is the author of *Scotland and its First American Colony 1683–1765* (1985) and *From Colonials to Provincials: Thought and Culture in America 1680–1760* (1997), and the editor of *Nation and Province in the First British Empire: Scotland and the Americas, 1600–1800* (2001).

James H. Merrell is Lucy Maynard Salmon Professor of History at Vassar College. His work on the early American frontier includes *The Indians' New World: Catawbas and Their Neighbors from European Contact Through the Era of Removal* (1989), and *Into the American Woods: Negotiators on the Pennsylvania Frontier* (1999).

Philip D. Morgan is Professor of History at Johns Hopkins University. He is the author of *Slave Counterpoint: Black Culture in the Eighteenth-Century Chesapeake and Lowcountry* (1998).

Margaret Newell is Associate Professor of History at the Ohio State University. She is the author of *From Dependency to Independence: Economic Revolution in Colonial New England* (1998).

Greg Nobles is Professor of History at the Georgia Institute of Technology. He has been a research fellow at the American Antiquarian Society, the Charles Warren Center at Harvard University, the Huntington Library, and Princeton University. He has also held two Fulbright positions, as Senior Scholar in New Zealand (1995) and as John Adams Chair in American History in The Netherlands (2002). His most recent book is *American Frontiers: Cultural Contact and Continental Conquest* (New York, 1997).

Carleen Payne is Lecturer in Caribbean History at the Clarence Fitzroy Bryant College in the West Indies. She is also a Ph.D. candidate in history with the University of the West Indies in Mona, Jamaica. Her research is concerned with the labor movements in the twentieth-century eastern Caribbean — particularly the emergence and heroic construction of labor/national leaders before and since political independence.

Peter Pope is Associate Professor of Anthropology and History at the Memorial University of Newfoundland. He received Memorial's President's Award for Outstanding Research in 2001 and is the author of *Fish into Wine: The Newfoundland Plantation in the Seventeenth Century* (forthcoming).

Carole Shammas is the John R. Hubbard Chair in History at the University of Southern California. She has produced studies of the beginnings of English colonization of the Americas, the history of inheritance in Britain, British America, and the United States, and transatlantic consumer patterns 1500–1800. Her book *The History of Household Government in America* (2002) is a reinterpretation of the household's importance as an institution in American life.

Verene Shepherd is Professor of Social History at the University of the West Indies, Mona Campus, Jamaica. She is the author, editor, compiler, and co-editor of several publications, including *Transients to Settlers: The Experience of Indians in Jamaica* (1994), *Caribbean Slavery in the Atlantic World* (co-edited with Hilary Beckles, 2000), and *Questioning Creole: Creolization Discourses in Caribbean Culture* (with Glen Richards, 2002).

Marvin T. Smith is Professor of Anthropology at Valdosta State University. He is the author of more than 70 scholarly publications, including *The Archaeology of Aboriginal Culture Change in the Interior Southeast: Depopulation during the Early Historic Period* (1987) and *Coosa: The Rise and Fall of a Southeastern Mississippian Chiefdom* (2000). In 1992, he received the C. B. Moore Award for Excellence, by the Lower Mississippi Survey.

Darren Staloff is Associate Professor of History at the City College of New York and the

Graduate Center of the City University of New York. He is the author of *The Making of an American Thinking Class: Intellectuals and Intelligentsia in Puritan Massachusetts* (1998).

Alan Tully is currently Professor of History and Chair of the History Department at the University of Texas at Austin. He is the author of *Forming American Politics: Ideals, Interests, and Institutions in Colonial New York and Pennsylvania* (1994).

Daniel H. Usner, Jr. is a Professor of History at Vanderbilt University. Usner taught for more than two decades at Cornell University, where he served as Director of the American Indian Program from 1999 to 2002. His publications include *Indians, Settlers, and Slaves in a Frontier Exchange Economy* (1992) and *American Indians in the Lower Mississippi Valley* (1998).

Daniel Vickers is Professor of History at the University of California San Diego. He is the author of *Farmers and Fisherman: Two Centuries of Work in Essex County, Massachusetts* (1994).

Marilyn Westerkamp is Professor of History, University of California at Santa Cruz. She has published extensively in early American religious history, including *Triumph of the Laity: Scots-Irish Piety and the Great Awakening 1625–1760* (1988) and *Women and Religion in Early America, 1600–1850: The Puritan and Evangelical Traditions* (1999).

Michael Zuckerman is Professor of History at the University of Pennsylvania. He is the author of *Peaceable Kingdoms: New England Towns in the Eighteenth Century* (1983), the editor of *Friends and Neighbors: Group Life in America's First Plural Society* (1982), and co-editor of *Beyond the Century of the Child* (2002).

Introduction

Daniel Vickers

The colonial period is at once the most disparate and collective field of study in America's past. Certainly, it is disparate in the number of colonies, cultures, countries, continents, and concerns that now constitute its subject area. Colonial historians study and teach a dizzying variety of different people – no longer just the residents of Beacon Hill and Broad Street or the settlers on the Welsh Tract in Pennsylvania and the shores of Chesapeake Bay, but now also the indigenous peoples of the Mississippi, St. Lawrence, and Colorado River Valleys, as well as Europeans and Africans from Bordeaux and Bristol to Barbados and the Bight of Benin. Yet, it is also collective as an academic project in which the density of scholarly interaction – concentrated around a relatively small number of graduate programs, a few extremely active historical institutes, and a dominant periodical, the *William and Mary Quarterly* – cannot be matched by any other period of American history. Colonial historians read one another with focused energy, meet together frequently in conferences and colloquia, cite one another endlessly, and publish books that manage to garner a remarkable number of prestigious prizes every year. By any measure, the intensity of interest in those few million pre-revolutionary people, the merest fraction of all historical Americans who ever lived, is nothing short of astounding. Edmund Morgan suggested many years ago that we already knew "more about the Puritans than sane men should want to know."[1] Historians of other periods and places would today almost certainly extend that quip to American colonial society as a whole. As the essays in this volume bear witness, this field continues to recruit fine historians in numbers quite out of proportion to the number of subjects under study.

This extraordinary fact is rooted more than anything in the blossoming of a fruitful interdependence between history and anthropology. Not too long ago, it was common to celebrate the interconnectedness of colonial history with *all* the social sciences, but in the past twenty years, anthropology has come to influence far more historical enquiry in the early American field than has any other discipline. Colonialists may still practice demography, trace the course of political events, and attempt to chart economic growth, but it is the study of gender, race, politics, capitalism, religion, and so forth as cultural constructions that drives the liveliest thinking and research in the field. This is not really surprising, for the study of culture has always been at the core of the greatest history. All good historians are anthropologists operating across time; their training is to become ethnographers of particular societies in particular ages. Many things about the past they are not particularly well equipped to study: they cannot systematically excavate ruins, perform econometric acrobatics, or deconstruct medieval plainsong. But historians do understand better than anyone else, as R. G. Collingwood once reminded us, how to think oneself into the action of the past and "to discern the thought of its agent."[2] That is why they are better equipped than economists or sociologists to recognize the meaning that their subjects attached to the world of that day.

Historians – like anthropologists but unlike sociologists, psychologists, or economists – are particularly adept at understanding cultural *difference*, and this is why so many of the best of them feel at home in the period of American history (for which there exists a documentary record) that is most remote from our own. We gain the longest historical perspective on the most significant issues that Americans face today when we study these problems in their chronologically deepest American context. Do we possess any communitarian tradition worthy of the name? How deeply imbedded is the subordination of women in our culture? Where exactly do the roots of racism lie? Perhaps most important of all, wherein sit the origins of the global, sometimes imperial, pre-eminence that the United States occupies today? Americans do well to revisit often the period when they inhabited colonies dominated by a distant power and when they themselves carried terror into the homelands of a foreign, indigenous people. The past can teach patriotism; it should also teach humility.

Twenty years ago, Jack P. Greene and J. R. Pole published a book of essays entitled *Colonial British America* in which they attempted to assess the state of early American history by recruiting some of the most talented historians of the day to write a series of fourteen topical essays on the major themes that had occupied scholarly attention in the field over the previous two or three decades. This fine collection has served a generation of colonialists as a creative and remarkably thorough survey of the state of the field as it stood in the mid-1980s. In their introduction, Professors Green and Pole drew attention to the explosion of new interest in the colonial period over the previous twenty or thirty years and tried to account for it principally in terms of two important external stimuli. One was the influence of the social sciences, especially sociology, psychology, economics, and anthropology, to whose language, concepts, methods, and concerns historians were increasingly drawn. The other was the example of historical inquiry carried on across the Atlantic by the French Annales school and Cambridge Population Group in England. "If the social sciences turned the attention of colonial historians in the direction of socioeconomic and cultural history," Pole and Greene contended, "the work of early modern historians in France and Britain taught them the virtues of endeavoring to recreate past societies in their own integrity, within their own terms of reference, and, insofar as possible, without the distortions of teleology."[3] Twenty years later, it is not hard to imagine other forces that may have borne equally on the writing of colonial history. Social unrest within the United States during the 1960s and 1970s is relegated to a condescending footnote in the introduction to *Colonial British America*, but it undoubtedly influenced many historians. So too did the challenge of the new British Marxist history practiced by E. P. Thompson and his followers, which Greene and Pole chose to ignore entirely. Feminism and a new interest in those whom Eric Wolf termed "the people without history" were also beginning to redirect the course of colonial historiography during the late 1970s and early 1980s in ways that were only marginally recognized in this volume.

Yet, from twenty years' perspective, it is not the omissions that stand out for this reader as much as the spirit of enormous confidence that suffuses the work. Although Greene and Pole worried about the narrowness of much of the new scholarship, they believed that in sum it really did begin to add up to the sort of *histoire totale* to which the French *annalistes* had aspired. Not only did they feel they could identify a list of shared characteristics that bound all of British Americans together; they also believed it was possible to construct for the colonies a general developmental framework that could encompass the entirety of this colonial world. That they advanced their particular conceptions in a "tentative and enquiring spirit," claiming these were nothing more than "an interim report on progress," diminishes not a whit the faith they possessed in the "underlying coherence of the field."[4]

Colonial British America reflected a general confidence in the cohesion of early American history that has since fractured. Historians of that day may have fought over the models in which they believed, but at least they believed their models were worth fighting over. At the dawn of the twenty-first century, notwithstanding the remarkable vigor of the colonial field, the chimera of one coherent master narrative seems more remote than ever. This is true mainly because so much of the important historical scholarship of the past twenty years has been advanced in the spirit of criticism. Though characteristically moderate in its attachment to the newer strands of critical theory, much of the freshest new work in colonial history aims either to deconstruct common sense interpretations of the past, undermine more and more of our national myths, construct new narratives to compete with the old, or at the very least complicate the old ones sometimes to the point of collapse. Colonial peoples are now the subjects of multiple perspectives with separate logics that seem impossible completely to reconcile. Their actions can be understood simultaneously from the perspectives of class, race, or gender, looking west from the European metropoles or the shores of Africa, "facing east from Indian country," or sitting in the mid-Atlantic looking all around at the swirl of humanity trading, warring, negotiating, settling, and working their lives away.[5] For most of the twentieth century, historians believed in an interpretive center to colonial American history – or at least in their own version of such a thing. Such no longer seems the case. And yet, the centrifugal course of this historiography is no indication of weakness; indeed, the reverse is true. While the multiplication of perspectives cuts against the grain of any aspiration towards an *histoire totale* and may sometimes cause historians to talk past one another, it also forces them into a habit of continual self-reflection, and in particular to question their reliance on common sense.

This volume attempts to explain the issues that have defined the historiography of colonial America, and in particular what distinguished it culturally from other parts of the early modern world and from subsequent periods in American history. Some of the chapters are organized topically. The history of colonial politics, religion, and migration, for example, are sub-fields with well-established literatures possessing many internally contested issues. Other chapters focus on specific historical debates. Class and the origins of the American Revolution, for instance, have in themselves been hotly argued issues since the revival of early American history in the 1950s, and they both deserve treatments of their own. Still other chapters are defined geographically. Here the attempt has been made to describe the historiography of areas external to the mainland colonies that eventually became the United States in an attempt to set the concerns of American colonialists in some comparative perspective. Not every corner of the pre-revolutionary past has been covered, and this volume will undoubtedly show its age as years roll by. If, in general, it serves to provide readers with an introduction to the current state of studies in colonial American history, with a view not to achieve some coherent vision of colonial history upon which we can all agree but rather to investigate the problem of cultural difference – that which ultimately distinguished them from us – across the greatest span of historical time available to Americans, it will have served its purpose.

NOTES

1   Morgan, Edmund S.: "The Historians of Early New England." In Ray Allen Billington, ed., *The Reinterpretation of Early American History* (San Marino, CA: Huntingdon Library, 1966), p. 41.
2   Collingwood, R. G.: *The Idea of History* (New York: Oxford University Press, 1956), p. 213.
3   Greene, Jack P. and Pole, J. R., eds.: *Colonial British America: Essays in the New History of the Early Modern Era* (Baltimore and London: Johns Hopkins University Press, 1984), p. 7.
4   Greene, Jack P. and Pole, J. R., eds.: *Colonial British America: Essays in the New History of the Early Modern Era* (Baltimore and London: Johns Hopkins University Press, 1984), p. 16.
5   The quotation is the title of a new book by Richter, Daniel: *Facing East From Indian Country: A Native History of Early America* (Cambridge, MA: Harvard University Press, 2001).

CHAPTER ONE

Pre-Contact: The Evidence from Archaeology

DAVID G. ANDERSON AND MARVIN T. SMITH

Human beings have been present in the New World for perhaps 15,000 years, a span of time thirty times longer than the five centuries since AD 1492. During the pre-Columbian period, profound technological and social advances occurred, and population levels over the hemisphere grew from a few hundred to millions of people. The changes that occurred in these societies, and the remains they left behind, have long held a fascination for archaeological researchers in eastern North America. The first monograph produced by the Smithsonian Institution, in fact, was devoted to the mounds and earthworks of the Mississippi and Ohio River Valleys (Squier and Davis, 1848). While this early literature provided valuable descriptions of sites since destroyed or modified by the growth of our own civilization, many of the ideas advanced about the mound builders themselves were quite fanciful, invoking peoples from all over the world (Silverberg, 1968). By the 1880s, however, technical monographs and papers documenting archaeological investigations in the East were appearing every year, by individuals in institutions like the Smithsonian's Bureau of American Ethnology and the Harvard Peabody Museum, as well as through the efforts of many private citizens. A major triumph of late nineteenth-century American archaeology was the demonstration, based on survey and excavation data from hundreds of sites, that the mounds and earthworks were the work of American Indians (Thomas, 1892; Willey and Sabloff, 1974, pp. 49–50).

Archaeological research in the East grew dramatically throughout the twentieth century. The discipline has been the beneficiary of major federal support since the earliest years of the Great Depression, when huge field projects were funded to provide relief to unemployed workers, support continuing with the reservoir salvage programs of the 1940s and 1950s (Lyons, 1996). The passage of the National Historic Preservation Act in 1966, mandating archaeological survey and excavation in cases where significant historic properties are threatened by federally funded or licensed activities, has prompted a vast amount of fieldwork and reporting in recent years (Fagan, 2000; Smith and Ehrenhard, 1991). As a result, a massive technical literature documents the development of North American Indian culture, much of it in the form of highly specialized archaeological reports, encompassing far more information than any one person can readily access or read. Accordingly, our goal in this chapter is to provide a broad general synthesis of this research, and let the reader know where to go to find more specific data. Our discussion spans the period of initial human colonization in the late Pleistocene through the mid-seventeenth century, and focuses on changes within American Indian societies. Major research findings from the 150 years of archaeological investigation that has occurred in eastern North America are emphasized, as well as the kinds of questions that remain to be answered. Several detailed syntheses on eastern North American prehistoric and early historic period archaeology exist, to which the interested reader is referred (Anderson and Mainfort, 2002; Anderson and Sassaman, 1996; Bense, 1994; Brown, 1994; Fagan, 2000; Grumet, 1995; Sassaman and Anderson, 1996; Smith, 1986, 1992a; Snow, 1980; Steponaitis, 1986; Willey and Sabloff, 1974).

In the course of presenting the results of archaeological research in the East, we will also outline some of the major research topics and questions that occupy the attention of contemporary scholars, as well as various competing positions when no clear agreement exists. For some of these subjects, such as the date of initial human colonization, or why complex agricultural societies arose in some areas and not in others, there are no clear answers, and the debate can be highly contentious, with research going in a number of directions. In chronological order, we discuss: (1) the peopling of the New World, (2) the beginnings of sedentary life, (3) increasing ceremonialism, (4) the rise of cultivation, (5) the beginnings of political complexity, and (6) the effects of European contact. In our discussion we will frequently refer to major time periods that also correspond to major periods of cultural development across the region. Briefly, these include (1) the Paleoindian period, which lasted from the unknown date of initial colonization until approximately 11,000 BP (years before present) or 9000 BC, and encompassed the highly mobile hunting and gathering ice-age inhabitants of the region; (2) the Archaic period from 9000 to 1000 BC, which included populations adapted to hunting and gathering, yet that also witnessed the beginnings of plant domestication, the construction of ceremonial mounds and earthworks, and the establishment of long-distance exchange networks across the region; (3) the Woodland period, which lasted from 1000 BC to AD 1000 in the Southeast, and until European contact in the Northeast, and was characterized by the widespread adoption of pottery, simple agriculture, earthen mound construction, and settled village life; and (4) the Mississippian period, which lasted from AD 1000 to 1650 in the Southeast, and was characterized by the emergence of chiefdoms, societies with hereditary rulers supported by tribute-based economies, and in many areas highly dependent on intensive maize agriculture.

The Peopling of the Americas

Archaeologists have long been interested in beginnings . . . what are the first stone tools like, where did plant and animal domestication occur, what is the earliest evidence for the use of fire, or artwork, or language, and so on. Careers have been made and in some cases tarnished by this quest for primacy. While it has become fashionable and indeed correct to say that the goals of archaeology include the resolution of broad adaptational patterns and historical processes, as well as the reconstruction of specific events and lifeways, great renown still accrues to the earliest sites of a particular type and, of course, to their discoverers. Resolving the origins of the first Americans, or Paleoindians, is no exception to this trend. While hundreds of archaeological sites are excavated in the New World every year, the popular media typically devotes considerable attention to those few for which a great antiquity has been advanced. While sites dating back 15, 20, and even 30 thousand years have been reported from time to time, until quite recently the evidence in support of these claims was almost invariably found to be deficient in some respect (e.g., Dincauze, 1984). Until a few years ago, in fact, no sites more than roughly 13,000 years old were accepted by more than a few members of the profession. In 1997, however, after years of debate, a site in Chile that had been dated to 15,000 years ago was accepted as valid by many archaeologists (Meltzer et al., 1997). With this finding, it became apparent that people were present in the New World much longer than previously thought, a somewhat revolutionary interpretation.

Throughout prehistory, Indians across the Americas made spear and arrow points of stone, bone, or ivory. These tools exhibit appreciable stylistic and technological variability, and as a result many forms can be dated to within a few hundred or at the most a thousand or so years. As such, the occurrence of diagnostic projectile points is one way archaeologists can quickly identify the approximate age of particular sites. Most sequences of cultural development in the Eastern Woodlands, particularly prior to the development of radiocarbon and other dating procedures, in fact, have been based on sequences of projectile point forms and, after about 3,000 years ago, when the use of ceramics became widespread, pottery types.

In 1926 a distinctive type of projectile point, characterized by a pronounced thinning flake scar running upward from the base on each face, was found in association with an extinct form of bison at Folsom, New Mexico. While these points had been reported in the technical literature prior to this, their great antiquity had not been recognized. With the Folsom discovery, which was witnessed by some of the prominent archaeologists of the day, "fluted" points were recognized as a signature of early human occupation, and they were soon found to occur throughout North America in areas that had not been covered with ice sheets or glacial lakes during the Late Pleistocene. A number of stylistic variants or types of fluted points were soon recognized, of which the earliest stratigraphically was called Clovis, after a town in eastern New Mexico near where this antiquity was demonstrated.

From the 1920s onward fluted points were found in great numbers – more than 12,000 have now been reported in the literature from the United States and Canada – sometimes in direct association with the butchered remains of large, extinct animals such as mammoth, mastodon, ground sloth, and a giant form of bison (Anderson and Faught, 1998, 2000). By the 1960s Clovis points had been radiocarbon dated to around 13,000 years ago, and were assumed to represent the first wave of colonization by people from the Old World, big game hunters that were so successful that they drove many species to extinction (Haynes, 1992). Whether what is now called the "overkill" model is correct remains a subject of heated debate among paleontologists and archaeologists, but there is one compelling piece of evidence to support it. Over the past two million years upwards of ten complete glacial-interglacial cycles have occurred worldwide, on a periodicity of about 100,000 years, and only at the end of the last one, about the time the first peoples arrived, did massive extinctions occur in North and South America. How humans may have brought about or contributed to such a dramatic event in the history of life is unknown, although superb hunting abilities, the introduction of new diseases, or the uncontrolled or widespread use of fire have all been suggested mechanisms, none of which are widely accepted. Some archaeologists, in fact, question whether these people hunted big game very often or in many areas, particularly in eastern North America, suggesting instead that they were likely more generalized foragers, exploiting a wide range of animals and plants (Meltzer and Smith, 1986). Unfortunately, few sites yielding well-preserved subsistence remains have been found anywhere in the East at present, so this argument remains unresolved.

Throughout most of the twentieth century, efforts to document earlier, pre-Clovis cultures in the Americas were singularly unsuccessful. While many such sites were proposed, and sometimes received great fanfare, as each came to be carefully examined doubts would emerge. Learned papers were written on the rigorous standards of evidence needed to unequivocally demonstrate pre-Clovis occupations, and each new discovery was evaluated by them and debunked or deemed questionable (e.g., Dincauze, 1984; Fidel, 2000). As a result, by the 1960s it became conventional wisdom that the makers of Clovis points were the first people in the hemisphere, and that they arrived around 13,000 years ago. Earlier sites continued to be announced, and since no diagnostic projectile points were found at these locations, it was thought by some archaeologists that pre-Clovis sites would be "pre-projectile point" as well, that is, with simple flaked stone tool industries.

Eastern North America produced its share of these possible pre-Clovis sites. The most controversial was Meadowcroft Rock shelter in Pennsylvania, where nondescript tools were found in strata with associated radiocarbon dates as early as 17,650 BC (Adovasio et al., 1978). The Meadowcroft dates were immediately questioned, and an extensive and sometimes acrimonious debate has been fought back and forth in the journals for almost 20 years with no end in sight (e.g., Haynes, 1992). Meadowcroft was not alone, however. At the Page-Ladson site in northern Florida, several radiocarbon dates between 14,000 and 14,500 BP were obtained from a level containing a mastodon tusk with possible cut marks on it (Dunbar and Webb, 1996). A radiocarbon date of 12,030±200 (c.14,000 BP) was obtained from the Little Salt Springs site in southern Florida on a wooden spear apparently used to kill a giant Pleistocene tortoise (Clausen et al., 1979).

But the nail in the coffin for the view of the primacy of the Clovis culture did not come from eastern North America, but from excavations at the Monte Verde site in Chile (Dillehay, 1989, 1997). Here in the extreme end of the hemisphere, an occupation dating back to around 14,000 years ago was found and extensively documented. Like the original Folsom discovery, Monte Verde was visited by a blue ribbon panel of experts, including some of the top proponents of the "Clovis First Model," who pronounced it authentic (Meltzer et al., 1997). The one difference, however, is that this time the visit occurred after the excavations were over, and so a few skeptics remain unconvinced (i.e., Fiedel, 1999, 2000). Their position, however, is now viewed about the same way that scholars advancing pre-Clovis sites were received previously. Breaking the "Clovis Barrier" however, took archaeologists almost three-quarters of a century, and in the new frontier we no longer have any clear idea as to when people actually did arrive, although most scholars think 15,000 years ago is a probable minimum age.

If people could reach lower South America by 14,000 years ago, they could have likely reached most other areas by then or even earlier, including eastern North America. It is now widely accepted that there were people in the Americas prior to the Clovis culture, and the hunt is on for their sites. At both the Cactus Hill site in Virginia and the Topper site in South Carolina, stone tool industries have been found stratigraphically below Clovis, although dating and associations remain somewhat uncertain (Goodyear, 2000; McAvoy and McAvoy, 1997). Interestingly, at Cactus Hill large triangular stone projectile points were found in the lowest levels which have been traditionally assumed to date much later in time. Pre-Clovis, accordingly, may not necessary have been pre-projectile point. Instead, the points that were used by these first peoples resembled later forms, and are only now being recognized. The fact these early remains are so few and far between, however, suggests that they likely represent visits by very small groups who died without issue, so-called "failed migrations," or else the remains of early continuous settlement, by such low numbers of people that the archaeological record they produced is nearly invisible.

Where the distinctive Clovis fluted point manufacturing technology itself originated remains unknown, however, and appreciable effort has been directed to locating source areas, in places as far removed as extreme northeastern Asia, Alaska, on the High Plains, in the Southeast, or even the Upper Paleolithic of western Europe. To this day we don't know where the "first" fluted points were made. Even though by far and away the greatest numbers of fluted points occur in eastern North America – almost ten times as many occur east of the Mississippi than west of this drainage – only a few scholars have argued that Clovis technology could have originated in this region. It remains identified, perhaps incorrectly, as a High Plains/southwestern culture, a lingering legacy of the fact that this was where the first major sites were found. Perhaps the most important archaeological development in recent years has been the profession's shift away from the Clovis first model. A major research focus for the foreseeable future, however, will continue to be "When and how were the Americas first peopled?"

Settling In: Beginnings of Sedentism in Eastern North America

The end of Clovis culture occurred about 12,500 BP, about the same time that the major Late Pleistocene extinctions were over. The last 1,500 years of the Paleoindian period, from 12,500 to 11,000 BP, witnessed a diversification of point forms across the Eastern Woodlands, and a dramatic increase in the number of sites. Populations were clearly growing, although we remain uncertain about the rate. Many of the new point forms were restricted to fairly small areas, no more than a few hundred miles in extent, and it is thought that these marked the beginnings of distinctive subregional cultures. Projectile point use changed as well, from lanceolate-shaped forms used primarily for spearing game, to serrated forms that were used as combination spear points and knives. Point edges were sharpened over and over by the removal of small flakes until some showed distinct beveling along their margins. The change in point forms is thought due, in part, to an increased need to kill and process large numbers of small animals, such as deer, rather than the occasional larger animals like mammoth or mastodon that were taken previously. While this trend toward smaller game is undoubtedly correct, it is also likely that human populations at all time levels, including the earliest Paleoindian peoples, ate whatever they could get when food supplies were low.

The Archaic period, which begins after 11,000 BP, was traditionally thought to have been the time when human populations in eastern North America became fully adapted to post-glacial climate, vegetation, and animal populations. Over time, and as human populations grew, group ranges became progressively smaller, first perhaps along one or more river systems, then to within a single drainage, and finally to within portions of single drainages. Until recently, conventional wisdom had it that Archaic peoples were primarily mobile hunters and gatherers. There was little evidence for sedentism, the permanent, year-round occupation of specific locations. As group ranges contracted, and peoples spent more and more time in smaller and smaller areas, some places came to be visited over and over again. In some areas, both on the coast and along rivers in the interior, massive piles of shellfish and other debris ("midden" in archaeological parlance) accumulated, suggesting extended occupations. These sites only rarely produced evidence for substantial structures that could have been used year round, however, and examination of the plant and animal remains (to determine what season they were collected) suggested that many interior sites were seasonal rather than year-round occupations (Marquardt and Watson, 1983).

Existing models of settlement during the Early Archaic period, from *c*.11,000 to 8500 BP, include appreciable seasonal movement of small band-level societies (i.e., small groups of *c*.25–50 people related by kinship and marriage ties), with annual fall aggregation events by multiple bands for trade and marriage purposes. That extensive group movement occurred is accepted by everyone, although appreciable debate centers on the details, such as how often and how far people may have moved from season to season, where aggregation events may have occurred and how many people may have participated, and what species of plants and animals were exploited. Wild plant and animal foods made up the entire diet, although local populations were undoubtedly growing increasingly familiar with their natural environment, and some plant species that were later domesticated may have begun to be collected intensively at this time.

By the Middle Archaic period, from *c*.8500 to 5500 BP, there is evidence for more restricted mobility in many parts of the region, something unquestionably brought on, in part, by increasing population levels. Post-glacial warming was at its peak at this time, with average temperatures warmer than at any point in the last 10,000 years, save perhaps for the past decade. As such, this mid-Holocene warm interval may offer clues to what climate might be like in a few decades if global warming trends continue (Anderson, 2001). Some areas in eastern North America appear to have been abandoned or greatly depopulated, particularly portions of the southeastern Gulf and Atlantic coastal plains, where pine forests replaced hardwoods, providing less food for both game animals and the human groups that preyed upon them. What conditions were like for human populations over the region, in fact, is the subject of appreciable research and debate. Large sites characterized by dense accumulations of occupational debris, particularly shellfish, for example, appeared in a number of the major river valleys in the Southeast and Midwest, and towards the end of the period large shell middens were present along the coast as well. The occurrence of these sites has long been thought to have been due, in part, to a retrenchment of populations into particularly favored areas during the mid-Holocene.

Large sites continued to occur in many areas of the Southeast and Midwest throughout the Late Archaic period, from approximately 5500–3000 BP. In many cases the accumulated deposits were several feet thick, and had large numbers of firepits, human burials, and postholes from structures. Appreciable research has been directed to delimiting whether these were occupied seasonally or year round, and hence reflect the beginnings of true sedentism. While most occupations continued to be seasonal, some sites do indeed appear to have been occupied throughout the year, at least in coastal areas, such as at Horr's Island in southern Florida (Russo, 1991). Conversely, there is little evidence of sedentary life in New England during the Middle Archaic, although there are some (seasonally?) occupied shell middens (Snow, 1980).

During the Middle and Late Archaic periods across much of eastern North America, appreciable evidence appears for substantial house construction activity (Sassaman and Ledbetter, 1996), the beginnings of violent conflict between groups (Maria Smith, 1996), the establishment of long-distance trading networks spanning much of the region (Johnson, 1994) and, as will be detailed in the next section of this chapter, increasing ceremonialism manifested in large-scale earthwork construction. Wild plants were utilized extensively, and by the Late Archaic, some local plants were being culti-vated for their starchy or oily seeds, such as chenopodium, sunflower, and maygrass, as well as a local squash (B. Smith, 1992a; Cowan, 1997). The Late Archaic also wit-nessed the so-called "container revolution" in which pottery or stone vessels appeared from Florida through the Carolinas, but this technology did not spread very far until the subsequent Woodland period (B. Smith, 1986; Sassaman, 1993). How sedentism ties in with all of these other changes that were occurring is a topic that will receive much more research in the near future. Crucial to this will be the careful analysis of seasonal indicators found in archaeological sites, such as plant and animal resources available only at certain times of the year.

IV Ceremonialism, Warfare, and Exchange

While all modern human groups engage in religious and ritual activity, in many hunt-ing and gathering societies archaeological evidence for this kind of behavior tends to be rare. The same is true in eastern North America, at least during the Paleoindian and Early Archaic periods. Few clearly ritual or ceremonial artifacts are known, although in some areas unusually large and well-made projectile points have been found that are thought to have been used in some kind of ritual behavior, possibly intended to pro-mote interaction and alliances between groups (Walthall and Koldehoff, 1998). Typi-cally, burials tend to have few associated grave goods, as was the case at the terminal Early Archaic/initial Middle Archaic period Windover site in Florida, where bodies were wrapped in cloth and placed in pond/bog deposits, offering excellent preserva-tion of the textiles, but also showing little else was present (Doran and Dickel, 1988). Exceptions sometimes do occur, such as at the Sloan site late Paleoindian period cem-etery area in northeast Arkansas, where a number of burials were found with clusters of finely made stone tools, many in mint condition (Morse, 1997). Caches of unusually well-made stone tools are also sometimes found with no evidence for an associated burial, which may also reflect some kind of ceremonial behavior. Elaborate artwork on cave or rockshelter surfaces, or rock art in general, however, has not been well docu-mented until the Woodland period and after in eastern North America (Simak et al., 1997).

Beginning in the Middle Archaic, evidence for extensive ceremonial behavior ap-pears in a number of parts of eastern North America. Burials with elaborate grave goods of worked shell, bone, stone, and copper, signaling individual status and in some cases group affiliation, appeared in many parts of the region. Many of these goods were exchanged over great distances, suggesting increased interaction between groups. Not all of this interaction was friendly, as many burials resulted from violent death, as evidenced by broken bones, embedded projectile points, and scalping marks. As populations grew and mobility decreased, competition and interaction between groups appears to have increased, perhaps as people were forced closer and closer together on the landscape. This competition was held in a number of arenas, such as for personal status items as indicated by the growth in exchange networks, for food or other natural resources as suggested by the increased evidence for warfare, and in collective ceremonial behavior, as reflected in the construction and use of elaborate mound centers. Some of these processes may have been mutually exclusive while others worked in tandem.

While some scholars might argue that ceremonialism would more likely have increased following the adoption of a sedentary lifestyle, complex ceremonialism in the form of mound building is actually earlier than any conclusive evidence for sedentism in many parts of eastern North America. Years ago, James Tuck (McGhee and Tuck, 1977) demonstrated burial mound construction at the L'Anse Amour site in Labrador dating back to 8000 BP. This was a small mound constructed of stone and earth covering the burial of a 12-year-old child. The people who constructed this monument were seasonally mobile hunters and gatherers.

In the lower Mississippi Valley, the conventional archaeological wisdom until quite recently held that earthen mound construction was first practiced by the Poverty Point culture of the Late Archaic period, from around 4200 to 3000 BP. Poverty Point is an elaborate site located in northeast Louisiana with a massive bird effigy mound some 70 feet high, making it the second tallest earthen mound in Eastern North America. In addition, a number of smaller mounds are nearby, and the primary mound fronts on an elaborate complex of six concentric earthen rings some 1,200 meters (¾ mile) in diameter. There is an abundance of occupational debris, suggesting many people lived at the site, although at present it is not known whether residence was year-round or less permanent. Poverty Point was the largest of a number of contemporaneous mound centers in the vicinity of the lower Mississippi Valley, and these peoples exchanged a wide range of materials back and forth, and obtained raw materials from across much of the lower Southeast and into parts of the Midwest. That such an elaborate culture could seemingly spring up so quickly, however, puzzled archaeologists for many years (Gibson, 1996b).

We now know that massive earthen mound complexes were being built at a much earlier time in parts of the region, well back into the Middle Archaic period prior to 5000 BP (Russo, 1994a). In Louisiana, the Frenchman's Bend site has radiocarbon dates between 5100 and 5600 BP, the Hedgepeth site has dates from 4900 to 7500 BP, and the Watson Brake site has dates from 5300 to 5900 BP (Saunders et al., 1994, 1997; Gibson, 1996a). These are not isolated mounds, but are huge complexes with multiple mounds in some cases connected by earthen embankments. One of the most complex sites is Watson's Brake, where the main period of construction occurred between about 5400 to 5000 BP (Saunders et al., 1997). This site consists of 11 mounds, seven of which are connected by a circular ridge/midden deposit. The largest mound is over 7 meters high, and the entire complex extends almost 300 meters across. Analyses of plant and animal remains from the site suggest seasonal occupation, in the spring, summer, and fall. The recognition of these large, complex Middle Archaic mound sites, dating up to 2,000 years earlier than Poverty Point, has been another revolutionary change in our understanding of eastern North American prehistory in recent years, comparable to the implications of the Monte Verde dating (Russo, 1994a).

These Louisiana sites are not alone in their antiquity. Mound sites from Florida are also very early, although in this region both shell and earth were used as construction materials (Russo, 1994b). At the Horr's Island site on the southwest Florida coast, a complex arrangement of mounds was constructed between 4600 and 5000 BP. Analysis of subsistence remains indicates that this site was occupied year around, furthermore, indicating true sedentism, the earliest evidence for this in the region. Apparently the abundant marine resources allowed an early sedentary lifestyle. Excavations at Horr's Island found minimal evidence for social differentiation, suggesting the mound building was likely the work of an egalitarian society, albeit one in which some groups may have had higher status or prestige than others (Russo, 1991). Other societies were also building elaborate mounds at an early date. The Tick Island mound site in northeastern Florida, for example, was built about 5,000 to 5,500 years ago (Russo, 1994b, pp. 106–8). Rock and earthen mounds were also built in the Nebo Hill culture of the lower Missouri River valley, and in the Helton and Titterington phase cultures of Illinois and Missouri from 5000 to 4000 BP (Claassen, 1996, p. 243).

Other elaborate Middle and Late Archaic cultures are known from across eastern North America, among which perhaps the best known archaeologically are the Shell Mound Archaic cultures of the mid-South and lower Midwest (Claassen, 1996; Marquardt and Watson, 1983), the Benton Interaction Sphere in the lower mid-South (Johnson and Brookes, 1989), the Stallings Island Culture of Georgia and South Carolina (Sassaman, 1993), the Mount Taylor culture of the St. Johns river valley of northeastern Florida (Piatak, 1994), and the Old Copper culture of the Great Lakes region (Stoltman, 1986). All appear to have been involved at varying levels of participation in the long-distance exchange networks spanning much of the region at this time. While still considered egalitarian societies, it is clear that some were fairly complex, and that some individuals had much higher status than others, and likely competed with other such individuals in their own and other societies for recognition and leadership in warfare, exchange, and probably the direction of public construction episodes and ceremony.

What is the significance of mound building activity? Mike Russo (1994b: 108) believes that the early mounds served the same purposes as later mound constructions, that is, they were built as "sacred places, as burial places, as centers of ceremony and ritual, and as territorial markers" and that mound building may have been a "mechanism for integrating the society." Were these populations sedentary? Jon Gibson (1994) points out that many of these sites are located in highly favorable ecological niches that might have promoted a sedentary lifestyle. He goes on to note, however, that we simply do not have firm archaeological data, in the form of sufficient food remains, house remains, and trash deposits, to determine if many early mound builders were sedentary or mobile hunter-gatherers. Research will continue on this problem of the relationship of sedentism and mound building, as well as how these factors tie in to evidence for exchange, warfare, and more complex forms of social organization.

The Emergence of Agriculture

Eastern North America represents one of the few areas on earth where the independent domestication and subsequent extensive cultivation of a number of native plant species is thought to have occurred. Between 4000 and 3000 BP, at the close of the Late Archaic period, morphological changes indicative of domestication are observed in a number of local plants whose remains have been found on archaeological sites (Smith, 1992a, p. 287). These changes include an increase in seed size to well beyond the average occurring in wild populations in sunflower (*Helianthus annus*) and sumpweed (*Iva annua*), and a decrease in seed coat thickness in goosefoot (*Chenopodium berlandieri*). Other plants that were domesticated include maygrass (*Phalaris caroliniana*), knotweed (*Polygonum erectum*), little barley (*Hordeum pusillum*), and local cucurbits or gourds. Knotweed, maygrass, and little barley are assumed to have been cultivated since they are found in archaeological settings far outside their natural range. It has recently been argued that a local variety of squash was also domesticated (Cowan, 1997). Taken together, these species are sometimes referred to as the "Eastern Agricultural Complex." This was apparently a true independent domestication of local plants by indigenous populations, who had been collecting them for millennia prior to this in their wild state.

Tropical species like maize, tobacco, and beans appear to have come into the East appreciably later, well into the Woodland period. These introductions occurred well after local domestication was under way, although evidence for earlier contact has not been unequivocally ruled out. It should be noted in passing that these tropical domesticates are the only "artifacts" of unequivocal, albeit very indirect Mesoamerican origin known from eastern North America. That is, there is no evidence at present for direct contact between the two regions, although over time agricultural products appear to have moved across the intervening areas, probably as they were adopted from group to group. The nutritional value of the Eastern Agricultural Complex plants is extremely high, with some "oily seeds" like sunflower and marshelder proving to be excellent sources of fat, and other "starchy seeds" like goosefoot, maygrass, and knotweed excellent sources of carbohydrates. Harvest yields comparable to those for maize can be obtained from some of these plants, on the order of 500 to 1,000 or more kg of seeds per hectare, although whether yields of this magnitude were obtained in the prehistoric Eastern Woodlands remains unknown (Smith, 1992a, p. 177). The role of these plants in the economies of eastern North American populations has become an important area of research. Bruce Smith (1986) has suggested that Woodland peoples in some parts of the mid-South and lower Midwest may have grown large fields of Chenopodium and other crops, and were true agriculturists, not simple gardeners. Human paleofeces recovered from Salts Cave in Kentucky show that some of these plants made a substantial contribution to the diet of Woodland peoples in this area. Pollen analyses suggest that fairly extensive forest clearing was taking place in some parts of the region by the middle portion of the Woodland period, additional evidence for possible cultivation. Taken together, these lines of evidence suggest that cultivation of plants was growing increasingly important (Smith, 1992b, pp. 108–11).

Two competing theories about how the process of domestication occurred are now debated. The first, the "weedy floodplain" hypothesis, suggests that these plants were first collected from and then encouraged to grow in the disturbed habitats in and near major earth and shell mound sites of the mid-South and lower Midwest (Smith, 1992a). An alternative hypothesis suggests that these plants were collected in adjoining upland areas, or in more hilly and mountainous parts of the Southeast like the Ozarks and the Cumberland Plateau, since that is where many of the domesticated specimens are found

(Gremillion, 1996, 2002). These two perspectives may be complementary, related more to factors of preservation, which are better in upland dry caves and rockshelters than in damp floodplain areas, although this remains to be fully explored.

While steps toward domestication were being taken in some parts of the region, and cultigens were assuming increasing importance in the diet, in other areas the hunting and gathering of wild foods continued well into the Woodland period (Fritz, 1993; Fritz and Kidder, 1993; Gremillion, 2002). Evidence for the use of domesticates during the Archaic and Woodland periods is rare on the Atlantic and Gulf Coastal Plain and in Florida, and in the lower Mississippi Valley. Why this is the case is uncertain, although it is thought that in areas of low population density such resources were not needed, while in ecologically rich areas they were unnecessary.

With regard to this latter point, in the 1950s, Joseph Caldwell (1958) coined the phrase "Primary Forest Efficiency" to describe the economic basis of eastern North American populations that made only minimal use of agriculture. In his view, after dozens of generations of experimentation with plants and hunting strategies during the Archaic period, by the Late Archaic or Woodland period local populations had achieved the ability to maximize the subsistence potential of wild plant and animal resources. Caldwell had excavated archaeological sites in parts of the Midwest and Southeast with large storage pits full of acorns, hickory nuts, and other local resources, and believed that efficient use of wild resources, along with well-developed storage techniques, could enable people to live a sedentary lifestyle in permanent villages. This process, he thought, had taken thousands of years. We now know that far back into the Archaic local peoples were aware of the subsistence potential of many of the plant and animal species around them, yet chose to avoid a sedentary life (e.g., Ford, 1985; Smith, 1992a). Given a low regional population density, they did not need to turn to these resources, or intensify their production, or settle at one location for very long, except perhaps during times of stress.

Eastern North America is thus an important area to study the beginnings of plant domestication and the shift from a primarily hunting and gathering economy to one based largely on domesticated plants. Questions that are being explored include how the process of plant domestication proceeded, and how agricultural food production may be related to population pressure, decreased group mobility, local and regional environmental conditions, or sociopolitical complexity. A particularly promising area for research encompasses the signatures various diets leave behind in human skeletal remains. People ingesting appreciable quantities of tropical cultigens such as maize, for example, have different ratios of stable carbon isotopes than people who ate local wild or domesticated plants. Because of this, we know that although maize was introduced into the East some time around 2,000 years ago, it did not contribute much to the diet of local peoples until a thousand years later, in the Mississippian period in the Southeast and Midwest, and not until appreciably later in parts of the Northeast. In some areas, in fact, maize agriculture was never adopted, or else played a minor role in subsistence. Why this was the case is unknown, as are the reasons why most of the Eastern Agricultural Complex species were apparently largely replaced by maize during the Mississippian period. Was maize easier to grow, harvest, or process, or more nutritious when used in combination with other species like beans and squash? All of these questions will be the subject of appreciable research in the years to come.

✓II✓ Rise of Political Complexity

Anthropologists have been interested in understanding how complex societies developed since the very beginnings of the field in the mid-nineteenth century. Many early anthropologists were avowed evolutionists, as exemplified by works like Lewis Henry Morgan's (1877) *Ancient Society*, which classified human societies into a series of successive stages from Savagery to Barbarism to Civilization. Interest in cultural evolution has waxed and waned within the broader discipline of anthropology over the past century, but within archaeology itself there has always been strong interest in first recognizing cultural change and then trying to understand the circumstances and processes that brought it about. Given archaeology's subject matter, the material remains of past human behavior that typically accumulated over long periods of time, it is not surprising that appreciable effort should be directed toward learning how and why the archaeological record formed the way it did. That is, to understand the behavior that produced the sites and assemblages that we find, we need to consider what past settlement, subsistence, and political systems were like, and the changes they may have undergone over time.

Eastern North America is an ideal laboratory to explore the evolution of cultural complexity. Complex tribal and perhaps chiefdom level societies are assumed to have emerged in parts of the region during the Woodland period, from about 1500 BC to AD 1000, and continued into the Mississippian period. During the Paleoindian and earlier parts of the Archaic period, in contrast, populations in the East likely lived in small bands of from 25 to 50 people. These groups met from time to time and interacted over large areas, but each was autonomous in subsistence production. All were essentially egalitarian, with no formal leadership positions beyond those individuals could achieve through their own abilities. Sometime in the Archaic, and certainly by the Woodland period, more complex, tribal-level social formations emerged. Tribes are groupings of numerous bands or somewhat larger sized social segments that are fused together through the existence and operation of institutions such as systems "of intermarrying clans, of age grades, or military or religious societies, which cross cut the primary segments" (Sahlins, 1961, pp. 93–4). Exactly when tribal organizations emerged in eastern North America is unknown, and they are particularly difficult to recognize archaeologically (Braun and Plog, 1982; Parkinson, 2002). The large mound complexes of the Middle Archaic are, however, increasingly thought to have been built by peoples with this kind of social organization (Anderson, 2002).

Chiefdoms are much easier to recognize archaeologically. These societies were characterized by hereditary leadership classes, and typically extended across a number of communities, with decision-making centralized in the hands of elites. Individual communities in chiefdoms, like those in tribal and band-level societies, were economically self-sufficient. Access to resources within local populations, however, was unequal. The chiefly elites could mobilize tribute from commoners to fuel their social, religious, or political agendas, although their ability to do so appears to have been scale-dependent, that is, related to the size and complexity of the chiefdom (Feinman and Neitzel, 1984, p. 57). A substantial literature documents the archaeological recognition of chiefdoms, with procedures including the analyses of site distributions for the presence of settlement hierarchies, the inspection of burials for evidence of different social strata, and examination of housing, settlement size, and artifact categories for status markers or other evidence indicating unequal access to resources.

Woodland societies across much of eastern North America are considered to have been predominantly tribal-level societies, while Mississippian societies in the Southeast and lower Midwest were chiefdoms. How did these social forms emerge and evolve over time? Competition between individuals and societies in the region for prestige goods, natural resources, and status, we have seen, dates back thousands of years, well back into the Archaic period. The fact that monumental construction activity, long-distance exchange, and warfare were all occurring upwards of 5,000 years ago in parts of the region suggests that societies more complex than simple bands had emerged (Anderson, 2002; Bender, 1985). Perhaps the clearest evidence for the emergence of tribal societies during the Archaic period is monumental architecture, whose construction was likely conducted by a great many cooperating people linked together by common ritual or purpose. How to recognize the existence of pan-tribal social institutions linking tribal segments together over large areas, of course, is a major challenge. It is also possible that the earliest tribal forms were the most weakly integrated, making their recognition even more difficult. The major centers of the Middle and Late Archaic, however, may well have been formed by the actions of one or more tribal-level groups, whose segments were ordinarily dispersed across the landscape, but that periodically came together for exchange, ritual, and cooperation in construction.

During the early part of the Woodland period after about 1500 BC, pottery, which had appeared about 1,000 years earlier in Florida, Georgia, and the Carolinas, was widely adopted and used across the region. Long-distance exchange declined markedly, however, and across the region people appear to have been living in small, more-or-less egalitarian groups, with community size on the order of a few dozen people, or several families. Earthen burial mounds occur in many areas, and for much of the twentieth century archaeologists considered the Woodland period to be the time when mound building and pottery use originated, something we now know to be incorrect. Mortuary facilities were often located away from settlements, suggesting they served to bring together peoples from a number of communities (Clay, 1998). Over time and in some areas, mound burial came to be reserved for fewer, presumably higher status individuals.

By the Middle Woodland period, from about 300 BC to AD 400, long-distance exchange networks had re-emerged, spectacular mounds and earthwork complexes were built in many areas, similarities in iconography and ritual behavior are evident across wide areas, and some individuals were buried in elaborate tombs within or under massive mounds. This behavior has come to be known as Hopewellian interaction, after the type site in Ohio where spectacular remains where found late in the nineteenth century (Brose and Greber, 1979; Pacheco, 1996). Many differing societies were present within the region, of course, whose participation in this interaction network varied greatly. Native cultigens are thought to have played a major role in the diet in some areas, although this remains to be well documented. Maize, while present in some areas, was not used extensively. Tribal societies are assumed to have been present, since there is no evidence for hereditary leadership positions. Besides enhancing individual status, tribal-scale interaction and exchange likely helped reduce the possibility of warfare and subsistence uncertainty for everybody, by creating ties between different groups.

The spectacular individual burials and associated grave assemblages are assumed to commemorate highly successful individuals, who were able to enlist the help of their communities in the pursuit of their social and ritual agendas. These have been called "Big Man" societies (B. Smith, 1986), a form of social organization best known from Melanesia. It must be noted, however, that the ethnographic examples offered of Big Man societies are nowhere near as complex as some of the Hopewellian societies of the Eastern Woodlands appear to have been (Sahlins, 1963, 1972, pp. 248–55). In the ethnographic cases, the Big Men typically had reputations for generosity and gift giving, while many of the Eastern Woodlands folks apparently "took it with them" when they died. Likewise, monumental construction is absent or minimal in most of the ethnographic cases. Accordingly, if Big Men (and Women) were present, how these individuals participated in the collective ceremony and monumental construction that characterize the more elaborate Middle Woodland societies needs to be determined.

During the Late Woodland period from *c.* AD 400 to 1000, a marked decline in interaction occurred, evidence for warfare increased, and major population growth is indicated in many areas, with settlements found scattered over the landscape. The bow and arrow appeared and spread rapidly over the region. While the bow was once thought to have contributed to the collapse of Hopewellian interaction, by making warfare more advantageous than exchange or ritual, we now know the actual introduction of this technology dates several hundred years later in many areas, to between *c.* AD 600 and 800 (Blitz, 1988; Nassaney and Pyle, 1999). By the end of the Woodland period, chiefdoms are thought to have emerged in the central and lower Mississippi Valley, and intensive maize agriculture was practiced in some areas. Major civic–ceremonial centers characterized by temple/mortuary mounds arranged around plazas appeared at this time in the lower Mississippi Valley. This site type is the hallmark of chiefly centers in the ensuing Mississippian period, from *c.* AD 1000 to 1550, when they occurred widely across the Southeast and lower Midwest.

During the Mississippian period, chiefdoms based on intensive maize agriculture were present in many parts of the region, long-distance exchange networks reemerged, and warfare was endemic in many areas. Chiefdom societies formed, expanded, and collapsed across the region, with the growth of one society typically at the expense of others. Regional maps constructed covering this interval at century by century intervals show whole areas being occupied and abandoned, in pattern akin to blinking Christmas tree lights (Anderson, 1991; Milner et al., 2001). Few of these societies appear to have lasted more than a century or two (Hally, 1993). The emergence and collapse of these societies at a regional scale, in fact a process that has come to be called chiefly cycling, has become the focus of appreciable research in eastern North America and beyond (Anderson, 1994a; Blitz; 1999; Earle, 1991).

How did chiefdoms emerge? Theories about the emergence of complex societies in the Eastern Woodlands have emphasized the importance of population pressure, intensive agriculture, warfare, the pivotal role specific individuals might have played, historical conditions, and the control over the exchange of desired items or "prestige goods." A massive literature, in fact, explores this question, and grows yearly (e.g., Anderson, 1994a; Knight, 1990; Muller, 1997; Pauketat and Emerson, 1997; Scarry, 1996; Smith, 1990). While it would be comforting if there were a simple answer to the evolution of cultural complexity, that does not appear to be the case. All of these factors, and many more, appear to have played a role in the changes observed in the Eastern Woodlands, albeit some were more important than others in specific cases.

How did the chiefdom organizational form spread? In part, peacefully through a process known as competitive emulation (e.g., Clark and Blake, 1994) and, in a less tranquil manner, through the threat of warfare (Carneiro, 1981). That is, attractive characteristics of chiefdoms may have been copied by neighboring societies. In the Eastern Woodlands the most dramatic Mississippian society in terms of size and complexity was also one of the earliest, at Cahokia in the central Mississippi Valley. It undoubtedly attracted a great deal of attention, and exerted a lot of both direct and indirect influence on other societies in the region (Anderson, 1997; Pauketat and Emerson, 1997). At the same time, the military advantage a chiefdom would have over a less complex society likely prompted a defensive reaction and reorganization among its neighbors, who would have had to adopt or be absorbed. Warfare was a major part of Mississippian life and, given the fact that warfare was already widespread in the late Woodland, appears to have shaped both the emergence and subsequent development of chiefdoms in the region (DePratter, 1983; Dye, 1990).

Why were chiefdoms in the Eastern Woodlands seemingly so unstable and short-lived? The primary reason appears to be the unstable nature of the chiefdom organizational form itself. The fact that leadership was determined by genealogy meant that there were likely a number of potential claimants for the position of chief. Unless these individuals were co-opted or eliminated, they could prove a threat. Factional competition is, in fact, rife in chiefdom societies, and the Southeast was no exception (Anderson, 1994b; Brumfiel and Fox, 1994; Hally, 1993). Changes in climate also appear to have played a role. In societies heavily dependent on intensive agriculture, repeated crop failures brought on by prolonged drought or other factors would have had disastrous effects. Most of these societies, however, appear to have developed elaborate cropping and storage strategies to reduce the effects of drought, but they were not always successful (Anderson et al., 1995).

Political complexity evolved in a different direction in the Northeast. Instead of hereditary chiefdoms, northeastern peoples developed elaborate confederacies. Bruce Trigger (1985, pp. 86–110) has documented changes from approximately AD 1000 to European contact. During the Early Iroquoian period, Native northeasterners lived in villages of 100–400 occupants. Trigger suggests that these communities were "continuations of the hunting bands of the Middle Woodland period" (1985, p. 86). We must remember that Trigger's perspective is from Canada, where there is no evidence for agriculture during the Middle Woodland. The Middle Iroquoian period of the fourteenth century saw major changes take place. There was a shift to larger communities, as apparently separate bands joined together in aggregate settlements. Villages were fortified, suggesting conflict. Conflict may have been one way males could obtain social status, something that may have been important given these were matrilineal societies where women provided much of the subsistence through horticulture. The joining together of several clans would necessitate increasing complexity of political organization – probably the formation of more formal village councils made up of clan representatives. Trigger also suggests that there may have been peace and war chiefs at this time.

By the Late Iroquoian period, AD 1400–1600, Trigger argues that the historically known tribes such as the Huron, Neutral, and Five Nation Iroquois had developed in the areas where Europeans found them. Community size continued to increase, as amalgamation reduced the number of villages but increased their size. Communities of 1,500 people became relatively common, greatly outnumbering the populations of typical Mississippian communities in the Southeast. Some villages, such as the Draper Site in Ontario, may have reached populations as large as 3,000. These large communities used appreciable quantities of natural resources (fertile soil, firewood, etc.), necessitating frequent village relocation.

Trigger also notes that there was a tendency of several villages to settle near one another, forming the "Tribes" known in the historic period. Tribal councils must have been formed to deal with these multicommunity settlements. Towns may have been linked by clan ties and medicine society membership. According to the Iroquois oral tradition, confederacies, such as the Huron and Five Nation Iroquois, were formed prior to European contact. Trigger sees these formations as natural extensions of the evolution of political complexity in the region.

European Contact and Culture Change

A tremendous amount of research has been expended on attempts to understand the effects of European contact on Native American groups, which were for the most part devastating in eastern North America. Early research by Henry Dobyns (1966) and Alfred Crosby (1972) focused research on the timing and intensity of the introduction of Old World infectious diseases. Dobyns (1983) suggested sweeping "pandemics" that spread across the North American continent from introduction points such as Mexico or Spanish Florida. In a largely theoretical study, George Milner (1980) suggested that Native polities and the uninhabited buffer zones that separated them would have inhibited the spread of disease in the southeastern United States. Later archaeological studies in the Mississippi Valley (Ramenofsky, 1987) and the interior of Georgia and Alabama (M. Smith, 1987) suggested major population reduction in the sixteenth century. The Southeast was traversed by a number of large Spanish expeditions, which could and in all likelihood did introduce deadly infectious diseases directly to the Native American inhabitants of the region. Smith in particular thought that there was evidence for the continuing introduction of disease into the interior Southeast even after the period of initial Spanish exploration. He saw a rapid destruction of Native political organization following the wake of initial contact.

While researchers in the Southeast suggested early and devastating effects of contact, conditions in the Northeast appeared to be significantly different. There, the first evidence for epidemic disease in the Iroquois area dated to the mid-1630s (Snow and Starna, 1989; Snow and Lanphear, 1988). From that time on, epidemics ravaged the Iroquois periodically. Why was there such a delay in the introduction of disease, compared with the Southeast? Both general areas saw European exploration in the mid-sixteenth century (e.g., De Soto in the Southeast and Jacques Cartier in the Northeast, followed by relatively constant coastal contacts in both areas). Both areas had societies that lived in compact villages; indeed, the northeastern tribal societies actually had larger settlements than many chiefdoms of the Southeast. Perhaps one important difference was in long-distance trade connections. The Southeast had a long tradition of long-distance trade, while most northeastern Woodland societies were just beginning to focus on long-distance trade, especially in marine shell, about the time of European contact (Pendergast, 1989). Perhaps this emphasis on trade, as well as more frequent direct contact with Europeans, explains the seemingly different timing of early epidemics.

It may also be relevant that the northeastern groups had a practice of incorporating vanquished enemies into their tribes by adoption. Thus, as warfare increased following European contact, if one group obtained European weapons prior to its enemies, wholesale adoptions (rather than the killing of defeated enemies) may have augmented populations suffering from European diseases (see Snow, 1996 for a discussion of the Mohawk; Bradley, 1987, p. 119 on the Onondaga). Thus, powerful groups such as the Five Nation Iroquois and the Susquehannocks may appear to have maintained large populations, even in the face of severe epidemics. When research is conducted on a regional scale, it becomes apparent that the Ohio Valley and much of the central Great Lakes area were being depopulated while Iroquoian groups were maintaining their size. Population loss from disease may be more significant than was readily apparent. More research is needed in this area.

Many other areas of aboriginal culture changed as a result of contact. Smith (1987, 2000) has demonstrated that for the Coosa valley of Georgia and Alabama, there was rapid disintegration of political complexity from hereditary chiefdoms to simpler tribal organization from c. AD 1540 to 1650. However, Knight (1994) has suggested that southeastern societies of the late seventeenth and early eighteenth centuries maintained more of their chiefly organizational heritage than has been recognized by most researchers. By way of contrast, the League of the Iroquois, assumed to have formed in the late prehistoric era, appears to have grown stronger in the century after European contact. Contemporaneous societies that were not organized into strong confederacies (and even some who were such as the Huron and Neutral) were unable to withstand the onslaught of the Five Nation Iroquois. The Iroquois remained strong, while their competitors all but vanished from the scene, some either joining or being adopted into the confederacy, while others fled to the west.

In the Northeast, European technology quickly replaced its aboriginal counterpart. Metal tools quickly replaced their stone counterparts, aboriginal ceramics were replaced by European metal cooking containers in many cases by the middle of the seventeenth century, and Indian reliance on firearms came as early as the 1640s (Bradley, 1987; Kent, 1984; Wray, 1973). In contrast, the century following European contact in the Southeast saw relatively little technological change (Smith, 1987). While metal axes and hoes were introduced by the Spaniards, metal cooking pots and firearms were all but absent in the Southeast prior to the founding of Charleston and the subsequent expansion of English trade in 1670.

Major changes in subsistence occurred after this time across the region. The fur trade in the North and the deerskin trade in the South made commercial hunting a way of life for many Native men. In both areas there were competing European powers to bid for the Native furs and hides. New crops were added to Native horticulture, such as peach and watermelon, which spread quickly across the Southeast. With the possible exception of chickens, Old World domesticated animals were not a fixture in either area until the eighteenth century. Efforts to understand the full effects of European contact remain a continuing theme of research.

 **Conclusions**

This chapter has attempted, in a few pages, to give some sense of the great time depth to Indian settlement in eastern North America, and the dramatic changes in culture that occurred over this interval. Regional population grew from the hundreds to the hundreds of thousands, and egalitarian hunting groups were transformed into complex agricultural societies. Archaeology explores evidence for these changes, and attempts to develop explanations for them. While our knowledge of the past is far better than it was a century ago, our understanding of what happened in prehistoric eastern North America is still far from complete or certain.

As new information becomes available, even our most fundamental assumptions and interpretations are subject to change. In recent years, for example, the date of initial human entry into the New World has been pushed back appreciably in time, and the origins of agriculture, mound building, and complex society in eastern North America are now known to have occurred much deeper in the past than we once thought. For every question archaeology has been able to answer, however, new questions have emerged. While we now know people were here 15,000 years ago, we still don't know when they first arrived, or how much of a role they played in the massive animal extinctions that occurred after this time. Likewise, while we now know that people in eastern North America had domesticated a number of local plants by roughly 4,000 years ago, we still don't understand the details of the process, or how important these foods were in subsistence. Did initial domestication occur in floodplain settings along major drainages, or in the hilly uplands of what may have been backwater areas? Did agriculture emerge because of population pressure, and why did some people adopt it while others did not?

These questions are signs of a healthy discipline, one whose information base is growing at a rapid rate, forcing the continual evaluation and refinement of our ideas. This research has a great deal of value to our modern world, particularly regarding the effects of long-term climate change, and why cultures change over time. The end of the ice age and the mid-Holocene warm interval were fairly dramatic episodes, and we now may be entering a third period of fairly rapid climate change. The eastern North American archaeological record indicates that while pronounced changes in climate did sometimes occur, local cultures were able to adapt and continue, to prevail and not merely to endure (Anderson, 2001).

From a purely intellectual or academic perspective, eastern North America is an exciting place to study broad patterns of historical development. Within the region the domestication of plants and the evolution of complex societies occurred, and we now know that this was no simple unilineal process of ever-increasing complexity or change within societies progressing in lockstep through time. Instead, the landscape was highly varied, characterized by societies of differing (albeit generally similar) levels of technology and organizational complexity. We now have dozens of well-documented cases dating back over the millennia of the emergence, expansion, and collapse of individual societies within the larger regional political landscape, and are beginning to understand why they changed the way they did. At an even broader scale, we are beginning to recognize much longer cycles of interregional exchange, warfare, and monumental construction. Both for its ability to provide information about specific events in the past, as well as broad general explanations, archaeology provides a valuable complement to history in the study of the Native peoples of eastern North America.

BIBLIOGRAPHY

Adovasio, James, Gunn, Joel, Donahue, J., and Stuckenrath, R.: "Meadowcroft Rockshelter, 1977: An Overview." *American Antiquity* 43 (1978), pp. 632–51.

Anderson, David G.: "Examining Prehistoric Settlement Distribution in Eastern North America." *Archaeology of Eastern North America* 19 (1991), pp. 1–21.

Anderson, David G.: *The Savannah River Chiefdoms: Political Change in the Late Prehistoric Southeast* (Tuscaloosa, AL: University of Alabama Press, 1994).

Anderson, David G.: "Factional Competition and the Political Evolution of Mississippian Chiefdoms in the Southeastern United States." In Elizabeth M. Brumfiel and John W. Fox, eds., *Factional Competition in the New World* (Cambridge: Cambridge University Press, 1994), pp. 61–76.

Anderson, David G.: "The Role of Cahokia in the Evolution of Mississippian Society." In Pauketat and Emerson (1997), pp. 248–68.

Anderson, David G.: "Climate and Culture Change in Prehistoric and Early Historic Eastern North America." *Archaeology of Eastern North America* 29 (2001), pp. 143–86.

Anderson, David G.: "The Evolution of Tribal Social Organization in the Southeastern United States." In William A. Parkinson, ed., *The Archaeology of Tribal Societies* (Ann Arbor, Michigan: International Monographs in Prehistory, 2002), pp. 291–327.

Anderson, David G. and Faught, Michael K.: "The Distribution of Fluted Paleoindian Projectile Points: Update 1998." *Archaeology of Eastern North America* 26 (1998), pp. 163–87.

Anderson, David G. and Faught, Michael K.: "Paleoindian Artifact Distributions: Evidence and Implications." *Antiquity* 74 (2000), pp. 507–13.

Anderson, David G. and Hanson, Glen: "Early Archaic Settlement in the Southeastern United States: A Case Study from the Savannah River." *American Antiquity* 53 (1988), pp. 262–86.

Anderson, David G. and Mainfort, Robert C., Jr., eds.: *The Woodland Southeast* (Tuscaloosa, AL: University of Alabama Press, 2002).

Anderson, David G. and Sassaman, Kenneth E., eds.: *The Paleoindian and Early Archaic Southeast* (Tuscaloosa, AL: University of Alabama Press, 1996).

Anderson, David G., Stahle, David W., and Cleaveland, Malcolm R.: "Paleoclimates and the Potential Food Reserves of Mississippian Societies: A Case Study from the Savannah River Valley." *American Antiquity* 60 (1995), pp. 258–86.

Bender, Barbara: "Emergent Tribal Formulations in the American Midcontinent." *American Antiquity* 50 (1985), pp. 52–62.

Bense, Judith A.: *Archaeology of the Southeastern United States: Paleoindian to World War I* (San Diego: Academic Press, 1994).

Blitz, John H.: "Adoption of the Bow in Prehistoric North America." *North American Archaeologist* 9 (2, 1988), pp. 123–45.

Blitz, John H.: "Mississippian Chiefdoms and the Fission–Fusion Process." *American Antiquity* 65 (1999), pp. 577–92.

Bradley, James W.: *Evolution of the Onondaga Iroquois* (Syracuse, NY: Syracuse University Press, 1987).

Braun, David and Plog, Stephen: "Evolution of 'Tribal' Social Networks: Theory and Prehistoric North American Evidence." *American Antiquity* 47 (1982), pp. 504–25.

Brose, David S. and Greber, N'omi, eds.: *Hopewell Archaeology: The Chillicothe Conference* (Kent, OH: Kent State University Press, 1979).

Brown, Ian W.: "Recent Trends in the Archaeology of the Southeastern United States." *Journal of Archaeological Research* 2 (1994), pp. 45–111.

Brumfiel, Elizabeth M. and Fox, John W., eds.: *Factional Competition in the New World* (Cambridge, England: Cambridge University Press, 1994).

Caldwell, Joseph R.: *Trend and Tradition in the Prehistory of the Eastern United States* (Menasha, WI: Memoirs of the American Anthropological Association No. 88, 1958).

Carneiro, Robert L.: "The Chiefdom: Precursor to the State." In Grant D. Jones and Robert R. Kautz, eds., *The Transition to Statehood in the New World* (Cambridge, England: Cambridge University Press, 1981), pp. 37–79.

Claassen, Cheryl P.: "A Consideration of the Social Organization of the Shell Mound Archaic." In Sassaman and Anderson (1996), pp. 235–58.

Clark, John E. and Blake, Michael: "The Power of Prestige: Competitive Generosity and the Emergence of Rank Societies in Lowland Mesoamerica." In Elizabeth M. Brumfiel and John W. Fox, eds., *Factional Competition in the New World* (Cambridge, England: Cambridge University Press, 1994), pp. 17–30.

Clausen, C. J., Cohen, A. D., Emeliani, C., Holman, J. A., and Stipp, J. J.: "Little Salt Spring, Florida: A Unique Underwater Site?" *Science* 203 (1979), pp. 609–14.

Clay, R. Berle: "The Essential Features of Adena Ritual and Their Implications." *Southeastern Archaeology* 17 (1998), pp. 1–21.

Cowan, C. Wesley: "Evolutionary Changes Associated with the Domestication of *Cucurbita pepo*: Evidence from Eastern Kentucky." In Kristen Gremillion, ed., *People, Plants, and Landscapes: Studies in Paleoethnobotany* (Tuscaloosa, AL: University of Alabama Press, 1997), pp. 63–85.

Crosby, Alfred: *The Columbian Exchange* (Westport, CT: Greenwood Press, 1972).

DePratter, Chester B.: *Late Prehistoric and Early Historic Chiefdoms in the Southeastern United States* (Ph.D. dissertation., University of Georgia, 1983).

Dillehay, T. D.: *Monte Verde: A Late Pleistocene Settlement in Chile: Paleoenvironment and Site Context* (Washington, DC: Smithsonian Institution Press, 1989).

Dillehay, T. D.: *Monte Verde: A Late Pleistocene Settlement in Chile: The Archaeological Context* (Washington, DC: Smithsonian Institution Press, 1997).

Dincauze, Dena F.: "An Archaeo-Logical Evaluation of the Case for Pre-Clovis Occupations." In F. Wendorf and A. Close, eds., *Advances in World Archaeology* (New York: Academic Press, 1984), pp. 275–323.

Dobyns, Henry F.: "Estimating Aboriginal American Population: An Appraisal of Techniques with a New Hemispheric Estimate." *Current Anthropology* 7 (1966), pp. 395–415.

Dobyns, Henry F.: *Their Number Become Thinned* (Knoxville, TN: University of Tennessee Press, 1983).

Doran, Glen H. and Dickel, David N.: "Multidisciplinary Investigations at the Windover Site." In Barbara A. Purdy, ed., *Wet Site Archaeology* (Caldwell, New Jersey: Telford Press, 1988), pp. 263–89.

Dunbar, James S. and Webb, S. David: "Bone and Ivory Tools from Submerged Paleoindian Sites in Florida." In Anderson and Sassaman (1996), pp. 331–53.

Dye, David H.: "Warfare in the Sixteenth Century Southeast: The De Soto Expedition in the Interior." In David H. Thomas, ed., *Columbian Consequences,* vol. 2, *Archaeological and Historical Perspectives on the Spanish Borderlands East* (Washington, DC: Smithsonian Institution Press, 1990), pp. 211–22.

Earle, Timothy K.: "Chiefdoms in Archaeological and Ethnohistorical Perspective?" *Annual Review of Anthropology* 16 (1987), pp. 279–308.

Earle, Timothy K., ed.: *Chiefdoms: Power, Economy, and Ideology* (Cambridge, England: Cambridge University Press, 1991).

Fagan, Brian M.: *Ancient North America: The Archaeology of a Continent*, third edition (New York: Thames and Hudson, 2000).

Feinman, Gary and Neitzel, Jill: "Too Many Types: An Overview of Sedentary Prestate Societies in the Americas." In Michael B. Schiffer, ed., *Advances in Archaeological Method and Theory* (Orlando: Academic Press, 1984), pp. 39–102.

Fiedel, Stuart J.: "Artifact Provenience at Monte Verde: Confusion and Contradictions." *Scientific American Discovering Archaeology* 1, no. 6 (1999), Special Report: Monte Verde Revisited, pp. 1–12.

Fiedel, Stuart J.: "The Peopling of the New World: Present Evidence, New Theories, and Future Directions." *Journal of Archaeological Research* 8 (2000), pp. 39–103.

Ford, Richard I.: "Patterns of Prehistoric Food Production in North America." In Richard I. Ford, ed., *Prehistoric Food Production in North America* (Ann Arbor: University of Michigan, Museum of Anthropology Anthropological Papers 75), pp. 341–64.

Fritz, Gayle J.: "Early and Middle Woodland Paleoethnobotany" In C. Margaret Scarry, ed., *Foraging and Farming in the Eastern Woodlands* (Tuscaloosa, AL: University of Alabama Press, 1993), pp. 39–56.

Fritz, Gayle J. and Kidder, Tristram R.: "Recent Investigations into Prehistoric Agriculture in the Lower Mississippi Valley." *Southeastern Archaeology* 12 (1993), pp. 1–14.

Gibson, Jon L.: "Before Their Time? Early Mounds in the Lower Mississippi Valley." *Southeastern Archaeology* 13 (1994), pp. 162–86.

Gibson, Jon L.: *Ancient Earthworks of the Ouachita Valley in Louisiana* (Tallahassee, TN: Southeast Archeological Center, 1996a).

Gibson, Jon L.: "Poverty Point and Greater Southeastern Prehistory: The Culture That Did Not Fit." In Sassaman and Anderson (1996b), pp. 288–306.

Goodyear, Albert C.: "The Topper Site 2000. Results of the 2000 Allendale Paleoindian Expedition." *Legacy: Newsletter of the South Carolina Institute of Archaeology and Anthropology, University of South Carolina, Columbia* 5, no. 2 (2000), pp. 18–25.

Gremillion, Kristen J.: "The Paleoethnobotanical Record for the Mid-Holocene Southeast." In Sassaman and Anderson (1996), pp. 99–114.

Gremillion, Kristen J.: "The Development and Dispersal of Agricultural Systems in the Woodland Southeast." In Anderson and Mainfort (2002), pp. 483–501.

Grumet, Robert S.: *Historic Contact: Indian People and Colonists in Today's Northeastern United States in the Sixteenth Through Eighteenth Centuries* (Norman, OK: University of Oklahoma Press, 1995).

Hally, David J.: "The Territorial Size of Mississippian Chiefdoms." In James B. Stoltman, ed., *Archaeology of Eastern North America Papers in Honor of Stephen Williams* (Jackson, MS: Mississippi Department of Archives and History, Archaeological Report No. 25, 1993), pp. 143–68.

Haynes, C. Vance: "Contributions of Radiocarbon Dating to the Geochronology of the Peopling of the New World." In R. E. Taylor, A. Long, and R. S. Kra, eds., *Radiocarbon after Four Decades* (New York: Springer-Verlag, 1992), pp. 219–36.

Johnson, Jay K.: "Prehistoric Exchange in the Southeast." In Timothy Baugh and Jonathan Ericson, eds., *Prehistoric Exchange Systems in North America* (New York: Plenum Press, 1994), pp. 99–126.

Johnson, Jay K. and Brookes, Samuel O.: "Benton Points, Turkey Tails and Cache Blades: Middle Archaic Exchange in the Southeast." *Southeastern Archaeology* 8 (1989), pp. 134–45.

Kent, Barry C.: *Susquehanna's Indians* (Harrisburg: The Pennsylvania Historical and Museum Commission, 1984).

Knight, Vernon J., Jr.: "Social Organization and the Evolution of Hierarchy in Southeastern Chiefdoms." *Journal of Anthropological Research* 46 (1990), pp. 1–23.

Knight, Vernon J., Jr.: "The Formation of the Creeks." In Charles M. Hudson and Carmen Chaves Tesser, eds., *The Forgotten Centuries* (Athens, GA: University of Georgia Press, 1994), pp. 373–92.

Lyon, Edwin A.: *A New Deal for Southeastern Archaeology* (Tuscaloosa, AL: University of Alabama Press, 1996).

Marquardt, William and Watson, Patty Jo: "The Shell Mound Archaic of Western Kentucky." In James Phillips and James Brown, eds., *Archaic Hunters and Gatherers in the American Midwest* (New York: Academic Press, 1983), pp. 323–39.

McAvoy, Joseph M. and McAvoy, Lynn D.: *Archaeological Investigations of Site 44SX202, Cactus Hill, Sussex County, Virginia* (Richmond: Virginia Department of Historic Resources, Research Report Series No. 8, 1997).

McGhee, R. and Tuck, James: "An Archaic Indian Burial Mound in Labrador." *Scientific American* 235 (1977), pp. 122–29.

Meltzer, David J. and Smith, Bruce D.: "Paleo-Indian and Early Archaic Subsistence Strategies in Eastern North America." In Sarah Neusius, ed., *Foraging, Collecting, and Harvesting: Archaic Period Subsistence and Settlement in the Eastern Woodlands* (Carbondale: Center for Archaeological Investigations, Southern Illinois University, 1986), pp. 1–30.

Meltzer, David, Grayson, Donald K., Ardila, Gerardo, Barker, Alex, Dincauze, Dena, Haynes, C. Vance, Mena, Francisco, Nunex, Lautaro, and Stanford, Dennis: "On the Pleistocene Antiquity of Monte Verde, Southern Chile." *American Antiquity* 62 (1997), pp. 659–63.

Milner, George R.: "Epidemic Disease in the Postcontact Southeast: A Reappraisal." *Midcontinental Journal of Archaeology* 5 (1980), pp. 39–56.

Milner, George R., Anderson, David G., and Smith, Marvin T.: "The Distribution of Eastern Woodlands Peoples at the Prehistoric and Historic Interface." In David Brose and Robert Mainfort, eds., *Societies in Eclipse* (Washington, DC: Smithsonian Institution Press, 2001), pp. 9–18.

Morgan, Lewis Henry: *Ancient Society* (New York: World Publishing Company, 1877).

Morse, Dan F.: *Sloan: A Paleoindian Dalton Cemetery in Arkansas* (Washington, DC: Smithsonian Institution Press, 1997).

Muller, Jon L.: *Mississippian Political Economy* (New York: Plenum Press, 1997).

Nassaney, Michael S. and Pyle, Kendra: "The Adoption of the Bow and Arrow in Eastern North America: A View from Central Arkansas." *American Antiquity* 64 (1999), pp. 243–63.

Pacheco, Paul J., ed.: *A View from the Core: A Synthesis of Ohio Hopewell Archaeology* (Columbus, OH: The Ohio Archaeological Council, Inc., 1996).

Parkinson, William A.: *The Archaeology of Tribal Societies* (Ann Arbor, Michigan: International Monographs in Prehistory, 2002).

Pauketat, Timothy R. and Emerson, Thomas E., eds.: *Cahokia: Domination and Ideology in the Mississippian World* (Lincoln, NE: University of Nebraska Press, 1997).

Pendergast, James F.: "The Significance of Some Marine Shell Excavated on Iroquoian Archaeological Sites in Ontario." In Charles Hayes and Lynn Ceci, eds., *Proceedings of the 1986 Shell Bead Conference* (Rochester: Rochester Museum and Science Center Research Records 20, 1989), pp. 97–112.

Piatak, Bruce J.: "The Tomoko Mound Complex in Northeast Florida." *Southeastern Archaeology* 12 (1994), pp. 109–18.

Ramenofsky, Ann F.: *Vectors of Death* (Albuquerque, NM: University of New Mexico Press, 1987).

Russo, Michael: *Archaic Sedentism on the Florida Coast: A Case Study from Horr's Island.* (Ph.D. dissertation., Department of Anthropology, University of Florida; Ann Arbor, MI: University Microfilms, 1991).

Russo, Michael: "A Brief Introduction to the Study of Archaic Mounds in the Southeast." *Southeastern Archaeology* 13 (1994a), pp. 89–93.

Russo, Michael: "Why We Don't Believe in Archaic Ceremonial Mounds and Why We Should: The Case from Florida." *Southeastern Archaeology* 13 (1994b), pp. 93–109.

Sahlins, Marshall D.: "The Segmentary Lineage: An Organization of Predatory Expansion." *American Anthropologist* 63 2, 1961), pp. 332–45.

Sahlins, Marshall D.: "Poor Man, Rich Man, Big Man, Chief: Political Types in Melanesia and Polynesia." *Comparative Studies in Society and History* 5 (3, 1963), pp. 285–303.

Sahlins, Marshall D.: *Stone Age Economics* (New York: Aldine Publishing Company, 1972).

Sassaman, Kenneth E.: *Early Pottery in the Southeast: Tradition and Innovation in Cooking Technology* (Tuscaloosa, AL: University of Alabama Press, 1993).

Sassaman, Kenneth E. and Anderson, David G., eds.: *Archaeology of the Mid-Holocene Southeast* (Gainesville, FL: University Presses of Florida, 1996).

Sassaman, Kenneth and Ledbetter, Jerald: "Middle and Late Archaic Architecture." In Sassaman and Anderson (1996), pp. 75–96.

Saunders, Joe, Allen, Thurman, and Saucier, Roger: "Four Archaic? Mound Complexes in Northeast Louisiana." *Southeastern Archaeology* 13 (1994), pp. 134–53.

Saunders, Joe W., Mandel, Rolfe D., Saucier, Roger T., Allen, E. Thurman, Hallmark, C. T., Johnson, Jay K., Jackson, Edwin H., Allen, Charles M., Stringer, Gary L., Frink, Douglas S., Feathers, James K., Williams, Stephen, Gremillion, Kristen J., Vidrine, Malcolm F., and Jones, Reca: "A Mound Complex in Louisiana at 5400–5000 Years Before the Present." *Science* 277 (1997), pp. 1796–9.

Scarry, John R., ed.: *Political Structure and Change in the Prehistoric Southeastern United States* (Gainesville, FL: University Presses of Florida, 1996).

Service, Elman R.: *Primitive Social Organization* (New York: Random House, 1971).

Silverberg, Robert: *The Mound Builders of Ancient America: The Archaeology of a Myth* (Greenwich, CT: New York Graphic Society, Ltd, 1968).

Simak, Jan F., Faulkner, Charles H., Frankenberg, Susan R., Klippel, Walter E., Ahlman, Todd M., Herrmann, Nicholas P., Sherwood, Sarah C., Walker, Renee B., Wright, W. Miles, and Yarnell, Richard: "A Preliminary Report on the Archaeology of a New Mississippian Cave Art Site in East Tennessee." *Southeastern Archaeology* 16 (1997), pp. 51–73.

Smith, Bruce D.: "The Archaeology of the Southeastern United States: From Dalton to De Soto, 10,500–500 BP." *Advances in World Archaeology* 5 (1986), pp. 1–92.

Smith, Bruce D.: *The Mississippian Emergence* (Washington DC: Smithsonian Institution Press, 1990).

Smith, Bruce D.: *Rivers of Change: Essays on Early Agriculture in Eastern North America* (Washington DC: Smithsonian Institution Press, 1992a).

Smith, Bruce D.: "Prehistoric Plant Husbandry in Eastern North America." In C. W. Cowan and Patty Jo Watson, eds., *The Origins of Agriculture: An International Perspective* (Washington, DC: Smithsonian Institution Press, 1992b), pp. 101–19.

Smith, George S. and Ehrenhard, John E., eds.: *Protecting the Past* (Boca Raton, FL: CRC Press, 1991).

Smith, Maria O.: "Biocultural Inquiry into Archaic Period Populations of the Southeast: Trauma and Occupational Stress." In Sassaman and Anderson (1996), pp. 134–54.

Smith, Marvin T.: *Coosa: The Rise and Fall of a Southeastern Mississippian Chiefdom.* (Gainesville, FL: University Press of Florida, 2000).

Smith, Marvin T.: *Archaeology of Aboriginal Culture Change: Depopulation During the Early Historic Period* (Gainesville, FL: University Press of Florida, 1987).

Snow, Dean R.: *The Archaeology of New England* (New York: Academic Press, 1980).

Snow, Dean R.: "Mohawk Demography and the Effects of Exogenous Epidemics on American Indian Populations." *Journal of Anthropological Archaeology* 15 (1996), pp. 160–82.

Snow, Dean R. and Lanphear, Kim: "European Contact and Indian Depopulation in the Northeast: The Timing of the First Epidemics." *Ethnohistory* 35 (1988), pp. 15–33.

Snow, Dean R. and Starna, William: "Sixteenth Century Depopulation: A View from the Mohawk Valley." *American Anthropologist* 91 (1989), pp. 142–9.

Squier, Ephraim G. and Davis, E. H., eds.: *Ancient Monuments of the Mississippi Valley* (Washington, DC: Smithsonian Contributions to Knowledge, no. 1, 1848).

Steponaitis, Vincas: "Prehistoric Archaeology in the Southeastern United States, 1970–1985." *Annual Review of Anthropology* 14 (1986), pp. 363–404.

Stoltman, James B.: "The Archaic tradition." In W. Green, J. B. Stoltman, and A. B. Kehoe, eds., Introduction to Wisconsin Archaeology. *Wisconsin Archaeologist* 67 3–4, 1986), pp. 207–38.

Thomas, Cyrus: *Report of the Mound Explorations of the Bureau of Ethnology* (Washington, DC: Bureau of American Ethnology Annual Report 12, 1894).

Trigger, Bruce G.: *Natives and Newcomers: Canada's "Heroic Age" Reconsidered* (Kingston: McGill-Queen's University Press, 1985).

Walthall, John A. and Koldehoff, Brad: "Hunter-gatherer Interaction and Alliance Formation: Dalton and the Cult of the Long Blade." *Plains Anthropologist* 43 (1998), pp. 257–73.

Willey, Gordon R. and Jeremy A. Sabloff: *A History of American Archaeology* (London: Thames and Hudson, 1974).

Wray, Charles F.: *Manual for Seneca Iroquois Archaeology* (Honeoye Falls: Cultures Primitive, 1973).

CHAPTER TWO

The Origins of Transatlantic Colonization

CAROLE SHAMMAS

For thousands of years, up to about AD 1500, the Americas were populated almost exclusively by Pacific migrants and their descendants. That situation changed in the sixteenth and seventeenth centuries as several million people from western Europe and western Africa arrived in what to them was a New World. Beginning in the Caribbean, sailing on towards Mexico and the Andes, creeping along the coasts of the Atlantic and even the Pacific, prowling along the major waterways of the North American and South American interiors were boatload after boatload of sword, Bible, and charter-bearing Portuguese, Spanish, English, French, and Dutch, followed by indentured workers or slaves imported from Africa. What prompted this colonization from the Atlantic is the subject of this chapter.

Technology versus Biology

Often textbooks refer to this period as the "Age of Discovery," commencing with explorations by Vasco da Gama, Columbus, Magellan, and Balboa and slowly evolving into conquest over Indians and colonization for purposes of religion and trade. They rely on a master narrative that links the European expansion into the Americas with a Renaissance spirit of advancement. Probably the most widely read book of this genre over the past half-century and still worth reading today is J. H. Parry's elegantly concise *The Establishment of the European Hegemony 1415–1715: Trade and Exploration in the Age of the Renaissance* (1949). Parry covers the overseas activities of all the major expansionist powers around the globe. After reminding his readers of the cultural superiority of China and the military might of the Ottoman Turks during the fifteenth century, he goes on to recount how western Europeans, by adopting new Renaissance knowledge in navigation and shipbuilding, laid the foundation for their later dominance of the globe. The Portuguese led the way, benefiting from the royal support of Prince Henry the Navigator and King John II and the learning of Jewish astronomers driven out of the Islamic world and Christian Spain. In his narrative, Portuguese tolerance was rewarded with the information necessary to calculate a ship's latitude from the placement of the stars and the height of the sun at midday. The new, improved square and lateen rigged sailing vessels marked another advance due to their versatility in handling winds. And finally, the placing of guns on the broadside of the ship rather than just the fore and aft made it difficult for the enemy to come close enough for his archers and soldiers to attack without severe damage to his own vessel. Outfitted with these tools, an international cadre of wily but fearless Renaissance men changed the course of world history. This theme of underdogs using technology and ingenuity on the high seas to become masters of the globe can also be found in other treatments of European expansion including Jones (1964), Cipolla (1965), Boxer (1969), and Morison (1971).

This story, however, did not survive the 1990s' quincentennial celebration of America's "discovery" intact and unscathed. As one reviewer phrased it, "Columbus was mugged on the way to his own party" (Mancall, 1998, p. 31 quoting Kenneth Maxwell). Rather than a story about Europeans relying on Renaissance smarts to take over a near-empty land from primitive peoples and, in the process, making something actually worthwhile out of the resources of the Americas, the European miracle, if it could be called that, seemed now to come from biological and geographic sources. At this point, the efforts of a generation of scholars working on American Indian history and demography (Jennings, 1975; Thornton, 1987; Daniels, 1992) together with the strikingly original work of Alfred Crosby (1972, 1986) provided much of the scholarly ammunition for a new text about the early encounter between the Europeans and the Indians. Literary scholars reinterpreted the discovery narratives of the Renaissance explorers (Greenblatt, 1991), while J. M. Blaut (1993) produced a less nuanced account of their latter-day chroniclers in *The Colonizer's Model of the World*.

The fact that contact brought disease and death to many Indian societies hardly counted as news, but what really made a difference was the swing in scholarly opinion about the pre-conquest size of the aboriginal Western Hemisphere population. In the first half of the twentieth century, the low estimates of Kroeber and Mooney – 8,400,000 for the Americas and less than 1,000,000 for North America above the Rio Grande – predominated in the textbooks. In the last half of the century, views shifted and estimates that range from double to ten times those of the two American pioneers of Indian demography now enjoy much more popularity. While small villages consisting of impermanent dwellings spaced widely apart may have characterized much of early America, other areas contained inhabitants living in large cities producing written records and impressive structures. That an ecological imperialism had eradicated such complex cultures made it difficult to see the *Pinta*, *Nina*, and *Santa Maria* as anything more than ships of death. Contributing to the general funereal tone was the recognition that the European invasion was also associated with a major upheaval within the African population, whereby 12 million men, women, and children had been forced to emigrate as slaves.

The biological and demographic approach to the study of European expansion, however, goes beyond the Columbian exchange of microbes that proved so catastrophic for the Indian populations. It extends to plants and animals. Physiologist Jared Diamond (1997) revisits some of the same incidents as found in the Age of Discovery literature but attributes the outcomes to very different circumstances. Relying on the research of scholars in a variety of disciplines, he argues that much of human history can be explained by (1) the presence or absence of large seeded cereals suitable for cultivation and (2) large mammals amenable to domestication. The establishment of agricultural societies, of course, is on almost everyone's list of critical elements necessary for the building of complex societies. The limitations of certain extreme environments – deserts and polar caps – for cultivation and the raising of stock are obvious. Diamond's contribution is to point out that even some seemingly fertile areas – such as the Western Hemisphere – had significant drawbacks as sites for human food production until flora and fauna from other continents could be transferred there. The Americas had comparatively few indigenous cereals and even fewer that actually merited cultivation. The large population of Meso-America had the advantage over other Western Hemisphere cultures in being able to cultivate a good mix of crops – corn, beans, and squash. It took thousands of years for these plants to migrate up to the Atlantic seaboard of North America, and once there, they encountered a shortened growing season, due to the colder temperatures. The Americas, also, suffered from a shortage of large mammals, having lost most of them prior to human migration. Only the llama and alpaca in South America and the dog in the North remained. In contrast, Eurasia had at least eleven varieties – including horses, cows, sheep, goats, pigs – that could provide food, work, transportation, and manure. The large number of cereals and mammals available in Europe and Asia could in part be attributed to their geography. Those continents spread horizontally, meaning they shared the same latitudes. Crops and animals well adapted in one area more often could also flourish in another. The Americas and Africa had vertical axes making diffusion much more difficult. Cultivation of crops resulted in a denser population, making it easier for microbes to move from host to host. Domesticated animals brought with them their own diseases that could be carried by insects from beast to human. Europeans had a long exposure to these diseases as well as a more reliable food supply that allowed them to support a larger non-agricultural sector. Thus, the American Indian population not only lost out in food production and animal power but also fell prey to new diseases introduced by the invaders and their animals.

Little doubt remains that the factors focused upon by Crosby, Diamond, and others interested in ecological issues go a long way towards explaining the hegemonic position enjoyed by Europeans over the conquered Indians. They do not, however, explain the question raised at the beginning of this chapter: why all of a sudden did people and resources from the Atlantic pour into the Western Hemisphere?

Glory, Gold, and Gospel versus the Capitalist World System

Almost anyone who has completed elementary school in the United States can rattle off some of the stock responses to this question. In addition to the Renaissance spirit argument, the other traditional textbook explanations are based heavily on the promotional literature of the time (Wright, 1970). That literature exhorted contemporaries to bring glory to themselves and their monarchs through conquests over Indians and rival European colonial powers, win riches and wealth in the process, and spread the true Christian faith to the heathen. While the stated motives do not ring false, they do ring hollow, when text is taken simply as fact. All of the items mentioned may well have been on the typical western European's wish list c.1500, but the reader of the "gold, glory, and gospel" histories is given little assistance in connecting these coveted objectives to societal processes that would actually put bodies and equipment in boats.

In the early 1970s, as part of a new receptivity in western Europe and North America to Marxist and materialist explanations for European expansion and aggression, two major historical studies appeared, both of which focused more on societal processes than on the Renaissance man characteristics of the colonizing elite. Fernand Braudel's work on capitalism and world civilization (1973) and Immanuel Wallerstein's initial volume on the modern world system (1974) emphasized the material and economic interests at stake and stressed the global ramifications of expansion. These works masterfully fit the various geographical pieces together and placed them in a long multi-strand chronology. Wallerstein, operating within a Marxist framework, argued at the beginning of his first book that capitalism captured the world, beginning in the sixteenth century, because Europe's upper stratum appropriated surplus from the lower strata more efficiently than tribute-collecting empires could do. Thus Europe had the advantage over the technologically and governmentally more sophisticated China. Not having to deal with an elaborate imperial structure allowed its capitalist bourgeoisie to operate more freely and create the new order.

In the following chapters, however, Wallerstein's narrative turns into a general description of the social classes and political economy of Europe, and it becomes difficult to discern those elements critical to expansion. Like the subtitle of the volume, "capitalist agriculture and the origins of the European world-economy," the text offers the traditional explanation for economic development within Europe as well as overseas trade and colonization. While certainly agricultural surpluses, whether produced by enclosure or technological innovation, were a pre-condition for transatlantic activities, a capitalist farming system does not explain why Europeans first went to the Americas rather than digging canals or inventing power looms. Wallerstein was determined to find the answer to change in the means of production rather than in consumption. As he stated at one point, when critiquing Henri Pirenne and Paul Sweezy for attributing too much of the change to trade in luxuries, "I am skeptical . . . that the exchange of preciosities, however large it loomed in the conscious thinking of the European upper classes, could have sustained so colossal an enterprise as the expansion of the Atlantic world, much less accounted for the creation of a European world-economy" (Wallerstein, pp. 41–42). For a long time, the equation of non-essentials with luxuries, and the assumption that only the rich participated in the trade, interfered with connecting consumer demand to early modern European expansion.

Putting Bodies in Boats

Globally oriented historians like Wallerstein and Braudel were also hampered by the submersion of most European and American historians in a social history largely based on in-depth studies of communities. So important for the development of a more societal approach to historical research, community studies have had the shortcoming of seldom connecting their locales with national subjects much less transnational ones. The nature of the records tends to privilege the stories of those who stayed over those who left. And one thing that can be said about the study of the Atlantic world and European overseas expansion is that it is very much about those and that which left.

The application of social history techniques to overseas migration took some time. A substantial amount of research, however, has now been published and collections summarizing the state of scholarship have also appeared (Altman and Horn, eds., 1991; and Canny, ed., 1994). More than the traditional gold, glory, and gospel narratives or the global systems literature, the migration studies give a much better idea of the scale of the migration and demographic composition of the migrants, information that can then be more easily linked to developments in the country of origin.

It makes some sense to think of American colonization as the product of two somewhat separate phenomena, which, at the end of the sixteenth century, after nearly a hundred years of "discovery" and settlement, overlapped with one another. The invasions of the first half of the sixteenth century – the ones conquering Indian nations and ultimately decimating those populations, christianizing continents, and generating new ethnic groups – involved relatively small numbers of people from very restricted areas of Europe and Africa, and elicited very small amounts of interest from European heads of state and merchant communities (Kicza, 1992). The impetus for these efforts can be traced back to medieval preoccupations that were refocused on the Americas, after Catholicism's victory in Iberia and defeats in eastern Europe at the hands of the Ottoman Turks. This colonization gradually gave way to a much different recruitment and funding formula that put much bigger smiles on the faces of those in overseas trade and in charge of the royal coffers and greatly increased the numbers of those with a stake in the Americas. The stimulus for this activity had very different roots, however, from the first phase of colonization.

Table 2.1 provides some rough indication of the numbers involved in the Atlantic colonization effort between 1492 and 1700, in 50-year segments. The first segment, up to 1550, shows migration numbers of about 60,000 Spanish, 15,000 Portuguese, and 41,000 Africans. Europeans exceeded Africans by significant numbers. The African immigration grew fourfold in the next 50 years, and then by the seventeenth century outstripped European numbers. If these figures are correct, fewer numbers of Europeans arrived in the last half of the seventeenth century than had come in during the first half, despite the much larger number of colonial destinations.

Phase I: Military Adventurers and the Brothers

Much of the migration of Europeans to the Americas in the pre-1550 period can in one way or another be traced to expeditions of military adventurers. The successful ones we call conquistadors, the unsuccessful, explorers or discoverers. The Spanish leaders – Cortés, Pizarro, De Soto, Alvarado – claimed lesser gentry backgrounds and hailed from Estremadura in the southwestern portion of the Kingdom of Castile (Boyd-Bowman, 1973; Lockhart, 1972; Altman, 1989). They drew on kin and neighbors for their followers, and their servants traveled in retinues rather than under indentures. Males, mostly young, constituted 85–95 percent of this early migration. The major conquests in Mexico and Peru stimulated the increased migration from the conquerors' home town areas. The Spanish Crown sent some functionaries, both lay and religious, and encouraged in vain the development of sugar plantations in the Spanish Caribbean islands (Blackburn, 1997, p. 137). Africans first entered Spanish America as part of the entourage of those coming from Spain or the Canaries, where slavery had existed for some time, and they more often performed domestic or public works jobs in town than agricultural labor on plantations.

Scholars have noted the close correspondence between the unification of a Christian Spain under Ferdinand and Isabella and the availability of young lesser gentry and their followers from their own localities or Andalusian port towns to go on overseas expeditions. Because so many of the conquistadors had tried various occupations,

Table 2.1   Estimate of Atlantic immigration to Americas, 1492–1700 (in 000s)

Origin	to 1550	1551–1600	1601–50	1651–1700	Total
West Africa	41	161	396	615	1,212
Western Europe					
Spain	60	157	195	40	
Portugal	15	35	50	50	
Netherlands	–	*	15	10	
France	–	*	25	50	
Britain	–	*	161	197	
Ireland	–	–	10	20	
Total	75	192	456	367	1,090
Total					2,302

* under 1,000

Source: McEvedy, Colin and Jones, Richard: *Atlas of World Population History* (New York, Penguin, 1978); Lovejoy, Paul E.: "The Volume of the Atlantic Slave Trade: A Synthesis." *Journal of African History* 23 (1982), pp. 478–81; Eltis, David: "The Volume and Structure of the Transatlantic Slave Trade: A Reassessment." *William and Mary Quarterly* 3rd ser., 58 (2001), p. 45 (Table III); Morner, Magnus: "Spanish Migration to the New World prior to 1810: A Report on the State of Research." In Fredi Chiappelli, ed., *First Images of America: The Impact of the New World on the Old*, vol. 2 (Berkeley: University of California Press, 1976), p. 767; Godinho, Vitorino Magalhaes: "Portuguese Emigration from the Fifteenth to the Twentieth Century: Constants and Changes." In P. C. Emmer and Magnus Morner, eds., *European Expansion and Migration* (New York: Berg, 1992), pp. 13–48; Altman, Ida and Horn, James: "Introduction." In Ida Altman and James Horn, eds., *To Make America: European Emigration in the Early Modern Period* (Berkeley: University of California Press, 1991), p. 3; Blackburn, Robin: *The Making of New World Slavery: From the Baroque to the Modern 1492–1800* (London: Verso, 1997), pp. 168, 173; Lucassen, Jan: "The Netherlands, the Dutch, and Long Distance Migration, in the Late Sixteenth to Early Nineteenth Centuries." In Canny, N., ed., *Europeans on the Move*, pp. 175, 178, 179; Choquette, Leslie: "Recruitment of French Emigrants to Canada, 1600–1760." In Altman and Horn, eds., *To Make America*, p. 161; de Lemps, Christian Hertz: "Indentured Servants Bound for the French Antilles." In Altman and Horn, eds., *To Make America*, pp. 172–203; Canny, Nicholas: "Conclusion." In Canny, N., ed., *Europeans on the Move*, pp. 275–6; Canny, Nicholas: "English Migration," in Canny, N., ed., *Europeans on the Move*, p. 64; Smout, T. C., Landsman, N. C. and Devine, T. M.: "Scottish Emigration in the Seventeenth and Eighteenth Centuries." In Canny, N., ed., *Europeans on the Move*, p. 90; Cullen, L. M.: "The Irish Diaspora of the Seventeenth and Eighteenth Centuries," in Canny, N., ed., *Europeans on the Move*, p. 139.

seldom observed the protocols of the military, and ended up settling permanently in the Americas, Latin America historians do not characterize these men as professional soldiers (Kicza, 1992, pp. 250–253). On the other hand, the conquistadors did expect to use force or the threat of force as a means to conquer territory and claim lordship. They may not have fit the emerging concept of military adventurer as mercenary, but they did fit the traditional one of gentleman adventurer, the sort who looked to the sword as the appropriate means to distinguish oneself and benefit from the kind of social mobility laid out in the chivalric pulp fiction of the time.

Many other Europeans, aside from the Spanish, organized expeditions of this nature. We know most about the English gentleman adventurers, whose heyday extended from the 1560s through the early stages of the Virginia colony. Elizabeth I happily passed off the cost of military endeavors to the aggressive young men who graced her court. The leadership of these colonization efforts came disproportionately from the English West Country, sons of obscure gentry, such as Ralegh, his half-brother, Humphrey Gilbert, Francis Drake, and Richard Grenville, who hoped for advancement through military exploits (Shammas, 1978). They alternated their activities in America with soldiering on the Continent and in Ireland, the primary area of colonization for the English in the sixteenth century (Quinn, 1974; Canny, 1976). Their followers came from the coastal towns of the West Country and the nation's major port, London. Although some merchants funded these expeditions in the hope of commercial gain, the promise of looting the silver galleons of the Spanish is what attracted the most capital, and it came heavily from Elizabethan courtiers willing to gamble on piracy carried out against their most hated enemy in hopes of rich rewards (Rabb, 1967; Andrews, 1984). Elizabeth's successor, while retaining an interest in young men, had much less tolerance for provocative naval actions in the Atlantic. After James I executed Walter Ralegh in 1619 for an unauthorized expedition to South America, interest in military adventurers in the Americas declined precipitously.

The military adventurer phase of the Atlantic migration derived its impetus more from political and religious developments in Europe and the Near East than from commercial enterprise. Christian Europeans were no strangers to expansionary schemes. During the latter half of the medieval period, serious Christians, both lay and clerical, directed their energies towards the capture of Jerusalem and the defeat of the Muslim infidels. European colonists, perhaps a quarter of a million, settled in the Crusader states and held on to them for about two hundred years (Phillips, 1994, pp. 18–19). The battles of the Pope and Christian princes with Muslim princes over the centuries gave meaning and direction to the lives of European military adventurers as well as many in religious orders (Prawer, 1972). In no place was this perhaps more true than in Iberia, the southern portion of which Muslims controlled during the Middle Ages. The struggle to make the peninsula safe for Christianity lasted for hundreds of years.

The Pope's inability to reclaim the Holy Land, the spread of Islam into the Balkans, and then the 1453 taking of Constantinople by the Ottoman Turks left not only military adventurers but many religious orders all dressed up with no place to go. When in 1492 the Spaniards, winning one for the Vatican, completed the Reconquest by forcing all Muslims and Jews to convert or leave, the need to channel the energies of these new militants in a new direction intensified. Even before Luther began shaking up the Church by advertising his doubts in conspicuous places, the victory in Spain combined with the defeats at the hands of the Ottomans to encourage a millenarian frame of mind among the Christian brotherhoods and a new resolve to save souls. The Portuguese had an early triumph by successfully engineering the conversion of the Kongo Kingdom in West Central Africa (Thornton, 1983). That coup, however, was just the beginning.

Attention to the Protestant Reformation and the setbacks suffered by the Pope in northern Europe, as well as doubts raised by historians of American Indians over the sincerity of the newly converted (Trigger, 1985, ch. 5), have to some extent obscured the incredible successes of the Catholic Church worldwide in the sixteenth and seventeenth centuries. A recent trend in historiography to consider the Counter-Reformation more as a global Catholic Reformation, however, suggests a reassessm⁻ under way (Hsia, 1998). The missionary activities of the evangelical religio among them Augustinians, Dominicans, but especially Franciscans an(

represent about the only long-term successes Europeans have ever had in christianizing non-Europeans around the globe. It could be argued that it was the Orders, with their promiscuous baptizing and mission building, that transformed a military conquest into Spanish cultural hegemony in much of North America, South America, and the Philippines. They accomplished this task with very few people. The Franciscans' spiritual invasion of Mexico took off with the "Twelve Apostles" who walked from Veracruz to Mexico City in 1524 for the saving of souls (Ricard, 1933, Eng. tr. 1966; Phelan, 1956 rev. ed. 1970). The power of the Franciscans was greatest in frontier areas. The sprawl of the empire northward depended on friars going into New Mexico and later California and establishing settlements around missions (Gutiérrez, 1991). The military adventurers came and went, but the missions and small bands of evangelists remained.

The story of the Jesuits is still controversial and underdeveloped, although new studies are finally appearing, most notably Dauril Alden's *The Making of an Enterprise: The Society of Jesus in Portugal, its Empire, and Beyond 1540–1750* (1996). The principal founder of the order, Inigo Lopez de Recaldo, a contemporary of both Cortés and Luther, began life as a Spanish military man from the Basque region. A French cannonball in 1521 put an end to his career as a glory-seeking, "amorous knight." Turning to the spiritual life, he tried meditation, pilgrimages, and university studies. Rejecting the new Protestant movement, he organized around him a group of young followers, changed his surname to reflect the place of his birth, Loyola, and pushed for papal approval of his circle, the Society of Jesus, in 1540. Dedicating themselves to education, the Jesuits spread out over the globe, even though their numbers were small. The order in Spain consisted of fewer than 2,000 men during the sixteenth and seventeenth centuries, yet they sent missionaries to Angola, Mozambique, Ethiopia, Goa, China, Moluccas, Japan, Philippines, Macao, and perhaps most prominently to Brazil. In the seventeenth century they became the most dynamic element in the French colonies, even though the earliest secular leaders there were typically Huguenot (Lippy, Choquette, and Poole, 1992). The Jesuits managed to have those provisions in the Edict of Nantes granting limited toleration to Protestants eliminated in New France to get rid of their critics. From Canada the missionaries expanded into the Great Lakes and traveled down the Mississippi River.

Western European heads of state showed less enthusiasm for the conquest of American bodies and souls than did their militant knights and priests. These monarchs directed themselves more towards solidifying control over contiguous territory and eliminating rival forces than to building far-flung empires. The Hapsburgs and the Tudors might allow a region or principality to retain some unique traditional right or custom, but they had little tolerance for independent armies within their own realms (Elliott, 1963; Stone, 1965; Ohlmeyer, 1998). Without crusades or civil wars, opportunities for lordship and tributes were nil. Patron–client relationships deteriorated, producing what some have called a crisis of the aristocracy. Not only did the political landscape change but so did the nature of warfare itself. What Geoffrey Parker (1996, 2nd ed.) has dubbed the "Military Revolution" changed fighting from individual combat on horse to large infantries, the replacement of bows, pikes, and swords with firearms and the increased reliance on cannons both on land and sea. Warfare on the Continent was an enterprise for a head of state with a bureaucratized army bolstered by mercenaries. On sea, heavy guns ran up the cost of a navy, although a small window of opportunity existed for the privateer in the sixteenth century. The English put cheap guns on small ships, enabling West Country native, Francis Drake, and others like him to achieve fame and fortune (Rodger, 1998). The size of the vessels engaged in these activities, however, ill suited the needs of colonization projects.

The Americas were the last crusade for this warrior class. During the first half of the sixteenth century, these Spanish military adventurers covered an enormous amount of territory and spread an impressive array of microbes over the Americas, but as land developers they left something to be desired. When the Indian population dwindled to nothing, as it did in the Caribbean, the Spanish exited en masse. Very small numbers of Spanish women migrated, making the reproduction of a Spanish population abroad difficult. Merchants and Crown had limited interest in their activities. The Crown, tired of destructive behavior, turned against the adventurers and in proclamations beginning in 1542 removed the Indians from the colonists' direct supervision and later gave authority in "discoveries" to the religious orders. What renewed the enthusiasm of the Spanish Crown was the discovery of large silver deposits followed by a mining boom in the late sixteenth century (Barrett, 1990, pp. 230–238).

Ironically, the same mining boom that ended the era of the conquistador allowed a whole new crop of military adventurers from other countries to obtain funding from their monarchs or merchants to plunder the ships of the Spanish. Eager to be rid of these potentially dangerous subjects, monarchs for a time happily authorized their expeditions. Yet, as mentioned above with Ralegh in 1619 and earlier with the royal proclamations against the conquistadors, heads of state happily abandoned them when they proved troublesome. Then of course these military adventurers required a sedentary society to conquer. The men that had found such societies often settled with Indian women, but those who found no appropriate cultures to conquer left. The relatively limited numbers of Spanish and the prevalence of small-scale communities of Indians in the Americas suggest that over time the European identity of the conquistadors would have disappeared within the still large Indian population. Fabulously rich silver mines rekindled the interest of the Spanish but such sites surfaced only slightly more often than civilizations on the scale of the Aztec and Inca. In short, the long-term viability of this group serving as a catalyst for large-scale emigration and propagation seems questionable. Europeans would need something else to insure a continual stream of bodies in boats.

Phase II: European Consumer Demand and the Planters' Complex

That something else began to show its potential in the late sixteenth century, steadily grew in consequence during the seventeenth century, and remained the most important element in transatlantic migration and investment up to the American Revolution. In Table 2.1 on immigration, the steady increase in the numbers from Africa and a significant proportion of the influx from Europe can be attributed to the growth of what Philip Curtin (1998) has termed the "plantation complex." These highly capitalized agricultural enterprises produced sugar, cacao, coffee, and tobacco, relying in turn on Indians, European indentured servants, and finally African slaves for labor. Curtin's pathbreaking analysis of slave trade statistics (1969) forced the academy to deal with the importance of the African Atlantic migration. His work is now being augmented and re-analyzed by a group of scholars associated with the W. E. B. DuBois database project (Eltis and Richardson, eds., 1997; Eltis, 2001).

What had happened? European consumer demand for tobacco smoked in pipes, for sugar, used as a sweetener or to make molasses or rum, and caffeine drinks – chocolate in Iberia, coffee on the Continent, and eventually tea in the English-speaking world – rose at phenomenal rates in the seventeenth century and made the cultivation and trade in these commodities as well as the traffic in slaves among the most lucrative businesses in the world. The promotional literature of the time stressed the importance of the Indies both West and East as a market for woolen cloth, but apparently most merchants entered these trades because of the demand for tropical goods by western Europeans (Brenner, 1993). There is little evidence that, initially, governments encouraged this consumption. In fact, with tobacco, monarchs tried to suppress it (Braudel, 1973, p. 190). Only when royal authorities grasped the value of the import duties these commodities could provide did they become more enthusiastic. Rather the support came initially from merchant–planter alliances formed to profit from the popularity of these high energy and appetite-appeasing tropical goods among elites, town dwellers, and even eventually the rural population (Mintz, 1985; Shammas, 1990; Steensgaard, 1990; Goodman, 1993). Seemingly trivial commodities changed the dietary habits of the western European population.

This development, however, began gradually. Before Columbus set sail, the Genoese had collaborated with the Portuguese in Madeira and with the Spanish in the Canary Islands to set up sugar plantations worked by African slaves (Verlinden, 1970). While the Spanish, early in the sixteenth century, tried developing a sugar crop in both the West Indies and then Mexico, these efforts either failed or captured no more than a local market. It was the Portuguese colonies in Brazil that ultimately made the breakthrough, although this did not happen overnight either. Brazilian Indians showed little interest in the kind of employment opportunities offered on Iberian sugar plantations. The Portuguese of this period considered the East Indies more promising than the Americas, and so very small numbers migrated to Brazil. Not until Portuguese merchants and their Italian and Flemish partners experienced problems with sugar production in Madeira and San Tome did the Brazilian plantation economy grow. The late sixteenth-century rise in production and the importation of African slaves went hand in hand (Schwartz, 1985; Phillips, 1990, pp. 57–63). From 1600 to 1650 over 180,000 Africans entered Brazil, mainly to plant sugar. The profitability of the sugar plantations attracted the Dutch, always stalking Portuguese enterprises, and led to the first plantation complex war, a struggle in the mid-seventeenth century over Portuguese holdings in both Brazil, the site of production, and Angola, the source of labor (Blackburn, 1997, pp. 166–215).

Since Brazil, like the Atlantic Islands, was situated relatively close to Lisbon and to the western coast of Africa, and since the Portuguese had extensive experience by the sixteenth century with sugar cultivation and trade, that country's emergence as a leader in plantation production is not surprising. What mostly requires explanation about the Brazilian boom is the African side of things. How was it, in an age when most cultures had developed elaborate social mechanisms to restrict the mobility of labor, that so many Africans involuntarily became available for work thousands of miles away?

Historians have often explained the volume of slave sales as being a result of African desperation and ignorance as well as European slave-catching expeditions. Walter Rodney in *How Europe Underdeveloped Africa* (1981 rev. ed.) argued that an economically aggressive and technologically superior Europe set the terms of trade for

Africa. Africans responded to "*external* factors." While many African societies attempted to stay out of this commerce in flesh, their leaders, "when bamboozled by European goods," had little choice but to "raid outside their societies as well as to exploit internally by victimizing some of their own subjects" (pp. 79–82). One line of research, therefore, has looked at the history of West African politics and war to measure the dramatic "transformation" produced by a trade of unprecedented capitalist intensity (Lovejoy, 1989). An alternative interpretation, advanced by John Thornton (1998 rev. ed., chapter 3) maintains that sixteenth-century Africa should not be confused with its nineteenth-century self. Africans of the early modern era had a well-developed economic system with many commodities to trade, including iron and textiles. Specifically, he has challenged the notion that Africans were not full participants in the global economy and did not understand slave markets. Ownership in labor rather than ownership of land formed the basis of their system of wealth. "Slavery was widespread in Atlantic Africa because slaves were the only form of private, revenue-producing property recognized in African law" (p. 74). The economy of many African nations, before the European trade commenced, depended heavily on selling men and especially women, often enemies captured in wars but also convicts and debtors, to obtain goods. Europeans tapped into this system. European and African cultures, in his view, jointly produced the plantation complex. The economic dependency characteristic of Africa in the later colonial period should not be projected back into this earlier time.

The success or at least the viability of nearly all colonial ventures of the seventeenth century depended on the commerce in tropical goods. The most successful seventeenth-century colonies in terms of immigration and mercantile investment were those that cultivated tropical goods on plantations. The first permanent English colony, Virginia, was not successful until it traded in its military adventurers for tobacco planters (McCusker and Menard, 1985, ch. 6). Maryland adopted the same staple. These plantation colonies primarily employed indentured servants until the end of the century, when a declining supply of such labor combined with increasing English participation in the slave trade produced a shift to Africans. The profits from the trade enabled planters to make this investment in a more stable workforce. English possessions in the West Indies also started out with tobacco but switched to sugar in the mid-seventeenth century and began importing large numbers of African slaves. The London port books in 1686 indicate the dominant position of these two commodities in transatlantic trade: 88 percent of the value of imports from the West Indies and 86 percent from the 13 colonies derived from tobacco or sugar products, with the West Indian sugar far outstripping everything else (Zahedieh, 1998, p. 410). Out of approximately 360,000 seventeenth-century British immigrants to America, over 80 percent went to the plantation colonies of the West Indies or the southern mainland.

To some economic historians, these tropical goods dominated the societies of the Caribbean and the southern mainland in the same way that extractive commodities such as fur, fish, and silver ruled areas of Canada, Mexico, and South America. Consequently, they advocate a "staple thesis" approach to studying the development of their societies, where the characteristics and fortunes of the crop determine not only the growth rate but such things as the composition of the workforce, and the degree of urbanization (McCusker and Menard, 1985, ch. 1).

Reformation Era Christianity and the Securing of European Cultural Hegemony

Given the overwhelming importance of plantation colonies in terms of immigration and trade, should we infer that the Reformation and militant Protestantism had little significance once the trade in tobacco, sugar, and other lucrative commodities developed? Not necessarily. As noted in the case of the Catholic religious orders, sheer numbers do not tell the whole story. Chartered trading companies financed the migration of an unfree labor force and a transient maritime community, but what proved extremely important in producing a free migrant class and natural population growth were the upheavals in the ecclesiastical establishment of western European countries. The English, of particular relevance here because they are always cited as the most successful in sending out colonists to America, relied heavily on Protestant sectarians – Puritans, Separatists, Huguenots, Quakers, Anglo-Catholics, and, during the period of Cromwellian dominance, Anglican Cavaliers – to build provincial societies abroad during the seventeenth century (Fischer, 1989).

Many sectarians actually settled in plantation colonies, including the Caribbean. As A. P. Newton (1914) pointed out many years ago and as Karen Kupperman's book *Providence Island 1630–1641: The Other Puritan Colony* (1993) has so effectively reminded us, leading Puritan political figures of the 1630s created not only a City on a Hill in the stony soil of Massachusetts but also a West Indies settlement where plantation slavery and privateering predominated. By 1641, Kupperman observes, when the Spanish invaded Providence Island, they found more slaves than whites. In the later seventeenth century, Quaker merchants set up shop in the West Indies. Even those sectarians who went to the northern colonies and founded the major port cities of Boston, Philadelphia, and New York prospered mainly by provisioning the West Indies (Bailyn, 1955; Tolles, 1948, p. 87; Wilkenfeld, 1978, pp.112–13 and 140–1). In the much smaller migrations of the Dutch and the French, the numbers going to the West Indies greatly exceeded those headed for the colder climes of New York and Canada. Religious motivation did not conflict necessarily with participation in the plantation complex. Huguenots, fleeing to the Americas after Louis XIV's reversal on toleration, settled in both northern cities and southern plantations (Butler, 1983).

Historians continue to debate whether the New England migration of the 1630s, the most famous of the sectarian movements across the Atlantic, occurred for strictly religious reasons (Anderson, 1991, ch. 1) or whether a combination of religious, political, and socioeconomic concerns provoked the move (Breen and Foster, 1973; Cressy, 1987). At the very least, however, being at odds with the religious establishment of one's nation-state seemed to provide that extra push onto a ship and also to serve as an incentive for investment in the New World, whether in support of sectarian or non-sectarian undertakings (Sacks, 1991; Brenner, 1993).

One of the most important characteristics of migrating Protestant sects, wherever they alighted, was that they involved families. All the other major European migrant classes – military adventurers, religious orders, merchant planters, and indentured servants – were typically 90 percent or more male, usually young adults. A recent analysis of the seventeenth-century settler population in the two Puritan colonies of Massachusetts Bay and Providence Island shows that young adult men were also over-represented in the migration, but males exceeded females by a much lower ratio, about

60:40, than in plantation colonies (Archer, 1990; Games, 1999). The greater presence of women allowed sectarian populations to grow at a faster pace than those in other colonies. Massachusetts Bay inhabitants even registered higher fertility rates than their seventeenth-century British counterparts at home (Smith, 1972). The willingness of the English to allow sectarian settlement by their own and by their neighbors' troublesome Protestants secured the northern portion of North America for the British Crown and boosted the population of their southern and West Indian colonies as well.

A new historiography on the ideology and language of national identity has argued for a strain of militant Protestantism that sustained British colonization efforts. The great popularity of theories of imagined national communities and shared public spheres (combined with work on the building of national strength and feelings in the eighteenth century by scholars such as Linda Colley [1992]) has recently prompted intellectual and literary historians of Tudor–Stuart England to renew acquaintance with the promotional tracts and policy papers used so extensively by the gold, glory, and gospel scholarship of a generation ago. Accordingly, these scholars have gone back to the words of Tudor–Stuart expansionists such Hakluyt, Purchas, and Ralegh as well as dramatists and poets (Helgerson, 1992, ch. 4; Armitage, 2000; Bach, 2000) to find the origins of transatlantic imperial thought. The strongest evidence for a militant Protestant–Imperial link comes in the "Western Design" of the Puritan Commonwealth's head of state, Oliver Cromwell (Armitage, 1992). There is not much of a consensus, however, as to the role that should be assigned to nation-state building in the creations of western European empires.

Western European Nation-State Building and American Colonization

Generally, the transatlantic migrations of the sixteenth and seventeenth centuries were not state projects. Nations farmed out the task of colonization to private groups (Greene, 1994). Politically, the period seemed a propitious time for building nation-states but not empires. Monarchs emptied their treasuries to defend or extend their European boundaries, and they began to encourage a territorial sense of nation, an endeavor that conflicted with the concept of a transatlantic realm. Furthermore, the Reformation seemingly announced that the Protestants at least had abandoned their connections with a medieval universal empire of Christians (Pagden, 1995). Two recent authors of books on early modern English imperial thought and behavior argue essentially that a distinct idea of an empire built on trade and Protestantism did not exist prior to the Glorious Revolution of 1688, and even the Cromwellian period presents a mixed picture (Armitage, 2000; Lenman, 2001). Those in the British Isles inclined toward imperial thought in the sixteenth and early seventeenth centuries could think no further than Ireland. Even the Cromwellian period presents a mixed picture. His Western Design ran counter to the emerging republican ideology among the English revolutionaries, who feared that empire might bring luxury, dissolute manners, standing armies, tyrants, and ultimately destruction. When eighteenth-century imperial theory did evolve, it came from provincials – Irish unionists, merchant–planter lobbies, and colonial officials – not the metropolitan center of the state.

By focusing so closely on the underdevelopment of imperial theory during the first two centuries of American colonization, does one risk obscuring the belligerent nature of early modern European states in the Atlantic world? Those viewing the situation from a global perspective to determine why western Europeans, rather than the subjects of more substantial empires, came to dominate American colonization, invariably come back to the role of nation-state building in encouraging aggressive behavior overseas (Levenson, ed., 1967; Abernethy, 2000). The divergent paths taken by China and western Europe in overseas expansion were not due to big gaps in living standards or technology but were heavily influenced by the objectives of the ruling dynasties. The Qing rulers of the Chinese empire took a jaundiced view of any migration unrelated to the shoring up of its imperial boundaries and the protection of its ancestral homelands in Manchuria (Pomerantz, 2000)

By contrast, in western Europe, the existence of culturally homogeneous yet autonomous states, it is theorized, led to heightened competition among them. This competitive environment is seen as promoting colonization, especially after one kingdom, the Spanish, had been so successful in its transatlantic endeavors. Examination of the political behavior, as opposed to the political treatises, of those around royal courts, in the armies, and on the seas as well as the tolerance, if not the bankrolling, of expansionist interests by supposedly insular-minded monarchs results in an alternative interpretation of state intentions. In the case of England, attention is drawn to the strong anti-Spanish, pro-expansion lobby beginning with the sixteenth-century West Country privateers and continuing with the forces behind the Virginia Company that not only helped put bodies in boats but offered an alternative foreign policy much more dedicated to transatlantic conquest than the official views of Elizabeth, James I, and Charles I. Disruptive military adventurers and religious sects were allowed, albeit at their own expense, to expand the realm into America. Puritan politicians pressured the Crown to build a naval force that could counter the Catholic powers of Spain and France and secure plantation trade. The alternative policy became the official policy with Cromwell's assumption of power during the Interregnum, when he funded a state navy and implemented navigation acts. After the Restoration, these policies continued with the Stuart kings incorporating American proprietaries into the royal patronage system (Webb, 1979; Braddick, 1998; Israel, 1998; Pestana, forthcoming). England had become a major colonial power, still behind Spain but vying with Portugal for second place in terms of American subjects and land occupied. When the expansionist lobby is considered as part of the polity and comparisons are made with the activities of empires in Asia and Africa, the aggressive pursuit of transatlantic territory appears to be part and parcel of the western European nation-state building process.

Conclusion

The dominance of the Atlantic migrants over the descendants of the Pacific does not have one explanation. The emphasis of the traditional historians of discovery on the Renaissance spirit of European colonizers has invoked serious criticism, especially from those studying American Indian societies. Disease rather than technological superiority is now given much more importance in explaining the inability of the indigenous population to repel or subject the European invaders. The way Indian nations shaped the settlement patterns of European colonies has also emerged as an important area of study.

Just as crucial as the decline of the Indian population is the question of what prompted the continual shiploads of Europeans and Africans setting sail for the Americas during the sixteenth and seventeenth centuries. The work of historians such as Fernand Braudel and Immanuel Wallerstein in the 1970s emphasized that it was a global narrative. Centuries-old conflicts with the Muslim world had encouraged the expansionary tendencies of certain social groups, especially military adventurers and militant religious orders. The stalemate that developed after the rise of the Ottomans and the success of the Spanish Reconquest meant that the traditional Christian target for expansion had disappeared. The growth of centralized monarchies in western Europe precluded adventuring and proselytizing at home unless one aimed at a civil war and in Europe unless sanctioned by one's prince. So the conquistadors and the brothers made their physical and spiritual conquests across the Atlantic. For historians to get at the sources of migration and investment, however, required the application of social or community history techniques. The heavily male character of the migration and its dependence on the discovery of affluent sedentary cultures suggests that over the long term, the great conquests may have left little behind them in the Americas but myths about the origins of men on horses and great plagues. The activities of the religious orders provided greater institutional permanence, but the brothers numbered few as well.

The discovery of silver mines in the mid-sixteenth century kept the Spanish imperial project afloat. For the rest of the Europeans – Portuguese, British, Dutch, French – however, it was the consumer demand for tropical goods and the availability of a bound labor force that ultimately assured the continued expansion. Historians of Africa, Europe, and the American colonies have uncovered the importance of the plantation complex in the creation of an Atlantic world. Demand among European consumers lured merchants and planters to the Americas to realize profit margins unavailable from other pursuits. The need for a steady supply of labor gave African slave traders the edge, since their bound workers were just what European commercial interests saw as appropriate for hard labor in the distant Americas. The parts of the story most underdeveloped at this point and most likely to change as more research on African nations appears are the conditions along the western portion of the sub-continent that contributed to the increased levels of slave sales.

The cultural identity of the European population might well have been subsumed through ethnogenesis, if it had not been for the Protestant Reformation and the endless variations of sectarians who traveled to English colonies, frequently with their families and usually with more wealth than other transplanted Europeans. Their demographic success, out of all proportion to their original migration numbers, gave a peculiar cast to the northern British colonies. The Puritans' political importance in England and Scotland and their capture of the government in the mid-seventeenth century insured support for expansion and even military intervention in the Americas. In answering the frequently asked question of why western Europe rather than the more developed portions of Asia came to dominate the Americas, opinions are split as to the importance of the nation-building process in encouraging imperial structures. More consensus exists concerning the reasons for the growth and permanence of the settlements. It appears that mercantile efforts to satisfy consumer cravings and political developments in Africa guaranteed a constant stream of Atlantic migrants, but that various forms of early modern Christian zealotry were what assured cultural hegemony for Europeans.

BIBLIOGRAPHY

Abernethy, David B.: *Dynamics of Global Dominance: European Overseas Empires, 1415–1980* (New Haven: Yale University Press, 2000).

Alden, Dauril: *The Making of an Enterprise: The Society of Jesus in Portugal, its Empire, and Beyond 1540–1750* (Stanford: Stanford University Press, 1996).

Altman, Ida: *Emigrants and Society: Extremadura and America in the Sixteenth Century* (Berkeley: University of California Press, 1989).

Altman, Ida and Horn, James, eds.: *"To Make America": European Emigration in the Early Modern Period* (Berkeley: University of California Press, 1991).

Anderson, Virginia Dejohn: *New England's Generation: The Great Migration and the Formation of Society and Culture in the Seventeenth Century* (Cambridge, Eng.: Cambridge University Press, 1991).

Andrews, K. R., Canny, N. P., and Hair, P. E. H., eds.: *The Westward Enterprise: English Activities in Ireland, the Atlantic, and America, 1480–1650* (Liverpool: Liverpool University Press, 1979).

Andrews, Kenneth R.: *Trade, Plunder, and Settlement: Maritime Enterprise and the Genesis of the British Empire, 1480–1630* (Cambridge, Eng.: Cambridge University Press, 1984).

Archer, Richard: "New England Mosaic: A Demographic Analysis for the Seventeenth Century." *William and Mary Quarterly* 3rd ser., 47 (1990), pp. 477–502.

Armitage, David: "The Cromwellian Protectorate and the Language of Empire." *Historical Journal* 35 (1992), pp. 531–555.

Armitage, David: *The Ideological Origins of the British Empire* (Cambridge, Eng.: Cambridge University Press, 2000).

Bach, Rebecca Ann: *Colonial Transformations: The Cultural Production of the New Atlantic World, 1580–1640* (New York: Palgrave, 2000).

Bailyn, Bernard: *The New England Merchants in the Seventeenth Century* (Cambridge, MA: Harvard University Press, 1955).

Barrett, Ward: "World Bullion Flows." In Tracy, ed., *Rise of Merchant Empires* (1990), pp. 224–54.

Blackburn, Robin: *The Making of New World Slavery: From the Baroque to the Modern 1492–1800* (London: Verso, 1997).

Blaut, James M.: *Colonizer's Model of the World: Geographical Diffusionism and the Eurocentric View of the World* (New York: Guilford Press, 1993).

Boxer, C. H.: *Portuguese Seaborne Empire 1415–1825* (New York: Knopf, 1969).

Boyd-Bowman, Peter: *Patterns of Spanish Emigration to the New World 1493–1580* (Buffalo: Council on International Studies, 1973 typescript).

Braddick, Michael J.: "The English Government, War, Trade and Settlement 1625–1688." In Canny, ed., *Oxford History of the British Empire: Origins of Empire* (1998), pp. 286–308.

Braudel, Fernand: *Capitalism and Material Life, 1400–1800*, trans. Miriam Kochan (London: Weidenfeld and Nicolson, 1973).

Breen, T. H. and Foster, Stephen: "Moving to the New World: The Character of Early Massachusetts Immigration." *William and Mary Quarterly* 3rd. ser., 30 (1973), pp. 189–222.

Brenner, Robert: *Merchants and Revolution: Commercial Change, Political Conflict, and London's Overseas Merchants 1550–1653* (Princeton: Princeton University Press, 1993).

Butler, Jon: *The Huguenots in America: A Refugee People in New World Society* (Cambridge: Harvard University Press, 1983).

Canny, Nicholas: *The Elizabethan Conquest of Ireland: A Pattern Established, 1565–1576* (New York: Barnes and Noble, 1976).

Canny, Nicholas, ed.: *Europeans on the Move: Studies on European Migration, 1500–1800* (Oxford: Clarendon Press, 1994).

Canny, Nicholas, ed.: *The Oxford History of the British Empire: The Origins of Empire* (Oxford: Oxford University Press, 1998).

Cipolla, Carlo: *Guns, Sails, and Empires: Technological Innovation and the Early Phase of European Expansion 1400–1700* (New York: Pantheon Books, 1965).

Colley, Linda: *Britons: Forging the Nation, 1707–1837* (New Haven: Yale University Press, 1992).

Cressy, David: *Coming Over: Migration and Communication between England and New England in the Seventeenth Century* (Cambridge: Cambridge University Press, 1987).

Crosby, Alfred: *The Columbian Exchange: Biological and Cultural Consequences of 1492* (Westport, CT: Greenwood Press, 1972).

Crosby, Alfred: *Ecological Imperialism: the Biological Expansion of Europe 900–1900* (New York: Cambridge University Press, 1986).

Curtin, Philip D.: *The Atlantic Slave Trade: A Census* (Madison: University of Wisconsin Press, 1969).

Curtin, Philip D.: *The Rise and Fall of the Plantation Complex: Essays in Atlantic History* (New York: Cambridge University Press, 1990, rev. ed. 1998).

Daniels, John D.: "The Indian Population of North America in 1492." *William and Mary Quarterly* 3rd ser., 49 (1992), pp. 298–320.

Diamond, Jared: *Guns, Germs, and Steel: The Fates of Human Societies* (New York: Norton & Co., 1997).

Elliott, J. H.: *Imperial Spain 1469–1716* (London: St. Martin's Press, 1963).

Eltis, David: "The Volume and Structure of the Transatlantic Slave Trade: A Reassessment." *William and Mary Quarterly* 3rd ser., 58 (2001), pp. 17–46.

Eltis, David and Richardson, David, eds.: *Routes to Slavery: Direction, Ethnicity, and Mortality in the Atlantic Slave Trade* (London: Frank Cass, 1997).

Fischer, David Hackett: *Albion's Seed: Four British Folkways in America* (New York: Oxford University Press, 1989).

Games, Alison: *Migration and the Origins of the English Atlantic World* (Cambridge, MA: Harvard University Press, 1999).

Goodman, Jordan: *Tobacco in History: The Cultures of Dependence* (London: Routledge, 1993).

Greenblatt, Stephen: *Marvellous Possessions: The Wonder of the New World* (Chicago: University of Chicago Press, 1991).

Greene, Jack P.: *Negotiated Authorities: Essays in Colonial Political and Constitutional History* (Charlottesville: University Press of Virginia, 1994), ch. 1, pp. 1–24.

Gutiérrez, Ramon: *When Jesus Came, the Corn Mothers Went Away: Marriage, Sexuality, and Power in New Mexico, 1500–1846* (Stanford: Stanford University Press, 1991).

Helgerson, Richard: *Forms of Nationhood: The Elizabethan Writing of England* (Chicago: University of Chicago Press, 1992).

Hsia, R. Po-Chia: *The World of Catholic Renewal 1540–1770* (New York: Cambridge University Press, 1998).

Israel, Jonathan: "The Emerging Empire: The Continental Perspective, 1650–1713." In Canny, ed., *The Oxford History of the British Empire: The Origins of Empire* (1998), pp. 423–44.

Jennings, Francis: *The Invasion of America: Indian Colonization and the Cant of Conquest* (Chapel Hill: University of North Carolina Press, 1975).

Jones, Howard Mumford: *O Strange New World, American Culture: The Formative Years* (New York: Viking Press, 1964).

Kicza, John E.: "Patterns in Early Spanish Overseas Expansion." *William and Mary Quarterly* 3rd ser., 49 (1992), pp. 229–253.

Kupperman, Karen: *Providence Island 1630–1641: The Other Puritan Colony* (Cambridge: Cambridge University Press, 1993).

Lenman, Bruce P.: *England's Colonial Wars 1550–1688: Conflicts, Empire, and National Identity* (Harlow, Essex: Longman, 2001).

Levenson, Joseph R., ed.: *European Expansion and the Counter-Example of Asia, 1300–1600* (Englewood Cliffs, NJ: Prentice-Hall, 1967).

Lippy, Charles H., Choquette, Robert, and Poole, Stafford: *Christianity Comes to the Americas 1492–1776* (New York: Paragon House, 1992).

Lockhart, James: *The Men of Cajamarca: A Social and Biographical Study of the First Conquerors of Peru* (Austin: University of Texas Press, 1972).

Lovejoy, Paul: "The Impact of the Atlantic Slave Trade on Africa: A Review of the Literature." *Journal of African History* 30 (1989), pp. 365–94.

Mancall, Peter: "The Age of Discovery." *Reviews in American History* 26 (1988), pp. 26–53.

Martin, John Frederick: *Profits in the Wilderness: Entrepreneurship and the Founding of New England Towns in the Seventeenth-Century* (Chapel Hill: University of North Carolina Press, 1991).

McCusker, John and Menard, Russell: *The Economy of British America 1607–1789* (Chapel Hill: University of North Carolina Press, 1985).

Mintz, Sidney: *Sweetness and Power: The Place of Sugar in Modern History* (New York: Viking Press, 1985).

Morison, Samuel Eliot: *The European Discovery of America: The Northern Voyages* (New York: Oxford University Press, 1971).

Newton, Arthur Percival: *The Colonising Activities of the English Puritans* (Port Washington, NY: Kennikat Press, 1966, orig. pub. 1914).

Ohlmeyer, Jane H.: "'Civilizinge of these rude partes:' Colonization within Britain and Ireland 1580–1640." In Canny, ed., *Oxford History of British Empire: Origins* (1998), pp. 124–147.

Pagden, Anthony: *Lords of all the World: Ideologies of Empire in Spain, Britain and France c. 1500–c.1800* (New Haven: Yale University Press, 1995).

Parker, Geoffrey: *Military Revolution: Military Innovation and the Rise of the West 1500–1800* (Cambridge: Cambridge University Press, 1988, rev. ed. 1996).

Parry, J. H.: *The Establishment of the European Hegemony 1415–1715: Trade and Exploration in the Age of the Renaissance* (New York: Harper and Row, 1961, orig. pub. 1949).

Pestana, Carla: *The Revolutionary Atlantic World, 1642–1661* (Cambridge, MA: Harvard University Press, forthcoming).

Phelan, John Leddy: *The Millennial Kingdom of the Franciscans in the New World: A Study of the Writings of Geronimo de Mendieta, 1525–1604* (Berkeley: University of California Press, 1956, rev. ed. 1970).

Phillips, Carla Rahn: "The Growth and Composition of Trade in the Iberian Empires, 1450–1750." In Tracy, ed., *Rise of Merchant Empires* (1990), pp. 34–101.

Phillips, Seymour: "The Medieval Background." In Canny, ed., *Europeans on the Move* (1994), pp. 13–25.

Pomerantz, Kenneth: *The Great Divergence: China, Europe, and the Making of the Modern World Economy* (Princeton: Princeton University Press, 2000).

Prawer, Joshua: *The Latin Kingdom of Jerusalem: European Colonialism in the Middle Ages* (London: Weidenfeld and Nicolson, 1972).

Quinn, David B.: *England and the Discovery of America, 1481–1620* (New York: Knopf, 1974).

Rabb, T. K.: *Enterprise and Empire: Merchant and Gentry Investment in the Expansion of England, 1575–1630* (Cambridge, MA: Harvard University Press, 1967).

Ricard, Robert: *The Spiritual Conquest of Mexico*, trans. Lesley Byrd Simpson (Berkeley: University of California Press, 1966, English trans. of 1933 ed.).

Rodger, N. A. M.: "Guns and Sails in the First Phase of English Colonization 1500–1650." In Canny, ed., *Oxford History of British Empire: Origins* (1998), 79–98.

Rodney, Walter: *How Europe Underdeveloped Africa* (Washington, DC: Howard University Press, 1981 rev. ed.).

Sacks, David: *The Widening Gate: Bristol and the Atlantic Community 1450–1700* (Berkeley: University of California Press, 1991).

Schwartz, Stuart B.: *Sugar Plantations in the Formation of Brazilian Society: Bahia 1550–1835* (Cambridge: Cambridge University Press, 1985).

Shammas, Carole: "English Commercial Development and American Colonization 1560–1620." In Andrews et al., *The Westward Enterprise* (1979), pp. 151–74.

Shammas, Carole: *The Preindustrial Consumer in England and America* (Oxford: Clarendon Press, 1990).

Smith, Daniel Scott: "The Demographic History of Colonial New England." *Journal of Economic History* 32 (1972), pp. 165–83.

Steensgaard, Niels: "The Growth and Composition of the Long-Distance Trade of England and the Dutch Republic before 1750." In Tracy, ed., *Rise of Merchant Empires* (1990), pp.102–52.

Stone, Lawrence: *Crisis of the Aristocracy 1558–1641* (Oxford: Clarendon Press, 1965).

Thornton, John K.: *The Kingdom of Kongo: Civil War and Transition 1641–1718* (Madison: University of Wisconsin Press, 1983).

Thornton, John: *Africa and Africans in the Making of the Atlantic World, 1400–1800* (New York: Cambridge University Press, 2nd ed., 1998).

Thornton, Russell: *American Indian Holocaust and Survival: A Population History Since 1492* (Norman, OK: University of Oklahoma Press, 1987).

Tolles, Frederick B.: *Meeting House and Counting House: The Quaker Merchants of Colonial Philadelphia 1682–1763* (Chapel Hill: University of North Carolina Press, 1948).

Tracy, James, ed.: *Rise of Merchant Empires: Long-Distance Trade in the Early Modern World 1350–1750* (Cambridge: Cambridge University Press, 1990).

Trigger, Bruce G.: *Natives and Newcomers: Canada's "Heroic Age" Reconsidered* (Kingston and Montreal: McGill-Queen's University Press, 1985).

Verlinden, Charles: *The Beginnings of Modern Colonization*, trans. Yvonne Freccaro (Ithaca, NY: Cornell University Press, 1970).

Wallerstein, Immanuel: *The Modern World System: Capitalist Agriculture and the Origins of the European World-Economy in the Sixteenth Century* (New York: Academic Press, 1974).

Webb, Stephen Saunders: *The Governors General: The English Army and the Definition of Empire, 1569–1681* (Chapel Hill: University of North Carolina Press, 1979).

Wilkenfeld, Bruce Martin: *The Social and Economic Structure of the City of New York 1695–1796* (New York: Arno Press, 1978).

Wright, Louis B.: *Glory, Gold, and Gospel: The Adventurous Times of the Renaissance Explorers* (New York: Atheneum, 1970).

Zahedieh, Nuala: "Overseas Expansion and Trade in the Seventeenth Century." In Canny, ed., *Oxford History of the British Empire: Origins of Empire* (1998), pp. 398–422.

CHAPTER THREE

Ecology

JOHN BROOKE

The post-Columbian expansion of Europe unleashed vast ecological transformations in North America and the wider Atlantic world, transformations that propelled the societies of the North Atlantic world into global hegemony in the early modern era. This essay sketches the place of the founding of North American settler and slave-labor societies in the wider ecological history of the early modern Atlantic, itself a fragment of a wider, global history. In North America, an evolving relation of native human societies and the biosphere was utterly destroyed in a series of shock radiations paralleled only in the farming diasporas of the Neolithic period and the trade-borne confluences of disease that had swept the Old World in ensuing millennia. Expropriated to the purposes of commercial empires and settler societies, these resources laid the groundwork for a national economy that would surpass all others in its capacity for subduing nature.

Such a circum-Atlantic ecological history is a vast collective undertaking, comprehending the geography and climatology of complex tropical and temperate biomes, the movement of peoples across ocean and landmass, the explosive shock radiations of microbial and macrobial flora and fauna, the expropriation and transformation of biome into new agroecologies and new landscapes, the flow of natural biomass as commodity and living organism, and the evolving relationship between culture and nature. The concept of an ecological history may disturb many historians, who never have been comfortable with any interpretative approach that permits natural forces to impose limits on human agency. Thus a review of the ecological history of early North America immediately raises difficulties of definition, difficulties that are manifested in the awkward relation of an ecological history to its putative parent discipline, environmental history. Environmental history, as defined by Donald Worster (1990) and William Cronon (1990), incorporates four uneasily associated domains: the reconstruction of past natural environments, the study of human societies' material interactions with these environments, the history of political and legal actions bearing on the environ-

John Brooke has been an observer of ecological history ever since studying environmental biology, archaeology, and demography as an undergraduate and working as a survey archaeologist in the mid-1970s. From 1994 to 2000 he taught an annual course in global ecological history at Tufts. He is obliged to John Komlos and Kenneth Pomeranz for generously sharing their unpublished manuscripts, and to Robert Gross, Jeanne Penvenne, Jack Ridge, David Stahle, and especially Daniel Vickers for valuable comments and suggestions.

ment, and the study of cultural understandings and perceptions of nature. An ecological history certainly gives priority to the first two of these domains, decidedly leaning toward a materialist frame of reference, and committed to an understanding as scientific as possible of the relationship of humanity and nature. But at the heart of this materialism lies the fundamental centrality of human agency. An ecological history assumes that human societies are shaped by natural forces, but it also assumes an innately human agency in resisting these forces, a resistance that both sustains those societies – and profoundly shapes nature.

This question of human agency has shaped an epistemological crisis in the scientific field of ecology, a shift in understanding that has engendered fundamental problems in the rise of an American ecological history. When this sub-field first emerged in the late 1960s, the story seemed relatively simple. European settlers encountered and destroyed a pristine primal wilderness, the final cumulative summation of forest succession, the orderly and systemic outcome of mature natural systems. The primary mission of American environmental history was to describe both this natural baseline in time past and the ways in which human impacts had changed it. An American wilderness was recoverable in history, and hopefully in conservation and restoration. Unfortunately, just as historians were turning their sights toward this discipline, ecology was historicizing its understanding of nature. Since 1970 ecological science has abandoned its model of nature as a stable system ever returning to a steady state of mature succession. Nature is now seen as being in unsystemic disequilibrium, a shifting and changing congery of individual species, battered by contingent disturbance. In great measure, this understanding has brought ecological science into line with emerging understandings in evolutionary science, particularly that of punctuated equilibrium (Eldredge, 1999). This epistemological shift has been very disturbing to American environmental historians, particularly in their activist personas. Old absolute measures suddenly become slippery and relative, stability gives way to chaos, human environmental disturbances suddenly share the stage with equally important natural disturbances (Cronon, 1996; Demeritt, 1994; Worster, 1994, pp. 388–433). But if American historians, with our deeply rooted assumption of a primal wilderness, shuddered at this new relativity, Europeans shrugged their shoulders; theirs was and is a landscape profoundly "anthropogenic" – shaped for tens of millennia by human action (Schama, 1995; Dunlap, 1999).

This chapter is grounded in this European sensibility and is shaped by two Europeans, Thomas Malthus and Ester Boserup, whose thinking allows us to put the question of human sustainability and agency at the center of an ecological history. It argues that ecological resources around the Atlantic circuit, many very fragile and delicate, were put to new purposes starting in the sixteenth century, with profound consequences in a world-historical accounting of survival and sustainability. It is this problem of the ecological sustainability of societies and economies that provides the most comprehensive approach to the material history of the peoples and biomes of the early modern Atlantic world. The consequences of the age of exploration – the shock radiation of diseases on populations without immunities and the expropriation of territory and biomass – cut through the separate histories of the regional societies around the Atlantic basin, profoundly altering regional vectors of change, while stitching them together into a new transoceanic eco-system that would help to underwrite the ensuing industrial revolution. Here a Malthusian perspective on population and resources is most useful, as modified by the understandings developed thirty years ago by Boserup (Malthus, 1970 [1798, 1830]; Boserup, 1965, 1981; Newman et al., 1990). In essence, Malthus argued that population growth only follows heroic leaps in technological change: otherwise populations are subject to either the social, preventive checks on fertility or the catastrophic positive checks of crisis mortality. Boserup reversed the logic of his formula, arguing that the press of population growth has long been inherent in the human condition, constantly forcing incremental innovations and resource substitutions in productive technologies and their supporting social systems. These intensifications have been a constant feature of the deeper rhythms of human history, Boserup argued, as societies struggled to "run in place," to avoid "falling behind" in the sense of a Malthusian crisis, and occasionally to "get ahead" in the struggle to sustain and to nurture their growing numbers.

This simple understanding of population growth driving intensification, with due attention to soil depletions and long-range climate change, provides a useful frame of reference in an examination of the ecological trajectories and disruptions of the post-Columbian Atlantic world. Around this oceanic circuit, between the fourteenth and the eighteenth centuries, Old and New World societies in Europe, North America, and Africa all were moving along Boserupian trajectories of growing population and increasing intensification. These centuries were also marked by a general climatic deterioration, as the Medieval Warm Period gave way to the Little Ice Age, bringing cold hard winters to northern Europe, and desertification to the African Sahel and the American West. Ultimately, it was the historically more crowded Europe, pressed by population and crisis, that initiated the process that transformed Atlantic ecologies.

There are differing opinions about the inevitabilities of this process. Recently Jared Diamond, in a widely hailed grand synthesis, has argued that the ecological "endowments" of the various continents fundamentally shaped these outcomes (1997). Thus in a swath of the Old World running from Europe and the Mediterranean east to India, China, and Japan, the lack of ecological barriers to the east–west spread of domesticable plants and animals at the end of the Pleistocene ice ages has determined the basic shape of the modern world. Eric Jones has argued that Europe's temperate climate and multi-alluvial terrain provided the ground for Europe's narrow window of per-capita prosperity and competitive advantage relative to Asia (1987, pp. 3–44). But others might not be so convinced of Europe's inherent edge over the rest of the world. If North America and western Africa historically had low population densities, populations were growing dramatically in the centuries prior to the impact of European trade, settlement, and empire, a growth underwriting significant social change. But they were resting on fragile foundations, and the first encounters with European imperialism set off dynamic spirals of adverse change, in effect exogenously induced Malthusian crises, which would have both regional and global consequences running down to the present. And in North America, settler populations would temporarily escape the imperatives of both Malthusian restraint and Boserupian innovation, to flourish in lands emptied by disease and temporarily reverting to so-called wilderness.

* * * * *

The encounter of peoples and biologies from three continents requires that a review of the ecological history of colonial America begin with the briefest of sketches of the pre-Columbian circumstances of Native American, African, and European societies. In North America, one of the most fundamental assumptions about the ecology of the colonial era has been undermined by a vast body of research over the past thirty years. The classical story was one of Europeans encountering a wilderness and engaging with that wilderness's few savage inhabitants across a frontier. A revolution in the study of the Native people of North America has overturned the assumptions informing this story on almost every front, one of the most profound contributions of the new environmental history of colonial America – equally in terms of a broader cultural approach and a more precisely ecological approach.

The centerpiece of the past decades' revolutionary reinterpretation of Native American society and ecology has been the debate over numbers. The traditional understanding was of the Native peoples as nomadic, few in number, and thinly scattered across a pristine natural landscape. These assumptions framed the traditional estimate of about one million Native North Americans at Columbian contact. Since 1966, however, estimates of pre-contact New World populations have surged upward and downward, ranging between Henry Dobyns's high of 18 million and Douglas Ubelaker's recent estimate of 1.894 million, a figure that many see as more realistic (Dobyns, 1966; Ubelaker, 1993; Daniels, 1992). If there is a consensus, it is that the older literature seriously underestimated the regional variability of population densities in the New World in general and North America in particular.

The debate will not be resolved soon, but it has had a powerful effect on the understanding of the social ecology of Native America. Whether or not the pre-contact populations were as large as some have argued, the debate has contributed to a resituating of Native America in global history, from noble savagery in a state of nature to complex societies undergoing historical change. If the traditional metaphor painted America as a "virgin land," the new understanding is of a "widowed land" (Jennings, 1975). The recent literatures in history and archaeology describe a New World with significant regions of dense sedentary population, with productive technologies and cultural landscapes shaped by centuries of adaptation to changing environmental conditions, and shattered by the impact of Old World epidemic diseases. All of this, incidentally, has contributed to the epistemological crisis caused by the new ecology of chaos and disturbance; not only was nature not a stable structure, but non-Europeans had their own history of life on the land. The wilderness that Americans assumed lay before their time, recoverable by conservation, turns out to have been "anthropogenic," shaped by human hands for millennia (Peacock, 1998; Butzer, 1992; Sauer, 1966).

The higher populations of the new pre-contact North America, even if they were only twice that thought before, require a rethinking of pre-contact ecological adaptations. Low, mobile populations had meant a light usage of the landscape, few impacts on local ecologies, a high sustainability of adaptation – and little change over time. Higher, more sedentary populations, even if they were only regional, mean the reverse: more intense land-use, more severe impacts, lower sustainability, and accelerating change. The question is of course one of degree. Many scholars have argued that Native peoples were "natural ecologists," carefully conserving the landscape in a cultural symbiosis (White, 1984). Certainly Native systems of foraging and hunting were sustainable over very long periods. But broad climate shifts toward cooler weather after roughly 3000 BC, warming at around AD 800 and again cooling around AD 1300, acted powerfully on Native American ecological adaptations (Pielou, 1991; Kutzbach and Webb, 1991). And in the populations that had shifted to agricultural production there are also signs of crisis; late prehistoric population growth was contributing to Malthusian impacts on subsistence and health.

The most significant means of environmental manipulation that Native North American peoples had at hand were agriculture and fire. The cooling at the close of the so-called "Hypsothermal" climatic optimum between roughly 5000 and 3000 BC contributed to the domestication of local seed plants in the American Southeast, and after 2000 BC to the development of the fire-governed landscapes that French explorers and English settlers found on the New England coast (Smith, 1995, pp. 185–201). Indian fires fundamentally shaped the natural environments of North America in the ensuing millennia, working locally to improve hunting and to prepare grounds for agriculture, and on a continental level to slow the southward advance of the boreal forest into the deciduous oak zone, and the westward advance of the forest into the prairie (Bragdon, 1996, pp. 55–79; Whitney, 1994; McAndrews, 1988).

Eventually, fire would play a role in preparing corn-planting grounds, though more than a thousand years elapsed between the availability of corn and its emergence as a significant crop in eastern North America in the centuries after AD 800, as new varieties emerged that grew well in shorter North American growing seasons. Broadly speaking, intensive corn cultivation was associated with the emergence of the stratified societies of the "Mississippian" complex – and with rising populations. In the Mississippi and Ohio Valleys evidence suggests that population pressure was the driving force behind the transition to maize cultivation on the shifting swidden system of long forest fallow, as wild resources were depleted. Such trajectories toward higher populations, agricultural economies, and hierarchical chiefly societies were in motion across the Southeast and casting "Mississippian" influences to the Northeast, where corn cultivation was developing among the Owasco proto-Iroquois and the southern New England Algonquin about AD 1000–1100. With this linked population growth and increased dependence on agriculture, paleopathologists have found skeletal evidence of declining health and nutrition. Their findings suggest that Native American populations from the Ohio Valley into the greater Southeast experienced malnutrition with the transition to corn cultivation, and variable levels of nutrition but increased levels of disease as population densities grew (Johannessen and Hastorf, 1994; Larsen and Milner, 1994; Verano and Ubelaker, 1993).

Certainly the bounty of North American environments allowed the delay of a Native American dependence on agriculture for millennia. But a dynamic of sedentism, agriculture, rising populations, and declining health took hold across wide regions after AD 1000, a dynamic that had its roots in the Hopewellian exchange networks of 1000 BC–AD 400. Many Native American populations were thus "running in place," as most Old World populations had been for millennia – intensifying production to keep up with rising populations. Some might ask whether Malthus's limits eventually might have been reached in parts of native North America, as suggested by the trajectories toward declining health and by the collapse of the proto-state of Cahokia around 1250. More likely, Native American societies were averting Malthusian crisis by Boserupian means but falling into a deadlock of growth and intensification (Bragdon, 1996, pp. 85–88; Mulholland, 1988).

In the context of the debate about Native American populations, there are two corollaries to high pre-contact populations: a greater ecological impact on American biomes, and a more catastrophic loss of life in the centuries following contact. European imperialism carried with it a secret and unconscious weapon: the shock radiation of Old World diseases. Smallpox, influenza, chicken pox, measles, diphtheria, typhoid, scarlet fever, malaria, yellow fever – a long list of pathogens flowed out from the Old World, killing between 70 and 90 percent of the Native populations and emptying vast stretches of land (Cook, 1998). Recent studies are suggesting that the post-Columbian epidemics need to be seen as long-term processes rather than sudden events. Malnutrition may have undermined disease resistance: paleopathologists conclude that in the great interior valleys declining diet and nutrition left Native peoples with weakened immune systems, potentially contributing to their susceptibility to Eurasian diseases (Buikstra, 1993; Perzigian et al., 1984). While these conclusions might suggest an early impact of Old World diseases, other scholars are emphasizing a complex mosaic of disease impacts, with variable exposures and chronologies of infection unfolding over centuries. Disease movement came in "spurts and bursts," as it ripped through dense settlements and then slowed at "buffer zones" until spreading to other population centers (Larsen and Milner, 1994; Verano and Ubelaker, 1993).

Landform, climate, and disease also shaped the trajectory of societies of western Africa that would be caught up in the destructive compass of the early modern Atlantic world. Here a series of paradoxes grounded in regional ecology set the stage for a catastrophic spiral. Where dense and growing European populations struggled over small amounts of young, glacially tilled, and highly productive soils, African populations were spread more thinly on a larger landscape leached by millennia of tropical rains, where in many places the tsetse fly undermined any significant expansion of animal traction by horses or cattle. In these circumstances, as in the Americas, labor itself was at a premium, and social and political organization was driven not by the imperatives of legal title to real property but by the mobilization of human energies. Slavery, as an extension of the lineage system or in chattel form, was a pervasive answer to the problem of marshaling labor. It was also, as African historians have demonstrated, a solution to periodic subsistence crises, as droughts led to famine in drier regions, sending refugees in flight to slavery in societies entrenched in well-watered lowlands. Along the great ecological boundary separating the Sahara from the Sahel, the global effect of the Little Ice Age operated to drive the desert south for hundreds of miles between 1600 and 1850, undermining the great west African empires and setting off a struggle for resources between small warring states just as the Atlantic slave trade began to compete with the slave trade running north to the Islamic Mediterranean. As the trade in slaves emerged and grew, periodic drought and famine only increased the volume of the tens of thousands sent into the maw of the Atlantic economy, and ensuing disease mortality in the slave camps paradoxically drove up the demand for more slaves. Conversely, as prices for slaves rose, so too did the incentive for slavers to capture and sell even more people into the Atlantic world. By the late seventeenth century these processes brought a stagnation of population growth in western African societies, where, paradoxically, labor-poor societies continued to export their young adults. But if African societies had been historically labor-poor, population growth in the centuries before the slave trade in parts of west Africa had laid the ground for significant agricultural intensification and market growth. This platform for internal economic and political development was undermined by the slave trade. The early modern encounter with

Europe thus deflected western African societies from a Boserupian trajectory of internal change and potential dynamism, from the possibility of getting ahead on their own terms (McCann, 1999, pp. 23–31; Webb, 1995; Brooks, 1993).

The launching of this encounter was shaped by a sequence of crises in sustainability in Europe. The entire Eurasian state domain moved from Malthusian crisis in the fourteenth century – the century of the Black Death/the bubonic plague – to recovery in the fifteenth and sixteenth centuries to renewed Malthusian pressures in the seventeenth century. And as in the case of North American and West African societies, these population pressures were felt in the context of the incrementally colder temperatures of the Little Ice Age. Over the past twenty years historians have elaborated on the framework of a general seventeenth-century crisis, first advanced by Eric Hobsbawm and Hugh Trevor-Roper. Jack Goldstone has described the trajectory from post-plague recovery to seventeenth-century crisis in a global framework, arguing that, from Stuart England to Ottoman Turkey to Ming China, population growth overwhelmed state finances, set off elite conflict and popular unrest, and engendered new ideologies of restoration and transformation (Goldstone, 1991). David Fischer describes the period for Europe in much the same terms, setting the seventeenth-century crisis into a sequence of four price revolutions, general crises, and ensuing equilibria running from the thirteenth century to the present (Fischer, 1996; Parker and Smith, 1997). These pressures were particularly alarming in England, with a domain precisely circumscribed by salt waters. Between 1541 and 1636 the population of England and Wales grew by almost 80 percent. Although populations had not quite recovered from the fourteenth-century collapse from famine and plague, contemporary observers were alarmed at the rising numbers of the wandering poor, and the potential that they posed for social and political disorder.

* * * * *

These were the circumstances of the societies around the Atlantic circuit, poised for an encounter on North American coasts. The ecology of this encounter must also be seen in terms of the circum-Atlantic perspective. William McNeill (1976) and Alfred Crosby (1972) stand as the great synthesizers of the first of four great paradigms in this Atlantic eco-history: the radiation and impact of Old World organisms in the New World. Both also view this process as an exchange, as New World organisms flowed back to the Old in a backwash that had powerful effects on global food supply. William Cronon (1983) and Donald Worster (1990) established two more central paradigms for Atlantic eco-history. Neatly encapsulating and reversing the subject matter of economic history, their conceptions of a "commodification" of nature and of "agroecology" provide frameworks for analyzing the ways in which European economies consumed the biomass of the imperial periphery (Cronon, 1983, 1991; Worster, 1990). The vehicles of this metabolism were twofold, both the agricultural practices and ecological impacts of settling peoples, but also the merchant networks that organized the wider extraction of resources around an imperial circuit. Crosby added a fourth basic paradigm, that of "demographic takeover," in which settler societies established "Neo-Europes" in global zones of moderate temperate climate that most resembled Old Europe, a pattern of great consequence in the world-historical accounting of ecological resources (1986). A corollary of Crosby's demographic takeover is what can be called the problem of "feral colonial ecologies": the altering and degrading of species diversity and soil integrity of New World regions even just brushed by colonial encounters, transformed not just by micro-organisms but by cattle, pigs, rats, and weeds (Crosby, 1986; Cronon, 1983; Curtin, 1990, pp. 92–6). Yet another paradigm, running back to Frederick Jackson Turner but also evident in contemporary cultural studies, reverses the causal arrow, stressing the impact of nature on colonizing peoples, the natural bounty and the natural constraints that shaped the ecological adaptations of the new settler societies. In what follows, these adaptations will be discussed in terms of a "creolization" – an exchange of cultures and biologies among the peoples meeting in North America.

Environmental historians have provided at least two broad synthetic approaches to the specific ecological histories of the early modern Atlantic empires. Timothy Weiskel proposes a five-stage drama of 1: biotic encounter, 2: unstable population explosions, 3: a coterminous niche formation, 4: intrusion of settler societies into a disturbed ecosystem, and 5: the restabilization of altered regional ecologies on the settler's terms (1987). His stages 1 to 3 correspond to the pre-settlement history of post-Columbian native American history reviewed above; his fourth and fifth to the period 1609–1775 to be discussed below. Weiskel's concept of an ecological restabilization is very useful, suggesting that colonizing societies reorganized ecologies and landscapes to suit the agroecological and aesthetic purposes. But Weiskel's scenario brings an open-ended process to a premature closure: a restabilized colonial ecology was subject to new forces of change. Carolyn Merchant's model of two grand ecological revolutions probably provides our best overview perspective (1987). First, Merchant's "colonial ecological revolution" describes the transition from native American to settler agroecology, encompassing McNeill and Crosby's radiations, Cronon's commodifications, Weiskel's stages 1–4, and Crosby's demographic takeover. But her second, the "capitalist ecological revolution," provides an ongoing dynamic, lacking in Weiskel's formulation. Stretching some of her terms, this perspective allows us to look beyond the colonial agricultural world out into the wider Atlantic basin, to the accelerating forces of the market and the demography of the emerging world economy that shaped and intensified Cronon's commodification of nature, rapidly entangling native and colonist in the web of material production flowing from the shops and mills of the incipient industrial revolution. These frameworks are here reformulated in terms of Ester Boserup's intensifications, and the ecological contexts and outcomes of a continual struggle to "get ahead."

* * * * *

Merchant trade networks operating around the Atlantic perimeter were the fundamental agents in the direct commodification of nature in the New World. Fishing fleets were financed, fur traders dispatched, and lumbering and ship-building camps set up, all through the efforts of partnerships of merchant capitalists, all the agents of a progressive erosion of the natural bounty of the New World.

Of the three, commercial lumbering had the least impact during the colonial period. Forest historians are agreed that the rate of deforestation was extremely slow in the seventeenth century, as small settling populations occupied savanna-like Indian clearings, and began to whittle away at the surrounding woods. The rate of deforestation

accelerated toward the mid-eighteenth century, with population growth and penetration of settlement far beyond the Indian old-fields. Exports of timber as masts, barrel
staves, shingles, and potash and pine resin as naval stores were far less of a factor in
deforestation than the clearing of land for fields, construction lumber, and fuel. Settlement brought local deforestation within fifty to one hundred years. Well before that,
however, the prime first quality trees were long gone, cut through for construction or
export to the West Indies. The issue is further complicated by the rapid regrowth of
temperate deciduous forest in roughly twenty to thirty years, regrowth that provided
some of the necessary lumber and fuel wood (Whitney, 1994, pp. 131–35; Williams,
1989, pp. 53–110).

The contrast between the rapid destruction of the massive first quality trees, and the
scrubby regrowth of old-fields might be viewed though the evolutionary categories of
r-selection and K-selection. In "r-selection," a species broadcasts eggs or seeds in hope
that more will survive predation to maturity. "K-selected" species, usually relatively
larger animals, have limited annual litters, and nurture these few offspring for relatively
long dependent periods. Here then, we might conceive of massive ancient oaks and
white pines as K-selected, and the thickets of maples and chestnuts that replaced them
as r-selected. If the composition of the second-growth forest changed, the endowment of the North American temperate climate and soils has meant that significant
exploitation of the woodlands would be sustainable over the long term (Whitney,
1994, pp. 156–61, 313–14). These selection alternatives were far more significant for
the key animal species commodified by the merchant networks: fish and fur-bearing
animals. Recent studies of cod fisheries suggest that even in the seventeenth century,
hand-line fishing caused local collapses in the Grand Banks fisheries, along sections of
the Newfoundland coast. Such depletions had already occurred from overfishing in
the eastern Atlantic. But the vast schools of cod breeding in the offshore ocean – a
classically r-selected species – meant that the Grand Banks fishery would be sustainable
until the advent of modern high-volume fish factories (Vickers, 1996). Beaver, by
contrast, was a vulnerable K-selected species. With amazing rapidity, beaver and other
fur-bearing animals were eliminated from eastern forests, in a merchant-organized fur-
trapping frontier that soon receded far into the north (Curtin, 1984, pp. 207–29;
Wolf, 1982, pp. 158–94). More mobile, if not necessarily more prolific, the southern
white-tailed deer managed to rebound cyclically during periods of warfare (Silver, 1990,
pp. 91–4). Both of these exploitations formatively shaped and reshaped the ecological
"new world" of Native American peoples, leading to cultural and ecological changes
that progressively drew their surviving descendants toward the livestock and plow-
based agricultural systems of the settler societies (Merrell, 1989).

* * * * *

The seventeenth-century emigrations from England to Ireland and the New World set
off a vast expropriation of global biomes, not for the temporary purposes of simple
resource extraction, but for the transfer and propagation of entire populations. The
result of this population transfer, combined with the deadly impact of Old World
diseases, would be a radical expansion of peoples of European origin relative to global
population, a trajectory reversed only in the past half-century (Demeny, 1990). Thus,
two great surges of population have been driven by world-historical changes in eco-

logical condition: the modern expansion of non-European people by massive post-World War II public health initiatives, and the earlier surge of European peoples by their selective appropriation of favored regions of moist temperate climate. As Crosby stressed with such effect, the colonized "Neo-Europes" were strategically situated on virtually all of the global temperate domains, ensuring the easy replication of familiar modes of agriculture and social life (1986). Eric Jones (1987, pp. 3–44), Jared Diamond (1997, pp. 176–91), and most recently David Landes (1998, pp. 3–28) all have argued that for millennia the benefits of young, recently glaciated soils, multiple river systems, regular but moderate rainfall, and easy access to the unique domesticated species of the Levant gave the peoples of Europe a cumulative advantage over those in less favored situations. For most of these millennia, the expanding populations of Europe were accommodated by internal frontiers (Phillips, 1994); with the sixteenth and seventeenth centuries they began to spill across global frontiers. If many Europeans went to the tropics in both the New World and island Southeast Asia, many more set their sights immediately to the west, where vast stretches of temperate biome faced them across the Atlantic, an ecological coincidence that has no parallel elsewhere in the world.

In some small measure, a seventeenth-century crisis in England was mitigated by creative responses – Boserupian innovations – avoiding a possible encounter with Malthus. The revenue demands of a war-making monarch were challenged by Puritan revolutionaries, coal replaced wood in the hearth-fires of London and the great towns, and scientific improvements began to raise agricultural productivity. There were radical responses to the seventeenth-century crisis; Gerald Winstanley and the Diggers took agricultural improvement into their own hands, attempting an agricultural commune in the winter of 1648–49 (Skipp, 1978). But Atlantic empire provided the critical innovation.

Here England followed the example of Spain and Portugal in a colonial expropriation of "windfall" of biomass in the New World. But the English took the process one step further, thinning their population in an artificial plague through a "swarming" to the New World, mimicking the impact of a Malthus positive check. Of any colonizing country, England exported far and away the greatest share of its population: half a million people in the seventeenth century. Of these, 400,000 crossed to the New World; others went to Ireland or into military or naval service. Some 220,000 were shipped to the West Indies where they died in great numbers; roughly 175,000 landed on the North American mainland (Gemery, 1980; Menard, 1991; Canny, 1994). With the exception of the predominantly family migrants who went to New England, the majority of these were young men, and their departure left thousands of young women without marital prospects (Wrigley and Schofield, 1981, pp. 201, 219–33, 469–71, 528–29). The result was in a sense an "overshoot" – English population growth stalled and indeed reversed for several decades. But in relieving population pressures, seventeenth-century emigration allowed an orderly movement toward the eighteenth century, when England would begin an economic transformation with profound ecological implications. If they set aside the Digger dream of land in common, English emigrants to the New World achieved something of the hopes and aspirations of English economic radicals, redirected from English to American "wastes."

The successful implantation of these migrant peoples, and the establishment of the first of Crosby's Neo-Europes, required that they pay close attention to Richard

Hakluyt's stipulation that they "use the natural people there with all humanity." Put in ecological language, the least successful species to invade the New World was the human species – at least in the short term. In any process of "radiation," invasive species must adapt to niches in local ecosystems to sustain themselves. Often they are pre-adapted, or local organisms lack the mechanisms to fend them off. Certainly northern European peoples were pre-adapted to the general temperate biomes of eastern North America (Sauer, 1981). But they were not pre-adapted to the specific ecological conditions prevailing in those biomes, particularly in their warmer latitudes, and until they could make the necessary cultural and biological adjustments and adaptations, invading Europeans suffered crises of sustainability on North American coasts. Further south, in the tropical conditions of the West Indies, European invaders and colonizers faced perpetual crises in sustainability. And as they occupied lands only partially emptied of native occupants by Old World disease and purchased African laborers to work their plantations, sustainable adaptations emerged in an ongoing set of intercultural exchanges. For better or worse, a new New World was emerging in a process that contemporary historians are describing as a "creolization." This creolizing of old into new had fundamental ecological dimensions.

The story of starving times and adjustments to American natural environments is literally the oldest story in the history of the United States, and deeply embedded in the intellectual origins of American environmental history. It is here that Frederick Jackson Turner's insights on the role of nature and the frontier on American culture are particularly salient. Richard White (1985) and Alfred Crosby (1995, p. 1185) see in Turner's frontier tradition the historiographical roots of American environmental history. Paradoxically Turner's frontier thesis, imputing a causal arrow from nature to culture as his wilderness transformed Old World peoples into Americans, has had less influence on more materialist ecological histories than it has on more cultural ones. One school of environmental history, drawing its vision from Henry David Thoreau, John Muir, Aldo Leopold, and Carl Sauer, stresses the transformative impact of European commodification on American landscapes (Worster, 1993, pp. 16–44). But recent cultural histories of the environment turn the causal arrow in the other direction, echoing Turner in subtle ways. Here the encounter with New World climate, flora, and fauna provides a ground for the redefinition of European and American identities (Kupperman, 1984a, 1984b; Parish, 1997; Dunlap, 1999). Indeed, in the first century or so of the colonial experience, it is the Turnerian causal arrow from nature to culture that offers the most parsimonious perspective upon the ecological history of eastern North America. European culture had to be altered in the New World. Where Turner would have called this a process of Americanization, historians have adopted the idea of "creolization" to describe the adjustments and adaptations requisite for colonial survival in the New World (Breen, 1984). These adjustments were indeed the first steps toward making Americans.

Here lies a great paradox. The cultural and ecological creolizing of Old World peoples was a form of "adaptive innovation," but in a sense that violated Ester Boserup's meaning. Rather than *intensifying* innovations forced by population pressure, these were *counter-intensive* innovations, permitted by the release of population pressure. The creolizing settler societies implanted along the North American coastline could afford – for over a century – to be *extensive* rather than intensive in their use of land. Colonial creolization would establish the ground for a "demographic takeover," but in its adoption of the New World it did surprisingly little damage to New World environments. In ways that we creatures of the twenty-first century can only dimly imagine, these extensive agroecologies, so pervasive in life routines, left the white majorities of the settling peoples far less "European" than they appeared on the surface. It would be only in the middle of the eighteenth century, with massive additions to population, an accelerating involvement in the Atlantic economy, and a conscious emulation of Old World norms, that Americans began to intensify in the classical Boserupian sense, and to do serious damage to North American environments.

The first and most basic set of adjustments that had to be made were agricultural. Between 1585 and 1629 English settlers arrived at the Outer Banks, on the Maine coast, on the James River, and along the Massachusetts Bay without sufficient food provisions. Many soon died of starvation, and if they did not quickly adapt to American soils, species, and diets, they continued to die. At Roanoke, apparently, the adaptation was complete: the survivors of the final 1587 expedition probably disappeared into the Native peoples of the southern Chesapeake (Quinn, 1985). At Jamestown, Plymouth, Salem, and Shawmut, the English died in the first winters of settlement before they began to plant American corn, maize, under the instruction of Native informants. Dutch and Swedish settlers on the Hudson and the Delaware similarly took up corn. When in 1630 Governor John Winthrop wrote that "our Indian Corne answers for all," he spoke for all settling Old World peoples (McMahon, 1985, p. 31).

The adoption of corn was not temporary, but permanent, and systemic. And, though not without cultural resistance and regional variation, settlers took up the Indian horticultural system with the corn. Native agriculture was based on shifting patterns of planting and long-fallow abandonment, in which fields were carved out of the woods by girdling trees and planting in hills among the stumps. These circumstances and the lack of domesticated animal traction dictated that the hoe, rather than the plow, would be the central implement of agricultural labor. In different degrees and for different durations, all settling peoples adopted these agricultural methods.

In New England, the recent collapse of the Native population left relatively unoccupied thousands of acres of old planting fields, fresh meadows, salt marshes, and fire-cleared uplands. Puritan settlers rapidly developed a livestock economy on the hay resources of meadow and marsh, but sustenance required grain crops. At least through the 1630s corn grown by Native methods prevailed; by the 1640s some localities, particularly in the Connecticut Valley, were plowing to plant wheat (Cronon, 1983, pp. 128–43; Wood, 1997, pp. 9–52). New England creolization thus soon turned modified "English Ways" of agriculture to producing an American diet (Allen, 1981). In the Chesapeake, by contrast, such "English Ways" were delayed for a century and a half. When the early settlements in Virginia and Maryland began to fall into a viable routine in the 1630s and expanded their productivity in the 1640s, they were practicing a fundamentally New World agriculture. Revolving around the Native species of corn and tobacco, with cattle and pigs run loose to graze in the woods, Chesapeake farming practiced a shifting long-fallow form, as planters, with their servants and slaves, took up and abandoned scattered plots of ground suitable to tobacco cultivation. Land rotated from tobacco to corn and occasionally wheat for five to eight years before being left fallow for twenty years or more. Tobacco and corn both were best worked with hoes, with the result that plows did not appear on a majority of Chesapeake farms until late in the eighteenth century (Earle, 1975, pp. 27–30; Carr et al., 1991, pp. 33–43; Morgan, 1998, 29–58).

Settling peoples survived in the New World by cultivating Native plants with Native practices. Corn, attuned to the drier, sandier soils in temperate North America, would provide a bountiful sustenance for centuries of American expansion (Crosby, 1994). For much of the seventeenth century the abundance of land allowed a continuance of fallow-farming, with a sparsity of labor and of draft animals impeding the re-adoption of Old World plowing traditions. And it was Native labor, ironically, which allowed plowing. In New England, traditional English agricultural practices re-emerged more rapidly and completely in great measure because so much cleared land along the coast had been maintained by centuries of Indian burning and horticulture. In the Chesapeake, settlers gained access to equivalent old-fields after the 1622 Powhatan War, and if these lands could not support an expanding and depleting tobacco cultivation for very long, they must have played a key role in getting the tobacco economy under way. Thus two broad modes of agricultural creolization emerged along the North American coast over the seventeenth century. In New England, settlers grazed cattle and, increasingly with plows, grew corn and rye on Indian-created openings onto the forest; in the Chesapeake, settlers moved from Indian fields into the woods with axes and hoes to grow tobacco and corn.

These modes of creolization were shaped, indeed profoundly reinforced, by colonial adaptations to the climatological and microbial environments of the New World. Here the creolization of populations, their "seasoning," was fundamentally shaped by the environmental regime: quick in the temperate Northeast, slow in the southern borderline sub-tropics, and disastrous in the tropical West Indies. Karen Kupperman has carefully chronicled the way in which climate shaped the configuration of English settlement in the New World: driven out of Newfoundland by the cold, attracted to dangerous hot climates by the lure of profits from exotic commodities, replicating the familiar in New England's moderate latitudes (1982, 1984a&b). The English in the West Indies escaped some of the European diseases only to die in large numbers from tropical disease, yaws, sleeping sickness, but most importantly yellow fever and the gradual degradations of poor diet, excessive drinking, and malaria. African slaves, subjected to far worse conditions of diet and labor, died in vast numbers (Dunn, 1972, pp. 300–34; Kiple, 1984). Malaria was established in endemic form along the seventeenth-century North American coast. The high mortality in the earliest Chesapeake settlement at Jamestown was rooted in a different environmental circumstance, the brackish conditions of the salt–fresh water transition in the James River at Jamestown, leading to epidemics of typhoid, dysentery, and salt poisoning (Earle, 1979; Childs, 1940). These conditions were shaped by intense droughts in the Tidewater and south to the Lowcountry sea islands from the 1650s to roughly 1612, which had particular impact on the Spanish settlements at Santa Elena begun in 1565, the Roanoke settlement of 1587, and the Jamestown settlement in 1606–1612. Ongoing drought conditions seem to have plagued the Chesapeake from the early 1640s into the 1670s (Stahle et al., 1998). The Puritan settlements of temperate New England, as the research of the past thirty years has demonstrated, entirely escaped both these conditions and diseases circulating in Europe, and boasted life expectancies that exceeded not just the islands and the Chesapeake, but that of England itself (Wells, 1992). Though droughts would eventually ease, feral disease environments would persist, shaping different regions in different ways. Conditions in New England would begin to worsen in the 1670s, while those in the Chesapeake would begin to moderate, and those in the

Caribbean would continue to be deadly down through the end of slavery and the discovery of the microbial basis of disease. Everywhere subtle environmental differences of heat, humidity, and non-lethal microbes required a period of seasoning by newly arriving immigrants (Greene, 1988, pp. 56–57, 82–99).

These conditions of disease and environment were tied in complex ways to the agricultural adaptations sustaining the settling populations. For the entire era of sugar-producing plantation slavery, the islands and the northern coasts were irrevocably tied in a mutual ecological dependence: islands planted shore to shore in sugar survived only by importing fish and farm commodities from first New England and then the mid-Atlantic. Here the healthy conditions in early New England contributed to the vigorous supply of commodities to the islands. It also must have shaped the degree of transformation of the agricultural system. If healthy conditions encouraged the birth of a creole generation of American-born Puritans, it also allowed the survival of the elders. Conversely, the conditions in the Chesapeake shortened life spans, and gave young men unusual authority over household and plantation. These conditions may well have contributed on the one hand to the relatively conservative, perhaps involutionary, re-establishment of "English Ways" in New England, and on the other hand to youthful agro-innovation in the Chesapeake, forging a rapid creolization of agriculture among a people whose own transition to creole status would have taken far longer (Kulikoff, 1986, pp. 60–63, 167–72; Tate and Ammerman, 1979, pp. 126–82, 243–96; Smith, 1978).

Such biological adaptions in agriculture, diet, and microbial seasoning were set in a wider complex of material creolization, shaped by evolving patterns of social circulation and household ecology, a complex that can be most simply defined as a "landscape." In the widest terms, changing landscapes set the terms of the wider mediation between nature and culture in early America. Most specifically, these landscapes shaped the disease regimes that determined the immediate fate of these settling peoples.

Perhaps the most fundamental condition of early American landscapes was that of relative dispersion. Health in the early modern world was fundamentally shaped by disease exposures, and Old World settlers reaped the benefits of taking up a distant and depopulated land. Regional societies that could establish and maintain an open-country settlement pattern could achieve remarkably favorable conditions of life, depending upon local conditions and their isolation from metropolitan diseases. There were unhealthy conditions in the Islands, the Lowcountry, and in the seaport towns, but these were the exceptions to the wider American rule. Into the nineteenth century the vast majority of Americans reaped the health benefits of life in open-country neighborhoods, from the southern upcountry and the emerging Appalachian frontier to the mid-Atlantic and New England countrysides. Population dispersion, an ample diet, good water, and temperate climate all worked to shape an exceptionally healthy people.

Ultimately, these determinants of human health were forged into a critical synthesis by the ecological work of women in households. This domain has been conceptualized by Carolyn Merchant under the rubric of "reproduction" (1989, pp. 167–72), and made tangible in Laurel Ulrich's study of the life of a Maine midwife, Martha Ballard (1990). It seems highly likely that the differences in mortality that continued to distinguish New England from the Chesapeake through the 1670s were shaped in some measure by the relative presence and absence of women, and the "environmental services" that women's work contributed to the welfare of these societies. Similarly, as Americans became consumers of larger and larger quantities of manufactured commodities – cotton cloth, soap, candles, glazed ceramics – the British Industrial Revolution itself began to provide "environmental services" for American populations, lightening work and improving health (Breen, 1986; Bushman, 1992, pp. 63–78; Shammas, 1990; Carson et al., 1994). Tea itself, Alan McFarlane has suggested, may have contributed to improved health conditions (1997). Imports of Old World seeds were also intimately connected with gardens, in which women's work enhanced the nutritional and aesthetic conditions, while literally reshaping American biomes (Yentsch, 1994). Women's cultural and ecological work inside the household and across the neighborhood landscape offers American ecological historians a fertile field for fresh research.

The outcomes of women's ecological work of reproduction manifested itself in both the demographic and phenotypical size of American populations. In an explosion of growth unique in the early modern world, American peoples grew both in numbers and in physical size, testament to the ecological value of the land that they had appropriated.

The phenomenal growth of continental American populations was grounded in an ecological dynamic: the establishment and rapid proliferation of family households in healthy temperate environments. Such a regime was never established in the West Indies and took hold with great difficulty in the sub-tropical coastal south, both the Tidewater and the Lowcountry. It thrived from New England south to the southern upcountry, anywhere that the landscape would support an open-neighborhood settlement pattern. American populations grew far faster than that of England for two reasons: American women were more likely to get married, and to get married sooner. English population growth was bound by Malthusian preventive checks before the mid-eighteenth century, whereas the availability of land released Americans from these checks (Wrigley and Schofield, 1981). The result was large families: American completed families had from six to eight children; English completed families had five to six. Combined with lower rates of mortality, these high fertility rates produced high rates of natural increase (Wells, 1992; Galenson, 1996). The result was a rapid increase in total population – what has been rightly called a repopulation of eastern North America. Settler populations had reached a total of 250,000 in 1700, and between 1710 and 1720 they probably surpassed Native population totals east of the Mississippi. By the opening of the Revolution in 1775 American populations, white and black, had topped 2.5 million. Doubling by 1800, settler Americans had achieved half the population total of England and Wales. In another half-century they would exceed it.

If the numerical size of the American population had not exceeded that of the old country by the end of the colonial period, the physical size of these people certainly had. Recent inquiries have firmly established that colonial Americans grew to adult heights that significantly exceeded those of Europeans. This difference is the most striking result of two decades of ongoing analysis of records of military enlistments, apprenticeships, runaway ads, and slave records. Low population densities, and easy access to fertile soils, shaping both isolation from disease and good diet, with plenty of protein, gave all Americans, propertied and unpropertied, a nutritional advantage – translating into adult height – over Old World populations in both Europe and Africa, particularly the poor (Steckel, 1999). The evidence would seem to suggest that living standards were rising significantly across the board in the eighteenth-century colonies, marked only by the stresses of the revolutionary economy, which bore particularly heavily on slaves. Overall, however, the eighteenth-century American experience provides a vivid example of what can happen when Malthusian pressures are lifted. As demographer Massimo Livi-Bacci has argued, changes in nutrition translate into variations in the sheer biomass of human populations, rather than in their mortality. Clearly eighteenth-century Americans were already "a people of plenty," taking up more than their share of ecological matter (Livi-Bacci, 1991; Potter, 1954).

* * * * *

Such were the evolving ecological circumstances of the settler populations along the Atlantic coast of British North America. Having outlined these human outcomes, the inverse question – central to an ecological history – remains: what were the ecological circumstances of the land itself? What was the nature and the scale of the impact of these settling and rapidly growing populations on the North American lands that they so quickly came to occupy? Having already sketched the impact of colonization on directly extractable biomass, fur, fish, and timber, it remains to assess the impact of colonization on soils, the effect of new colonial agroecologies supporting growing populations of increasingly large people.

Timothy Weiskel has proposed a global model for the archaeology of colonization: everywhere a stratum of large sedimentary deposits should appear, caused by the sudden impact of new, intensive, extractive agricultures established in the colonial periphery. Hypothetically, the prismatic impact of the global market on colonized lands would be sudden and intense soil erosion (Weiskel, 1988, pp. 170–1). Traditionally historians have pointed to the mineral depletion inflicted by tobacco and corn on Chesapeake soils, and William Cronon's *Changes in the Land* provides a powerful account of the impact of plows and cattle on thin New England soils (1983). While there is every reason to assume that soil depletion and erosion have, indeed, followed upon colonial expansions, more recent work on the Chesapeake and New England suggests a series of caveats to this global model. The simple presence of settlers practicing an extractive agroecology was not necessarily enough to really compromise the integrity of local American soils. Rather, serious impacts were a function of a series of variables: the technology employed, the scale of population growth, and even the slope of the land itself. Ironically, the evidence suggests that for more than a century an extractive monocrop agriculture had done little to compromise the soil ecologies of the greater Chesapeake. The establishment of a general agriculture in New England, however, may have had serious impacts but only in certain localities. In both cases, arguments are now being advanced for the sustainability of early American agricultural practices into the middle of the eighteenth century.

The traditional story of early southern agriculture was advanced by Avery Craven in the 1920s, on the ground of dismissive English travelers' accounts: tobacco and corn worked in tandem to mine the soil of its mineral content, leaving a desolate wasteland of scrubby abandoned fields (Craven, 1925). But for at least a quarter of a century specialists have agreed that the creolized agroecology that developed in the early Chesapeake did not have the unsustainable impacts that the traditional interpretation ascribed to it (Papenfuse, 1972; Silver, 1990, pp. 163–5; Whitney, 1994, pp. 227–41). Rather, the adoption of hoes and long-fallow cultivation cycles established an agricultural system that had remarkably little impact on the soil. The partially cleared patchwork of fields, with stumps in place and tangles of brush on the field margins, worked lightly with hoes, resisted runoff and soil erosion. This was a system adopted from Native American sources in the mid-seventeenth century, but its ongoing viability must have been enhanced by African familiarity with similar long-fallow swidden systems. Tobacco and corn were certainly depleting, but the twenty to thirty years' rotations of the long-fallow systems allowed a sufficient restoration of minerals. European travelers condemned the seeming disorder and sloppiness of American agriculture, with its piles of brush and rotting stumps, but it may have had the soil-conserving functions of modern "trash farming" (Miller, 1986; Brush, 1986).

The sustainability of this system had its limits, and those were a minimum ratio of roughly 50 acres of land per laborer. A planter would need sufficient land to maintain a rotation, or need access to new lands. The system began to break apart during the middle decades of the eighteenth century, as growing population in the Chesapeake undermined the chronology of the fallow system, and shorter rotations indeed began to seriously deplete the soil. Two strategies ensued: migration to new lands in the Piedmont and the Shenandoah Valley to continue the production of tobacco, and a transition to wheat cultivation in the Tidewater (Kulikoff, 1986, 45–54; Clemens, 1980). Starting in some areas in the 1760s, Tidewater wheat cultivation expanded rapidly in the 1780s. Recent studies have amply demonstrated that the shift to wheat had serious ecological consequences. Wheat production required the abandonment of the hoe and the shifting system, already under some stress by the 1750s, for the plow-cultivation of extensive fields on old low-lying tobacco lands and more exposed uplands. The result was rapid and massive soil erosion and the siltation of streams, harbors, and parts of the Bay itself (McClelland, 1997, pp. 41–52; Percy, 1992; Miller, 1986; Brush, 1986).

The rapid destruction of soils in the late eighteenth-century Chesapeake was certainly driven by the explosive expansion of population, from 98,000 in 1700 to 377,000 in 1750 to 786,000 in 1780 to 1,150,000 in 1800. In no small degree, however, this transition was implicated with the broad shift from creole to Anglicized modes of culture that bore such a powerful if ambiguous relation to the forging of the American republic. As Timothy Breen (1985), Carville Earle (1988), and Richard Bushman (1991) have stressed, this ecologically disastrous transition to wheat had ideological as well as economic implications. The tobacco crop, its shifting creolized agroecology, and the scrubby look that this "trash farming" gave to the landscape all were associated with the dependencies of the old colonial relationship. Wheat would be the emblem of virtue and independence, and the adoption of an improved agriculture, deep plowing, and an orderly landscape would allow Chesapeake planters to take their rightful place in the ranks of Atlantic nations. Thus it was a belated Europeanizing of the Chesapeake that accelerated the destruction of this American environment.

There is some debate over the impact of another European agroecology, to the north, in early New England. The question of the agricultural sustainability of early New England agriculture depends upon whether it can be interpreted as creole or English, subsistence or commercial. William Cronon has argued that commercial English farming planted on the shores of Massachusetts Bay had an immediate and serious impact on the local ecologies. Cattle and pigs trampled and rooted up delicate soils, compounding the erosion caused by plowing, all to the purpose of an extractive commodification of nature (1983). Carolyn Merchant has painted a very different picture, shifting the focus of impact from settlement to the expansion of the capitalist market. New England farmers, in her analysis, developed a creolized synthesis of native and English agroecologies for the purpose of a simple subsistence (1989, pp. 149–56). Most recently, Brian Donahue, in a careful analysis of the agricultural history of Concord, has argued for a third interpretation: New England farmers slowly constructed an ecologically sustainable American version of traditional English husbandry, based on a careful balancing of plowland, hay-marsh, and wood-lots (1995). Donahue's emphasis on the importance of hay-marshes in New England agriculture is reinforced by Joseph Wood's recent discussion of the role of salt and fresh-water marshes in the siting and ecology of early New England towns (1997, pp. 22–51).

Each of these interpretations has unique and shared qualities and emphases. Cronon, Wood, and Donahue focus on the eastern Massachusetts towns settled in the seventeenth century, Merchant on upland towns settled in the eighteenth century. Where Cronon sees unsustainable impacts stemming from the settling of an alien culture, Merchant and Donahue – for different reasons – defer these impacts into the eighteenth century. Where Merchant sees a New World synthesis, Donahue sees a fully articulated English agriculture, complete with efforts to manure fields from the earliest decades.

Among these three studies directly addressing the problem of the ecological viability, Donahue's dissertation presents the most careful ethnographic analysis of local records, and may well prove to be the decisive interpretation. The resolution of this debate, however, will require careful paleoecological analysis of seventeenth- and eighteenth-century sediments, in studies analogous to those that have so successfully defined the ecological history of the Chesapeake Bay. Hypothetically, Cronon's, Donahue's, and Merchant's models may all describe the agroecologies of colonial New England, if we apply Cronon to the towns first settled on the coast, Donahue to the towns settled at lush fresh-water meadows in the immediate interior and along the Connecticut Valley, and Merchant to the upland towns of the eighteenth-century frontier.

The relatively light touch of the seventeenth-century settlements on American soils was also grounded in a lost, open landscape. All along the Atlantic coast terrible epidemics, shattering Native peoples, had left relatively unoccupied tens of thousands of acres of old planting fields, fresh meadows, salt marshes, and fire-cleared uplands: an open landscape maintained by Native American labor for centuries, lightly overgrown in the early seventeenth century. Eric Jones has estimated that these open lands comprised a capital endowment equivalent to a century of labor by the settling populations, "improvements" assumed without payment and vital to the founding of colonial societies (Jones, 1996, 1974). Here in southern New England, on the Hudson, the Delaware, and around the Chesapeake these relatively open lands would for decades be more than sufficient for the needs of the colonial settlements – and competition over these unforested intervals lay at the heart of genocidal warfare with surviving Native peoples in 1622, 1637, 1642, and 1675.

If Puritans fought Native peoples for control of ancient open lands at the end of the seventeenth century, Yankees plunged into the woods in the eighteenth century.

Merchant and Donahue may differ over the nature of a sustainable, traditional New England agroecology, but they agree about when the system began to break down. For Donahue, the keystone of a traditional sustainable agriculture was a balance of cattle and natural haylands; when market demand increased the number of cattle being grazed, the forests were assaulted for conversion to upland pasture, and the towns began to suffer from lack of timber and fuel as well as accelerated soil erosion. Merchant and Donahue agree with the general picture painted by Robert Gross in *The Minutemen and their World*: the expansion of the cattle trade in the middle decades of the century marked the collapse of a sustainable agricultural system (Donahue, 1995, pp. 244–74; Merchant, 1989, pp. 185–90; Gross, 1976, pp. 68–109). In new and old towns alike there was a surge in forest clearance to open up pasturage for cattle destined for the West Indian trade, a market that would fuel the New England economy before and after the Revolution, indeed down to the Embargo years of 1807–1815 (Whitney, 1994, pp. 151–4, 252–5). The expansion of the cattle trade, giving rise to specialized upland-grazing, lowland stall-feeding, and series of cattle droving trunk-roads (Garrison, 1987), coincides with the integration of prices and wages that Winifred Rothenberg (1992) has detected emerging in the 1750s. In these decades New Englanders learned the skills they would require to open the forested frontiers to the north and the west after the Revolution (Taylor, 1998).

This gathering assault upon the wooded ecologies of New England and the mid-Atlantic was driven by surging populations and changing culture. If the initial stages of the settlement of the uplands and the development of grazing comprised a "low-intensity agriculture," the older coastal settlements were adopting a high-intensity agriculture, clearing land for farms and fuel and continuous cropping in ways that mirrored the evolving agricultural history of the Chesapeake. By the 1740s stretches of countryside around Boston were "open and pleasant"; by the time of the Revolution they were on the verge of the American agricultural revolution. As Richard Bushman has suggested, this "opening of the countryside" was both a manifestation and vehicle of the Anglicization of American life in the mid-eighteenth century (1991); Carolyn Merchant calls it the "capitalist ecological revolution" (1989, pp. 198–231); Brian Donahue sees a transition from sustainability to unsustainability as Concord farmers changed their priorities from meadow to market (1995, pp. 344–74); Robert Gross has called attention to the linkages between "culture and cultivation" in this transition (1982). And, as Timothy Silver has put it, this "more civil landscape" came at a "price." Qualitative changes in the relationship of Americans to a wider Atlantic market and culture, as much as their simple presence in the New World, set the stage for the cumulative environmental impacts that are their legacy (1990, p. 185).

Beyond the Chesapeake and New England, which for reasons of space must be the limit of this discussion, the dynamic of the market and soil degradation was evident but not fundamental at the end of the colonial era. In the great alluvial valleys of the Hudson and the Delaware, settlement was relatively recent and ongoing, the soils were deep, and the ground surface generally flat enough to resist erosion. In the Virginia Piedmont the planting of corn and tobacco in hilly land was resulting in serious erosion, but to the south along the coast and the uplands processes of erosion and depletion were only beginning (Silver, 1990, pp. 165–8).

The most striking environmental change along the coast from southern Maine to the Albemarle Sound was the near total stripping of the forest cover, as burgeoning populations linked together the seventeenth-century openings in the forests for farm clearance, iron works, and fuel wood (Whitney, 1994, pp. 209–26; Williams, 1989, pp. 79–81). In as much as it was a function of clearing for farms and fuel, this impact was driven by population density, and here clearly southeastern New England led the way. This circumstance requires a brief reconsideration of the argument for a Malthusian crisis in eighteenth-century New England and, more generally, the question of a Malthusian interpretation of population growth and ecological sustainability in the colonies at large.

In the largest sense, the American colonies were a place where Europeans might escape from Malthusian positive checks. Their export from seventeenth-century England mitigated the possibility of a Malthusian crunch in England, and American bounty – soils and biomass – and American isolation allowed most colonists to forget both positive and preventive checks. With the exception of the Islands, the seventeenth-century Tidewater and the eighteenth-century Carolina Lowcountry, Americans evaded the European disease regimes, lowered their age at marriage, ate increasingly protein-rich diets, and avoided the workload of improved agriculture by pursuing a counter-intensive, long-fallow trash farming. The results were expanding populations, expanding body size, and an expansive consumption of American biomes. Into the nineteenth century many Americans would continue to escape Malthusian constraints by migration to frontiers, and by an expansion of a staple mono-crop – tobacco in the eighteenth century and cotton in the nineteenth. Across the south these Euro-American peoples sustained their standard of living by expropriation of native American land and African labor – in effect externalizing their ecological costs. Where in the seventeenth century mono-crop agriculture pursued in the swidden system had done little fundamental damage to the land, the more intensive cropping on southern and western frontiers that followed the "First American Agricultural Revolution" would take a much greater toll. Eventually, nineteenth-century rural Americans of all regions would begin to restrict their fertility, but in the closing decades of the colonial era the peoples of the frontier and the agrarian backcountry reproduced with wild abandon (Easterlin, 1976).

* * * * *

Among free Americans, two populations were left behind, perhaps to confront the implications of Malthus. The poor and the propertyless in the expanding seaport towns were in increasingly difficult circumstances (Nash, 1979). And then there were the rural peoples of the old counties of eastern New England, especially Massachusetts, where population densities were highest in all of North America. It was for this region that Kenneth Lockridge, Robert Gross, and Daniel Scott Smith twenty to thirty years ago developed variants of a Malthusian model of declining resources, crowding, and growing poverty. If Lockridge posited a crisis (1968), Gross "scarcity" (1976), and Smith a frontier solution (1980), the implications were the same: European ecological conditions had caught up with these New World settlers. Challenged in the early 1980s, the Malthusian thesis will not disappear. Daniel Vickers, in his account of the ongoing struggle of Essex County fishing and farming people to make a living, feels required to announce that "no genuine Malthusian crisis descended on coastal Massachusetts prior to 1775" (1994, p. 205); Brian Donahue distances himself from Gross's theme of a "world of scarcity" but then announces that eighteenth-century Concord was "a world of limits, . . . feeling . . . the earliest touch of a good old Malthusian positive check" (1995, pp. 344, 367–70). There were, as Donahue here notes, three paths out of such a condition: crisis and collapse, emigration, and adjustment. While New Englanders did emigrate in large numbers, they also adjusted. In the language of Ester Boserup, spurred by population – and motivated by culture – New Englanders were the first Americans since the native peoples adopted agriculture to escape Malthus by intensifying their economy, pursuing artisanal by-employment, the fisheries, and the livestock trade in ways which may even have raised the standard of living (McMahon, 1985; McMahon, 1989; Main and Main, 1999).

If a Malthusian crisis did not materialize in eighteenth-century New England, some of the credit must go to the region's ecology itself. The cold winters and resilient vegetation of a moist temperate biome was an important asset, indeed an environmental service to the settling peoples. Woods cleared for farming or fuelwood regrew in twenty years of fallow, and although soils might erode, they healed over relatively quickly. Relative, that is, to the tropical alternative. Timothy Flannery has noted that the impact of European agroecologies was fundamentally different in North America and Australia, where dry, leached tropical soils and erratic rainfall patterns made British agroecological colonization much more difficult (Flannery, 1997; McKibbon, 1996). Similarly, in the New World, tropical soils cleared of their forest contained few nutrients and proved extremely delicate and fragile under colonial assault. Soil exhaustion was apparent in the tobacco and cotton fields of Barbados and St. Kitts by the 1640s, and on the smaller sugar islands generally by the 1660s, leaving only Jamaica and St. Domingo as large enough to sustain large-scale sugar cultivation into the nineteenth century. In northeast Brazil, as in the islands, sugar was produced on the shifting system, followed by coffee, inexorably consuming coastal forest ecosystems, left to scrub grazing after the soil played out (Watts, 1987; McNeill, 1986). In Spanish Mexico and New Mexico, the introduction of large-scale sheep-grazing in the sixteenth and eighteenth centuries led to devastating erosion of arid and semi-arid soils (Melville, 1994; MacCameron, 1994).

If the delicate but often richly productive tropics brought a short-lived bonanza for European empires, the temperate north provided longer-term ecological benefits for settler peoples. Not just in New England, but throughout eastern North America, the resilience of temperate biomes provided a buffer against the severest forms of environmental deterioration, a tangible asset – an environmental service – to the empire.

* * * * *

As elements of empire, these tropical and temperate regimes were set in a wider Atlantic ecological and political circuit, to which we must finally turn to complete an analysis of the ecological history of colonial North America. Here key concepts in the work of William Cronon (1983) and Carolyn Merchant (1987) come to bear, those of a commodification of ecologies and of a capitalist ecological revolution. The British North American colonies were part of a wider circum-Atlantic ecosystem, or rather one of several continental ecosystems stitched together by an empire that centered on the movement of natural life forms – peoples and organic biomass commodities – politically determined for the benefit of certain emerging European nations, principally Britain itself. The empire was grounded on an exchange of resources: an exchange that was growing increasingly complex in the mid-eighteenth century and that can be visualized as an ecological system – or at least a system with ecological drivers and consequences. What were in economic terms simply commodities were also in ecological terms "services," whereby life-enhancing values of biomass were directed to the benefit of certain populations, allowing them to get ahead, while others in the system fell behind (Wallerstein, 1974; Demeny, 1990, pp. 44–45). In the specific context of the Anglo-Atlantic, this process brought a realization of the Hakluyts' dream that the old country would reap the rewards of colonization, rising in prosperity and in numbers, from having planted peoples in the New World.

In great measure, of course, the ecological exchanges following Columbus had global reach, transcending specific empires. The globalization of food crops following the discovery of the New World played a critical role in stabilizing and expanding Old World populations (Crosby, 1972; Langer, 1975; Pelto and Pelto, 1985). American foods could be grown in situations where traditional Old World foods could not, increasing the complexity, resilience, and density of Old World agroecologies. Corn, potatoes, cassava/manioc, and peppers were the most important of these crops, and variously contributed to fundamental population increases around the Mediterranean, in West Africa, in China, and notoriously in Ireland. Slave-raiding in West Africa was enabled by the adoption of American food crops. But the renewed population growth in eighteenth-century Britain was less a function of new sources of nutrition than it was of new sources of employment. The great staples of the British empire – cheap sugar, American tobacco and cocoa, as well as Asian tea and coffee – were nutritionally dubious, but they provided a psychological and physiological boost as this new industrial workplace – and the bourgeois respectability benefiting from it – began to take shape (Mintz, 1974; Austen and Smith, 1992).

The results of thirty years of work by the Cambridge School have determined that it was employment in the first phases of the Industrial Revolution that began to drive up British population levels in the 1740s, ending the stagnation that had persisted from the 1660s. Opportunities to work in the expanding cottage industries, particularly when the work was regular rather than casual, allowed British men and women the opportunity to flaunt the preventive checks that had restrained population expansion in England for centuries, and most powerfully since the 1650s. The proportion of women marrying rose and their age at first marriage dropped, resulting in larger completed families (Wrigley and Schofield, 1981, pp. 417–35; Wrigley, 1983; Goldstone, 1986). The Industrial Revolution, whether a gradual process or a true revolution (Temin, 1997), was, John Komlos has argued, a Boserupian escape from the Malthusian trap, in which growing productivity allowed the British people to relax the rigors of preventive checks without having to fear the positive (1993).

Here there is an interesting parallel. On both sides of the Atlantic peoples under the umbrella of the British empire were – for diametrically opposite reasons – escaping the dictates of Malthus's demographic law. In North America the independence provided by free land was encouraging low ages of marriage and high birth rate, as the independence provided by wage labor in proto-manufacturing was in England. On one side of the Atlantic independence was gained in a counter-intensified extensive economy, on the other in a classically Boserupian intensification. Recently, but only that, historians have begun to sketch the relationships that illustrate how these population expansions were part of a single system, woven in interdependence by the ecology of Hakluyt's empire.

The debate runs back to Eric Williams's thesis in *Capitalism and Slavery*. Williams originally argued that the profits from the slave-based production of sugar funded the British Industrial Revolution, an argument that was easily refuted and then buried, as economic historians reacted to dependency theory by stressing the endogenous sources of economic development during the Industrial Revolution (Williams, 1944; Engerman, 1972; O'Brien, 1982; Bairoch, 1993, pp. 57–125). But in the past decade the terms of the debate have been redefined, and a solid body of work has demonstrated the importance of the markets that an empire provided for the British economy, particularly its emerging manufacturing sector. By the late seventeenth century London already was seeing an expansion of manufacturing from the demand of colonial consumers, particularly those in the West Indies (Zahedieh, 1994). Over the course of the eighteenth century, and particularly in the third quarter, while British exports doubled in value and increased their share of total British output, the slave trade and American markets emerged as a critical fraction of the British export markets, rising from 12–15 percent between 1700 and the 1740s to 35 percent in the early 1770s. A variety of key products – wrought iron, copper and brass, cotton checks, linen, and Yorkshire woolens – were exported almost entirely to the American and African markets. The expansion in these exports after 1750 was funded by an expanding production of tobacco, rice, indigo, and especially sugar, the growing volume and profitability of the slave trade, and the secondary supply trade of livestock, fish, and wood products from New England to the West Indies (Solow and Engerman, 1987; Solow, 1991; Inkori, 1992). Detailed analysis of the local configurations of British industrial export production and population growth clearly demonstrates that the first shaped the second (Levine, 1977). And, if slave labor underwrote the prosperity of white populations throughout British America, the prosperity and expansion of these populations would continue to fuel the dynamic of population and export manufacturing in Britain. Kenneth Pomeranz argues that British industrial growth – as compared to the failure of core areas in China to industrialize – was fundamentally shaped by the local availability of coal and the colonial expropriation of New World land and African labor (2000). Most generally then, this colonial expropriation of biomass was thus a key engine of two fundamental revolutions beginning in eighteenth-century Britain: demographic and industrial.

Returning to British North America, we might consider briefly the health implications of the ecological exchanges around this Atlantic circuit. Broadly speaking, the evidence both of traditional economic history and standards of living as measured by adult height suggests that in the long run sustainability and human outcomes were shaped by a relative sharing of environmental services and costs. In some sectors of this early modern world, these services were meager and costs were high; in others these services were abundant and costs were low. If adult heights may serve as a proxy for human ecological outcomes, they suggest that white southerners, from the eighteenth through the nineteenth centuries fared the best, slaves fared particularly badly during the revolutionary era, while white northerners and especially the British working class fell between, marked by the stresses of accelerated work routines and perhaps poorer diets in the trajectory toward an urban-industrial world.

These patterns suggest that white southern men, surviving to be measured at military enlistment, fared the best ecologically of all early Americans. We might suggest that their advantage came through a remarkable externalization of ecological cost. Southern populations spreading across the eighteenth-century upcountry occupied a favorable temperate biome at very low densities. The available land allowed free grazing for livestock, which provided high levels of protein. It also allowed a form of the old swidden, shifting agricultural system that had first emerged in the seventeenth-century Tidewater. Labor costs were reduced in avoiding agricultural improvement, and externalized onto unfree black Americans. And in consuming manufactured imports, southerners externalized the ecological costs of industrialization, which were experienced in lower standards of living and adult height. This world, of course, was the Jeffersonian ideal, a slave-based agrarianism that directed health and prosperity to the white male head of household. It was also, given enough land, an ecologically sustainable world. Southerners could continue to escape both Malthusian checks and Boserupian intensification by simply reproducing an extensive extractive agriculture on successive frontiers, and by ensuring that tariffs would not disrupt a favorable balance between export and import prices. Both these strategies would reach a political limit in the 1850s.

Northern society, first in eastern New England, could not follow this model of sustainability through externalization. Rather than escaping Malthus by dispersion and expansion on the model of seventeenth-century England, northern society would follow the eighteenth-century British route, escaping through Boserupian intensification – classically seen as development, rather than growth. The result was an internalization of cost. Whether through teenage labor or poor nutrition, northern men would be shorter. Higher population densities required more intense labor, and extracted a greater toll on the land. The result would be more effort required to manage limited resources, and to manage the ecological impacts of industrialization and urbanization (Fogel, 1989, pp. 301–12; Steinberg, 1991). The challenges of intensification and internalization fed upon and encouraged a complex civil life.

These are some of the key dimensions of an ecological approach to colonial America, set in a wider Atlantic setting. The story involves a vast struggle for resources as the peoples of three continents collided on unequal terms. I leave this story unfinished in the middle of the eighteenth century, as an accelerated commerce was one symptom of the emergence of an evolving oceanic process of interconnected change in populations, exchanges, and land-use. If I have stressed the counter-intensive agroecologies of the seventeenth-century colonies, completing this story would require a careful exploration of the reversal of this ecological regime. Starting in New England by the 1690s, and advancing as far south as the older Chesapeake settlements by the 1760s, rising populations, land pressures, warfare, and economic opportunity drove a progressive re-intensification of the economy – with significant and possibly measurable adverse effects on local ecologies. And such an exploration would argue that the return of these Americans to the stresses, the demands, and the possibilities of "getting ahead" embedded in Boserupian innovation were building deep strains in the imperial relation. The coming of the American Revolution in the 1760s was certainly grounded in constitutional issues, but it also was profoundly shaped by the incompatibility of competing centers of intensification within a single empire. That Revolution would set the stage for a shift of world-historical consequence, as the early internalizations of American industrial ecology gave way in the late nineteenth century to profound externalizations of environmental cost.

* * * * *

Where might the study of the ecological history of colonial North America move in the next decade or so? Certainly there is room for more studies of regional ecologies, most especially for the mid-Atlantic. These studies will undoubtedly exploit the emerging potential of computer-mapping and geographic information systems, allowing an increasingly powerful integration of historical and scientific data. Such studies can conceivably be attempted for entire colonies, coastlines, and eventually for the Atlantic as a whole. On a more traditional scale, the unfolding textual, cultural history of the environment may sharpen or obscure my suggestion that first nature and then culture prevailed in colonial America.

But beyond these two approaches, the close analysis of the ecology of material life set in cultural landscapes comprises one of the most promising domains of ongoing and prospective research in this entire historical field. Grounded in a fruitful synthesis of demography, paleoecological studies, archaeology, geography, quantitative social history, and cultural analysis, such studies can explore questions of ecological services, cultural construction, ethnic difference, and gender role. This work requires a reinvigorated attention to material things as the critical point of mediation between culture and nature, between constructed identity and ecological circumstance. Potentially, such studies will provide the ground for a new American historical narrative.

BIBLIOGRAPHY

Allen, David Grayson: *In English Ways: The Movement of Societies and the Transferral of English Local Law and Custom to Massachusetts Bay in the Seventeenth Century* (Chapel Hill: University of North Carolina Press, 1981).

Austen, Ralph A. and Smith, Woodruff D.: "Private Tooth Decay as Public Economic Virtue: The Slave-Sugar Triangle, Consumerism, and European Industrialization." In Joseph E. Inkori and Stanley L. Engerman, eds., *The Atlantic Slave Trade: Effects on Economies, Societies and Peoples in Africa, the Americas, and Europe* (Durham: Duke University Press, 1992), pp. 183–204.

Bairoch, Paul: *Economics and World History: Myths and Paradoxes* (Chicago: University of Chicago Press, 1993).

Boserup, Ester: *The Conditions of Agricultural Growth: The Economics of Agrarian Change under Population Pressure* (Chicago: Aldine, 1965).

Boserup, Ester: *Population and Technological Change: A Study of Long-Term Trends* (Chicago: University of Chicago Press, 1981).

Bragdon, Kathleen J.: *Native Peoples of Southern New England, 1500–1650* (Norman: University of Oklahoma Press, 1996).

Breen, Timothy H.: "Creative Adaptations: Peoples and Cultures." In Jack P. Greene and J. R. Poles, eds., *Colonial British America: Essays in the New History of the Early Modern Era* (Baltimore: Johns Hopkins University Press, 1984), pp. 195–232.

Breen, Timothy H.: *Tobacco Culture: The Mentality of the Great Tidewater Planters on the Eve of the Revolution* (Princeton: Princeton University Press, 1985).

Breen, Timothy H.: "An Empire of Goods: The Anglicization of Colonial America, 1690–1776." *Journal of British Studies* 25 (1986), pp. 467–99.

Brooks, George E.: *Landlords and Strangers: Ecology, Society, and Trade in West Africa, 1000–*

1630 (Boulder, CO: Westview Press, 1993).

Brush, Grace S.: "Geology and Paleoecology of Chesapeake Bay: A Long-Term Monitoring Tool for Management." *Journal of the Washington Academy of Sciences* 76 (1986), pp. 146–60.

Buikstra, Jane E.: "Diet and Disease in Late Prehistory." In John W. Verano and Douglas H. Ubelaker, eds., *Disease and Demography in the Americas* (Washington, DC: Smithsonian Institution Press, 1993), pp. 87–102.

Bushman, Richard L.: "Opening the American Countryside." In James A. Henretta et al., eds., *The Transformation of Early American History: Society, Authority, and Ideology* (New York: Knopf, 1991), pp. 237–56.

Bushman, Richard L.: *The Refinement of America* (New York: Knopf, 1992).

Butlin, Robin A. and Roberts, Neil, eds.: *Ecological Relations in Historical Times* (Oxford: Blackwell, 1995).

Butzer, Carl: "The Americas before and after 1492." *Annals of the Association of American Geographers* 82 (1992), pp. 345–368.

Canny, Nicholas: "English Migration into and across the Atlantic during the Seventeenth and Eighteenth Centuries." In Nicholas Canny, ed., *Europeans on the Move: Studied on European Migration, 1500–1800* (Oxford: Clarendon, 1994), pp. 39–75.

Carr, Lois Green, Menard, Russel R., and Walsh, Lorena: *Robert Cole's World: Agriculture & Society in Early Maryland* (Chapel Hill, NC: University of North Carolina Press, 1991), pp. 33–43.

Carson, Cary, Hoffman, Ronald, and Albert, Peter J., eds.: *Of Consuming Interests: The Styles of Life in the Eighteenth Century* (Charlottesville, VA: University Press of Virginia, 1994).

Childs, St. Julien R.: *Malaria and Colonization in the Carolina Low Country, 1526–1696* (Baltimore, MD: Johns Hopkins University Press, 1940).

Clemens, Paul G. E.: *The Atlantic Economy and Colonial Maryland's Eastern Shore: From Tobacco to Grain* (Ithaca, NY: Cornell University Press, 1980).

Cook, David Noble: *Born to Die: Disease and New World Conquest, 1492–1650* (New York: Cambridge University Press, 1998).

Craven, Avery O.: *Soil Exhaustion as a Factor in the Agricultural History of Virginia and Maryland, 1606–1860* (Urbana, IL: University of Illinois, 1925).

Cronon, William: *Changes in the Land: Indians, Colonists, and the Ecology of New England* (New York: Hill and Wang, 1983).

Cronon, William: "Modes of Prophecy and Production: Placing Nature in History." *Journal of American History* 76 (1990), pp. 1122–31.

Cronon, William: *Nature's Metropolis: Chicago and the Great West* (New York: W. W. Norton, 1991).

Cronon, William: "The Trouble with Wilderness: Getting Back to the Wrong Nature." In William Cronon, ed., *Uncommon Ground: Rethinking the Human Place in Nature* (New York: W. W. Norton, 1996), pp. 69–90.

Crosby, Alfred W.: *The Columbian Exchange: Biological and Cultural Consequences of 1492* (Westport, CT: Greenwood, 1972).

Crosby, Alfred W.: *Ecological Imperialism: The Biological Expansion of Europe, 900–1900* (New York: Cambridge University Press, 1986).

Crosby, Alfred W.: "Demography, Maize, Land, and the American Character." In *Germs, Seeds, & Animals: Studies in Ecological History* (Armonk, NY: M. E. Sharpe, 1994), pp. 148–79.

Crosby, Alfred W.: "The Past and Present of Environmental History." *American Historical Review* 100 (1995), pp. 1177–89.

Curtin, Philip D.: *Cross-Cultural Trade in World History* (New York: Cambridge University Press, 1984).

Curtin, Philip D.: *Rise and Fall of the Plantation Complex: Essays in Atlantic History* (New York:

Cambridge University Press, 1990).

Daniels, John D.: "The Indian Population of North America in 1492." *William and Mary Quarterly* 3rd ser., 49 (1992), pp. 298–320.

Demeny, Paul: "Population." In B. L. Turner II, William Clark, Robert W. Kates, John F. Richards, Jessica T. Matthews, and William B. Meyer, eds., *The Earth as Transformed by Human Action: Global and Regional Changes in the Biosphere over the Past 300 Years* (New York: Cambridge University Press, 1990), pp. 41–54.

Demeritt, David: "Ecology, Objectivity, and Critique in Writings on Nature and Human Societies," with a reply by William Cronon, "Cutting Loose or Running Aground?" *Journal of Historical Geography* 20 (1994), pp. 22–43.

Diamond, Jared: *Guns, Germs, and Steel: The Fates of Human Societies* (New York: Knopf, 1997).

Dobyns, Henry F.: "Estimating Aboriginal American Populations: An Appraisal of Techniques with a New Hemispheric Estimate." *Current Anthropology* 7 (1966), pp. 395–416.

Donahue, Brian: "Plowland, Pastureland, Woodland and Meadow: Husbandry in Concord, Massachusetts, 1635–1771" (Ph.D. dissertation, Brandeis University, 1995).

Dunlap, Thomas R.: *Nature and the English Diaspora: Environment and History in the United States, Canada, Australia, and New Zealand* (New York: Cambridge University Press, 1999).

Dunn, Richard S.: *Sugar and Slaves: The Rise of the Planter Class in the English West Indies, 1624–1713* (Chapel Hill, NC: University of North Carolina Press, 1972).

Earle, Carville V.: *The Evolution of a Tidewater Settlement System: All Hollow's Parish, Maryland, 1650–1783* (Chicago: University of Chicago Dept. of Geography, 1975).

Earle, Carville V.: "Environment, Disease, and Mortality in Early Virginia." In Thad W. Tate and David L. Ammerman, eds., *Colonial Chesapeake in the Seventeenth Century: Essays in Anglo-American Society & Politics* (Chapel Hill, NC: University of North Carolina Press, 1979), pp. 96–125.

Earle, Carville V.: "The Myth of the Southern Soil Miner: Macrohistory, Agricultural Innovation, and Environmental Change." In Donald Worster, ed., *The Ends of the Earth: Perspectives on Modern Environmental History* (New York: Cambridge University Press, 1988), pp. 175–210.

Easterlin, Richard A.: "Factors in the Decline of the Farm Family Fertility in the United States: Some Preliminary Research Results." *Journal of American History* 63 (1976), pp. 609–14.

Eldridge, Niles: *The Pattern of Evolution* (New York: W. H. Freeman, 1999).

Engerman, Stanley L.: "The Slave Trade and British Capital Formation in the Eighteenth Century: A Comment on the Williams Thesis." *Business History Review* 46 (1972), pp. 430–43.

Fagan, Brian: *The Little Ice Age: How Climate Made History, 1300–1850* (New York: Basic Books, 2000).

Fenn, Elizabeth A.: *Pox Americana: The Great Smallpox Epidemic of 1775–82* (New York: Hill and Wang, 2001).

Fischer, David Hackett: *The Great Wave: Price Revolutions and the Rhythm of History* (New York: Oxford University Press, 1996), pp. 65–102.

Flannery, Timothy F.: "The Fate of Empire in Low- and High-Energy Ecosystems." In Tom Griffiths and Libby Robin, eds., *Ecology & Empire: Environmental History of Settler Societies* (Seattle: University of Washington Press, 1997), pp. 46–59.

Fogel, Robert W.: *Without Consent or Contract: The Rise and Fall of American Slavery* (New York: W. W. Norton, 1989), pp. 301–12.

Galenson, David W.: "The Settlement and Growth of the Colonies: Population, Labor, and Economic Development." In Stanley L. Engerman and Robert E. Gallman, eds., *The Cambridge Economic History of the United States*, vol. 1, *The Colonial Era* (New York: Cambridge University Press, 1996), pp. 135–208.

Garrison, J. Ritchie: "Farm Dynamics and Regional Exchange: The Connecticut Valley Beef Trade, 1670–1850." *Agricultural History* 61 (1987), pp. 1–17.

Gemery, Henry A.: "Emigration from the British Isles to the New World, 1630–1700." In Paul Uselding, ed., *Research in Economic History* 5 (1980), pp. 179–231.

Goldstone, Jack A.: "The Demographic Revolution in England: A Re-examination." *Population Studies* 49 (1986), pp. 5–33.

Goldstone, Jack A.: *Revolution and Rebellion in the Early Modern World* (Berkeley: University of California Press, 1991).

Greene, Jack P.: *Pursuits of Happiness: The Social Development of Early Modern British Colonies and the Formation of American Culture* (Chapel Hill, NC: University of North Carolina Press, 1988).

Gross, Robert A.: *The Minutemen and their World* (New York: Hill and Wang, 1976).

Gross, Robert A.: "Culture and Cultivation: Agriculture and Society in Thoreau's Concord." *Journal of American History* 69 (1982), pp. 42–61.

Inkori, Joseph E.: "Slavery and the Revolution in Cotton Textile Production in England." In Joseph E. Inkori and Stanley L. Engerman, eds., *The Atlantic Slave Trade: Effects on Economies, Societies and Peoples in Africa, the Americas, and Europe* (Durham: Duke University Press, 1992), pp. 145–82.

Jennings, Francis: *The Invasion of America: Indians, Colonialism, and the Cant of Conquest* (Chapel Hill, NC: University of North Carolina Press, 1975).

Johannessen, Sissel and Hastorf, Christine A., eds.: *Corn and Culture in the Prehistoric New World* (Boulder, CO: Westview, 1994).

Jones, Eric L.: "Creative Disruptions in American Agriculture, 1620–1820." *Agricultural History* 48 (1974), pp. 510–28.

Jones, Eric L.: *The European Miracle: Environments, Economies, and Geopolitics in the History of Europe and Asia*, 2nd ed. (New York: Cambridge University Press, 1987).

Jones, Eric L.: "The European Background." In Stanley L. Engerman and Robert E. Gallman, eds., *The Cambridge Economic History of the United States*, vol. 1, *The Colonial Era* (New York: Cambridge University Press, 1996), pp. 95–135.

Kiple, Kenneth F.: *The Caribbean Slave: A Biological History* (Cambridge: Cambridge University Press, 1984).

Komlos, John: "The Industrial Revolution as the Escape from the Malthusian Trap." Paper presented at the Social Science History Association Meeting, 1993.

Kulikoff, Allan: *Tobacco and Slaves: The Development of Southern Cultures in the Chesapeake, 1680–1800* (Chapel Hill, NC: University of North Carolina Press, 1986).

Kupperman, Karen O.: "The Puzzle of Climate in the Early Colonial Period." *American Historical Review* 87 (1982), pp. 1262–89.

Kupperman, Karen O.: "Fear of Hot Climates." *William and Mary Quarterly* 3rd ser., 41 (1984a), pp. 213–40.

Kupperman, Karen O.: "Climate and Mastery of the Wilderness in Seventeenth-Century New England." In David D. Hall and David G. Allen, eds., *Seventeenth-Century New England* (Charlottesville, VA: University Press of Virginia, 1984b), pp. 3–39.

Kutzbach, John E. and Webb, Thompson, III: "Late Quaternary Climatic and Vegetational Change in Eastern North America: Concepts, Models, and Data." In Linda C. K. Shane and Edward J. Cushing, eds., *Quaternary Landscapes* (Minneapolis, MN: University of Minnesota Press, 1991), pp. 175–218.

Landes, Davis S.: *The Wealth and Poverty of Nations: Why Some Nations are so Rich and Some so Poor* (New York: W. W. Norton, 1998).

Langer, William: "American Foods and Europe's Population Growth." *Journal of Social History* 8 (1975), pp. 51–66.

Larsen, Clark Spencer and Milner, George R., eds.: *In the Wake of Contact: Biological Responses to Conquest* (New York: Willey-Liss, 1994).

Levine, David: *Family Formation in an Age of Nascent Capitalism* (New York: Academic Press,

1977).

Livi-Bacci, Massimo: *Population and Nutrition: An Essay on European Demographic History*, trans. Tania Croft-Murray with the assistance of Carl Ipsen (New York: Cambridge University Press, 1991).

Lockridge, Kenneth: "Land, Population and the Evolution of New England Society, 1630–1790." *Past & Present* 39 (1968), pp. 62–80.

MacCameron, Robert: "Environmental Change in Colonial New Mexico." *Environmental History Review* 18 (1994), pp. 17–40.

MacFarlane, Alan: *The Savage Wars of Peace: England, Japan, and the Malthusian Trap* (Oxford: Blackwell, 1997).

Main, Jackson T. and Main, Gloria L.: "The Red Queen in New England?" *William and Mary Quarterly* 3rd ser., 56 (1999), pp. 121–50.

Malthus, Thomas: *An Essay on Population and A Summary View of the Principle of Population* (1798, 1830; Harmondsworth: Penguin, 1970).

McAndrews, John H.: "Human Disturbance of North American Forests and Grasslands: The Fossil Pollen Record." In Brian J. Huntley and Thompson Webb III, eds., *Vegetation History* (Boston, MA: Kluwer, 1988), pp. 673–97.

McCann, James: *Green Land, Brown Land, Black Land: An Environmental History of Africa, 1800–1990* (Portsmouth: Heinemann, 1999).

McClelland, Peter D.: *Sowing Modernity: America's First Agricultural Revolution* (Ithaca, NY: Cornell University Press, 1997).

McKibbon, Bill: "Future Old Growth." In Mary Byrd David, ed., *Eastern Old Growth Forests: Prospects for Rediscovery and Recovery* (Washington, DC: Island Press, 1996), pp. 344–58.

McMahon, Sarah: "A Comfortable Subsistence: The Changing Composition of Diet in Rural New England." *William and Mary Quarterly* 3rd ser., 42 (1985), pp. 26–65.

McMahon, Sarah: "'All Things in their Proper Season': Seasonal Rhythms of Diet in Nineteenth-Century New England." *Agricultural History* 63 (2) (1989), pp. 130–51.

McNeill, John R.: "Agriculture, Forests, and Ecological History: Brazil, 1500–1984." *Environmental Review* 10 (1986), pp. 123–33.

McNeill, William H.: *Plagues and Peoples* (Garden City: Anchor, 1976).

Melville, Elinor G. K.: *A Plague of Sheep: Environmental Consequences of the Conquest of Mexico* (New York: Cambridge University Press, 1994).

Menard, Russell R.: "Migration, Ethnicity, and the Rise of an Atlantic Economy: The Re-Peopling of British America, 1600–1790." In Rudolph J. Vecoli and Suzanne M. Sinke, eds., *A Century of European Migrations, 1830–1903* (Urbana, IL: University of Illinois Press, 1991), pp. 58–77.

Merchant, Carolyn: "The Theoretical Structure of Ecological Revolutions." *Environmental Review* 11 (1987), pp. 265–74.

Merchant, Carolyn: *Ecological Revolutions: Nature, Gender, and Science in New England* (Chapel Hill, NC: University of North Carolina Press, 1989).

Merrell, James H.: *The Indian's New World: Catawbas and their Neighbors from European Contact through the Era of Removal* (Chapel Hill, NC: University of North Carolina Press, 1989).

Miller, Henry M.: "Transforming a 'Splendid and Delightsome Land': Colonists and Ecological Change in the Chesapeake, 1607–1820." *Journal of the Washington Academy of Sciences* 76 (1986), pp. 173–87.

Mintz, Sydney W.: *Sweetness and Power: The Place of Sugar in World History* (New York: Viking, 1974).

Morgan, Philip D.: *Slave Counterpoint: Black Culture in the Eighteenth-Century Chesapeake and Lowcountry* (Chapel Hill, NC: University of North Carolina Press, 1998), pp. 29–58.

Mulholland, Mitchell T.: "Territoriality and Horticulture: A Perspective for Prehistoric Southern New England." In George P. Nicholas, ed., *Holocene Human Ecology in Northeast America*

(New York: Plenum Press, 1988), 137–66.

Nash, Gary B.: *The Urban Crucible: Social Change, Political Consciousness, and the Origins of the American Revolution* (Cambridge, MA: Harvard University Press, 1979).

Newman, Lucile F. et al.: "Agricultural Intensification, Urbanization, and Hierarchy." In Lucile F. Newman et al., eds., *Hunger in History: Food Shortage, Poverty, and Deprivation* (Cambridge, MA: Blackwell, 1990), pp. 101–25.

O'Brien, Patrick: "European Economic Development: The Contribution of the Periphery." *Economic History Review* 35 (1982), pp. 1–18.

Papenfuse, Edward C., Jr.: "Planter Behavior and Economic Opportunity in a Staple Economy." *Agricultural History* 66 (1972), pp. 297–311.

Parish, Susan Scott: "The Female Possum and the Nature of the New World." *William and Mary Quarterly* 3rd ser. (1997), pp. 475–514.

Parker, Geoffrey and Smith, Leslie M., eds.: *The General Crisis of the Seventeenth Century*, 2nd ed. (London: Routledge and Kegan Paul, 1997).

Peacock, Evan: "Historical and Applied Perspectives on Prehistoric Land Use in Eastern North America." *Environment and History* 4 (1998), pp. 1–29.

Pelto, Gretel H. and Pelto, Pertti J.: "Diet and Delocalization: Dietary Changes since 1750." In Robert I. Rotberg and Theodore K. Rabb, eds., *Hunger in History: The Impact of Changing Food Production and Consumption Patterns on Society* (New York: Cambridge University Press, 1985), pp. 309–30.

Percy, David O.: "Ax or Plow?: Significant Landscape Alteration Rates in the Maryland and Virginia Tidewater." *Agricultural History* 66 (2) (1992), pp. 66–9.

Perzigian, Anthony J. et al.: "Prehistoric Health in the Ohio River Valley." In Mark N. Cohen and George J. Armelagos, eds., *Paleopathology at the Origins of Agriculture* (New York: Academic Press, 1984), pp. 347–66.

Phillips, Seymour: "The Medieval Background." In Nicholas Canny, ed., *Europeans on the Move: Studies on European Migration, 1500–1800* (Oxford: Clarendon Press, 1994), pp. 9–25.

Pielou, E. C.: *After the Ice Age: The Return of Life to Glaciated North America* (Chicago: University of Chicago Press, 1991).

Pomeranz, Kenneth: *A Great Divergence: China, Europe, and the Making of the Modern European Economy* (Princeton, NJ: Princeton University Press, 2000).

Potter, David M.: *People of Plenty: Economic Abundance and the American Character* (Chicago: University of Chicago Press, 1954).

Quinn, David B.: *Set Fair for Roanoke: Voyages and Colonies, 1584–1606* (Chapel Hill, NC: University of North Carolina Press, 1985).

Rothenberg, Winifred: *From Market-places to a Market Economy: The Transformation of Rural Massachusetts, 1750–1850* (Chicago: University of Chicago Press, 1992).

Sauer, Carl O.: *The Early Spanish Main* (Berkeley, CA: University of California Press, 1966).

Sauer, Carl O.: "European Backgrounds of American Agricultural Settlement." In Sauer, *Selected Essays, 1963–1975* (Berkeley: Turtle Island Press, 1981), pp. 16–44.

Schama, Simon: *Landscape and Memory* (New York: Knopf, 1995).

Shammas, Carole: *The Pre-industrial Consumer in England and America* (Oxford: Clarendon, 1990).

Silver, Timothy: *A New Face on the Countryside: Indians, Colonists, and Slaves in the South Atlantic Forests, 1500–1800* (New York: Cambridge University Press, 1990).

Skipp, Victor: *Crisis and Development: An Ecological Case Study of the Forest of Arden, 1570–1694* (Cambridge: Cambridge University Press, 1978).

Smith, Bruce: *The Emergence of Agriculture* (New York: Freeman, 1995), pp. 185–201.

Smith, Daniel Blake: "Mortality and Family in the Colonial Chesapeake." *Journal of Interdisciplinary History* 7 (1978), pp. 408–15.

Smith, Daniel Scott: "A Malthusian-Frontier Interpretation of United States Demographic History Before c. 1815." In Woodrow Borah et al., eds., *Urbanization in the Americas: The Background in Comparative Perspective* (Ottawa: National Museum of Man, 1980), pp. 15–24.

Solow, Barbara ed.: *Slavery and the Rise of the Atlantic System* (New York: Cambridge University Press, 1991).

Solow, Barbara, and Engerman, Stanley L., eds.: *British Capitalism and Caribbean Slavery: The Legacy of Eric Williams* (New York: Cambridge University Press, 1987).

Stahle, David W. et al.: "The Lost Colony and Jamestown Droughts." *Science* 240 (1998), pp. 564–68.

Steckel, Richard H.: "Nutritional Status in the Colonial Economy." *William and Mary Quarterly* 3rd ser., 56 (1999), pp. 31–52.

Steinberg, Theodore: *Nature Incorporated: Industrialization and the Waters of New England* (New York: Cambridge University Press, 1991).

Tate, Thad W. and Ammerman, David L., eds.: *Colonial Chesapeake in the Seventeenth Century: Essays in Anglo-American Society & Politics* (Chapel Hill, NC: University of North Carolina Press, 1979).

Taylor, Alan: "'Wasty Ways': Stories of American Settlement." *Environmental History* 3 (1998), pp. 291–310.

Temin, Peter: "Two View of the British Industrial Revolution." *Journal of Economic History* 57 (1997), pp. 63–82.

Ubelaker, Douglas H.: "North American Indian Population Size: Changing Perspectives." In John W. Verano and Douglas H. Ubelaker, eds., *Disease and Demography in the Americas* (Washington, DC: Smithsonian Institution Press, 1993), pp. 169–77.

Ulrich, Laurel Thatcher: *A Midwife's Tale: The Life of Martha Ballard, based on her Diary, 1785–1812* (New York: Knopf, 1990).

Verano, John W. and Douglas H. Ubelaker, eds.: *Disease and Demography in the Americas* (Washington, DC: Smithsonian Institution Press, 1993).

Vickers, Daniel: *Farmers and Fishermen: Two Centuries of Work in Essex County, Massachusetts, 1630–1850* (Chapel Hill, NC: University of North Carolina Press, 1994).

Vickers, Daniel, ed.: *Marine Resources and Human Societies in the North Atlantic Since 1500* (St. John's, Newfoundland: The Institute of Social and Economic Research, Memorial University, 1997).

Wallerstein, Immanuel: *The Modern World System: Capitalist Agriculture and the Origins of the European World-Economy in the Sixteenth Century* (New York: Academic Press, 1974).

Watts, David: *The West Indies: Patterns of Development, Culture, and Environmental Change since 1492* (Cambridge: Cambridge University Press, 1987).

Webb, James L.: *Desert Frontier: Ecological and Economic Change along the Western Sahel, 1600–1850* (Madison, WI: University of Wisconsin Press, 1995).

Weiskel, Timothy C.: "Agents of Empire: Steps toward an Ecology of Imperialism." *Environmental Review* 11 (1987), pp. 275–88.

Weiskel, Timothy C.: "Toward an Archaeology of Colonialism: Elements in the Ecological Transformation of the Ivory Coast." In Donald Worster, ed., *The Ends of the Earth: Perspectives on Modern Environmental History* (New York: Cambridge University Press, 1988), pp. 141–171.

Wells, Robert V.: "The Population of England's Colonies in America: Old English or New Americans?" *Population Studies* 46 (1992), pp. 85–102.

White, Richard: "Native Americans and the Environment." In W. R. Swagerty, ed., *Scholars and the Indian Experience: Critical Reviews of Recent Writing in the Social Sciences* (Bloomington, IN: Indiana University Press, 1984), pp. 179–204.

White, Richard: "Historiographical Essay: American Environmental History: The Development of a New Historical Field." *Pacific Coast Review* 54 (1985), pp. 297–335.

Whitney, Gordon G.: *From Coastal Wilderness to Fruited Plain: A History of Environmental Change in Temperate North America, 1500 to the Present* (Cambridge: Cambridge University Press, 1994).

Williams, Eric: *Capitalism and Slavery* (Chapel Hill, NC: University of North Carolina Press, 1944).

Williams, Michael: *Americans and Their Forests: A Historical Geography* (New York: Cambridge University Press, 1989).

Wolf, Eric R.: *Europe and the People Without History* (Berkeley, CA: University of California Press, 1982).

Wood, Joseph S.: *The New England Village*, with a contribution by Michael Steinitz (Baltimore, MD: Johns Hopkins University Press, 1997).

Worster, Donald: "Transformations of the Earth: Toward an Agroecological Perspective in History." *Journal of American History* 76 (1990), pp. 1087–107.

Worster, Donald: *The Wealth of Nature: Environmental History and the Ecological Imagination* (New York: Oxford University Press, 1993).

Worster, Donald: *Nature's Economy: A History of Ecological Ideas*, 2nd ed. (New York: Cambridge University Press, 1994).

Wrigley, E. A.: "The Growth of Population in Eighteenth-Century England: A Conundrum Resolved." *Past & Present* 98 (1983), pp. 21–51.

Wrigley, E. A. and Schofield, R. S.: *The Population History of England, 1541–1871: A Reconstruction* (Cambridge, MA: Harvard University Press, 1981).

Yentsch, Anne E.: *A Chesapeake Family and their Slaves: A Study in Historical Archaeology* (New York: Cambridge University Press, 1994).

Zahedieh, Nuala: "London and the Colonial Consumer in the Late Seventeenth Century." *Economic History Review* 47 (1994), pp. 239–61.

CHAPTER FOUR

Migration and Settlement

NED LANDSMAN

For students of a land whose inhabitants have proclaimed themselves a nation of immigrants almost from the beginning, historians of early America were long strangely silent about the subject of migration. Just a few decades ago, one looking to survey the literature in that area would have found little to consider, beyond a few short treatments of servant migration to the Chesapeake concerned principally with such questions as whether or not those groups were best described as "middling people" or "common sort" (Campbell, 1959; Galenson, 1978), some discussion of whether the "Great Migration" to New England was motivated principally by spiritual or secular impulses, and a few straightforward and uninspiring narratives of ethnic migration. There was markedly little in the way of detailed discussion of the transatlantic crossing, except as a part of the almost timeless experience of uprooting broadly sketched by Oscar Handlin. The closest we came to obtaining a full treatment of early migration, by Marcus Hansen (1940), was never completed and offered little coverage before the nineteenth century. What was already emerging as a remarkably nuanced portrait of African migration in the slave trade was rarely considered a part of that literature at all.

Perhaps that lack of attention was not so strange after all. Part of the problem was methodological: few historians then were capable of applying the sophisticated quantitative techniques upon which much of the recent discussion has depended. An even greater obstacle was conceptual: a still-pervasive belief in American exceptionalism and a consequent lack of interest in integrating migration into the mainstream of early American history. From the portrait of the "American farmer" by the French-born J. Hector St. John de Crèvecoeur through the frontier thesis of Frederick Jackson Turner and his followers, it was the confrontation with the new land and the new situation more than the backgrounds of the inhabitants or how they came to be there that rendered Americans distinctive. Migration was thus reduced to America's pre-history, interesting for what it said about how far Americans had come but, like such other elements of American pre-history as the pre-Columbian inhabitants, not really determinative of what had followed.

A second aspect of American exceptionalism that discouraged the study of migration was the assumption that if the details of the Atlantic crossing mattered little, its result – the turning of Europeans into Americans – was of paramount importance. In that view, the transatlantic migration was radically different from other geographic movements. Thus, American historians saw little reason to examine or even to think about migration within Europe. Where such migrations were noticed at all, they were viewed as mere shufflings of population lacking the profound transformative effects that followed the transatlantic migration – reinforcements of the old order rather than facilitators of the new. Neither did the voluntary migration of European settlers seem to bear much relationship to the forced migration of Africans, nor to the regular, often seasonal movements of American Indians, which – like the seemingly circular movements of Europeans at home – seemed to partake less of the migrant than the migratory.

During the past several decades the situation changed considerably. Much more information is now available; historians influenced by European historians of the Annales school and the Cambridge Group for the History of Population and Social Structure undertook detailed examinations of many of the social groups that migrated to, or within, the Americas. Others have employed complex quantitative methods derived from historical demography and migration studies to map out usable estimates of the scale, paths, and pace of migration. Early Americanists have begun to enter seriously into comparative history and are far more likely than their predecessors both to consider and to examine for themselves the backgrounds of American migrants, not only from England but from other parts of Britain and western Europe, as well as Africa and North America. In addition, Bernard Bailyn, Jack P. Greene, and David Hackett Fischer all attempted major syntheses concerned largely with the general topics of migration and settlement.

The assumptions of those historians have changed as well. As Americans have come to see themselves as ever more enmeshed within global networks of communication, American historians have paid more attention to transnational links in the past. They have begun to consider American colonization as a part of a larger and often interconnected migration system involving domestic, international, and transoceanic population movements. Historians have come to recognize that the movements of Africans and Native Americans were far more closely interwoven with the transatlantic migration of Europeans than they hitherto had supposed. Moreover, they have discovered that the styles and even cultures of migration have varied significantly with the circumstances and the historical traditions of the groups involved and have begun to consider how those distinct migration cultures affected the developing societies of colonial British America. The result has been a considerable reintegration of migration into early American history, the completion of which still occasionally runs afoul of a lingering exceptionalism.

The leader in this field has been Bernard Bailyn, who has made migration into the centerpiece of his recent work on early American history, both in his two books on what he calls the "peopling" of early America and in the seminar on the Atlantic world that he has created for younger scholars at Harvard. In his book-length survey of *The Peopling of British North America: An Introduction* (1986), Bailyn offered four general propositions about early American migration. These can serve as useful benchmarks for evaluating how the literature had evolved to that point, and how it has continued to develop.

Measuring Migration

Bailyn's first proposition was that the peopling of British North America represented "an extension outward and an expansion in scale of domestic mobility in the lands of the immigrants' origins" (p. 20). Much of that has become commonplace, and European historians have made it abundantly evident that, far from having lived in the static and immobile world historians used to imagine, early modern Europe was rife with movement. There were two partially separate streams of movement. The larger one consisted of a system of local moves by individuals and families, while the smaller was a variable proportion of longer movements, principally of young people seeking employment and the ambitious searching for opportunity (Clark, 1979; Houston, 1992; Canny, 1994).

Transatlantic migrations, as Bailyn suggests, were often set up by those internal flows. In England, London became a great magnet for population, drawing to it something on the order of a fifth of the English population (Wrigley, 1967). A fraction of that moving population decided to venture farther, and both London and Bristol served as funnels for transatlantic migration (Horn, 1994, pp. 39–44). Amsterdam and Rotterdam served similar functions for Continental migrants, a portion of whom subsequently took ship for America.

It is less often recognized by American historians how regularly Europeans moved outside of their homelands, even to places other than America. Amsterdam attracted Protestant populations from all over Europe, some of whom ventured onward to the Dutch overseas empires, especially the East Indies, which may have absorbed as much as 20 percent of the young men of the Netherlands in the seventeenth and eighteenth centuries (De Vries, 1985). Germans migrated northward to the Low Countries and eastward into eastern Europe (Fertig, 1994). Some English men and women moved to the Continent, while more went to Ireland, which drew close to 200,000 during the seventeenth century (Games, 1997; Canny, 1994). Scots left their homeland at an even greater rate per capita, for Ireland, the Netherlands, Scandinavia, and Poland. Abroad, they established regular places for themselves, including a group of semi-permanent overseas communities in Ulster, Scandinavia, and Rotterdam, to which they would regularly go and from which they would often return (Smout et al., 1994).

So extensive were some of those movements that they may compel us to reconsider the last part of Bailyn's first proposition: that the American colonization "ultimately . . . introduced a new and dynamic force in European population history, which permanently altered the traditional configuration" (p. 20). That may, indeed, have been true in the long run; it probably was not so until the nineteenth century. Instead, the transatlantic migration remained but one part of a diverse, ongoing, and irregular flow. During the seventeenth century, migration to America was of limited interest to most European peoples. Thus, New France was never a well-populated colony; even among those who ventured there, the majority apparently chose not to remain (Moogk, 1989). New Netherlands had to get settlers from wherever it could get them – English, German, Scots, and Walloons, as well as Dutch – and it never drew the numbers that traveled to other parts of the Dutch commercial empire, including the East Indies and Brazil (Lucassen, 1994). The small settlements in Nova Scotia attracted so few Scots that a small band of English settlers there probably constituted a majority of the colonists (Griffiths and Reid, 1992), even though tens of thousands of Scots departed for Ulster, the Netherlands, and Poland during those same years. Whether it was the lure of riches in the Dutch East Indies, or the traditional opportunities that Scots merchants, mercenaries, and peddlers found on the European Continent, the immediate influence of traditional European patterns of migration for many groups was to inhibit movement to the New World.

The principal exceptions to that trend were Spain (to the whole of its American possessions and not principally North America) and England. Why the English proved such an exception among northern Europeans has not been fully explored, largely because the English experience has too often been taken for the norm. It does seem that England may have had fewer links to other European destinations than some of its competitors, such as Scotland, Ireland, or the Netherlands, although it had many (Canny, 1994). It certainly directed a much larger proportion of its emigrants towards North America than did its neighbors.

Even the English movements were less than a permanent dynamic force in migration history. English migration to the New World peaked during the first half of the seventeenth century but declined thereafter, apparently quite considerably (Canny, 1994). The migrations of other peoples also tended to ebb and flow. Transatlantic migration from the Rhineland, insignificant before 1700, increased substantially towards the middle of the eighteenth century but fell off dramatically thereafter (Wokeck, 1989). Only Ireland and especially Scotland among European nations were increasing their transatlantic traffic towards the end of the colonial period, but that hardly represented a new dynamic in migration. Indeed, the overall rate of emigration from Scotland was much lower in the eighteenth century than it had been the century before, when Scots had rarely traveled to America (Smout et al., 1994).

None of this would be readily apparent had historians not developed reasonable estimates for the size of those movements. Three decades ago, there was little more to work from than the often-unreliable estimates of contemporaries or the fragmentary records kept at a few European or American ports. More recently, some historians have tried to establish the magnitude of migration through a complex quantitative process that involves calculating backwards from the best population figures for each of the British colonies, from which they subtract an estimate of natural increase based upon presumed fertility and mortality rates for each region. The remainder is attributed to migration. The leader in this field has been Henry Gemery (1980), who estimated that close to 400,000 English men and women migrated to North America during the seventeenth century, of whom more than half went to the Caribbean. Gemery matched those numbers against the estimate of English historical demographers that that nation lost about half a million people to emigration over the same period (Wrigley and Schofield, 1981).

Nicholas Canny (1994) has recently raised some new questions about Gemery's numbers. Estimating that close to 200,000 persons migrated from England to Ireland during the century, Canny points out that if Wrigley and Schofield's calculations of total emigration from England of half a million during that period are accurate, then Gemery's projection of 400,000 English migrants to British America must be too high. He suggests making up the shortfall in English migration by recognizing that a substantial number of Irish also migrated to the West Indies (Cullen, 1994). Here we may have reached the point beyond which aggregate numbers of this sort can be pushed. Canny's argument does highlight the danger of assuming that all or even most emigration from Europe was directed towards North America, as well as the fact that our estimates of all of those migration flows are of necessity strongly interconnected. It also reinforces the contention that Canny and other followers of

D. B. Quinn have made for including Ireland within the 'westward enterprise' (Andrews et al., 1979).

Canny's discussion hints at a bigger problem that emerged in attempting to offer overall projections of eighteenth-century migration: the later colonies derived their populations from more varied migration streams. Thus historians have had to work closely with the records of the many diverse groups who arrived during the eighteenth century in what were largely separate migrations, compiling totals from the bottom up. The only comprehensive data derive from the very end of the period, when a flood of migration from Scotland, Ireland, and northern England following the end of the Seven Years' War led landowners in those areas to fear a mass exodus, and authorities to record all departures. Working backwards from those registers, which were kept only for the period from 1773 to 1775, Bailyn has suggested a total of more than 55,000 Irish and 40,000 Scots during the brief interval between the end of the Seven Years' War and the outbreak of Revolution in 1775, and a total of more than 140,000 European migrants during those same years (1986a, p. 26). Several historians who have worked closely with the records of some of those groups have suggested lower numbers (Wokeck, 1989, p. 137; Fogelman, 1996, p. 2).

The best work on any one group is that on German-speakers, part of a vast flow of migrants, only a minority of whom headed for North America. Most of these arrived in Philadelphia, organized by an active group of merchant entrepreneurs in Rotterdam, Amsterdam, London, and Philadelphia (Wokeck, 1986; Beiler, 1997). From the records of the last port, Marianne Wokeck (1989) has detailed a cycle of flow and ebb in German immigration, beginning in earnest in 1727 and reaching a peak during the 1740s and 1750s, when as many as 37,000 migrants from the Rhineland reached the Quaker city. Migration was largely halted by the outbreak of war in 1754 and never regained its former level, as an increasing proportion of migrants were drawn instead towards eastern Europe. Thus, the migration of German-speakers was waning on the eve of the American Revolution just as that for other non-English groups accelerated. Wokeck projects about 100,000 German-speaking migrants to North America overall, although others have offered figures either somewhat higher (Roeber, 1993, p. ix) or lower (Fogelman, 1996, p. 2).

Scottish migration poses a considerably greater problem. Not only were usable emigration records almost wholly lacking before the 1770s; they would not be very revealing in any event, since nearly all Scots migrants traveled as individuals on regular commercial ventures rather than in emigration parties. Moreover, the traditionally high rate of out-migration from Scotland meant that many transatlantic migrants sailed not from Scotland but from England or Ireland. Thus Ian Graham (1956) estimated 25,000 Scottish emigrants between 1763 and 1775 by relying entirely upon reports of the departures or arrivals of emigrants, but others have suggested higher numbers (Bailyn, 1986a; Smout et al., 1994). Port records from the north of Ireland are better, and estimates from those have included 100,000–120,000 by R. J. Dickson (1966) and the 55,000 Bailyn suggested for the period after the Seven Years War, although Marianne Wokeck's tabulations from the port records of Philadelphia, the largest point of entry, would suggest a lower figure (1989, p. 137).

The Irish estimates would include any Scots who departed from Ulster, which may have been a considerable number. That there was a relationship between those migrations is clear; during the 1690s, a substantial famine in parts of Scotland led to catastrophic mortality and a migration to Ulster generally reckoned above 40,000 persons (Smout et al., 1994). Over the next half-century, while emigration from Scotland, with its lower population, was vastly reduced, Ulster and its expanded population became one of the leading sources of emigration to North America.

Adding up the estimates for European migrants to British North America during the colonial period would give a figure of 700,000 to 800,000, including the Caribbean. That was far exceeded by the migration of Africans in the slave trade, which included about 660,000 to mainland North America and more than two and a half million to the West Indies, as tabulated by Philip Curtin three decades ago and revised only modestly since then (1969; Lovejoy, 1982; Fogel, 1989). Even that represented only a fraction of the nearly ten million slaves in the Atlantic slave trade and an even smaller proportion of the forced migration of Africans to all parts of the world (Manning, 1996). Only in the first half of the seventeenth century did migration to North America from England, or, indeed, from all of Europe, exceed that from Africa.

All of these calculations are for net migration only; they do not consider those immigrants who may have returned to Britain. In a few cases, the number of return migrants may have been substantial. During the Civil War of the 1640s, with civil war in Britain, more New Englanders may have returned to England than ventured to New England, some of those to fight on behalf of the Parliamentary cause. David Cressy has estimated that as many as a sixth of all New England migrants may have returned to England (1987, p. 192), although that figure is calculated on the assumption that some 21,000 English men and women ventured there during the Great Migration, which is probably too high an estimate (Anderson, 1991, pp. 15–16). A high proportion of Scots also may have been return migrants, for reasons that will be discussed below. Nearly everywhere there was some return migration; how much is as yet anyone's guess.

The largest proportion of European migrants probably traveled as indentured servants. In what remains the most comprehensive examination of the scale of colonial servitude, David Galenson estimated a total of 300,000 to 400,000 to all of the colonies after 1650 out of a total European migration of 600,000 during those years (1981, p. 17). In addition, Roger Ekirch has found in the neighborhood of 50,000 convicts exported to the colonies from Britain and Ireland over the course of the eighteenth century (1987, pp. 25–7).

Although historians have yet to calculate overall rates of emigration by gender, two facts emerge from the literature. Male migrants outnumbered female virtually everywhere, but by a ratio that varied considerably over time and from region to region. In the Chesapeake, men outnumbered women by more than three to one until almost the end of the seventeenth century, after which female migrants began to appear in proportionally greater numbers even as the rate of English migration fell off (Menard, 1988). The migration to New England was more family-oriented, with a more even sex ratio, although Richard Archer, who has analysed records pertaining to more than 9,000 migrants to New England before 1650, finds many more males and single persons than have historians who have worked from town records or smaller samples (Archer, 1990; Anderson, 1991; Breen and Foster, 1973). Among German, Scots, and Irish settlers, young, single, and male migrants predominated during periods of lighter migration, but free families – and a relatively large number of females – apparently formed the bulk of the migrants during peak periods: the 1740s and early 1750s

for German-speakers, and the 1770s for Scots and Irish. The reasons for those variations are complex and can only be understood within the context of each group's
story. In the aftermath of the Seven Years' War, for example, migration from the
Rhineland was becoming more male, and falling, just as that from Scotland and Ireland was becoming more family-oriented and rising. Overall, Galenson suggests that
among servants, women may have comprised in the neighborhood of 20 percent of
the arrivals during the seventeenth century but only half of that a century later (1981,
pp. 23–6). The sex ratio among free passengers, including families, would of course
have been much closer.

The work of Russell Menard on British migration to the Chesapeake (1988) illustrates clearly how close attention to migration flows can illuminate the history of a
region. Building upon the work of scholars in migration studies and the history of
European migration as well as the methods of Henry Gemery, Menard not only provides the best data we have for total immigration into that region but carefully places
it within the context of economic and demographic developments on both sides of the
Atlantic. Like Bailyn, Menard views that migration as the direct outgrowth of England's various domestic migration systems, although the latter's nuanced portrayal
suggests that throughout the period, the Chesapeake remained just one element of a
complex transatlantic system rather than the dynamic element.

After starting slowly early in the seventeenth century, English migration to the
Chesapeake peaked in the middle decades at 2,000 to 3,000 per year and then declined rapidly after 1680. The dropping pace of migration was affected both by local
factors, such as the fall in tobacco prices, which made the Chesapeake less attractive,
and – at least as important – by a general decline in the overall rates of long-distance
migration and of emigration within England itself. Moreover, with the emergence of
new English colonies in the Carolinas and the mid-Atlantic, the Chesapeake now faced
increased competition in a contracting labor market. The result was a decline in English settlement in the Chesapeake, an apparent increase in the proportion of seemingly
less sought-after servants – including very young men, women, Irish, Welsh, and Scots
– and a shift in the Tidewater labor force from English servants to African slaves. The
Chesapeake planters were certainly not the dynamic force driving overseas migration.

Europeans were not the only ones moving. Native Americans also undertook both
short- and long-distance migrations. Historians are still debating the size of native
populations and the rate of mortality caused by European diseases, and they lack any
of the data used to estimate migration for other groups. Yet the numbers surely were
substantial. The story of many Indian nations during the period of colonization is a
story of movement: sometimes to escape from either European or Indian enemies; at
other times to improve their trading opportunities. Historians have detailed the migration of the Susquehannocks, for example, from their homes in what would become
Pennsylvania to settle near the English settlements on the Chesapeake early in the
seventeenth century possibly in pursuit of trade, only to flee northward again after
1675 away from hostile neighbors (Jennings, 1984). Richard White (1991) described
the flight of Indian refugees from numerous nations facing brutal wars in the east, and
their reconstitution into mixed nationalities in the midwestern region known as the
pays d'en haut. James Merrell (1989) has examined the incorporation by the Catawbas
in the Carolina backcountry of a variety of Indian nations that moved into their vicinity. Thus, Europeans were not the only peoples whose migrations resulted in their

melting together into new peoples in the Americas. Indeed, transatlantic population movements probably introduced even more of a new dynamic element into the migration histories of native North Americans and, as we shall see, Africans.

Cultures of Migration and Regional Cultures

The existence of varied or "highly differentiated" patterns of emigration to the New World is the essence of Bailyn's second and third propositions, and, with an eye towards the burst of emigration that broke out after the Seven Years' War that he described so vividly in *Voyagers to the West*, Bailyn identifies two patterns in particular: that resulting from the high demand for labor, and that motivated by the widespread availability of land (1986, pp. 49–50, 60). On the eve of the American Revolution, those represented nearly separate streams of emigration. One was composed chiefly of artisans and laborers from the south of England, often young and single, traveling as servants and seeking work in the well-established central colonies of Virginia, Maryland, and Pennsylvania. The other was dominated by farm families, mostly from Scotland and the northern parts of Ireland and England, heading for available land in more distant locations on the peripheries of New York and Carolina, in Georgia and on the southern frontiers, as well as in Nova Scotia and Quebec. The main exception to this pattern was Pennsylvania, which was the principal site of immigration to the North American mainland for most of the eighteenth century. That colony attracted immigrants from both streams at a far greater rate than *Voyagers* suggests (Bailyn, 1986a, pp. 206–18).

Bailyn derived those two forces – the demand for labor and the lure of land – from an analysis of registers compiled during the 1770s to track persons intending to emigrate. In other situations, emigration was often less clearly separated from other kinds of movements, as when migrants sought to profit from commercial opportunities. One should not assume that all of those who left for America necessarily had emigration in mind. It is therefore worth investigating the particular migration cultures of the various groups that traveled to British America, and the different regions within which they settled.

The first such region to attract significant migration was the Chesapeake, which drew as many as 100,000 migrants from Britain during the seventeenth century and formed the most populous section of the mainland plantation economy. Virginia and Maryland depended heavily upon a stream of young, predominantly male, single migrants from England. Three decades ago, one of the most important questions in Chesapeake history was that of the social class or quality of these emigrants. Mildred Campbell, in an article based upon several emigration registers for English servants, revised the earlier claim by Abbot Emerson Smith that most servants were of the lowest social backgrounds and argued instead that they were predominantly of respectable, middle class origin (1959). That position was challenged in turn by David Galenson, who used the same registers to contend that servants were more often of lower middling or common background (1978). For each of these historians, the characteristics of the migration had important implications for the character of those colonies.

During the past three decades, that debate has given way to far more nuanced treatments by a new generation of social historians. These scholars have made intensive use of economic and demographic records to depict the experience of the migrants once they arrived, especially the frightful prospects of mortality that awaited them. Several characteristics of the migration have been fundamental to that analysis: the youth of the migrants, their predominantly unmarried status, and the high ratio of males to females. Yet, despite the fact that these studies have contained some of the most detailed investigations of emigration to any early American region, the initial effect of that literature was often to distract attention from the migration itself, since the prevalence of mortality seemed to have foreclosed the possibility of establishing coherent settlements. Thus, Edmund S. Morgan's *American Slavery, American Freedom* (1975), which explored the effects upon Virginia of a predominantly young and male immigrant labor force, described conditions so unsettled and foreboding as to make a civil lifestyle nearly impossible. Gloria Main depicted a Maryland landscape of ramshackle dwellings placed down with no particular order or sense of permanence (1982, pp. 140–1). Lois Green Carr and Lorena Walsh (1977) described the dramatic effects such a situation had upon the lives of that minority of women who managed to survive the early years. The implication seemed to be that demographic conditions within the region far outweighed the particular effects of the migration.

More recent studies have emphasized the degree of settlement migrants were able to achieve in spite of the inhospitable environment, providing a basis for reconnecting Chesapeake society with the characteristics of the cultures the migrants brought with them. Darrett and Anita Rutman's *A Place in Time* (1984) looked for both the inward- and outward-facing threads of community that settlers were able to establish in Middlesex County, Virginia. Jack P. Greene's *Pursuits of Happiness* (1988) found so regular a process of social maturation in the Chesapeake, from initial disorder toward a growing stability, that he used it as a model of social development not only for the other early American regions, but even for Britain! And David Hackett Fischer's massive *Albion's Seed* (1989) described a Chesapeake culture able to reproduce a wide variety of "folkways" from southern England virtually without alteration. This he attributed to the predominance of migrants from that region – although many historians remain sceptical of that description, either for the Chesapeake or for any of the other regional cultures he has chosen to depict (Horn, 1991).

The most sustained treatment of the relationship of migration to the development of the Chesapeake is James Horn's *Adapting to a New World* (1994). To Horn, the most important condition of life in the seventeenth-century Chesapeake was continual migration of both servants and free passengers, from the environs of Bristol as well as London, linking the region to several of England's migration cultures. The constant presence of immigrants made the Chesapeake not less but more like England, full of settlers who were never far removed from their homeland and who adapted, without slavishly replicating, English ways and a semblance of English order to life in the New World.

One important Chesapeake institution that had little counterpart in England was slavery, which was rare in the region for most of the seventeenth century but grew rapidly in the last few decades. This occurred largely because the stream of migrant English labor began to dry up, partly as a result of the overall decline in English emigration in the second half of the seventeenth century, and partly owing to new opportunities in other colonies. Russell Menard has calculated from price levels of servants that the white labor supply dwindled before planters began their shift toward slave labor (Menard, 1977). Thus, the change to African labor constituted part of an increasing differentiation of migration within the Atlantic world.

The character of the slaveholding societies that emerged in the Chesapeake and elsewhere in British America has been linked to the nature of the migration, not only of Europeans but of Africans as well. Some historians have argued that the background of Africans themselves proved crucial in determining the kind of society that was created; Peter Wood, for example, long ago considered the significance of West African experience in cattle-raising and the cultivation of rice upon early South Carolina (1974). More recently, John Thornton described the many ways in which African cultural patterns may have shaped the contours of African American culture, from religion to language to community (1992). Others have explored in some depth the increasingly well-mapped paths of slave importations and the extent to which the "ethnicity" of African migrants affected the development of the various regional slave cultures (Eltis and Richardson, 1997; Morgan, 1997; Morgan, 1998). Still others have examined how the presence of predominantly African-born or creole slave populations – including slaves imported from the West Indies or elsewhere in the coastal Atlantic, from North America to Africa – influenced a slaveholding society. Philip Morgan and Michael Nicholls (1989) have examined the effects of the importation of a high proportion of young and female slaves upon the rapid development of the slave community in Piedmont Virginia. And in *Slave Counterpoint* (1998), Morgan has considered how the manner of migration to Carolina – the importation of slaves along with their masters at the outset, along with the substantial importation of slaves from the same regions of Africa thereafter – allowed them to develop a coherent slave community and slave culture. The migration experience of slaves continued to affect local cultures after their arrival in the New World. Most Africans came to the mainland colonies from the Caribbean, where they had undergone a period of seasoning. Africans thus inhabited all of the major points in the world of colonial commerce, from the African coast to the Caribbean to the colonial port cities to the plantation regions, helping to disperse a wide array of African and African American influences throughout the Atlantic world. Some slaves traveled regularly within that world. Thus, Olaudah Equiano's life encompassed an African childhood, the middle passage, a life in slavery, and service on ships engaged in all sorts of imperial commerce, including the West Indian–North American slave trade itself. Equiano's career, along with those of others who moved among various parts of the British colonial world, gives real substance to Paul Gilroy's notion of the formation of a Black Atlantic culture transcending the particulars of place (1993).

Africans were not the only ones whose experiences ranged widely across the Atlantic world. The reason Equiano visited all of those varied places was his employment as a seaman. In *Between the Devil and the Deep Blue Sea*, Marcus Rediker has described the Anglo-American seaman as a "man of the world" (1987, p. 10), removed from the traditions and affiliations of particular places. If he remained subject to the laws imposed upon him by imperial authorities, he could occasionally eliminate that burden by removing himself, through desertion or, at the margins, piracy. The seaman was the most mobile of that group who, lacking the property needed to give them a place in their original homes, undertook long-distance movements within Britain or its empire, helping to create what unities existed in the larger British Atlantic culture.

A focus on migration offers an especially compelling case for reintegrating the West

Indies and their island neighbors into the British colonial world. Movement between the colonies on the mainland and those in the islands was frequent, and merchant firms in all of the major colonial cities had extensive ties to the islands. Even Quakers, among whom were found virtually the only voices in the colonial world to attack the institution of slavery, had substantial interests in the sugar plantations on the islands and in the slave trade between the Caribbean and the mainland (McCusker and Menard, 1985, pp. 193–4).

The transition to slavery came more quickly to the Caribbean region and to its offshoot in Carolina than it had in the Chesapeake; slaves outnumbered white servants on Barbados as early as the 1640s. Unlike the Chesapeake, the shift was not the result of a decline in European migration, which did not occur until later in the century; rather, heavy mortality there created a perpetual demand for labor beyond what white migrants could supply, and the high profits of sugar allowed planters to bid for slaves. White servants continued to migrate in considerable numbers nonetheless – especially Irish servants, who were considered less desirable by planters and may have had fewer opportunities elsewhere than their English counterparts. Their migration introduced an often-unruly element into white society on the islands (Beckles, 1990; Cullen, 1994; Burnard, 1996, pp. 777–8).

Very different from the plantation colonies was New England, which drew upon a different strand of English migration, comprising not only young, single persons but also established families of the sort less often found on the migration trail. Three or four decades ago the principal question about migration into that region was whether the primary motive was a religiosity distinctive to the Puritans or an economic necessity common to most migrants. Beginning with the appearance of the first major New England town studies around the year 1970, the discussion began to center on the extent to which the social facts of land, population, family, and economy in colonial New England, rather than religious ideology, determined the character of the settlement and development of the region. As was the case in the historiography of the Chesapeake, the initial effect of the move towards social history was to de-emphasize the importance of cultural inheritances brought over in the migration in favor of American conditions. Nonetheless, the shift did at least place domestic migration at the center of discussion, with historians using the surprisingly low rate of out-migration in some early towns as an index of New England distinctiveness, and its later rise as an indicator of social transformation and a reversion to English norms (Lockridge, 1968).

Subsequent discussions gave considerably more weight to the migration itself. In a 1973 article, T. H. Breen and Stephen Foster, relying upon an analysis of emigration registers from 1637, explored the relationship between the kind of settler that migrated to New England – with a predominance of families and persons of at least modest means, including an unusual number from urban, artisanal backgrounds – and the character of the villages they established. More recently, Christine Heyrman (1984) and Daniel Vickers (1994) have both explored the effects upon coastal Massachusetts of the early influx of working fisherman largely outside of the Puritan errand. And David Cressy, in *Coming Over* (1987), has looked at the very substantial contacts New England's settlers maintained with England after their arrival in the New World, including the decision of a significant number to return home.

The most intensive exploration of the social characteristics that migrants brought to New England has been David Grayson Allen's *In English Ways* (1982). Allen follows the migrations of groups of English men and women from their English homes to their towns of settlement, contending that in that process, those groups almost invariably recreated the local or regional environments with which they were familiar. Such a finding would account for the considerable variety that existed among New England towns while returning migration to the center of the story. Yet, in suggesting that New England settlers created wholly distinctive regional English communities, Allen comes close to implying that transatlantic migration had mattered not at all, and that communities in New England differed little from those that existed before the migration. No other scholar with the exception of David Hackett Fischer (1989) has found such intense loyalty to local origins in settlement or such distinct and stable communities thereafter. Indeed, most recent works have pointed out the tendency of New Englanders to continue their movements one or more times in the wake of the migration, often intermixing in the process (Archer, 1990; Martin, 1991).

The most comprehensive effort to consider the meaning of migration in the early history of New England is Virginia DeJohn Anderson's *New England's Generation* (1991). Examining the 693 passengers on the seven ships for whom complete emigration lists are available, Anderson finds that group to have been very ordinary English men and women, quite unlike early emigrants to almost any other colony. New Englanders were older, less predominantly male, more prosperous, and far more likely to travel in family units than migrants elsewhere. In short, they look less like England's typical migrating population and more like the people of England itself. For such a group, Anderson concludes – one so unlike the typical migrating population – only so compelling a reason as a firm religious commitment could have provoked a departure from their homes.

Anderson's data may not settle the question of the migrants' motives. Richard Archer, who has examined a larger sample of migrants, suggests that early New Englanders differed less from other emigrants than she allows, not only in their demographic characteristics but perhaps in their motivations as well (1990). Nonetheless, Anderson does offer some striking observations about the role that the Great Migration played in New England culture. The fact that the region was settled within little more than a decade by a group of families approximating a single generation strongly shaped the course of the region's history. Indeed, the legend that New England was distinctive because of the manner of its creation became one of the foundational myths of American culture. One might add that the atypical character of the migrating population and its substantial religious motivation helped insure that once the Puritan moment had passed, New England would find no other significant migrant stream upon which to draw.

If both New England and the Chesapeake experienced declines in English migration in the latter part of the seventeenth century, part of the reason was that a large proportion of those who migrated were diverted toward newer colonies, especially those in the mid-Atlantic. For no other region have historians devoted so much attention to the varied patterns of migration than the middle colonies. From the founding of Pennsylvania in 1681 through the end of the colonial era, the mid-Atlantic replaced the Chesapeake as the principal magnet for European migrants seeking economic opportunity under conditions of substantial toleration in what came to be widely known within the emigration literature as the "best poor man's country in the world."

The first part of that phrase constitutes the title of James Lemon's pathbreaking historical geography of southeastern Pennsylvania (1972). The principal characteristics of this region, in Lemon's view, were a function of the pattern of migration: a late seventeenth-century movement dominated by aspiring farmers seeking land and opportunity and ignoring the constrictions posed by rigid social hierarchies or intensive communal ties that had limited earlier settlements. The result was the creation of a uniform landscape of single family farms in open-country neighborhoods. While the religious and national backgrounds of the settlers were diverse, there was a striking uniformity in their motivations and in the communities they created.

Recent literature has devoted far more attention to those differences than Lemon allowed. Two decades ago, Michael Zuckerman characterized the mid-Atlantic as "America's first plural society" (1982). In the intervening years, it has become increasingly clear that diversity itself took very different forms in the several colonies. New York was divided into largely separate and sometimes antagonistic Dutch- and English-speaking communities deriving from two separate migrations. Pennsylvania was composed of a heterogeneous collection of English Quakers and Anglicans, German Reformed, Lutherans, and sectarians, and Scots and Irish Presbyterians – any of which might be intermixed within a single settlement. New Jersey lay somewhere in between both geographically and culturally. So different were the migrations upon which those colonies drew that an important question has become whether or not mid-Atlantic society possessed sufficient unity to be classified as a single region at all (Gough, 1983; Bodle, 1989).

The settlement of New Netherland developed as a rather modest side venture in a Dutch commercial empire dominated by the far more lucrative East Indian trade. Even within the Western Hemisphere, New Netherland was a limited effort, and migration there was limited to whatever small groups the colony was able to persuade to go. There were many of these upon which to draw, since the seventeenth-century Netherlands housed an abundance of Protestant refugees seeking opportunity and security in an age of religious wars. Thus the colony was settled by German-speakers, Walloons, English, and Scots, along with Jews, Africans brought in by Dutch traders, often from other parts of the Dutch overseas empire, as well as some actual "Dutch" (Rink, 1986). The primacy of commercial motives in the colony determined much about the nature of settlement, which at the outset was established in a series of commercial outposts at various stages along the Hudson Valley, with similar smaller settlements along the Delaware (Merwick, 1990). The continuous importation of African slaves, another offshoot of Dutch activity elsewhere, would make New Netherland and then New York into the leading slaveholding colony north of the Chesapeake.

After the seizure of New Netherland by an English fleet in 1664 the migration stream through the Netherlands was cut off, and the growth of the colony stagnated. The remaining inhabitants divided in their loyalties. Some of the elite among the old inhabitants, mostly in New Amsterdam, worked closely with the newcomers to forge a prominent Anglo-Dutch commercial community. Others remained quite separate, some migrating further into the Hudson Valley or New Jersey, where they established Dutch-speaking communities that were sometimes more orthodox in religion and culture than were the migrant communities from which they came. The divided migration into New York produced a divided colony (Goodfriend, 1992; Roeber, 1991).

The attraction of migrants seeking to profit from commercial enterprise gave the fur-trading capital at Albany a central role in imperial affairs. That, in turn, meant that some of the most important migrations in late seventeenth-century New York were Indian rather than European. During the 1670s, Governor Edmund Andros negoti-ated an offer of protection with the Five Nations that allowed the Susquehannocks, then under attack from Chesapeake settlers during Bacon's Rebellion, to move within the bounds of New York. About the same time, the Mohawk were able to drive their Mohican rivals out of their Hudson Valley homes north and east into Connecticut and Massachusetts. Four decades later, more than 1,500 Tuscarora moved northward from their North Carolina homes to become the sixth nation of the Iroquois League. The result of all of those movements was to buttress the Five Nations, which had been severely weakened by disease and warfare, and to tie their fortunes more closely to those of British imperial authorities in New York (Jennings, 1984; Richter, 1992, pp. 135–6, 237–9).

Part of the reason for the sluggish growth of New York was that potential migrants were attracted to nearby Pennsylvania, which provided more ample opportunities, along with the prospect of peace and security under a Quaker leadership that was devoting unprecedented efforts to promoting settlement throughout the mid-Atlantic. Begin-ning with the scattered arrivals of English and New English Quakers on Long Island and New York in the 1650s and 1660s and continuing through the aggressive settle-ment of West Jersey and Pennsylvania in the following decades, the Society of Friends established itself as an important transatlantic force that would help determine the patterns of settlement that would prevail in the region for the next century.

Barry Levy's *Quakers and the American Family* (1988) helps account for the will-ingness of Friends to migrate. Following groups of Quakers from their homes in north-western England and Wales to their eastern Pennsylvania destinations, Levy's work well demonstrates the interconnections between the manner of migration and the settlements that were created. Living in several of the poorer regions of the British Isles, and having adopted a Quaker ethic of spiritualized household relations that de-manded keeping children close within the family and the faith, Quaker families from northwestern England and Wales were attracted to the option of emigration as one of the few means available to provide for their children without sending them out for employment away from their homes. The mid-Atlantic colonies thus drew upon a largely untapped migration stream. In Pennsylvania, those same domestic goals prompted Quakers to opt for what became the characteristic mid-Atlantic form of modest but profitable grain farms that would allow a sufficient accumulation over time to secure the livelihoods of their children.

Another group to migrate to the middle colonies were German-speaking families from village societies in the Rhineland, where economic and demographic pressures had produced a large outward migration north into the Netherlands and eastward into eastern Europe in search of economic and religious security. Although German migra-tion to Pennsylvania began with the arrival of a few sectarians recruited by William Penn during the 1680s, German-speaking migrants rarely followed that route until the 1720s. About that time, merchant promoters in Rotterdam began aggressively sponsoring migration to Pennsylvania, where the combination of toleration and op-portunity appealed to German families. The great bulk of the migrants arrived over the next quarter-century, mostly in family groups and most settling in Pennsylvania, al-though younger migrants in particular extended German settlement into the backcountries of Maryland, Virginia, and Carolina. German-speakers comprised perhaps a third of the population of Pennsylvania by mid-century (Wokeck, 1989; Fogelman, 1996). The predominance of families helped create stability within German-speaking communities, whose leaders assisted their countrymen in assimilating enough of English culture to use the legal and political systems to defend their family goals of security of religion and property (Roeber, 1993).

Scotland was a relative latecomer to transatlantic migration, despite having one of the most mobile populations in Europe. Migration was embedded in the very structure of Scottish society, as the continual movements of friends and family members within distinct geographical areas served to link the inhabitants together in small regional communities. Thus individuals and families moved regularly within extended territories without abandoning the ties of community. Scots also maintained longstanding overseas communities in several parts of Europe, where they would regularly go and often return. The presence of such familiar sites meant that relatively few Scots were tempted to venture to the New World before the middle of the eighteenth century.

The first permanent Scottish settlement in the New World, in eastern and central New Jersey, was the subject of *Scotland and its First American Colony 1683–1765* (Landsman, 1985). Scottish emigration to East Jersey was less the result of a new-found commitment to emigration in the 1680s than a response by commoners to a substantial initiative among Scotland's improvement-minded elites to develop national commercial ventures abroad to compete with those of their English neighbors. Scots not only established a presence in the region but also a system of expansive commercial, community, and family networks, which were well suited to extending Scottish settlement and trade across the central Jersey corridor from New York to Philadelphia.

Scots had a distinct style of migration. While their overall rate of migration to the Americas was modest before 1760, that of skilled and professional groups, such as merchants, physicians, clergymen, educators, and imperial officials, was much higher. Those groups had long sought out places abroad, in overseas communities, at Continental universities, or in the Scottish regiments. They had to; Scotland regularly produced a greater number of such persons than the impoverished domestic economy could support. Moreover, Scottish overseas trade depended upon the efforts of Scottish merchants to travel abroad and seek it out, since few foreign traders worked actively to pursue Scottish commerce (Landsman, 1999).

Alan Karras (1992) has argued that Scots in the West Indies and the Chesapeake were mostly sojourners, persons who ventured abroad intending only to make their fortunes and return home. Such a label may be too rigid and certainly does not encompass the intentions of all Scots who moved overseas, some of whom clearly aspired to return to Scotland, some of whom did not, and many of whom had less firm plans for their ultimate destinations. The situation was not unlike that of Scots in the north of Ireland or in Rotterdam, where some families remained for generations, while others moved back and forth with some regularity.

One group of migrants whose settlements have been curiously neglected were those from Ireland, most of whom were Protestants from Ulster, the so-called Ulster Scots or Scots-Irish, although Catholics may have comprised up to a quarter of the immigrant pool (Cullen, 1994). As a group they have been seriously misunderstood. Those Scots and English who settled in Ulster during the seventeenth century did not move all at once during the original plantation period, as most descriptions imply (Leyburn,

1962), but in successive waves during the 1620s, 1650s, 1670s, and especially the 1690s. Throughout the century there was considerable movement across the twenty-mile crossing between Ulster and the Scottish Lowlands. Thus those who migrated from Ulster to North America were often not so far removed from a Scottish background, and scattered evidence suggests the frequent presence among them of travelers directly from Scotland.

Ulster natives are often viewed as natural frontiersmen willing to forsake former homes in favor of the wilds of undeveloped borderlands. In North America, they were notorious for their willingness to settle on the frontiers, where they frequently came into conflict with their Indian neighbors. Yet they also created a formidable array of institutions in their settlements, including schools and Presbyterian churches. The form of those churches – neither national and hierarchical nor purely local – was particularly suited to linking the inhabitants of dispersed congregations together. Thus the movements of Ulster Scots, like those of their Scottish neighbors, may have allowed them to move to the frontiers without leaving their principal ties behind, a possibility reinforced by Marion Winship's recent portrayal of the close connections maintained between "movers" and "stayers" who ventured westward into the Kentucky backcountry at the end of the eighteenth century (Winship, 1997).

The Scots-Irish were among the principal settlers of what came to be known as the backcountry. Understanding the role of migration within that region is surely one of the keys to comprehending its place in American culture. In the days of Frederick Jackson Turner, the usual assumption was that the frontiers were settled from east to west, as inhabitants of the older settled regions trekked westward in successive waves to search for opportunity. Historians now recognize a more complex pattern to backcountry settlement, which included migrations not only from east to west, but northward or southward, as well as directly from overseas (Bailyn, 1986a).

In *Albion's Seed* (1989), David Hackett Fischer portrayed backcountry culture as a perfect reflection of that migration, dominated by north British emigrants who were typical borderers: wild, unruly, short on learning and temper, and long on aggression and violence. Such a portrayal does not do justice to the complexity of border life in either place. In Britain, the intensive involvement of Scots on the Continent, especially among the skilled and educated, introduced markedly cosmopolitan and enlightened elements into Scottish culture (Landsman, 1999). A similar result occurred in northern Ireland from the close connections that Ulster Scots maintained with Glasgow and its flourishing commercial sector, its university, and its Presbyterian Enlightenment.

Throughout the American backcountries, conditions of instability and violence were often accompanied by such seemingly contrary elements as the establishment of regular stores and commercial networks, the building of churches and academies of religion and enlightenment, and the quest for order. These regions housed migrants from many places, who often came face to face in the borderlands. Some settlers came from a variety of European backgrounds, including immigrants and native-born, intending either to settle or to pursue trading opportunities across the backcountry. Others came from various Indian nations, some of them also recent migrants to those lands, often in the process of combining with others and synthesizing new nationalities. In the southern backcountries, they all confronted westward-moving plantation owners and increasing numbers of African slaves from the Tidewater, the Caribbean, or Africa. There is now a rapidly expanding literature on those areas, much of it examining the difficult process those groups encountered in creating common or negotiated meanings for their interactions (Nobles, 1989; Morgan and Nicholls, 1989; Klein, 1990; White, 1991; Usner, 1992; Cayton and Teute, 1998). While it would be difficult to reduce that situation to the effects of just two migration streams, or indeed, to apply an emigration model to those complex movements at all, the backcountry experience does emphatically reinforce Bailyn's insistence that highly differentiated patterns of migration produced great diversity among the early American regions.

Centers and Peripheries of Migration

The complexity of the borderlands suggests the need to consider further Bailyn's fourth proposition, that American culture is best viewed as an "exotic far western periphery, a marchland, of the metropolitan European culture system" (1986, p. 112). That contention is useful in that it links migrations to North American colonies with simultaneous movements to such other places as Ireland's borderlands, the peripheries of eastern Europe, or the East Indies. But its perspective is decidedly metropolitan, even though for much of the period, most migrants did not derive from the metropolis. To portray those migrants as intentionally heading to a world at "constant risk" (1986a, p. 5) is to slight the motivations of those whose primary quest was not only for opportunity but also for security. The attraction of Pennsylvania before the middle of the eighteenth century resulted from its promise of toleration, economic opportunity, and peace. The insecurity produced by war after mid-century was substantially responsible for the decline in German emigration into Pennsylvania.

For many of the migrants from Scotland and Ireland, or even parts of the Continent, the sense of living in proximity to the peripheries was nothing new. North Britons as well as Americans were likely to see themselves as surrounded by barbarity. Glasgow commentators, for example, often noted the dangers that lay close at hand just beyond the Highland line; Glasgow itself was attacked by a Highland army in 1745. None of that stopped Glaswegians from portraying their city as a center of commerce, progress, and Enlightenment. Americans also were well able to separate the insecurity of life on the frontiers during the wars of mid-century from the conditions of opportunity and security that existed elsewhere in peacetime.

To Bailyn, the proliferation of transatlantic migration that followed upon the conclusion of the Seven Years' War was something novel and dramatic: an accelerating enthusiasm for migration, especially in Britain's outlying provinces, inspired by the nearly universal yearning to "live independent." Such a portrayal may be the product of a determination to view the American migration as fundamentally different from anything that came before. It rests in part upon an incomplete picture of the migration cultures of northern Britain and in part upon a counterfactual: the assumption that only the intervention of the American Revolution prevented the enthusiasm for emigration from accelerating to the point that it might have caused the near depopulation of northern Britain (1986a, pp. 3–5).

In Britain's northern peripheries, or in the German Palatinate, population movements that approached mass migration were not without precedent. In the early decades of the seventeenth century, a member of England's Parliament expressed the fear that the Union of Crowns would lead to the southward migration of so many Scots that "we shall be over-run with them, . . . witness the multiplicities of the Scots in

Polonia." Scottish migration to Poland continued to increase thereafter (Smout et al., 1994, p. 81). The famine years of the 1690s led to real concerns for the depopulation of northern Scotland. During the 1720s immigration from Ulster to Pennsylvania reached the point that James Logan, among the first promoters of the movement, now worried that Ireland was about to send "all her inhabitants hither" (Jones, 1991, p. 297). A similar movement from the Scottish Highlands to British North America occurred during the first two decades of the nineteenth century (Bumsted, 1982). None of those led to the feared depopulation. In each case, as in the British migrations of the 1770s or the German emigrations before mid-century, those movements lasted only until a change in circumstances, such as war or political transformation, altered either the direction or the magnitude of the flow.

What did cause the eventual depopulation of much of Britain's Highland zones was not the lure of America but the joint influences of industrialization, underemployment, and deliberate clearances by ambitious landlords, which combined to drive the great majority off the land. Highlanders then sought refuge not only in America, but in Australia, New Zealand, and even London and Glasgow (Richards, 1982).

What was new after the middle of the eighteenth century was the increasing focus of those emigrants on North America and the appearance of emigration in public discussion on an unprecedented scale in the form of promotional pamphlets, literary publications, and letters and reports in the public prints (De Wolfe, 1997). These included the warnings about the dangers of depopulation that Bailyn cited in *Voyagers to the West* (1986a, pp. 36–66). They also included much that was promotional, fostered largely by merchants, ministers, and emigration agents, who were able to link emigration and American liberty to contemporary political discussions, using it to criticize the greed and corruption they saw emanating from the centers of power. That theme was sounded especially by a network of provincials and dissenters on both sides of the Atlantic and was prominent in both the Scottish and Scots-Irish emigrations (De Wolfe, 1997; Landsman, 1994).

Had the Revolution not intervened, it may be that the social dislocations caused by continuing mass migration would have intensified nativist themes already hinted at in such contemporary discussions as Benjamin Franklin's mid-century warnings about German migration and in frequent complaints about Scots and Irish settlers. Instead, the rhetorical link among liberty, prosperity, and migration was left substantially intact. Thus later commentators were free to fuse those ideas with an emerging nationalism and fix the notion of an American migration that was utterly unlike any other (Crèvecoeur, 1782). So successful would they be that it has taken two hundred years for historians to begin to reinsert the transatlantic migration into the broader field of migration history.

BIBLIOGRAPHY

Akenson, Donald: "Why the accepted estimates of the ethnicity of the American people, 1790, are unacceptable." *William and Mary Quarterly* 3rd ser., 41 (1984), pp. 102–18.

Allen, D. G.: *In English Ways: The Movement of Societies and the Transferal of English Local Law and Custom to Massachusetts Bay in the Seventeenth Century* (Chapel Hill, NC: University of North Carolina Press, 1982).

Altman, I. and Horn, J., eds.: *"To Make America"*: *European Emigration in the Early Modern Period* (Berkeley: University of California Press, 1991).

Anderson, V. D.: *New England's Generation: The Great Migration and the Formation of Society and Culture in the Seventeenth Century* (New York: Cambridge University Press, 1991).

Andrews, K. R., Canny, N. P. et al.: *The Westward Enterprise: English Activities in Ireland, the Atlantic, and America 1480–1650* (Detroit: Wayne State University Press, 1979).

Archer, R.: "New England Mosaic: A Demographic Analysis for the Seventeenth Century." *William and Mary Quarterly* 3rd ser., 47 (1990), pp. 477–502.

Armitage, D.: "Making the Empire British: Scotland in the Atlantic World 1542–1707." *Past and Present* 155 (1997), pp. 34–63.

Bailyn, B.: *The Peopling of British North America* (New York: Alfred A. Knopf, 1986).

Bailyn, B.: *Voyagers to the West: A Passage in the Peopling of America on the Eve of the Revolution* (New York: Alfred A. Knopf, 1986a).

Bailyn, B. and Morgan, P. D., eds.: *Strangers within the Realm: Cultural Margins of the First British Empire* (Chapel Hill, NC: University of North Carolina Press, 1991).

Beckles, H. M.: "A 'Riotous and Unruly Lot': Irish Indentured Servants and Freemen in the English West Indies: 1644–1713." *William and Mary Quarterly* 3rd ser., 47 (1990), pp. 503–22.

Beiler, R. J.: "Distributing Aid to Believers in Need: The Religious Foundations of Transatlantic Migration." In N. Canny, J. E. Illick et al., eds., *Empire, Society and Labor: Essays in Honor of Richard S. Dunn. Pennsylvania History* 64 (1997), pp. 73–87.

Berlin, Ira: "From Creole to African: Atlantic Creoles and the Origins of African-American Society in Mainland North America." *William and Mary Quarterly* 3rd ser., 53 (1996), pp. 251–88.

Bodle, W.: "The 'Myth of the Middle Colonies' Reconsidered: The Process of Regionalization in Early America." *Pennsylvania Magazine of History and Biography* 113 (1989), pp. 527–48.

Breen, T. H. and Foster, S.: "Moving to the New World: The Character of Early Massachusetts Immigration." *William and Mary Quarterly* 3rd ser., 30 (1973), pp. 189–222.

Bumsted, J. M.: *The People's Clearance: Highland Emigration to British North America, 1770–1815* (Edinburgh: Edinburgh University Press, 1982).

Burnard, T.: "European Migration to Jamaica, 1655–1780." *William and Mary Quarterly* 3rd ser., 53 (1996), pp. 769–94.

Butler, J.: *The Huguenots in America: A Refugee People in New World Society* (Cambridge, MA: Harvard University Press, 1983).

Campbell, M.: "Social origins of some early Americans." In James Morton Smith, ed., *Seventeenth-Century America: Essays in Colonial History* (Chapel Hill, NC: University of North Carolina Press, 1959), pp. 63–89.

Canny, N., ed.: *Europeans on the Move: Studies on European Migration, 1500–1800* (Oxford: Clarendon Press, 1994).

Canny, N.: "English Migration into and across the Atlantic during the Seventeenth and Eighteenth Centuries." In Canny (1994), pp. 39–75.

Carr, L. G. and Walsh, L. S.: "The Planter's Wife: The Experience of White Women in Seventeenth-Century Maryland." *William and Mary Quarterly* 3rd ser., 34 (1977), pp. 542–71.

Cayton, A. R. L. and Teute, F. J.: *Contact Points: American Frontiers from the Mohawk Valley to the Mississippi, 1750–1830* (Chapel Hill, NC: University of North Carolina Press, 1998).

Chambers, D. B.: "'My Own Nation': Igbo Exiles in the Diaspora." In Eltis and Richardson (1997), pp. 72–97.

Clark, P.: "Migration in England during the Late Seventeenth and Early Eighteenth Centuries." *Past and Present* 83 (1979), pp. 57–90.

Clark, P. and Souden, D., ed.: *Migration and Society in Early Modern England* (Tiptree, Essex: Anchor Brendon Ltd., 1987).

Cressy, D.: *Coming Over: Migration and Communication Between England and New England in the Seventeenth Century* (New York: Cambridge University Press, 1987).

Crèvecoeur, J. Hector St. John de: *Letters from an American Farmer* (1782; Harmondsworth, Middlesex: Penguin, 1981).

Cullen, L. M.: "The Irish Diaspora of the Seventeenth and Eighteenth Centuries." In Canny (1994), pp. 113–49.

Curtin, P. D.: *The Atlantic Slave Trade: A Census* (Madison, WI: University of Wisconsin Press, 1969).

De Vries, J.: "Population and Economy of Preindustrial Netherlands." *Journal of Interdisciplinary History* 15 (1985), pp. 661–82.

De Wolfe, B., comp.: *Discoveries of America: Personal Accounts of British Emigrants to North America During the Revolutionary Era* (New York: Cambridge University Press, 1997).

Dickson, R. J.: *Ulster Emigration to Colonial America, 1718–1775* (London: Routledge & Kegan Paul, 1966).

Dobson, D.: *Scottish Emigration to Colonial America, 1607–1785* (Athens, GA: University of Georgia Press, 1994).

Ekirch, A. R.: *Bound for America: The Transportation of British Convicts to the Colonies 1718–1775* (Oxford: Clarendon Press, 1987).

Eltis, D. and Richardson, D., eds.: *Routes to Slavery: Directions, Ethnicity and Morality in the Transatlantic Slave Trade* (London: Frank Cass Publications, 1997).

Equiano, O.: *The Interesting Narrative of the Life of Olaudah Equiano* (1791), ed. R. J. Allison (New York: St. Martin's Press, 1995).

Fertig, G.: "Transatlantic Migration from the German-Speaking Parts of Central Europe, 1600–1800: Proportions, Structures, and Explanations." In Canny (1994), pp. 192–235.

Fischer, D. H.: *Albion's Seed: Four British Folkways in America* (New York: Oxford University Press, 1989).

Flinn, M., ed.: *Scottish Population History from the 17th Century to the 1930s* (New York: Cambridge University Press, 1977).

Fogel, R. W.: *Without Consent or Contract: The Rise and Fall of American Slavery* (New York: W. W. Norton & Co., 1989).

Fogelman, A. S.: *Hopeful Journeys: German Immigration, Settlement, and Political Culture in Colonial America, 1717–1775* (Philadelphia: University of Pennsylvania Press, 1996).

Galenson, D. W.: "'Middling People' or 'Common Sort'? The Social Origins of Some Early Americans Re-examined." *William and Mary Quarterly* 3rd ser., 35 (1978), pp. 499–524.

Galenson, D. W.: *White Servitude in Colonial America: An Economic Analysis* (New York: Cambridge University Press, 1981).

Games, A.: "The English Atlantic World: A View from London." In Canny, Illick et al., *Pennsylvania History* 64 (1997), pp. 46–72.

Gemery, H. A.: "Emigration from the British Isles to the New World, 1630–1700: Inferences from Colonial Populations." *Research in Economic History* 5 (1980), pp. 179–231.

Gemery, H. A.: "European Emigration to North America, 1700–1820: Numbers and Quasi-numbers." *Perspectives in American History*, n.s. 1 (1984), pp. 283–342.

Gilroy, P.: *The Black Atlantic: Modernity and Double Consciousness* (Cambridge, Mass.: Harvard University Press, 1993).

Goodfriend, J. D.: *Before the Melting Pot: Society and Culture in Colonial New York City, 1664–1730* (Princeton, NJ: Princeton University Press, 1992).

Gough, R. J.: "The Myth of the 'Middle Colonies': An Analysis of Regionalization in Early America." *Pennsylvania Magazine of History and Biography* 108 (1983), pp. 93–419.

Graham, I. C. C.: *Colonists from Scotland: Emigration to North America, 1707–1783* (Ithaca, NY: Cornell University Press, 1956).

Greene, J. P.: *Pursuits of Happiness: The Social Development of Early Modern British Colonies and the Formation of American Culture* (Chapel Hill, NC: University of North Carolina Press, 1988).

Griffiths, N. E. S. and Reid, J. G.: "New Evidence on New Scotland, 1629." *William and Mary Quarterly* 3rd ser., 49 (1992), pp. 492–508.

Hansen, M. L.: *The Atlantic Migration 1607–1860: A History of the Continuing Settlement of the United States* (Cambridge, MA: Harvard University Press, 1940).

Heyrman, C. L.: *Commerce and Culture: The Maritime Communities of Colonial Massachusetts 1690–1750* (New York: W. W. Norton, 1984).

Horn, J.: "Cavalier Culture? The Social Development of Colonial Virginia." *William and Mary Quarterly* 3rd ser., 48 (1991), pp. 238–45.

Horn, J.: *Adapting to a New World: English Society in the Seventeenth-Century Chesapeake* (Chapel Hill, NC: University of North Carolina Press, 1994).

Houston, R. A.: *The Population History of Britain and Ireland 1500–1700* (London: Macmillan, 1992).

Houston, R. A. and Withers, C. W. J.: "Migration and the Turnover of Population in Scotland, 1600–1900." *Annales de Demographie Historique* (1990), pp. 285–308.

Jennings, F.: *The Ambiguous Iroquois Empire: The Covenant Chain Confederation of Indian Tribes with English Colonies* (New York: W. W. Norton, 1984).

Jones, M. A.: "The Scotch-Irish in British America." In Bailyn and Morgan (1991), pp. 284–313.

Karras, A. L.: *Sojourners in the Sun: Scottish Migrants in Jamaica and the Chesapeake, 1740–1800* (Ithaca, NY: Cornell University Press, 1992).

Klein, R. N.: *The Unification of a Slave State: The Rise of the Planter Class in the South Carolina Backcountry, 1760–1808* (Chapel Hill, NC: University of North Carolina Press, 1990).

Klepp, S. E., ed.: *The Demographic History of the Philadelphia Region, 1600–1800.* In Proceedings of the American Philosophical Society, 133 (1989).

Kulikoff, A.: "Migration and Cultural Diffusion in Early America, 1600–1860." *Historical Methods* 19 (1986), pp. 153–89.

Landsman, N. C.: *Scotland and its First American Colony 1683–1765* (Princeton, NJ: Princeton University Press, 1985).

Landsman, N. C.: "The Provinces and the Empire: Scotland, the American Colonies, and the Development of British Provincial Identity." In L. Stone, ed., *An Imperial State at War: Britain from 1689 to 1815* (London: Routledge, 1994), pp. 258–87.

Landsman, N. C.: "Nation, Migration, and the Province in the First British Empire: Scotland and the Americas 1600–1800." *American Historical Review* 104 (1999), pp. 463–75.

Lemon, J. T.: *The Best Poor Man's Country: A Geographical Study of Early Southeastern Pennsylvania* (Baltimore: Johns Hopkins University Press, 1972).

Levy, B.: *Quakers and the American Family: British Settlement in the Delaware Valley* (New York: Oxford University Press, 1988).

Leyburn, J. G.: *The Scotch-Irish: A Social History* (Chapel Hill, NC: University of North Carolina Press, 1962).

Lockhart, A.: *Some Aspects of Emigration from Ireland to the North American Colonies between 1660 and 1775* (New York: Arno Press, 1976).

Lockridge, K.: "Land, Population, and the Evolution of New England Society, 1630–1790." *Past and Present* 39 (1968), pp. 62–80.

Lovejoy, P.: "The Volume of the Atlantic Slave Trade: A Synthesis." *Journal of African History* 23 (1982), 473–501.

Lucassen, J.: "The Netherlands, the Dutch, and Long-Distance Migration in the Late Sixteenth to Early Nineteenth Centuries." In Canny (1994), pp. 153–91.

Main, G. L.: *Tobacco Colony: Life in Early Maryland* (Princeton, NJ: Princeton University Press, 1982).

Manning, P., ed.: *Slave Trades 1500–1800: Globalization of Forced Labor* (Brookfield, VT: Variorum, 1996).

Martin, J. F.: *Profits in the Wilderness: Entrepreneurship and the Founding of New England Towns* (Chapel Hill, NC: University of North Carolina Press, 1991).

McCusker, J. J. and Menard, R. R.: *The Economy of British America 1607–1789* (Chapel Hill, NC: University of North Carolina Press, 1985).

McDonald, F. and E. S.: "The Ethnic Origins of the American People, 1790." *William and Mary Quarterly* 3rd ser., 37 (1980), pp. 179–99.

Menard, R. R.: "From Servants to Slaves: The Transformation of the Chesapeake Labor System." *Southern Studies* 16 (1977), pp. 355–90.

Menard, R. R.: "British Migration to the Chesapeake Colonies in the Seventeenth Century." In L. G. Carr, P. D. Morgan et al., eds., *Colonial Chesapeake Society* (Chapel Hill, NC: University of North Carolina Press, 1988), pp. 99–132.

Menard, R. R.: "Migration, Ethnicity, and the Rise of an Atlantic Economy: The Re-peopling of British America, 1600–1790." In R. J. Vecoli and S. M. Sinke, eds., *A Century of European Migrations, 1830–1930* (Urbana: University of Illinois Press, 1991), pp. 58–77.

Merrell, J. H.: *The Indians' New World: Catawbas and their Neighbors from European Contract Through the Era of Removal* (Chapel Hill, NC: University of North Carolina Press, 1989).

Merwick, D.: *Possessing Albany, 1630–1710: The Dutch and English Experiences* (New York: Cambridge University Press, 1990).

Miller, K. A.: *Emigrants and Exiles: Ireland and the Irish Exodus to North America* (New York: Oxford University Press, 1985).

Moogk, P.: "Reluctant Exiles: Emigrants from France in Canada before 1769." *William and Mary Quarterly* 3rd ser., 46 (1989), pp. 463–505.

Moogk, P.: "Manon's Fellow Exiles: Emigration from France to North America before 1763." In Canny (1994), pp. 236–60.

Morgan, E. S.: *American Slavery, American Freedom: The Ordeal of Colonial Virginia* (New York: W. W. Norton, 1975).

Morgan, P. D.: "British Encounters with Africans and African-Americans, circa 1600–1780." In Bailyn and Morgan (1991), pp. 157–219.

Morgan, P. D.: "The Cultural Implications of the Atlantic Slave Trade: African Regional Origins, American Destinations, and New World Developments." In Eltis and Richardson (1997), pp. 122–45.

Morgan, P. D.: *Slave Counterpoint: Black Culture in the Eighteenth-Century Chesapeake & Lowcountry* (Chapel Hill, NC: University of North Carolina Press, 1998).

Morgan, P. D. and Nicholls, M. L.: "Slaves in Piedmont Virginia, 1720–1790." *William and Mary Quarterly* 3rd ser, 46 (1989), pp. 211–51.

Nobles, G. H.: "Breaking into the Backcountry: New Approaches to the Early American Frontier, 1750–1800." *William and Mary Quarterly* 3rd ser., 46 (1989), pp. 641–70.

Purvis, T. L.: "The European Ancestry of the United States Population, 1790." *William and Mary Quarterly* 3rd ser., 41 (1984), 85–101.

Rediker, M.: *Between the Devil and the Deep Blue Sea: Merchant Seamen, Pirates, and the Anglo-American Maritime World, 1700–1750* (New York: Cambridge University Press, 1987).

Reid, J. G.: *Acadia, Maine, and New Scotland: Marginal Colonies in the Seventeenth Century* (Toronto: University of Toronto Press, 1981).

Rich, E. E.: "The Population of Elizabethan England." *Economic History Review* 2nd ser., 2 (1950), pp. 247–65.

Richards. E.: *A History of the Highland Clearances* (London: Croom Helm, 1982).

Richter, D. K.: *The Ordeal of the Longhouse: The Peoples of the Iroquios League in the Era of European Colonization* (Chapel Hill, NC: University of North Carolina Press, 1992).

Rink, O. A.: *Holland on the Hudson: An Economic and Social History of Dutch New York* (Ithaca,

NY: Cornell University Press, 1986).

Roeber, A. G.: "'The Origin of Whatever is not English among us': The Dutch-Speaking and the German-Speaking Peoples of Colonial British America." In Bailyn and Morgan (1991), pp. 220–83.

Roeber, A. G.: *Palatines, Liberty, and Property: German Lutherans in Colonial British America* (Baltimore, MD: Johns Hopkins University Press, 1993).

Rutman, D. B. and A. H.: *A Place in Time: Middlesex County, Virginia 1650–1750* (New York: W. W. Norton & Co., 1984).

Salinger, S. V.: *"To Serve Well and Faithfully": Labor and Indentured Servants in Pennsylvania, 1682–1800* (New York: Cambridge University Press, 1987).

Smith, A. E.: *Colonists in Bondage: White Servitude and Convict Labor in America, 1607–1776* (Chapel Hill, NC: University of North Carolina Press, 1947).

Smout, T. C., Landsman, N. C. et al.: "Scottish Emigration in the Seventeenth and Eighteenth Centuries." In Canny (1994), pp. 76–112.

Soderlund, J. R.: "Black Importation and Migration into Southeastern Pennsylvania, 1682–1810." In Klepp (1989), pp. 144–53.

Thornton, J.: *Africa and Africans in the Making of the Atlantic World, 1400–1680* (New York: Cambridge University Press, 1992).

Usner, D. H., Jr.: *Indians, Settlers, and Slaves in a Frontier Exchange Economy: The Lower Mississippi Valley Before 1783* (Chapel Hill, NC: University of North Carolina Press, 1992).

Vickers, D.: *Farmers & Fishermen: Two Centuries of Work in Essex County, Massachusetts, 1630–1830* (Chapel Hill, NC: University of North Carolina Press, 1994).

Walsh, L. S. and Menard, R. R. "Death in the Chesapeake: Two Life Tables for Men in Early Colonial Maryland." *Maryland Historical Magazine* 69 (1974), pp. 11–27.

Wells, R. V.: *The Population of the British Colonies of America Before 1776: A Survey of Census Data* (Princeton, NJ: Princeton University Press, 1975).

White, R.: *The Middle Ground: Indians, Empires, and Republics in the Great Lakes Region, 1650–1815* (New York: Cambridge University Press, 1991).

Winship, M. N.: "The Land of Connected Men: A New Migration Story from the Early Republic." In N. Canny, J. E. Illick et al., eds., *Pennsylvania History* 64 (1997), 88–104.

Wokeck, M. S.: "Promoters and Passengers: The German Immigrant Trade." In R. S. Dunn and M. M. Dunn, eds., *The World of William Penn* (Philadelphia: University of Pennsylvania Press, 1986), pp. 259–81.

Wokeck, M. S.: "German and Irish immigration to Colonial Philadelphia." In Klepp (1989), pp. 128–43.

Wood, P. H.: *Black Majority: Negroes in Colonial South Carolina from 1670 through the Stono Rebellion* (New York: Alfred A. Knopf, 1974).

Wrigley, E. A.: "A Simple Model of London's Importance in Changing English Society and Economy 1650–1750." *Past and Present* 37 (1967), pp. 44–70.

Wrigley, E. A. and Schofield, R. S.: *The Population History of England 1541–1871: A Reconstruction* (Cambridge, MA: Harvard University Press, 1981).

Zuckerman, M. W., ed.: *Friends and Neighbors: Group Life in America's First Plural Society* (Philadelphia: Temple University Press, 1982).

CHAPTER FIVE

Empire

RICHARD R. JOHNSON

The theme of "empire," unlike many of the analytical categories that modern scholars have discerned in Anglo-American colonial history, was one familiar to the colonists themselves, part of an interpretative tradition extending back through sixteenth-century England to ancient times. The term itself has long played many parts. First deployed, as in Parliament's renowned 1533 declaration that "this Realm of England is an Empire," to assert a sovereign nationalism, it only slowly took on the characteristics of geographical breadth and expansive ambition associated with a "British" world empire. Its rightful form and function remained matters for debate. With America settled, seventeenth-century royal administrator William Blathwayt's vision of the king's "real Empire in those parts" in terms of colonial union and strict subordination to the Crown stood in sharp contrast to the colonists' conceptions of a looser, confederative imperium. But colonial views, too, could shift with circumstance: Benjamin Franklin could proclaim the colonies part of Britain's "empire of liberty" in arguing for the Crown's responsibility for the costs of their defense, only for John Adams to deny any such membership because of what he saw as empire's implications for subjecting Americans to an inherently despotic, Roman style of rule. These are but a sampling of the large literature of the term's use charted by modern scholars (Koebner, 1961; Pagden, 1995; Armitage in Canny, 1998; Armitage, 2000).

Through much of the modern historiography of empire, therefore, runs a dialogue between past and present. Historians have reassessed the components, contexts, and perspectives that contemporaries identified with empire and added their own layers of meaning, especially as the course of modern events has entangled the term with its more recently coined and decidedly more pejorative offspring, imperialism. Central to the debate – and, hence, to the discussion in this chapter – has been a series of evolving definitions and questions. Given that empire can embody a spectrum of meaning ranging from geopolitical entity to mode of dominance, how is its expression in British America prior to 1760 best defined: in terms of conquest, government, commerce, consumption, culture, or community? Is its essence seaborne, land based, or amphibious, national or transnational? And within which timeframe should its workings – and its significance as an analytical category – be assessed: the span culminating in the British empire's seeming dissolution in 1783 or one that includes its subsequent resurgence, thereby contrasting the majority of colonists who seceded with the majority of colonies that remained? The pages that follow attest that matters of structure, policy, and governance, with the question of their relationship to the onset of American independence, still dominate discussion. Equally apparent, however, is a turn towards investing empire with broader and more explicitly comparative social and cultural meanings in ways that have the capacity to transcend the boundaries of political and national American history.

This dialogue of past and present has been slow to assume its modern form. Through much of the nineteenth century, the matter of empire and the story of the founding years of what had become the United States remained largely distinct in historical writing. American historians chronicled the years before the Revolution in terms of a saga of European settlement shaped by the manifest destiny of impending nationhood. British scholars found empire better defined and defended in its nineteenth-century growth than in its faltering beginnings or its eighteenth-century schism. Moreover, the essential materials for the study of Britain's government of America remained secluded in London's archives, with access to them inhibited by the individual consent needed from British Foreign Secretaries still doubtful of the propriety of allowing all and sundry to read their predecessors' mail and apprehensive lest research rekindle such issues as the status of Canada's boundary with northern New England. After mid-century, however, a series of publications began to open up the subject. Several American state historical bodies commissioned transcripts of the London records, and the indefatigable Benjamin Franklin Stevens copied and printed other public documents of the revolutionary era. In England, the appearance after 1860 of a succession of volumes summarizing early colonial materials and published by London's Public Record Office – most notably the series extending to the year 1738, of *Calendars of State Papers, Colonial Series* – provided what is still the greatest single stimulus ever given to scholarly study of early English overseas expansion. A fresh perspective for their use emerged in Sir John Seeley's breezy and best-selling *The Expansion of England*, first published in 1883 and repeatedly reprinted on both sides of the Atlantic during an era of Anglo-American rapprochement. Seeley pictured Anglo-American history as a coherent whole before (and even after) 1776 and argued that the Revolution – that "schism in Greater Britain" – was more the consequence of a flawed colonial system than any cosmic contest between liberty and tyranny. His work helped give an enduring imperial dimension to the academic study of history then taking shape in Britain, a trend later given institutional form by the endowment (with fortunes dug out of colonial South Africa) of professorships of imperial history at several leading English universities.

The stage was set for the pioneering work of three American historians, Herbert L. Osgood, his student, George Louis Beer, and Charles M. Andrews. All strove with crusading fervor and in the name of a more scientific and factually based history, to reorient the study of early America away from what they saw as its existing provincialism and towards its true nature as a phase of European and, especially, British history. Beer, before his early death in 1920, produced four well-researched volumes on British colonial policy (1907, 1908, 1912) and Osgood published a more synthetic seven-volume opus detailing the structure and workings of American colonial government (1904–7, 1924–5). Andrews, the most prolific, long-lived, and influential member of the group, was also the most insistent that he was not an "imperial" historian. He avoided use of the term and criticized those such as Osgood who applied it to British measures before the 1760s. His goal, he declared, was "to put the 'colonial' back into colonial history . . . a colony must have a mother country and a mother country a colony and each is bound to be influenced by whatever that relationship demands" (1920, pp. 159–60). But Andrews was at one with his fellow scholars in holding to a vision that was certainly imperial in scope, one that comprehended both Britain's Caribbean and its North American mainland colonies and encouraged their assessment both comparatively and as a whole, and from a predominantly metropolitan, London-based perspective. As such, though without any formal acknowledgment, it echoed the "metrocentric" interpretation of later European imperialisms then being advanced by such scholars as J. A. Hobson in Europe (Doyle, 1986, pp. 22–4). The great importance of Andrews lay in his dual legacy – the writings that culminated in his great four-volume work, *The Colonial Period of American History* (1934–38), and, of even greater value for later scholars, the thousands of pages he compiled in the form of guides and lists cataloguing the materials for American colonial history contained in British archives (1912–14).

The great bulk of these materials dealt with London's political administration of the American colonies, and they formed the basis of several notable studies that grew out of work begun in Andrews' doctoral seminar at Yale. These included Frank Pitman's analysis of the British West Indian development (1917), Viola Barnes' account of the Dominion of New England (1923), Gertrude Jacobsen's biography of Blathwayt (1932), Lawrence Gipson's multi-volume history, *The British Empire Before the American Revolution* (1939–70), and a monumental, and still unmatched, dissection of the structure of royal government in America by Leonard W. Labaree (1930). Similar in approach, and strongly influenced by Andrews' methods, was Lawrence Harper's massive examination of English commercial regulation as embodied in the acts of trade (1939).

All these works shared Andrews' commitment to a tradition of historical scholarship that employed careful institutional analysis to construct a predominantly political narrative. All more or less explicitly subscribed to a scenario of impending imperial disruption outlined by Osgood and cogently summarized by Andrews in his *The Colonial Background of the American Revolution* (1931), by which England's essentially benevolent (or, at least, well-intentioned) authority began to seem at variance with colonial ways, especially as shown in the encroachment upon the powers of royal governors by local representative assemblies. Almost insensibly, England and America grew apart, so that Whitehall's belated attempt in the 1760s to impose truly imperialistic policies of control ran headlong into the colonists' now-accustomed habits of self-government.

Even as Andrews and his students wrote, they encountered criticism suggesting that their limited vision of what constituted history could not adequately account for the changes they described. Skeptics pointed to the colonies' social, economic, and intellectual development, and to internal divisions and frontier expansion, as more important factors than structural divergence and political infighting in the coming of the Revolution. History vaunted as scientific and definitive now seemed deficient both in its content and its insight into human motivation. English commercial regulation was more exploitative than simple exposition of its structure revealed; and to portray its opponents, the colonial radicals, as terrorists driven by blind unreason (the words are those of Andrews) was to ignore their popular support and the real threat posed by British measures. The years during and after World War II, with America locked in hot and cold struggles with various expansive "empires," only heightened this reaction.

New accounts of the coming of the Revolution, such as Edmund and Helen Morgan's *The Stamp Act Crisis* (1953), lauded the accuracy and efficacy of the colonists' principled objections to British policy. Others studied the growth of resistance in individual colonies and its consequence for the years after 1776. By setting rebellion in the context of what Americans were about to accomplish – as the first act in the creation of a new order of the ages rather than the curtain coming down on empire – historians of the 1950s turned away from an imperial perspective. The multi-volume series of the post-war period celebrated, not empire, but the lives and papers of the great white founders of the American republic.

In the face of such reassessment, scholars who persisted in studying the course of empire in British America before 1783 pulled back from presenting overarching explanations for its schism. They made no perceptible effort to attune their work to the lively debate over the nature and evolution of imperialism then emerging among historians of its later, Victorian phase (Doyle, 1986, pp. 141–8). Instead, they looked to particular elements of British colonial governance. In particular, they attached a new importance, one plainly influenced by the work of Sir Lewis Namier on eighteenth-century British politics, to understanding the informal workings as much as the structural processes of these bodies. A succession of monographs explored the workings of the Crown's vice-admiralty courts, the careers of a variety of royal officials, the shaping of frontier policy, and colonial administration during the early years of the Board of Trade and the Duke of Newcastle's long tenure as Secretary of State (Ubbelohde, 1960; Hall, 1960; Leder, 1961; Sosin, 1961; Steele, 1968; Henretta, 1972). Together, these books gave new substance to the operation of the imperial system, especially for the period of the eighteenth century relatively neglected by Andrews and his colleagues. Following a path blazed by Namier's scholarship, they moved beyond an earlier generation's focus on the materials of London's Public Record Office by utilizing the many collections of personal and family papers now open to scholars, often by means of the new research tool of microfilm, on both sides of the Atlantic.

But the figure most responsible for giving study of the imperial connection fresh inspiration and legitimacy has been Bernard Bailyn. Over a span of forty years, Bailyn's scholarship has proved far too protean to be tied to the wheels of any "imperial" school. But his 1953 doctoral thesis on New England's merchant community early alerted him to the importance of an Atlantic context for early American colonization and to the implications for colonial politics of the extension of royal authority in the late seventeenth century. By the 1960s, the graduates of his seminar at Harvard included several whose work re-evaluated the transatlantic connections underlying eighteenth-century Anglo-colonial government: Stanley Katz's account of London's administration of the province of New York (1968), Michael Kammen's examination of the work of the agents appointed to represent colonial interests in London (1968), and Thomas Barrow's still definitive study of the British Customs service in America (1967).

Bailyn's own accompanying scholarship has at once subverted and yet given new validity to this work. In 1967, he published his renowned *The Ideological Origins of the American Revolution*, a work that effectively subordinated the study of imperial governance to the more glittering task of recovering the patterns of thought whereby Americans came to conceive of imperial measures, howsoever intended, as a deliberate conspiracy against their liberties. Just one year later, however, appeared his elegant short study entitled *The Origins of American Politics*. The book began by tracing further back into the eighteenth century the influence on colonial thought of the English opposition literature that Bailyn saw as energizing patriot perceptions of London's policies. Yet he then found this to be but one ingredient of a more fundamental, institutionally based disjuncture between the formal structure of imperial government in America and its actual workings. As a consequence, and by contrast with a stable British polity where these elements were more compatible, early American politics were uniquely plagued with a factionalism so unstable as to be "latently revolutionary" (Bailyn, 1968, p. 160). Ideological perceptions configured and exacerbated but grew out of institutional and political realities.

Bailyn's argument has, in its turn, been undermined by recent scholarship on both sides of the Atlantic that finds both a growing stability in colonial politics and a more volatile British political arena than his broad brush-strokes had portrayed. Nonetheless, his approach has done much to revive – and endow with new explanatory power – the insistence of Andrews and his colleagues on setting early American history within a larger transatlantic context. It has given a new vitality to the comparative study of Anglo-American political culture, drawing upon the scholarly legacy of earlier institutional and Namierist approaches but reconceptualizing it in pursuit of such broader cultural themes as the origins of a republican ideology, the iconography of political protest, traditions of collective violence, and the dynamic and delegitimizing effects of an emerging transatlantic belief in a governmental conspiracy against British liberties. And it has refurbished the concept of an emerging British empire by replacing the model predicating a progressive divergence of British America from Britain (with its sub-theme of the early formation of an incipient American nationalism) with one suggesting an increasing social and political convergence with the mother country, a process that John Murrin has aptly characterized as one of colonial "anglicization" (1966). It was the colonists' pride in, and determination to preserve, their rights, status, and ways of life as Englishmen – couched in language drawn from the vocabulary of English political protest – that fueled and legitimized the mounting resentment of London's measures. The imperial connection, instead of being marginalized as a short-lived and mildly disreputable phase that the colonists discarded on their way to nationhood, now took its place as an essential and enduring component of the development and eventual reconstitution of British America.

The late 1960s, therefore, witnessed a notable surge of interest in the political culture of empire, one capped by the publication of a wide-ranging volume of essays on Anglo-American political relations edited by Alison Gilbert Olson and Richard Maxwell Brown (1973). Yet this momentum was not sustained. It is tempting, but perhaps too facile, to ascribe the loss of interest to the turbulence of a decade in America's history during which any manifestation of empire, whether on campus or in Southeast Asia, was tarred with the brush of imperialism. Students of Europe's legacy in Asia and Africa would use these years to explore how colonized groups both received and resisted colonialism. For historians of the United States, however, other paths of study, and especially those involving a search for the roots of family and community, plainly exerted a greater appeal, bringing history as well as the war "back home." In particular, the wave of studies of Puritan town life published in the early 1970s added an appealing new precision in the form of sophisticated quantitative techniques for demographic and societal analysis to the long-standing scholarly interest in the formation of specifically American ways of life and belief. Simultaneously, within and outside the United States, the study of its history was shaped by the proliferation of American Studies programs whose format likewise gave a special emphasis to identifying the exceptional characteristics, good or evil, of American life. Undeniably, too, the study of society and people in the mass, and over the span of generations – of history from the bottom up, in a famous phrase – appeared to possess a greater potential than a chronicling of the mechanisms of imperial governance for exploring the issues of race, gender, and class now coming to the forefront of American historiography.

The response of Americanists who remained committed to an "imperial" perspective has ranged from something resembling defiance to a more subtly collaborative attitude. In the first mode stands Stephen Saunders Webb's substantial and powerfully original book, *The Governors-General: The English Army and the Definition of the Empire, 1519–1681* (1979). Building upon his doctoral dissertation, which had documented the large numbers of English army officers who served as colonial governors between 1660 and 1730, Webb now advanced a much broader argument for the prevalence of a system of "garrison government" in the British Isles and, from the late seventeenth century, in England's American colonies. Webb followed Andrews in stressing the view from London and the need to include colonies such as Jamaica in any account of English rule, but viewed him as quite mistaken in seeing English colonial policy as predominantly commercial and mercantile prior to the 1760s. To the contrary, English rule was from the first both militant and imperial, seeking to impose state control on dependent people by force, and by means of the soldier-governors who "were the instruments of an overweening prerogative power, the agents of an actual executive conspiracy" (Webb, 1979, pp. xvi–xxii, 459, 4). Webb has since published a second book, *1676: The End of American Independence*, that gives a somewhat lower profile to the thesis of "garrison government" but develops the theme of the growth of empire in America through chronicling the Crown's suppression of Bacon's Rebellion in Virginia and the forging of a diplomatic and military alliance between two "empires" – English and Iroquois Indian – against the threat of a third, the outcome of French expansion in North America. The spirit of a seventeenth-century '76, he suggests, thereby helps us to face up to "the contemporary fact of American empire" (Webb, 1984, p. xv).

Webb's interpretation remains controversial. Reviewers, including this writer, have found little evidence for Whitehall's formulation of any deliberate policy of militant imperialism. They have pointed to the weaknesses of the later Stuart army, the civilian character of many of those Webb dubs military autocrats, and the absence of any effective English military presence in America (Johnson, 1986). Webb's depiction of the decade following 1676 as an era in which the crown established an enduring empire in America appears more rhetorical than substantive, and his portrayal of the Glorious Revolution of 1688–9 as "a military coup" presaging a further expansion of militant empire in America runs counter to more traditional – and better documented – explanations of the Revolution as a defeat for Stuart autocracy and as the basis of an enduring constitutional settlement combining royal executive authority with the power of locally elected legislatures. David Lovejoy's *The Glorious Revolution in America* (1972) and Robert Bliss' *Revolution and Empire* (1990) remain more reliable guides to these events. This said, Webb's work continues to provide a valuable and bracing riposte to scholars lacking his breadth of vision, depth of research in neglected materials, and jugular instinct for the realities of power politics. His insistence on the efficacy of executive power counters the long-standing, Whiggish tradition of looking to the colonial legislatures as the effective instruments of political development. Finally, too, Webb's depiction of the steady extension of imperial intervention from the marchlands of the British Isles to the near corners of North America, from the Irish to the Iroquois, has helped foster several of the most prominent themes of recent imperial historiography, such as the attention given to the role of war in state formation and the continuities and contrasts between different areas of English colonization.

For all its originality, Webb's work still holds tightly to the older orthodoxy of viewing early America and its inhabitants through the eyes of the Crown and its servants. The role assigned to the colonists scarcely exceeds that of feeling gratitude for the introduction to empire that rescues them from incompetent local leadership and shepherds them towards the dawn of modern imperial America. A different perspective, and one more attuned to recent studies of Anglo-American "connections" and the colonies' social development, shapes the work of Alison Gilbert Olson, David Lovejoy, and Richard Johnson. Olson, a scholar with an exceptional knowledge of both British and American archives, has written two books tracing the links between British and colonial political groupings. The first, *Anglo-American Politics* (1973), is an extended and densely illustrated essay suggesting the existence of coherent colonial factions or "parties" parallel to those emerging in late seventeenth-century England. While the ties between these factions flourished, as in the years up to 1714, an integrated transatlantic political community seemed to be forming, but the subsequent Whig monopoly of power in England eroded these connections in ways that would eventually turn leaders back upon their own local interests and electorates, and leave the imperial system incapable of resolving the crises of the revolutionary period. Olson's argument may overstate both the mutuality of transatlantic "party" issues and the abruptness of their decay; and her second book, *Making the Empire Work* (1992), takes a different road (and periodicization) towards the same destination by focusing on the role of interest groups within the imperial community. These groups are located more in London than on both sides of the ocean, and it is now the three decades after 1720 that Olson finds to be the heyday of interest group cooperation and influence. Not until after the mid-1750s did English and colonial lobbyists begin to lose their voice in the shaping of policy, as their collaborative, backstairs approach gave way to the more vociferous, confrontational, and insufferably principled tactics of the 1760s. *Making the Empire Work* remains especially valuable for its meticulous reconstruction of the (often overlapping) work of two species of hitherto neglected political groupings – the merchants involved in different imperial trades, and the religious organizations – Quaker, Jewish, Anglican, Huguenot, and Presbyterian being the most prominent – who not only lobbied for protection and privilege in sectarian matters but took an active role in influencing policy decisions and appointments to colonial office. We gain a fresh appreciation of the range and diversity of groups with vested interests in the security, prosperity – and continuance – of empire.

Lovejoy's *The Glorious Revolution in America* (1972) adopts a different though equally creative approach to imperial issues by combining a broad comparative analysis of the origins and impact of the events of 1689–92 within the various British American colonies with the stated intent of exploring what these events meant for the colonists themselves. His conclusion, that much of the Glorious Revolution's significance lay in providing particular colonial groups with the opportunity to advance their own local ambitions, re-emphasizes the necessity of an imperial dimension for any adequate explanation of early eighteenth-century colonial political development; and his accompanying argument, that the colonists sought to realize a conception of empire based on an equality between Englishmen on both sides of the Atlantic, provides a suggestive, if more speculative, theme for examining some of the perceived constitutional ambiguities that would later bedevil imperial relations.

A still more explicit argument for the formative role in both colonial and imperial development played by the colonists' relations with England appears in Johnson's *Adjustment to Empire* (1981), a study of the region, New England, most intransigently opposed to late seventeenth-century Stuart regulation. The book finds a gradual accommodation, during and after the Glorious Revolution, to a greater measure of royal authority, and one that fostered a new interdependence with an England now perceived, by its resumed leadership of the Protestant cause, as once more worthy of the colonists' allegiance. Simultaneously, Johnson suggests, New England's leaders learned how to use their agents and allies in England to manipulate the channels of official action to their own advantage, winning military aid and influencing the appointment of royal governors. Collaboration replaced confrontation. Throughout these three authors' work, therefore, runs the theme of an early eighteenth-century imperial polity constituted by willing and "interested" participation on both sides of the ocean. War, politics, and commerce dictated a closer connection with the mother country as a majority of Britain's American colonies passed under direct rule by London-appointed executives. Within this connection, however, groups and individuals were enabled to pursue a multitude of personal or sectarian ambitions in ways that preserved much of the colonists' sense of founding mission and local autonomy. A greater attachment to English ways of life and government did not extend to unconditional allegiance to the Crown.

This theme, of the calculated, many-handed construction of an Anglo-American empire, one shaped by forces as much centripetal as centrifugal, remains central to modern scholarship. But it is now less often expressed in terms of British America's political development. There have been few recent book-length studies of colonial politics, and those that have appeared conspicuously lack an imperial dimension. A distinguished exception, though one looking less to the everyday workings of politics than to its theoretical underpinnings, is Jack P. Greene's *Peripheries and Center: Constitutional Development in the Extended Polities of the British Empire and the United States, 1607–1788* (1986). In nine tightly written chapters, Greene traces the course of contemporary debates over the relationship between metropolitan core and colonial peripheries, from their seventeenth-century beginnings to their reincarnation in republican form in the Confederation period of the 1780s. At the heart of these debates, he suggests, lay not the fears of ministerial conspiracy advanced in Bailyn's *Ideological Origins* but legal questions concerning the nature of political authority and its necessary component of consent. Seen in these terms, and here reviving an old debate among constitutional scholars about the legitimacy of Parliament's policies in the 1760s, the colonists could justly cite usage, custom, and habits of localist, consensual government as good law – an informal "imperial constitution" – that justified their rebellion and then shaped their own attempts to construct alternative authorities.

Peripheries and Center reminds us of the centrality of constitutional and legal issues in the minds and writings of contemporaries. Its persuasive depiction of overlapping constitutional legitimacies within a single "extended polity" resonates with the ongoing debate among historians as to the "composite," confederal nature of many of the early modern European states (Elliott, 1992). It points to the continuity linking "imperial" and "federal" issues in North American history. Yet these very insights also suggest the extent to which the book ties the issue of empire to the formation of a post-imperial order. The years before 1776 become an extended prelude to revolution. Colonists are grouped together on the periphery, confronting and contesting rather than contributing to the construction of empire taking place at the core. Plainly, the huge gravitational pull exerted by our foreknowledge of the eventual implosion of Britain's empire still makes it difficult for historians of early American politics to assess the period before 1760 on its own terms.

In place of political history, the course of "explaining empire" has taken other paths. In particular, empire has enlarged its social, spatial, and transnational dimensions – and thereby shed some of the burden of pejorative implications it had carried in the 1960s – by reappearing under the blander, maritime aegis of "Atlantic history." The term is not new: back in 1949, Michael Kraus had written of the origins of an Atlantic civilization and others, subsequently, of the rise of Europe's "seaborne empires" (Bailyn, 1996, pp. 24–7). Two contributions to multi-volume surveys of the modern world, Ralph Davis' *The Rise of the Atlantic Economies* (1973) and K. G. Davies' *The North Atlantic World in the Seventeenth Century* (1974), demonstrated the explanatory potential of the new approach, as in the latter's organization by chapters given to such transnational topics as people, products, government, and relations with native populations. Stimulated by scholarly debate over the emergence of modern "world systems," this "atlanticism" has grown to encompass the comparative analysis of all aspects of the formation of early modern seagoing societies, and especially the economic and demographic components of their overseas expansion. The explosive growth of the Atlantic slave trade, for example, with the staple economies derived from the cultivation of sugar and tobacco by enslaved labor, have become recognized as worldwide phenomena and not just peculiarly North American institutions. This, in turn, has given new prominence to the complex interplay *between* empires – to the struggle to dominate the Caribbean sugar islands and the northern cod fisheries, the competition to supply Spanish America with slaves and continental Europe with tobacco, and the impact of piracy and privateering. Books such as Jacob Price's *France and the Chesapeake* (1973), Sidney Mintz's *Sweetness and Power* (1985), and James Walvin's *Fruits of Empire* (1997) reveal "empires" of trade, production, and consumption transcending national boundaries.

Within the narrower realm of British colonization, meanwhile, the infusion of social history with an Atlantic perspective has encouraged scholars to recast their basic categories of analysis. The governance-based distinctions between different kinds of colonies – royal, proprietorial, corporate – that underpinned the old imperial history have given way to comparisons between geographical regions identified by their settlement patterns, land-use and labor systems, economic ties, and cultural orientation (Greene and Pole, 1984, pp. 12–13). The resulting literature is assessed elsewhere in this volume. But we should note in passing that its incorporation of such matters as the influence of the English Caribbean colonies on the settlement of Carolina or the parts played by the Atlantic slave and tobacco trades in the transformation of the late seventeenth-century Chesapeake now assumes the necessity of an "imperial" perspective extending beyond individual colonies or those that became the United States (as Greene, 1988; Morgan, 1975; Clemens, 1980).

Intrinsic to this re-categorization has been a greater recognition of the early forma-tion, broad dimensions, and enduring impact of British America's multi-ethnicity. New questions combined with painstaking demographic analysis have revealed what older accounts failed to perceive, let alone credit, that those traditionally labeled "minori-ties" – immigrant Africans and Native American Indians – were in fact majorities in many parts of pre-revolutionary British America in terms of lives lived, as opposed to power exercised and communities established. Philip Morgan concludes that nearly three-quarters of the migrants to the British Caribbean and mainland colonies be-tween 1630 and 1780 were of African rather than European origin, a fact plainly stretching the cultural and spatial horizons for the study of the formation of empire far beyond those envisioned by Charles M. Andrews (Morgan in Bailyn and Morgan, 1991, pp. 161–2). There is a black as well as a white Atlantic. Once arrived, we now know from the literature discussed elsewhere in this volume, these African migrants found very different lives, with a terrible first-generation mortality in the Caribbean sugar plantations but with the slow emergence in the mainland colonies, by the mid-eighteenth century, of native-born, African American communities and cultures. Si-multaneously, the Indian population of the Caribbean and eastern North America was suffering a death rate, due mainly to the ravages of imported Old World infections, that scholars set as high as 90 percent during the first hundred years of contact. In sum, the reassessment of the processes of colonization to give fuller account to the transatlan-tic trade in peoples, germs, and products has greatly enhanced our understanding of the human components of empire. To the traditional agents for imperial growth – gold, glory, gunpowder, and the gospel – have been added others that reveal its costs and consequences, especially the ravages of disease and a death toll among both migrants and aboriginal inhabitants on a scale unparalleled in modern human history.

The reappraisal of the patterns of transoceanic movement has also reshaped the traditional narrative of European migration to British America. A succession of studies (Bailyn, 1986; Fischer, 1989; Roeber, 1993) have challenged old assumptions about the domestic formation of American culture by chronicling how particular migrant groups transmitted and preserved their Old World heritages, propagating what might be described as small-scale cultural empires in America. Others have enriched our un-derstanding of the seaborne character of migration and its configuration of subse-quent settlement. Ian Steele (1986) shows how the faster pace and greater security of transoceanic travel and communication accelerated the creation of a multifaceted Eng-lish Atlantic community. Donald Meinig (1986) portrays the making of "a vast Atlan-tic circuit" through the eyes of an historical geographer. Cole Harris's *Historical Atlas of Canada: The Beginning to 1800* (1987) maps the patterns of New World settlement with a creative imagination that enriches both history and the visual arts.

Most of this "Atlantic" scholarship is best characterized as broad-scale social history. Matters of policy and politics are seldom allowed to complicate stories centered on the movement of bodies. Even as this work appeared, however, scholars such as J. G. A. Pocock and David Fieldhouse were urging that it be set in a more specifically imperial and interactive context. They called for the writing of a new, "Greater British" history, one that would extend both throughout and beyond the British Isles and do justice to an expansive past obscured by Britain's modern retreat from empire and turn towards a European identity. Such history would look beyond viewing empire as an organism directed from the center to recognize it as "a double-ended process," one of continuous interaction within the framework of an evolving British identity between a diversity of nationalities, institutions, and cultures (Pocock, 1982; Fieldhouse, 1984). Several studies have followed this lead. T. H. Breen exemplifies the process of interaction in an article visualizing "an empire of goods," the part played by the consumption of imported products in anglicizing American colonial society (Breen, 1986). In *The Refinement of America* (1992), Richard Bushman paints a still broader picture in showing the reception and infusion of a culture of metropolitan gentility, ranging from architectural forms to the ceremony of "taking tea." David Shields' *Oracles of Empire* (1990) demonstrates the strength of "British" and "imperial" concerns and loyalties in a wide range of colonial poetry and prose hitherto slighted by scholars committed to discovering the origins of a distinctively "American" literature. Conversely, we are learning more about the colonies' "imperialization" of Britain through the transmission of tropical products, plant life, scientific knowledge, and fortunes made across the sea (Draper in Marshall, 1998; Bowen, 1996).

But the single work that, more than any other, has embodied the new meaning and future possibilities of a more broadly conceived but specifically imperial perspective is the volume of essays, *Strangers within the Realm: Cultural Margins of the First British Empire* (1991), edited by Bailyn and Philip Morgan. In a wide-ranging and thoughtful introduction, the two editors acknowledge inspiration from the scholarship of the 1980s. But, as they note, what emerges from their volume pushes further. It includes superbly crafted essays by Morgan and James Merrell on the intersection of Africans and American Indians with the Atlantic world, depicting the first impelled into the maelstrom of slave and slaveholding societies, and the second struggling with the complexities of a shifting political and cultural frontier along the fringes of empire. It gives equal place to Irish and Scottish contributions to imperial formation, and to the parts played by Scots-Irish, Dutch, and German settlers in British America. Taken together, the volume's essays turn attention away from the traditional (and predominantly political and institutional) relationship between metropolitan English core and colonial periphery towards the construction of empire by groups hitherto deemed "strange" and marginal. They highlight the social and cultural interplay within and between peripheries or, more particularly and as an eighteenth-century empire took shape, between England's first peripheries – the Celtic lands and the earliest American colonies – and newer ones being settled across the seas, with such older peripheries as Scotland and Massachusetts developing over time their own metropolitan character and influence.

The sparks struck by this volume are still setting fires. Scholars continue to explore the many facets of Scotland's politically subordinate but culturally distinctive role in the formation of empire, as in the spread of Enlightenment thought and religious evangelism, migration projects, and the personnel of the Hudson Bay Company and the British army overseas (Landsman, 1985; Bayly, 1989; Sher and Smitten, 1990; Colley, 1992; Landsman in Stone, 1994; Robertson, 1995). David Hancock's superbly researched and aptly titled *Citizens of the World* (1995) details the careers of a group of Scots merchants who prospered mightily in Atlantic commerce and entered Britain's landed gentry. Contrary to Dr. Johnson's slur, we may now conclude, the best sight that an eighteenth-century Scotsman could see was not the high road to England but the ship taking him – or his writings, his goods, or those he had trained – overseas. Nor did this imply any subversion of metropolitan authority. Just as Welsh and Scots writers had been among the first to speak of a British empire, so their descendants continued to emphasize, for their own purposes, the range and legitimacy of Great Britain's power: "Rule Britannia," it has been noted, came from a Scottish pen, and Highlanders exiled to America would rally in support of King George in 1776.

Stepping westward, to mid-continent, a second group of studies have uncovered the networks of negotiation, exchange, and – in Richard White's phrase – "creative misunderstanding" that formed in the shifting, intersecting borderlands of European expansion in North America (White, 1991; Hinderaker, 1997; Calloway, 1997). Indian peoples such as the Iroquois and Cherokee are revealed as active, calculating participants in the clash of empires, as much by their pursuit of their own "imperial" aspirations within an irreversibly altered Indian world as by their dealings with colonists and royal officials. Individuals dislocated by changing circumstances fashion hybrid lives as traders, mercenaries, and cultural brokers. It is here that early Americanists are best responding to the challenge posed by scholars of European colonialisms in other continents, that of building complex, layered analyses that question the traditional dualism of colonizer and colonized, perceive how each was reconfigured by their mutual engagement, and accord agency to both in the new worlds that emerged (as Cooper and Stoler, 1997). It is in this field, too, that scholars such as White and Eric Hinderaker are most creatively considering and comparing different forms and outcomes for American empire. In revising the older, simplistic scenarios of deepening racial hatred and collision, they show these empires – Spanish, French, British, and of an independent United States – to be still more many-handed, and multi-ethnic, constructs than we had previously perceived.

A third focus of recent scholarship returns to a more traditionally British and metropolitan setting but with a perspective colored by the new methodologies of literary and non-materialist cultural studies. These methodologies' strong theoretical content have led imperialists elsewhere into the complexities associated with "postcolonial" and "subaltern" perspectives (Kennedy, 1996). For the years before 1760, however, debate has so far centered on the more specific issue of the part played by empire in Britain's sudden rise to world power. Scholars have derived new insights from analyzing contemporary literary and political discourse. But they have also held to the interpretive framework established by several influential attempts to explain the growth of what John Brewer has termed the eighteenth-century "fiscal-military" English state (Brewer, 1989; Stone, 1994).

From this convergence have come several distinctive interpretations that study the emergence of empire as a function of Britain's national history. Brewer's brilliant sketch of the English state's growing capacity to raise money and wage war has noted the tensions thereby aroused between groups competing to direct the expansion of state power, others seeking to profit from its military and commercial success, and still others fearing a subversion of cherished traditions of limited government and constitutional liberty. Several writers have winnowed the literature of this debate to assess empire's contribution to the shaping of British national identity. Linda Colley finds that it helped forge a more cohesive, royalist, and self-consciously patriotic state. Kathleen Wilson counters with a more nuanced argument that, to the contrary, the vision of empire emerging by the 1740s owed much to oppositionist arguments against perceived corruption and authoritarianism at home. Britain's empire, unlike those of her European rivals, could be a force for liberty and benevolence both at home and abroad – providing that it remain Protestant not popish, commercially not autocratically ordered, and "blue-water"-based and seaborne rather than territorial and militaristic. Not until the crisis of the 1770s, Wilson suggests, did this conceptual marriage of empire and nation break asunder, prompting a more conservative patriotism and forceful imperialism on the one hand and the rise of populist and extra-parliamentary protest on the other (Colley, 1992, pp. 132–45; Wilson, 1995, pp. 157, 282, 277, 436–7). Two recent books by Peter Miller (1994) and Eliga Gould (2000) likewise present the late eighteenth-century debate over empire as a defining moment in reformulating the conceptual foundations and moral bonds of the early modern British state. David Armitage (2000) traces the lineage and gradual coalescence of the commercial, libertarian, Protestant, and maritime elements of a specifically British ideology of empire back to the experiences of sixteenth-century state-building within the British Isles. Literary scholars, by contrast, emphasize the part played by European encounters with the overseas "other" in giving linguistic and conceptual form to national identity (Hulme, 1986; Cheyfitz, 1991). A massive two-volume study of British imperialism between 1688 and 1914 looks to the habits of economic behavior that sparked the nation's dramatic growth and argues for the sustained power of "gentlemanly capitalism," a fluid alliance of urban merchants and landed gentry within the British domestic economy, in fostering an expansive overseas presence (Cain and Hopkins, 1993).

These assessments of empire in terms of a British national history have necessarily embodied a metrocentric perspective reminiscent of older interpretations, though one now taking cultural representation and process throughout British society as formative rather than events in Westminster and Whitehall. Empire and early America assume peripheral, contributory roles not unlike those assigned to them by scholars searching for the roots of American nationality. Yet this work has forged a closer connection between American colonial and early modern European studies, narrowing the divide that, as noted earlier, long isolated the study of Britain's pre-1776 American empire from the lively debates surrounding European imperialism. This divide was in part a consequence of the differences seen between colonies of "settlement" (as, usually but not exclusively, in the Americas) and those of "occupation" and "exploitation" (as in Asia and Africa). But it also stemmed from the blinkered vision endemic in a historical narrative tied to the service of an emerging American nationalism and, on the other side of the pond, from the long-standing reluctance of European historians to acknowledge upstart American history as a legitimate pedagogical subject. The methodology of cultural studies, insistently transnational and as fervent in its claims to explanation as in censuring the very topics it chooses to dissect, is proving a useful solvent of these provincialisms. Empire and imperial issues are revealed as shared and essential components of both early America's and modern Britain's self-representation. Many more scholars trained outside the United States now write on early American matters, and an interest in "empire" often serves as their *Mayflower* in entering the field.

In addition, the breadth of this scholarship opens a way to the field's reintegration with more traditional approaches. For in defining empire as cultural construct rather than social process, and redirecting attention from the movement of bodies to the shaping of minds and the structuring of identity, it is resurrecting, by way of such issues as state formation and the genesis of early modern political culture, many of the institutional and political concerns central to an earlier generation of scholars.

A final benefit of this new work for students of early American empire is – or should be – the global, if still predominantly British, context in which their subject becomes sited. From this viewpoint, the impetus of empire was redirected, not ended, by the defeat of 1783: Britain's "imperial meridian," in Christopher Bayly's phrase, would come in the half-century that followed, in Asia, Africa, and the Antipodes. This has prompted new attempts to understand the changes and continuities linking the "first" and the "second" British empires. In a succession of already classic articles, P. J. Marshall has re-examined the periodicization and perceived implications of British imperial policy. If there was a turning point in the rise of a more forceful and deliberately imperial policy, he suggests, it occurred, not in 1763 or 1783, but in mid-century, as London dramatically increased the men and resources assigned to the defense of British America and laid plans for a closer supervision of its governments. The global triumphs of the Seven Years' War then produced "a new kind of empire, which directly challenged earlier ideals," one territorial rather than maritime and growing by conquest rather than settlement. It aroused fears by its overtones of "Asiatic" authoritarianism, complete with foreign mercenaries and standing armies. Equally, it alarmed settler elites by its comprehension of new, non-British populations – Bengalis, American Indians, and French Catholics (Marshall, 1987, pp. 106, 114–15). This debate continues: looking at the forms of government created in eighteenth-century British North America, Elizabeth Mancke (1997) finds a turn in policy as early as the postwar settlement of 1713; at the other end of the spectrum, Philip Lawson (1997) suggests that such measures as the Quebec Act reshaped British political culture (and alienated settler leadership) precisely because they presaged an empire more diverse in its politics, societies, and religions, and more protective of its exploited peoples. In this light, American rebellion takes on some of the character of a defense of "Herrenvolk settler" privilege and aspiration, sustaining Marc Egnal's argument that British policy threatened the interests of colonial expansionists intent on founding their own American empire (van den Berghe, 1967; Egnal, 1988). At the least, these wide-ranging questions should revive interest in the work begun several years ago by Jack Greene and Alison Olson, of deciphering the changes that began to reshape London's relationship with the American colonies during the eighteenth century's neglected middle years.

Huw Bowen's *Elites, Enterprise, and the Making of the British Overseas Empire, 1688– 1775* (1996) provides a lucid summary of this debate. But Bowen goes further. Drawing upon extensive reading and his own work on British India, he shows that "gentlemanly capitalism" was not simply a metropolitan phenomenon. As the eighteenth century unfolded, genteel, entrepreneurial elites formed in every province of the empire, transforming what had been dominated from England into a multinational, multilateral business and military enterprise. The interdependent but increasingly contentious relationships between provincial and metropolitan elites then shaped the development and eventual splintering of empire. In pulling together the recent work assessing empire for its part in national histories with that which sees it as a subject with a life and reach transcending nationalism, Bowen has provided the best single-volume introduction to the eighteenth-century empire, and one that plots a course for further research into the interactive formation of empire in its peripheries no less than at its core.

This brings us to the present – and empire's future. Armitage's recent volume (2000), and another by James Muldoon (1999), enlarge our understanding of the legal and conceptual underpinnings of empire, revising the classic studies by Klaus Knorr (1944) and Richard Koebner (1961), and supplementing Anthony Pagden's *Lords of all the World: Ideologies of Empire in Spain, Britain, and France* (1995). Pagden's treatment, though brief, has the great merit of taking a comparative approach, one sorely missing in recent work, save in some general surveys (Fieldhouse, 1966; Lang, 1975; McFarlane, 1994). We must await the appearance of John Elliott's planned comparative study of the American realms of Britain and Spain. The first half of the seventeenth century, a relatively uncharted world for modern British imperial scholarship since the days of Charles M. Andrews, promises to gain fresh visibility from Armitage's work and Alison Games' account (1999) of the period's transatlantic migration. These, too, may spur comparison with the unduly neglected topics of early Dutch and French relations with their fledgling colonies in North America.

Until then, the best evidence of the field's vitality and direction is contained in the first two volumes of *The Oxford History of the British Empire* (1998), edited by Nicholas Canny (*The Origins of Empire*) and P. J. Marshall (*The Eighteenth Century*) – volumes planned as one, but then expanded to two, matching the number allotted to the empire after 1800. The contrast with the old *Cambridge History of the British Empire* (1929) is profound. In place of a predominantly chronological and institutional treatment, the forty-seven essays in the Oxford volumes engage such topics as literature, science, naval technology, finance, religion, the black and Indian experiences, and the slave trade, all matters hardly dreamt of in the philosophies of Charles Andrews and George Louis Beer. Essays dealing with Ireland, Africa, and Asia stand alongside those on the Americas. Much greater space is given to the formation of empire within the colonies themselves, even if the reader may wonder that this emerges as so singularly masculine a process. The absence of gender studies aside, the two volumes demonstrate the ways in which "empire" has re-emerged as a vibrant aspect of the study of early American history, and one with the added capacity to link students to an exceptional range of transnational and global issues.

So vibrant and far-reaching, perhaps, that "empire" now risks following "republicanism" into being a term invoked so much as to mean very little. We must remain alert to how we use the term, and to ways in which different questions and contexts continue to rework our dialogue between past and present. In particular, we must strive to hold a balance between our filtered knowledge of empire's outcome and our attempts to recover the complex but temporally restricted horizons of its creators. More than a century ago, Sir John Seeley famously suggested that the British Empire had been acquired "in a fit of absence of mind." Recent scholarship has demonstrated that, on the contrary, empire in its many forms was very much on the minds of contemporaries. We are now realizing how the themes of these envisionings can lead to a richer explanation of events.

BIBLIOGRAPHY

Andrews, Charles M.: *Guide to the Materials for American History, to 1783, in the Public Record Office of Great Britain*, 2 vols (Washington, DC: Carnegie Institute of Washington, 1912–14).

Andrews, Charles M.: "How American Colonial History Should be Written." Publications of the Colonial Society of Massachusetts, 20, *Transactions, 1917–1919* (1920), 159–63.

Andrews, Charles M.: *The Colonial Background of the American Revolution: Four Essays in American Colonial History*, rev. ed. (New Haven: Yale University Press, 1931).

Andrews, Charles M.: *The Colonial Period of American History*, 4 vols (New Haven: Yale University Press, 1934–8).

Andrews, K. R.: *Trade, Plunder, and Settlement: Maritime Enterprise and the Genesis of the British Empire, 1480–1630* (Cambridge: Cambridge University Press, 1984).

Armitage, David: *The Ideological Origins of the British Empire* (Cambridge: Cambridge University Press, 2000).

Bailyn, Bernard: *The Ideological Origins of the American Revolution* (Cambridge, MA: Harvard University Press, 1967).

Bailyn, Bernard: *The Origins of American Politics* (New York: Alfred A. Knopf, 1968).

Bailyn, Bernard: *Voyagers to the West: A Passage in the Peopling of America on the Eve of the Revolution* (New York: Alfred A. Knopf, 1986).

Bailyn, Bernard: "The Idea of Atlantic History." *Itinerario* 20, no. 1 (1996), pp. 19–44.

Bailyn, Bernard and Morgan, Philip D.: *Strangers within the Realm: Cultural Margins of the First British Empire* (Chapel Hill: University of North Carolina Press, 1991).

Barnes, Viola F.: *The Dominion of New England: A Study in British Colonial Policy* (New Haven: Yale University Press, 1923).

Barrow, Thomas: *Trade and Empire: The British Customs Service in Colonial America, 1660–1775* (Cambridge, MA: Harvard University Press, 1967).

Bayly, C. A.: *Imperial Meridian: The British Empire and the World, 1780–1830* (London: Longman, 1989).

Beer, George L.: *British Colonial Policy, 1754–1765* (New York: Macmillan, 1907).

Beer, George L.: *The Origins of the British Colonial System, 1578–1660* (New York: Macmillan, 1908).

Beer, George L.: *The Old Colonial System, 1660–1754,* part 1, *The Establishment of the System, 1660–1688,* 2 vols (New York: Macmillan, 1912).

Bliss, Robert: *Revolution and Empire: English Politics and the American Colonies in the Seventeenth Century* (Manchester: Manchester University Press, 1990).

Bowen, H. V.: *Elites, Enterprise, and the Making of the British Overseas Empire, 1688–1775* (London: Macmillan Press, 1996).

Breen, T. H.: "An Empire of Goods: The Anglicization of Colonial America, 1690–1776." *Journal of British Studies* 25 (1986), pp. 467–99.

Brewer, John: *The Sinews of Power: War, Money, and the English State, 1688–1783* (New York: Alfred A. Knopf, 1989).

Bushman, Richard L.: *The Refinement of America: Persons, Houses, Cities* (New York: Alfred A. Knopf, 1992).

Cain, P. J. and Hopkins, A. G.: *British Imperialism: Innovation and Expansion, 1688–1914* (London: Longman, 1993).

Calloway, Colin G.: *New Worlds for All: Indians, Europeans, and the Remaking of Early America* (Baltimore, MD: Johns Hopkins University Press, 1997).

Canny, Nicholas, ed.: *The Oxford History of the British Empire*, vol.1, *The Origins of Empire* (Oxford: Oxford University Press, 1998).

Cheyfitz, Eric: *The Poetics of Imperialism: Translation and Colonization from The Tempest to Tarzan* (New York: Oxford University Press, 1991).

Clemens, Paul: *The Atlantic Economy and Maryland's Eastern Shore: From Tobacco to Grain* (Ithaca, NY: Cornell University Press, 1980).

Colley, Linda: *Britons: The Forging of a Nation, 1707–1837* (New Haven: Yale University Press, 1992).

Cooper, Frederick and Stoler, Ann Laura: *Tensions of Empire: Colonial Cultures in a Bourgeois World* (Berkeley, CA: University of California Press, 1997).

Davies, K. G.: *The North Atlantic World in the Seventeenth Century* (Minneapolis, MN: University of Minnesota Press, 1974).

Davis, Ralph: *The Rise of the Atlantic Economies* (Ithaca, NY: Cornell University Press, 1973).

Doyle, Michael W.: *Empires* (Ithaca, NY: Cornell University Press, 1986).

Egnal, Marc: *A Mighty Empire: The Origins of the American Revolution* (Ithaca, NY: Cornell University Press, 1988).

Elliott, J. H.: "A Europe of Composite Monarchies." *Past and Present* 137 (1992), 48–71.

Fieldhouse, David: *The Colonial Empires: A Comparative Survey from the 18th Century* (London: Weidenfeld and Nicolson, 1966).

Fieldhouse, David: "Can Humpty-Dumpty be Put Together Again? Imperial History in the 1980s." *Journal of Imperial and Commonwealth History* 12, no. 2 (1984), pp. 9–23.

Fischer, David Hackett: *Albion's Seed: Four British Folkways in North America* (New York: Oxford University Press, 1989).

Games, Alison: *Migration and the Origins of the English Atlantic World* (Cambridge, MA: Harvard University Press, 1999).

Gipson, Lawrence Henry: *The British Empire before the American Revolution*, 15 vols (1–3 rev.) (New York: Alfred A. Knopf, 1939–1970).

Gould, Eliga H.: *The Persistence of Empire: British Political Culture in the Age of the American Revolution* (Chapel Hill, NC: University of North Carolina, 2000).

Greene, Jack P.: *Peripheries and Center: Constitutional Development in the Extended Polities of the British Empire and the United States, 1607–1788* (Athens, GA: University of Georgia, 1986).

Greene, Jack P.: *Pursuits of Happiness: The Social Development of Early Modern British Colonies and the Formation of American Culture* (Chapel Hill, NC: University of North Carolina, 1988).

Greene, Jack P. and Pole, J. R. eds.: *Colonial British America: Essays in the New History of the Early Modern Era* (Baltimore, MD: The Johns Hopkins University Press, 1984).

Hall, Michael Garibaldi: *Edward Randolph and the American Colonies, 1676–1703* (Chapel Hill, NC: University of North Carolina, 1960).

Hancock, David: *Citizens of the World: London Merchants and the Integration of the British Atlantic Economy, 1735–1785* (New York: Cambridge University Press, 1995).

Harper, Lawrence A.: *The English Navigation Laws: A Seventeenth-Century Experiment in Social Engineering* (New York: Columbia University Press, 1939).

Harris, R. Cole, ed.: *Historical Atlas of Canada*, vol. 1, *From the Beginning to 1800* (Toronto: University of Toronto Press, 1987).

Henretta, James A.: *"Salutary Neglect": Colonial Administration under the Duke of Newcastle* (Princeton, NJ: Princeton University Press, 1972).

Hinderaker, Eric: *Elusive Empires: Constructing Colonialism in the Ohio Valley, 1673–1800* (New York: Cambridge University Press, 1997).

Hulme, Peter: *Colonial Encounters: Europe and the Native Caribbean, 1492–1787* (London: Methuen, 1986).

Jacobsen, Gertrude: *William Blathwayt: A Late Seventeenth Century English Administrator* (New Haven, CT: Yale University Press, 1932).

Johnson, Richard R.: *Adjustment to Empire: The New England Colonies, 1675–1715* (New Brunswick, NJ: Rutgers University Press, 1981).

Johnson, Richard R.: "The Imperial Webb: The Thesis of Garrison Government in Early America Considered." *William and Mary Quarterly* 3rd ser., 43 (1986), pp. 408–30.

Kammen, Michael G.: *A Rope of Sand: The Colonial Agents, British Politics, and the American Revolution* (Ithaca, NY: Cornell University Press, 1968).

Katz, Stanley Nider: *Newcastle's New York: Anglo-American Politics, 1732–1753* (Cambridge, MA: Harvard University Press, 1968).

Kennedy, Dane: "Imperial History and Post-Colonial Theory." *Journal of Imperial and Commonwealth History* 24 (1996), pp. 345–63.

Knorr, Klaus E.: *British Colonial Theories, 1570–1850* (Toronto: University of Toronto Press, 1944).

Koebner, Richard: *Empire* (Cambridge: Cambridge University Press, 1961).

Kraus, Michael: *The Atlantic Civilization: Eighteenth-Century Origins* (Ithaca, NY: Cornell University Press, 1949).

Labaree, Leonard W.: *Royal Government in America: A Study of the British Colonial System before 1783* (New Haven: Yale University Press, 1930).

Landsman, Ned C.: *Scotland and Its First American Colony, 1683–1765* (Princeton, NJ: Princeton University Press, 1985).

Lang, James: *Conquest and Commerce: Spain and England in the Americas* (New York: Academic Press, 1975).

Lawson, Philip: *A Taste for Empire and Glory: Studies in British Overseas Expansion, 1660–1800* (London: Ashgate Publishing, 1997).

Leder, Lawrence H.: *Robert Livingston, 1654–1728, and the Politics of Colonial New York* (Chapel Hill, NC: University of North Carolina, 1961).

Lovejoy, David S.: *The Glorious Revolution in America* (New York: Harper and Row, 1972).

Mancke, Elizabeth: "Another British America: A Canadian Model for the Early Modern British Empire." *Journal of Imperial and Commonwealth History* 25 (1997), pp. 1–36.

Marshall, P. J.: "The First and Second British Empire. A question of demarcation." *History* 49 (1964), 13–23.

Marshall, P. J.: "The British Empire in the Age of the American Revolution." In William J. Fowler, Jr. and Wallace Coyle, eds., *The American Revolution: Changing Perspectives* (Boston: Northeastern University Press, 1979), pp. 189–212.

Marshall, P. J.: "Empire and Authority in the Later Eighteenth Century." *Journal of Imperial and Commonwealth History* 15 (1987), pp. 105–22.

Marshall, P. J., ed.: *The Oxford History of the British Empire*, vol. 2, *The Eighteenth Century* (Oxford: Oxford University Press, 1998).

McFarlane, Anthony: *The British in the Americas, 1480–1815* (London: Longman, 1994).

Meinig, Donald William: *The Shaping of America: A Geographical Perspective on Five Hundred Years of History*, vol. 1, *Atlantic America, 1492–1800* (New Haven, CT: Yale University Press, 1986).

Miller, Peter M.: *Defining the Common Good: Empire, Religion, and Philosophy in Eighteenth-Century Britain* (Cambridge: Cambridge University Press, 1994).

Mintz, Sidney W.: *Sweetness and Power: The Place of Sugar in Modern History* (New York: Viking, 1985).

Morgan, Edmund S.: *American Slavery, American Freedom: The Ordeal of Colonial Virginia* (New York: W. W. Norton and Company, 1975).

Morgan, Edmund S. and Helen M.: *The Stamp Act Crisis: Prologue to Revolution* (Chapel Hill, NC: University of North Carolina Press, 1953).

Muldoon, James: *Empire and Order: The Concept of Empire, 800–1800* (New York: St. Martin's Press, 1999).

Murrin, John M.: "Anglicizing an American Colony: The Transformation of Provincial Massachusetts" (Ph.D. dissertation, Yale University, 1966).

Olson, Alison Gilbert: *Anglo-American Politics, 1660–1775: The Relationship Between Parties in England and Colonial America* (New York: Oxford University Press, 1973).

Olson, Alison Gilbert: *Making the Empire Work: London and American Interest Groups, 1690–1790* (Cambridge, MA: Harvard University Press, 1992).

Olson, Alison Gilbert and Brown, Richard Maxwell, eds.: *Anglo-American Political Relations, 1675–1775* (New Brunswick, NJ: Rutgers University Press, 1970).

Osgood, Herbert L.: *The American Colonies in the Seventeenth Century*, 3 vols (New York: Columbia University Press, 1904–7).

Osgood, Herbert L.: *The American Colonies in the Eighteenth Century*, 4 vols (New York: Columbia University Press, 1924–5).

Pagden, Anthony: *Lords of all the World: Ideologies of Empire in Spain, Britain, and France, c. 1500 to c. 1800* (New Haven, CT: Yale University Press, 1995).

Pitman, Frank W.: *The Development of the British West Indies, 1700–1763* (New Haven, CT: Yale University Press, 1917).

Pocock, J. G. A.: "The Limits and Divisions of British History: In Search of the Unknown Subject." *American Historical Review* 87 (1982), pp. 311–36.

Price, Jacob M.: *France and the Chesapeake: A History of the French Tobacco Monopoly, 1674–1791, and of its Relationship to the British and American Tobacco Trades*, 2 vols (Ann Arbor, Mich.: University of Michigan Press, 1973).

Robertson, John, ed.: *A Union for Empire: Political Thought and the British Union of 1707* (Cambridge: Cambridge University Press, 1995).

Roeber, A. G.: *Palatines, Liberty, and Property: German Lutherans in Colonial British America* (Baltimore, MD: Johns Hopkins University Press, 1993).

Rose, J. Holland, Newton, A. P. et al.: *The Cambridge History of the British Empire*, vol. 1, *The Old Empire from the Beginnings to 1783* (Cambridge: Cambridge University Press, 1928).

Seeley, J. R.: *The Expansion of England: Two Courses of Lectures* (London: Macmillan, 1883).

Sher, Richard and Smitten, Jeffrey R., eds.: *Scotland and America in the Age of the Enlightenment* (Princeton, NJ: Princeton University Press, 1990).

Sheridan, Richard: *Sugar and Slavery: An Economic History of the British West Indies, 1623–1775* (Baltimore, MD: The Johns Hopkins University Press, 1973).

Shields, David: *Oracles of Empire: Poetry, Politics, and Commerce in British America, 1690–1750* (Chicago: University of Chicago Press, 1990).

Sosin, J. M.: *Whitehall and the Wilderness: The Middle West in British Colonial Policy, 1760–1775* (Lincoln: University of Nebraska Press, 1961).

Steele, Ian K.: *Politics of Colonial Policy: The Board of Trade in Colonial Administration, 1696–1720* (Oxford: Clarendon Press, 1968).

Steele, Ian K.: *The English Atlantic, 1675–1740: An Exploration of Communication and Community* (New York: Oxford University Press, 1986).

Stone, Lawrence, ed.: *An Imperial State at War. Britain from 1689 to 1815* (London: Routledge, 1994).

Ubbelohde, Carl: *The Vice-Admiralty Courts and the American Revolution* (Chapel Hill, NC: University of North Carolina Press, 1960).

van den Berghe, Pierre: *Race and Racism: A Comparative Perspective* (New York: Wiley, 1967).

Walvin, James: *Fruits of Empire: Exotic Produce and British Taste, 1660–1800* (New York: New York University Press, 1997).

Webb, Stephen Saunders: *The Governors-General: The English Army and the Definition of the Empire, 1519–1681* (Chapel Hill, NC: University of North Carolina Press, 1979).

Webb, Stephen Saunders: *1676: The End of American Independence* (New York: Alfred A. Knopf, 1984).

Webb, Stephen Saunders: *Lord Churchill's Coup: The Anglo-American Empire and the Glorious Revolution Reconsidered* (New York: Alfred A. Knopf, 1995).

White, Richard: *The Middle Ground: Indians, Empires, and Republics in the Great Lakes Region, 1650–1815* (Cambridge: Cambridge University Press, 1991).

Wickwire, F. B.: *British Sub-Ministers and Colonial America, 1763–1783* (Princeton, NJ: Princeton University Press, 1966).

Wilson, Kathleen: *The Sense of the People: Politics, Culture, and Imperialism in England, 1715–1785* (Cambridge: Cambridge University Press, 1995).

CHAPTER SIX

Indian History During the English Colonial Era

JAMES H. MERRELL

During the past generation study of the Indian experience in early America has finally come into its own. Before Francis Jennings published *The Invasion of America: Indians, Colonialism, and the Cant of Conquest* twenty-five years ago (1975), few students of the colonial era paid much attention to Native peoples, and fewer still considered them important actors on the American stage. Jennings's book – with its provocative title and contentious, even belligerent tone – marked the onset of an unprecedented interest in Natives and their place in the larger colonial saga. Since then, scholars borrowing insights from anthropology, archaeology, linguistics, folklore, and other fields have been combing the archives and digging in the ground to retrieve Indian voices from times long past.

The results of their inquiries have shed new light on Native history, challenged prevailing notions of who belongs in the chronicle of America's formative years, and aspired to alter our understanding of all peoples living in North America before 1800. With the pages of the premier journal of colonial American studies, *The William and Mary Quarterly*, regularly featuring articles about Indians, with many practitioners in the field now working on their second or even third book, and with graduate student interest still on the rise, the scholarly pursuits set in motion in the 1970s show no sign of diminishing.

Tracking this development is easier than explaining it. It is clear enough, now, that – as friend and foe, trader and neighbor, fellow diplomat and fellow Christian – Natives were a powerful presence in early America, not just during a colony's first years and not just somewhere "out there," beyond the frontier. No less clear, today, is the abundance of evidence available to tell their story, from treaty minutes, missionary letters, oral traditions, and travelers' accounts to postholes, potsherds, baskets, and portraits. Less self-evident is why it took students of American history so long to realize all this. True, before Jennings a handful of people began to explore the Indian experience with colonists, and these pioneers often called on other scholars to do the same (Merrell, 1989a, p. 94). But few heeded the call until more recent times. It seems reasonable to ask why.

Some possible explanations can be dismissed out of hand. The trend cannot be accounted for by the sudden arrival of Iroquois, Cherokee, Delaware, or other Native Americans in the scholarly community; few of those writing about Indians have been

Indians themselves. Nor can the renaissance be explained by a higher profile of contemporary Native peoples in eastern North America, a profile that would have drawn attention and, perhaps, directed scholarly interest toward the ancestors of these nations. The recent lawsuits by Penobscots, Oneidas, Catawbas, and others to reclaim their lands, like the Pequot, Mashpee, and Lumbee battles for federal acknowledgment of their status as Indians, did not reach their full force and fame until the redirection of scholarly energies was already well under way. Similarly, the Pequots' renowned Connecticut casino (and, more recently, their impressive museum), which resulted from their winning federal recognition in 1983, came after, not before, this dramatic change in the currents of historical inquiry.

This is not to say that contemporary events had nothing to do with the return of the Native to the early American scene. Indians were more visible in 1975 than they were in, say, 1965 or 1955: the founding of the American Indian Movement (AIM) in 1968, the Indian takeover of Alcatraz Island a year later, the armed standoff at Wounded Knee in 1973, the provocative, popular writings of activists and scholars such as Vine Deloria, Jr. – these and other developments drew attention to America's original peoples, their past fortunes as well as their present condition and future prospects.

Still, even these events, which focused on current or recent trends and on western Indian nations, cannot explain the growing attention to Indians of the East in much more remote times. Most of those coming to study Iroquois and Massachusetts, Cherokees and Delawares, Creeks and Powhatans before 1800 have approached this historical terrain not from modern social movements or from study of the Great Plains peoples over the past century but from other corners of colonial America; they have come out of conventional graduate programs in early American history.

Here lies the principal source of the interest in Indians: it is part of the more general turn in colonial studies – a development shaped by political and intellectual demands for greater attention to America's forgotten or oppressed peoples, past and present – toward social history, toward the historically silent, toward history from the bottom up. This *Zeitgeist* has captured the imagination of students of colonial America – indeed, of the historical profession more generally. Hence the same intellectual impulses pushing scholars to look past John Winthrop and John Smith to consider pirates and poor folk, Puritan women and African slaves have also propelled scholars toward the Native peoples that virtually everyone in colonial America encountered.

Some scholars insist that the impetus for the renewed interest in Indian history can be traced not from colonial American studies more generally but from the growth of a hybrid methodology termed *ethnohistory* (Axtell, 1978, 1981; Martin, 1978). The term, popular at least since the foundation of the American Society for Ethnohistory in 1954, has had various meanings over the years (Krech, 1991). Still, consensus remains elusive beyond an avowed commitment to a multidisciplinary approach: Is it only for study of Native groups? Non-literate peoples? How does it differ from cultural or historical anthropology, or from social history? Indeed, there is considerable debate as to whether the term should be used at all. Arguing that changes in historical studies toward new sources and new, more inclusive subjects make the term unnecessary, some wonder whether it tends to segregate and ghettoize, rather than advance, understanding of the Native American experience (Merrell, 1989a; Richter, 1993).

Given the provenance of most scholars in the field, it seems safe to say that ethnohistorical theory did less to shape their eclectic approach than did developments in colonial studies, developments that led scholars interested in the heretofore shad-owy corners (and characters) of the early American landscape to examine old docu-ments with a fresh eye, and to consider other evidence – probate inventories, folklore, archaeological finds – long overlooked or spurned.

Crucial to this enterprise was the growing acknowledgment, indeed the celebration, of how much could be done with very little, of what webs of deep meaning and large significance could be spun from a few strands of evidence or from intense scrutiny of a small place. The burst of colonial community studies offered one source of inspiration; many of the works on Indians have been, essentially, studies of one community or tribe. Another came from historical archaeologists arguing for the significance of "small things forgotten," urging the curious to hold those fragments from the past up to the light and ponder them from many angles (Deetz, 1977).

More important still – both for Indianists and for others working on similarly ob-scure subjects in early America – has been work in anthropology that argued the same thing for texts and human performance. Clifford Geertz's technique of "thick descrip-tion" – analyzing small moments and gestures, asides and nuances, to unpack their meaning about the way a society functions, the way it arranges itself – has been instru-mental in this (Geertz, 1973). For students of Indians, often faced with cryptic evi-dence, intellectual license to reconstruct the worlds of significance contained within a single person, a single document, even a single sentence, has been enormously liberat-ing.

Similar license has come from a trend in literary studies called the "new historicism." With its devotion to what one of its leading practitioners, Stephen Greenblatt, calls "representative anecdotes" and "ethnographic thickness," with its "intensified will-ingness to read all of the textual traces of the past" as well as other "cultural objects," with its focus on "cultural negotiation and exchange" as well as on what might con-ventionally (and, Greenblatt argues, incorrectly) "seem bizarre," this way of thinking has obvious appeal to those working on Indian history. That Greenblatt's interests lie in the early modern era, and particularly in the European encounter with the Ameri-cas, has made this approach that much more congenial (Greenblatt, 1990, pp. 5, 14, 164, 169, 176; 1991, pp. 2–3).

Less congenial, and less noticed, is Greenblatt's belief that, however much the new historicism lays bare fresh facets of European thought and culture, it cannot help us understand Indians. Because the texts studied are from European pens, Greenblatt asserts, even those that deal with Native peoples are too deeply "embedded" in the European worldview – reflecting explorers' preconceptions and concerns – to reveal much about the Native peoples they purport to describe. To think otherwise, accord-ing to this argument, is to perpetuate the ignorance and arrogance of the original colonial authors (the *authorities*), who – across a yawning linguistic and cultural chasm – blithely believed that they could understand, capture, and convey the essence of Native life. "We can be certain," Greenblatt concludes, "only that European represen-tations of the New World tell us something about the European practice of represen-tation . . . And so most of the people of the New World will never speak to us" (Greenblatt, 1990, pp. 27, 32; and see 1991, pp. 7, 95, 186; Murray, 1991; Richter, 1993, p. 386).

Obviously such a view, if accepted, would put students of Indian history out of business. More, it would put most *historians* out of work by confining examination of texts only to study of authors who actually penned them, thereby leaving out vast crowds of people in the past, not only Indians and Africans in America but also most colonial women and, indeed, many colonial men as well. Few students of Indian history have responded to this critique. Most feel that the sources, while certainly suspect, nonetheless can convey something of the Indian experience – either through colonial descriptions of Indian peoples or colonial rendition of Indian speeches – and that reading them with care while buttressing (or revising) them with oral, archaeological, and linguistic evidence is a wiser course than merely discarding them (Richter, 1993, pp. 384–6; Schwartz, 1994, pp. 1–2, 7, 19).

An even bolder challenge to the new work on Indian history has come from Calvin Martin. "Despite our profusion of monographs [on native history]," Martin wrote in 1987, "we have in truth largely missed the North American Indians' experience and meaning of it." The problem, Martin asserted, is that European and Indian ways of thinking are so fundamentally different that "those of us in the majority society who scrutinize the past have very little idea of *the Indian mind, of the Indian thought-world* . . ." Europeans think of time as linear, Natives as cyclical; Europeans believe in history, Natives myth; and European cosmology is anthropological, with humans at the center of the universe, while the Native worldview is biological, placing us amid, not above, the rest of the world. The result of this intellectual divide is, Martin insisted, "ideological colonization": "the traditional historian colonizes the Indian's mind, like a virus commandeering a cell's genetic machinery." Armed with "a kind of ethnocentric righteousness," scholars operating with Western constructs produce a "destructive" "caricature" of the Native experience that "surely strangles these people" (Martin, 1987, pp. 6, 7, 9, 15, 16, 27; and see Martin, 1992).

Martin is correct to remind us of the vast differences in ways of thinking and being between Natives and newcomers in North America, and his call for greater attention to the Indians' habits of thought – about time, ritual, and myth – is warranted. But it can be argued that his Indians – static, generic creatures whose attachment to nature and myth renders them superior to Europeans and their American descendants – also bear the stamp of stereotype, if not caricature. There is little room in Martin's creation for Native variety, for change of habit, change of clothing, change of belief, or change of mind. He asserted that "the mythic world once fully occupied by American Indians . . . [is] obviously still exerting a tremendous magnetic pull on them," but the implication is that an Indian who converts to Christianity, moves into a city, drives a pick-up truck, and takes on other untraditional trappings cannot be truly Indian unless he still somehow "subscribes to the promptings and messages of the mythic world of his ancestors . . ." (Martin, 1987, p. 31).

Nor does Martin offer much guidance for developing a research methodology to solve the problems he sees. Arguing that Indians exist "in eternity," he believes "that we historians need to get out of history, as we know it, if we wish to write authentic histories of American Indians." How to escape? Martin quotes men and women who find language itself an impediment, and books not particularly useful, especially compared to dreaming, surrendering "to the magic and mystery" of the animate universe, and taking drugs (Martin, 1987, pp. 15, 18, 23, 217). Imaginative attention to myth and ritual? Yes. Recognition that Natives arranged their world, viewed their world, explained their world differently, in ways that Europeans and historians might find nonsensical? Absolutely. But other than communing with nature and with "traditional"

Natives, Martin offers no clear directions on how to proceed from such assumptions. No wonder few have followed him, and fewer still have bothered to rebut him (Merrell, 1989a, p. 115, n. 95; Trigger, 1991; Richter, 1993, pp. 383, 386; and see Sahlins, 1995).

What Martin, Greenblatt, and other skeptics have achieved, however, is to imbue in students of the Native experience an even deeper sense of humility about what can (and cannot) be retrieved from the Indian countries of two or three centuries ago. Even the Iroquois, among the best-documented and most thoroughly studied peoples in eastern North America, remain elusive. "We must admit ultimately that we will never truly see through seventeenth-century Iroquois eyes . . .," Matthew Dennis states, "nor can we ever really speak for them" (Dennis, 1993, p. 13). "As a Euro-American of the late twentieth century," Daniel K. Richter agrees, "I do not pretend to have plumbed the mind of seventeenth-century native Americans, for most of the mental world of the men and women who populate these pages is irrevocably lost." Nor, Richter goes on, can anthropologists or contemporary Indians do much better than historians; no one, ultimately, can "more than partially recover it" (Richter, 1992a, pp. 4–5; and see Dowd, 1992, pp. xxiii–xxiv).

But to say that we cannot know everything we would like is not to say that we can know nothing at all. By sifting and weighing a wide range of sources, scholars attempt what Richter terms a "flawed triangulation," "a tenuous tripod" of evidence and inference, to explore the Indian experience after European contact (Richter, 1992a, pp. 5, 31). Probing the far corners and remotest reaches of that strange land, they have scrutinized everything from trade to treaties, from wars to missions, from Native treatment of captives and pigs to Native reaction to smallpox and rum, from the cultural significance of Indians' frock coats and menstrual huts to the hidden meaning of their rumors and dreams.

The guiding light directing these wide-ranging inquiries has tended to shift, over the past generation, from a penchant for seeing the colonial frontier as a dark and bloody ground, a clash of cultures, toward a tendency to point out areas of commonality, of agreement, of coming together in a clearing where peoples sought to overcome or overlook their differences in order to get along. Ironically, the celebrated power of metaphor in Native American speeches – paths bloody or clear, hatchets taken up or buried – has been replicated in the power that metaphors – *Invasion, Middle Ground* – have in our own day to shape scholarly patterns of thought.

The first of these metaphors exploded on the scene in 1975 with Jennings's *The Invasion of America*. Divided into two parts – the first on disease, trade, and other topics in Indian history, the second on relations between Natives and Puritans in seventeenth-century New England – the work told a grim tale of deceit, destruction, and dispossession. Starting with "the cant of conquest" promulgated by the victors in the contest for the continent, Jennings launched a scorched-earth campaign that spared no one. Historians of the American frontier were little better than apologists for colonial, and especially Puritan, misdeeds. "[Francis] Parkman and others like him had been willfully and consistently misleading," Jennings insisted, while even modern historians – often reared and trained in New England – offered little better than a "filiopietist portrayal" of Puritans. But Jennings reserved his sharpest words for colonists themselves. From "swaggering Virginians" and "backcountry Euramerican thugs" to sanctimonious Puritans, these invaders, with "sometimes stupendous arrogance" and a habit of hiding their tracks by altering or shredding documents, launched an American "reign of terror" against Indians clinging to "the naive view that they were entitled to rule themselves in their own lands" (Jennings, 1975, pp. v, 105, 110, 150, 164, 180–82, 277).

Along with sarcasm and scorn, Jennings offered a whole new way of looking at early America. He exposed common words and phrases as a biased, imperialist "cant of conquest." *The colonial era?* "From the Indian viewpoint, . . . it is the period of invasion of Indian society by Europeans." America a *virgin land?* Hardly: given the diseases Europeans brought to the continent, *widowed land* is more apt. *European settlement?* Wrong again: "The so-called settlement of America was a *re*settlement, a reoccupation of a land made waste . . ." *Civilized Europeans confronting Indian savages?* Mere semantic legerdemain: "Civilized war is the kind *we* fight against *them* (in this case, Indians), whereas savage war is the atrocious kind that they fight against us. . . . Europeans were at least as savage as Indians" (Jennings, 1975, pp. v, 15, 30, 146, 160). Shaped by the tumultuous times in which he researched and wrote, Jennings's criticism of European colonialism found a receptive audience among Americans preoccupied with, and shaken by, what he called "the Watergate deceits" and "the ministrations of nice young American boys in Vietnam" (Jennings, 1975, pp. vii, 163). *Invasion* quickly became a watchword, a sort of shorthand for a much less celebratory view of European adventures and misadventures in North America, marking a tectonic shift in perceptions of Indian and colonist alike.

Yet while *The Invasion of America* had a profound impact on the field, in the early 1990s it had to compete with a new and powerful metaphor developed by Richard White in his book *The Middle Ground* (1991). White's evocative, arresting take on the American frontier stressed not the clash of cultures but their convergence, not senseless slaughter but sophisticated and subtle means of bridging, crossing, or otherwise eliminating the cultural divide. White, exploring the French *pays d'en haut* ("upper country") of the Great Lakes region, found it "a place in between: in between cultures, peoples, and in between empires and the nonstate world of villages. . . . It is," he argued, "the area between the historical foreground of European invasion and occupation and the background of Indian defeat and retreat" (1991, p. x).

But White's middle ground was not merely a place; it was also a means by which "diverse peoples adjust their differences through what amounts to a process of creative, and often expedient, misunderstandings." That process, that place, was the product of a balance of power: Natives and newcomers, unable to "gain their ends through force," had, by "eternally negotiating," to "find a means, other than force, to gain the cooperation and consent of foreigners." Constructed on two levels – "everyday life" in which alien peoples came together to swap stories or swap goods, to make deals or make love, and "formal diplomatic relations" between leaders – the middle ground, forged by French and Indians in the late seventeenth century, endured beyond the French expulsion in 1763 only to end when the British, and then the Americans, became powerful enough to pursue conquest rather than settle for cooperation (White, 1991, pp. x, 52, 53, 148).

This metaphor, as subtle as *Invasion* is blunt, has had wide appeal. In an age when an ethos of multiculturalism contends with enduring ethnic and racial hostility both in the United States and abroad, the story of how alien peoples constructed a polyglot world out of a "common humanity" has exerted a tremendous pull on the scholarly imagination. Moreover, in a postmodern era that questions fixity and "Truth," either in language or in ethnic and racial groups, a book illustrating how groups deconstructed and reconstructed boundaries, how people shifted identities so that "a person could become someone else," won wide attention. Spurred on by White's assertion that "the processes of the middle ground were not confined to the groups" he considered, that the same sort of "accommodation" can be found elsewhere "for long periods of time in large parts of the colonial world," scholars since have scoured early America for other, similar sites (White, 1991, pp. x, xiv, 389; Cayton and Teute, 1998).

The Invasion of America. The Middle Ground. The two phrases seem to posit diametrically opposed views of Indian history. In fact, however, the books that coined these regnant metaphors are more subtle, and more similar, than their titles suggest. "The 'conquest of America,'" Jennings wrote in *Invasion*, "was a mingling of conflict and cooperation," a "reciprocal discovery," an "unstable symbiosis" in which "specific situations required particular Europeans to cooperate with particular Indians." "Europeans," he concluded, "went through a far more complex historical process than just fighting their way into the New World. What they did was to enter into symbiotic relations of interdependence with Indians (and Africans), involving both conflict and cooperation . . ." (1975, pp. 32, 39, 105, 173; and see Jennings, 1984). Similarly, White was careful to insist that his middle ground "was not an Eden, and it should not be romanticized. Indeed, it could be a violent and sometimes horrifying place" (1991, p. x).

Despite such warnings, readers usually ignore the genuine similarities between Jennings and White; the tendency has been to tell a book by its cover, to embrace the title without paying close attention to the nuanced explication of that title lying buried in the book's pages. The result is a somewhat Manichæan take on Indian history in the colonial era. In a very real sense, the scholarly conversation revolves around these two notions, these two ultimate conclusions about how to understand the Native experience. A look at the treatment of key arenas of contact – what might be called the frontiers of exchange, of spirituality, and of gender – reveals the lay of the interpretive landscape.

A generation ago, the interpretation of Native exchange with Europeans tended to stress the power of the new goods and of the Atlantic economic world to undermine Native life. Jennings, while pointing to the "cooperation" and "compatible traits" that helped "to draw Indians and Europeans together" in order to swap goods, nonetheless concluded that this new economic regime "transformed intertribal relations" from "cooperation . . . into competition and conflict" over furs while it also "metamorphosed the tribes' internal economies." The result was not only dependence on these new technologies – and on those who furnished them – but also the "decay" of Native society amid a "self-destructive frenzy" of intertribal warfare (Jennings, 1975, pp. 39–41, 85–8).

Calvin Martin, approaching the trade via ecology and spirituality rather than economics and diplomacy, reached much the same conclusion. Arguing that Native taking of game was "a *holy occupation*," a "balanced system" surrounded by "traditional safeguards" against overhunting, Martin asked how Indians came, so quickly, to hunt beaver and other fur-bearing creatures almost to extinction in order to meet the demands of the European trade. His answer involved the onset of new diseases, the onslaught of missionary endeavors, and the corrosive nature of alien trade goods: together these set in motion "a lockstep process," "a series of chain reactions" that succeeded in "breaking native morale and . . . cracking their spiritual edifice." Natives "apostatized," surrendering traditional attitudes toward the natural world to "a kind of mongrel outlook which combined some native traditions and beliefs with a European rationale and motivation." Crucial to this metamorphosis were European trade items. Each gun, each kettle, each shirt came, Martin argued, with ideological or spiritual strings attached. "In accepting the European material culture," then, "the natives were impelled to accept the European abstract culture, especially religion, and so, in effect, their own spiritual beliefs were subverted as they abandoned their implements for those of the white man. . . . Western technology made more 'sense' if it was accompanied by Western religion" (Martin, 1974, pp. 5, 11, 16, 17, 23, 25).

Even before White's notion of the Middle Ground took hold, studies of trade began to question this bleak view. The emerging consensus is now that the trading frontier was more evolutionary in its effects than revolutionary. Natives controlled the terms of exchange for a long time, trade goods entered Native communities slowly, and Indians reshaped those items they did accept to suit customary needs and expectations. Far from seeing quick decline or dependency, scholars find little or no change in Native ways; some even posit an enrichment of Native culture, a florescence of material – and therefore of ideological and social – lifeways as a result of European goods. Instead of hapless dupes tricked by sophisticated colonial traders, Natives have become shrewd customers, picking and choosing merchandise – hoes of a particular length and heft, beads of a certain size and color, cloth of the "right" texture and hue – that suited them. Even alcohol, infamously destructive in Indian country, is now seen as a commodity handled more carefully, and more successfully, than previously thought (Axtell, 1988, pp. 144–81; White, 1991, ch. 3; Braund, 1993; Dennis, 1993, ch. 5; Hatley, 1993, chs. 3–4; Mancall, 1995, chs. 3–4; Calloway, 1997a).

Part of this new view has been a more sophisticated and subtle understanding of exchange as Natives might have viewed it. While some scholars still talk of Indians as "customers" and "consumers" and of trade as involving "the simple exchange of goods" (Merrell, 1989b, p. 33; Axtell, 1992, ch. 5; Braund, 1993, p. 61), others insist that exchange was anything but simple and that Natives were much more than mere customers. The exchange of material items was not commercial: those objects, as gifts, formed a social bond between individuals and, as diplomatic currency, between groups (White, 1991, ch. 3; Dennis, 1993). More, they were "metaphors" for relationships between people and between the visible and invisible world. Examining the Natives' strong desire, initially, for beads, mirrors, and other objects Europeans scornfully dismissed as "toys," "trinkets," and "trash," Christopher Miller and George Hamell insist that "Indians did not think of trade in the same way Europeans did." Natives' attraction to "nonutilitarian" items stemmed from a desire to acquire powerful, spiritually charged objects that resembled those they already knew. Once acquired, these goods took their place – sometimes literally, as when glass beads joined quartzite pebbles in a shell rattle – in the established Native cosmology (Miller and Hamell, 1986; B. White, 1994). Hence what Europeans took to be ignorance and *naïveté* about an item's worth was in fact merely a different set of values operating in Native America during the early years of contact with colonists.

Whether approaching the subject from a spiritual or material direction, then, scholars now consider trade with Europeans far less destructive than previously thought. A similar shift has occurred in the scholarship on missionaries. Here the inquiries have been wide-ranging, considering Jesuit missions in Canada and Iroquoia, Dutch and Anglican efforts among Mohawks, and Moravian work among Delawares (Ronda, 1979; Axtell, 1985; Richter, 1992b; Merritt 1997). But the focus of debate centers upon the Puritan missionary enterprise in New England.

A generation ago, scholars painted that mission field in dark hues. Reacting against a long tradition of celebrating John Eliot and his fellow Puritan missionaries as selfless, courageous souls bringing Christian light to pagan darkness, Jennings and others depicted these men as scheming self-promoters bent on coercing Native peoples and obliterating Native culture for the sake of England's imperial designs. Convinced that Christian conversion had to follow, not precede, "civilization," between 1650 and 1675 Eliot established fourteen "Praying Towns" in Massachusetts Bay that were designed to "kill the Indian" in order to redeem the person, to change everything from clothing and housing to sexual mores and haircuts. The Natives collected in those locations and subjected to this harsh curriculum were, according to these scholars, a "pathetic," "dispirited" lot. "Alienated" from their traditional ways and with "no meaningful personality," the missionary's charges were "frightened, disillusioned, and confused," given to "melancholia" and "utter powerlessness" because Puritanism compelled them to "renounce their individual and collective pasts" and destroyed their "sources of collective identity and individual social stature," leaving them neither Indian nor English. It is a grim story indeed (Morrison, 1974, pp. 81, 84, 85, 89, 90; Salisbury, 1974, pp. 47, 50, 52).

Things look very different now. Around 1980 scholars intent on making Indians actors rather than victims and aware of new work on Puritanism stressing that faith's emotional richness and communal character began to depict a kinder, gentler mission scene in New England. Although missionaries seem to us arrogant and misguided, even hardliners like Eliot – not to mention the moderates such as the Mayhews on Martha's Vineyard – were genuinely committed to the biblical dictum of saving souls for Christ and to their Native charges (Naeher, 1989; Vaughan, 1995; Cogley, 1999).

And Indian converts, in this new view, were not committing cultural suicide; rather, they were as clever about adopting Christianity as they were about buying guns and coats. Some historians portray conversion as a calculated move by savvy Natives conquered by colonists, a form of "protective coloration" that enabled remnant Indian groups to blend into the now-hostile environment of their homeland (Axtell, 1988, p. 114; O'Brien, 1997, pp. 51–8). Other scholars insist that Native conversions were genuine. For Indians as for English folk, Puritanism was a faith, a way of life, promising personal solace and communal comfort to those cast adrift by wrenching change. Moreover, Natives remained selective consumers of civility and Christianity, shaping what they did adopt in order to suit their own needs. It appears that the phrase *Christian Indian* is not, after all, an oxymoron (Brenner, 1980; Ronda, 1981; Axtell, 1988, chs. 3, 7; and see Richter, 1992b; Shoemaker, 1995; but see Van Lonkhuyzen, 1990; Tinker, 1993, ch. 2).

The same two lines of interpretation evident in studies of trade and missions are, if anything, even more prominently on display in the burgeoning literature on Native American women. Here the metaphor is less often explicitly posed as *Invasion* or *Middle Ground*, but the point of contention remains the destruction or resilience of Indian culture. Were Indians victims of swift and terrible havoc wreaked by Europeans, or

were they actors able to work within a new order of things, to adapt to rapidly changing conditions?

Whatever scholars' differing views on the fortunes of Indian women after 1492,
almost everyone agrees that before colonization these women had high status. Few go
so far as Judith K. Brown, who in 1970 argued that "Iroquois matrons enjoyed unusual authority in their society, perhaps more than women have ever enjoyed anywhere
at any time" (Brown, 1970, p. 156); but most depict an America that was, for women,
almost Edenic. It was a world of balance and harmony between the sexes, a world filled
with creation stories that gave women starring roles, a world where women controlled
houses and fields, chose chiefs, and pushed for wars, a world where premarital sex was
accepted, childbirth relatively painless, and divorce easy. Though there are darker hints
in the scholarship, overall in the aboriginal world constructed by scholars "women and
men had complementary roles of equal importance, power, and prestige" (Braund,
1990; Anderson, 1991, chs. 6–7, and p. 163; Shoemaker, 1995, pp. 5, 7, 8, 19; Perdue,
1998, part 1).

Where scholars differ is in what happened once Europeans showed up. Some studies
paint a bleak picture indeed, arguing that the fur trade and Christian missions combined to promote male dominion. Hunters (always male) were now more important
than farmers (almost always female); meanwhile, Christianity's patriarchal ethos
prompted Indian men, with missionary encouragement, to turn on women in a battle
of the sexes. In what Karen Anderson, studying Indians in New France, called an
"astonishing" reversal of fortune, in a generation "men began to dominate women by
chastising them, physically punishing them and by controlling their decisions"
(Anderson, 1991, p. 162). Other historians believe that female subordination was
more gradual, that women offered stiffer resistance, yet they agree that European commerce and religion had a "negative impact on women." "Friction between men and
women," concludes Carol Devens, "is in fact the bitter fruit of colonization" (Devens,
1992, pp. 5, 27).

Most recent scholars find this view overly simplistic and grim. Noting that Indian
women were not a monolithic group following a single "script" after European contact (Harkin and Kahn, 1996, pp. 564–5), stressing the "plurality of women's responses, along with their richness and open-endedness" (Brown, 1996, p. 714), this
new approach stresses flexibility and ambiguity, resilience and persistence. Determining whether "women lost power or gained power" is no easy task, argues Nancy Shoemaker. "Power is not tangible, measurable, immediately observable and knowable
...[;] the many different manifestations of power need to be situated and contextualized
to be understood. . . . Indian women," Shoemaker concludes, "could have simultaneously lost and gained power." Overall, however, the scholarship stresses the positive,
focuses on how "Indian women continually worked to enhance their position within
native societies" (Shoemaker, 1991, p. 39; 1995, p. 13).

This was true for women in both trade and religion. Countering the notion that the
European trade regime automatically elevated men's status, Theda Perdue and others
insist that commerce "did not significantly alter the world of women. Women had
their own arena of power over which they retained firm control." Indeed, Perdue
suggests, "the growing involvement of men in the world beyond [the village and na-
tion] may, in fact, have enhanced the power of women within Cherokee society"
(Perdue, 1998, p. 10; and see Braund, 1990). Scholars examining other Native

nations find that women were actively involved in trade with colonists in ways that enhanced, rather than undermined, their customary status (White, 1999).

Studies of Christianity's impact on gender roles make a similar point. Whatever the intentions of missionaries and their Indian male converts, however dramatic the tales of beating or shaming women, Shoemaker and others, building on the insights of scholars who draw parallels between Christianity and Native spirituality, have found that some women embraced Christianity and shaped it to fit their needs, finding in it a "toolkit of symbols, stories, and rituals" for sustaining, and even enhancing, their position in Native society. Catholic converts in particular had devices – the cult of the Virgin Mary, female saints, celibacy, nunneries – that enabled them to challenge Christian patriarchy. Iroquois "women turned Christianity to their advantage," Shoemaker argues, found a way of "establishing a firmer place for themselves in a changing Iroquois society" (Shoemaker, 1995, pp. 52, 60; and see Ronda, 1981, pp. 384–8; Bragdon, 1996).

From gender to missions to trade, then, a split can be found between those who consider early America a battleground and those who find there a middle ground. These points of view are not sufficiently articulated to be considered formal schools of thought, with interpretive battle lines drawn, scholarly troops recruited and rallied, bombardments of articles and books launched against the other side. Nor, it could be argued, are they diametrically opposed. Some of the difference might be only a matter of emphasis. In a recent book of essays on the colonial frontier, for example, one scholar, coming upon an Iroquois-English word list compiled by an Indian and a colonist at a Pennsylvania fort during the Seven Years' War, cites it as proof of "peace and harmony," of "the fabric of understanding and common experience" there. In the very next chapter another historian, noting that this "vocabulary list ends abruptly" with "the translation of 'You lye,'" uses the same document to suggest how "the very act of trying to communicate with each other paradoxically fueled new misunderstandings that could just as easily turn violent" (Merrell, 1998, p. 41; Merritt, 1998, p. 70).

Similar shifts in emphasis occur in the numbers game scholars play with one 1674 census of Praying Indians, which reported that John Eliot had established fourteen Praying Towns containing "about" 1,100 Indians who were "subjected to the gospel," some 74 of those 1,100 full church members. What are we to make of 1,100 and 74? Of "subjected"? Scholars stressing the missionaries' "failure" and their "meager" harvest of souls write that "only 1100" Natives joined and point out that, since "most of them [were] not full church members," Indian saints comprised "a tiny minority" (Jennings, 1975, pp. 250–1; Cohen, 1993, p. 234). Others, impressed by "Christian success (from the missionary viewpoint)," remove the less christianized half of the fourteen Praying Towns from the count "(because they were founded too recently to bear spiritual fruit)," mention that 125 of the 500 Indians in the remaining villages were baptized, then add those 74 full communicants to arrive at "figures [of Christian devotion] that compare favorably with the older church-oriented English towns of the Bay Colony" (Axtell, 1985, p. 240; 1988, pp. 49–50, 108; Naeher, 1989, p. 346).

Still, not all the differences of opinion can be explained away as mere matters of emphasis. It might be possible to narrow the distance between battleground and middle ground; it is not possible to close that distance altogether. There remains a fundamental difference in sensibility, in how to read American history after 1492; ultimately there is, one might say, no interpretive middle ground in the scholarship on Indians; there is, rather, a contest that no amount of blurring and overlapping in lines of thought can altogether eliminate.

And those positing a Middle Ground are, at the moment, winning that contest, in the process refashioning prevailing notions about the very character of the American frontier. The recent work, seeking to banish the ghost of Frederick Jackson Turner, has gone a long way toward erasing the frontier line – the barrier, the divide – between *white* and *Indian*, between *civilized* and *savage*. In its stead is a "fluid," "flexible" place, a "porous," "permeable" membrane that peoples, goods, and ideas crossed easily and often (Usner, 1992, p. 210; Calloway, 1997a, p. 152; Perkins, 1998, p. 214). "The essence of a frontier," this sketch has it, "is the kinetic interactions among many peoples, which created new cultural matrices . . ." (Cayton and Teute, 1998, p. 2).

This "messier" picture has profound, and in many respects beneficial, implications; it fosters what might be called constructive confusion, overturning long-held assumptions about the American past (Calloway, 1997a, p. xiv; Aron, 1998, p. 175). Indian country, conventionally populated by famous Native nations, turns out in fact to consist of a kaleidoscopic array of peoples migrating and merging in dizzying profusion. *Choctaw, Catawba, Cherokee, Iroquois,* and the rest, far from stable polities anchored in ancient times, shifted dramatically in shape and meaning over the years, from scattered towns to nascent tribes to, sometimes, large confederacies or chiefdoms – and often back again into their constituent parts. Moreover, even the most basic unit of tribe or town was often a melting pot, as Iroquois absorbed Hurons, Catawbas adopted Cheraws, Creeks welcomed Yuchis, and so on in a bewildering, and all but hidden, welter of combination and recombination (Merrell, 1989b; Richter, 1992a; Hatley, 1993; Galloway, 1995).

The latest work further confuses things by mussing up the tidy American tricolor of *Red, White, and Black,* which has graced the covers of so many books as it has so profoundly shaped thinking on American history. In its place is a lively multicultural theater where natives of Europe, America, and Africa mix and mingle, producing a polyphonic, even cacophonous, medley where strange things can happen. Tuscaroras in North Carolina, preparing for war against their colonial neighbors, build a European-style fort – complete with portholes, moat, and bastions – following a design taught them by a runaway African slave (Wright, 1999, pp. 83, 277). Natives in New England live in wigwams furnished with tea tables and feather beds (Calloway, 1995, pp. 1–2). An Indian sends a letter to a colonist and receives a string of wampum beads in return (Merrell, 1999, pp. 46, 48, 51–2).

Gone, too, or at least crowded to the edge of the stage, are the standard stock characters of America's master narrative: the hardy pioneer, the doomed Indian, and the abject slave. In their place stand hybrids such as the mulatto Seneca, the Sun Fish, fluent in many languages (Hart, 1998, pp. 92, 101–2), and the Métis Andrew Montour (Oughsara), a man equally at home in an Iroquois council chamber or a provincial governor's dining room (Hagedorn, 1994; Merrell, 1997b). Capsule biographies of such obscure, culturally agile figures have been a cottage industry in recent years; most stress people's facility to make and remake themselves in the frontier's shifting, malleable terrain (Clifton, 1989; Karttunen, 1994; Szasz, 1994; Grumet, 1996).

Prominent, too, are strange new sites, places where such culturally adept individuals felt most at home. At Sir William Johnson's Georgian mansion on the Mohawk frontier, visitors found the lord of the manor living like "an English gentleman at his country seat" in summer, while at another season he might don Native "dress and ornaments" to become "Warraghiyagey." Whatever the name or the garb, Johnson presided over a household that included his Indian wives and Métis children, a German butler, a mustee waiter, and an Irishman who was overseer for fifteen black slaves (dressed in Iroquois outfits) and dozens of white workers (Hart, 1998). South of Johnson Hall stood Shamokin, an Indian town along the Susquehanna River that in the 1740s was home to Iroquois, Delawares, Tutelos, and Germans, and that frequently hosted passing war parties, diplomatic delegations, colonial land seekers, even "Delaware Negroes" (Merrell, 1998). Across the Allegheny Mountains to the west sat Kekionga, where "French, English, and Miami lived together," breakfasted together, took tea together, and saw in the New Year together. There things were so confused that during one crisis "British and French traders acted as cultural interpreters for an American [captive] about to become a Shawnee [adoptee] to replace another American [adopted] Shawnee killed by Americans"! Bewildering? Yes. But in that very confusion lies much of the power of the new tales being told about Indians in early America (White, 1991, pp. 448–53).

So far has this scholarly trend toward borrowing and blending been pushed that even Indians long considered most traditional, most vocal about rejecting what Europeans offered – from ideas to weapons to hoes – were, it turns out, thoroughly influenced by a wider Atlantic world. The Delaware Prophet, Neolin, whose visions in the 1760s demanded Indian rejection of white ways and a return to a Native past, in fact borrowed heavily from whites, speaking from a "book" of pictures he had drafted and from a house with a "stone cellar, stairway, stone chimney, and fireplace" that resembled "an English dwelling." His message, too, with its "references to the Christian God, to heaven and hell, to sin," was deeply syncretic – as indeed were the preachings of all Nativists (White, 1991, pp. 279–83; Aron, 1998, p. 187; and see Dowd, 1992; Merritt, 1997).

This portrait of a "mixed and mixed-up world where frontier cultures coincided as well as collided" has, then, done much to move us past outmoded habits of thought about Indians in early America (Aron, 1998, p. 175). But all the talk of "correspondence" and "convergence," of "crossroads" and "conjunctions" can be taken too far (Dennis, 1993, p. 2; Aron, 1998, pp. 175–6); it can obscure the hard truth that every harmony contained its dissonance, every coincidence its collision. Every middle ground – however lively, however fascinating – nonetheless was always *between*; it required for its very existence the powerful presence of two or more societies in contact.

Certainly those constructing that middle ground, or inhabiting it, never forgot this simple truth; early Americans of all stripes knew well enough where "English ground" ended and "the Indian countries" began (Merrell, 1999, p. 19). A closer look at the frontier's mixture suggests that lines were clearly drawn. People like the Sun Fish and Andrew Montour can be recovered from the documentary record precisely because they stood out from the crowd in early America and therefore were, quite literally, remarkable. William Johnson, who knew both of these men and who could don Indian ways as easily as he shrugged on a matchcoat, had no doubt about his true cultural loyalties: he was – first and foremost – an imperial administrator and colonial land speculator. At Shamokin, meanwhile, Tutelos married Oneidas and Cayugas wed

Shawnees, but the town saw no celebration of a German–Indian wedding. Kekionga, too, remained "a place where clearly separate groups" endured, where people got together "only at certain points and in a certain manner," where "an unseen line" always existed (White, 1991, pp. 450–1). The middle ground, then, if not an illusion, was at least a convenient fiction, an arrangement that enabled people to focus on superficial similarities while ignoring deeper structural differences, the bedrock of Indian and colonial societies (Tinker, 1993, pp. 34–5; Salisbury, 1999).

What was the nature of that different bedrock? Scholars properly eschewing racial essentialism – innate savagery vs. high civilization – have only begun to attempt an answer. However, it seems clear that Indian and colonist considered several differences fundamental. One of these was the different arrangement of relations between the sexes: European men and women in this era had nothing close to the "complementary roles of equal importance, power, and prestige" (Anderson, 1991, p. 163) scholars have found in Native America. Another was the distinction between societies grounded in kinship and those grounded in the nation-state, and related to this the Natives' emphasis on individual freedom from coercive forms of restraint. A third was European notions of permanent individual property rights, especially in land, which contrasted so sharply with Indian ideas about usufruct and collective ownership (White, 1991, pp. 392–4; Hatley, 1993, p. 62; Aron, 1998, pp. 194–8).

Even as the search for more middle grounds continues apace, then, murmurs of doubt and dissent can be heard. Some of those murmurs are metaphorical, as scholars purport to detect the frontier's "fault lines" (Merrell, 1998, p. 42; Aron, 1998, p. 177; Perkins, 1998, pp. 209, 234). Others are more sweeping and more blunt, insisting that "in most times and places of early American history, Indians and Europeans failed to create a lasting middle ground" (Richter, 1993, p. 390; and see Hatley, 1993, p. 228; Dowd, 1998, p. 118, n. 3).

More tightly focused studies of early English adventures with Indians suggest the limited possibility of getting along. Examining Virginia's first two years, Martin Quitt found in the intercultural encounters "flexibility" and "receptivity," but also an unhappy education that ultimately led each party to grasp all too well what the other was about – and to conclude that coexistence was impossible. "Neither side could go far enough to satisfy the other," argues Quitt; their "core values" were too different. The moral of this story is that "mutual understanding does not necessarily engender mutual respect, tolerance, or civility" (Quitt, 1995, pp. 227, 237, 258). Chronicling Indian adoption of livestock in seventeenth-century New England, meanwhile, Virginia Anderson found that "colonists . . . liked the Indians less the more like the English they became." Indeed, newcomers and natives discovered between them "differences so profound as to defy peaceful solution" (Anderson, 1994, pp. 617, 621). In many corners of colonial America, it turns out, familiarity bred, not concord but contempt (Dowd, 1998, pp. 116, 119; Merritt, 1998, p. 84; Merrell, 1999, pp. 123, 276).

The scholarly treatment of Indians in colonial times is, then, at a transitional – not to say confused – moment. For all their merits and accomplishments, neither of the prevailing metaphors offers an entirely satisfactory take on the course of colonial events. *Invasion* is overly simplistic in its stress on conflict and conquest. Yet *Middle Ground* has problems of its own, for, as Richter warns, "an exclusive stress on the arenas in which people from different cultures were able to work with . . . each other runs the risk of obscuring the very real conflicts that must remain central to the tale" (Richter, 1993, p. 390).

Finding some way past this metaphorical conundrum is one challenge facing students of Indian history. Another is recognizing that, for all the claims about burying Turner and demolishing the grand narrative of American progress and triumph, historians have not altogether shed past paradigms. However fresh this scholarship, however alert to bias in the European sources and attuned to Native voices, it remains to a surprising degree trapped within old habits of thought and expression.

Take words, for example. Jennings's assault on the "cant of conquest" and historians' loaded language continues, but it has a long way to go (Axtell, 1988, pp. 34–46; Clifton, 1989, p. 22). While terms such as *primitive* and *virgin* land have gone the way of *civilized* and *savage*, other words remain – even in work by specialists on Indians – distorting every story we tell. *Settlement* and *settlers*, used without adjectives, imply that America was unsettled before Europeans arrived, though Natives, too, could settle a spot. *Wilderness* always denotes Indian America, even though – since "wilderness" is anywhere one feels bewildered – from the Native point of view Europeans made a wilderness in America. *Backcountry*, which in the modern lexicon denotes the borders of Indian country, is another misnomer, since to Indians, the *backcountry* was Philadelphia or Boston (or London). The word list could go on – *trinkets* adopts a European scale of value; *pre-contact* or *pre-history* assumes that the only contact of note was with Europeans, who started American history – and on. Some scholars argue that even words such as *trade* and *war*, *male* and *female* need to be handled with care, for they contain the seeds of Eurocentric assumptions (Bragdon, 1996, p. 506; Gleach, 1997, p. 5). Political correctness run amok? Perhaps; following this critical line too far risks being able to say nothing at all about the American encounter. Still, such exercises in restraint and skepticism, in cleaning up our language, are valuable reminders of how far that very language itself remains an obstacle rather than a vehicle to understanding.

Another sign that scholars remain more bound by older notions than they like to admit lies in the focus of their inquiries. For all their imaginative use of an astonishing range of sources, most explorers of Indian country still linger at those places where European colonists tended to gather – and where, therefore, the evidential light is best; scholars are most preoccupied by the very subjects – trade, diplomacy, warfare, missions – that most interested the men keeping the records. What might be called Indian "social history," examining the contours of Native life away from the prying eyes of Europeans, is only just now beginning to emerge as a field of inquiry. The obstacles are formidable, of course, for by definition these realms lie deep in the evidential shadows. But studies of gender – which European men keeping the records noticed little and understood less – and of relations between Indian groups suggest that this sort of work is possible (Richter and Merrell, 1987; Dowd, 1992). That it is also important to head deeper into Indian country, away from the mission stations, trading posts, and treaty grounds, is clear; after all, as late as the early nineteenth century fully three-quarters of the supposedly "civilized" Cherokees saw little of, and apparently cared less about, the white world (McLoughlin, 1984, p. 22, n. 30).

Similar evidential obstacles and Eurocentric biases have stunted the scholarship chronicling Indian life "behind the frontier" (Mandell, 1996; O'Brien, 1997; Calloway, 1997b; Rountree 1990). Time and again, scholars tracing the fortunes of a Native people stop at the threshold of that chapter in the Indian experience (White, 1991; Dowd, 1992; Richter, 1992a). The reasons are obvious, and compelling. Triumphant colonists tended to ignore these tiny remnant groups, which were no longer a military threat, an economic opportunity, or a valuable ally; hence the conventional documentary record – travelers' accounts, traders' reports, treaty councils – is sparse. More, as these Natives adopted the English language and colonial customs, married colonists or Africans, sometimes lost their lands, and otherwise changed their profile to blend into their new surroundings, they ceased being "Indian" in ways recognizable to their conquerors.

If it is not surprising that scholars, too, have overlooked these peoples, it is unfortunate. For one thing, since all Indians in North America eventually ended up behind one frontier or another, the examination of those tribes who landed there sooner rather than later has significant implications that reach well beyond the relatively few people involved. Study of these people also raises important – if, nowadays, uncomfortable – questions about the nature of Indian identity. What made a person – speaking English, working in a local shop, praying to Jesus, dressing in English clothes, and marrying an African – still an Indian? Perhaps one reason scholars lose interest in Natives behind the frontier is to avoid this difficult, awkward question. Whatever the reason, histories of Indian communities usually halt with their subjects still in full possession of the "core values of their traditional culture," "keeping intact the core of their ancient culture." What happened when that old "core of . . . identity" – land, language, religion, whatever – disappeared? What formed a new core? Historians of Indians in early America would rather not say (Merrell, 1989a, p. 271; Richter, 1992a, pp. 256, 276; and see Hatley, 1993, p. 232). Yet here, too, the question has powerful resonance beyond the colonial era. Ignoring it not only follows the biased lead of the Indians' white conquerors, but prevents students of Natives in early America from joining a conversation with profound political and social implications.

But perhaps the surest proof that the study of Indians in early America has not yet broken the mold of the national narrative is the degree to which the field remains isolated from the rest of American historical studies (Merrell, 1989a; Richter, 1993). Those preaching the need to include Indians in that narrative are, to date, preaching to the choir, if not to the deaf. Surveys, syntheses, and most college courses remain wedded to a narrative that – save for bits of Indian color here and there – is not very different from the conventional wisdom of a generation or two ago. And Indian history remains what it was two decades ago, a sidebar to the lead article, while students in the field remain a tribe, a sect of true believers who have not found a way to win large numbers of converts. Whether that will change in the years to come remains to be seen; but there is reason to doubt it, even for treatment of that long span of time – from 1492 until at least 1800 – when most of the North American continent was Indian country.

BIBLIOGRAPHY

Anderson, Karen: *Chain Her By One Foot: The Subjugation of Women in Seventeenth-Century New France* (New York: Routledge, 1991).

Anderson, Virginia DeJohn: "King Philip's Herds: Indians, Colonists, and the Problem of Livestock in Early New England." *William and Mary Quarterly* 3rd ser., 51 (1994), 601–24.

Aron, Stephen: "Pigs and Hunters: 'Rights in the Woods' on the Trans-Appalachian Frontier." In Cayton and Teute (1998), pp. 175–204.

Axtell, James: "The Ethnohistory of Early America: A Review Essay." *William and Mary Quarterly* 3rd ser., 35 (1978), pp. 110–44.

Axtell, James: *The European and the Indian: Essays in the Ethnohistory of Colonial North America* (New York: Oxford University Press, 1981).

Axtell, James: *The Invasion Within: The Contest of Cultures in Colonial North America* (New York: Oxford University Press, 1985).

Axtell, James: *After Columbus: Essays in the Ethnohistory of Colonial North America* (New York: Oxford University Press, 1988).

Axtell, James: *After 1492: Encounters in Colonial North America* (New York: Oxford University Press, 1992).

Bailyn, Bernard: *The Peopling of British North America: An Introduction* (New York: Alfred A. Knopf, Inc., 1986).

Bragdon, Kathleen: "Gender as a Social Category in Native Southern New England." *Ethnohistory* 43 (1996), pp. 573–92.

Braund, Kathryn E. Holland: "Guardians of Tradition and Handmaidens to Change: Women's Roles in Creek Economic and Social Life during the Eighteenth Century." *American Indian Quarterly* 14 (1990), pp. 239–58.

Braund, Kathryn E. Holland: *Deerskins and Duffels: The Creek Indian Trade with Anglo-America, 1685–1815* (Lincoln, NE: University of Nebraska Press, 1993).

Brenner, Elise M.: "To Pray or to be Prey: That is the Question: Strategies for Cultural Autonomy of Massachusetts Praying Town Indians." *Ethnohistory* 27 (1980), pp. 135–52.

Brown, Jennifer S. H.: "Reading beyond the Missionaries: Dissenting Responses." *Ethnohistory* 43 (1996), pp. 713–19.

Brown, Judith K.: "Economic Organization and the Position of Women among the Iroquois." *Ethnohistory* 17 (1970), pp. 151–67.

Calloway, Colin G.: *The American Revolution in Indian Country: Crisis and Diversity in Native American Communities* (New York: Cambridge University Press, 1995).

Calloway, Colin G.: *New Worlds for All: Indians, Europeans, and the Remaking of Early America* (Baltimore, MD: Johns Hopkins University Press, 1997a).

Calloway, Colin G., ed.: *After King Philip's War: Presence and Persistence in Indian New England* (Hanover, NH: University Press of New England, 1997b).

Cayton, Andrew R. L. and Teute, Fredrika J., eds.: *Contact Points: American Frontiers from the Mohawk Valley to the Mississippi, 1750–1830* (Chapel Hill, NC: University of North Carolina Press, 1998).

Clifton, James A.: *Being and Becoming Indian: Biographical Studies of North American Frontiers* (Prospect Heights, IL: Waveland Press, 1993 [orig. pub. 1989]).

Cogley, Richard W.: *John Eliot's Mission to the Indians Before King Philip's War* (Cambridge, MA: Harvard University Press, 1999).

Cohen, Charles L.: "Conversion among Puritans and Amerindians: A Theological and Cultural Perspective." In Francis J. Bremer, ed., *Puritanism: Transatlantic Perspectives on a Seventeenth-Century Anglo-American Faith* (Boston: Massachusetts Historical Society, 1993), pp. 233–56.

Deetz, James: *In Small Things Forgotten: The Archaeology of Early American Life* (New York: Anchor Books, 1977).

Dennis, Matthew: *Cultivating a Landscape of Peace: Iroquois–European Encounters in Seventeenth-Century America* (Ithaca, NY: Cornell University Press, 1993).

Devens, Carol: *Countering Colonization: Native American Women and Great Lakes Missions, 1630–1900* (Berkeley, CA: University of California Press, 1992).

Dowd, Gregory Evans: *A Spirited Resistance: The North American Indian Struggle for Unity,*

1745–1815 (Baltimore, MD: Johns Hopkins University Press, 1992).

Dowd, Gregory Evans: "The Panic of 1751: The Significance of Rumors on the South Carolina–Cherokee Frontier." *William and Mary Quarterly* 3rd ser., 53 (1996), pp. 527–60.

Dowd, Gregory Evans: "'Insidious Friends': Gift Giving and the Cherokee–British Alliance in the Seven Years' War." In Cayton and Teute (1998), pp. 114–50.

Galloway, Patricia: *Choctaw Genesis, 1500–1700* (Lincoln, NE: University of Nebraska Press, 1995).

Geertz, Clifford: *The Interpretation of Cultures: Selected Essays* (New York: Basic Books, 1973).

Gleach, Frederic W.: *Powhatan's World and Colonial Virginia: A Conflict of Cultures* (Lincoln, NE: University of Nebraska Press, 1997).

Greenblatt, Stephen J.: *Learning to Curse: Essays in Early Modern Culture* (New York: Routledge, Chapman and Hall, 1990).

Greenblatt, Stephen J.: *Marvelous Possessions: The Wonder of the New World* (Chicago: The University of Chicago Press, 1991).

Grumet, Robert S., ed.: *Northeastern Indian Lives, 1632–1816* (Amherst, MA: University of Massachusetts Press, 1996).

Hagedorn, Nancy: "'Faithful, Knowing, and Prudent': Andrew Montour as Interpreter and Cultural Broker." In Szasz (1994), pp. 43–60.

Harkin, Michael and Kahn, Sergei: "Introduction." Special Issue on Native American Women's Response to Christianity, *Ethnohistory* 43 (1996), pp. 564–68.

Hart, William B.: "Black 'Go-Betweens' and the Mutability of 'Race,' Status, and Identity on New York's Pre-Revolutionary Frontier." In Cayton and Teute (1998), pp. 88–113.

Hatley, Tom: *The Dividing Paths: Cherokees and South Carolinians Through the Era of Revolution* (New York: Oxford University Press, 1993).

Jennings, Francis: "Goals and Functions of Puritan Missions to the Indians." *Ethnohistory* 18 (1971), pp. 197–212.

Jennings, Francis: *The Invasion of America: Indians, Colonialism, and the Cant of Conquest* (Chapel Hill, NC: University of North Carolina Press, 1975).

Jennings, Francis: *The Ambiguous Iroquois Empire: The Covenant Chain Confederation of Indian Tribes with English Colonies from Its Beginnings to the Lancaster Treaty of 1744* (New York: W. W. Norton and Company, 1984).

Karttunen, Frances: *Between Worlds: Interpreters, Guides, and Survivors* (New Brunswick, NJ: Rutgers University Press, 1994).

Krech, Shepard, III, ed.: *Indians, Animals, and the Fur Trade: A Critique of Keepers of the Game* (Athens, GA: University of Georgia Press, 1981).

Krech, Shepard, III: "The State of Ethnohistory." *Annual Review of Anthropology* 20 (1991), 345–75.

Leacock, Eleanor: "Montagnais Women and the Jesuit Programme for Colonization." In Mona Etienne and Eleanor Leacock, eds., *Women and Colonization: Anthropological Perspectives* (New York: Praeger, 1980), pp. 25–42.

Mancall, Peter C.: *Deadly Medicine: Indians and Alcohol in Early America* (Ithaca, NY: Cornell University Press, 1995).

Mandell, Daniel R.: *Behind the Frontier: Indians in Eighteenth-Century Eastern Massachusetts* (Lincoln, NE: University of Nebraska Press, 1996).

Martin, Calvin: "The European Impact on the Culture of a Northeastern Algonquian Tribe: An Ecological Interpretation." *William and Mary Quarterly* 3rd ser., 31 (1974), pp. 3–26.

Martin, Calvin: *Keepers of the Game: Indian–Animal Relationships and the Fur Trade* (Berkeley, CA: University of California Press, 1978).

Martin, Calvin, ed.: *The American Indian and the Problem of History* (New York: Oxford University Press, 1987).

Martin, Calvin: *In the Spirit of the Earth: Rethinking Time and History* (Baltimore, MD: The

Johns Hopkins University Press, 1992).

McLoughlin, William G.: *The Cherokee Ghost Dance: Essays on the Southeastern Indians, 1789–1861* (Macon, GA: Mercer University Press, 1984).

Merrell, James H.: "Some Thoughts on Colonial Historians and American Indians." *William and Mary Quarterly* 3rd ser., 46 (1989a), pp. 94–119.

Merrell, James H.: *The Indians' New World: Catawbas and Their Neighbors from European Contact through the Era of Removal* (Chapel Hill, NC: University of North Carolina Press, 1989b).

Merrell, James H.: "Dreaming of the Savior's Blood: Moravians and the Indian Great Awakening in Pennsylvania." *William and Mary Quarterly* 3rd ser., 54 (1997a), pp. 723–46.

Merrell, James H.: "'The Cast of his Countenance': Reading Andrew Montour." In Ronald Hoffman et al., eds., *Through a Glass Darkly: Reflections on Personal Identity in Early America* (Chapel Hill, NC: University of North Carolina Press, 1997b), pp. 13–39.

Merrell, James H.: "Shamokin, 'the Very Seat of the Prince of Darkness': Unsettling the Early American Frontier." In Cayton and Teute (1998), pp. 16–59.

Merrell, James H.: *Into the American Woods: Negotiators on the Pennsylvania Frontier* (New York: W. W. Norton and Company, 1999).

Merritt, Jane T.: "Metaphor, Meaning, and Misunderstanding: Language and Power on the Pennsylvania Frontier." In Cayton and Teute (1998), pp. 60–87.

Miller, Christopher L. and Hamell, George R.: "A New Perspective on Indian–White Contact: Cultural Symbols and Colonial Trade." *Journal of American History* 73 (1986), pp. 311–28.

Morrison, Kenneth M.: "'That Art of Coyning Christians': John Eliot and the Praying Indians of Massachusetts." *Ethnohistory* 21 (1974), pp. 77–92.

Murray, David: *Forked Tongues: Speech, Writing and Representation in North American Indian Texts* (Bloomington, IN: Indiana University Press, 1991).

Naeher, Robert James: "Dialogue in the Wilderness: John Eliot and the Indian Exploration of Puritanism as a Source of Meaning, Comfort, and Ethnic Survival." *New England Quarterly* 62 (1989), pp. 346–68.

O'Brien, Jean M.: *Dispossession by Degrees: Indian Land and Identity in Natick, Massachusetts, 1650–1790* (New York: Cambridge University Press, 1997).

Perdue, Theda: *Cherokee Women: Gender and Culture Change, 1700–1835* (Lincoln, NE: University of Nebraska Press, 1998).

Perkins, Elizabeth A.: "Distinctions and Partitions amongst us: Identity and Interaction in the Revolutionary Ohio Valley." In Cayton and Teute (1998), pp. 205–34.

Quitt, Martin H.: "Trade and Acculturation at Jamestown: The Limits of Understanding." *William and Mary Quarterly* 3rd ser., 52 (1995), pp. 227–58.

Richter, Daniel K.: *The Ordeal of the Longhouse: The Peoples of the Iroquois League in the Era of European Colonization* (Chapel Hill, NC: University of North Carolina Press, 1992a).

Richter, Daniel K.: "'Some of Them . . . Would Always Have a Minister with Them': Mohawk Protestantism, 1683–1719." *American Indian Quarterly* 16 (1992b), pp. 471–84.

Richter, Daniel K.: "Whose Indian History?" *William and Mary Quarterly* 3rd ser., 50 (1993), pp. 379–93.

Richter, Daniel K. and James H. Merrell, eds.: *Beyond the Covenant Chain: The Iroquois and their Neighbors in Indian North America, 1600–1800* (Syracuse, NY: Syracuse University Press, 1987).

Ronda, James P.: "The Sillery Experiment: A Jesuit–Indian Village in New France, 1637–1663." *American Indian Culture and Research Journal* 3 (1979), pp. 1–18.

Ronda, James P.: "Generations of Faith: The Christian Indians of Martha's Vineyard." *William and Mary Quarterly* 3rd ser., 38 (1981), pp. 369–94.

Rountree, Helen C.: *Pocahontas's People: The Powhatan Indians of Virginia through Four Centuries* (Norman, OK: University of Oklahoma Press, 1990).

Sahlins, Marshall: *How "Natives" Think: About Captain Cook, For Example* (Chicago: University of Chicago Press, 1995).

Salisbury, Neal: "Red Puritans: The 'Praying Indians' of Massachusetts Bay and John Eliot." *William and Mary Quarterly* 3rd ser., 31 (1974), pp. 27–54.

Salisbury, Neal: "'I Loved the Place of my Dwelling': Puritan Missionaries and Native Americans in Seventeenth-Century Southern New England." In Carla Pestana and Sharon Salinger, eds., *Inequality in early America* (Hanover, NH: University Press of New England, 1999), pp. 111–33.

Schwartz, Stuart B., ed.: *Implicit Understandings: Observing, Reporting, and Reflecting on the Encounters Between Europeans and Other Peoples in the Early Modern Era* (New York: Cambridge University Press, 1994).

Shoemaker, Nancy: "The Rise or Fall of Iroquois Women." *Journal of Women's History* 2 (1991), 39–57.

Shoemaker, Nancy, ed.: *Negotiators of Change: Historical Perspectives on Native American Women* (New York: Routledge, 1995).

Szasz, Margaret Connell, ed.: *Between Indian and White Worlds: The Cultural Broker* (Norman, OK: University of Oklahoma Press, 1994).

Tinker, George E.: *Missionary Conquest: The Gospel and Native American Cultural Genocide* (Minneapolis, MN: Fortress Press, 1993).

Trigger, Bruce G.: "Early Native North American Responses to European Contact: Romantic versus Rationalistic Interpretations." *Journal of American History* 77 (1991), pp. 1195–215.

Usner, Daniel H., Jr.: *Indians, Settlers, and Slaves in a Frontier Exchange Economy: The Lower Mississippi Valley before 1783* (Chapel Hill, NC: University of North Carolina Press, 1992).

Van Lonkhuyzen, Harold W.: "A Reappraisal of the Praying Indians: Acculturation, Conversion, and Identity at Natick, Massachusetts, 1646–1730." *New England Quarterly* 63 (1990), pp. 396–428.

Vaughan, Alden T.: *New England Frontier: Puritans and Indians, 1620–1675*, 3rd ed. (Norman, OK: University of Oklahoma Press, 1995).

White, Bruce M.: "Encounters with Spirits: Ojibwa and Dakota Theories about the French and Their Merchandise." *Ethnohistory* 41 (1994), pp. 369–405.

White, Bruce M.: "The Woman Who Married a Beaver: Trade Patterns and Gender Roles in the Ojibwa Fur Trade." *Ethnohistory* 46 (1999), pp. 109–45.

White, Richard: *The Middle Ground: Indians, Empires, and Republics in the Great Lakes Region, 1650–1815* (New York: Cambridge University Press, 1991).

Wright, J. Leitch, Jr.: *The Only Land They Knew: The American Indians of the Old South* (Lincoln, NE: University of Nebraska Press, 1999).

CHAPTER SEVEN

African Americans

PHILIP D. MORGAN

I Essay/Overview

No aspect of early American history has been as vibrant as the study of African Americans. Predictions that the subject is played out, that there is little left to say are constantly being confounded. The sheer profusion of new work is staggering. A torrent of books, articles, essay collections, CD-ROMs, and conference papers overwhelms even the casual reader. The most comprehensive bibliography of slavery (Miller, 1999; Miller and Holloran, 2000) reveals that in the past decade alone the number of books and articles on early British American slavery has roughly doubled. In 1999, well over 400 books and articles were published on slavery or the slave trade in North America and the British Caribbean. Hardly a month goes by without one – sometimes two or three – international conferences on slavery, the slave trade, or race relations. Various specialized research centers now exist to explore aspects of the subject: the Gilder Lehrman Center for the Study of Slavery, Resistance, and Abolition at Yale University, the Nigerian Hinterland Project at York University in Canada, and the International Centre for the History of Slavery at the University of Nottingham in England. A dedicated journal, *Slavery and Abolition*, in existence since 1979, disseminates the latest scholarship, although tracking journal articles on slavery and African Americans in early America means perusing a huge array of periodicals, for almost every discipline has relevant material.

Slaves have been probed, dissected, and examined from almost every possible angle and disciplinary perspective. The sheer mass of information (both quantitative and qualitative) now available is no better illustrated than in a couple of databases – one on 27,233 transatlantic slaving voyages, and the other on more than 100,000 Louisiana slaves (Eltis et al., 1999; Hall, 2000). Physical anthropologists have measured slave heights, weighed bodies, inspected bones and teeth. Evidence has accumulated on everything from comparative stature to the effects of late weaning, from lead content to congenital syphilis. Archaeologists have sifted faunal remains to explore diet; exhumed trash, pots, and pipes to provide clues to material life; discovered ritual objects to illuminate spiritual life; and pried open graves and subfloor pits to reveal the slaves' innermost secrets (e.g. Handler and Lange, 1978; Ferguson, 1992; Samford, 1996; Higman, 1998; Singleton, 1999; Haviser, 1999). DNA testing, which will surely become more widely used, has already suggested that Thomas Jefferson fathered at least one of Sally Hemings's children, and, by implication, all of them ("Forum," 2000). To get inside the slaves' minds as well as their bodies, literary scholars and cultural historians have perused autobiographies and memoirs, plumbed court trials, combed newspaper advertisements, and deconstructed songs and folktales. Art historians and semioticians are beginning to take the imagery of slavery and the iconography of race seriously. Everything from slave hairstyles to gestures, from statuary to musical instruments, from embroidery to ceramics, from broadsides to oil paintings has been subjected to close inspection (see, for example, Vlach, 1978; Lacey, 1996; White and White, 1998; Patton, 1998; Wood, 2000). The minutiae are by turns fascinating, intriguing, and mind-boggling. As a result, slaves seem in danger of supplanting Puritans in our historiography: we almost know more about them than sane people would want to know.

Academic interest in slavery is matched and fueled by growing popular fascination in the subject. Many people, from ordinary folk to artists and novelists, seem more willing to confront slavery than ever before – whether by placing a plaque at the site of a sunken slave ship off Key West; constructing a replica of the ship *Amistad*, a symbol of the fight against slavery; commemorating the African Burial Ground in lower Manhattan; designating the 500th anniversary of the arrival of the first African slave in the New World, at Hispaniola on September 16, 1501, as a Sankofa Observance; displaying publicly the connections to slavery, as in the permanent exhibition, which opened in 1994, at Liverpool's Merseyside Maritime Museum, dedicated to the history of the slave trade; building museums such as Cincinnati's National Underground Railroad Center which is scheduled to open in 2003; making films such as *Glory* and *Amistad* (although neither were box-office successes); or producing television programs such as the PBS series on Africans in America and the CBS miniseries on Sally Hemings. Contemporary novelists of all kinds have mined slavery, to much popular acclaim – whether Toni Morrison's *Beloved* (1987), Charles Johnson's *Middle Passage* (1990), Barry Unsworth's magnificent *Sacred Hunger* (1992), Caryl Phillips's *Cambridge* (1992) and *The Atlantic Sound* (2000), Fred D'Aguiar's *The Longest Memory* (1994) and *Feeding the Ghosts* (1997), or Connie Briscoe's *A Long Way from Home* (1999). Other popular writers have explored slavery in other genres: one in the form of a personal memoir and history of his slaveowning family, which also served as catharsis for a crime not fully acknowledged and act of public penance; another as a dual family saga, tracing the intertwined lives of whites and blacks, descendants of a North Carolina slaveholding planter and his slaves, which was also a parable of redemption (Ball, 1998; Wiencek, 1999).

Slavery and its racial legacy also continue to convulse American politics. Many blacks believe that it is time that America took responsibility for the crime of slavery by compensating the heirs of slaves for the unpaid forced labor of their ancestors. They argue that the plight of contemporary black America is a direct result of slavery. They also point out that the case for reparations rests on a bedrock American principle, one applied to Native Americans and Japanese Americans: those (including their heirs) who were exploited and maltreated by a government deserve monetary redress. Legislation sponsored by Representative John Conyers of Michigan calling for a commission to study the subject of reparations has been submitted to the House floor every year since 1989. A National Reparations Convention has drafted proposals to compensate present-day African Americans for the enslavement of their ancestors, and many city councils have passed resolutions urging federal hearings on the lasting effects of slavery. Inspired by German corporations compensating people who worked as slave laborers in Germany during World War II, a group of prominent black lawyers, organized as the Reparations Assessment Group, have proposed class-action lawsuits against modern-day corporations that have connections to slavery. A California law, passed in 2000, requires insurance companies that offered slave insurance policies to publicize the fact. Also in 2000 the Hartford *Courant*, the oldest continuously published newspaper in the nation, and Aetna Inc. apologized for publishing advertisements about or issuing insurance policies on slaves. Conversely, conservative commentators rebut these arguments and actions by emphasizing, among other things, that no single group is responsible for the crime of slavery (Africans and Arabs as well as Europeans were involved, they point out), that no one group benefited exclusively from slavery, that blacks have done much better in America than their counterparts in Africa, and that blacks do not deserve redress because white Christians ended slavery. Other arguments against reparations stress the difficulties of determining who would be eligible to receive restitution, how to quantify the debt, who should pay for it, and whether it is wise to invoke perpetual victimhood with reference to terms such as "post-slavery trauma syndrome." Slavery is no simple academic matter, but has divisive and explosive political implications.

Perhaps the most notable popular development of the past decade or so is African Americans' willingness to engage with, rather than ignore, slavery. For too long, most American blacks, in Toni Morrison's memorable words, preferred to forget the unforgettable and leave the unspeakable unspoken. That stance has been changing, although slowly and with notable setbacks, as in 1995 when black employees at the Library of Congress managed to remove an exhibition about slave housing because they claimed it was humiliating. But, at plantations all across America, descendants of slaves are now honoring their ancestors. On January 1, 2001, for example, exactly two hundred years after Martha Washington freed her husband's slaves, their descendants gathered at Mount Vernon to share stories and pay tribute to the men and women who "helped build a nation." When news reports revealed that 400 of the 650 workers who built the White House and the first phase of the Capitol in the 1790s were black slaves, two black representatives (one Republican, the other a Democrat) immediately called for a memorial to recognize their achievements. Powerful new gene technology is being enlisted in black Americans' search for their African ancestry. The aim is to find out the probable African region of origin and restore the specifics of identity lost under slavery. Seeking cultural, as opposed to genetic, roots inspires a form of heritage tourism – to the former slave castles and forts along the west coast of Africa. When the Association of Black Psychologists held its first overseas conference in Ghana, one of its organizers touted the therapeutic value of reconnecting to a painful past. Many black churches in the nation have been replacing white with black figures in biblical art and stained glass. Perhaps most striking is the growing number of African Americans who collect relics of slavery – shackles, neck collars, branding irons, bills of sale, emancipation papers, and the like. For these African Americans, laying claim to, and making sense of, America's most shameful legacy are prime motivations. Slavery has become a subject of pride, not shame; the slaves' survival skills, despite the restraints placed on them, are emphasized. Individuals are taking their collections to schools and colleges to make sure that the "Black Holocaust" – for many activists, the preferred term for slavery – is never forgotten.

Largely in response to this widespread fascination with slavery and early black life, the historiography of African Americans in colonial America is extraordinarily lively and creative. Some of the most promising lines of research into the lives of early African Americans derive from perfectly simple yet fundamental historical inquiries, from the obvious yet sometimes ignored questions of where, when, with whom, and how slaves lived – the all-important contextual questions that encourage us to recover the full texture of any people's lives. This essay will focus, then, upon the spatial (considered first from an African and then an American perspective), chronological, social, and cultural dimensions of African American life.

Africa and the Atlantic

In the early modern era, an integrated and cohesive Atlantic world began to emerge. The Atlantic was, after all, the first ocean to be regularly crossed from all directions, and the lands that bordered it came to have a common history. Over time, a variety of links, bonds, and connections drew the territories around the Atlantic more closely together. People, goods, and ideas circulated in ever wider and deeper flows between the pan-Atlantic continents. As a result, scholars of Africa have turned their sights toward the diaspora, while historians of the Americas have gradually realized that they must understand Africa as much as Europe.

Slavery existed in sub-Saharan Africa long before the Atlantic slave trade. In some – perhaps most – places, slavery tended to be a minor institution, with the slave able to pass in time from an alien to a kin member; in others, most notably a number of Islamicized regimes, slavery was more central, with violence, economic exploitation, and lack of kinship rights more evident. A broad spectrum of dependent statuses, with slavery just one variant, existed in Africa; and slaves played a wide range of roles from field workers to soldiers, from domestics to administrators. In addition to domestic slavery, a long-standing export trade delivered many millions of Africans across the Sahara Desert, Red Sea, and Indian Ocean to North Africa, the Mediterranean, and Persian Gulf. It began in the seventh century and lasted into the twentieth. The Atlantic trade built on existing institutions, therefore, but revolutionized them (Miers and Kopytoff, 1977; Manning, 1990; Klein, 1999; Lovejoy, 2000). The effects were highly varied, because the character and policies pursued by African societies differed markedly, not only spatially but also chronologically. The Atlantic trade was divided among a large number of African ports, some more prominent than others at any particular time, and drew its victims from different parts of their respective hinterlands. Generalizing broadly, two major patterns of response can be discerned. The increase in the demand for slaves led to the formation of highly militarized states, such as Oyo, Asante, Futa Jallon, Segu Bambara, and Dahomey. These centralized states conducted wars to acquire slaves to trade for European commodities (Roberts, 1987; Law, 1991; Searing, 1993; Barry, 1998; Klein, 1998). The impact of slaving on decentralized or stateless societies was also important. People in acephalous societies were not merely victims of raids but actively shaped their futures often by developing fortified villages, moving to more secure locations, entering into tributary arrangements with centralized states, and engaging in slaving of their own (Northrup, 1978; Harms, 1981; Baum, 1999; Nwokeji, 1999; Hawthorne, 1999, 2001; Klein, 2001).

The dominant trend in the recent historiography of the transatlantic slave trade – the largest involuntary migration known to history – has been the emphasis on African agency. Africans are no longer seen as passive pawns or unwitting dupes of Europeans;

rather, in the recent scholarly literature Africans have assumed the role of active shap-
ers, if not originators, of the despicable traffic in humans, and equal partners with
Europeans. It is even possible to argue that Africans exploited European support, playing off rival Europeans against each other (Hair and Law, 1998). Of course, all historians recognize that Europeans were the prime movers in the transatlantic slave trade,
that it operated for their benefit, that the trade was anchored in ports such as London,
Liverpool, and Nantes, and that it depended on European shipping technology. But
the large role of African merchants and political leaders and even ordinary Africans in
molding the trade is also increasingly emphasized (Eltis and Richardson, 1997;
Thornton, 1998a; Eltis, 2001).

The specialization involved in the slave trade owed much to African agency. Ships
leaving on a slave voyage would normally trade in only one African region. Only about
one in twenty ships traded across regional boundaries in Africa. Indeed, about three-
quarters of all slaves shipped from Atlantic Africa left from fewer than twenty ports. In
sending ships to the African coast, European merchants selected cargoes for specific
markets because Africans had regionally distinct preferences. Africans were selective,
discriminating customers, and goods that would sell well in one region were often
undesired in another. Thus, African consumer choices dictated regional assortments of
goods on the part of European merchants. European ship captains usually returned to
the same African region many times to trade with the same African merchants, who
lived in coastal communities and developed strong commercial links to the Europeans.
Valuable contacts, long-standing business ties, relationships of trust such as pawnship,
once established, were important to maintain. Furthermore, each region had its own
idiosyncratic patterns of trade that took time to learn – when was the best time to
arrive, when were food supplies most abundant, and so on. The ability of African
merchants to deliver slaves in a timely fashion also determined much about the trade.
In general, European merchants sent small ships to politically decentralized coastal
markets with intermittent slave supplies and larger ships to places that had the requisite political centralization and commercial infrastructure to maintain large-scale slave
shipments. European merchants and ship captains had to fit out vessels of the right
size for specific African regional markets (Law and Mann, 1999; Lovejoy and
Richardson, 1999, 2001; Behrendt, 2001; Eltis, 2001; Sparks, forthcoming).

Africans had considerable influence over who entered the transatlantic slave trade, as
both aggregate and regional patterns reveal. European slave traders sought primarily
men but overall were forced to buy more women and children than they wanted. West
Central Africa consistently exported more children than any other African region,
forming always about a fifth or more of the slaves sold into the trade. In the Bight
of Biafra women were almost as numerous as men among slaves carried to the Americas. The age and sex of captives varied far more by African region than by European
nation buying the slaves. Overall, women and children accounted for a greater proportion of slave migrants from Africa than they did of free migrants from Europe, and,
indeed, forced migrants from Africa were more demographically representative of the
societies they left behind than were European indentured servants (Eltis, 2000; Nwokeji,
2001).

Patterns of slave revolts on board ships at the African coast and in the Atlantic
crossing are the most direct evidence of African agency. About one in ten slave ships
experienced an insurrection. Nevertheless, almost all of the ships affected still man-

aged to reach the Americas with a large proportion of their original captives: the average number of slaves killed in insurrections was about 25. Overall, the loss of slaves through revolts represented a fairly modest cost to slave traders compared to deaths of slaves through other causes. Between 1500 and 1867 perhaps 100,000 slaves entering the transatlantic slave trade died in revolts; this number represents one-fifteenth of all those who died in the Middle Passage. Disease was a greater threat to mercantile interests than revolts. Yet slave revolts were common enough to induce traders to invest in preventative measures. About 20 percent of Middle Passage costs can be attributed to the perceived need for deterrence. If enslaved Africans had been more quiescent, shipping costs would have been lower, the price of Africans cheaper, and more Africans would have been transported. Thus, shipboard or coastal resistance by slaves probably saved about a million Africans from being shipped to the Americas during the entire history of the trade.

Revolts, like so much else in the trade, reveal striking regional variations. Upper Guinea – that is, Senegambia, Sierra Leone, and the Windward Coast – had much higher incidences of revolts than other parts of the African coast. Compared to ships trading in West Central Africa or the Bight of Biafra, those trading in Upper Guinea were more than fourteen times more likely to experience a revolt. Forty percent of all violent incidents occurred in Upper Guinea, and yet it accounted for less than 10 percent of the transatlantic slave trade. Upper Guinea was closest to Europe and passage times to the Americas were the shortest of any African region. This proximity to both Europe and the Americas should have guaranteed a robust trade, but the reputation the region gained for rebellion helped to hinder such a development. Senegambia, the region with the highest rate of shipboard insurrection and shore-based attacks, experienced a simultaneous breakdown in political authority, an increase in enslavement of people from near-coastal areas, and the presence of many soldiers among its captives. Disorder spread from shore to ship (Richardson, 2001; Behrendt, Eltis, and Richardson, 2001).

African agency also has a bearing on the memory of the slave trade. African oral tradition suggests that a moral economy existed among Africans about the trade. It revolved about ideas of witchcraft, in which individuals became rich by consuming the life force of others. Conceiving of the world as a zero-sum universe, Africans thought the amount of wealth in the world was ultimately limited. Anyone who prospered was suspected of having siphoned off the property and the vital energies of others. Such a belief system helps explain the prevalence of stories about cowry shells being fished from the ocean by using slave corpses as bait, about dead Congolese being transported to the New World as zombies, and about red cloth being used by European slave traders to lure slaves onto ships. It is often said that Africans felt no kinship or moral responsibility for the slaves being sold, because they were foreign or alien, but the wide circulation of beliefs linking the slave trade to witchcraft suggests that, for some, participation in this commerce was tainted with intense moral opprobrium (Shaw, 1997; Baum, 1999; Austen, 2001).

As Africans are now portrayed as active participants in the making of the Atlantic world, increasingly the aim is to trace connections between specific homelands in the Old World and particular destinations in the New. Linking regions in Africa to regions in the Americas seems a realistic possibility. The recent work on the transatlantic slave trade, with its emphasis on its specialized, patterned character, is crucial to such endeavors. Many Africans undoubtedly arrived in a particular New World setting along-side Africans from the same coastal region. Particularly early in the history of many slave societies, one or two African regions supplied most slaves, creating a basis for shared communication. A number of scholars now see slaves in the Americas forming identifiable communities based on their ethnic or national pasts. John Thornton, for example, maintains that "an entire ship might be filled not just with people possessing the same culture, but with people who grew up together"; and, once in the Americas, most slaves "on any sizeable estate were probably from only a few national groupings." Michael Gomez believes that it is possible to identify "African ethnic enclaves" in North America: thus "Virginia and Maryland were the preserve of the Igbo" and West Central Africans were foundational in South Carolina and Georgia. The development of rice culture in the Americas, Judith Carney argues, involved not just the transfer of a plant from Africa across the Atlantic but "an indigenous knowledge system," a cultural complex of productive techniques, processing skills, and modes of consumption (Thornton, 1998a, pp. 195–97, and 1998b; Gomez, 1998, pp. 150–51; Carney, 2001, p. 2).

Nevertheless, while many Africans arriving in the Americas shared a distinctive local ethnic identity, the conception of homogenous peoples being swept up on one side of the ocean and set down en masse on the other is problematic. Ethnic mixing and the reconstitution of identity started well before the coerced migrants ever set foot on a ship. Ethnicity was not a constant, but was subject to constant redefinition. Because many African slaves came in tortuous and convoluted ways from the interior to the coast, whatever ethnic identity they originally had was in flux. Identities were reshaped as slaves moved to the coast, a process often taking months, occasionally years, and as they awaited shipment in the barracoons and in the holds of ships as loading proceeded. Africans employed pidgin and even creole languages on the coast as they tried to communicate with one another. Many slaves became identified by their port of origin – Calabars, Coromantees [from Kormantin], Whydahs [Ouidah], Popos [Popo] – but such labels masked diversity (Thornton, 1998c, 2000). Even when New World ethnonyms such as "Lucumi" and "Nago" (both used to describe the Yoruba) can be traced to particular African groups or places, they were not alternative names for the same people; as Law (1997) demonstrates, Lucumi referred primarily to southern, and Nago to western, Yorubaland.

Just as identities were in flux in Africa, inevitably they were extraordinarily fluid in the Americas. Ethnogenesis did occur but in extremely complicated ways. Thus, for example, many Africans from the Bight of Biafra who had never heard the name Ibo in their own lands and identified themselves instead by their villages or districts, yet came to accept – at least to some degree – the term abroad. They may even have incorporated people and cultural traits from places far remote from the Bight of Biafra. Perhaps the most famous Ibo of the eighteenth century, Olaudah Equiano, seems to have participated in the invention or reconstitution of his identity. Equiano may well have been a native of South Carolina rather than of the Bight of Biafra. That he chose to become an Ibo says much about the importance of that group in his life. Similarly, consciousness of Yoruba ethnicity first emerged among the displaced African diaspora, and the "Lucumi" of Cuba included some non-Yoruba groups. Ethnic identities in America were more wide-ranging and inclusive than they had been in Africa (Law, 1997; Carretta, 1999; Northrup, 2000).

E.

Borrowing, adaptation, modification, and invention characterize social and cultural development, as well as identity formation, among African American slaves. Slaves were ruthless *bricoleurs*, picking and choosing from a variety of cultural strains, precisely because they came from such diverse origins. If one or two African coastal regions often dominated the early history of a New World slave society, over time more mixing occurred. Increasing heterogeneity is the dominant feature of African migration into most North American and Caribbean regions. The time a vessel spent acquiring a full consignment of captives increased markedly after the mid-eighteenth century, and in response merchants greatly expanded the range of their African operations. New regions rose to prominence as suppliers of slaves. With increasingly heterogeneous arrivals, slaveowners could rarely pick and choose between different ethnicities. They generally bought whoever was available and in sufficiently small lots that plantations perforce became forcing houses of cultural fusion and syncretism among a variety of African cultures (Mintz and Price, 1992; Morgan, 1997; Burnard, 2000; Price, 2001; Burnard and Morgan, 2001).

The spatial focus in this resurgence of interest in Africa is on flows, dispersals, mixtures, and movements of people. This is diaspora history. Just as no self-respecting study of European migration fails to explore the Old World background, so now African American history is discovering in great particularity and specificity its African roots.

American Regions and the Atlantic

At the same time as the study of New World slavery now looks back to Africa, so increasingly it encompasses the whole of the Americas, the broader Atlantic region, and indeed the world. Certainly, North American slavery is no longer seen as wholly southern; in the colonial period, it was as much northern. Slavery was in fact ubiquitous, and a multinational view of its origins is becoming better appreciated. This synoptic view in turn encourages the search for differences and uniformities across space ("AHR Forum," 2000).

American slavery has been studied comparatively more than any other Atlantic institution, and provides by far the most extensive and sophisticated comparative literature in American historiography. Frank Tannenbaum (1946) and Stanley Elkins (1959) were the pioneers; and Tannenbaum, in particular, is still setting the terms for debate for more localized studies that seek to explore the relative severity of slave systems. Historians are still grappling with Tannenbaum's original claim that the law and the Church allowed for greater recognition of the slaves' humanity in the Spanish, Portuguese, and French colonies than in their English and Dutch counterparts (see, for example, Landers, 1999, and Ingersoll, 1999). Following the lead of these two pathbreaking comparativists, the bilateral comparisons have been systematic and varied, contrasting slavery in Virginia and Cuba, race relations in North and South America, two plantations in Virginia and Jamaica, white supremacy in the United States and South Africa, unfree labor in America and Russia, the slaves' economy and material culture on sugar plantations in Jamaica and Louisiana, acculturation in the American South and the British Caribbean, and black life in the Chesapeake and Lowcountry (Klein, 1967; Degler, 1971; Dunn, 1977; Fredrickson, 1981; Kolchin, 1987; Mullin, 1992; McDonald, 1993; Morgan, 1998).

American slavery has also to be understood in its full European, Atlantic, and global context. The Old World background to New World slavery – the extension of slave trading from the Mediterranean to the Atlantic islands, the rise of sugar and racial slavery on the Canary Islands, Madeira, and Sao Tome, the place of African slaves in Europe, the early construction of race, the critical relations with North African Muslims or "Moors," the various institutional precedents and parallels, such as villeinage, Mediterranean galleys, Barbary captivity, penal servitude – all need to be fully known (Phillips, 1985; Blackburn, 1997; "Constructing Race," 1997; Matar, 1999; Aylmer, 1999; Guasco, 2000). Large-scale enslavement of Europeans occurred as the African slave trade got under way: between 1580 and 1680, for example, the Barbary states enslaved about 850,000 Christians (Davis, 2001). Furthermore, American slavery's constituent elements, its special characteristics, its inner core can be grasped only in the largest context. The essence of slavery, as Patterson (1982) demonstrates, lies in the relation of human domination. For Patterson, the slave state is a power relation, one of the most extreme forms of domination, with three central features: the threat of naked force, the loss of ties of birth in both ascending and descending generations, and the degree of powerlessness and dishonor. Patterson offers the most comprehensive analysis of the institution of slavery, notable for its comparative breadth and erudition, although his depiction of New World slavery can be faulted in two competing respects: first, for failing to capture its true horror, by minimizing the property element and the labor exploitation; second, for being excessively pessimistic, by failing to take into account the slaves' perspective, their subjective sense of lineage and honor.

In the Americas, just as in Africa, slavery is increasingly differentiated by region. In early North America, about eight distinct regional slave systems can be identified, with as many, if not more, in the closely connected Caribbean. It is always possible to lump or split even further, but the major regional units comprise New England, the mid-Atlantic, the Chesapeake, the Lowcountry, Spanish and briefly British Florida, French and later Spanish Louisiana, the Upper South interior of Kentucky and Tennessee, and the Deep South interior. In the Caribbean, arguably, each island was a separate slave system, but conventional groupings differentiate Greater from Lesser Antilles, Leeward from Windward Islands, first-phase from second- and third-phase sugar colonies, and sugar from non-sugar colonies (Higman, 1984).

Major defining features of these various slave systems are now evident, because, for most, at least one major book, often more than one, and many specialized articles provide rich portraits of the respective black experiences. The two major regions in the North have been well explored, even though slavery was never central to the economies of either. For New England, as Piersen (1988) notes, "family slavery" was ubiquitous, masters and slaves lived closely together, slaves were put to diversified work, and a form of black government arose, with the annual "Negro election" representing, in the words of Melish (1998, p. 47), a combination of "black empowerment, white control, [and] reinforcement of Africanity" (see also White, 1994). Despite some unusual legal, religious, and political opportunities for New England blacks, no longer is it possible to argue that slavery was benign in the region (Greene, 1942). For one thing, family formation was often difficult for most New England slaves, living as they generally did isolated in white households. Also, as a sign of the depersonalization present even in New England's "family slavery," only two of the roughly 2,500 slaves advertised for sale in two Boston newspapers between 1704 and 1760 were identified by name (Desrochers, forthcoming). The mid-Atlantic region was more committed to slavery than New England. For a long time, New York had a larger black population that any other North American city, and gave rise to a major slave revolt in 1712 and a famous slave conspiracy of 1741. In such cities as New York and Philadelphia, African Americans built a rich community life, even as they faced harsh demographic conditions; as Berlin (1998, p. 62) puts it, "the graveyard became the first truly African-American institution," but it was soon followed by churches, dance halls, taverns, and schools (Nash, 1987; Klepp, 1994; Hodges, 1997, 1999; Linebaugh and Rediker, 2000). In the mid-Atlantic region, a middle ground between North and South, as Waldstreicher (1999) shows, mixed forms of slavery and servitude led to fluid and hybrid racial categories.

The most intensely studied slave systems are the Chesapeake and Lowcountry, the two most dominant slave societies on the North American mainland. The two had much in common: slaves in both regions lived on ever larger plantations, and in many locales they increasingly outnumbered whites; most slaves in both regions worked in staple agriculture, with a growing minority of slaves, particularly men, working at crafts, on the water, as supervisors, in manufacturing, and as domestics; family life became more robust for both regions' slaves; slaves elaborated similar styles in the way they spoke, danced, made music, and worshipped their gods. Yet the parallels were in many respects overshadowed by the differences. The Chesapeake slave system is arguably most notable for its self-reproducing slave population – the first and fastest growing in the New World. By the 1720s, the fertility of the region's slave population produced a majority who had never seen Africa (Kulikoff, 1986; Sidbury, 1997; Walsh, 1997). A generation later, the Lowcountry's slave population too became more native-born than immigrant, but Africans were always a significant minority in this region throughout the century. A large part of the Lower South was a black world; most of the Upper South was a white world. The relationship between masters and slaves in the Chesapeake was less harsh and adversarial than in the Lowcountry. Slaves worked at different crops, experienced different labor arrangements, and had different craft opportunities in the two regions. Slaves faced greater oppression and had greater autonomy in the Lowcountry than in the Chesapeake (Wood, 1984, 1995; Morgan, 1998; Olwell, 1998).

Some of the most exciting recent work on the early black experience has been in the borderlands. The Lower Mississippi Valley was a rough-and-tumble, violent world of military outposts, slave fugitives, and occasional maroon bands, extensive slave conversions, and interracial alliances, arguably one of the most racially fluid societies in the Americas (cf. Hall, 1992 with Ingersoll, 1999). For long a frontier economy, slaves hunted, fished, cut timber, herded cattle, defended the colony as soldiers, and raised a range of crops. Early on, lower Louisiana became a full-fledged slave society, with a black majority, a significant free black sector, but it did not find a highly profitable export commodity until the end of the eighteenth century (see also Usner, 1992; Hanger, 1997; Clark, 1998; Din, 1999; Spear, 1999). Black society in early Florida too, as Landers (1999) has brilliantly shown, was racially flexible. Fugitives from South Carolina and later Georgia found an asylum in Florida; newly freed slaves for a while lived in their own town, Gracia Real de Santa Teresa de Mose; many blacks in the colony were town-dwellers, carried arms, professed Catholicism, and became property-owners (see also Weber, 1992). One borderland that requires greater attentic

Upper, Deep South, and even Northwest interiors; the little that is known would suggest a measure of fluidity and malleability in race relations in this early frontier setting, although not on the scale of the lower Mississippi Valley or Florida (Lucas, 1992; Eslinger, 1994; Perkins, 1998; Hart, 1998; Taylor, 1998).

As Richard Dunn (1972, p. 224) put it, "Slavery in one form or another is the essence of West Indian history." No British Caribbean colony, Barbara Solow (1991, p. 3) emphasizes, "ever founded a successful society on the basis of free white labor." Over a half of the books and two-thirds of the articles published on the region in the past twenty-five years have focused upon the institution of slavery, the life of slaves, and the experience of freed people. Elsa Goveia (1965) pioneered the study of a slave society, arguing strongly for the role of coercion by law and force in her work on the Leeward Islands, and soon after Patterson's (1967/9) even bleaker study emphasized the alienation and distortion produced by slavery in Jamaica. By contrast, Edward Brathwaite (1971) stressed the creative features of a creole society in his investigation of late eighteenth-century Jamaica. Since those pathbreaking works, a few general and thematic studies of slavery in the seventeenth- and eighteenth-century British Caribbean now exist – e.g., Craton (1982), Sheridan (1985), Ward (1988), Mullin (1992) – but regional and island studies are largely absent, except for a few marginal places, e.g., Olwig (1985), Craton and Saunders (1992), and Kupperman (1993). There are no comprehensive studies of slavery, for example, in eighteenth-century Barbados or the Windward Islands. The best general introduction to slavery in the Caribbean can be found in the individual essays in the UNESCO *General History of the Caribbean* edited by Knight (1997), although many were quite dated when the volume was finally published (see also Shepherd and Beckles, 2000).

Another way of exploring slavery spatially is to focus on the work that slaves performed – arguably the crucial defining feature of most forms of the institution, as Berlin and Morgan (1993) suggest. Slavery knew no limits; it penetrated every economic activity. Slaves who worked in the non-agricultural sector have now begun to receive the attention always afforded field hands. One spotlight has fallen on maritime slaves, forever moving along the edges of the plantation world and connecting one to the other: from the Kru, *grumettes*, and canoe men of the African coast; through the Bermudians and Bahamians who fished the Grand Banks, pursued whales in the North Atlantic, raked salt, salvaged wrecks, and traded in the Caribbean; to the coastal boatmen and offshore seamen who plied up and down the North American coast. In some ways, black mariners were always disadvantaged; in others, as Bolster (1997, p. 91) notes, "Atlantic maritime culture included strong egalitarian impulses that frequently confounded the strict racial etiquette of slave societies" (see also Scott, 1991, 1996). Differences are becoming clearer between locally anchored, community-based seafarers from smaller ports (see especially Jarvis, forthcoming) and the more anonymous, rootless maritime proletariat working out of large urban places. Closely connected to maritime slavery was urban slavery. Urban chimney sweeps, fishermen, specialist tradesmen, female higglers, washerwomen, concubines, slaves who hired their own time, who established community institutions – the panorama of urban slave life is being recovered (Morgan, 1984; Nash, 1987; Knight and Liss, 1991; Gilje and Rock, 1994; Welch, 1995). Another group moving from the shadows into the sunlight are slaves who worked in manufacturing – whether ironworks, chemical works, sugar mills, artisanal trades of all kinds (e.g., Lewis, 1979; Whitman, 1993; Bezis-Selfa, 1997).

The attention to the non-plantation world is welcome, attesting to slavery's flexibility and adaptability. The shops, ships, and manufacturing enterprises may be likened to safety valves that helped govern and regulate the plantations – the engines that drove the Atlantic slave system.

Investigations of single locales – whether a colony, a county, a town or city, a plantation – are especially valuable because of the heightened specificity that such microscopic studies permit. Some of the best studies of Caribbean slavery focus on single plantations – whether Codrington, Worthy Park, Egypt, Drax Hall, and Montpelier, just to mention a few (Bennett, 1958; Craton, 1978; Hall, 1989; Armstrong, 1990; Higman, 1998). A community history of Carter's Grove plantation, Virginia (Walsh, 1997), shows how enslaved Africans became Afro-Virginians. A study of Monmouth County, New Jersey, reveals slaves working on small family farms and forming an integral part of the local economy (Hodges, 1997). A local study can sometimes obscure typicality and broader significance; the greater the attention to regional context, the more these dangers can be avoided.

The spatial awareness of slavery studies ranges widely – from microscopic explorations of a single locale to wide-ranging transnational, comparative analyses. Whatever the angle of vision, the aim must be to examine the links, exchanges, parallels, and differences between interrelated segments of an increasingly unified if extended Atlantic system, to integrate the whole and the parts, the general and particular.

Time

For too long slavery in North America has been seen as an antebellum institution. But the institution is now recognized to have had a long history in the Americas, dating back to 1501 when the first African slave arrived in Hispaniola and to 1519 when the first known vessel carrying slaves directly between Africa and the Americas arrived in Puerto Rico. The year 1619 – when African slaves first reached British North America at Jamestown – is not quite the canonical date it once was. After all, the first Africans to land in North America arrived at Sapelo Sound in present-day Georgia in 1526 and the first slave set foot in a British American colony in Bermuda in 1616 (Wood, 1974; Bernhard, 1999). It is even possible that some African slaves were in Virginia earlier than 1619. Recognizing that slavery has had a *longue durée* also goes hand in hand with an acknowledgment that it changed greatly over time. A series of watersheds or critical disjunctures, it is now understood, frame the development and evolution of black life in North America. No longer is slavery viewed statically (Kolchin, 1993).

One vital turning point that many, though not all, colonial societies experienced was the shift from a slaveowning society to a slave society, from a society with slaves to a society based on slaves, akin to the distinction that some economists make between marketplace economies where commerce occurs and true market economies where commerce reigns supreme (Morgan, 1991; Turley, 2000). Race relations tended to be more fluid in slaveowning than in slave societies. The early slaveowning phase was a plastic period, a soft moment, a time of malleability that would later rigidify and harden. A slave generally could pass more readily from bondage to freedom and work at a wider range of tasks within a hybrid labor force in a society where slavery was a marginal, rather than central institution (Menard, 1988–89; Beckles, 1989a; Menard and Schwartz, 1993). In these early Atlantic settings, blacks, dubbed "Atlantic creoles" by

Ira Berlin (1998, pp. 17, 24), because of their "linguistic dexterity, cultural plasticity, and social agility," possessed more de facto freedom and range of choice than did later African slaves. In shaping cultural patterns, the earliest migrants enjoyed certain advantages over later arrivals. They invented many of the rules, created languages, and learned how to deal with one another. The emergence of a true slave society was usually accompanied by a large influx of Africans, restrictive and regimented forms of labor, a distancing of white and black, a battery of harsh legal codes, and a battening down of any escape hatches out of slavery.

Another crucial transition is rather more difficult to pinpoint but is perhaps even more important to document. The glitter of first contact inevitably catches the eye, but the long-term historical processes of interracial negotiation of power and meaning, while less glamorous, are absolutely vital to an understanding of an emerging slave society. As masters and slaves became familiar with one another, they found ways to live together. A major turning point was the emergence of a critical mass of creole or native-born slaves, sometimes with self-sustaining families reproducing themselves demographically and culturally. At the workplace, customary rules and routines emerged. A growing minority of men escaped field labor and began to assume managerial, artisanal, and domestic posts, while slave women increasingly dominated field labor. A code, as much unwritten as written, arose to govern the sexual exploitation of slave women: it ranged from open concubinage in some societies to furtive interracial liaisons in others. Access to freedom, almost non-existent in the early years of most full-fledged slave societies, inched wider as time passed, in large part because some white fathers freed their mulatto offspring. An interpenetration of Western and African values took place (Sobel, 1987).

A major landmark in the history of early American slavery is the era of revolutions, not just political, important as they were, but economic, religious, and intellectual transformations that reshaped the world of white and black and redefined race. For the first time, slavery faced serious challenge: in unprecedented fashion, slaves attacked the general principles justifying their enslavement; and the northern states gradually put the institution on the road to extinction. At the same time as the era marked a new birth of freedom, it also witnessed a great expansion of slavery: the Atlantic slave trade peaked at the end of the eighteenth century, a huge territorial growth of slavery occurred, and racial thought crystallized. A gradual sea-change affected master–slave relations as masters began to emphasize solicitude rather than authority, sentiments rather than severity in the governance of their slaves (Ward, 1988; Berlin, 1998; Morgan, 1998).

Another watershed occurred when a slave system began to falter. The nature of Barbadian slavery changed – although it has not yet been fully documented – once the white-hot fury of the initial seventeenth-century sugar revolution cooled. Other islands underwent the same process at later times. By the early eighteenth century, parts of the Chesapeake had shifted from tobacco to grains, with all sorts of repercussions for slaves, both at the workplace, in family organization, and in community life. Diversification – cultivating foodstuffs, producing for internal consumption, engaging in local manufacturing, increased hiring of slaves – was among the most obvious responses to downturns in a region's primary staple. Slavery in the northern colonies was never central, but it became progressively marginal in many places. Diversification almost certainly improved the slaves' material well-being, but slave family life, for example, was subject to new pressures and strains with increased hiring and sales.

Narrating linear sequences is not easy. Certain cyclical or broad repeating patterns seem to characterize the ways in which slavery expanded, as, say, the movement from a frontier to a settled state, or from pioneer farming to monocultural production, or from specialized monoculture to diversified farming, or from creole to African, or from a predominantly immigrant to a predominantly native-born slave population, all of which occurred in successive stages to some degree in one slave society to the next. Or perhaps a helix is a more appropriate metaphor than a repeating circle, for slavery's progression from one society to another (often direct, as from Barbados to South Carolina, or from the Leewards to the Windwards, or from Virginia to Kentucky) could compress, skip almost entirely, perhaps even elongate elements of earlier stages. A continuous and expanding spiral may be the best way to see slavery expanding from one zone to another. Similarly, cultural development followed no straightforward trajectory of attenuation, death, or survival. Rather, complex processes of appropriation, subversion, masking, invention, and revival took place. The transmission of ethnicity involved reinvention and reinterpretation, discontinuities as much as continuities. In short, the stages of slavery's development were never simple or clear-cut, even if they were part of one overall historical process.

Whatever the narrative complexities, the overall aim must be to historicize slavery, to abandon static analyses of the institution, and to render slaves a people with a history, not outside history, as a people with agency, shaping their own experiences and thereby molding the structures that also victimized them.

⊅ White–Black Relations

Simplistic dichotomies have tended to govern how relations between masters and slaves, whites and blacks have been portrayed. The binary opposites – negotiation or mastery, patriarchalism or commercialism, viewing slaves as humans or animals, racism or proto-racism, race or class – are not so much wrong as incomplete. They do not fully capture the complexity of human relationships under slavery. The best studies transcend and reconcile these neat formulations.

If there is one concept that has dominated recent characterizations of white–black relations under slavery, it is negotiation. Slavery was, Ira Berlin (1998, p. 2) insists, a "negotiated relationship." The master–slave relationship was a complex give-and-take, of incentives, subversion, exchanges, concessions, and bargaining. No matter how unevenly matched, the parties, masters and slaves, whites and blacks, balanced needs and wills, contested and compromised, renegotiated and redefined the terms of their existence in the myriad processes of daily life. Negotiation emphasizes subaltern agency in the interactions between masters and slaves; slaves "held cards of their own," Berlin emphasizes (see also Ingersoll, 1999, p. xvi)

Slavery was less a tug-of-war, others argue, than a state of war. The savagery of the slave regime, the sheer coercive power available to masters must never be underestimated. Rather than reciprocity involved in negotiation, stark conflict and sharply opposed battle lines constitute slavery's essence. Masters committed arbitrary violence; slaves engaged in unceasing guerrilla warfare. The whip was the ubiquitous reality and symbol of authority under slavery. Masters and overseers were schooled in "the diplomacy of the lash," as one Jamaican governor put it, not in the arts of persuasion.

From this vantage point, physical punishment – the fact of it and the threat of it – incidental cruelties, despotic whimsy, callous brutishness, family breakups must be located at the center of any discussions of slavery. The concept of mastery is required to understand slavery (Kay and Cary, 1995; Greene, 1999).

Both of these perspectives have a point, and only a combination of the two is likely to penetrate to slavery's essence. A focus on slavery from an institutional perspective – perhaps a study of slave laws (as in the best recent study by Morris, 1996), or of slave crime (by Schwarz, 1988), or an investigation of slave patrols (by Hadden, 2001) – is likely to emphasize oppression and domination. A look at the extensive daily contacts that occurred across the racial divide (as in Sensbach, 1998) is likely to uncover unlimited permutations of human emotions, infinitely subtle moral entanglements. The slave market (Johnson, 1999) should be studied for its oppressions and subversions, objectifications and negotiations. Similarly, sexual encounters between masters and slaves – the very term encounter may be too anodyne and euphemistic – ranged from deep commitments to the most outrageous forms of sexual abuse, from forced embraces to tender affection. Sex between whites and blacks created, in one historian's words, "a tangled web of love and hatred, of pride and guilt, of passion and shame" (Clinton and Gillespie, 1997; Lewis and Onuf, 1999, p. 76 [quote]; Hodes, 1999).

The appropriateness of patriarchalism or paternalism to describe master–slave relations is contentious. Was it not more myth than fact? Were not masters hypocrites, merely capitalist wolves in patriarchal clothing? Surely, selling so-called children cannot be reconciled with any conception of familial governance and must represent the triumph of the marketplace over any conceivable ethic of paternal responsibility. Of course, slaves were chattel, and masters thought of and acted toward them using the language of property. Early Anglo-American masters were profit-conscious, operated in a market economy, and employed the language of commercial capitalism. Yet at the same time, masters thought of slaves as dependants. Slaves were part of households. Patriarchalism cannot be dismissed as mere propaganda or apologetics; it was rather an authentic, if deeply flawed, worldview. Like all ideological rationalizations, it contained its share of self-serving cant, but its familial rhetoric was not just a smokescreen for exploitation because it offered no guarantee of benevolence. Furthermore, an economically acquisitive mentality was not incompatible with the ethics and customs of patriarchy. After all, slavery in the New World, as Robin Blackburn (1997, p. 19) notes, "was above all a hybrid mixing ancient and modern, European business and African husbandry, American and Eastern plants and processes, elements of traditional patrimonialism with up-to-date bookkeeping and individual ownership." Paternalism and capitalism went hand in hand (Olwell, 1998; Morgan, 1998; Ingersoll, 1999; Johnson, 1999; cf. Kay and Cary, 1995).

Similarly, the basic humanity of the slave could hardly be denied, yet slaves were easily thought of and treated as animals. A slave's status varied along a broad spectrum of rights, powers, and protections. A few individual slaves enjoyed considerable privileges. Perhaps the most widely claimed right was that of creating and sustaining families, even though slaveowners always could, and did, break up families through sale and bequest – as if they were buying, selling, or transferring livestock. Similarly, many slaves had customary claims to property, in some cases considerable amounts, although once again masters legally owned everything a slave possessed. At any moment, slaves could be stripped of their privileges. They could be sold, whipped, even killed at the whim of an owner. Radical uncertainty, vulnerability, and sheer unpredictability were the essence of the slave condition, contributing to its dehumanization, and making comparisons to domestic animals commonplace. To control domesticated beasts, human beings devised collars, chains, prods, whips, and branding irons. They castrated males. Slaveowners applied similar means of control to human captives, treating slaves in many respects like dogs, horses, or cattle: beasts of burden to be driven and inventoried, animals to be tamed and domesticated. An emphasis on human ascendancy encouraged the assumption that people who seemingly lived most like animals – eating improper foods, engaging in sexual promiscuity, going naked – must be something like beasts. Conversely, the undermining of notions of human uniqueness, the narrowing of the chasm between the human and animal kingdoms that occurred during the early modern era, paved the way for the argument that some people were really more animal than human (Jacoby, 1994; Morgan, 1995; Davis, 1996).

The dichotomy in scholarly assessments of white attitudes toward blacks is essentially about continuity versus change. Some scholars emphasize contingency and marked shifts in how Africans were viewed. In the pre-colonization period, they argue, whites often admired sub-Saharan Africans or at least viewed them neutrally and pragmatically. Dislike and fear of strangers were of course commonplace, but Africans, it is claimed, were not always singled out for opprobrium. Some of the same stereotypes later applied to Africans were first developed for peasants, the poor, and aliens. Medieval Europeans, as Benjamin Braude has demonstrated (in "Constructing Race," 1997) did not associate the biblical Ham with Africa. There was no linear or inevitable progression to racism. Until well into the eighteenth century, physical attributes such as skin color, shape of nose, and texture of hair were less important to the assessment of others than religion, civility, and rank. The term "race" initially meant lineage, clan, or species. Modern notions of race, defined by hereditarian determinism, did not come into being until the late eighteenth century (Davis, 1975; Barker, 1978; Bartels in "Constructing Race," 1997; Hudson, 1996; Hannaford, 1996; K. Brown, 1999; Wheeler, 2000).

Conversely, other scholars emphasize the fateful association of blackness with evil, danger, and filth. They note how revulsion toward Africans has a long pedigree, stretching back at least into medieval times. Africans, they point out, were always held in special contempt as a people associated with slavery, sin, and bestiality. Quite how far back to go is a question. Representations of sub-Saharan Africans circulating in sixteenth-century England, Alden Vaughan and Virginia Mason Vaughan insist (in "Constructing Race," 1997, and see also Vaughan, 1995), focused on skin color and unfamiliar customs to "set them apart in English eyes and imaginations as a special category of humankind." The contrast between the first English depictions of Indians, to whom they likened themselves, and of Africans, from whom they differentiated themselves, is also especially striking. Others point to the importance of mid-fifteenth-century Portuguese voyages to sub-Saharan Africa as a time when the "combining of black skin and pagan faith in the bodies of significant numbers of enslaved captives," notes Malcolmson (2000, pp. 150, 152), "was the beginning of what one might call modern blackness." Iberian racial ideologies had a much longer history, James Sweet argues (in "Constructing Race," 1997), for although they crystallized in fifteenth-century Castile and Andalusia, their antecedents can be traced to the development of African slavery in the Islamic world as far back as the eighth century. Indeed, scholars now recognize the large role played by Arabic science and philosophy in the development of Western thought, helping shape a racial archetype based on ideas about blood, physiognomy, and climate. When western Europeans began to think of themselves as one, as insiders, for whom enslavement was no longer an alternative to death – even when strictly economic principles argued for cheaper European than African slavery in the New World – is an interesting question. No doubt the Crusades and Reconquest of Iberia did much to create a sense of common Christian brotherhood (Jordan, 1968; Lewis, 1990; Hall, 1995; Davis, Kupperman, and Chaplin in "Constructing Race," 1997; Goldenberg, 1999; Eltis, 2000).

Race is always bound up with class. How Africans came to be enslaved used to be couched as a matter of race versus class – either racial ideology identified Africans as potential candidates for enslavement even before there was a need for slaves, or economic necessity mediated through class considerations largely accounts for the process. Racial prejudice, however inchoate, does seem to have been sufficient to single out Africans as potential victims, but the question then remains of how the process of debasement occurred. To answer it in turn raises issues of power, economic force, and, perhaps above all, class. Prejudice often existed, but the historian needs to ask what was made of it – particularly by different social groups (see Morgan, 1975; Wood, 1997). Furthermore, racial attitudes and race relations varied according to class. The triangular relationship of non-slaveowners, slaveowners, and slaves deserves much more investigation. Linebaugh and Rediker (2000) posit alliances between slaves and religious radicals, sailors, and various oppressed groups throughout the early modern Atlantic world. Setting such people in motion, they claim, created a new class of working people, the first modern proletariat, a multi-ethnic, interracial motley crew, committed to cooperation and subversion. Too little is said of the divisions among these workers – how sailors, for example, preyed on slaves in the Middle Passage and how not one mutiny, involving sailors and slaves, has surfaced among the records of the over 27,000 recorded transatlantic slaving voyages (cf. Bolster, 1997). Although too romanticized and too neat a division of this Atlantic world into heroes and villains, their account tells fascinating personal stories about the "Atlantean proletarian," Francis, an influential black member of a Baptist congregation in mid-seventeenth-century Bristol, or Catherine and Edward Despard, a mixed-race couple who lived in the Caribbean and Central America during the War of Independence and then became involved in a radical plan to capture London. Attitudes also varied according to class location – whether in the metropolis or periphery, for example. An enlarged British empire after the Seven Years' War, Christopher Brown (1999) argues, stimulated some far-seeing imperial thinkers, particularly those concerned with imperial administration, to envision a stronger empire, with blacks as full British subjects, no longer as slaves. Meanwhile, in New England, out on the margins, undercurrents of popular anti-slavery sentiment have been discovered as early as the 1730s (Minkema, 1997).

As with many of the dichotomies used to depict white–black relations, elements of both positions will need to be taken into account. Teasing out the subtle and complicated interplay between negotiation and mastery, patriarchalism and commercialism, humanity and animalization, long-standing racial prejudices and positive attitudes toward Africans, race, and class, will be necessary to capture the full complexity of early white–black relations.

Interior of Black Life

The material standards of most slaves, particularly in the Caribbean region, were far worse than that of free workers. Africans experienced worse mortality and more crowded conditions – by a factor of three or four in each case – than any other transatlantic traveler. Once on American soil, slaves worked extraordinarily hard, with labor participation rates at least twice as great as those for free laborers, with children being put to work at young ages and women placed in whip-driven field gangs. Slaves, especially on sugar plantations, toiled for many more hours than free workers, although the heightened intensity of labor associated with gang-driven slave labor was more important than the actual number of hours worked. The killing work regimen of sugar helps explain the high rates of natural decrease experienced by Caribbean slave populations. Slaves were forced to live in the flimsiest, most cramped quarters; wear the cheapest, most drab, uncomfortable clothes, often going naked and barefoot; and eat a diet high in starch, low in protein, and extremely monotonous in content (Fogel, 1989; Prude, 1991; Vlach, 1993; Engerman et al., 2001).

At the same time, many poor whites experienced material conditions not all that dissimilar to slaves, particularly slaves living on the mainland. One indicator of relative well-being is the speed at which mainland slave populations grew – faster from natural increase than contemporary European populations, for example. Another indicator is the amount of protein that slaves consumed. The diet of mainland slaves in particular seems little different from that of poor whites; slaves probably ate more chicken, fish, and wild animals and somewhat less beef and pork than free laborers. Furthermore, by the time of the Revolution native-born North American blacks were almost the same height as whites – on average less than an inch shorter. The physical stature of native-born slaves on the late colonial mainland puts them on a par with contemporary European aristocrats, not peasants. Slaves born in North America were taller than those born in the Caribbean, who in turn were generally taller than those born in Africa. Although there were variations, slaves on the mainland seem to have worked fewer hours than free workers in the northern colonies (Komlos, 1996; Bowen, 1996; Steckel, 1999; Walsh, 2000).

No longer can it be argued that the family was unthinkable or that the nuclear unit was unknown to early American slaves. Slavery undoubtedly subjected slaves' familial aspirations to enormous stress, often to breaking point: owners generally recognized only the mother–child tie, bought mostly men who then had difficulty finding partners, separated slave families by sale and transfer, and committed their own sexual assaults on slave women. Yet an emphasis on the instability, promiscuity, casual mating, disorganization, or near anarchy of slave family life is overdrawn. Historians now emphasize the resilience of slave families, the strength of kinship bonds, evident, for example, in naming patterns, and the depth of parent–child affection (on naming, see Cody, 1987; Thornton, 1993; Handler and Jacoby, 1996; Burnard, 2001). Nevertheless, this more positive view of slave family life rests on fragmentary evidence; much more is known of the structure of slave families than the quality of family relations; and the information is invariably cross-sectional, providing snapshots of slave families at a point in time, rather than the serial life-cycle of slave families. Two studies of slave children (by Wilma King, 1995 and Marie Jenkins Schwartz, 2000) in the antebellum South now exist, but none for the eighteenth century. In short, much is unknown about slave family life, and it is best to underscore the formidable obstacles facing slaves as they struggled to create and then maintain families (Gutman, 1976; Higman, 1978, 1984b; Craton, 1979; Kulikoff, 1986; Kay and Cary, 1995; Morgan, 1998).

Women experienced slavery differently from men, but how much so? In work, women labored alongside men in the fields, and even predominated in some field gangs. Few women escaped fieldwork because skilled opportunities were largely the preserve of slave men. Many slave women brought up their children alone; in that sense, many slave families were matrifocal, although this pattern cannot be traced to Africa where patriarchal authority was strong. If slavery bred strong women, it hardly emasculated black men who headed most households, tended to be much older than their female partners, monopolized privileged positions, traveled more than women, and dominated most rebellions, petit and grand marronage, and conspiracies. Slave women may therefore be considered doubly exploited – both in their productive and reproductive capacities. Most obviously, slave women were vulnerable to rape and sexual harassment by whites and blacks. Yet slave women were not just victims. Slave women enjoyed better health, secured more household positions (domestics, washerwomen, occasional seamstresses, midwives, and nurses), marketed more produce, anchored more families (because in many divided-residence households, women brought up the children most of the time), converted more readily to Christianity, and were manumitted more frequently than men (Beckles, 1989b; Bush, 1990; Brown, 1996; Gaspar and Hine, 1996).

A flurry of interest in the religious lives of African Americans has not quite overtaken early American historians' fascination with Puritanism, but the time may be nigh. For one thing, African religious history has come of age, and it is possible to trace connections between homeland and diaspora as never before. In the sixteenth and seventeenth centuries, Catholic missionaries were remarkably successful in some parts of Africa, particularly West Central Africa (see, for example, MacGaffey, 1994) although by the beginning of the eighteenth century, as Adrian Hastings (1994, p. 127) notes, the "likelihood of any enduring Catholic presence in black Africa of more than miniscule size had become extremely slight" (cf. Thornton, 1998a, 253–271). The role of Islam among African forced migrants to the New World has now been well documented, although perhaps exaggerated for the Anglo-American world (see Austin, 1997, pp. 2–62; Gomez, 1998, pp. 59–87; Diouf, 1998, 1999). Evangelical revivalism's extensive church records and missionary journals have been tapped to make clear that Protestant proselytizing made significant inroads into African American communities in both the Caribbean and North America from the mid-eighteenth century onward. Gender analysis has also helped: women's spiritual leadership was perhaps even more evident among blacks than whites, as Frey and Wood (1998) suggest, because white men feared black male preachers. West African women, Emily Clark and Virginia Meacham Gould (2002) demonstrate, were much more likely than men to participate in the ritual of Catholic baptism in early eighteenth-century New Orleans. A fascinating look at the margins of Protestantism is offered by a study of those few African Americans who became full members of several North Carolina Moravian churches in the late eighteenth century. For a time, Afro-Moravians experienced a rare measure of spiritual equality; membership was sealed with the "kiss of peace" (Sensbach, 1998). Other margins include the ways in which New England African Americans drew on Euro-American evangelical idioms (Seeman, 1999), a study of the first black abolitionists, who attacked the slave trade and slavery (Saillant, forthcoming), and those slaves who became Baptists in the late eighteenth century (Sobel, 1979). The biggest question still to be resolved is the degree to which slavery transformed traditional African religious practices and beliefs. What was the balance between losses and retentions? (Butler, 1990, pp.129–63; Morgan, 1998, pp. 610–58).

Perhaps the best term to describe cultural development among African Americans is creolization, and models for the process are often taken from language development (Brathwaite, 1971; Palmie, 1995; Buisseret and Reinhardt, 2000). Thus, it is argued, like the grammar that orders a language, a set of deep structural principles shared by most West and West Central Africans provided slaves with a common foundation on which creolized cultural systems could develop. A good survey now exists of the languages spoken by African Americans across the Atlantic region, as do some in-depth studies of early black languages (Holm, 1988–9; Lalla and D'Costa, 1990; Rickford and Handler, 1994; Bernstein et al., 1997). Dance and music were certainly woven into the very fabric of early African American life. Distinctive African American forms of dance and music can be glimpsed, such as the emphasis on percussion, carrying the body's center of gravity low, and syncopation (Epstein, 1977; Abrahams, 1992; Rath, 1993, 2000; White and White, 1999; Heckscher, 2000). How much interpretation depends on small scraps of information is no better indicated than the many variant readings of the dance and musical scene depicted in the watercolor, *The Old Plantation*, said to have been painted in the 1790s and almost certainly set in the Lowcountry, perhaps the Julianton plantation in Georgia (see, for example, Kay and Cary, 1995, p. 182; Franklin, 1997, pp. 227–35; Morgan, 1998, pp. 585–6).

Some insight into the interior black experience can be gained by visual analyses. The black servant in eighteenth-century domestic portraits, Beth Fowkes Tobin (1999) notes, moves over time from being an emblem of the exotic – often turbaned and suggesting sexuality – to incorporation into everyday family life, placed closer to mother and children, for example. Afro-Caribbean women, painted by the Italian, Agostino Brunias, in the 1770s, with their many forms of dress, undress, varied head coverings, and lively market participation, assume agency, even as they are rendered according to taxonomic and ethnographic conventions. Images of slaves put up for sale or as fugitives in broadsides and newspaper advertisements generally depict Africans and African Americans as partially clad, often in loincloths. Associating slaves with nudity and sensuality was commonplace, although some African newcomers are depicted with jewelry and bandannas – an interesting visual clue to what they brought with them. Slaves for sale are often depicted with spears, fugitives with walking sticks. Visual representations of the fugitive slave, as Marcus Wood (2000, pp. 80, 87) notes, developed from earlier conventions for advertising runaway, strayed, or missing persons, primarily white servants. Similarly, the feathered skirts and headdresses, with which some Africans are represented, derived from standard Native American iconography; and represented a trope for savagery (Bugner, 1976–9; Lacey, 1996; Patton, 1998; Erickson and Hulse, 2000). Even images of artifacts, with no slaves present, can reveal much about colonial power relations, as Kriz (2000) demonstrates.

Literary scholars too have added much to our understanding of the black experience. Excellent scholarly editions, particularly those by Vincent Carretta, now exist of some of the earliest black writers. His annotations of the works of Olaudah Equiano and Phillis Wheatley (Equiano, 1995; Wheatley, 2001) are models of scholarly detective work. Valuable anthologies, including Potkay and Burr (1995), two by Carretta (one co-edited with Gould) (1996, 2001), now exist. In one collection of Caribbean English literature can be found one of the earliest representations of slave speech (1709) and the speech of Moses Bon Saam (1735), purportedly a maroon leader, who delivers a fascinating abolitionist oration to his fellow blacks (Krise, 1999, pp. 93–107; see also Greene, 2000). Literary scholars have put the works of black writers into a range of contexts – spiritual autobiographies, captivity narratives, travel books, adventure tales, narratives of slavery – and introduced us, for example, to the trope of the "talking book" (Andrews, 1988; Gates, 1988, pp. 127–69).

Few historians since Elkins have probed what slavery did to the personality of the slave. Bertram Wyatt-Brown (2001, pp. 3–55) is one of the few, and in a suggestive essay has explored the nature of male slave psychology (noting that the pyschological effects of overlordship on African American women remains to be examined). His survey runs the gamut of melancholy, paralysis of will, repression, self-deprecation, to verbal dexterity, satire, resentment, anger, and sturdy self-identification. Even more notable is the exploration by Alex Bontemps (2001, pp. ix, 41) of "how enslavement implicated survivors in the initiation and perpetuation of their own oppression." He explores advertisements for runaway slaves who had difficulty looking people in the face, had various nervous disorders, or were sensible, bold, brazen, impertinent. He analyzes planter correspondence where the sheer invisibility of slaves reduced their rebelliousness merely to the ability to "frustrate, irritate, anger, and perplex." To preserve a sense of self, Bontemps argues, slaves had to play a self-denying role – acting like a Negro without becoming one. Survival was never without its costs.

Creating a distinctive language, music, and religion – in short, a culture – had political implications of profound ambivalence. On the one hand, it was an act of resistance, perhaps the greatest act of resistance accomplished by blacks. By carving out some independence for themselves, by creating something coherent and autonomous, by forcing whites to recognize their humanity, slaves triumphed over circumstances. They opposed the dehumanization inherent in their status and demonstrated their independent will and volition. On the other hand, their cultural creativity eased the torments of slavery, gave them a reason for living, thereby encouraging accommodation to the established order. This ambivalence is evident in interpretations of slave resistance (Mintz, 1995). Concentrate on all the plots and rebellions that slaves mounted and slave resistance appears structurally endemic (Craton, 1982; Gaspar, 1985; Kea, 1992). Recall the bitter fact that the vicious system of Anglo-American slavery lasted for hundreds of years without serious challenge, and its stability seems paramount. Slave resistance was always more than collective violence; individual, and sometimes collective, flight was its most common form (Mullin, 1972: Franklin and Schweninger, 1999). Even maroons, the ultimate symbol of rebellion, were forced to accommodate to slavery, often proving effective allies to whites, tracking down slave runaways and rebels, living in an uneasy symbiosis with their white neighbors, seeking arms, tools, pots, and cloth, as well as employment (Price, 1979). Blacks were found on opposite sides of most political disputes. Masters and states, particularly in emergencies, placed slaves under arms. In the islands free blacks became an important part of the militia. During the American Revolutionary War, slaves were used as soldiers by both sides (Brown and Morgan, forthcoming).

Rewards for military service, as well as gratis manumission or some form of self-purchase, were common mechanisms by which slaves gained freedom. Before the American Revolution, only a small number of African Americans were able to take advantage of such strategies to become free. They tended to be mulatto or colored, female, and children. The few who did secure their freedom often signaled their status by assuming a new name, by changing location, by putting their families on a more secure footing, by creating associations to strengthen community life, by actively buying and selling property, even slaves, and by resorting to courts to protect their hard-won gains. But throughout the colonial period, freed persons were generally too few to separate themselves markedly from other slaves, and many of their closest contacts were still with their enslaved brethren. In the 1770s free coloreds and free blacks were about 6 percent of Louisiana's African American population, 2 percent of Jamaica's and Virginia's and less than 1 percent of Barbados's and South Carolina's (Cohen and Greene, 1972; Landers, 1996; Hanger, 1997).

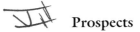 Prospects

As the twenty-first century begins, the study of African Americans in early America is as vibrant and vigorous as ever. Major works have appeared in the past decade or so, and more are in the offing. The range of disciplinary perspectives brought to the subject has never been greater. Perhaps the greatest challenge will be to connect developments in Africa to events in the Americas with as much spatial and chronological specificity as possible. The story of how Africans passed aspects of their heritage to the native-born, and how creoles in turn transferred that cultural heritage to succeeding generations, has still not been fully told. Many spatial dimensions of the black experience need to be explored – most Caribbean islands deserve much closer study, as does the mainland interior, from the Piedmont westward; more comparative studies, say of particular subgroups of slaves, whether artisans, domestics, drivers, or those living in urban places or engaged in manufacturing, across a range of slave societies would be useful – but perhaps the biggest goal will be to put North American slavery into its full Atlantic and global context. The largest gap in our knowledge of white–black relations concerns encounters between black and white in the households of farmers and small planters rather than the elite. How various ethnic groups (such as the Irish, Scots-Irish, or Jews) interacted with blacks would be helpful; and a comprehensive study of relations between African Americans and Native Americans still awaits its historian (for the best studies, see McLoughlin, 1974; Perdue, 1979; Merrell, 1984; Braund, 1991; Usner, 1995; Saunt, 1998, 1999). The interior of slave life is still cast in shadows – whether it is relations between kinfolk, or magical beliefs, or musical styles, or the meaning of dance. The effects on slaves of nearly absolute power, the extent of the psychic damage, the impact of the pathology of racism – all require more subtle probing. Visual analyses of black life are still in their infancy, and literary investigations not much further along. Archaeology, material culture, DNA studies, and many other disciplines can be counted on to illumine aspects of black life.

Slavery's powerful grip on the imagination of so many varied scholars from so many different perspectives is surely not all that hard to explain. Racial slavery is the grim and irrepressible theme governing the settlement of much of the Western Hemisphere. Much of the wealth of early America derived from slave-produced commodities. Slavery defined the structure of a majority of New World societies, underpinning not just their economies but their social, political, cultural, and ideological systems. In classical and Judeo-Christian traditions, slavery was the central paradigm for understanding the nature of liberty (Patterson, 1991). In large measure, conceptions of freedom were the creation of slavery. Many claims have been made for the single key to understanding America, the one bedrock on which all else rests – the frontier, the desire for personal freedom, land speculation, affluence – but there is little dispute about America's nightmare, its dark underside. Racial slavery is America's haunting original sin. Depriving people of liberty in a land devoted to freedom was the country's greatest atrocity, its deepest evil – "a monstrous injustice," in Abraham Lincoln's words. And the crime of slavery created a national wound of racial grievance that has continued to fester and that has failed to heal. The legacy of slavery is a permanent stain on the United States. Laying its ghosts to rest may never be possible. It is why some call for a National Atonement Day, necessary, they claim, for forgiveness. It is why some believe it is a disgrace that Washington DC has a Holocaust Museum and Museum of the American Indian, but no national slavery museum. It is why the movement for reparations, compensating African Americans for slavery, is gaining momentum. It is why the subject of slavery continues to fascinate. Each generation has to come to terms with it.

BIBLIOGRAPHY

Books, Editions, and Dissertations

Abrahams, Roger D.: *Singing the Master: The Emergence of African-American Culture in the Plantation South* (New York: Pantheon Books, 1992).

Andrews, William L.: *To Tell a Free Story: The First Century of Afro-American Autobiography, 1760–1865* (Urbana, IL: University of Illinois Press, 1988).

Armstrong, Douglas V.: *The Old Village and the Great House: An Archaeological and Historical Examination of Drax Hall Plantation, St. Ann's Bay, Jamaica* (Urbana, IL: University of Illinois Press, 1990).

Austin, Allan D.: *African Muslims in Antebellum America: Transatlantic Stories and Spiritual Struggles* (New York: Routledge, 1997) and for a fuller, but more dated, version, see *African Muslims in Antebellum America: A Sourcebook* (New York: Garland Publishing, 1984).

Ball, Edward: *Slaves in the Family* (New York: Farrar, Straus, and Giroux, 1998).

Barker, Anthony J.: *The African Link: British Attitudes to the Negro in the Era of the Atlantic Slave Trade, 1550–1807* (London: Frank Cass, 1978).

Barry, Boubacar: *Senegambia and the Atlantic Slave Trade* (New York: Cambridge University Press, 1998).

Baum, Robert M.: *Shrines of the Slave Trade: Diola Religion and Society in Precolonial Senegambia* (New York: Oxford University Press, 1999).

Beckles, Hilary: *White Servitude and Black Slavery in Barbados, 1627–1715* (Knoxville, TN: University of Tennessee Press, 1989a).

Beckles, Hilary: *Natural Rebels: A Social History of Enslaved Black Women in Barbados* (New Brunswick, NJ: Rutgers University Press, 1989b).

Bennett, J. Harry: *Bondsmen and Bishops: Slavery and Apprenticeship on the Codrington Plantations of Barbados, 1710–1838* (Berkeley and Los Angeles: University of California Press, 1958).

Berlin, Ira: *Many Thousands Gone: The First Two Centuries of Slavery in North America* (Cambridge, Mass.: Harvard University Press, 1998).

Berlin, Ira and Morgan, Philip D., eds.: *Cultivation and Culture: Labor and the Shaping of Slave Life in the Americas* (Charlottesville, VA: University Press of Virginia, 1993).

Bernhard, Virginia: *Slaves and Slaveholders in Bermuda, 1616–1782* (Columbia, MO: University of Missouri Press, 1999).

Bernstein, Cynthia, Nunnelly, Thomas, and Sabino, Robin, eds.: *Language Variety in the South Revisited* (Tuscaloosa, AL: University of Alabama Press, 1997).

Blackburn, Robin: *The Making of New World Slavery: From the Baroque to the Modern 1492– 1800* (London: Verso, 1997).

Bolster, W. Jeffrey: *Black Jacks: African American Seamen in the Age of Sail* (Cambridge, MA: Harvard University Press, 1997).

Bontemps, Alex: *The Punished Self: Surviving Slavery in the Colonial South* (Ithaca, NY: Cornell University Press, 2001).

Brathwaite, Edward: *The Development of Creole Society in Jamaica, 1770–1820* (Oxford: Clarendon Press, 1971).

Brown, Christopher L. and Morgan, Philip D., eds.: *The Arming of Slaves: From Classical Times to the Modern Age* (New Haven, CT: Yale University Press, forthcoming).

Brown, Kathleen M.: *Good Wives, Nasty Wenches, and Anxious Patriarchs: Gender, Race, and Power in Colonial Virginia* (Chapel Hill, NC: University of North Carolina Press, 1996).

Bugner, Ladislas, ed.: *The Image of the Black in Western Art*, vol. 1, *From the Pharaohs to the Fall of the Roman Empire*, ed. Jean Vercoutter et al.; vol. 2, *From the Early Christian Era to the "Age of Discovery"*, pt. 1, *From the Demonic Threat to the Incarnation of Sainthood*, ed. Jean Devisse, pt. 2, *Africans in the Christian Ordinance of the World (Fourteenth to the Sixteenth Century)*, ed. Jean Devisse and Michel Mollat; vol. 3, *Africa and Europe: Sixteenth to Eighteenth Century* (forthcoming); vol. 4, *From the American Revolution to World War I*, pt. 1, *Slaves and Liberators*, pt. 2, *Black Models and White Myths*, ed. Hugh Honour (Lausanne, Switz.: Menil Foundation, 1976–1979 (vols 1–2); Cambridge, MA: Menil Foundation and Harvard University Press, 1989 (vol. 4)).

Buisseret, David, and Reinhardt, Steven G., eds.: *Creolization in the Americas* (College Station, TX: Texas A&M Press, 2000).

Bush, Barbara: *Slave Women in Caribbean Society, 1650–1838* (London: James Currey Ltd, 1990).

Butler, Jon: *Awash in a Sea of Faith: Christianizing the American People* (Cambridge, MA: Harvard University Press, 1990).

Carney, Judith A.: *Black Rice: The African Origins of Rice Cultivation in the Americas* (Cambridge, MA: Harvard University Press, 2001).

Carretta, Vincent, ed.: *Unchained Voices: An Anthology of Black Authors in the English-Speaking World of the Eighteenth Century* (Lexington, KY: University Press of Kentucky, 1996).

Carretta, Vincent and Gould, Philip, eds.: *"Genius in Bondage": A Critical Anthology of the Literature of the Early Black Atlantic* (Lexington, KY: University Press of Kentucky, 2001).

Clark, Emily: "A New World Community: The New Orleans Ursulines and Colonial Society, 1727–1803" (Ph.D. dissertation, Tulane University, 1998).

Clinton, Catherine and Gillespie, Michele, eds.: *The Devil's Lane: Sex and Race in the Early South* (New York: Oxford University Press, 1997).

Cohen, David W. and Greene, Jack P., eds.: *Neither Slave Nor Free: The Freedmen of African Descent in the Slave Societies of the New World* (Baltimore, MD: Johns Hopkins University Press, 1972).

Craton, Michael: *Searching for the Invisible Man: Slaves and Plantation Life in Jamaica* (Cambridge, MA: Harvard University Press, 1978).

Craton, Michael: *Testing the Chains: Resistance to Slavery in the British West Indies* (Ithaca, NY: Cornell University Press, 1982).

Craton, Michael and Saunders, Gail: *Islanders in the Stream: A History of the Bahamian People*, vol. 1, *From Aboriginal Times to the End of Slavery* (Athens, GA: University of Georgia Press, 1992).

Davis, David Brion: *The Problem of Slavey in Western Culture* (Ithaca, NY: Cornell University Press, 1975).

Degler, Carl: *Neither Black nor White: Slavery and Race Relations in Brazil and the United States* (New York: Macmillan, 1971).

Din, Gilbert C.: *Spaniards, Planters, and Slaves: The Spanish Regulation of Slavery in Louisiana* (College Station, TX: Texas A&M University Press, 1999).

Diouf, Sylviane: *Servants of Allah: African Muslims Enslaved in the Americas* (New York: New York University Press, 1998).

Dunn, Richard S.: *Sugar and Slaves: The Rise of the Planter Class in the English West Indies, 1624–1713* (Chapel Hill, NC: University of North Carolina Press, 1972).

Elkins, Stanley M.: *Slavery: A Problem in American Institutional and Intellectual Life* (Chicago: University of Chicago Press, 1959).

Eltis, David: *The Rise of African Slavery in the Americas* (New York: Cambridge University Press, 2000).

Eltis, David and Richardson, David, eds.: *Routes to Slavery: Direction, Ethnicity and Mortality in the Transatlantic Slave Trade* (London: Frank Cass, 1997).

Eltis, David, Behrendt, Stephen D., Richardson, David, and Klein, Herbert S., eds.: *The Trans-Atlantic Slave Trade: A Database on CD-Rom* (New York: Cambridge University Press, 1999).

Epstein, Dena J.: *Sinful Tunes and Spirituals: Black Folk Music to the Civil War* (Urbana, IL: University of Illinois Press, 1977).

Equiano, Olaudah: *The Interesting Narrative and Other Writings*, ed. Vincent Carretta (New York: Penguin Putnam Inc., 1995).

Erickson, Peter and Hulse, Clark, eds.: *Early Modern Visual Culture: Representation, Race, and Empire in Renaissance England* (Philadelphia: University of Pennsylvania Press, 2000).

Essah, Patience: *A House Divided: Slavery and Emancipation in Delaware, 1638–1865* (Charlottesville, VA: University Press of Virginia, 1996).

Ferguson, Leland: *Uncommon Ground: Archaeology and Early African America, 1650–1800* (Washington, DC: Smithsonian Institution Press, 1992).

Fogel, Robert William: *Without Consent or Contract: The Rise and Fall of American Slavery* (New York: W. W. Norton, 1989).

Franklin, John Hope and Schweninger, Loren: *Runaway Slaves: Rebels on the Plantation* (New York: Oxford University Press, 1999).

Franklin, Maria: "Out of Site, Out of Mind: The Archaeology of an Enslaved Virginian Household, ca. 1740–1778" (Ph.D. dissertation, University of California, Berkeley, 1997).

Fredrickson, George M.: *White Supremacy: A Comparative Study in American and South African History* (New York: Oxford University Press, 1981).

Frey, Sylvia R. and Wood, Betty: *Come Shouting to Zion: African American Protestantism in the American South and British Caribbean to 1830* (Chapel Hill, NC: University of North Carolina Press, 1998).

Gaspar, David Barry: *Bondsmen and Rebels: A Study of Master–Slave Relations from Antigua with Implications for Colonial British America* (Baltimore, MD: Johns Hopkins University Press, 1985).

Gaspar, David Barry and Hine, Darlene Clark, eds.: *More than Chattel: Black Women and Slavery in the Americas* (Bloomington, IN: Indiana University Press, 1996).

Gates, Henry Louis, Jr.: *The Signifying Monkey: A Theory of African–American Literary Criticism* (New York: Oxford University Press, 1988).

Gomez, Michael A.: *Exchanging Our Country Marks: The Transformation of African Identities in the Colonial and Antebellum South* (Chapel Hill, NC: University of North Carolina Press, 1998).

Goveia, Elsa V.: *Slave Society in the British Leeward Islands at the End of the Eighteenth Century* (New Haven, CT: Yale University Press, 1965).

Greene, Lorenzo Johnston: *The Negro in Colonial New England* (New York: Columbia University Press, 1942).

Guasco, Michael J.: "Encounters, Identities, and Human Bondage: The Foundations of Racial Slavery in the Anglo-Atlantic World" (Ph.D. dissertation, College of William and Mary, 2000).

Gutman, Herbert G.: *The Black Family in Slavery and Freedom, 1750–1925* (Oxford: Blackwell, 1976).

Hadden, Sally E.: *Slave Patrols: Law and Violence in Virginia and the Carolinas* (Cambridge, MA: Harvard University Press, 2001).

Hall, Douglas: *In Miserable Slavery: Thomas Thistlewood in Jamaica, 1750–86* (London: Macmillan, 1989).

Hall, Gwendolyn Midlo: *Africans in Colonial Louisiana: The Development of Afro-Creole Culture in the Eighteenth Century* (Baton Rouge, LA: Louisiana State University Press, 1992).

Hall, Gwendolyn Midlo: *Databases for the Study of Afro-Louisiana History and Genealogy 1699–1860: Computerized Information from Original Manuscript Sources* (Baton Rouge, LA: Louisiana State University Press, 2000).

Hall, Kim F.: *Things of Darkness: Economies of Race and Gender in Early Modern England* (Ithaca, NY: Cornell University Press, 1995).

Handler, Jerome S. and Lange, Frederick: *Plantation Slavery in Barbados: An Archaeological and Historical Investigation* (Cambridge, MA: Harvard University Press, 1978).

Hanger, Kimberly: *Bounded Lives, Bounded Places: Free Black Society in Colonial New Orleans, 1769–1803* (Durham, NC: Duke University Press, 1997).

Hannaford, Ivan: *Race: The History of an Idea in the West* (Washington, DC: The Woodrow Wilson Center Press and Johns Hopkins University Press, 1996).

Harms, Robert: *River of Wealth, River of Sorrows: The Central Zaire Basin in the Era of the Slave and Ivory Trade, 1500–1891* (New Haven, CT: Yale University Press, 1981).

Hastings, Adrian: *The Church in Africa, 1450–1950* (Oxford: Clarendon Press, 1994).

Haviser, Jay B., ed.: *African Sites: Archaeology in the Caribbean* (Princeton, NJ: Markus Wiener Publishers, 1999).

Heckscher, Jurretta Jordan: "'All the Mazes of the Dance': Black Dancing, Culture, and Identity in the Greater Chesapeake World from the Early Eighteenth Century to the Civil War" (Ph.D. dissertation, George Washington University, 2000).

Higman, B. W.: *Slave Populations of the British Caribbean 1807–1834* (Baltimore, MD: Johns Hopkins University Press, 1984a).

Higman, B. W.: *Montpelier, Jamaica: A Plantation Community in Slavery and Freedom, 1739–1912* (Kingston: The University Press of the West Indies, 1998).

Hodes, Martha, ed.: *Sex, Love, Race: Crossing Boundaries in North American History* (New York: New York University Press, 1999).

Hodges, Graham Russell: *Slavery and Freedom in the Rural North: African-Americans in Monmouth County, New Jersey, 1665–1865* (Madison, WI: Madison House, 1997).

Hodges, Graham Russell: *Root & Branch: African Americans in New York & East Jersey, 1613–1863* (Chapel Hill, NC: University of North Carolina Press, 1999).

Holm, John A.: *Pidgins and Creoles, I, Theory and Structure* and *II, Reference Survey* (Cambridge: Cambridge University Press, 1988–89).

Ingersoll, Thomas N.: *Mammon and Manon in Early New Orleans: The First Slave Society in the Deep South, 1718–1819* (Knoxville, TN: University of Tennessee Press, 1999).

John, Ann Meredith: *The Plantation Slaves of Trinidad, 1783–1816* (Cambridge: Cambridge University Press, 1988).

Johnson, Walter: *Soul by Soul: Life inside the Antebellum Slave Market* (Cambridge, MA: Harvard University Press, 1999).

Jordan, Winthrop D.: *White over Black: American Attitudes toward the Negro, 1550–1812* (Chapel Hill, NC: University of North Carolina Press, 1968).

Kay, Marvin L. Michael and Cary, Lorin Lee: *Slavery in North Carolina, 1748–1775* (Chapel Hill, NC: University of North Carolina Press, 1995).

King, Wilma: *Stolen Childhood: Slave Youth in Nineteenth-Century America* (Bloomington, IN: Indiana University Press, 1995).

Klein, Herbert S.: *Slavery in the Americas: A Comparative Study of Cuba and Virginia* (Chicago: University of Chicago Press, 1967).

Klein, Herbert S.: *The Atlantic Slave Trade* (New York: Cambridge University Press, 1999).

Klein, Martin A.: *Slavery and Colonial Rule in French West Africa* (Cambridge: Cambridge University Press, 1998).

Knight, Franklin W., ed.: *The Slave Societies of the Caribbean*, vol. 3, *General History of the Caribbean* (London: Unesco Publishing/Macmillan, 1997).

Knight, Franklin W. and Liss, Peggy K., eds.: *Atlantic Port Cities: Economy, Culture, and Society in the Atlantic World, 1650–1850* (Knoxville, TN: University of Tennessee Press, 1991).

Kolchin, Peter: *Unfree Labor: American Slavery and Russian Serfdom* (Cambridge, MA: Harvard University Press, 1987).

Kolchin, Peter: *American Slavery, 1619–1877* (New York: Hill and Wang, 1993).

Komlos, John: *The Biological Standard of Living in Europe and America, 1700–1900: Studies in Anthropometric History* (Aldershot, England: Variorum, 1996).

Kopytoff, Igor and Miers, Suzanne, eds.: *Slavery in Africa: Historical and Anthropological Perspectives* (Madison, WI: University of Wisconsin Press, 1977).

Krise, Thomas W., ed.: *Caribbeana: An Anthology of English Literature of the West Indies, 1657–1777* (Chicago: University of Chicago Press, 1999).

Kulikoff, Allan: *Tobacco and Slaves: The Development of Southern Cultures in the Chesapeake* (Chapel Hill, NC: University of North Carolina Press, 1986).

Kupperman, Karen Ordahl: *Providence Island, 1630–1641: The Other Puritan Colony* (New York: Cambridge University Press, 1993).

Lalla, Barbara and D'Costa, Jean: *Language in Exile: Three Hundred Years of Jamaican Creole* (Tuscaloosa, AL: University of Alabama Press, 1990).

Landers, Jane G., ed.: *Against the Odds: Free Blacks in the Slave Societies of the Americas* (London: Frank Cass, 1996).

Landers, Jane: *Black Society in Spanish Florida* (Urbana, IL: University of Illinois Press, 1999).

Law, Robin: *The Slave Coast of West Africa: The Impact of the Atlantic Slave Trade on an African Society* (Oxford: Clarendon, 1991).

Lewis, Bernard: *Race and Slavery in the Middle East: An Historical Enquiry* (New York: Oxford University Press, 1990).

Lewis, Jan Ellen and Onuf, Peter S., eds.: *Sally Hemings and Thomas Jefferson: History, Memory, and Civic Culture* (Charlottesville, VA: University Press of Virginia, 1999).

Lewis, Ronald L.: *Coal, Iron, and Slaves: Industrial Slavery in Maryland and Virginia, 1715–1865* (Westport, CT: Garland Press, 1979).

Linebaugh, Peter and Rediker, Marcus: *The Many-Headed Hydra: Sailors, Slaves, Commoners, and the Hidden History of the Revolutionary Atlantic* (Boston, MA: Beacon Press, 2000).

Lovejoy, Paul E.: *Transformations in Slavery: A History of Slavery in Africa*, 2nd ed. (Cambridge: Cambridge University Press, 2000).

Lucas, Marion B.: *A History of Blacks in Kentucky*, vol. 1, *From Slavery to Segregation, 1760–1891* (Frankfort, KY: The Kentucky Historical Society, 1992).

Malcolmson, Scott L.: *One Drop of Blood: The American Misadventure of Race* (New York: Farrar, Straus, Giroux, 2000).

Manning, Patrick: *Slavery and African Life: Occidental, Oriental, and African Slave Trades* (Cambridge: Cambridge University Press, 1990).

Matar, Nabil: *Turks, Moors, and Englishmen in the Age of Discovery* (New York: Columbia University Press, 1999).

McDonald, Roderick A.: *The Economy and Material Conditions of Slaves: Goods and Chattels on the Sugar Plantations of Jamaica and Louisiana* (Baton Rouge, LA: Louisiana State University Press, 1993).

Melish, Joanne Pope: *Disowning Slavery: Gradual Emancipation and "Race" in New England, 1780–1860* (Ithaca, NY: Cornell University Press, 1998).

Miers, Suzanne and Kopytoff, Igor, eds.: *Slavery in Africa: Historical and Anthropological Perspectives* (Madison, WI: University of Wisconsin Press, 1977).

Miller, Joseph C., ed.: *Slavery and Slaving in World History: A Bibliography, 1900–1996*, 2 vols (Armonk, NY: M. E. Sharpe, 1999).

Mintz, Sidney W. and Price, Richard: *The Birth of African-American Culture* (Boston, MA: Beacon Press, 1992).

Morgan, Edmund S.: *American Slavery, American Freedom: The Ordeal of Colonial Virginia* (New York: W. W. Norton, 1975).

Morgan, Philip D.: *Slave Counterpoint: Black Culture in the Eighteenth-Century Chesapeake and Lowcountry* (Chapel Hill, NC: University of North Carolina Press, 1998).

Morris, Thomas D.: *Southern Slavery and the Law, 1619–1860* (Chapel Hill, NC: University of North Carolina Press, 1996).

Mullin, Gerald W.: *Flight and Rebellion: Slave Resistance in Eighteenth-Century Virginia* (New York: Oxford University Press, 1972).

Mullin, Michael: *Africa in America: Slave Acculturation in the American South and the British Caribbean, 1736–1831* (Urbana, IL: University of Illinois Press, 1992).

Nash, Gary B.: *Forging Freedom: The Formation of Philadelphia's Black Community, 1720–1840* (Cambridge, MA: Harvard University Press, 1987).

Northrup, David: *Trade Without Rulers: Pre-Colonial Economic Development in South-Eastern Nigeria* (Oxford: Clarendon Press, 1978).

Nwokeji, G. Ugo: "The Biafran Frontier: Trade, Slaves, and Society, c. 1750–1905" (Ph.D. dissertation, University of Toronto, 1999).

Olwell, Robert: *Masters, Slaves, & Subjects: The Culture of Power in the South Carolina Low Country, 1740–1790* (Ithaca, NY: Cornell University Press, 1998).

Olwig, Karen Fog: *Cultural Adaptation and Resistance on St. John: Three Centuries of Afro-Caribbean Life* (Gainesville, FL: University of Florida Press, 1985).

Palmie, Stephan, ed.: *Slave Cultures and the Cultures of Slavery* (Knoxville, TN: University of Tennessee Press, 1995).

Patterson, Orlando: *The Sociology of Slavery: An Analysis of the Origins, Development, and Structure of Negro Slave Society in Jamaica* (Rutherford, NJ: Farleigh Dickinson University Press, 1969 [1967]).

Patterson, Orlando: *Slavery and Social Death: A Comparative Study* (Cambridge, MA: Harvard University Press, 1982).

Patterson, Orlando: *Freedom*, vol. 1, *Freedom in the Making of Western Culture* (New York: Basic Books, 1991).

Patton, Sharon F.: *African-American Art* (New York: Oxford University Press, 1998).

Perdue, Theda: *Slavery and the Evolution of Cherokee Society, 1540–1866* (Knoxville, TN: University of Tennessee Press, 1979).

Perkins, Elizabeth A.: *Border Life: Experience and Memory in the Revolutionary Ohio Valley* (Chapel Hill, NC: University of North Carolina Press, 1998).

Phillips, William D. Jr.: *Slavery from Roman Times to the Early Transatlantic Trade* (Minneapolis, MN: University of Minnesota Press, 1985).

Piersen, William D.: *Black Yankees: The Development of an Afro-American Subculture in Eighteenth-Century New England* (Amherst, MA: University of Massachusetts Press, 1988).

Potkay, Adam and Burr, Sandra, eds.: *Black Atlantic Writers of the 18th Century: Living the Exodus in England and the Americas* (New York: St. Martin's Press, 1995)

Price, Richard, ed.: *Maroon Societies: Rebel Slave Communities in the Americas*, 2nd ed. (Baltimore, MD: Johns Hopkins University Press, 1979).

Roberts, Richard: *Warriors, Merchants, and Slaves* (Stanford, CA: Stanford University Press, 1987).

Saillant, John: *Black Puritan, Black Republican: Faith and Antislavery in the Life of Lemuel Haynes, 1753–1833* (New York: Oxford University Press, forthcoming).

Saunt, Claudio: *A New Order of Things: Property, Power, and the Transformation of the Creek Indians, 1733–1816* (New York: Cambridge University Press, 1999).

Schwartz, Marie Jenkins: *Born in Bondage: Growing up Enslaved in the Antebellum South* (Cambridge, MA: Harvard University Press, 2000).

Schwarz, Philip J.: *Twice Condemned: Slaves and Criminal Laws of Virginia, 1705–1865* (Baton Rouge, LA: Louisiana State University Press, 1988).

Searing, James F.: *West African Slavery and Atlantic Commerce: The Senegal Valley, 1700–1860* (New York: Cambridge University Press, 1993).

Sensbach, Jon F.: *A Separate Canaan: The Making of an Afro-Moravian World in North Carolina, 1763–1840* (Chapel Hill, NC: University of North Carolina Press, 1998).

Shepherd, Verene, and Hilary McD. Beckles, eds.: *Caribbean Slavery in the Atlantic World: A Student Reader* (Princeton, NJ: Markus Wiener, 2000).

Sheridan, Richard B.: *Doctors and Slaves: A Medical and Demographic History of Slavery in the British West Indies, 1680–1834* (New York: Cambridge University Press, 1985).

Sidbury, James: *Ploughshares into Swords: Race, Rebellion, and Identity in Gabriel's Virginia, 1730–1810* (New York: Cambridge University Press, 1997).

Singleton, Theresa A.: *"I, Too, Am America": Archaeological Studies of African-American Life* (Charlottesville, VA: University of Virginia Press, 1999).

Sobel, Mechal: *Trabelin' On: The Slave Journey to an Afro-Baptist Faith* (Westport, CT: Greenwood Press, 1979).

Sobel, Mechal: *The World They Made Together: Black and White Values in Eighteenth-Century Virginia* (Princeton, NJ: Princeton University Press, 1987).

Solow, Barbara L., ed.: *Slavery and the Rise of the Atlantic System* (New York: Cambridge University Press, 1991).

Spear, Jennifer M.: *"'Whiteness and the Purity of Blood': Race, Sexuality, and Social Order in Colonial Louisiana"* (Ph.D. dissertation, University of Minnesota, 1999).

Tannenbaum, Frank: *Slave and Citizen: The Negro in the Americas* (New York: Alfred A. Knopf, 1946).

Taylor, Quintard: *In Search of the Racial Frontier: African Americans in the American West, 1528–1990* (New York: W. W. Norton, 1998).

Thornton, John: *Africa and Africans in the Making of the Atlantic World, 1400–1800*, 2nd ed. (Cambridge: Cambridge University Press, 1998a).

Tobin, Beth Fowkes: *Picturing Imperial Power: Colonial Subjects in Eighteenth-Century British Painting* (Durham, NC: Duke University Press, 1999).

Turley, David: *Slavery* (Oxford: Blackwell, 2000).

Usner, Daniel: *Indians, Settlers, and Slaves in a Frontier Exchange Economy: The Lower Mississippi Valley before 1803* (Chapel Hill, NC: University of North Carolina Press, 1992).

Vaughan, Alden T.: *Roots of American Racism: Essays on the Colonial Experience* (New York: Oxford University Press, 1995).

Vlach, John Michael: *The Afro-American Tradition in Decorative Arts* (Cleveland, OH: Cleveland Museum of Art, 1978).

Vlach, John Michael: *Back of the Big House: The Architecture of Plantation Slavery* (Chapel Hill, NC: University of North Carolina Press, 1993).

Walsh, Lorena S.: *From Calabar to Carter's Grove: The History of a Virginia Slave Community* (Charlottesville, VA: University of Virginia Press, 1997).

Ward, J. R.: *British West Indian Slavery, 1750–1834: The Process of Amelioration* (Oxford: Clarendon Press, 1988).

Weber, David: *The Spanish Frontier in North America* (New Haven, CT: Yale University Press, 1992).

Welch, Pedro V.: "The Urban Context of the Slave Plantation System" (Ph.D. dissertation, University of the West Indies, Cave Hill, 1995).

Wheatley, Phillis: *Complete Writings*, ed. Vincent Carretta (New York: Penguin Putnam, 2001).

Wheeler, Roxann: *The Complexion of Race: Categories of Difference in Eighteenth-Century British Culture* (Philadelphia: University of Pennsylvania Press, 2000).

White, Shane and White, Graham: *Stylin': African American Expressive Culture from its Beginnings to the Zoot Suit* (Ithaca, NY: Cornell University Press, 1998).

Wiencek, Henry: *The Hairstons: An American Family in Black and White* (New York: St. Martin's Press, 1999).

Williams, William H.: *Slavery and Freedom in Delaware, 1639–1865* (Wilmington, DE: Scholarly Resources, Inc., 1996).

Wood, Betty: *Slavery in Colonial Georgia, 1730–1775* (Athens, GA: University of Georgia Press, 1984).

Wood, Betty: *Women's Work, Men's Work: The Informal Slave Economies of Lowcountry Georgia* (Athens, GA: University of Georgia Press, 1995).

Wood, Betty: *The Origins of American Slavery: Freedom and Bondage in the English Colonies* (New York: Hill and Wang, 1997).

Wood, Marcus: *Blind Memory: Visual Representations of Slavery in England and America, 1780–1865* (New York: Routledge, 2000).

Wood, Peter H.: *Black Majority: Negroes in Colonial South Carolina from 1670 through the Stono Rebellion* (New York: Alfred A. Knopf, 1974).

Wyatt-Brown, Bertram: *The Shaping of Southern Culture: Honor, Grace, and War, 1760s–1880s* (Chapel Hill, NC: University of North Carolina Press, 2001).

Articles and Essays

"AHR Forum: Crossing Slavery's Boundaries." With contributions from David Brion Davis, Peter Kolchin, Rebecca J. Scott, and Stanley L. Engerman. *American Historical Review* 105 (2000), pp. 451–84.

Austen, Ralph A.: "The Slave Trade as History and Memory: Confrontations of Slaving Voyage Documents and Communal Traditions." *William and Mary Quarterly* [hereafter, *WMQ*] 3rd ser., 58 (2001), pp. 229–51.

Aylmer, G. E.: "Slavery under Charles II: The Mediterranean and Tangier." *English Historical Review* 114 (1999), pp. 378–88.

Behrendt, Stephen D.: "Markets, Transaction Cycles, and Profits: Merchant Decision Making in the British Slave Trade." *WMQ* 3rd ser., 58 (2001), pp. 171–204.

Behrendt, Stephen D., Eltis, David, and Richardson, David: "The Costs of Coercion: African Agency in the Pre-modern Atlantic World." *Economic History Review* 14 (2001), pp. 454–76.

Bezis-Selfa, John: "Slavery and the Disciplining of Free Labor in the Colonial Mid-Atlantic Iron Industry." *Pennsylvania History* 64, special supplemental issue (Summer, 1997), pp. 270–86.

Bowen, Joanne: "Foodways in the Eighteenth-Century Chesapeake." In Theodore R. Reinhart, ed., *The Archaeology of Eighteenth-Century Virginia* (Richmond, VA: Archaeological Society of Virginia, 1996), pp. 87–130.

Braund, Kathryn E. Holland: "The Creek Indians, Blacks, and Slavery." *Journal of Southern History* 57 (1991), pp. 601–37.

Brown, Christopher L.: "Empire without Slaves: British Concepts of Emancipation in the Age of the American Revolution." *WMQ* 3rd ser., 56 (1999), pp. 273–306.

Brown, Kathleen: "Native Americans and Early Modern Concepts of Race." In Martin Daunton and Rick Halpern, eds., *Empire and Others: British Encounters with Indigenous Peoples, 1600–1800* (London: University College London Press, 1999), pp. 79–100.

Burnard, Trevor: "E Pluribus Plures: African Ethnicities in Seventeenth- and Eighteenth-Century Jamaica." *Jamaican Historical Review* (forthcoming, 2000).

Burnard, Trevor: "Slave Naming Patterns: Onomastics and the Taxonomy of Race in Eighteenth-Century Jamaica." *Journal of Interdisciplinary History*, 31 (Winter 2001), pp. 325–46.

Burnard, Trevor and Morgan, Kenneth: "The Dynamics of the Slave Market and Slave Purchasing Patterns in Jamaica, 1655–1788." *WMQ* 3rd ser., 58 (2001), pp. 205–28.

Carretta, Vincent: "Olaudah Equiano or Gustavus Vassa? New Light on an Eighteenth-Century Question of Identity." *Slavery and Abolition: A Journal of Slave and Post-Slave Studies* [hereafter *Slavery & Abolition*] 20 (1999), pp. 96–105.

Clark, Emily and Gould, Virginia Meacham: "The Feminine Face of Afro-Catholicism in New Orleans, 1727–1852." *WMQ* 3rd ser., 59 (2002), pp. 409–48.

Cody, Cheryl Ann: "There was no 'Absalom' on the Ball Plantations: Slave-Naming Practices in the South Carolina Low Country, 1720–1865." *American Historical Review* 92 (1987), pp. 563–96.

"Constructing Race: Differentiating Peoples in the Early Modern World." With contributions from David Brion Davis, Alden T. Vaughan and Virginia Mason Vaughan, Emily C. Bartels, Robin Blackburn, Benjamin Braude, James H. Sweet, Jennifer L. Morgan, Karen Ordahl Kupperman, and Joyce E. Chaplin: *WMQ* 3rd ser., 54 (1997).

Craton, Michael: "Changing Patterns of Slave Families in the British West Indies." *Journal of Interdisciplinary History* 10 (1979), pp. 1–35.

Davis, David Brion: "At the Heart of Slavery." *New York Review of Books* (Oct. 17 1996), pp. 51–4.

Davis, Robert Charles: "Counting European Slaves on the Barbary Coast". *Past and Present* 172 (Aug. 2001), pp. 87–124.

Desrochers, Robert E.: "Souls for Money: Slave-for-sale Advertisements and Slavery in Massachusetts, 1704–1760." *WMQ* (forthcoming).

Diouf, Sylviane A.: "*Sadaqa* among African Muslims Enslaved in the Americas." *Journal of Islamic Studies* 10 (1999), pp. 22–32.

Dunn, Richard S.: "A Tale of Two Plantations: Slave Life at Mesopotamia in Jamaica and Mount Airy in Virginia 1799 to 1828." *WMQ* 3rd ser., 34 (1977), pp. 32–65.

Eltis, David: "The Volume and Structure of the Transatlantic Slave Trade: A Reassessment." *WMQ* 3rd ser., 58 (2001), pp. 17–46.

Engerman, Stanley L., Haines, Robin, Klein, Herbert S., and Shlomowitz, Ralph: "Transoceanic Mortality: The Slave Trade in Comparative Perspective." *WMQ* 3rd ser., 58 (2001), pp. 93–117.

Eslinger, Ellen: "The Shape of Slavery on the Kentucky Frontier, 1775–1800." *Register of the Kentucky Historical Society* 92 (1994), pp. 1–23.

"Forum: Thomas Jefferson and Sally Hemings redux." With contributions from Jan Lewis, Joseph J. Ellis, Lucia Stanton, Peter S. Onuf, Annette Gordon-Reed, Andrew Burstein, and Fraser D. Neiman: *WMQ* 3rd ser., 57 (2000), pp. 121–210.

Gilje, Paul A. and Rock, Howard B.: "'Sweep O! Sweep O!': African-American Chimney Sweeps and Citizenship in the New Nation." *WMQ* 3rd ser., 51 (1994), pp. 507–38.

Goldenberg, David M.: "The Development of the Idea of Race: Classical Paradigms and Medieval Elaborations." *International Journal of the Classical Tradition* 5 (1999), pp. 561–70.

Greene, Jack P.: "Beyond Power: Paradigm Subversion and Reformulation and the Re-creation of the Early Modern Atlantic World." In Darlene Clark Hine and Jacqueline McLeod, eds., *Crossing Boundaries: Comparative History of Black People in Diaspora* (Bloomington: Indiana University Press., 1999), pp. 319–42.

Greene, Jack P.: "'A Plain and Natural Right to Life and Liberty': An Early Natural Rights
Attack on the Excesses of the Slave System in Colonial British America." *WMQ* 3rd ser., 57
(2000), pp. 793–808.

Hair, P. E. H. and Law, Robin: "The English in Western Africa to 1700." In Nicholas Canny,
ed., *The Oxford History of the British Empire*, vol. 1, *The Origins of Empire: British Overseas
Enterprise to the Close of the Seventeenth Century* (Oxford: Oxford University Press, 1998), pp.
241–63.

Handler, Jerome S. and Jacoby, JoAnn: "Slave Names and Naming in Barbados, 1650–1830."
WMQ 3rd ser., 53 (1996), pp. 685–728.

Hart, William B.: "Black 'Go-Betweens' and the Mutability of 'Race,' Status, and Identity on
New York's Pre-Revolutionary Frontier." In Andrew R. L. Cayton and Fredrika J. Teute,
eds., *Contact Points: American Frontiers from the Mohawk Valley to the Mississippi, 1750–1830*
(Chapel Hill, NC: University of North Carolina Press, 1998), pp. 88–113.

Hawthorne, Walter: "The Production of Slaves Where There Was No State: The Guinea-Bissau
region, 1450–1815." *Slavery & Abolition* 20 (1999), pp. 97–124.

Hawthorne, Walter: "Nourishing a Stateless Society during the Slave Trade: The Rise of Balanta
Paddy-Rice Production in Guinea-Bissau." *Journal of African History* 42 (2001), pp. 1–24.

Higman, B. W.: "African and Creole Slave Family Patterns in Trinidad." *Journal of Family
History* 3 (1978), pp. 163–80.

Higman, B. W.: "Terms for Kin in the British West Indian Slave Community: Differing Perceptions of Masters and Slaves." In Raymond T. Smith, ed., *Kinship Ideology and Practice in
Latin America* (Chapel Hill, NC: University of North Carolina Press, 1984b), pp. 59–81.

Hudson, Nicholas: "From 'Nation' to 'Race': The Origin of Racial Classification in Eighteenth-
Century Thought." *Eighteenth-Century Studies* 29 (1996), pp. 247–64.

Jacoby, Karl: "Slaves by Nature? Domestic Animals and Human Slaves." *Slavery & Abolition*,
15 (1994), pp. 89–97.

Jarvis, Michael: "Maritime Masters and Seafaring Slaves: Race, Family, and Labor on Bermuda,
1680–1783." *WMQ* (forthcoming).

Kea, Ray: "'When I Die, I Shall Return to My Own Land': An 'Amina' Slave Rebellion in the
Danish West Indies, 1733–1734." In John Hunwick and Nancy Lawler, eds., *The Cloth of
Many Colored Silks: Papers on History and Society Ghanian and Islamic in Honor of Ivor Wilks*
(Evanston: Northwestern University Press, 1992), pp. 159–93.

Klein, Martin A.: "The Slave Trade and Decentralized Societies." *Journal of African History* 42
(2001), pp. 40–65.

Klepp, Susan E.: "Seasoning and Society: Racial Differences in Mortality in Eighteenth-Century
Philadelphia." *WMQ* 3rd ser., 51 (1994), pp. 473–506.

Kriz, Kay Dian: "Curiosities, Commodities, and Transplanted Bodies in Hans Sloane's 'Natural
History of Jamaica.'" *WMQ* 3rd ser., 57 (2000), pp. 35–78.

Lacey, Barbara E.: "Visual Images of Blacks in Early American Imprints." *WMQ* 3rd ser., 53
(1996), pp. 137–80.

Law, Robin: "Ethnicity and the Slave Trade: 'Lucumi' and 'Nago' as Ethnonyms in West Africa.' *History in Africa*, 24 (1997), 205–219.

Law, Robin and Mann, Kristin: "West Africa in the Atlantic Community: The Case of the Slave
Coast." *WMQ* 3rd ser., 56 (1999), pp. 307–34.

Lovejoy, Paul E. and Richardson, David: "Trust, Pawnship, and Atlantic History: The Institutional Foundations of the Old Calabar Slave Trade." *American Historical Review* 104 (1999),
pp. 333–55.

Lovejoy, Paul E. and Richardson, David: "The Business of Slaving: Pawnship in Western Africa,
c. 1600–1810." *Journal of African History* 42 (2001), pp. 67–89.

MacGaffey, Wyatt: "Dialogues of the Deaf: Europeans on the Atlantic Coast of Africa." In
Stuart B. Schwartz, ed., *Implicit Understandings: Observing, Reporting, and Reflecting on the*

Encounters between Europeans and Other Peoples in the Early Modern Era (New York: Cambridge University Press, 1994), pp. 249–67.

McLoughlin, William G.: "Red Indians, Black Slavery, and White Racism: America's Slaveholding Indians." *American Quarterly* 26 (1974), pp. 366–83.

Menard, Russell R.: "Transitions to African Slavery in British America, 1630–1730: Barbados, Virginia, and South Carolina." *Indian Historical Review* 15 (1988–89), pp. 33–49.

Menard, Russell R. and Schwartz, Stuart B.: "Why African Slavery? Labor Force Transitions in Brazil, Mexico, and the Carolina Lowcountry." In Wolfgang Binder, ed., *Slavery in the Americas* (Wurzburg: Konigshausen & Neumann, 1993), pp. 89–114.

Merrell, James H.: "The Racial Education of the Catawba Indians." *Journal of Southern History* 50 (1984), pp. 363–84.

Miller, Joseph C. and Holloran, John R.: "Slavery: Annual Bibliographical Supplement (1999)." *Slavery & Abolition* 21 (2000), pp. 176–283.

Minkema, Kenneth P.: "Jonathan Edwards on Slavery and the Slave Trade." *WMQ* 3rd ser., 54 (1997), pp. 823–34.

Mintz, Sidney W.: "Slave Life on Caribbean Sugar Plantations: Some Unanswered Questions." In Stephen Palmie, ed., *Slave Cultures and the Culture of Slaves* (Knoxville, TN: University of Tennessee Press, 1995), pp. 12–22.

Morgan, Philip D.: "Black Life in Eighteenth-Century Charleston." *Perspectives in American History*, 1 n.s. (1984), pp. 187–232.

Morgan, Philip D.: "British Encounters with Africans and African-Americans, circa 1600–1780." In Bernard Bailyn and Philip D. Morgan, eds., *Strangers within the Realm: Cultural Margins of the First British Empire* (Chapel Hill, NC: University of North Carolina Press, 1991), pp. 157–219.

Morgan, Philip D.: "Slaves and Livestock in Eighteenth-Century Jamaica: Vineyard Pen, 1750–1751." *WMQ* 3rd ser., 52 (1995), pp. 47–76.

Morgan, Philip D.: "The Cultural Implications of the Atlantic Slave Trade: African Regional Origins, American Destinations and New World Developments," In David Eltis and David Richardson, eds., *Routes to Slavery* (London: Frank Cass Publishers, 1997), pp. 122–45.

Northrup, David: "Igbo and Myth Igbo: Culture and Ethnicity in the Atlantic World, 1600–1850." *Slavery & Abolition* 21 (2000), pp. 1–20.

Nwokeji, G. Ugo: "African Conceptions of Gender and the Slave Traffic." *WMQ* 3rd ser., 58 (2001), pp. 47–67.

Price, Richard: "The Miracle of Creolization, A Retrospective." *New West Indian Guide*, 75 (2001), pp. 35–64.

Prude, Jonathan: "To Look upon the 'Lower Sort': Runaway Ads and the Appearance of Unfree Laborers in America." *Journal of American History* 78 (1991), pp. 124–60.

Rath, Richard Cullen: "African Music in Seventeenth-Century Jamaica: Cultural Transit and Transmission." *WMQ* 3rd ser., 50 (1993), pp. 700–26.

Rath, Richard Cullen: "Drums and Power: Ways of Creolizing Music in Coastal South Carolina and Georgia, 1730–90." In David Buisseret, ed., *Creolization in the Americas* (College Station, TX: Texas A&M University Press, 2000), pp. 99–130.

Richardson, David: "Shipboard Revolts, African Authority, and the Atlantic Slave Trade." *WMQ* 3rd ser., 58 (2001), pp. 69–92.

Rickford, John R. and Handler, Jerome S.: "Textual evidence on the nature of early Barbadian speech, 1676–1835." *Journal of Pidgin and Creole Languages*, 9 (1994), pp. 221–55.

Samford, Patricia: "The Archaeology of African-American Slavery and Material Culture." *WMQ* 3rd ser., 53 (1996), pp. 87–114.

Saunt, Claudio: "'The English Has Now a Mind to Make Slaves of Them All': Creeks, Seminoles, and the Problem of Slavery." *American Indian Quarterly* 22 (1998), pp. 157–80.

Scott, Julius S.: "Afro-American Sailors and the International Communication Network: The

Case of Newport Bowers." In Colin Howell and Richard J. Twomey, eds., *Jack Tar in History: Essays in the History of Maritime Life and Labor* (Fredericton, New Brunswick: Acadiensis Press, 1991), pp. 37–52.

Scott, Julius S.: "Crisscrossing Empires: Ships, Sailors, and Resistance in the Lesser Antilles in the Eighteenth Century." In Robert L. Paquette and Stanley L. Engerman, eds., *The Lesser Antilles in the Eighteenth Century* (Gainesville, FL: University Press of Florida, 1996), pp. 128–43.

Seeman, Erik R: "'Justise Must Take Plase': Three African Americans Speak of Religion in Eighteenth-Century New England." *WMQ* 3rd ser., 56 (1999), pp. 393–414.

Shaw, Rosalind: "The Production of Witchcraft/Witchcraft as Production: Memory, Modernity, and the Slave Trade in Sierra Leone." *American Ethnologist* 24 (1997), pp. 856–76.

Sparks, Randy: "The Two Princes of Calabar: An Atlantic Odyssey from Slavery to Freedom." *WMQ* (forthcoming).

Steckel, Richard H.: "Nutritional Status in the Colonial American Economy." *WMQ* 3rd ser., 56 (1999), pp. 31–52.

Thornton, John: "Central African Names and African-American Naming Patterns." *WMQ* 3rd ser., 50 (1993), pp. 727–42.

Thornton, John: "The African Experience of the '20 and odd Negroes' Arriving in Virginia in 1619." *WMQ* 3rd ser., 55 (1998b), pp. 421–34.

Thornton, John: "The Coromantees: An African Cultural Group in Colonial North America and the Caribbean." *Journal of Caribbean History*, 32 (1998c), pp. 161–78.

Thornton, John K.: "War, the State, and Religious Norms in 'Coromantee' Thought: The Ideology of an African American Nation." In Robert Blair St. George, ed., *Possible Pasts: Becoming Colonial in Early America* (Ithaca, NY: Cornell University Press, 2000), pp. 181–200.

Usner, Daniel H., Jr.: "Indian–Black Relations in Colonial and Antebellum Louisiana." In Stephen Palmie, ed., *Slave Cultures and the Culture of Slaves* (Knoxville, TN: University of Tennessee Press, 1995), pp. 145–61.

Waldstreicher, David: "Reading the Runaways: Self-Fashioning, Print Culture, and Confidence in Slavery in the Eighteenth-Century Mid-Atlantic." *WMQ* 3rd ser., 56 (1999), pp. 243–72.

Walsh, Lorena S.: "The African American Population of the Colonial United States." In Michael R. Haines and Richard H. Stecke, eds., *A Population History of North America* (Cambridge: Cambridge University Press, 2000), pp. 191–240.

White, Shane: "'It Was a Proud Day': African Americans, Festivals and Parades in the North, 1741–1834." *Journal of American History* 81 (1994), pp. 13–50.

White, Shane and White, Graham: "'Us Likes a Mixtery': Listening to African-American Slave Music." *Slavery & Abolition* 20 (1999), pp. 22–48.

Whitman, Stephen T: "Industrial Slavery at the Margin: The Maryland Chemical Works." *Journal of Southern History* 59 (1993), pp. 31–62.

CHAPTER EIGHT

Economy

MARGARET NEWELL

America in the twenty-first century stands as the lone superpower in more ways than one. Of its economic rivals from the last half of the twentieth century, only China seems poised to challenge America's dominance in the foreseeable future. Some look on our prosperity with envy and admiration and burn to emulate it; others express scorn for our materialism and resent our reckless, outsized consumption of global resources. Nonetheless, for people around the globe America remains the sine qua non of sustained economic development in the modern era.

It is tempting to frame a study of the colonial economy with these present-day successes in mind. But a celebratory narrative of America's march to economic success ignores the fact that growth and development are not inevitable; they are historical contingencies that need explaining. For proof, we have only to look at the efforts of so-called developing nations in the contemporary era to diversify their economies and deliver an acceptable standard of living to their citizens. In much of Africa, Asia, and Latin America today, politicians and entrepreneurs face the difficult task of establishing new industries and creating an infrastructure in the context of an extremely competitive global economy in which more developed nations have a head start. As producers of raw materials, many face an uphill battle. Resource-rich countries such as Brazil and Nigeria still struggle to reduce their neo-colonial dependence on shifting First World markets and to meet domestic demand for consumer goods without incurring crippling trade deficits or hyperinflation. They know that foreign investment capital often comes at a high price – the sacrifice of some local sovereignty. And, even those nations that most eagerly embrace the market must cope with the mobility, diversity, and challenges to cultural traditions that often accompany capitalism.

We shake our heads at their failures, the persistent political corruption, the defaults on IMF and World Bank loans, and other deviations from the American model. Such problems seem foreign to America's experience. Yet, it is useful to remember that for nearly two centuries, mainland English America was an underdeveloped, dependent outpost of one of the most powerful commercial empires in Europe. According to historian Bernard Bailyn, "frontier" is too kind a word to apply to early America, since it assumes a certain developmental dynamism and future progress. Instead, he describes early America as a peripheral "marchland . . . a ragged outer margin of a central world, a regressive, backward-looking diminishment of metropolitan accomplishment" (Bailyn, 1986, pp. 112–13). North America was a marginal, somewhat unattractive destination even in colonial terms; as late as 1650, half of the English population in the

Americas in lived in a few tiny English-controlled islands in the Caribbean and the Atlantic.

In the seventeenth century, most English men and women (when they thought of America at all) viewed the colonies as objects of exploitation. After all, the English Crown carelessly used giveaways of colonial land and offices to reward political cronies. America represented a staging ground for economic experiments and a source of cheap land, extractable raw materials, and exotic new crops such as sugar and tobacco. At the same time, the colonies served as a dumping ground for potential enemies of social order in Europe: troublesome ethnic groups, religious dissidents, convicts, and the poor. America was a no-holds-barred place where immigrants could conceive of – and construct – societies based on exploiting hundreds of thousands of enslaved Africans, and displacing, enslaving, or killing hundreds of thousands of Native Americans. Violent, diverse, outlandish, exotic, and backward – the American colonies were no model to follow.

Moreover, they were *colonies* – and colonies justified their existence by bringing wealth and strategic advantages to the mother country. English policy presumed the subordination of the colonies to the superior claims of the metropolis in both political and economic terms. Adam Smith coined the term "mercantilism" in 1776 to describe the constellation of laws and regulations that Crown and Parliament devised between 1651 and 1696 to ensure that the benefits of colonial production and trade in key commodities remained an English monopoly. These so-called Navigation Acts also sought to secure for English ship owners all profits from shipping and freighting – the "invisibles" of trade. Other laws in the eighteenth century aimed to limit several nascent colonial industries. These policies reflected a growing conviction that it was in England's interest that America prosper, but not develop. The colonists should restrict themselves to economic endeavors that would not compete with the mother country, Sir Josiah Child wrote in 1804 [1693]. A useful American colony would remain an exotic borderland that produced "commodities of different natures from those of this Kingdom," one whose inhabitants consumed the output of British manufacturers rather than making finished goods themselves (Child, 1804 [1693], p. 199).

Conventional wisdom in the late sixteenth and early seventeenth century held that the English colonies could best serve the empire by blocking Spain and France in their respective colonial enterprises and by creating trading posts. Ideally, these Crown chartered private companies, or "factories of England," would extract profitable resources from the land and its native inhabitants, enriching England and arming its merchants with goods to re-export elsewhere. They would not seek self-sufficiency, but rather would depend on native peoples for food and on imports from England for all manufactured supplies. Most of the early experiments in colony-as-trading post – Sagadahoc in Maine, and Jamestown in Virginia, both founded in 1607 – failed disastrously. The settlers died at alarming rates from malnutrition, exposure, disease, and warfare. Indian trade garnered some profits, and Indian foodstuffs helped Virginia at least limp along, but neither trade nor mining realized the fabulous wealth that investors and planners had anticipated. Demographic crises, lack of economic success, and a devastating Indian attack ended the trading company stage of Virginia's development in 1624.

By the 1630s, successes with tobacco in the Chesapeake and sugar in the West Indies suggested a second path for colonial economies – more self-sufficiency in food and the cultivation of "staples" for export to Europe. It was the trade in these valuable plantation products, the so-called "enumerated" goods, that England sought to control through its Navigation Acts. The southern colonies and the West Indies – especially the latter – became archetypes of the ideal colony in the eyes of many policymakers. In the process of generating enormous wealth for plantation owners, they generated revenue for the Crown, profits for English merchants who re-exported plantation goods to other markets, and customers for English manufacturers. White immigrants to the Carolina Lowcountry, settled in the late seventeenth and early eighteenth centuries, would eventually follow a similar path. These successes came at a huge human cost, however; planter profits relied on the use of bound labor – first indentured white servants from Europe, and then enslaved Africans.

More ambiguous in the eyes of imperial planners were the middle colonies and New England. The first European settlements in the colonial northeast in the early 1600s – New Netherland, New Sweden, the English settlements of Salem and Dorchester, and even the early Pilgrims of Plymouth – followed the trading post model, at least initially. By mid-century, however, the English colonies were moving away from complete dependence on Indian trade and extractive industries. Their environments dictated different strategies from those available to the Chesapeake and the West Indies, and the English religious dissidents and European refugees who settled them brought their own cultural imperatives and goals. The white inhabitants of these colonies sought to replicate the institutions and economic activities they had known in Europe, with some improvements – more extensive landownership being one. They grew Indian corn, but they also cultivated European crops, planted orchards, built churches, and founded colleges. They largely relied on family labor, especially in New England, although white indentured servants and enslaved Africans were a significant presence in some areas. Lacking a staple export like tobacco or sugar, the northern colonies found an economic niche by supplying food to the staple colonies of the Southeast and the West Indies, using the plantation products or cash they received in return to buy needed goods in Europe. Fishing and timber composed New England's other key exchange commodities, while wheat became a prominent export from the mid-Atlantic. Since colonial-owned and -built ships counted as English carriers under the Navigation Acts, British regulation actually helped northern merchants by eliminating some of their foreign competition for the colonial carrying trade. Northern traders increasingly profited, not just from selling imports and exports, but by supplying other services to their southern and Caribbean customers. Likewise, many of the commodities that the northern colonies exported abroad required processing, which spawned industries such as lumber- and flour-milling and distilling. The extent to which the northern colonies replicated and even competed with England's own commerce concerned many policymakers, though at least through 1750 their active consumption of British-made goods was thought to compensate in part for these transgressions of the proper colonial role.

Thinking about colonial America as an underdeveloped place helps restore a sense of contingency to the story of its later success (Newell, 1998; Vickers, 1996). It turns early America's economic development into an historical problem: how and why did America go from being a violent, diverse, outlandish, exotic backwater to a powerful industrial nation in the post-independence era? It also highlights the many failures, miscalculations, reversals, and the unexpected twists and turns that are part of early America's economic history.

Sources, Methods, and Approaches

Characterizing this process and charting these changes presents both practical and conceptual problems. Perhaps the biggest obstacle to a more complete understanding of the colonial economy is the nature of the available evidence. Historians working on the late nineteenth and twentieth century have access to enormous quantities of data on population and on industrial and agricultural production. Even those working on the pre-1889 era, before the federal government began formally compiling figures on GDP and GNP, have access to census figures. By contrast, early American economic historians, especially in certain areas, must cull information from a haphazard group of archival sources. For example, we know much more about the colonies' overseas trade than we do about the contours of the domestic economy. Because of the Navigation Acts, imperial officials created voluminous records of imports and exports for inspection and taxation purposes, many of which have survived. The British Public Records office houses the so-called "Customs Series" – the records of the Inspectors General, which detail trade to and from the colonies in certain key years; historians have especially focused on the data from 1768–1772 (Shepherd and Walton, 1972; Walton and Shepherd, 1979; Price, 1984; McCusker and Menard, 1985). The US Bureau of the Census has published some of these trade figures (1975–6). Another group of documents, the "American Series," includes quarterly reports from naval officers and trade inspectors stationed in British North America and the West Indies for the century before the Revolution. Miscellaneous records from major colonial and English seaports – "port books" – provide some information on colonial trade even before the Navigation Acts went into effect. Despite gaps and lost materials, then, such records offer valuable insight into the North American colonies' trade with the Americas, Europe, and Britain.

In contrast, available data on the domestic economy is much more sparse and irregular. The colonial domestic economy remains the "final frontier" of early American economic history. This subject comprehends topics (some of which have merited entire chapters in this volume) such as household and rural economies, the working lives of ordinary whites, Africans, and Indians (both men and women), internal trade and distribution networks, consumption, manufacturing, the emergence of paper money and capital markets, demographic trends, land speculation, and town and farm creation.

There are no "benchmark" figures on domestic production for the colonial period of the kinds that economists delight in – uniform data sets from key years spanning all the colonies that would allow scholars to measure change over time and to identify larger patterns. Instead, we have patchworks of information about particular towns, regions, individuals, and industries, at different times. Extant public records include: occasional, on-demand reports from royal governors to the Board of Trade (officials responsible for implementing colonial policy and enforcing the Navigation Acts) or to the Privy Council (the Crown's own cabinet of advisors); the proceedings of colonial assemblies; local tax records; militia records; probate inventories; and the odd county census or colony population report. Colonial newspapers (containing advertisements and ship clearance notices), the private papers of merchants, planters, and entrepreneurs, and account books kept by small traders and farmers round out the currently available information. Indeed, a 1995 conference, "The Economy of Early British

America: The Domestic Sector," held at the Huntington Library proved just how hard
it is to measure and generalize about colonial economic growth, productivity, and
income. The organizer, John J. McCusker, and the participants had hoped to create
benchmarks for a systematic analysis of growth and development, but despite the excellent papers the conference raised as many questions as it answered.

Not all of the difficulties associated with writing colonial economic history stem
from evidentiary issues. Other problems are human and conceptual. Economic history
is a schizophrenic field. Trained in different disciplines, the historians and economists
who practice it sometimes work from completely different conceptual frameworks and
use completely different methods. There are a few rare economic historians who bridge
both fields – Jacob Price, who writes on Anglo-American trade, is one name that
comes to mind – but often economists and historians talk past one another.

Economists seek data that can be presented in graphic or tabular form. They pose a
problem, generate a time series based on benchmark evidence, interpolate (make an
educated guess) as to what happened between the benchmark figures, and devise theories
or models to characterize and explain the macroeconomic, long-term trends in an
economy. Economists are generally less concerned with issues of culture and context
than are historians. At the heart of liberal economic theory, dating back to Adam
Smith's *Wealth of Nations* (1776), is the assumption that human beings are rational
profit-maximizers and that economic behavior is natural and inherent. Economists
have a distinct vocabulary and assign very specific meaning to words like development,
market economy, capitalism, comparative advantage, and labor. These approaches work
less well for the colonial period, however, where, as Jacob Price notes, "the best trained
quantitative explorer . . . enter[s] a wilderness so ill provided with his sort of data that
he cannot proceed except with the most extraordinary caution" (Price, 1984, p. 19).

Historians rely heavily on more impressionistic textual evidence, including contemporaries' own perceptions of what was occurring; their evidence often consists of a few
examples rather than aggregate data. Many scholars of colonial America approach economic issues from the perspective of social and cultural history. Implicitly or explicitly,
they assume that religion, ethnicity, gender, worldview, political bodies, and other
ideologies and institutions affected individual and collective economic choices, and
that questions regarding the economy cannot be separated from this rich context. For
example, many view capitalism not as a "natural" system or set of behaviors, but rather
as learned behavior and the product of unique environmental, political and social circumstances. Thus, they explore topics such as "economic culture" or "economic
behavior," seeking to track shifts in these areas within a context of meaning as well as
material circumstances.

Historians pose questions that do not always lend themselves to quantification. Their
units of analysis vary from the individual to the household, from the community to the
colony, region, or empire. Historians stress specificity, uniqueness, contingency, and
the role of individual decision-makers. They tend to see change in whatever period
they study. Yet, they also tend to draw rather bold generalizations from limited case
studies. They often use the same terminology as economists, but without the same
precision. When historians discuss capitalism or growth, they may deploy these terms
in idiosyncratic ways that make methodologically rigorous economists shudder.

So, economists look at the work of social and cultural historians and rightly see
assertions unsupported by much data, and fuzzy conceptual frameworks. Historians

look at the work of economists and see intimidating statistics and Gini coefficients, overly abstract models that ignore the messy human element, and results that overstate limited data or run counter to the impressionistic evidence.

Given these evidentiary constraints and conceptual/methodological differences, it is not surprising that despite an outpouring of excellent research and writing about the early American economy in the past three decades, there remains considerable debate over basic questions of how to characterize the colonial economy (or, indeed, how to approach its study at all). One aspect of this debate centers on whether early America was a capitalist society. Before 1970 most history textbooks assumed that the answer was yes. As Adam Smith wrote, "the colony of a civilized nation which takes possession, either of a waste country, or one so thinly inhabited, that the natives easily give place to the new settlers, advances more rapidly to wealth and greatness than any other human society" (1976 [1776]). The classic re-statement of this sentiment in the mid-twentieth century appeared in Carl Degler's *Out of our Past* (1959) – Degler entitled his first chapter "Capitalism came in the First Ships" – but other historians endorsed it as well (Boorstin, 1958; Grant, 1961). The basic narrative asserted that immigrants brought with them the attitudes and behaviors of a commercializing society – England – and applied them to a resource-rich virgin wilderness. Once freed from the restraints imposed by feudal, anti-market institutions (guilds, monarchs, gentry engrossment of land, established churches), immigrants to America eagerly embraced widespread land ownership and market participation. Carving farms out of the frontier, they created a prosperous, egalitarian society that impressed later European observers the likes of Alexis de Tocqueville – and, in the process, created wealth. Similarly, colonial seaports provided the entrepreneurial and capital seedbeds not just for overseas trade but for future industrialization. The story of colonial America's economy matched the Whig political narrative of constant progress that the break with England only accelerated.

In the 1970s, however, a new generation of social and cultural historians challenged these notions. First, several studies focusing on New England towns argued that far from embracing capitalism, Puritan town fathers had consciously rejected individualistic, competitive economic behaviors in order to further other ethical, communal goals (Lockridge, 1970; Greven, 1970; Demos, 1970). The methods and conclusions of these early community studies soon came under attack (the foremost criticism being that the authors' reliance on church records and town focus had biased results against economic activity and extra-communal exchange). But their insistence that culture and institutions – as opposed to strictly material factors – affected economic behavior had a lasting impact on colonial economic history. Today, we take for granted that developing nations' political, educational, and legal institutions, as well as popular attitudes toward work, productivity, and consumption, affect their economic performance – sometimes more profoundly than the presence or absence of natural resources. Could the same have been true of early America?

Meanwhile, other scholars began to examine more closely the available data on population, prices, and household production. Several, notably James Henretta (1978) and Michael Merrill (1977), published works in support of the contention that many colonial households chose self-sufficiency and avoided market participation – not necessarily on moral grounds but rather because entrepreneurial behavior lay outside the scope of their pre-capitalist culture. Strategic considerations, such as the desire to maintain neighborly relations and to avoid the risk that accompanied participation in a global economy, also influenced the colonists' decision-making. These salvos prompted return fire in the form of studies that argued for the presence of market attitudes in colonial America. Examining land use and spatial organization in colonial Pennsylvania, James T. Lemon (1972) had found a "liberal" economic culture and farmers who were keenly attuned to export markets. In later articles he contended that such values existed elsewhere in the colonies as well, and questioned the hegemony of a pre-capitalist mentality. "Far from being opposed to the market," he noted, "'independent' farmers eagerly sought English manufactured goods and in other ways acted as agents of capitalism" (1984, p. 102; 1980). Even the founding of many New England towns, it seemed, was more the product of the efforts of entrepreneurial land speculators than of godly pilgrims (Innes, 1983; Martin, 1991).

A second major area of contention emerged around the morphology of colonial development. The new quantitative and demographic techniques that many in this generation of social historians employed led them to challenge other unexamined assumptions about the colonial economy. Did the economy actually "develop" in the classic sense of a real increase in income per capita over time? Was growth steady through the colonial period? Economists had mapped out stunning growth rates for nineteenth-century American economy, based on benchmark data from the 1840s, and most presumed that the foundation of this growth must lie in the colonial period (David, 1967; Gallman, 1972). Historian Marc Egnal (1975) re-examined these conjectures in the light of available information on prices and population, and concluded that colonial America had indeed experienced overall growth in the sense of aggregate economic expansion, albeit in fits and starts.

But, after examining probate records and population figures, several historians posited that far from enjoying unalloyed growth colonists in some areas confronted a European-style Malthusian crisis in the 1700s as population increases began to put pressure on resources and farm size (Henretta, 1973; Lockridge, 1973; Greven, 1970; Smith, 1980). Other authors exposed the existence of land tenancy in portions of the middle colonies, the Chesapeake, and New England (Earle, 1975; Innes, 1983). The persistence – even the conscious revival – of feudal institutions in colonial America belied its image as a land of widespread white landownership (Murrin and Berthoff, 1973). Gary Nash (1976, 1979) and others found similar trends in the colonial seaports. While rich merchants got richer in the eighteenth century, urban workers struggled (Smith, 1981). A sizable poor underclass emerged in cities such as Boston on the eve of the Revolution. Not only was early America not capitalist; perhaps it wasn't even growing and prospering.

Most of these early social histories centered on the northern colonies. But, several important works on colonial slave societies that appeared in the 1970s revealed economies that fit neither pattern. Although not direct participants in the market/development debate, Richard Dunn (1972) and Edmund Morgan (1975) exposed the paradoxical nature of plantation economies in the English West Indies and the Chesapeake. As producers of key agricultural staples, these regions were more integrated into the global economy than any others in the colonies, and accounted for the lion's share of colonial exports to Europe. They were sites of some of the most naked – and successful – profit-seeking in the colonial world. Yet, the majority of the population in the southern Lowcountry and the West Indies consisted of enslaved Africans, while Chesapeake planters brutally exploited the labor of white indentured servants for nearly a century before also turning to slave markets. Historians writing about the nineteenth century were already considering the question of whether hierarchical societies built on bound (as opposed to free) labor could be considered capitalist; what did links between colonial entrepreneurship and slavery mean for this debate (Genovese, 1974)?

Morgan's description of seventeenth-century Virginia society and economy indicated that the trajectory of southern development was marked by repeated failures and downturns, and enormous human costs. He portrayed a place of incredible death rates through the 1640s, caused in part by its planners' persistent miscalculations and the settlers' hostility towards the Native Americans on whom they depended for food. Even after tobacco put the colony on a sounder economic foundation, Morgan highlighted the boom and bust cycles of the tobacco economy, the appropriation of power and resources by an inner circle of political cronies, and the rapid waning of economic opportunities for poor whites – all of which sparked armed rebellion and eventually the transition to slavery in the late 1600s.

By the 1980s a fully fledged debate over the nature of the colonial economy, the extent of settlers' involvement in markets, and the timing of the "transition to capitalism" raged among American historians (Clark, 2000; Kulikoff, 1989). Some of the disagreements stemmed from the fact that scholars were looking at different colonial regions or sub-regions at different times. Indeed, this growing awareness of regional differences in the colonial era proved a beneficial side effect of the capitalism debates. Radically distinct economies distinguished the plantation societies of the West Indies from the marginal farms of western New England, and arguments that might fit one region simply failed to describe reality in others.

In addition, the contending sides often employed distinct definitions of capitalism, markets, and market behavior. Clearly, elements of nineteenth-century capitalism as Karl Marx defined it, such as a large pool of alienated labor and extensive industrialization, were absent or embryonic in the colonial period. The household largely remained the unit of production, except for the big plantations of the Caribbean and the Carolina Lowcountry. Yet, just as clearly, most colonists had to participate in a global exchange economy, since absolute self-sufficiency was beyond reach exactly because America was such a backward marchland (Shammas, 1982a). The irony of underdevelopment is that less-developed places (such as colonies) depend on external trade to supply many necessities. In the colonists' case, this meant manufactured goods such as clothing, weapons, and ironware, not to mention desirable foodstuff luxuries such as wine, sugar, and coffee.

And, in the end, both sides in the capitalism debate acknowledged the merits of creating a subtle, multi-variate portrait of early American society and culture as opposed to characterizing it in absolutes. Daniel Vickers has argued (1990) that most Euro-Americans, regardless of what motives brought them to the New World, sought to achieve both household economic independence and a degree of material comfort – what they would have termed "competency." Depending on one's larger goals, competency could be a means to an end, but for the mass of newcomers it was an end in itself. To secure a competent standard of living, families pursued a range of strategies: they might engage in neighborly, non-competitive exchanges locally, and yet still sell goods and services to external markets. Other historians came to agree that liberal economic attitudes and activity did not preclude community ties in the colonial period (in fact, they could create new ties) (Lemon, 1984). Likewise, values, structures, and strategies that looked "pre-capitalist" on the face of things, such as reliance on family business networks and household production, turned out to have relevance and utility not only in the colonial era but in an industrializing nineteenth-century capitalist society as well (Lamoreaux, 1999; Clark, 1990). In the meantime, the debates over the character of early American development had produced a huge body of useful empirical research at the micro-level of farm accounts, wills, town populations, etc. The debates had also reoriented attention away from an exclusive focus on external trade towards the domestic economy.

In the 1980s and 1990s economists and historians began to delve more systematically into questions of development and growth for the colonies as a whole while remaining sensitive to regional variation. Economists had new tools (the computer and statistical software), and new methods (econometrics) to aid their investigations. Lack of data had long frustrated efforts to compile solid figures on changing patterns of colonial GDP (Gross Domestic Product) and wealth, key measures of economic performance. In her 1980 book *Wealth of a Nation to Be*, however, Alice Hanson Jones proposed an ingenious solution. She valued the contents of a sample of probated estates and tax records from each region, divided this measure by estimated population figures, and arrived at figures for per capita wealth and income in all the colonial regions for the year 1774. Some critics attacked Jones' methods. Estate inventories measure the wealth of the deceased and, therefore are weighted towards the oldest (and richest) members of the population; they give hints about household wealth, but provide less information about the productive roles of household members. Colonial probate courts under-reported assets at both ends of the scale, and many areas outside of New England were lax about requiring that wills go through probate at all (Shammas, 1993). Because no complete census existed, Jones had to estimate the total population (the denominator for her income equations). Finally, since Jones compiled data only for a single year, this made temporal comparisons difficult. Still, her estimates remain widely used, and her research sparked many new investigations.

Jones' results included a number of surprises. First, although direct comparisons were complicated because of different bases of measurement, it appeared that wealth and income rates in America remained well below those in eighteenth-century England. The average per capita wealth for free white persons on the mainland colonies (excluding the value of slaves and indentured servants) was 37.4L, less than one-third of the figures for the mother country on the eve of Revolution. Including the value of slaves and servants brings the colonial average to approximately 74L, still below English levels. Even more intriguing were the regional variations she uncovered. Per capita wealth among the free white population in 1774 was 33L in New England, 51L in the middle colonies, and 132L in the South. Jones focused only on British North America, but the research of Richard B. Sheridan (1974) provided figures of 1,200L per free white capita for Jamaica (McCusker and Menard, 1985). In other words, if one included slaves and servants as capital, and excluded them as wealth-owners, planters in the West Indies owned more than 25 times the wealth of their northern colonial neighbors (Galenson, 1996).

These numbers gave many economic historians food for thought. First, several scholars used nineteenth-century figures and Jones' own estimates to offer conjectures on pre-1774 annual growth rates. Consensus estimates posited a rate of between 0.3 to 0.8

per annum – not nearly as high as America's growth in the nineteenth century nor as England's in the eighteenth century, but respectable by the standards of early modern Europe (McCusker and Menard, 1985; Gallman and Wallis, 1992). The average of these figures more or less matched earlier estimates made by Marc Egnal (1975). Jones herself downplayed the gap between colonial and English per capita wealth and insisted that it should not obscure the colonists' very real economic achievements. She noted that land in the colonies – a huge part of family wealth – was valued at a much lower rate than in England and that (despite the racial and regional inequities) wealth was distributed much more equally in the colonies than in the mother country. As an immigrant society, colonial America was full of people who were starting from scratch. Moreover, the colonists had many sources of "free" income – food sources, firewood, and other resources that Europeans had to pay more for – so colonial income might actually be a more accurate gauge of the health and growth of the economy than simple wealth.

But what had powered that growth? One theory focused on the driving influence of international trade. For many historians, the most eye-catching element of the new data on wealth was the staggering gap between the family-farm-centered northern colonies and the plantation colonies, particularly the West Indies. Since available export data showed that the plantation regions also dominated colonial exports, positing a relationship between economic growth and trade seemed plausible. In 1985, John McCusker and Russell P. Menard published a stunning synthesis of the economic history of British America. McCusker and Menard showcased a range of approaches to the colonial economy but in the end they concluded that the "staples approach" best explained the nature of colonial development. The staples approach assumes "the overriding importance of overseas trade." "The colonists wanted goods imported from abroad," the authors noted; "to buy them they had to produce goods for which an export market existed abroad." For small, dependent outposts like colonies, which lacked capital and labor yet boasted abundant resources, the comparative advantage lay in production of a staple resource, be it furs, fish, timber, tobacco, indigo, rice, or sugar, for export to a developed metropolitan economy – Europe. Expansion in production and export of the staple determined the rate of economic growth for a region. Initially, colonists enjoyed high prices for their staple exports, which helped them recoup the costs of establishing production on the periphery and pay for the high cost of labor. A successful staple also helped a colony attract immigrants eager for success. But if metropolitan demand for a colonial export flattened or was never strong in the first place, then increased production would begin to flatten the colonists' profits – and immigration rates – as well. For example, New England received few immigrants after 1640; nearly all the region's population growth thereafter depended on natural increase. If metropolitan demand grew, however, then production, immigration (and importation of forced labor), and the real incomes of colonists would grow in tandem. Thus, the staples thesis helped explain why certain colonial regions experienced different rates of growth and different overall standards of living.

In the hands of McCusker and Menard, the staples thesis proved a nuanced qualitative tool as well. Although they privileged expansion of the export sector, they emphasized the importance of "linkages" – "the process of economic diversification around the export base." They paid attention to how external trade could prompt internal economic development and manufacturing. Internal trade networks emerged to link producers of agricultural staples in order to transport goods to market centers for export and to bring imported consumer goods back along the same networks to customers in return. All staple commodities had to be packed for shipping, and some, such as wheat or sugarcane or rum or preserved meat, might require processing beforehand, which stimulated the construction of sugar-, saw- and flour-mills, barrel-making, distilling, and a host of other crafts and small industries. Some staple producers, notably the planters of tobacco, rice, and sugar in the Southeast and West Indies, relied on first Dutch and then British merchants to ship their goods, but northern ports developed shipbuilding industries to help supply their own fishing and trading fleets. Eventually, these northern-built ships would end up serving the Caribbean and the South as well.

Thus, the staples thesis offers a possible explanation not just for differences in wealth or migration streams among regions, but also for different developmental paths among them. The kind of staple that each region produced had an enormous impact on the quantity and character of the "linkages" that emerged. Certainly, tobacco, sugar, and the direct European markets that these goods secured produced more wealth for the plantation colonies. In contrast, the northern colonists had to scramble to find a staple; they had to aggressively pursue multiple regional and foreign markets. Eventually, however, this experience helped northern merchants become providers of shipping and other financial services throughout the colonies. Similarly, the exports of the mid-Atlantic and New England – flour, livestock, fish, timber and timber products like potash and turpentine, ships and shipping – required extensive processing and internal transportation. All these factors made for a more diversified, and in a sense, a more developed economy in the colonial North (Newell, 1998). The dominance of plantations in the South retarded the formation of towns – foreign ships literally sailed to the great planter's door to pick up and discharge cargoes. The implications of these differences were great for the independence era – the tension produced by northern development and England's efforts to restrict it were factors in the Imperial Crisis of the 1760s – but they become even clearer in the post-revolutionary era. We know that in the nineteenth century the northern states launched American industrialization, dominated internal transportation networks and capital markets, and attracted immigrants. We know that southern plantations produced great wealth for their owners, and yet the antebellum South developed much less in the way of industry and services, and had fewer urban centers and received fewer immigrants.

Despite these many analytical pluses, however, the staples approach has its drawbacks as a tool to explain colonial American growth and development. First, an emphasis on exports can create a distorted view of the colonial economy. Focusing on staples privileges certain regions (the staple colonies), certain products, and certain aspects of colonial production (and certain producers) at the expense of others. Likewise, focusing on "linkage" industries runs the risk of ignoring household and small-scale manufacturing and industrial efforts that lack an obvious link to staples processing – import-substitution in the form of cloth-making and shoemaking, for example. Manufactured goods themselves could be a kind of staple. For example, on the eve of the Revolution, American forges were turning out more iron than those in England and Wales combined, and some of this product the colonists exported to English cutlery makers. Capital goods – the tools of manufacture – formed an increasing proportion of the colonies' imports from abroad in the eighteenth century.

The attention brought to bear on the colonial household economy during the capitalism debate has revealed the extent to which farm families produced what they consumed. In other words, an apparently large but difficult-to-measure proportion of colonial output and income went straight to domestic consumers and never registered on the export records. Estimates range from a little less than one-half in a colony such as Barbados to three-fourths in Massachusetts, with additional variance by era and region (Eltis, 1995; Shammas, 1982b). Production for purposes of home consumption was especially common in the North, which makes their colonial economies particularly hard to analyze fully. James Lemon estimated that by the latter half of the eighteenth century nearly one-third of the adult male workforce in southern Pennsylvania were not engaged in growing that colony's staple – wheat – but rather followed non-agricultural occupations (1972).

Even the Caribbean, the Chesapeake, and South Carolina enjoyed more economic variety than a focus on sugar, tobacco, or rice might suggest. As Jacob Price points out, exports of tobacco from the Chesapeake tripled between the turn of the eighteenth century and the early 1770s, but at the same time the population grew sevenfold: "since there is no evidence of a decline in income per head, it is fairly obvious that a lot was going on . . . besides growing tobacco" (Price, 1984, p. 25). Most household studies focus on the North, but recent studies reveal that households of all sizes – and all races – in the southern colonies also engaged in production for home consumption and regional exchange. The household of moderately prosperous seventeenth-century tobacco planter Robert Cole grew tobacco for export, but income from tobacco composed only a little more than one-third of what the farm produced; local trade and production for home consumption generated the other two-thirds (Carr, Walsh, and Menard, 1991). In the absence of town centers, the largest plantations operated grain mills, joineries, brick-making facilities, and blacksmith shops that served both the immediate needs of the plantation and those of surrounding farmers. Through the mid-eighteenth century, some planters imported and distributed goods to smaller producers until Scottish and English merchants entered this trade and began to open local outlets in the colonies (Isaac, 1982). Lois Green Carr and Lorena S. Walsh found that small Chesapeake farm households, perhaps discouraged by falling export prices, began to redirect their labor away from tobacco by the early 1700s in favor of an increasingly diverse range of economic activities (1988). These included new crop mixes as well as petty manufactures: shoemaking, spinning yarn, dairying, cider- and beer-making – some for home use, but some for internal trade. Even the enslaved participated in this internal economy. As Philip Morgan notes in his essay for this volume, alongside their other duties slaves in the West Indies and the Carolina Lowcountry often bore responsibility for feeding themselves. They grew crops and raised livestock for their own families' consumption and marketed the surplus to whites in cities such as Kingston and Charleston.

An exclusive focus on exports also underestimates and marginalizes the contribution of key members of the domestic workforce – women and children. Marriage was an almost universal state for whites in colonial America, in part because men and women depended on each other's labor to survive. In the typical household, the adult male and female heads fulfilled rigidly distinct yet integrated work roles. Men engaged in public business (militia muster, jury duty, trade), worked the fields, and produced a variety of raw materials. Under certain circumstances colonial women – particularly widows in seaport towns – operated in this public commercial world, continuing their husbands' business ventures or operating small businesses and taverns on their own. Black women worked alongside men in the fields. Most white women in early America, however, confined their activities largely to the household and its immediate environs (garden, dairy), in part because childcare responsibilities consumed much of their time. Along with childcare, however, women's work consisted of processing for consumption the raw materials that men produced. This included baking flour into bread; growing and preserving fruits and vegetables; making cheese, butter, cider, and sometimes beer; spinning flax, cotton, or wool into thread, and either weaving it themselves or trading it for finished cloth (Ulrich, 1983, 1988, 1998).

Households consumed many of the commodities that women produced, but even in the seventeenth century traders' account books show that women exchanged their home-processed goods within local and regional networks in order to secure other comforts for the home (Newell, 1998). When eighteenth-century farm families diversified their output in order to compensate for falling tobacco prices in the Chesapeake or shrinking farm size in New England, they were mobilizing the labor of women for the domestic market (Clark, 1990; Carr and Walsh, 1988). Children's labor also played a crucial role in economic development, particularly in the North, where family labor took the place of scarce, expensive bound and wage workers (Vickers, 1994). In regions such as New England where immigration faltered early, in fact, the household literally reproduced the labor force.

Finally, the staples approach, like the records it is based on, privileges the relationship between colonies and metropolitan center, in this case, Britain. Yet, the colonists' trade networks were multivariate. The taxation and exportation restrictions of the Navigation Acts applied only to a list of "enumerated goods" that the Board of Trade published annually. The list tended to focus on plantation staples and goods seen as strategic, such as ships' masts. Thus, many of the goods produced in the North for export – fish, timber – remained unrestricted, which meant that the colonists could trade them freely with clients in Europe and elsewhere. We know the basic contours of this direct trade with Europe, Latin America, and the Wine Islands, but its extent – and therefore its role in and precise relationship to the domestic economy – remains more difficult to track.

Evidentiary challenges complicate our understanding of inter-colonial and intra-colonial trade even more. This is despite the fact that one study estimated that during the decade before the Revolution the coastal trade was worth nearly 70 percent of the value of foreign trade in that period (Shepherd and Williamson, 1972). Internal trade also generated profits for carriers – those mysterious "invisibles" of freight charges. British North America's lengthy coastline and many ports of departure meant that much of this trade went unobserved by customs officials and thus remained unrecorded – except in rare cases where the shipper's private accounts survive. Yet, the inhabitants of the Americas were each others' best customers in some respects. In the seventeenth century, a pattern emerged by which the northern colonies provisioned the plantation colonies, and in return the plantation colonies supplied them with cash and staples to exchange abroad or consume at home. Bermuda and the West Indies, not England, served as New England's first crucial export markets in the 1640s when the Puritan colonies teetered on the brink of economic collapse. The accounts of merchants, small traders, ship's captains, and farmers reveal that by the late seventeenth century inter-regional and inter-colonial trade involved a wide range of products and services – items of domestic growth and manufacture, as well as the re-exportation of imported manufactured goods, luxury foods, and wine.

Internal trade also comprehended exchanges between the hinterlands and port towns and between whites and Native Americans as well as exchanges among commercial towns and regions. And, as Bruce Daniels pointed out (1980), internal trade created its own "linkages" of services, transportation networks, and industries. Farmers and traders moved goods inland over surprisingly long distances (Rothenberg, 1981). By the late colonial period, merchants such as the Browns of Providence, Rhode Island, were sending locally made bricks, earthenware vessels, whale-oil candles, house frames, axes, shoes, furniture, and rum to other colonial markets.

One area that cries out for greater attention is the role of Native Americans in colonial economic development. We know the basic contours of the story. There were approximately 500,000 Indians living in the territory later occupied by the thirteen colonies at the beginning of the seventeenth century. Their numbers had dwindled to about 260,000 due to disease, warfare, and dislocation by 1700, but that was still close to half the population of British North America. The first English and French colonial settlements in North America simply could not have survived without the aid of indigenous peoples. The Indians' willingness to provide food – and, sometimes, the colonists' ability to appropriate it by force – kept the inhabitants of Plymouth and Jamestown from literally starving to death. Later, white colonists settled on or near Indian villages, farmed fields cleared by Indians, and adapted crops and techniques from native agriculture. In the first decades of settlement, the Indian fur trade provided colonists from Maine to the Carolinas with their only real export commodity with which to pay for desperately needed imports.

Too often, however, Indians disappear from the economic narrative once Virginians discover tobacco exports and New Englanders discover fishing and commerce. Indians and the Indian fur trade seem like "frontier" activities. In addition, some historians of Native American/European exchange tend to emphasize the symbolic, political nature of those exchanges rather than their economic quality (White, 1991). Yet, furs and deerskins still represented a healthy portion of the colonies' exports to Europe – just behind timber and grain – at the end of the colonial period, which suggests that the Indian fur trade remained vitally important. Indians served as a key internal market for domestic traders and seaport importers throughout the colonial era. Scattered evidence suggests that many storekeepers in coastal areas kept special inventories for Native Americans in the late seventeenth century, and that Indian households, like their white counterparts, engaged in cottage industries such as broom-making in order to exchange them for desired consumer goods. Merchant account books in areas of dense white settlement such as Maryland, Rhode Island, and Connecticut show voluminous transactions with Indians living "behind the frontier."

The lure of Indian trade, as much as land, drew white migrants and colonial officials into western areas to participate in a "frontier exchange economy" (Usner, 1992). One frustrated South Carolina official complained that there was a trader for every ten or twelve Indians living among the Creeks and Chickasaw by the 1760s. Indians also provided crucial labor as wage-workers and bound servants. Indian slaves were themselves a widely pursued and traded commodity, one that enriched early entrepreneurs from New England to Georgia. Indeed, enslaved Indians were a major export out of Charleston, South Carolina, through 1715.

These activities in the internal economy seem at least relevant to questions of colonial growth and development. So, although tracking exports can help illuminate much about trends in the growth and development of the colonial economy, the staples approach under-reports domestic production and exchange. It therefore complicates calculations of wealth and income. To put it yet another way, the quantity and value of exports from British America grew in absolute terms over the colonial period, but as a share of the overall colonial economy they declined in significance. They also changed in composition over time.

If exports were not the sole driving force behind the colonial economy, then what were the other important variables? In the 1980s, some scholars began to investigate the behavior of colonial buyers and consumers for answers. Scouring probate inventories, diaries, advertisements, account books, prices, and import schedules, scholars such as Carole Shammas, T. H. Breen, and Gloria Main traced changes in the material lives of the colonists and revealed the intimate relationship between colonial production and colonial consumption (Breen, 1986; Main, 1983; Shammas, 1982a, 1982b, 1990).

Consumption studies proved relevant to the analysis of colonial wealth that Alice Hanson Jones had initiated, as well as to discussions about colonists' economic behavior and choices and the general morphology of economic growth and development. By arguing that her own figures on wealth probably understated early American incomes and actual material well-being, Jones had raised an issue that economists and historians are still considering today: do classical economic definitions of wealth and income – or even measures of economic success – work for the colonial period? Consumption studies suggested that putting goods in the hands of consumers might be a better measure of success than growth rates or income. Income would only form part of this equation; the presence of peddlers, traders, and country stores to make goods available, as well as roads and inns for travelers and traders, would be important variables. Certainly, access to consumer goods varied regionally in colonial America, but the preponderance of studies published in the last two decades point to a rise in the variety and quantity of available goods.

Other evidence points to colonial Americans' rising willingness to consume for consumption's sake – to be fashionable, to claim higher status and gentility, or to signal one of the many other identities or social cues that consumption and display allow individuals to communicate (Bushman, 1992; Isaac, 1982; Carson, 1994). Probate records reveal the growing prevalence of luxury goods such as chairs, looking glasses, glassware, cutlery, china, and fine linens in coastal port households in the northern colonies as well as wealthy Chesapeake households in the late seventeenth century (Ulrich, 1983; Carson, 1994). By the mid-eighteenth century, Connecticut storekeeper Jonathan Trumbull and others like him were peddling tea sets, velvet dresses, and ribbons to farm customers in the hinterlands. Where distribution networks failed or prices remained high, consumers turned to local furniture makers, clock makers, and earthenware producers for import substitutes. This behavior certainly made it look as if many colonists willingly participated in a market economy – that they produced in order to afford consumer goods from outside the household. Thus, consumption became an important drive factor for growth and development. And, ironically, despite the fact that it frequently functioned as a class marker, consumption was also a great leveler in the sense that people of all classes and races in colonial America engaged in it. Women wove cloth so as to afford sugar and tea, slaves used extra income to buy ritual objects, ribbons, and mirrors as well as food, and Native Americans purchased not just utilitarian tools and weapons but also cloth and objects for personal ornamentation.

Diet and food formed another component of colonial consumption and offer other clues to colonial well-being. Exotic foods and wine represented a staggering proportion of colonial imports from abroad at points in the eighteenth century – perhaps as much as half. And food production, whether for home consumption, export, or exchange, remained the chief work of most colonial households. Most investigations of colonial diet conclude that although their per capita wealth might have been lower than that of Britons, the colonists as a whole ate better. Generally, income correlates to nutrition which in turn correlates to other measures of health. Yet, recent studies of human stature based on military records and skeletal remains suggest that white native-born eighteenth-century Americans were the tallest people in the world – taller and healthier than they had any right to be given existing income estimates (Steckel, 1995; Sokoloff and Villaflor, 1982). Even enslaved African Americans in British North America were taller than their Caribbean and South American counterparts. Several generations of colonists also reaped health benefits from the low population density, which hampered the spread of epidemic disease, and the relatively microbe-free environment that North America represented for European newcomers.

Just as the diet and height indicators suggest that current calculations of income and wealth probably understate colonial American "well-being," so the intensive studies of local probate records by scholars of consumption have had relevance for studies of the morphology of the colonial economy's growth and development. For example, the sudden appearance of new products in backcountry regions or in small households points to changes in production or improved transportation services. Similarly, most accounts of colonial growth stress that annual growth rates were not steady and even. Certain regions, such as New England, experienced flat or even negative growth at times. Studies indicate, however, that during periods when the economy seemed to be stagnant or growing only slowly in terms of exports – as in the case of New England *circa* 1750 – the inhabitants apparently enjoyed real improvements in purchasing power and standard of living because the goods they produced commanded higher prices abroad relative to prices of the goods that they consumed (Egnal, 1975; Main and Main, 1988, 1999).

The colonists consumed more than commodities. They consumed education, the professions, churches, representative government, and other elements that are hard to quantify in monetary terms but which contribute to "quality of life" – and they consumed them in increasing numbers as the colonial period wore on. By the eve of the Revolution, white colonial Americans had some of the highest literacy rates of their day (close to 90 percent for men), higher even than Britain. America had two colleges in 1700; by 1770 it had eight. Interestingly, access to education and clergy were inversely proportional to measured export and income levels. New England, which had the lowest per capita income and value of exports of any colonial region in British America in the mid-eighteenth century, had the highest rates of literacy and access to the professions; the middle colonies followed, and the South and West Indies trailed. Here again, income and wealth seem insufficient measures of colonial well-being. Moreover, these discrepancies in education and other elements of cultural "infrastructure" among colonial regions match diversification patterns identified earlier in this essay – patterns that had long-term economic consequences. Just as the elite planters of the Caribbean, the Carolina Lowcountry, and the Chesapeake "outsourced" much of their shipping and financial services, they also "outsourced" educational facilities, sending their children to service providers – Britain and the northern colonies – for schooling.

Economists remain divided over the significance of cultural elements such as political systems and education in accounting for economic growth and development. Factor endowments, such as climate, environment, and natural resources, are the traditional variables in calculations of "comparative advantage." Yet, just as historians have become more sensitive to the need for precision and quantitative evidence, so too have economists begun to appreciate the influence that institutions and culture exerted on early American economic development (McCusker and Menard, 1985; Engerman and Sokoloff, 1997; Temin, 2000).

Key among these institutional innovations were the representative governments common to all the thirteen colonies. Despite the restrictions and subordinate position that membership in the British empire imposed upon them, to varying degrees the colonists used their local governments to foster economic growth and development. In some colonies, that meant getting land into the hands of private owners and giving tax incentives to individuals willing to operate mills or other needed enterprises. It also meant requiring that able-bodied men contribute so many days to road construction each year. It meant empowering inspectors to enforce quality controls on tobacco, preserved meat, and other North American exports to Europe in order to protect their "brand" and market value. In the most extreme cases, it meant printing paper money and operating public mortgage banks in order to put investment capital into the hands of land-rich but cash-starved colonists (England forbade an American mint) (Newell, 1998).

Here again, the effects of such policy measures are hard to quantify, but their cumulative impact was significant. To reiterate the theme of the opening paragraphs of this chapter, the growth and development of the American economy was in some ways an atypical story. A comparison with other countries in our own hemisphere is suggestive. Mexico and Brazil boast enormous natural resources. In the late eighteenth century, both nations had established export markets and international trade relationships, transportation networks, educated elites, and pockets of manufacturing. In many ways, their economies looked even more promising than did that of the former British colonies. Yet, the post-independence trajectories of the US and Latin America look very different. In analyzing these differences, Stanley Engerman and Kenneth Sokoloff noted the importance of factor endowments, but they highlighted the crucial role of rights, literacy, and relative economic equality in fostering "the evolution of markets, institutions conducive to widespread commercialization, and technological change" in North America (1997).

This essay has limned a fairly positive portrait of colonial growth and development – positive both in the sense that growth and development did occur in the colonial period, and in the sense that most of the colonies' white inhabitants thereby secured a high level of material comfort. Still, it is important to keep in mind that although the northeastern colonies offered greater degrees of economic equality and opportunity than did most other contemporary societies, and that all the colonies delivered a relatively high standard of living, white immigrants of European extraction were the beneficiaries of these very real achievements. Enslaved Africans and Indians created a great deal of wealth in the colonies. Yet, a racial frontier increasingly isolated Africans and Indians from the benefits of American growth and development in the eighteenth century. For example, by many measures Native Americans became poorer as Euro-American society prospered. One recent study claims that the inclusion of Indians who lived within the boundaries of the thirteen colonies in national calculations of wealth and well-being changes the outcome dramatically, lowering overall figures for growth and income (Mancall and Weiss, 1999). Clearly, more research on the participation of Africans and Native Americans in the colonial economy is necessary. If it is difficult to calculate the wealth, product, and income of white colonists because of evidentiary and other reasons, it is doubly difficult to calculate these values for Native Americans – and even harder to conceptualize and define wealth and well-being for indigenous populations with distinct cultures and values.

Clearly there is a need for more research on topics such as the internal economy, the impact of culture and institutions in economic development, the participation of Native Americans, and the role of women as producers of wealth and goods. One other direction I would suggest is conceptual and methodological. Much of the best research in the past two decades has taken the form of micro-studies of households and individual industries, which frustrates those who revel in generally applicable models. Moreover, as the extent of regional differences has become apparent, the possibility of creating over-arching economic narratives or finding patterns that apply to all the colonies seems ever more remote (Egnal, 1996). Yet, there are patterns embedded in these micro- and regional studies that offer the means to construct trans-regional comparisons. The household focus, in fact, reveals Native Americans, Pennsylvanians, New England farm families, and Chesapeake yeomen engaged in diversified production for home consumption as well as for the market. A focus on slavery need not limit investigations to the South; recent studies point to the extent to which northern economic lives in New York and Rhode Island were embedded in the slave trade and related commercial activities. In addition, as scholars tackle studies of individual industries, households, and communities, the paucity of quantitative data will gradually become less of a handicap. It may soon become possible to create the kinds of benchmark sets that will allow historians and economists to formulate new paradigms of colonial American economic growth and development.

BIBLIOGRAPHY

Bailyn, Bernard: *The Peopling of British North America: An Introduction* (New York: Alfred A. Knopf, 1986).

Boorstin, Daniel J.: *Americans: The Colonial Experience* (New York: Vintage Press, 1958).

Breen, Timothy H.: "An Empire of Goods: The Anglicization of Colonial America, 1690–1776," *Journal of British Studies* 25 (1986), 467–99.

Bushman, Richard L.: *The Refinement of America: Persons, Houses, Cities* (New York: Alfred A. Knopf, 1992).

Carr, Lois Green and Walsh, Lorena S., "Economic Diversification and Labor Organization in the Chesapeake, 1650–1820." In Stephen Innes, ed., *Work and Labor in Early America* (Chapel Hill, NC: University of North Carolina Press, 1988), pp. 145–88.

Carr, Lois Green, Walsh, Lorena S., and Menard, Russell R.: *Robert Cole's World: Agriculture and Society in Early Maryland* (Chapel Hill, NC: University of North Carolina Press, 1991).

Carson, Cary: "The Consumer Revolution in Colonial British America: Why Demand?" In Cary Carson, Ronald Hoffman, and Peter J. Albert, eds., *Of Consuming Interests: The Style of Life in the Eighteenth Century* (Charlottesville: University Press of Virginia).

Child, Josiah: *A New Discourse of Trade* (London, 1804 [1693]).

Clark, Christopher: *The Roots of Rural Capitalism: Western Massachusetts, 1780–1860* (Ithaca, NY: Cornell University Press, 1990).

Clark, Christopher: "The Transition to Capitalism: Early American History and the Market Revolution." Paper presented at the Sixth Annual Conference of the Omohundro Institute of Early American History and Culture, June 2000.

Daniels, Bruce: "Economic Development in Colonial and Revolutionary Connecticut: An Overview." *William and Mary Quarterly* 3rd ser., 37 (1980), pp. 429–50.

David, Paul: "The Growth of Real Product in the United States before 1840: New Evidence, New Conjectures." *Journal of Economic History* 27 (1967), pp. 151–97.

Degler, Carl N.: *Out of Our Past: the Forces That Shaped Modern America* (New York: Harper & Brothers, 1959).

Demos, John: *A Little Commonwealth: Family Life in Plymouth Colony* (New York: Oxford University Press, 1970).

Dunn, Richard: *Sugar and Slaves: The Rise of the Planter Class in the English West Indies, 1624–1713* (Chapel Hill, NC: University of North Carolina Press, 1972).

Earle, Carville: *The Evolution of a Tidewater Settlement System: All Hallow's Parish, Maryland, 1650–1783* (Chicago: University of Chicago Press, 1975).

Egnal, Marc: "The Economic Development of the Thirteen Continental Colonies, 1720–1775." *William and Mary Quarterly* 3rd ser., 32 (1975), pp. 191–222.

Egnal, Marc: *Divergent Paths: How Culture and Institutions Have Shaped North American Growth* (New York: Oxford University Press, 1996).

Eltis, David: "The Total Product of Barbados, 1664–1701." *Journal of Economic History* 55 (1995), pp. 321–38.

Engerman, Stanley: "Economic Growth 1783–1860." *Research in Economic History* 8 (1981), pp. 1–46.

Engerman, Stanley L. and Gallman, Robert E., eds.: *The Cambridge Economic History of the United States*, vol. 1, *The Colonial Era* (Cambridge: Cambridge University Press, 1996).

Engerman, Stanley L. and Sokoloff, Kenneth L.: "Factor Endowments, Institutions, and Differential Paths of Growth Among New World Economies." In Stephen Haber, ed., *How Latin America Fell Behind* (Palo Alto: Stanford University Press, 1997).

Galenson, David: "The Settlement and Growth of the Colonies: Population, Labor, and Economic Development," in S. L. Engerman and R. E. Gallman, eds., *The Cambridge Economic History of the United States*, vol. 1, *The Colonial Era* (Cambridge: Cambridge University Press, 1996), pp. 135–208.

Gallman, Robert: "The Pace and Pattern of American Economic Growth." In Lance E. Davis et al., eds., *American Economic Growth: An Economist's History of the United States* (New York: Harper & Row, 1972).

Gallman, Robert E. and Wallis, John Joseph, eds.: *American Economic Growth and Standards of Living before the Civil War* (Chicago: University of Chicago Press, 1992).

Genovese, Eugene D.: *Roll, Jordan, Roll: The World the Slaves Made* (New York: Pantheon Books, 1974)

Grant, Charles S.: *Democracy in the Connecticut Frontier Town of Kent* (New York: Vintage Press, 1961).

Greven, Philip: *Four Generations: Population, Land and Family in Colonial Andover, Massachusetts* (Ithaca, NY: Cornell University Press, 1970).

Henretta, James: *The Evolution of American Society, 1700–1815: An Interdisciplinary Analysis* (Lexington, MA: D. C. Heath & Company, 1973).

Henretta, James: "Families and Farms: Mentalite in Pre-Industrial America." *William and Mary Quarterly* 3rd ser., 35 (1978), pp. 3–32.

Innes, Stephen: *Labor in a New Land: Economy and Society in Seventeenth Century Springfield* (Princeton, NJ: Princeton University Press, 1983).

Isaac, Rhys: *The Transformation of Virginia, 1740–1790* (Chapel Hill, NC: University of North Carolina Press, 1982).

Jones, Alice Hanson: *Wealth of a Nation to Be: The American Colonies on the Eve of the Revolution* (New York: Columbia University Press, 1980).

Kulikoff, Allan: "The Transition to Capitalism in Rural America." *William and Mary Quarterly* 3rd ser., 46 (1989), pp. 120–44.

Lamoreaux, Naomi: "Accounting for Capitalism in Early American History: Farmers, Merchants, Manufacturers, and their Economic Worlds," paper presented at the annual meeting of the Society for Historians of the Early American Republic in Lexington, KY, July 1999.

Lemon, James T.: *The Best Poor Man's Country: A Geographical Study of Southeastern Pennsylvania* (Baltimore, MD: Johns Hopkins University Press, 1972).

Lemon, James T.: "Early Americans and their Social Environment." *Journal of Historical Geography* 6 (1980), pp. 115–31.

Lemon, James T.: "Spatial Order: Households in Local Communities and Regions." In Jack P. Greene and J. R. Pole eds., *Colonial British America: Essays in the New History of the Early Modern Era* (Baltimore, MD: Johns Hopkins University Press, 1984).

Lockridge, Kenneth: *A New England Town: The First Hundred Years* (New York: W. W. Norton, 1970).

Lockridge, Kenneth: "Social Change and the Meaning of the American Revolution." *Journal of Social History* 6 (1973), pp. 403–39.

Main, Gloria L.: "The Standard of Living in Colonial Massachusetts." *Journal of Economic History* 43 (1983), pp. 101–8.

Main, Gloria L. and Main, Jackson T.: "Economic Growth and the Standard of Living in Southern New England, 1640–1774." *Journal of Economic History* 48 (1988), pp. 27–46.

Main, Gloria L. and Main, Jackson T.: "The Red Queen in New England?" *William and Mary Quarterly* 56 (1999), 121–150.

Mancall, Peter C. and Weiss, Thomas: "Was Economic Growth Likely in Colonial British North America?" *Journal of Economic History* 59 (1999), pp. 17–40.

Martin, John Frederick: *Profits in the Wilderness: Entrepreneurs and the Founding of New England Towns in the Seventeenth Century* (Chapel Hill, NC: University of North Carolina Press, 1991).

McCusker, John and Menard, Russell B.: *The Economy of British America, 1609–1789* (Chapel Hill, NC: University of North Carolina Press, 1985).

Merrill, Michael: "Cash is Good to Eat: Self-Sufficiency and Exchange in the Rural Economy of the United States." *Radical History Review* 3 (1977), pp. 42–71.

Morgan, Edmund: *American Slavery, American Freedom: The Ordeal of Colonial Virginia* (New York: W. W. Norton & Company, 1975).

Murrin, John M. and Berthoff, Roland: "Feudalism, Communalism, and the Yeoman Freeholder: The American Revolution Considered as a Social Accident." In Stephen G. Kurtz and James H. Hutson, eds., *Essays on the American Revolution* (Chapel Hill, NC: University of North Carolina Press, 1973).

Nash, Gary: "Urban Wealth and Poverty in Pre-Revolutionary America." *Journal of Interdisciplinary History* 6 (1975–76), pp. 545–84.

Nash, Gary: *The Urban Crucible: Social Change, Political Consciousness, and the Origins of the American Revolution* (Cambridge, MA: Harvard University Press, 1979).

Newell, Margaret Ellen: *From Dependency to Independence: Economic Revolution in Colonial New England* (Ithaca, NY: Cornell University Press, 1988).

Newell, Margaret Ellen: "The Birth of New England in the Atlantic Economy." In Peter Temin, ed., *Engines of Enterprise: The Economic History of New England* (Cambridge, MA: Harvard University Press, 2001).

Price, Jacob: "The Transatlantic Economy." In Jack P. Greene and J. R. Pole, eds., *Colonial British America: Essays in the New History of the Early Modern Era* (Baltimore, MD: Johns Hopkins University Press, 1984).

Rothenberg, Winifred B.: "The Market and Massachusetts Farmers, 1750–1855." *Journal of Economic History* 41 (1981), pp. 283–314.

Shammas, Carole: "Consumer Behavior in Colonial America." *Social Science History* 6 (1982), pp. 67–86.

Shammas, Carole: "How Self-Sufficient was Early America?" *Journal of Interdisciplinary History* 13 (1982), pp. 247–72.

Shammas, Carole: *The Pre-industrial Consumer in England and America* (Oxford: Clarendon Press, 1990).

Shammas, Carole: "A New Look at Long-Term Trends in Wealth Inequality in the United States." *American Historical Review* 98 (1993), pp. 412–32.

Shepherd, James and Walton, Gary: *Shipping, Maritime Trade, and the Economic Development of Colonial North America* (Cambridge: Cambridge University Press, 1972).

Shepherd, James and Williamson, Samuel H.: "The Coastal Trade of the British North American Colonies." *Journal of Economic History* 32 (1972), pp. 783–810.

Sheridan, Richard B.: *Sugar and Slavery: An Economic History of the British West Indies, 1623–1775* (St. Lawrence, Barbados: Caribbean Universities Press, 1974).

Smith, Adam: *An Inquiry into the Nature and Causes of the Wealth of Nations*, ed. R. H. Campbell, A. S. Skinner, and W. B. Todd, 2 vols (Oxford: Oxford University Press, 1976 [1776]).

Smith, Billy G.: "The Material Lives of Laboring Philadelphians, 1750–1800." *William and Mary Quarterly* 3rd ser., 38 (1981), pp. 163–202.

Smith, Daniel Scott: "A Malthusian-Frontier Interpretation of United States Demographic History before c. 1815." In Woodrow Borah, Jorge Hardoy, and Gilbert Stelter, eds., *Urbanization in the Americas: The Background in Comparative Perspective* (Ottawa: History Division, National Museum of Man, 1980), pp. 15–24.

Sokoloff, Kenneth L. and Villaflor, Georgia C.: "The Early Achievement of Modern Stature in America." *Social Science History* 6 (1982), pp. 453–81.

Steckel, Richard H.: "Nutritional Status in the Colonial American Economy: An Anthropological Perspective" (working paper, 1995).

Temin, Peter, ed.: *Engines of Enterprise: The Economic History of New England* (Cambridge, MA: Harvard University Press, 2000).

Ulrich, Laurel Thacher: *Good Wives: Image and Reality in the Lives of Women in Northern New England, 1650–1750* (New York: Vintage Press, 1983).

Ulrich, Laurel Thacher: "Martha Ballard and Her Girls: Women's Work in Eighteenth-Century Maine." In S. Innes, ed., *Work and Labour in Early America* (Chapel Hill, NC: University of North Carolina Press, 1988), pp. 70–105.

Ulrich, Laurel Thacher: "Wheels, Looms, and the Gender Division of Labor in Eighteenth Century New England," *William and Mary Quarterly* 55 (1998), 3–38.

US Bureau of the Census: *Historical Statistics of the United States, Colonial Times to 1970* (Bicentennial Edition: Washington, DC, 1975) {reprinted in 1976 as *The Statistical History of the United States, from Colonial Times to the Present*, ed. Ben J. Wattenberg [New York, 1976]}.

Usner, Daniel H.: *Indians, Settlers, and Slaves in a Frontier Exchange Economy: The Lower Mississippi Valley Before 1783* (Chapel Hill, NC: University of North Carolina Press, 1992).

Vickers, Daniel: "Competency and Competition: Economic Culture in Early America." *William and Mary Quarterly* 3rd ser., 47 (1990), pp. 3–29.

Vickers, Daniel: *Farmers and Fishermen: Two Centuries of Work in Essex County, Massachusetts, 1630–1830* (Chapel Hill, NC: University of North Carolina Press, 1994).

Vickers, Daniel: "The Northern Colonies: Economy and Society, 1600–1775." In Engerman and Gallman (1996), pp. 209–48.

Walton, Gary M., and Shepherd, James F.: *The Economic Rise of Colonial America* (Cambridge: Cambridge University Press, 1979).

White, Richard: *The Middle Ground: Indians, Empires, and Republics in the Great Lakes Region, 1650–1815* (Cambridge: Cambridge University Press, 1991).

CHAPTER NINE

Women and Gender

CAROL KARLSEN

Early American women's history can be considered an old or a new field. We tend to think of it, like women's history in other times and places, as a relatively recent practice, a product of the women's liberation and civil rights movements of the 1960s and 1970s. And for the most part it is. But for historians who initiated their studies in the 1970s, at least two earlier bodies of work beckoned, one on European Americans, the other on Native Americans. Because these literatures so profoundly influenced the assumptions, questions, challenges, and theoretical orientations of subsequent scholarship, assessment of the how the field has developed over the past three decades necessarily starts here.

Most widely recognized in 1970 were several books written earlier in the twentieth century by feminist writers interested in women who migrated from England (Earle, 1904; Abbot, 1910; Dexter, 1924; Spruill, 1938). Not all of these authors had academic credentials and their approaches and arguments varied, but they shared a passion for reclaiming a place for Anglo-American women in particular in early American history. As a group these scholars fostered the idea that skewed sex ratios, labor shortages, high mortality, and institutional instability worked to these women's advantage, whether as compared to their European counterparts or their nineteenth-century American descendants. Frontier conditions, in conjunction with pre-industrial work patterns and values, the argument went, enhanced women's status and opportunities in the New World; once these circumstances changed, especially with increased social and cultural complexity and the coming of the Industrial Revolution, women's status declined and women were relegated to the marginal positions they would occupy from then on.

Eventually each of these constructions – frontier, pre-industrial, women's status, New World, and most recently, women – would be contested, as would much of the larger argument. But in the early 1970s, this interpretation held, in part because it had received considerable support since the 1930s from established male historians. Less interested in women's lives per se than in re-creating early religious, legal, family, and community history, these scholars had stressed the harmony and mutuality of relations between women and men. Puritans in particular, they affirmed, with their emphasis on the centrality of marriage and the equality of souls before God, had accorded colonial women unusual respect and authority. Flexible legal practices and the family's role as a model for New England's social order also added to the rights these women could claim to protection and property. In 1970, writing about Plymouth colony, John Demos had articulated the prevailing view when he wrote that "this does *not* seem to have been a society characterized by a really pervasive, and operational, norm of male dominance" (Demos, 1970, p. 95).

If these early studies sometimes acknowledged restrictions European American women faced, when the second wave of colonial women's historians began their research in the 1970s, they found the possibilities foregrounded – and not only by their male counterparts. Contemporary feminist colleagues specializing in the nineteenth century had already begun publishing books and articles distinguishing gender relations in the industrial age from presumably more benign colonial forms (Flexner, 1959; Lerner, 1969; Buhle et al., 1971). For some, colonial women were not simply better off than their descendants; they were roughly equal to the men in their communities.

In 1970, seventeenth- and eighteenth-century Native American gender arrangements seemed even more egalitarian than those created by European Americans (Stites, 1905; Randle, 1951; Brown, 1970). Having been subjects of study even longer than colonial women, albeit among anthropologists primarily, Native American women evoked images of considerable autonomy and power as well as authority, respect, and high status. Some scholars had gone so far as to argue that these women had more control over resources and decision-making than the men in their communities. Although explanations for women's unusual position in Native societies focused on the production and distribution of food and matrilineal kinship practices, parallels to the accepted narrative on colonial women are striking. Relations between women and men were described as "traditional" rather than resulting from frontier conditions, but here too women enjoyed an enviable position at first, only to suffer its loss. In this case, European colonization, rather than internal social and cultural dynamics, catalyzed decline. This picture had more vocal critics than the one drawn for European American women, but for several reasons, including some rather persuasive evidence, it garnered considerable support. Based almost exclusively on anthropological studies of Iroquois people, however, and rarely distinguishing one century of "traditional" life from another, it was equally vulnerable to challenge.

By the mid- to late 1970s, when second wave feminist scholars began publishing their research on the seventeenth and eighteenth centuries, the dominant interpretations of both European American and Native American gender relations were already subjects of extensive debate. The first challenges to the accepted wisdom about colonial women came from male scholars, demographers and social historians primarily, whose quantitative research on marriage and fertility patterns, birth control, pre-marital pregnancy, widowhood, poverty, and literacy raised thoughtful and crucial questions about the rosy picture earlier studies painted and the evidence upon which it was based (Wells, 1972; Smith, 1973; Keyssar, 1974; Jones, 1974, Lockridge, 1974). Their studies highlighted striking gender differences in poverty levels, literacy rates, opportunities for remarriage, and other measures of social and economic power, suggesting that the actual conditions of colonial women's daily lives had been masked by too great a reliance of earlier scholars on the diaries, letters, sermons, and other literary sources left by European American men. Two provocative articles on Anne Hutchinson's battle with Boston's religious and secular leaders during the Antinomian crisis, moreover, indicated that Hutchinson may have been less anomalous in her defiance of male authority than previously thought, thereby raising questions about other exceptions to Puritan women's presumed acceptance of an enviable lot (Barker-Benfield,

1972; Koehler, 1974). If these revisionist studies focused mainly on New England, they also stimulated reassessments of other parts of British America.

The early 1970s objections to the dominant narrative about Native women came from within feminist anthropology not history. More theoretically oriented than historians, anthropologists tackled the question of whether societies with gender equality had ever existed or whether the subordination of women was universal (Rosaldo and Lamphere, 1974). The quality and persuasiveness of the arguments generated on both sides of this issue drew the attention of feminist scholars from other disciplines, history among them, but the research required to participate in this discussion was conducted largely by anthropologists. The debate raged into the early 1980s (Reiter, 1975; Etienne and Leacock, 1980; Ortner and Whitehead, 1981), with Native American gender relations cited as some of the strongest evidence that sexual equality once characterized societies generally, only to wane with the origins of private property, state formation, and European conquest, colonization, and missionization. Calling for a more historically informed anthropology, proponents of the gender egalitarianism position carried the day among women's historians. The Marxist orientation of so many women's studies scholars at the time surely enhanced its appeal. When historian Joan Jensen entered this debate with her analysis of Seneca women's experience in the late eighteenth and early nineteenth centuries (1977), she reinforced assumptions that prior to colonization, Native American women held extensive economic and political power and strongly resisted subsequent European efforts to diminish it.

Native women entered the historical discussion in two other important ways during these years. Well ahead of her time, Rayna Green (1975) deconstructed the Pocahontas image in American popular culture. Although her brief exploration ranged from the colonial period to the present, her attention to both literary and visual culture influenced later analyses of how Europeans represented indigenous women and gender relations in colonial discourse. Sylvia Van Kirk (1980) and Jennifer Brown (1980) also moved beyond the equality vs. subordination controversy with intercultural analyses of Native women's roles in northern fur trading societies. Addressing the emergence and perpetuation of Métis communities, they introduced questions of cultural hybridity into North American gender studies. Not until the 1990s, however, would these three scholars' methods and insights be fully appreciated.

In contrast to the very few who researched indigenous gender relations, second wave women's historians turned their attention to colonial women in large numbers. Articles began to appear regularly in the mid-1970s and full-length studies soon after. This work continued the focus on New England that had preoccupied male scholars, though substantial interest in Chesapeake region became apparent as well. Quantitative analyses still characterized much of this scholarship, especially on the Chesapeake, yet a palpable desire to reclaim the experiences of actual women drew researchers to more diverse sources as well as new readings of the old. If colonial women's status and roles remained crucial concerns, a growing feminist theoretical literature complicated them (Mitchell, 1971; Kelly-Godol, 1975; Rubin, 1975; Johansson, 1976), pushing colonial historians to rethink and reframe some questions and develop others. What did feminists mean by women's status? By spiritual equality? By production and reproduction? By sex and gender? Was gender a system created primarily by its male beneficiaries? What specifically shaped the way in which those systems were constructed in colonial communities? Could feminist scholars even talk about colonial women's lives, when they varied so much by region, ethnicity, religion, and class? How might an increasingly sophisticated understanding of the social relations of the sexes in the late twentieth century help us better unravel the gender dynamics of the past? Answers would emerge in time, but historical questions and research were decidedly shaped in the 1970s by the rapid growth of women's studies, the academic arm of the women's liberation movement.

Puritanism was one of the first concerns addressed by second wave colonial women's historians. Who was right, feminists asked, scholars who found Protestants, and especially Puritans, highly valuing and encouraging of colonial women or those who stressed the male dominance of Puritan culture and New England society? In their responses, however, they resisted polarizations of these two positions, arguing for more nuanced understandings of Puritanism and New England's social order. Still, some studies emphasized the positive, others the negative. Laurel Thatcher Ulrich (1976), for example, writing on ministerial literature, acknowledged the narrow frames of reference within which clergymen discussed women, but stressed the spiritual equality they accorded women and the similar qualities they praised in men and women. Careful to note that the evidence could be read in opposing ways, and reluctant to presume behavior from prescription, Ulrich nonetheless offered support for the idea that Puritan ministers fostered a respect for women who embodied the virtues they prescribed. Mary Maples Dunn (1978), on the other hand, in a study of Puritans and Quakers, found that both religious movements stimulated colonial women's activism in support of their beliefs, but that the men in the two groups differed in the level of spiritual autonomy they allowed women. Whereas Puritan men did not take spiritual equality among men and women to mean a shared ministry and church governance, Quaker men did. Social equality among Puritans remained a possibility during the early years of settlement, Dunn noted, but in the face of challenges to patriarchal authority by Anne Hutchinson and other independently minded women, religious and secular authorities had squelched that potential by the 1660s.

Quantitatively based studies of demography, marriage, family life, widowhood, and divorce were similarly cautious but affirming of one or the other position in the status debate. Lois Green Carr and Lorena Walsh (1977), for example, looking at early Maryland colonists, addressed a series of questions about single, married, and widowed women's experiences. If tentative in their conclusions, they found that single women were more vulnerable but less restricted than had they stayed in England, with marriage more likely. As planters' wives and widows, they and their families suffered higher death rates, although those who survived attained more respect, independence, and power. Still, the conditions of early settlement were temporary, they reminded readers; by the late seventeenth century life chances were better but the status women enjoyed had deteriorated. Studying divorce in eighteenth-century Massachusetts, Nancy Cott (1976) saw improvement over time. Colonial women found it easier to obtain a divorce than English women, she argued, but colonial husbands found it easier than colonial wives. A double standard of marital fidelity, higher illiteracy rates for women, and men's greater social and political power worked to women's disadvantage. Not until the end of the colonial period could wives expect roughly the same success attaining divorces as husbands. Cott concluded that gender inequality was built into the colonial marriage contract and did not disappear during the Revolutionary years, but that a heightened emphasis on male virtue and a new marital ideal may have worked to women's advantage.

Analysis of probate, divorce, and other court records led as well to initial forays into legal history and more general reassessment of long-established assumptions about how colonial women fared before the bar. Again, opposing analyses emerged. Joan Hoff Wilson (1976), in an attempt to show that the American Revolution benefited women very little, echoed earlier arguments that modifications of English common law practices and equity jurisprudence advanced the status of Anglo-American over British women in the colonial period. She noted certain losses in their legal power by the mid-eighteenth century, especially with less women-friendly inheritance practices, but found the most crucial changes during the years leading up to and following the Revolution. Marylynn Salmon disagreed (1979). Comparing the relative importance of common law and equity courts in Pennsylvania and looking specifically at marriage, dower rights, and property transactions, she found the evidence more mixed. Still, she held that the judicial system there, even the equity courts, fostered colonial women's dependence rather than independence.

Although critical transitions in European American women's lives occurred at different times in these studies, varying from region to region and driven by a range of different engines including industrialization, modernization, or the American Revolution, the late eighteenth century remained as central to second wave interpretations as it had been to feminist scholars of the early twentieth century. Privacy was rare during the colonial period; by the Victorian period it was sacrosanct. Early generations of women were denied advanced education; in the new republic, institutions were created especially for them. Both men and women contributed economically to their households in the seventeenth and eighteenth centuries; the nineteenth saw the emergence of a new ideology that masked women's ongoing participation in household economies by identifying men as providers and women as leisured. Once women controlled childbirth and midwifery; by 1800, neither was an exclusively female preserve.

Emphasis on the late eighteenth century as the most significant turning point in early American women's history received its strongest endorsement during this period with the publication of Nancy Cott's *The Bonds of Womanhood* (1977), Linda Kerber's *Women of the Republic* (1980), and Mary Beth Norton's *Liberty's Daughters* (1980). While Cott's main focus was the origins of the nineteenth-century "cult of domesticity" (1977, p. 1) and its relationship to the women's rights movement, and Kerber's the significance of political and intellectual changes for European American women's experiences in the new republic, all three spoke to the colonial period, Norton most thoroughly. Each affirmed that these women's educational prospects improved, but their assessments of the causes and significance of other ideological and material changes diverged considerably.

For Norton, who had already identified what she called the "myth of the golden age" in colonial scholarship (1979, p. 37), the American War of Independence was a milestone in the improvement of European American women's status. She characterized the colonial period as constraining these women's roles, choices, independence, and self-perceptions and the revolutionary era as enhancing them. Kerber concurred that colonial women suffered many political, legal, and familial restrictions and that the political ferment surrounding the war was crucial to understanding what lay ahead for their descendants. But she was much less sanguine, seeing these women's political activism only temporarily encouraged, their legal position fundamentally unchanged, and "Republican Motherhood" only a partial advance over the more overtly patriarchal ideology that preceded it (1980, p. 11). Cott, limiting her study to New England, identified the economic, social, and demographic transformations brought about by industrialization and modernization as key to comprehending changes in European American women's lives and the emergence of the ideology of domesticity in the late eighteenth and early nineteenth centuries. Beginning with eighteenth-century wives' legally defined dependence and subordination, in assessing changes in the work patterns of single and married women, for example, she saw continuities characterizing married women's experiences, while daughters benefited from increased economic as well as educational opportunities.

However much the status debate and emphasis on late eighteenth-century transitions shaped the literature on European American women during this period, women's historians were not sidetracked from their main task. On the contrary, these and other authors initiated an immensely creative effort to explore previously untapped sources and find theoretical frameworks that would foster historical re-creation of women's daily lives. Childbirth, mothering, and motherhood were simply three of several topics that had received little attention prior to the mid-1970s, but that would become integral to the field within a few years. The term social childbirth entered academic discussion as best describing the relations among colonial women during the birthing process, with efforts to comprehend this female world and its subsequent decline added to the scholarly agenda (Wertz and Wertz, 1977; Scholten, 1977). Mothering was also disentangled from motherhood, with the former recognized as social practice and the latter identified as an ideological construction that was loaded with symbolic meanings and linked to larger social and cultural changes in both Europe and the colonies (Bloch, 1978; Kerber, 1980). The socialist feminist theoretical underpinnings of so many women's history analyses were hardly lacking in these discussions, but other explanatory models gained momentum.

The 1970s also witnessed initial efforts to address African American women's lives in the seventeenth and eighteenth centuries. Historians of slavery, race relations, demography, and labor history, however, rather than women's historians, undertook the research and offered the first insights. Russell Menard (1975), Herbert Gutman (1976), Allan Kulikoff (1977), and others told of family formation in the Southeast, including how population growth, sex ratios, mortality rates, plantation size, and other factors influenced the marriage, childbearing, and child-rearing patterns of enslaved Africans and their creole descendants. These early studies also pointed to, but did not pursue very far, important questions about gender differences in sexual vulnerability, forms of slave resistance, access to skilled work, and relationships with children and other family members. During the early seventeenth century, these studies showed, freedom was still a legal possibility for men and women, but after mid-century, conditions simultaneously deteriorated and improved. As both plantations and slave populations enlarged, especially in the eighteenth century, slavery became a more deeply entrenched, restrictive, and brutal institution at the same time that isolation and alienation lessened as families and communities became easier to establish.

In the 1980s, early American women's history developed rapidly. Articles not only grew into books, but the scholars who initiated the field in the 1970s had been busy training graduate students to generate additional questions, unearth fresh sources, and expand into understudied regions. Not surprisingly, many of these students built upon, revised, or challenged the arguments of their mentors, though others struck out on their own. And as before, some new studies dealt specifically with the colonial period, while others only touched on the seventeenth or eighteenth centuries in analyses that focused on the nineteenth century. The results were exciting, though disappointing in that New England still drew more than its share of attention and research on European American women far outstripped the study of other groups.

Only a few historians considered African American women's early history worthy of their scholarly engagement. In 1986, Joan Gundersen investigated a single inland Virginia parish in the early eighteenth century, asking how gender and race intersected in the lives of both African American and European American women. Although her argument that gender fostered an interracial community of women sparked controversy, her emphasis on how race also divided women moved the discussion of slave women beyond the earlier though still dynamic demographic studies of the Chesapeake region. Gundersen also addressed the question of how female slaves' experiences differed from those of male slaves. In doing so, she allowed readers to compare her findings on colonial Virginia to arguments nineteenth-century scholars had made for the antebellum period.

Carole Shammas (1985) was another exception. While supporting previous scholarly arguments that most enslaved women in the eighteenth century were abused as field workers not as household laborers, Shammas focused on a growing tendency among some late eighteenth-century planters to move female slaves into domestic work, particularly the production of food and textiles. If Shammas's main achievement lay in her demonstration of variability and change in patterns of African American women's work prior to the antebellum period, her research into the social and economic history of slavery also undermined popular portrayals of domestic arrangements in the "big house" by showing that some of the main characters had been seriously miscast.

Free women in late eighteenth- and early nineteenth-century Petersburg, Virginia, drew the attention of Suzanne Lebsock. Like Deborah Gray White, who addressed similar questions about antebellum slave women (1982), she expressed annoyance at late twentieth-century policy makers' widespread assumption that African American women had historically been matriarchs. Lebsock combed local records for information on sex ratios, household structures, property ownership, work patterns, and other indicators of free women's status and familial relations in one urban center in the wake of the American Revolution. Finding documentation that these women outnumbered free men by 3:2 but had minimal opportunities for employment, she also located evidence showing that they headed more than half of the free households, and even occasionally held property. She concluded that "[t]he sex ratio, the law, poverty, and preference conspired to keep a great many free black women single, and to the extent that women remained single, they remained free agents in the economic realm" (1982, p. 282). By no means minimizing the weight of the first three factors or the level of exploitation these women suffered, she did argue that the lack of opportunities free men had to control their female counterparts, and the consequences of marriage for property-owning women working to purchase the freedom of family members, may have led some women to shun legal marriage in favor of some measure of autonomy. But that autonomy, she noted, fragile as it was, hardly constituted the power the word matriarch conveyed.

Although Jacqueline Jones's research interests lay in nineteenth- and twentieth-century African American history at this time, she undertook the first sustained attempt to synthesize the many fragments of information other scholars had unearthed on seventeenth- and eighteenth-century slave women's experiences in British North America (1989). She addressed questions about women's work and familial relations primarily and paid closest attention to the end of the colonial period. But she greatly enhanced her contribution by making regional comparisons and discussing the impact of colonists' struggle against England on black women's own fight for independence for themselves and their families. The nearly simultaneous publication of several full-length studies of enslaved women in the Caribbean (Beckles, 1989; Morrissey, 1989; Bush, 1990) furthered the value of Jones's comparative analysis. Together, they generated a formidable agenda for subsequent work on race and gender in the Americas.

The 1980s witnessed only minimal progress in developing Native American women's early history. Though Elisabeth Tooker offered a powerful challenge to the idea that Iroquois women once enjoyed unequaled power (1984), while Irene Silverblatt effectively reaffirmed the egalitarian position more generally in her study of gender ideologies and colonialism in Peru (1987), anthropologists generally lost interest in both Native American women and the equality vs. subordination debate. Sociologist Karen Anderson (1985) and historian Carol Devens (1986) entered it, however, with articles (and subsequently books) dealing with French–Native relations in the regions north of the Great Lakes and St. Lawrence River. Anderson's comparative analysis of French influence on Huron and Montagnais-Naskapi gender relations complicated the gender symmetry argument, while Devens's emphasis on female resistance to Christianization placed Native women more centrally within the power struggles European colonization fostered. Métis cultures of the Great Lakes region were further analyzed in this decade (Peterson, 1985). Pueblo gender systems in early New Mexico drew attention as well, especially as they were refigured in the wake of Spanish invasion and occupation (Foote and Schackel, 1986).

During the 1980s, other previously ignored regions and groups entered the scholarly conversation about early American women. Concern with colonialism and the fur trade stimulated interest in the gender systems French immigrants and their descendants had created among themselves along the Mississippi River (Boyle, 1987). Attention to Mexico, New Mexico, and Alta California brought Spanish Mexican women into the picture (Gutiérrez, 1985; Seed, 1988; Castañeda, 1990; Hernández, 1990; Rock, 1990). As initial forays into the sources, legal matters – most notably marriage, inheritance patterns, property exchanges – dominated this work, speaking as much perhaps to the accessibility of particular records as to the kinds of questions already raised about British colonials on the eastern seaboard. Some of these studies presented Spanish Mexican and French American women as having property rights and access to power they would later lose. Others directly or indirectly challenged that view, opening up newer questions about Spanish colonialism's effect on both colonizers and their descendants.

In addition to Patricia Seed's highly influential study of Mexico (1988), the most detailed study of Spanish Mexican gender relations came from Ramón Gutiérrez. In an important 1985 article on honor and marriage in eighteenth- and early nineteenth-century New Mexico, Gutiérrez portrayed a society steeped in patriarchy, where control over who married whom remained the primary way elite men established and maintained class, race, and gender hierarchies. Honor, however, was not the same for women and men, and was virtually non-existent for those who could not claim Spanish heritage. Gutiérrez defined honor in this time and place as "a prestige system based on principles of inherent personal worth." Elite men demonstrated that worth through honesty, loyalty, and authority over their families and lower ranking males, and by acting "con hombria (in a manly fashion)." Elite women, he added, embodied that worth in shame, diffidence, sexual propriety, and "feminine" behavior. While Gutiérrez was highly persuasive in recounting the symbolic power of marriage and men's honor in maintaining intricately layered social inequalities, his elision of the meanings this gendered system of honor might have had for Spanish Mexican women disappointed many readers. Still, he implied that whatever power these women attained through control of property (and apparently he found little of that), paled in comparison to the limits imposed on them before and during marriage. Though he suggested that "an increased preference for unions based explicitly on romantic love over those arranged by parents pursuing economic considerations" lessened the weight of patriarchy for these women by 1800, for the most part the picture he painted was grim (1985, pp. 84, 86, 101).

As before, European American women's history commanded the most attention in the 1980s. For the first time, second wave feminists published book-length studies on seventeenth-century immigrants or included the early decades of settlement in long-term analyses. The late eighteenth century still drew more attention, with transitions into the nineteenth century remaining a primary concern, but earlier indications that the pre-revolutionary period was hardly a seamless whole now also received considerable support. These new works tended to combine social and cultural history, much as their predecessors had in the 1970s, but the social still predominated and the theories and methods informing each became more explicit and even more broadly interdisciplinary. The law – and the women who either resorted to it or ran afoul of it – took center stage in this literature, but women's work and domestic worlds were highly visible. Article-length investigations treated many of the same concerns and theoretical orientations as longer interpretations, but they also prefigured topics, such as sexuality and politics, that would distinguish the 1990s more than the 1980s.

Debates about inheritance law and its impact on Euro-American women heated up during the 1980s, overshadowing most other scholarly concerns. Some reasons for this are not hard to discern. The lack of first-person narrative sources for the period before 1750, the availability of printed laws and probate and other court records for each of the British colonies, and widespread training in computer-based quantitative techniques fostered research on inheritance along with other matters of law. As if not more crucial, control of property was one of the most obvious indicators of economic position and power, and women's access to it was determined primarily by inheritance law and practice. However explained, inheritance studies became a cottage industry of sorts among women's and family historians; as a result, almost as many patterns emerged in the literature as there were places and times investigated.

Comparing New York and Virginia in the early eighteenth century, for example, Joan Gundersen and Gwen Gampel argued that coverture was largely a legal fiction, that legal restrictions on married women went unenforced or carried little weight in a system in which dower rights were protected, both during a woman's marriage and her widowhood (1982). Marylynn Salmon, on the other hand, found protection of women's inheritance rights weak in seventeenth-century New England and coverture strenuously enforced, with wives' property interests subordinated to those of their husbands and sons (1986). Looking at New York in the late seventeenth and early eighteenth centuries, David Narrett found that wives and widows there suffered extensive losses as the Dutch system of community property within marriage gave way to English colonial practices of restricting women's legal control of estates (1989), while Gloria Main found more continuity than change in the wills husbands wrote in rural Massachusetts in the mid- to late eighteenth century (1989). At the very least, these and other sharp differences in the arguments put forth in inheritance studies showed a marked diversity in practices and in the quality and quantity of the surviving records, not only across regions, but also within individual colonies over time.

The confusing array of patterns documented in the inheritance literature spoke as well to the continuation of two contradictory sets of assumptions about the position of European American women in the British colonies. By the 1980s, the basic structures of male domination had been identified and enough careful research conducted on the framing and fleshing out of those structures that very few historians openly articulated or defended a roughly egalitarian argument about gender relations, let alone an egalitarian one. As Gloria Main allowed, "[o]ne begins with the acknowledgment that women in Anglo-American culture occupied only a secondary status in their world, subordinate to their fathers and husbands and, in their widowhood, even to their grown sons" (1989, p. 68). Nonetheless, arguments that delineated the shape, extent, and significance of patriarchal control and its meaning for women met strong resistance – and not just from writers who deemed women's history irrelevant and feminist scholarship a contradiction in terms.

Among those who studied gender relations, some disagreements about colonial women's position vis-à-vis inheritance fell along lines dividing women's history from family and community history. Others suggest that fundamental differences in constructions of gender were at work. Even before publication of Joan Scott's widely regarded essay, "Gender: A Useful Category of Historical Analysis (1986)," feminist historians tended to construct gender as *relations of power*, with interactions among family members comprising one of several interconnecting sets of unequal relationships influencing how women negotiated their worlds. Scholars in the 1980s who challenged studies of the workings of power in early America generally were more likely to discuss gender as the *power of relations*, with family claims, bonds, and dynamics among the most crucial determinants of male/female interactions within and among households. These ways of seeing are not mutually exclusive, of course; but what scholars chose to foreground seems to have varied with the assumptions they brought to their sources about what gender means and why gender matters.

From this perspective, for instance, Lisa Wilson Waciega's upbeat portrayal (1987) of men's trust of their wives and generosity toward them as expressed in late eighteenth-century inheritance practices in southeastern Pennsylvania speaks at least in part to the profound importance she attributed to family connections and survival strategies. Similarly, Carole Shammas's decidedly less sanguine assessment (1989) of inheritance patterns in the same region appears to have been shaped to some degree by her tracing of the development of family capitalism and its influence on men's decisions about how to divide their property among potential heirs. This is not to say that definitions of gender fully explain the inheritance controversies of the 1980s, nor indeed, any of the other debates that characterized these years. It is to suggest, though, that perspectives on gender, like other assumptions scholars bring to their research, help us reconcile such divergent readings of the surviving evidence on inheritance law and practice.

Colonial women and men who came into court on criminal charges or who filed complaints against others were also featured in the 1980s literature. Here, too, the treatments seem intrinsically related to the gendered meanings authors brought to their evidence at this time. As the first book-length accounts of New England witch-craft to address questions about women's central roles in witchcraft cases, John Dem-os's *Entertaining Satan* (1982) and my own *The Devil in the Shape of a Woman* (1987) illustrate this point. Our arguments were based on the same core evidence, so the relationships among our analyses of that evidence, the additional sources we turned to, and our own constructions of gender are more apparent than in other discussions of women and the law.

Demos found that with few exceptions male dominance and control of women held little explanatory power in New England's witchcraft cases. Rather, early childhood experiences fostered widespread inner and interpersonal tensions that took pride of place in a multifaceted interpretation of why some men and women were accusers and others the targets of witchcraft accusations. Social and cultural dynamics were central to Demos's larger explanation, but unresolved oedipal and pre-oedipal conflicts were even more so. For my part, internal and external conflicts were vital to understanding New England's witchcraft beliefs and accusations, but I found those conflicts gener-ated less by the traumas of infancy than by social and cultural institutions, events, and processes. I argued that witchcraft trials were fostered by Puritan constructions of both women and witches and by the related power dynamics that played themselves out in seventeenth-century New England's emerging social structure. While our inter-pretations complemented one another in many respects, our differing views of gender help account for the divergences.

Colonial women's work emerged as the third main area of scholarly interest in the 1980s. Interpretive disagreements were hardly absent in this area of study but they were certainly more muted. Greater consistency among authors about what gender meant may explain much of the fit among interpretations, but consistency in the kind of evidence found also mattered. So too perhaps did the sense that reconstructing the everyday lives of colonial women was necessarily a tentative venture, given the paucity of diaries, letters, and other conscious articulations of personal experience, especially before the American Revolution.

Though long a subject of interest because of Nancy Cott's work on domesticity (1977) and Linda Kerber's on republican womanhood, explorations of colonial wom-en's work and domestic worlds in the 1980s aroused new questions about the content and cultural definitions of this work, about its value and significance, and about its visibility and invisibility. Growing sensitivity to differences among women, so force-fully urged and debated in women's studies programs, conferences, and theoretical literature, had not yet pushed colonial scholars to consider European American wom-en's racial identities significant enough to analyze. But age, marital status, religion, region, and class were increasingly differentiated, as were urban and rural patterns and different moments within the colonial and revolutionary periods.

Carole Shammas (1980–1) and Laurel Thatcher Ulrich (1982) led the way, sorting out what objects colonial women could and did surround themselves with and what they valued in things as well as relationships. Consumption, domestic rituals, sociability, oral contracts, and neighboring trading networks joined production and reproduction as scholarly concerns. Together, these two authors demolished the idea that colonial households were self-sufficient, either economically or socially. Shammas also prefigured later analyses by placing European American communities more firmly in the context of European colonialism, the eighteenth-century consumer revolution, and the larger Atlantic world.

Meanwhile, family-based labor systems among European Americans drew considerable attention, along with continuities and changes within regions as colonial economies became more cash and market oriented and more class-based (Dudden, 1983; Karlsen and Crumpacker, 1984; Jensen, 1986; Blewett, 1988; Boydston, 1990; Ulrich, 1990). The transition from girl to woman received further examination, as did the differences between single and married women's experiences. Some women's historians looked at the shift in young women's labor, from a time when virtually all European American females provided domestic help in their own and other households to the emergence of domestic service as a class- (and race-)based occupation. Others took issue with the notion that either single or married women's household work diminished in the late eighteenth-century households; rather, they argued, production actually increased for some, while for others it became more varied or moved to new locations.

Joan Jensen's *Loosening the Bonds* (1986) and Jeanne Boydston's *Home and Work* (1990) profoundly altered the way colonial historians talk about married women's work in the late eighteenth century. Studying Delaware and southeastern Pennsylvania, Jensen demonstrated the continued vitality and necessity of European American women's household production in rural areas well beyond the colonial period, reminding readers not only that industrial capitalism came a lot more slowly to the United States than prior attention to a few cities and towns would indicate but also that commercial capitalism increased rather than decreased many women's economic contributions to their households. Boydston concurred. Looking at the Northeast more broadly, at urban as well as rural areas, Boydston challenged not only the long-held assumption that married women's household work precreased over the course of the eighteenth and early nineteenth centuries but also the related presumption that that labor remained outside of capitalism's yoke. Instead, she submitted, women's work lost recognition *as* work, indeed was rendered invisible as work, precisely because married women's economic contribution to their households became more not less necessary to the developing economy.

The 1990 publication of Laurel Ulrich's pathbreaking book, *A Midwife's Tale,* cemented many of the insights and arguments of the previous decade about colonial women's work, while bringing one of those women to life, so to speak. Martha Ballard, now a household name among American historians, made her own labor visible, but it took Ulrich's skill to demonstrate its significance, given how the trivialization of women's work in our own time had blinded scholars to the content and meaning of household labor. Focusing on Ballard as housewife and midwife, Ulrich drew a vivid picture of how Ballard participated in separate worlds of female labor and commercial exchange while working "in tandem" with her husband and other men in her family and community. "There were really two family economies in the Ballard household," Ulrich argued, "the one managed by Martha, the other by [her husband] Ephraim" (1990, p. 80). Although much of Ballard's history, gleaned from her long neglected diary, took place after the American Revolution, scholars of early America recognized in Ulrich's analysis a useful model for coming to terms with the complexities of earlier colonial households. Along with the early chapters of Judith Hewitt's *Brought to Bed* (1986), *A Midwife's Tale* also showed that the work of bringing children into the world went well beyond the labor of the birthing mother.

In 1980, anthropologist Michelle Rosaldo had asked rhetorically whether the cross-cultural assumption that women inhabited a private sphere and men a public sphere might be simply a gendered construct, widely accepted as social reality but "merely reflecting the prevailing gender belief system" of a culture. During the next decade, directly or indirectly, books and articles dealing with colonial women's labor began addressing this question empirically. Like Laurel Ulrich, most of them found solid evidence that European American women and men lived in separate worlds much of the time, but not that those worlds corresponded in any way to an impermeable split between supposedly public and private realms. Jeanne Boydston took the discussion furthest, identifying the economic value of women's household work and how it was constructed as leisure, not work, in the eighteenth and early nineteenth centuries. Calling that process the "pastoralization of housework," she tied it firmly to the creation of "the ideology of gender spheres" in the Northeast (1990, p. 142).

The early 1980s also saw powerful cross-disciplinary critiques of white feminist assumptions about the universality of white middle-class women's experiences (Omolade, 1980; Hooks, 1981; Hull et al., 1982). Hazel Carby in particular argued forcefully (1982) that white feminist preoccupation with late eighteenth- and early nineteenth-century constructions of white womanhood and sisterhood erased black women from women's history. The 1980s saw little in the way of empirical responses to these charges from feminists studying colonial women. Nonetheless, in raising the specter of racism within women's history and women's studies more generally, black feminists laid the groundwork for subsequent research on white and black race formation.

Theoretical responses to Rosaldo, Carby, and other critics came more swiftly. Whether intentionally or not, during the rest of the decade historians and other feminist scholars more thoroughly deconstructed not only public and private spheres, but also the related concepts of sisterhood, true womanhood, and even "woman" (Mohanty, 1984; Hewitt, 1985; Carby, 1987; Kerber, 1988; Spelman, 1988; Riley 1988; Butler, 1990). Republican womanhood and domesticity, analytical frameworks formulated by women's and gender historians earlier (Kerber, 1980; Cott, 1977), also faced intense scrutiny and revision. By 1990, not only had the old public/private dichotomy been drained of its explanatory power, but many earlier arguments about late eighteenth- and early nineteenth-century transitions in women's lives crumbled under the weight of the question: for which women?

Conventional political history, one of the areas Joan Scott identified as needing rethinking among feminist scholars (1986), had drawn attention from colonial women's historians early on, especially those who studied the American Revolution. But the 1980s pushed that project forward as well (Baker, 1984; Kerber, 1985; Bloch, 1987; Lewis, 1987), increasingly in directions Scott envisioned. Ruth Bloch's "The Gendered Meanings of Virtue in Revolutionary America" may be most representative of this emerging literature in its exploration of the relationship between language, gender ideology, and political change. Bloch focused not on the impact of the American Revolution on European American women's lives – long a subject of concern – but on how virtue, as a gender-laden symbol, was transformed through the political discourse of the Revolution and new republic. As an intellectual historian, Bloch's interest in language and texts was not in itself unusual, but her essay signals the degree to which, by the late 1980s, cultural history was becoming as important as social history to feminist historians interested in how unequal power relations were created and maintained in early America. Literary theory had also joined anthropological theory in providing some of the most incisive tools women's historians brought to this project.

Since 1990, relationships among gender, power, politics, and law have dominated feminist interpretations of early American women's history. The late eighteenth century remains a critical moment for many scholars, especially though not exclusively for those interrogating the meanings of coverture for the long-term histories of citizenship, marriage, and divorce. But other studies have reached back long before the American Revolution, suggesting that close readings of earlier events and processes reveal political and legal turning points missed in the focus on industrialization, modernization, and the American Revolution. Women's work and household economies retain a significant place in 1990s scholarship, with recent studies in these areas furthering our understanding of the fit between the social relations of work and larger political, economic, and cultural developments. Religion, which had threaded itself through many earlier studies, especially on New England, has become more prominent and our understanding of its meanings for women has been greatly enhanced. Nation-building, colonialism, race formation, sexuality, and the body have emerged as the newest areas of interest, and those with the most potential for integrating race and gender and men's and women's history. Men and manhood have joined women and womanhood in a few post-1990 studies, and the lives of European American, African American, Mexican American, and Native American women have increasingly intersected, though for the most part, early American scholars have confined their analyses to one group or another.

Kathleen Brown's *Good Wives, Nasty Wenches, and Anxious Patriarchs* is an extraordinary exception to this last point. Concentrating on seventeenth- and early eighteenth-century Virginia, Brown examines the lives of men as well as women, of African Americans and Native Americans as well as European Americans, along what she identifies as "gender frontiers" created in the processes of conquest, colonization, and enslavement (1996, p. 33). Long called for in the women's studies theoretical literature, but rendered especially pressing in the early 1990s by powerful historically based arguments presented by Elsa Barkley Brown (1991), Evelyn Brooks Higginbotham (1992), and Antonia Castaneda (1992), *Good Wives, Nasty Wenches, and Anxious Patriarchs* offers one of the best analyses to date of race, class, and gender as overlapping and mutually constitutive categories of analysis. The book stands alone in building upon previous theoretical and empirical work on race, gender, and class to alter fundamentally how we understand power and politics in early America. It speaks as well to other long-term and more recent concerns of feminist historians, from marriage and marital status to work and consumption to constructions of identities, bodies, and sexualities.

Perhaps in response to heated debates in the late 1980s and early 1990s about whether the field should best be defined as the history of women or the history of gender (the latter usually but not always signaling a history of men as well as women), Kathleen Brown creates both: a study of patriarchal power in which men and manhood are as vital to the telling as women and womanhood. Mary Beth Norton's *Founding Mothers and Fathers* (1996) does the same. It also focuses, if not on race, on gender, power, and politics. She, too, looks at European American men and women as gendered subjects, and with a similar goal: to understand the distinctive forms patriarchy took in the British colonies, in her case by analyzing two regions, New England and the Chesapeake, in the years prior to 1670. A work of political philosophy as well as social and cultural history, Norton's agenda is almost as daunting as Brown's and its argument as complex. For the larger goals of women's history and women's studies, however, its strength lies in close analyses and comparisons of discursive relationships between the family and the state as well as in its detailed illustrations of colonial women's use of informal power to support or diminish official male power. Most useful theoretically, Norton delineates creative new ways of thinking about the concepts of public and, in particular, private, adding to as well as redirecting earlier theoretical discussions of these constructions.

Most other in-depth 1990s studies of gender, politics, and the law reinforce Brown's and Norton's emphasis on the growing difficulties colonial women faced as patriarchal power became more firmly entrenched. Tracing this process over the longest period of time, Cornelia Dayton's *Women before the Bar* (1995) matches Brown's and Norton's in the sweep of its argument and its command of early legal records. She makes a compelling case that in New Haven colony (later county) colonial women easily accessed the courts for most of the seventeenth century and could expect that most of their complaints would be given a fair hearing. After 1690, however, a combination of social, economic, and legal changes resulted in the diminished presence of women in the courts and, for many, a double standard of treatment when there. In cases of rape, for example, where European American women could once assume that their voices would be heard, after the seventeenth century they found that unless their assailants were African American or otherwise deemed marginal in the community their word no longer mattered.

Dayton, Norton, Brown, and other women's and gender historians writing since the early 1990s lend support to previous indications that the periodization of European American women's history needed reassessing. While the late eighteenth and early nineteenth century is likely to remain a crucial turning point (in part because the colonists' break from England carried so much political and social import for African Americans and Native Americans as well as European Americans), earlier transitions now draw increasing attention. The first years of settlement are emerging as the time of greatest flexibility in British American gender arrangements, a time when women's informal power was most apparent and their treatment by men in positions of official power most evenhanded. Crises of male authority vary in these and earlier studies – from the late 1630s to the early eighteenth century – with differences in timing only partially accounted for by class, regional, and religious variations. Not finding a simple declension pattern, some of these post-1990 gender studies have begun to explore how critical transformations in the experiences of colonial women during these years were related to class and race formation and to equally profound changes in the experiences of African Americans and Native Americans.

Analyses based on extensive use of court records have recently been challenged, however, albeit indirectly, for overstating the negative effects of coverture and other legal restrictions on colonial women, missing cases where these women's legal liabilities worked to their own or their families' advantage. In a study of seventeenth- and early eighteenth-century Virginia, for instance, Linda Sturtz concludes that the actions of European American women who held powers of attorney "demonstrate that a spectrum of possibilities was open to women under colonial law." Sturtz's evidence concerning some women's uses of powers of attorney *has* been overlooked by feminist historians, and therefore Sturtz adds nicely to our understanding of that "spectrum of possibilities" (2001, p. 253). But her implication that her findings fundamentally alter the big picture does not persuade, in part because she fails to acknowledge that Mary Beth Norton, Cornelia Dayton, Kathleen Brown, and others have also documented colonial (and in Brown's case, African American) women's creative use of the legal system on their own or their families' behalf. The real difference between Sturtz and the scholars with whom she takes issue lies in where they see this kind of evidence fitting into the much broader spectrum of women's experiences in colonial courts.

As in the 1980s, this and other recent quarrels with influential interpretations of European American women and the law may reflect an understanding of gender as the power of relations rather than relations of power. Sturtz's reading of her evidence certainly stresses the unity of interests among family members and collective strategies for attaining and maintaining family wealth and influence. But in her ignoring of contradictory evidence, her oversimplifying the legal histories she contests, and her reducing Laurel Ulrich's argument about women's roles as "deputy husbands" (1982, p. 9) to women following men's instructions, Sturtz suggests another pattern. The 1990s have witnessed increasing attacks, whether conscious or unconscious, on historians who affiliate themselves with women's studies and the contemporary women's movement by historians who seem intent on distinguishing their work on women or gender from feminist scholarship. I hesitate to identify these responses as one side of a debate because they too often exhibit a tendency, shared by Sturtz, to obscure who and what is being disputed.

In the more overt forms this trend has taken, the political agenda is striking, however inadvertent it might be. Consider, for instance, Hendrik Hartog's *Man and Wife in America* (2000) in the context of Nancy Cott's *Public Vows* (2000), Linda Kerber's *No Constitutional Right to Be Ladies* (1998), and Norma Basch's *Framing American Divorce* (1999). Although each of these books deals primarily with the century or two after the American Revolution, they all begin with the late eighteenth century. For Cott, Kerber, and Basch, the early republic marks a starting point for subsequent developments in American legal and political culture. Cott explores how marriage, usually conceptualized as the most private of institutions, has from the nation's beginning been defined, regulated, and politicized by the state. Kerber examines how and why certain obligations of citizenship were denied to women and how these developments relate to the law of coverture and the nation's refusal to women of certain rights. Basch traces changes in divorce law, the multifaceted debates that surrounded them, and their meanings for different groups of women and American society from the early reforms of the revolutionary period until 1870. In the depth of their research and complexity of their arguments, it would be hard to find three stronger or more compelling arguments about the ongoing politics of marriage and the state.

Hartog offers readers a powerful analysis as well, of how the history of marital law, separation, and divorce since the late eighteenth century shows that women could sometimes benefit from their legal subordination. He introduces his work, however, by setting it against what he calls two kinds of American marriage history, both sides, he laments, "shaped by explicit political and normative concerns." Although he does not say which histories he refers to, one side is clearly feminist, almost certainly the work of Cott, Kerber, and Basch, among others. Less apparent are the historians on the other side. Hartog suggests that their politics are right wing, but if so, locating right-wing scholarship on the legal history of marriage (as opposed to non-scholarly right-wing discussions of contemporary marriage) takes some doing. By placing "[n]early all recent scholarship on the legal history of American marriage" into one of these two categories, however, Hartog's characterization serves at least two interrelated purposes. First, it locates his own work in a balanced, apolitical middle between two un-identified but equally reprehensible political extremes. And, second, much like late twentieth-century attacks on liberals, it places most other historical studies of gender, marriage, and the law – by and large feminist – beyond the pale of respectable scholarship – and politics (2000, p. 3).

If Hartog's positioning of his own brand of scholarship vis-à-vis feminist history is difficult to miss, other strategies can be harder to detect. Richard Godbeer's 1992 misrepresentation and reworking of parts of my own witchcraft argument, for instance, puzzled me at first, in part because, like Hartog and Sturtz, Godbeer does not ac-knowledge whose work he is targeting. Only after reading David Hall's statement, in the introduction to the anthology in which the article appeared, that Godbeer "quietly corrects one of the assertions by a historian who has posited witch-hunting as embody-ing men's drive for domination over women" (1992, p. 15) did I fully grasp that my book *The Devil in the Shape of a Woman* (1987) was quietly being corrected. But why the hush-hush, in this or other oblique responses to early American (and other) femi-nist scholarship? One explanation lies in their most pronounced political effect: readers of quiet corrections rarely have a clue that this process is going on, so they have little opportunity to evaluate the evidence and merits of opposing positions.

Laura McCall and Donald Yacovone (1998) reveal yet another strategy in the recent backlash against feminist scholarship – the explicit distortion of respected arguments in order to diminish their influence. While several articles in the anthology they edited offer important contributions to both men's and women's history, the editors use their introduction to misconstrue for readers the early work of Nancy Cott (1977), Linda Kerber (1980), and other women's historians who initially traced the ideologies of domesticity and republican womanhood from the late eighteenth into the early nineteenth century. Cott must be flabbergasted to find that, in 1977, rather than charting the development of woman's sphere ideology and its meanings for New Eng-land's middle and upper class women, she became one of "the chief architects of the doctrine of separate spheres and the idea of true womanhood." Indeed, McCall and Yacovone assign Cott and Kerber much of the responsibility for a whole range of what they dismiss as "interpretive fictions." Under this guise, Cott and Kerber stand ac-cused, with others, of arguing the existence of "strict gender segregation" and wom-en's confinement to "a domestic sphere" (1998, pp. 1, 12n). Even if Cott and Kerber ever made these claims – which to my knowledge they never did – the by now nearly two decades of refinements and revisions, including their own, have profoundly trans-formed the way most women's historians understand separate spheres discourse.

Veiled hostility to feminist scholarship among historians who write about women or gender reflects, in part, the field's enormous growth since 1990. This growth has also fostered expressions of more explicit – and more productive – differences. In addition to race and racism, terminology and identity continue to generate debate, much as they did before 1990. Naming, for instance, causes conflict between those who see themselves as women's historians and those who identify themselves as gender historians. These arguments, part of a larger dispute about whether related interdisciplinary programs should be called women's studies or gender studies, may be as much generational as political. Scholars who have entered the field most recently seem to have less at stake in the debate, thus encouraging open reflection on what those labels mean as well as on the larger politics of history. That this essay is entitled "Women and Gender" rather than "Women's History" or "Gender History" (reflecting, in part, my own identity as a women's historian who sees gender, race, and class as primary categories of analysis) says something about the kind of compromises reached. That consensus about these meanings still so profoundly eludes us, however, suggests as well how deeply fraught the battle remains.

For scholars new to early American women's and gender history in the 1990s, as well as for their predecessors, early American politics and political culture still draw significant attention, even as new ways of addressing the topic have come to the fore (Smith-Rosenberg, 1992; Smith, 1994; Shammas, 1995; Klepp, 1998; Wulf, 2000; Branson, 2001). Susan Klepp, for example, directs us to a previously unnoticed political language articulated during and after the War of Independence. Middle- and upper-class European American women, she finds, "adapted a Revolutionary rhetoric of independence, self-control, sensibility, contractual equity, and numerical reasoning" to support their desires to limit the size of their families (1998, p. 911). Looking at less prosperous women's involvement in food riots during the American Revolution, Barbara Clark Smith analyzes female anger at merchants and shopkeepers who took advantage of shortages to charge exorbitant prices for their goods. Smith interprets these actions in the three contexts of merchant capitalism, "common people's politics," and a political culture of resistance that the Revolution "opened for women . . . as social and economic actors within household, neighborhood, and marketplace" (pp. 4–5). These arguments further complicate the old public/private discussion by pointing to women's own gendering of politics with respect to their reproductive lives and household economies.

Susan Branson's *These Fiery Frenchified Dames* (2001) and Karin Wulf's *Not All Wives* (2000), both studies of Philadelphia's European American women, present other ways of rethinking the relationship between gender and politics. Though her sources orient her toward the middle and upper classes, Branson follows Barbara Smith in expanding our knowledge of popular political culture, in her case in the two decades after the War of Independence. Her stories highlight parades and protests, play writing and theater going, salons and the political sociability of dinner table conversation – in short, a broader range of political practices and concerns than most other colonial women's historians have explored. Branson also points to widespread resistance in the city to women's political participation, especially in the wake of the French Revolution and growing divisions between political parties. But the unsettled political culture of the new nation's Capitol, she argues, enriched the very soil from which women's sense of themselves as political actors grew.

Karin Wulf's main storyline lies elsewhere. Hers is a multifaceted argument about the vitality and diversity of single women's experiences among Philadelphia's European American population prior to the American Revolution. She ranges from young educated women's evaluations of marriage to Quaker theology's encouragement of women's decisions to remain single to the economic and social benefits unmarried women found in the city's vibrant urban culture. Key to her larger interpretation are political and public policy changes instituted after mid-century – chiefly the withdrawal from property-owning women of the "freeman" status that allowed them access to local political authority and the withholding from impoverished women of the aid that supported their struggle for economic independence. In Wulf's telling, the mid-eighteenth-century discourse that increasingly equated men with independence and women with dependence lent legitimacy to these changes and fostered a "masculinization" of Philadelphia's political culture by the time of the Revolution (2000, pp. 186, 191). This argument may not contradict Branson's as much as it first appears, if we consider how little overlap exists between the two time frames and if, as Wulf avers, women's historians' greater attention to married than unmarried women has slanted our vision of both the gendering of politics and the politics of gender.

In documenting the employments available to the single urban women she studies and class differences in their opportunities for self-support, Wulf also contributes to post-1990s discussions of colonial women's work and household economies (Main, 1994; Cleary, 1995; Boydston, 1996; Hood, 1996; Crane, 1998; Ulrich, 1999; Norling, 2000; Wulf, 2000). With some exceptions, agreement more than disagreement continues to characterize research in this area, among historians who have recently joined the conversation as well as those engaged in it for some time. Especially noticeable is how much support new studies lend to earlier arguments about the importance of cities in European American women's economic and cultural history and about the increase rather than decrease in household production and female wage work over the course of the eighteenth century, among both single and married women. Evidence of higher rates of shop keeping, boarding, provisioning, money lending, economic independence, and poverty moreover, has been added to the mix. Women's historians vary in their timing of these developments, in their assessments of whether, how, and to what extent different groups of women benefited from them, and, of course, their significance.

Most compelling are studies that link this dramatic change with larger economic, political, and cultural transformations. Jeanne Boydston, building on her own earlier work (1990) and more recent research on Philadelphia, finds increased household production tied to an "expanded dependence on the market labor of women, performed both within and outside the household" as the groundwork was being laid for industrial capitalism in the mid- to late eighteenth century. Addressing why the cultural narratives articulated about that process, then and later, constructed women's market labor as absent – simply not there – she posits that it was precisely because women's paid (as well as unpaid) work was becoming more critical to their households, the larger economy, and even themselves. Indeed, women's "very aggressive presence" during this transition, and their political engagement, she thinks, may have created tensions within and beyond households, so threatening "the customary bases of manhood" that women were discursively disassociated from the work they did and their "public absence" affirmed. Meanwhile, men were more vigorously associated with "the status of producer" and the new civic culture fostered by the Revolution (1996, pp. 186, 191, 198, 202).

Laurel Ulrich's work dovetails nicely with Boydston's. Building on her own earlier book (1990), and Boydston's (1990), she confronts the relationship between growing class inequalities in Boston, increased household production of textiles in rural New England, among young single women primarily, and the "pastoralization" of rural life by aspiring urban elites. By transforming "rural labor into artful leisure," Ulrich contends, the embroidered pastoral imagery taught to the young daughters of this emerging elite bespeaks growing class as well as gender inequalities in the mid-eighteenth century, the importance of most young women's economic contribution to their families' support, primarily though not exclusively through the manufacture of their own dowries, and aspiring men and women's stake in "private property, companionate marriage, and female industry" (1999, pp. 195–6)

In the area of gender and religion, concurrence rather than discord also characterizes the recent literature on European American women – and a substantial body of work it has become in the past decade. Interestingly, some of the best analyses come from the edges of the field, not from opponents of women's history, but from scholars whose interest in gender seems to follow upon other, more central concerns. Apparent as well is a related pattern: gender analyses often comprise only one or two chapters in books that treat religion or another topic more broadly. And like some other areas of concern, scholars interested in gender and evangelical religion among colonists have begun to bring African Americans into their studies.

To emphasize congruity is not to minimize conflicting interpretations. Speaking about New England, my colleague Susan Juster, for example, argues that "[f]rom the evangelical insistence on the equality of all souls came the relative egalitarianism of the evangelical polity in matters of church governance in the mid-eighteenth century" (1994, p. 41). Looking at mid-eighteenth-century New England as well, Laurie Crumpacker and I found moments when evangelical women gained a significant measure of spiritual or social power, but no evidence that they enjoyed even a relative egalitarianism within their churches (Karlsen and Crumpacker, 1984). In *Ye Heart of a Man* (1999), a study of colonial New England manhood and domestic relations that relies heavily on the words of ministers, Lisa Wilson challenges studies like Juster's (1994) and my own (1987) that focus on gender and power in early American religious history; Wilson sees this kind of work portraying men as "one-dimensional power brokers," and thus "not allow[ing] for a nuanced portrait of colonial manhood" (Wilson, 1999, p. 2). Exploring the power relations embedded in male and female religious participation and institutional authority, Anne Braude (1997) argues against scholars who see early American religious history through a lens of declension or feminization. Differences such as these are overshadowed, however, by widespread agreement about the meanings of religion for colonial women.

Recent work confirms that the Society of Friends offered European American women the most spiritual autonomy in the colonial period, the most say in their religious organizations and communities, and the most opportunity to pursue their own ministries (Pestana, 1991; Brekus; 1998; Larson, 1999; Wulf, 2000). Before the 1990s, the skeletal outlines of these patterns were in place, but the portrait is now more finely drawn: the gendered reasons Quakers so threatened established authorities outside of Pennsylvania; the numbers and experiences of female ministers who traversed the colonies and the larger Atlantic world; the relationship between Quaker women's spiritual authority and their authority within their families and communities; and the distinctive lives of the women who chose to follow a spiritual rather than a marital path.

We now know even more about the eighteenth-century evangelical cultures European Americans created – New Light Congregationalist, New Side Presbyterian, Methodist, Baptist, and Moravian – as well as the kind of gender relations they fostered. The First Great Awakening, once associated exclusively with the 1730s and 1740s, has merged with the Second Great Awakening, usually seen more as a nineteenth- than an eighteenth-century phenomenon, revealing an ongoing series of smaller religious revivals generated at different times by one group or another. Enough varied practices have been uncovered to be wary of generalizing about evangelical culture as a whole, but sufficient parallels exist across groups and regions to see gendered patterns in the initial outpourings of religious feeling and in the transformations brought about as respectability beckoned.

Christine Heyrman and Dee Andrews offer two of the most persuasive analyses of European American evangelical worlds: Heyrman for southern Methodists and Baptists, Andrews for mid-Atlantic Methodists. Both studies treat the eighteenth into the nineteenth century and, in both, race as well as gender undergoes some scrutiny. In *Southern Cross* (1997), Heyrman tells us why so many European American women were attracted to southern evangelicalism and why itinerant ministers welcomed their support, however ambivalently. She departs from other works in also addressing the similarly gendered reasons why other women either resisted the spiritual pull of the revivals or soon fell away from the fold. Andrews's *The Methodists and Revolutionary America, 1760–1800* (2000) covers much the same ground on the opportunities available for European American women to create positions of power and authority for themselves within Methodism and the forms male opposition took, but she reveals more about what these women's faith meant to them and the spiritual associations they formed with other women. Both books speak to the familial language and imagery Methodists drew upon in creating what they called their "Family-Religion" (Andrews, 2000, p. 106), however divisive it could be at times within actual households. As her chapter title "Mothers and Others in Israel" implies, Heyrman places a bit more emphasis on married women (1997, p. 161). Andrews, in her "Evangelical Sisters" chapter, writes more about the young, single women who came to Methodism "on their own or in the company of one or another female relations" (2000, p. 99).

Susan Juster's *Disorderly Women* (1994) and Ann Taves's *Fits, Trances, and Visions* (1999) are the most theoretically sophisticated of these evangelical studies, while Marilyn Westerkamp's *Women and Religion in Early America, 1600–1850* (1999) provides the best synthesis. Juster brings a wide range of anthropological and literary theory to her reading of conversion narratives, discipline hearings, and other sources left by New England's Baptists primarily, making a persuasive case for the importance of gendered language in shaping evangelical experience. Looking more at the Methodists, Taves pays a different kind of attention to the language of spiritual devotion, interrogating the concept of religious experience itself. Although not a study of gender in the usual sense or solely about revivals, Taves's book fundamentally alters how we think about forms of spiritual expression more often associated with women than men. Westerkamp puts women and revivalism into the larger context of the Protestant Reformation and Puritan religious hegemony in New England.

The gender and religion literature as a whole points to initial periods of openness among all eighteenth-century evangelical groups to European American women charting their own spiritual journeys. It also indicates considerable internal as well as external male opposition as the strength women drew from ministerial encouragement, their own growing influence among the faithful, and their relationship with God became apparent. As spiritual euphoria subsided and the implications of women's independent religious thought and public expression sank in, ministers, as Christine Heyrman so aptly phrases it, "continued their delicate brinkmanship of encouraging public displays of female eloquence while denying that such show of virtuosity entitled women to any right to rule in the churches." Attesting to how complicated the gendered power dynamics within Methodism became by the beginning of the nineteenth century, Heyrman also wryly notes that "the exclusion of women from governing powers was less an accomplished fact than a continuing achievement" (1997, pp. 168–69).

As the field of women's history has matured in the past decade, we find increasingly creative attempts to interweave subject matter and approaches – such as literary and anthropological theory, religion and politics, social and cultural history, women's and men's history, and African American and European American women's history, for example. With an eloquence and wit that rivals Christine Heyrman's, Jane Kamensky's work is emblematic of some of these trends. In *Governing the Tongue* (1997), she interrogates the spoken word from several angles of vision, teaching us as much about ways of hearing Puritan sources as it does about the gendered meanings of speech and silence in early New England. With her usual aplomb, Carroll Smith-Rosenberg (1992) applies an array of rich theoretical frameworks to her assessment of how a presumably American national identity was forged out of the crucible of gender and race in the years before the Constitution was ratified. Toby Ditz (1994), building upon Smith-Rosenberg's insights, offers her own highly complex assessment of eighteenth-century Philadelphia merchants' deployment of gendered imagery in refashioning their identities as men in the face of personal financial failure.

As these three works attest, many women's and gender historians, along with so many of their colleagues, took the linguistic turn in the 1990s. Surprisingly, though, within early American history, the move has been relatively uncontroversial. Certainly, some women's historians continue to fight the theory wars and debate the merits of the new cultural history. But except for complaints about obscure language and trendiness that occasionally surface in conference sessions, book reviews, and online chat rooms, historians of women and gender in early America remain remarkably outside the fray. One explanation for the relative lack of controversy lies in the high quality of work potentially at issue. The above-mentioned studies by Kamensky, Ditz, and Smith-Rosenberg are cases in point. Notable also for drawing on a wide array of linguistic and performance theory as well as gender, race, and class formulations, Kathleen Brown's *Good Wives, Nasty Wenches, and Anxious Patriarchs* (1996) offers yet another.

A second reason for widespread acceptance of the linguistic turn among early American women's and gender historians may lie in a long-term interest in prescriptive literature: sermons, travel accounts, captivity narratives, origin stories, early novels and magazines, among others. Feminist historians had turned to them with great regularity in the 1970s and 1980s to understand what were then called ideological formulations or social or cultural constructions of womanhood. It has not required a really dramatic transformation, then, to re-read those same sources in terms of gender discourse or ritual performance or symbolic communication theory and supplement them with maps, prints, and other visual texts.

Still, the results have been transforming. Historian Jennifer Morgan's 1997 analysis of English constructions of African and Native American females in the sixteenth and seventeenth centuries, for example, draws on familiar travel narratives and conceptions of womanhood; but by reframing her study primarily in terms of an array of theories on race, gender, and colonial representations, she takes readers much further than most of her predecessors into the heart of European struggles to articulate national identities and racial hierarchies through stories of monstrous female bodies and animalistic sexual behavior. Studies such as these have profoundly changed the meaning of colonial history for many early American women's historians (among others). Increasingly, attention is being redirected to issues of gender and colonialism within the colonies and new nation, but situated within the context of the Americas more broadly and the larger Atlantic world. Feminist scholarship on colonialism and post-colonialism in African, Asian, and Pacific worlds undertaken in anthropology, geography, and cultural studies has also greatly encouraged and enriched this line of inquiry (Mohanty, 1984; Stoler, 1991; McClintock, 1995; Friedman, 1998).

The linguistic turn among American women's historians has been paralleled by the new historicism among early modern literary scholars that has also deeply influenced the past decade's early American gender analyses, at the same time further blurring lines between historical and literary sources and interpretations. In an essay that seems almost a companion piece to Jennifer Morgan's, literary scholar Susan Scott Parrish brings her substantial talent to the treatment of the bodies of female possums in travel narratives, natural histories, and maps, along with more conventional literary texts (1997). Arguing for the shifting symbolic importance of this "new world" animal, from a monstrous, fecund, devouring female beast to a protective, nurturing, still fertile female caretaker, Parrish sees European and European American men's fascination with the possum's anatomy expressing anxieties about an uncontrolled female generativity, an undomesticated womanhood, and an untamed mother nature in their newfound land.

The overlapping concern with texts and textuality among historians and literary scholars manifests itself as well in other recent studies of sexuality, gendered bodies, body language, and embodiment (Montrose, 1991; Hodes, 1997; Klepp, 1998; Lindman and Tarter, 2001); in analyses of European American men and manhood (Lockridge, 1992; Ditz, 1994; Smith, 1998); in studies of gendered identities, self-fashionings, rituals, and performances (Brown, 1996; Kamensky, 1997; Hoffman, Sobel, and Teute, 1997; St. George, 2000); in attention to dreams, emotions, sensibility, and sociability (Shields, 1997; Ellison, 1999; Sobel, 2000); and in treatments of gender, nation, and nationalism (Smith-Rosenberg, 1992; Waldstreicher, 1997; Nelson, 1998). Not everyone draws on the same theoretical frameworks, but the historians in this group have come to share with their literary colleagues the conviction that language tells us even more than we once thought about how gendered power relations are constructed, maintained, resisted, and subverted.

Certain topics stand out more than others for drawing both literary scholars and historians to them, even historians with little apparent enthusiasm for critical theory. Captivity and captivity narratives, for example, engaged the attention of both women's historians and feminist literary critics long before 1990, but the past decade or so has witnessed a surge of renewed interest, with historians June Namias (1993), John Demos (1994), James Brooks (1997), Jill Lepore (1998), and others joined by English professors such as Christopher Castiglia (1996) and Rebecca Blevins Faery (1999). Historians in this group are more likely to explore the gender-based experiences and identities of captives, while the literary critics demonstrate a greater concern with the meanings that captivity narratives convey about gendered power. Often, though, we find significant theoretical and methodological overlap.

Once considered the purview of American studies and women's studies programs, augmentation of interdisciplinary exchanges among women's historians and feminist literary scholars testifies as well to the unprecedented preoccupation with race and race formation since 1990. Among the already-mentioned studies that draw on literary and historical analyses, for example, a substantial number pay some attention to race. Works on gender and captivity in particular demonstrate this trend. So too do studies of early modern and modern writers, artists, propagandists, naturalists, and others who sexualized and racialized images of Africans and Native Americans to express and justify to themselves European conquest, colonization, and enslavement (Zamora, 1990–91; Montrose, 1991; Lubin, 1994; Morgan, 1997). Indeed, investigation of the intersection of race and gender within European colonial discourse has become one of the most visible trends of early American women's and gender history.

Unfortunately, too often these analyses stop with readings of the stories Europeans told themselves about their colonial ventures and the Africans and Native Americans they encountered. Only a few feminist scholars go beyond those stories to combine cultural histories of gender and race with the social histories of African Americans, Mexican Americans, and Native Americans. Hence, Europeans and European Americans remain at the center of most studies of these analyses. On a more positive note, this work has begun in the past decade, most of it within the context of local or regional studies. As mentioned above, Kathleen Brown (1996) has made the greatest strides, articulating a complex argument about how gender worked in Virginia to naturalize English conquest, racial categories, the institutionalization of slavery, and patriarchal power. On one level an argument about gender, race, and class formation, her book is simultaneously a social history of the interactions of English, African, and Native American women and men. Using Brown's book as entry point, let us turn finally to what the post-1990 scholarship has added to our understanding of the early history of African American, Mexican American, and Native American women.

Brown places African American women at the heart of her race formation analysis. Countering the absence of women or gender in explanations of slavery's origins, she argues that racial categories were created in a series of legal distinctions Virginia's ruling elites drew in the mid- to late seventeenth century between African American and colonial women. Passing laws declaring that African American women were tithable and that the children of slaves follow the status of their mother, Virginia's rulers fixed racial difference in law by symbolically marking it on women's bodies. Since neither statute applied to colonial women, Anglo-Virginians legally affirmed, to borrow Elsa Barkley Brown's formulation, that "all women do not have the same gender" (1992, p. 88). Kathleen Brown elaborates in some detail on the effects of this kind of gender difference on enslaved and free African American women. She delineates as well the legal and other strategies they devised to protect themselves and their children.

Although no book-length monograph has yet been published in which pre-nine-teenth-century African American women's history in North America is the central focus, other studies speak further to the how race and gender were legally inscribed on the bodies of African American women (Bardaglio, 1995; Fischer, 2001; Herndon, 2001). In *Suspect Relations*, for example, Kirsten Fischer looks at court cases dealing with illicit sex, sexual slander, and sexualized violence in eighteenth-century North Carolina. Whereas Kathleen Brown demonstrates how Anglo-Virginian planters con-structed race through the laws they passed, Fischer finds ordinary European Ameri-cans reinscribing class, race, and gender categories through the meanings they attached to consensual sexual encounters and sexualized violence. Although African American men appeared more frequently in court narratives about consensual sex across the color line, Fischer finds, African American women were more likely to be the subjects of other legal stories, for example, those emphasizing female immorality or the "black-ening" of "white" men's reputations. African American women's own stories rarely made it into court. Labeled black women not white, not even the violence regularly inflicted upon them attracted official notice. Describing eroticized whippings, mutila-tions, and rapes against African American women as ritual "performances of race" as well as of gendered power, Fischer argues that violence was "a social practice . . . that transformed official categories of race into a physical relationship: some people had rights to freedom from violation while others did not" (2001, pp. 150, 160–1).

Scholarship that does place early African American women's experience at the very center of historical inquiry is found in anthologies primarily. *The Devil's Lane* (1997), edited by Catherine Clinton and Michele Gillespie, is one of the most useful. While covering the whole colonial and revolutionary period and not limiting itself to a single group of women, this collection includes articles on African American women that deal with wide-ranging concerns, such as variations in work patterns, the impact of different systems of law on their ability to sue for legal rights, and the meaning of eighteenth- and early nineteenth-century evangelical religion to its enslaved adher-ents. David Barry Gaspar's and Darlene Clark Hine's *More than Chattel* (1996) is another vital source, especially for understanding the varied uses of slave women's labor, forms of sexual harassment, and opportunities for escape, self-purchase, and manumission. Treating women under slavery in Africa and the Americas more broadly, this book speaks to the growing trend in early American women's history to think comparatively about gender, race, and slavery across colonial regimes.

Comparative analyses are related to another significant scholarly development in African American women's history in the past decade, the growth of local studies. Together, these works point to enormous variations in the lives of African American women, both slave and free. For example, while violence against female slaves in eight-eenth-century Louisiana seems no less brutal than in Kirsten Fischer's North Carolina, from there the resemblance between the two regions begins to fade. Several factors distinguished Louisiana from most other North American slave-holding areas, most notably its French and Spanish colonial control prior to 1803 and the ethnic back-grounds and cultural resilience of its African-born populations. From these stemmed greater opportunities for slaves to move about, earn income, obtain freedom, hold property, and bring suits in court. In many cases, widespread public tolerance for long-term relationships between European American men and African American women advantaged these women. While African American men benefited from some of Louisiana's unusual conditions – more chances to develop marketable skills were available to them than in most other places, for instance – women could gain as well. Most notably, the possibility of purchasing their own or their children's freedom and passing on their status as *libres* to their descendants was greater in Louisiana, and in New Orleans in particular, than elsewhere (Hall, 1997; Gould, 1997; Hangar, 1997).

Recent attention to the opportunities New Orleans held for African American women has done more than simply register the number of manumissions or the extent of property holding among them or their children. It has implicitly and explicitly challenged earlier scholarly assumptions that enslaved women involved in long-term relationships with European American men were simply victims of sexual violence or profligate females eager and willing to use their bodies to gain freedom or wealth or both. While not denying that most New Orleans women were held in sexual as well as economic slavery, nor diminishing the psychological costs for either these women or their families, post-1990s New Orleans scholarship has greatly complicated our understanding of these relationships. Creating a picture of a highly complex creole culture in Louisiana that incorporated Native Americans, Europeans, and Africans of many ethnic backgrounds in the early eighteenth century, recent arguments highlight the permeability of certain racial categories throughout most of the colonial period. Although in some respects resembling British colonies in the early seventeenth century, eighteenth-century New Orleans underwent a racialization process that seems to have made it possible for some women to negotiate the meanings of concubinage for themselves and their children more effectively than in other parts of North America.

Nor was New Orleans the only urban environment that African American women navigated with some success in the late eighteenth and early nineteenth centuries. Although no two were alike, cities have recently emerged as featured sites of gendered analysis. When articles in *The Devil's Lane* and *More than Chattel* on Charlestown, South Carolina and several gulf ports are read alongside James Sidbury's discussion of Richmond in *Ploughshares into Swords* (1997), Betty Wood's analysis of eighteenth-century Savannah in *Women's Work, Men's Work* (1995), and Kimberly Hanger's New Orleans study, *Bounded Lives, Bounded Places* (1997), it becomes vividly clear that urban centers in general, and port cities in particular, fostered a wider range of legal and economic freedoms and fewer personal restrictions for enslaved women than did most rural districts. Here, too, the point is not to diminish the horrors of bondage anywhere. It is to say that early American scholars increasingly look to place and space as relevant categories in analyzing the variations and nuances of African American women's lives and gender relations.

Robert Olwell (1996), Virginia Gould (1997), James Sidbury (1997), and others lend strong support to earlier indications that late eighteenth- and early nineteenth-century southern cities offered African American women more opportunities to earn income, however limited they might be. Charleston, Savannah, New Orleans, and some other urban centers allowed enslaved women, though at times illegally, to market fruit, vegetables, eggs, poultry, and other commodities in plantation owners' stead, making it possible for some to trade plantation surplus or their own goods on what came to be known as the "black market" (Olwell, 1996, p. 103). In some cities, the trading skills of free women were valued as well, enabling them to run successful businesses from market stalls, vending carts, small shops, or their own dwellings. Even in cities like Richmond, which preferred European American control of urban markets, increasing demand for cooks, house cleaners, washerwomen, wet nurses, and spinners provided more paid employment possibilities for free women than in rural environments. Providing lodging and boarding offered another way for free urban females to support themselves and their families. Keeping "disorderly houses" was yet another (Sidbury, p. 169). The exceptionally high proportion of female-headed households Sidbury found in Richmond supports earlier findings (Lebsock, 1982) that free women were simultaneously valued and devalued as urbanization and commercialization altered southern social relations.

Post-1990s scholarship on African American gender relations also fosters the recognition of not one, but multiple, overlapping, and highly gendered black cultures. As James Sidbury points out, because their employments took them into the artisan shops or yards where commodities were produced or repaired, or onto the carts and boats that hauled materials or goods from one place to another, "[e]nslaved and free Black men in and around Richmond developed a masculine culture of the road and the river" (Sidbury, p. 245). Even on their customary trips to nearby plantations to visit wives and children, he adds, they walked roads that other men but few women traveled. For their part, Richmond's free and slave women worked primarily in households, their own and others, and in nearby work sites. Their worlds were largely shaped by the social and economic networks they established with other women, which generated both conflict and financial and other assistance during hard times. The different worlds of men and women did not preclude close relations between husbands and wives, or fathers and children, but they did encourage more assertive female behavior and more fluid gender practices among African Americans than among European Americans. From Sidbury's perspective, gender relations were not egalitarian – the trend in recent African American scholarship has been to modify that earlier argument considerably – only less hierarchical than those among Richmond's European American population.

Recent scholarship on enslaved and free men and women in the Gulf South also reveals distinctively gendered patterns of resistance to colonists' efforts to enforce white supremacy. Although it has long been understood that work patterns and separations from families made certain forms of resistance easier for males than females, both slaves and free, Virginia Gould suggests that Louisiana's distinctive eighteenth-century culture fostered an assertiveness among free black women that ranged from aggressive defense of their legal rights to subversive clothing styles. Gould offers a telling example of the latter. After the Spanish governor decided in 1786 that sumptuary restrictions were necessary to control what he saw as the extravagance and unhampered behavior of free women of color, he forbade them to dress their hair with jewelry and feathers and ordered them to cover their heads with the distinctive kerchief slave women used to keep their hair clean and away from their face when working. This symbolic effort to bind free women to slavery failed, Gould notes: free women defied the "tignon law" by wrapping and knotting such brilliantly colored fabrics around their heads that "the stylish and flattering tignon . . . became a badge or mark of distinction of their race, their status, and their gender" (1997, p. 238).

In the late eighteenth century, becoming a Christian could also convey early African American slave women's resistance to the absolute power of masters and mistresses, and even to the sexual abuse by slave men. According to Cynthia Lyerly (1996), both men and women were attracted to Methodism for the comfort they found in God in times of adversity, for the evangelical emphasis on the spiritual equality of all believers, and for the openly abolitionist sentiments many early Methodists espoused. Enslaved women were particularly drawn to Methodism, Lyerly argues, for more subtle reasons – the more positive gender identity offered as a daughter of Christ than the world beyond the Church allowed, the opportunity to establish bonds with other women, especially for women on small plantations, the possibility of bringing disciplinary charges against slave men who sexually abused them or their daughters, and the informal public roles they could take on within the church. Although the racism and sexism still embedded in church relations precluded their enjoying any official roles or making claims to social equality, they could, Lyerly maintains, affirm themselves and influence others through the power of their prayer, conversion, testimony, and exhortation.

While substantial progress has been made since 1990 in the writing of African American women's early history, the scholarship on pre-nineteenth-century Spanish Mexican women and gender relations in the West and Southwest has been slower to develop. In 1991, Ramón Gutiérrez published his monumental *When Jesus Came, the Corn Mothers Went Away*, which delves more deeply than prior studies, including his own, into the symbolic and practical meanings Spanish Mexican discourses on marriage and sexuality had for the families who migrated from Mexico to New Mexico before 1800. Though women's perspectives on these aspects of the colonizing process or their own experiences under Spanish patriarchal authority remain largely unexamined, Gutiérrez's analysis of the gendering and racialization of male power is impressive. At the same time, recent articles on inheritance (Venya, 1993; Leyva, 1997) lend support to his discussions of how early New Mexico's religious and secular elites viewed women with class backgrounds similar to their own. Together, these studies revise earlier upbeat portrayals of women's independent control of property in this region with more realistic glimpses into how the situations of widows, wives, and daughters differed by class.

However difficult, given the paucity of sources, some scholars have incorporated into their research Spanish Mexican women who migrated from Mexico to Alta California in the late eighteenth century. Antonia Castañeda (1998) has led the way here, raising questions about what class, race, and marital status may have meant for their role as colonizers as well as for their position as women under male rule in the California missions. Both she and Virginia Bouvier (2001) look at the daily work these women undertook in Spanish missions, from cooking and nursing the sick to policing the sexual behavior of Native American women to teaching their charges European-style domestic labor. Finding hierarchies among women as well as between women and men, and collusion with as well as resistance to official mission policies, both scholars speak to the problems of assuming too great a distinction between colonizer and colonized. Quoting Latin American scholar Florencia Mallon, Castañeda argues theoretically that "[no] subaltern identity can be pure and transparent; most subalterns are both dominated and dominating subjects, depending on the circumstances or location in which we encounter them" (Castañeda, p. 145). Bouvier makes virtually the same point with her empirical claim that the first women colonizers the Spanish sent to Alta California missions were christianized Indians from Baja California.

Highly complex social relations among groups, transculturation, race and class formation, and the multiple identities now recognized as inevitable in the Spanish Mexican/Native American borderlands must have been vital to the decisions Gutiérrez, Castañeda, Bouvier, and Albert Hurtado (1999) made to study Native American history's intersection with that of Spanish America. The clash of what Kathleen Brown would call "gender ways" along California's and New Mexico's "gender frontier" lies at the core of their interpretations (Brown, 1996, pp. 45, 55). Looking specifically at the Acoma Pueblo world in New Mexico, for example, Gutiérrez begins with Acoma religious beliefs about the world's origins, links those beliefs to Acoma gender arrangements, and asks questions about what happened when, in the wake of military conquest, the Spanish imposed their own religion and gendered worldview onto this very different culture. The response of feminist and Pueblo scholars and activists to this part of his interpretation has been mixed at best. Though acclaiming the power and sweep of his argument about New Mexico's Spanish conquerors and their male descendants, many of his critics take a dim view of his trust in non-Pueblo sources to convey Pueblo constructions of male and especially female sexuality. Just as problematic, *When Jesus Came, the Corn Mothers Went Away* disregards the meanings of rape and other violent assertions of gendered power for the women, men, and children Spaniards subjugated or enslaved.

While Virginia Bouvier benefits greatly from Gutiérrez's work on the Spanish invasion of New Mexico, her *Women and the Conquest of California, 1542–1840* finds the "mythic beginnings" of Spanish conquest possibly more significant than Native origin stories for assessing gendered power relations in and around the California missions (2001, p. 3). Sexuality and marriage are also crucial in Bouvier's narrative. Here, too, she takes as her main task the determination of not only Spanish constructions of Christian sexual and marital arrangements, but also the effects the imposition of alien values had on indigenous communities. Speaking to the paucity of Pueblo sources for the Spanish colonial period, Gutiérrez says that his book "gives vision to the blind, and gives voice to the mute and silent" (1991, p. xvii). Bouvier attempts a related strategy – interrogation of the various "codes of silence" that masked the daily violence inflicted on Native women in California. She points out that just as missionaries and secular officials enforced these codes in the eighteenth century, historians took over this task in the nineteenth and twentieth. Moreover, she finds women, both Spanish Mexican and Native American, sometimes complicit in the silencing (2001, pp. 93–96, 107, 170).

Neither Antonia Castañeda (1993), James Brooks (1997), nor Albert Hurtado (1999) yet offers as expansive a view of the pre-1800 years as Gutiérrez and Bouvier. But they, too, are interested in the gendered meanings of intercultural power dynamics. Castañeda asks why missionaries and colonial administrators regularly decried but officially tolerated Spanish Mexican soldiers' raping of indigenous women in and around the northern California missions in the late eighteenth century, especially given that stopping the assaults was in the interests of both. She proposes that the Spanish conquest was sexual as well as geographical, with Native American women the unnamed spoils of that conquest. Recurring rapes, Castañeda reasons, were acts of national more than individual terrorism, forms of virulence that reflected a cultural and political devaluation of Native women based on Spanish ideologies of both gender and race. Albert Hurtado concurs, affirming that "rape is an act of domination carried out by men who despise their victims because of their race and gender." In addition, he links sexual violence to efforts by Spanish clerics and administrators "to subdue, colonize, and convert." He also provides some evidence that missionaries may have had trouble distinguishing rape from consensual sex and that they presumed that Native women's free movement along public roadways provoked other, more disreputable men to rape them. Unfortunately, Hurtado seems to share some of that confusion: his rape, race, and gender argument gets muddled in his intermingling of words like seduction, sexual involvement, and a lack of sexual restraints with sexual conquest, rape, and sexual assault (Hurtado, 1999, pp. 13–15).

James Brooks addresses the violent trade in women between men of different cultures from the early eighteenth to the mid-nineteenth century. He asserts that the experience of captivity for Native American and Spanish Mexican women in New Mexico began with a terrifying wrenching from families and communities, their sale at trade fairs or more informal bartering sessions, and the likelihood of forced cohabitation or more brutal forms of rape. While such violence could easily destroy a woman's will to live, some of these captives, Brooks maintains, developed highly specialized survival skills that kept them and their children alive and integrated as "fictive kin" into clans of "host" societies. Though Brooks proposes that the exchange of captive women "provided European and native men with mutually understood symbols of power with which to bridge cultural barriers," he finds that the women themselves often negotiated "narrow fields of agency with noteworthy skill" (Brooks, 1997, pp. 99, 101).

Following upon Richard White's highly influential *The Middle Ground* (1991) and earlier studies of the distinctive Métis cultures that formed along the northern borderlands (Van Kirk, 1980; Brown; 1980; Peterson, 1985), two recent books feature intercultural collaboration rather than violence in analyzing early gender frontiers of the upper Midwest (Murphy, 2000; Sleeper-Smith, 2001). Both further our awareness of Native American women's centrality to the success of the French fur trade and render visible long invisible communities that formed through networks of economic exchange and cooperation.

Although "marriage after the custom of the country" between Native women and French men has long been recognized as providing French fur traders unusual access to Native communities (Van Kirk, 1980, p. 28), Susan Sleeper-Smith advances this argument well beyond women's roles as cultural intermediaries. Tracing familial and fictive kinship networks that several Catholic Native women created in the southern Great Lakes river basin in the eighteenth century, Sleeper-Smith reveals how intermarriage and godparentage, the obligations of which "controlled both entrance into the trade and access to peltry," also empowered women to extend these kin and fictive kin networks throughout the Great Lakes region over several generations. What is more, she shows that these women participated in virtually all aspects of the region's economy, occasionally even attaining independent fur trading licenses. These female networks fostered a "frontier Catholicism," Sleeper-Smith adds, that was integral to both their extended families' successful trading ventures and their collective sense of kinship-based identity. When removal threatened, their descendants resorted to "hiding in plain view" by constructing themselves as white (Sleeper-Smith, 2001, pp. 4–5, 116). Even more than James Brooks, Sleeper-Smith emphasizes how the sometimes porous boundaries between cultures could enhance women's opportunities and agency.

Like Sleeper-Smith, Lucy Eldersveld Murphy's investigation of what she sees as blended or creole cultures of the Fox-Wisconsin region, and particularly of the local economies of Green Bay and Prairie du Chien, stresses the possibilities for cooperation, negotiation, and adaptation between Native Americans and Europeans during the early stages of cultural contact. She finds a strong Métis presence among a diversified population, where women's work was vital to subsistence, to the fur trade, to production of lead for the market, and to the continuing autonomy of the Native American peoples in western Great Lakes. She focuses as well on gender frontiers. French fur traders adapted to gender-based cultural difference, she argues, but Anglo-American settlers refused to do so. With the colonists' takeover of the lead mines in the early nineteenth century, Murphy submits, cooperation gave way to the violence, exploitation, and fierce struggles over gender relations that colonization so often brought in its wake. Removal swiftly, though not inevitably, followed.

French colonial elites in eighteenth-century Louisiana resembled Anglo-American colonists more than French fur traders: they became deeply concerned, writes Jennifer Spear (1999), about the porous sexual boundaries between cultures. Sustained conjugal unions between French men and Native women in remote trading centers might be tolerable, but marriage after the custom of the country became sinful concubinage when Louisiana's colonial administrators and missionaries came face to face with it. Fear of the attractions indigenous cultures and female sexuality in particular held for French men, concern about the growing number of children of mixed parentage, and determination to keep property and inheritance in French male hands, Spear concludes, made secular officials more willing than religious authorities to accept mortal sin rather than legitimate marriages across the ideological barriers they had constructed. In this context colonial officials encouraged French women to migrate to Louisiana and gradually developed a discourse of race and gender to create greater "social and sexual distance between French and Native cultures" (Spear, 45). Probably foreshadowing a future argument, Spear closes her essay by drawing attention to Native American population decline and increasing enslavement of Africans. With new political and economic goals, she suggests, the colony's leaders would subsequently rework their race and gender discourses, this time to forestall European men cohabiting with African rather than Native women.

Interested even more in actual social practices among subaltern peoples than European proscriptions concerning them, Daniel Mandell (1999) considers intercultural intimacy as well, but between Native American women and African American men, and in southern New England. He finds Anglo Americans hindering ongoing relationships between these two groups in a number of ways, among them the racialization of both. If similar demographic, economic, and social experiences in the eighteenth century increasingly brought these women and men together in predominantly Native enclaves, tensions between partners over gender practices and among other members of communities over values, identities, and scarce communal resources could also break them apart. In describing the conditions and benefits that fostered these heterosexual unions and the many barriers to sustaining them, Mandell adds yet another level of complexity to the post-1990 treatment of intercultural gender relations.

So, too, does Ann Marie Plane, whose work Mandell parallels and to some extent is indebted. Less interested in intercultural unions *per se*, Plane devotes most of her research, and particularly *Colonial Intimacies*, to the intricate discursive and legal processes through which a notion of "Indian marriage" took shape in early New England (2000, p. 7). She begins by tackling the thorny linguistic problem of what to call enduring heterosexual intimacy and domestic relations within Native American communities prior to English colonization of the region, since the concept of marriage carries too many European signifiers to fit Native practices. From there, she argues that before the colonizers arrived, a spectrum of conjugal relations constituted the norm. She then addresses the more familiar question of what happened to these practices once English colonization began. Drawing on prior studies of the symbolic and material importance of marriage and family to Puritan notions of social order, Plane goes further than previous scholars in teasing out from recalcitrant sources the complex processes by which Puritans initially deployed religious, legal, and racializing strategies to change Native gender beliefs and practices and later, segregated Native Americans from Anglo-Americans. Among Plane's many achievements is keeping Native women and men at the center of her narrative, drawing a subtle portrait of resistance and adaptation.

Persistence lies at the heart of *Dispossession By Degrees*, Jean O'Brien's study of Natick, Massachusetts, the most prominent "Praying Town" that Puritan missionaries established for christianizing Native Americans. O'Brien's book advances a compelling challenge to the myth of Native American extinction in New England by reframing the Natick story as individual, family, and group perseverance in the face of "dispossession, displacement, and dispersal" (1997, pp. 11, 207). It does not advertise itself as a study of women and gender; nevertheless, in its interweaving of continuities and changes in conceptions of land, divisions of labor, and family and kinship forms into its larger narrative, this book offers many insights to readers interested in the gendered meanings of colonization for Native Americans who accepted Christianity in the seventeenth century. O'Brien's analysis dovetails nicely with Ann Plane's and Daniel Mandell's, especially in her tracing of both women's and men's participation in the "gendered mobile economy" and women's particular role in ensuring cultural as well as physical survival (O'Brien, p. 21).

Recent research on Iroquoian- and Algonquian-speaking communities in the North and Southeast rounds out a growing consensus that Native American gender systems were nowhere near as uniform as they appeared to feminist scholars in 1970 and the impact of European colonization upon them never as straightforward. Nancy Shoemaker made both of these points in her path-breaking essay "The Rise or Fall of Iroquois Women" (1991). She strengthened this argument in her introduction to her anthology, *Negotiators of Change* (1995), and in her essay on Mohawk saint Kateri Tekakwitha's motivations for embracing Catholicism that she included in this collection. Kathleen Brown lent considerable support to these conclusions in her examination of the gender frontiers created by the English colonization of indigenous lands in the Chesapeake region, which she first published in Shoemaker's book. So, too, did Natalie Zemon Davis, in her comparison of Native American women from the St. Lawrence region and their French counterparts in Europe (1994), and Kathleen Bragdon in her discussion of the impact of Christianity on indigenous groups in early New England (1996). Whether challenging established wisdom about cultural encounters between colonizers and colonized, simply offering more subtle readings of the surviving evidence, or insisting that scholars reframe the questions they ask, the relationship between gender and colonialism remains the dominant theme in the Native American women's history literature.

Theda Perdue's long-awaited *Cherokee Women* (1998) stands out as the most thorough reflection on the impact of colonialism on Native American gender systems. With the exception of race formation, about which she says little, Perdue's study sums up recent interests and approaches in the field, though her conclusions are not uncontested. She begins with the Cherokee origin story and how it speaks to the separate but linked worlds women and men shared in 1700, emphasizing the importance placed on complementarity within their sexual divisions of labor and their larger gender system. She finds women wielding considerable power within that system, primarily because of how kinship was structured. The arrival of Anglo-American traders did not destroy the balance established between men and women, she says, or the cultural recognition accorded women's activities. Nor did Cherokees merely adopt markers of the "civiliza-tion" that Europeans tried so hard to foist upon them. Instead Perdue finds subtle resistance and creative adaptation, especially with more intermarriage between Cherokee women and Anglo-American traders and increasing class, race, and gender differentia-tion. Like so many other current scholars, Perdue emphasizes cultural persistence and the part women played in keeping traditions alive in the midst of enormous pressures to conform to European American gender norms. Stopping short of the full story of Cherokee removal, Perdue leaves readers with a fairly positive portrayal of physical and cultural endurance in the face of tremendous adversity,

The entry of African American, Mexican American, and Native American women into the early American women's history – so gradual for so long – has picked up considerable speed since the early 1990s. And in no area are the implications for fur-ther study in the women and gender field more apparent. Concern with colonialism's impact on Native American women has a long history; but today awareness has broad-ened to questions about its many-layered effects on all women, and not just in the British, French, and Spanish colonies discussed here but in the larger Atlantic and Pacific worlds. The focus on intercultural relationships, intimate and not, has also made it clear that distinctions among groups have been too sharply drawn for too long. The related interest in how women and men have identified themselves in the past and how others have constructed them has similarly brought recognition of the over-compartmentalization of not only groups but also regions, religions, sexualities, bodies, even genders. Ironically, only by looking carefully at how different groups of women have been studied over the past three decades can we begin to learn ways to counter the still lingering tendency to think pious-New-England-matrons-in-their-saltbox-houses when the topic of early American women comes up. If research on European American women still predominates, the most recent publications in the field indicate that the tide is finally turning.

Still the biggest challenge, it seems, is to heed Elsa Barkley Brown's call to study women in relation to other women – "to recognize not only differences [among women] but also the relational nature of those differences. Middle-class white women's lives are not just different from working-class white, black, and Latina women's lives . . .," she adds, "mid-dle-class women live the lives they do precisely because . . ." working-class women and women of color "live the lives they do" (1991, p. 86). Occasionally early American wom-en's historians have demonstrated empirically how this worked in practice – think of Kathleen Brown's 1996 argument about how and why Virginia's lawmakers differently gendered African American and Anglo-American women in the seventeenth century.

But more often than not relational differences among groups of women have not been on the agenda. Barkley Brown suggested a decade ago that women's historians learn to think and write like jazz musicians rather than as classical musicians. Instead of many people continuing to tell one story at a time, with other stories held in abeyance, she urged the telling of many at the same time. Because history is "everybody talking at once, multiple rhythms being played out simultaneously," she argues, differences among women would be better understood if scholars allowed for how much their histories take place "in dialogue with" one another" (1991, p. 85). It may be wishful thinking, but early American historians of women and gender seem to be heading in that general direction.

BIBLIOGRAPHY

Abbot, Edith: *Women in Industry: A Study in American Economic History* (New York, 1910; reprint ed., New York: Arno Press, 1969).

Anderson, Karen: "Commodity Exchange and Subordination: Montagnais-Naskapi and Huron Women, 1600–1650." *Signs* 11 (1985), pp. 48–62.

Andrews, Dee: *The Methodists and Revolutionary America, 1760–1800: The Shaping of an Evangelical Culture* (Princeton, NJ: Princeton University Press, 2000).

Baker, Paula: "The Domestication of Politics: Women and American Political Society, 1780–1920." *American Historical Review* 89 (1984), pp. 620–47.

Bardaglio, Peter: *Reconstructing the Household: Families, Sex, and the Law in the Nineteenth Century* (Chapel Hill, NC: University of North Carolina Press, 1995).

Barker-Benfield, Ben: "Anne Hutchinson and the Puritan Attitude toward Women." *Feminist Studies* 1 (1972), pp. 65–96.

Basch, Norma: *Framing American Divorce: From the Revolutionary Generation to the Victorians* (Berkeley, CA: University of California Press, 1999).

Beckles, Hilary McD.: *Natural Rebels: A Social History of Enslaved Black Women in Barbados* (New Brunswick, NJ: Rutgers University Press, 1989).

Benes, Peter and Benes, Jane Montague, eds.: *Wonders of the Invisible World: 1600–1900* (Boston, MA: Dublin Seminar for New England Folklife Annual Proceedings, 1992).

Blewett, Mary: *Men, Women and Work: Class, Gender, and Protest in the New England Shoe Industry, 1710–1910* (Urbana, IL: University of Illinois Press, 1988).

Bloch, Ruth H.: "American Feminine Ideals in Transition: The Rise of the Moral Mother, 1785–1815." *Feminist Studies* 4 (1978), pp. 100–26.

Bloch, Ruth: "The Gendered Meanings of Virtue in Revolutionary America," *Signs* 13 (1987), pp. 37–58.

Bouvier, Virginia Marie: *Women and the Conquest of California, 1542–1840: Codes of Silence* (Tucson, AZ: University of Arizona Press, 2001).

Boydston, Jeanne: *Home and Work: Housework, Wages, and the Ideology of Labor in the Early Republic* (New York: Oxford University Press, 1990).

Boydston, Jeanne: "The Woman Who Wasn't There: Women's Market Labor and the Transition to Capitalism in the United States." *Journal of the Early Republic* 16 (1996), pp. 183–206.

Boyle, Susan C.: "Did She Generally Decide?: Women in Ste. Genevieve, 1750–1805." *William and Mary Quarterly* 3rd ser., 44 (1987), pp. 775–89.

Bragdon, Kathleen: "Gender as a Social Category in Native Southern New England." *Ethnohistory* 43 (1996), pp. 573–92.

Branson, Susan: *These Fiery Frenchified Dames: Women and Political Culture in Early National Philadelphia* (Philadelphia: University of Pennsylvania Press, 2001).

Braude, Ann: "Women's History *is* American Religious History." In T. A. Tweed, ed., *Retelling U.S. Religious History* (Berkeley, CA: University of California Press, 1997), pp. 87–107.

Brekus, Catherine A.: *Strangers and Pilgrims: Female Preaching in America, 1740–1845* (Chapel Hill, NC: University of North Carolina Press, 1998).

Brooks, James F.: "'This Evil Extends Especially to the Feminine Sex': Captivity and Identity in New Mexico, 1700–1846." In Elizabeth Jameson and Susan Armitage, eds., *Writing the Range: Race, Class, and Culture in the Women's West* (Norman, OK: University of Oklahoma

Press, 1997), pp. 97–121.

Brown, Elsa Barkley: "Polyrhythms and Improvisation: Lessons for Women's History." *History Workshop Journal* 31 (1991), pp. 85–90.

Brown, Jennifer S. H.: *Strangers in Blood: Fur Trade Company Families in Indian Country* (Vancouver: University of British Columbia Press, 1980).

Brown, Judith K.: "Economic Organization and the Position of Women among the Iroquois." *Ethnohistory* 17 (1970), pp. 151–67.

Brown, Kathleen M.: *Good Wives, Nasty Wenches, and Anxious Patriarchs: Gender, Race, and Power in Colonial Virginia* (Chapel Hill, NC: University of North Carolina Press, 1996).

Buhle, Mari Jo, Gordon, Ann G., and Schrom, Nancy: "Women in American Society: An Historical Contribution." *Radical America* 5 (1971), pp. 3–66.

Bush, Barbara: *Slave Women in Caribbean Society, 1650–1838* (Bloomington, IN: Indiana University Press, 1990).

Butler, Judith: *Gender Trouble: Feminism and the Subversion of Identity* (New York: Routledge, 1990).

Carby, Hazel V.: *Reconstructing Womanhood: The Emergence of the Afro-American Woman Novelist* (New York: Oxford University Press, 1987).

Carby, Hazel V.: "White Women Listen: Black Feminism and the Boundaries of Sisterhood." In *The Empire Strikes Back: Race and Racism in Seventies Britain* (London: Hutchinson, 1982), pp. 211–235.

Carr, Lois Green and Walsh, Lorena S.: "The Planter's Wife: The Experience of White Women in Seventeenth-Century Maryland." *William and Mary Quarterly* 3rd ser., 34 (1977), pp. 542–71.

Castañeda, Antonia I.: "Gender, Race, and Culture: Spanish-Mexican women in the Historiography of Frontier California." *Frontiers* 11 (1990), pp. 8–20.

Castañeda, Antonia I.: "Women of Color and the Rewriting of Western History: The Discourse, Politics, and Decolonization of History." *Pacific Historical Review* 61 (1992), pp. 501–33.

Castañeda, Antonia I.: "Sexual Violence in the Politics and Policies of Conquest: Amerindian Women and the Spanish Conquest of Alta California." In de la Torre and Pesquera (1993), pp. 15–33.

Castañeda, Antonia I.: "Engendering the History of Alta California, 1769–1848: Gender, Sexuality, and the Family." In Ramón A. Gutiérrez and Richard J. Orsi, eds., *Contested Eden: California before the Gold Rush* (Berkeley, CA: University of California Press, 1998), pp. 230–59.

Castiglia, Christopher: *Bound and Determined: Captivity, Culture-Crossing, and White Womanhood from Mary Rowlandson to Patty Hearst* (Chicago: University of Chicago Press, 1996).

Cleary, Patricia: "'She Will Be in the Shop': Women's Sphere of Trade in Eighteenth-Century Philadelphia and New York." *Pennsylvania Magazine of History and Biography* 119 (1995), pp. 181–202.

Clinton, Catherine and Gillespie, Michele, eds.: *The Devil's Lane: Sex and Race in the Early South* (New York: Oxford University Press, 1997).

Cott, Nancy F.: "Divorce and the Changing Status of Women in Eighteenth-Century Massachusetts." *William and Mary Quarterly* 3rd ser., 33 (1976), pp. 586–614.

Cott, Nancy F.: *The Bonds of Womanhood: "Woman's Sphere" in New England, 1780–1835* (New Haven, CT: Yale University Press, 1977).

Cott, Nancy F.: *Public Vows: A History of Marriage and the Nation* (Cambridge: Harvard University Press, 2000).

Crane, Elaine Forman: *Ebb Tide in New England: Women, Seaports, and Social Change, 1630–1800* (Boston, MA: Northeastern University Press, 1998).

Davis, Natalie Zemon: "Iroquois women, European women." In Margo Hendricks and Patricia

Parker, eds., *Women, "Race," and Writing in the Early Modern Period* (New York: Routledge, 1994), pp. 243–71.

Dayton, Cornelia Hughes: *Women before the Bar: Gender, Law, and Society in Connecticut, 1639–1789* (Chapel Hill, NC: University of North Carolina Press, 1995).

De La Torre, Adela and Pesquera, Beatriz M., eds.: *Building with Our Hands: New Directions in Chicana Studies* (Berkeley: University of California Press, 1993).

Demos, John Putnam: *A Little Commonwealth: Family Life in Plymouth Colony* (New York: Oxford University Press, 1970).

Demos, John Putnam: *Entertaining Satan: Witchcraft and the Culture of Early New England* (New York: Oxford University Press, 1982).

Demos, John: *The Unredeemed Captive: A Family Story from Early America* (New York: Alfred A. Knopf, 1994).

Devens, Carol: "Separate Confrontations: Gender as a Factor in Indian Adaptation to European Colonization in New France." *American Quarterly* 38 (1986), pp. 461–80.

Dexter, Elizabeth Williams Anthony: *Colonial Women of Affairs: Women in Business and the Professions in America before 1776* (1924; reprint ed., New York: A. M. Kelly, 1972).

Ditz, Toby: "Shipwrecked; or, Masculinity Imperiled: Mercantile Representations of Failure and the Gendered Self in Eighteenth-Century Philadelphia." *Journal of American History* 81 (1994), pp. 51–80.

Dudden, Faye E.: *Serving Women: Household Service in Nineteenth-Century America* (Middletown, CT: Wesleyan University Press, 1983).

Dunn, Mary Maples: "Saints and Sisters: Congregational and Quaker Women in the Early Colonial Period." *American Quarterly* 30 (1978), pp. 582–601.

Earle, Alice Morse: *Colonial Dames and Good Wives* (Boston: Houghton, Mifflin & Company, 1904).

Ellison, Julie: *Cato's Tears and the Making of Anglo-American Emotion* (Chicago: University of Chicago Press, 1999).

Etienne, Mona and Leacock, Eleanor, eds.: *Women and Colonization: Anthropological Perspectives* (New York: Praeger, 1980).

Faery, Rebecca Blevins: *Cartographies of Desire: Captivity, Race, and Sex in the Shaping of an American Nation* (Norman, OK: University of Oklahoma Press, 1999).

Fischer, Kirsten: *Suspect Relations: Sex, Race, and Resistance in Colonial North Carolina* (Ithaca, NY: Cornell University Press, 2001).

Flexner, Eleanor: *Century of Struggle: The Woman's Rights Movement in the United States* (Cambridge, MA: Harvard University Press, 1959).

Foote, Cheryl J. and Schackel, Sandra K.: "Indian Women of New Mexico, 1535–1680." In Joan M. Jensen and Darlis A. Miller, eds., *New Mexico Women: Intercultural Perspectives* (Albuquerque: University of New Mexico Press, 1986), pp. 17–40.

Friedman, Susan Stanford: *Mappings: Feminism and the Cultural Geographies of Encounter* (Princeton, NJ: Princeton University Press, 1998).

Gaspar, David Barry and Hine, Darlene Clark, eds.: *More Than Chattel: Black Women and Slavery in the Americas* (Bloomington, IN: Indiana University Press, 1996).

Godbeer, Richard: "Chaste and Unchaste Covenants: Witchcraft and Sex in Early Modern Culture." In Benes and Benes (1992), pp. 53–72.

Godbeer, Richard: "The Cry of Sodom: Discourse, Intercourse, and Desire in Colonial New England," *William and Mary Quarterly* 3rd ser., 52 (1995), pp. 250–86.

Gould, Virginia Meacham: "'A Chaos of Iniquity and Discord': Slave and Free Women of Color in the Spanish Ports of New Orleans, Mobile, and Pensacola." In Clinton and Gillespie (1997), pp. 232–46.

Green, Rayna: "The Pocahontas Perplex: The Image of Indian Women in American Culture." *The Massachusetts Review* 16 (1975), pp. 698–714.

Gundersen, Joan R.: "The Double Bonds of Race and Sex: Black and White Women in a Colonial Virginia Parish." *Journal of Southern History* 52 (1986), pp. 351–72.

Gundersen, Joan R. and Gampel, Gwen Victor: "Married Women's Legal Status in Eighteenth-Century New York and Virginia." *William and Mary Quarterly* 3rd ser., 39 (1982), pp. 114–34.

Gutiérrez, Ramón A.: "Honor Ideology, Marriage Negotiation, and Class–Gender Domination in New Mexico, 1690–1846." *Latin American Perspectives* 12 (1985), pp. 81–104.

Gutiérrez, Ramón A.: *When Jesus Came, the Corn Mothers Went Away: Marriage, Sexuality, and Power in New Mexico, 1500–1848* (Stanford, CA: Stanford University Press, 1991).

Gutman, Herbert G: *The Black Family in Slavery and Freedom, 1750–1925* (New York: Pantheon Books, 1976).

Hall, David: "Introduction and Commentary." In Benes and Benes (1992), pp. 11–16.

Hall, Gwendolyn Midlo: "African Women in French and Spanish Louisiana: Origins, Roles, Family, Work, Treatment." In Clinton and Gillespie (1997), pp. 247–61.

Hangar, Kimberly S.: *Bounded Lives, Bounded Places: Free Black Society in Colonial New Orleans, 1769–1803* (Durham, NC: Duke University Press, 1997).

Hartog, Hendrik: *Man and Wife in America: A History* (Cambridge, MA: Harvard University Press, 2000).

Hernández, Salomé: "No Settlement without Women: Three Spanish California Settlement Schemes, 1790–1800." *Southern California Quarterly* 72 (1990), pp. 203–33.

Herndon, Ruth Wallis: *Unwelcome Americans: Living on the Margin in Early New England* (Philadelphia: University of Pennsylvania Press, 2001).

Hewitt, Nancy: "Beyond the Search for Sisterhood: American Women's History in the 1980s." *Social History* 10 (1985), pp. 299–321.

Heyrman, Christine Leigh: *Southern Cross: The Beginnings of the Bible Belt* (New York: Alfred A. Knopf, 1997).

Higginbotham, Evelyn Brooks: "African American Women's History and the Metalanguage of Race." *Signs* 17 (1992), pp. 251–74.

Hodes, Martha: *White Women, Black Men: Illicit Sex in the Nineteenth-Century South* (New Haven, CT: Yale University Press, 1997).

Hoffman, Ronald and Albert, Peter J., eds.: *Women in the Age of the American Revolution* (Charlottesville, VA: University Press of Virginia, 1989).

Hoffman, Ronald, Sobel, Mechal, and Teute, Fredrika J., eds.: *Through a Glass Darkly: Reflections on Personal Identity in Early America* (Chapel Hill, NC: University of North Carolina Press, 1997).

Hood, Adrienne: "The Material World of Cloth: Production and Use in Eighteenth-Century Rural Pennsylvania." *William and Mary Quarterly* 3rd ser., 53 (1996), pp. 43–66.

Hooks, Bell: *Ain't I a Woman: Black Women and Feminism* (Boston, MA: South End Press, 1981).

Hull, Gloria T., Scott, Patricia Bell, and Smith, Barbara, eds.: *All the Women Are White, All the Blacks are Men, But Some of Us Are Brave: Black Women's Studies* (Old Westbury, NY: The Feminist Press, 1982).

Hurtado, Albert L.: *Intimate Frontiers: Sex, Gender, and Culture in Old California* (Albuquerque, NM: University of New Mexico Press, 1999).

Jensen, Joan M.: "Native American Women and Agriculture: A Seneca Case Study." *Sex Roles* 5 (1977), pp. 432–41.

Jensen, Joan M.: *Loosening the Bonds: Mid-Atlantic Farm Women, 1750–1850* (New Haven, CT: Yale University Press, 1986).

Johansson, Sheila Ryan: "'Herstory' as History: A New Field or Another Fad?" In Berenice A. Carroll, ed., *Liberating Women's History: Theoretical and Critical Essays* (Urbana: University of Illinois Press, 1976), pp. 400–30.

Jones, Douglas: "The Strolling Poor: Transiency in Eighteenth-Century Massachusetts." *Journal of Social History* 8 (1974), pp. 28–54.

Jones, Jacqueline: "'My Mother was much of a Woman': Black Women, Work, and the Family under Slavery." *Feminist Studies* 8 (1982), pp. 235–69.

Jones, Jacqueline: "Race, Sex, and Self-Evident Truths: The Status of Slave Women during the Era of the American Revolution." In Hoffman and Albert (1989), pp. 293–337.

Juster, Susan: *Disorderly Women: Sexual Politics & Evangelicalism in Revolutionary New England* (Ithaca, NY: Cornell University Press, 1994).

Kamensky, Jane: *Governing the Tongue: The Politics of Speech in Early New England* (New York: Oxford University Press, 1997).

Karlsen, Carol F.: *The Devil in the Shape of a Woman: Witchcraft in Colonial New England* (New York: W. W. Norton and Company, 1987).

Karlsen, Carol F. and Crumpacker, Laurie, eds.: *The Journal of Esther Edwards Burr, 1754–1757* (New Haven, CT: Yale University Press, 1984).

Kelly-Gadol, Joan: "The Social Relation of the Sexes: Methodological Implications of Women's History." *Signs* 1 (1976), pp. 809–23.

Kerber, Linda K.: *Women of the Republic: Intellect and Ideology in Revolutionary America* (Chapel Hill, NC: University of North Carolina Press, 1980).

Kerber, Linda K.: "The Republican Ideology of the Revolutionary Generation." *American Quarterly* 37 (1985), pp. 474–95.

Kerber, Linda K.: "Separate Spheres, Female Worlds, Woman's Place: The Rhetoric of Women's History." *Journal of American History* 75 (1988), pp. 9–39.

Kerber, Linda K.: *No Constitutional Right to be Ladies: Women and the Obligations of Citizenship* (New York: Hill and Wang, 1998).

Keyssar, Alexander: "Widowhood in Eighteenth-Century Massachusetts: A Problem in the History of the Family." *Perspectives in American History* 8 (1974), pp. 83–119.

Klepp, Susan E: "Revolutionary Bodies: Women and the Fertility Transition in the Mid-Atlantic Region, 1760–1820." *Journal of American History* 85 (1998), pp. 910–45.

Koehler, Lyle: "The Case of the American Jezebels: Anne Hutchinson and Female Agitation during the Years of Antinomian Turmoil, 1636–1640." *William and Mary Quarterly* 3rd ser., 31 (1974), pp. 55–78.

Kulikoff, Allan: "The Beginnings of the Afro-American Family in Maryland." In Aubrey Land, Lois Green Carr, and Edward C. Papenfuse, eds., *Law, Society, and Politics in Early Maryland* (Baltimore, MD: Johns Hopkins University Press, 1977), pp. 171–96.

Larson, Rebecca: *Daughters of Light: Quaker Women Preaching and Prophesying in the Colonies and Abroad, 1700–1775* (New York: Alfred A. Knopf, 1999).

Leavitt, Judith Walzer: *Brought to Bed: Childbearing in America, 1750–1950* (New York: Oxford University Press, 1986).

Lebsock, Suzanne: "Free Black Women and the Question of Matriarchy: Petersburg, Virginia, 1784–1820." *Feminist Studies* 8 (1982), pp. 271–92.

Lepore, Jill: *The Name of War: King Philip's War and the Origins of American Identity* (New York: Alfred A. Knopf, 1998).

Lerner, Gerda: "The Lady and the Mill Girl: Changes in the Status of Women in the Age of Jackson." *MidContinent American Studies Journal* 10 (1969), pp. 5–15.

Lewis, Jan: "The Republican Wife: Virtue and Seduction in the Early Republic." *William and Mary Quarterly* 3rd ser., 44 (1987), pp. 689–721.

Leyva, Yolanda Chávez: "'A Poor Widow Burdened with Children': Widows and Land in Colonial New Mexico." In Elizabeth Jameson and Susan Armitage, eds., *Writing the Range: Race, Class, and Culture in the Women's West* (Norman, OK: University of Oklahoma Press, 1997), pp. 85–96.

Lindman, Janet Moore and Tarter, Michele Lise, eds.: *A Centre of Wonders: The Body in Early*

America (Ithaca, NY: Cornell University Press, 2001).

Lockridge, Kenneth A.: *Literacy in Colonial New England: An Inquiry into the Social Context of Literacy in the Early Modern West* (New York: W. W. Norton, 1974).

Lockridge, Kenneth A.: *On the Sources of Patriarchal Rage: The Commonplace Books of William Byrd and Thomas Jefferson and the Gendering of Power in the Eighteenth Century* (New York: New York University Press, 1992).

Lubin, David M.: *Picturing a Nation: Art and Social Change in Nineteenth-Century America* (New Haven, CT: Yale University Press, 1994).

Lyerly, Cynthia Lynn: "Religion, Gender and Identity: Black Methodist Women in a Slave Society, 1770–1810." In Patricia Morton, ed., *Discovering the Women in Slavery: Emancipating Perspectives on the American Past* (Athens: University of Georgia Press, 1996), pp. 202–26.

Main, Gloria: "Widows in Rural Massachusetts on the Eve of the Revolution." In Hoffman and Albert (1989), pp. 67–90.

Main, Gloria L.: "Gender, Work, and Wages in Colonial New England." *William and Mary Quarterly* 3rd ser., 51 (1994), pp. 39–66.

Mandell, Daniel R.: "The Saga of Sarah Muckamugg: Indian and African American Intermarriage in Colonial New England." In Martha Hodes, ed., *Sex, Love, Race: Crossing Boundaries in North American History* (New York: New York University Press, 1999), pp. 72–90.

McCall, Laura and Donald Yacovone, eds.: *A Shared Experience: Men, Women, and the History of Gender* (New York: New York University Press, 1998).

McClintock, Anne: *Imperial Leather: Race, Gender and Sexuality in the Colonial Contest* (New York: Routledge, 1995).

Menard, Russell R.: "The Maryland Slave Population, 1658 To 1730: A Demographic Profile of Blacks in Four Counties." *William and Mary Quarterly* 3rd ser., 32 (1975), pp. 29–54.

Mitchell, Juliet: *Women's Estate* (New York: Pantheon, 1971).

Mohanty, Chandra Talpade: "Under Western Eyes: Feminist Scholarship and Colonial Discourses." *Feminist Review* 30 (1988), pp. 65–88.

Montrose, Louis: "The Work of Gender in the Discourse of Discovery." *Representations* 33 (1991), pp. 1–41.

Morgan, Jennifer L.: "'Some Could Suckle over their Shoulder': Male Travelers, Female Bodies, and the Gendering of Racial Ideology, 1500–1770." *William and Mary Quarterly* 3rd ser., 54 (1997), pp. 167–92.

Morrissey, Marietta: *Slave Women in the New World: Gender Stratification in the Caribbean* (Lawrence, KS: University Press of Kansas, 1989).

Murphy, Lucy Eldersveld: *A Gathering of Rivers: Indian, Métis, and Mining in the Western Great Lakes, 1737–1832* (Lincoln, NE: University of Nebraska Press, 2000).

Namias, June: *White Captives: Gender and Ethnicity on the American Frontier* (Chapel Hill, NC: University of North Carolina Press, 1993).

Narrett, David: "Men's Wills and Women's Property Rights in Colonial New York." In Hoffman and Albert (1989), pp. 91–133.

Nelson, Dana D.: *National Manhood: Capitalist Citizenship and the Imagined Fraternity of White Men* (Durham, NC: Duke University Press, 1998).

Norling, Lisa: *Captain Ahab Had a Wife: New England Women and the Whalefishery, 1720–1870* (Chapel Hill, NC: University of North Carolina Press, 2000).

Norton, Mary Beth: "The Myth of the Golden Age." In Carol Ruth Berkin and Mary Beth Norton, eds., *Women of America: A History* (Boston, MA: Houghton Mifflin Company, 1979).

Norton, Mary Beth: *Liberty's Daughters: The Revolutionary Experience of American Women, 1750–1800* (Boston, MA: Little, Brown, 1980).

Norton, Mary Beth: *Founding Mothers and Fathers: Gendered Power and the Forming of American Society* (New York: Alfred A. Knopf, 1996).

O'Brien, Jean M.: *Dispossession by Degrees: Indian Land and Identity in Natick, Massachusetts, 1650–1790* (Cambridge: Cambridge University Press, 1997).

Olwell, Robert: "'Loose, Idle, and Disorderly': Slave Women in the Eighteenth-Century Charleston Marketplace." In Gaspar and Hine (1996), pp. 97–110.

Omolade, Barbara: "Black Women and Feminism." In Hester Eisenstein and Alice Jardine, eds., *The Future of Difference* (New Brunswick, NJ: Rutgers University Press, 1980), pp. 247–57.

Ortner, Sherry B. and Whitehead, Harriet, eds.: *Sexual Meanings: The Cultural Construction of Gender and Sexuality* (New York: Cambridge University Press, 1981).

Parrish, Susan Scott: "The Female Opossum and the Nature of the New World." *William and Mary Quarterly* 3rd ser., 59 (1997), pp. 475–514.

Perdue, Theda: *Cherokee Women: Gender and Culture Change, 1700–1835* (Lincoln, NE: University of Nebraska Press, 1998).

Pestana, Carla: *Quakers and Baptists in Colonial Massachusetts* (New York: Cambridge University Press, 1991).

Peterson, Jacqueline: "Many Roads to Red River: Métis Genesis in the Great Lakes Region, 1680–1815." In Jacqueline Peterson and Jennifer S. H. Brown, eds., *The New Peoples: Being and Becoming Métis in North America* (Manitoba: University of Manitoba Press, 1985), 37–73.

Plane, Ann Marie: *Colonial Intimacies: Indian Marriage in Early New England* (Ithaca, NY: Cornell University Press, 2000).

Randle, Martha C.: "Iroquois Women, Then and Now." *Bulletin of the Bureau of Ethnography*, 149 (1951), pp. 167–80.

Reiter, Rayna R., ed.: *Toward an Anthropology of Women* (New York: Monthly Review Press, 1975).

Riley, Denise: *"Am I That Name?": Feminism and the Category of "Women" in History* (Minneapolis, MN: University of Minnesota Press, 1988).

Rock, Rosalind Z.: "'Pido y suplico': Women and the Law in Spanish New Mexico, 1697–1763." *New Mexico Historical Review* 65 (1990), pp. 145–59.

Rosaldo, Michelle Zimbalist: "The Use and Abuse of Anthropology: Reflections on Feminism and Cross-Cultural Understanding." *Signs* 5 (1980), pp. 389–417.

Rosaldo, Michelle Zimbalist and Lamphere, Louise, eds.: *Women, Culture, and Society* (Stanford, CA: Stanford University Press, 1974).

Rubin, Gayle: "The Traffic in Women: Notes on the 'Political Economy' of Sex." In Rayna R. Reiter, ed., *Toward an Anthropology of Women* (New York: Monthly Review Press, 1975), pp. 157–210.

Salmon, Marylynn: "Equality or Submersion? Feme Covert Status in Early Pennsylvania." In Carol Ruth Berkin and Mary Beth Norton, eds., *Women of America: A History* (Boston, MA: Houghton Mifflin, 1979), 92–113.

Salmon, Marylynn: *Women and the Law of Property in Early America* (Chapel Hill, NC: University of North Carolina Press, 1986).

Scholten, Catherine M.: "'On the Importance of the Obstetrick Art': Changing Customs of Childbirth in America, 1760 to 1825." *William and Mary Quarterly* 3rd ser., 34 (1977), pp. 426–45.

Scott, Joan Wallach: "Gender: A Useful Category of Historical Analysis." *American Historical Review* 91 (1986), pp. 1053–75.

Seed, Patricia: *To Love, Honor, and Obey in Colonial Mexico: Conflict over Marriage Choice, 1574–1821* (Stanford, CA: Stanford University Press, 1988).

Shammas, Carole: "The Domestic Environment in Early Modern England and America." *Journal of Social History* 14 (1980–81), pp. 3–24.

Shammas, Carole: "Black Women's Work and the Evolution of Plantation Society in Virginia."

Labor History 26 (1985), pp. 5–28.

Shammas, Carole: "Early American Women and Control over Capital." In Hoffman and Albert (1989), pp. 134–54.

Shammas, Carole: "Anglo-American Household Government in Comparative Perspective," *William and Mary Quarterly* 3rd ser., 52 (1995), pp. 104–44.

Shields, David S.: *Civil Tongues and Polite Letters in British America* (Chapel Hill, NC: University of North Carolina Press, 1997).

Shoemaker, Nancy: "The Rise and Fall of Iroquois Women." *Journal of Women's History* 2 (1991), pp. 39–57.

Shoemaker, Nancy, ed.: *Negotiators of Change: Historical Perspectives on Native American Women* (New York: Routledge, 1995).

Sidbury, James: *Ploughshares into Swords: Race, Rebellion, and Identity in Gabriel's Virginia, 1730–1810* (New York: Cambridge University Press, 1997).

Silverblatt, Irene: *Moon, Sun, and Witches: Gender Ideologies and Class in Inca and Colonial Peru* (Princeton, NJ: Princeton University Press, 1987).

Sleeper-Smith, Susan: *Indian Women and French Men: Rethinking Cultural Encounter in the Western Great Lakes* (Amherst, MA: University of Massachusetts Press, 2001).

Smith, Barbara Clark: "Food Rioters and the American Revolution." *William and Mary Quarterly* 3rd ser., 51 (1994), pp. 3–38.

Smith, Daniel Scott: "Parental Power and Marriage Patterns: An Analysis of Historical Trends in Hingham, Massachusetts." *Journal of Marriage and the Family* 35 (1973), pp. 419–39.

Smith, Daniel Scott: "Inheritance and the Social History of Early American Women." In Hoffman and Albert (1989), pp. 45–66.

Smith, Merril D., ed.: *Sex and Sexuality in Early America* (New York: New York University Press, 1998).

Smith-Rosenberg, Carroll: "Dis-covering the Subject of the 'Great Constitutional Discussion', 1786–1789." *Journal of American History* 79 (1992), pp. 841–73.

Sobel, Mechal: *Teach Me Dreams: The Search for Self in the Revolutionary Era* (Princeton, NJ: Princeton University Press, 2000).

Spear, Jennifer M.: "'They Need Wives': Metissage and the Regulation of Sexuality in French Louisiana, 1699–1730." In Martha Hodes, ed., *Sex, Love, Race: Crossing Boundaries in North American History* (New York: New York University Press, 1999), pp. 35–59.

Spelman, Elizabeth V.: *Inessential Woman: Problems of Exclusion in Feminist Thought* (Boston, MA: Beacon Press, 1988).

Spruill, Julia Cherry: *Woman's Life and Work in the Southern Colonies* (Chapel Hill, NC: 1938; New York: W. W. Norton, 1972).

St. George, Robert Blair: *Possible Pasts: Becoming Colonial in Early America* (Ithaca, NY: Cornell University Press, 2000).

Stites, Sara H.: *Economics of the Iroquois* (Lancaster, PA: New Era Printing Company, 1905).

Stoler, Ann Laura: "Carnal Knowledge and Imperial Power: Gender, Race, and Morality in Colonial Asia." In Micaela di Leonardo, ed., *Gender at the Crossroads of Knowledge: Feminist Anthropology in the Postmodern Era* (Berkeley, CA: University of California Press, 1991), pp. 51–101.

Sturtz, Linda L.: "'As Though I My Self was Pr[e]sent'": Virginia Women with Power of Attorney." In C. L. Tomlins and B. H. Mann, eds., *The Many Legalities of Early America* (Chapel Hill: University of North Carolina Press, 2001), pp. 250–71.

Taves, Ann: *Fits, Trances, and Visions: Experiencing Religion and Explaining Experience from Wesley to James* (Princeton, NJ: Princeton University Press, 1999).

Tooker, Elisabeth: "Women in Iroquois Society." In Michael K. Foster, Jack Campisi, and Marianne Mithun, eds., *Extending the Rafters: Interdisciplinary Approaches to Iroquoian Studies* (Albany, NY: State University of New York Press, 1984), pp. 109–23.

Ulrich, Laurel Thatcher: "Vertuous Women Found: New England Ministerial Literature, 1668–1735." *American Quarterly* 28 (1976), pp. 20–40.

Ulrich, Laurel Thatcher: *Good Wives: Image and Reality in the Lives of Women in Northern New England, 1650–1750* (New York: Knopf, 1982).

Ulrich, Laurel Thatcher: *A Midwife's Tale: The Life of Martha Ballard, Based on Her Diary, 1785–1812* (New York: Knopf, 1990).

Ulrich, Laurel Thatcher: "Sheep in the Parlor, Wheels on the Common: Pastoralism and Poverty in Eighteenth-Century Boston." In C. G. Pestana and S. V. Salinger, eds., *Inequality in Early America* (Hanover, NH: University Press of New England, 1999), pp. 182–200.

Van Kirk, Sylvia: *"Many Tender Ties": Women in Fur-Trade Society in Western Canada, 1670–1870* (Winnipeg: Watson and Dwyer, 1980).

Venya, Angelina F.: "'It Is My Last Wish that . . .': A Look at Colonial Nuevo Mexicans through Their Testaments." In de la Torre and Pesquera (1993), pp. 91–108.

Waciega, Lisa Wilson: "A 'Man of Business': The Widow of Means in Southeastern Pennsylvania, 1750–1850." *William and Mary Quarterly* 3rd ser., 44 (1987), pp. 40–64.

Waldstreicher, David: *In the Midst of Perpetual Fetes: The Making of American Nationalism, 1976–1820* (Chapel Hill, NC: University of North Carolina Press, 1997).

Wells, Robert V.: "Quaker Marriage Patterns in a Colonial Perspective." *William and Mary Quarterly* 3rd ser., 29 (1972), pp. 415–42.

Wertz, Richard W. and Wertz, Dorothy C.: *Lying-In: A History of Childbirth in America* (New York: Free Press, 1977).

Westerkamp, Marilyn J.: *Women and Religion in Early America, 1600–1850: The Puritan and Evangelical Traditions* (New York: Routledge, 1999).

White, Deborah Gray: "Female Slaves: Sex Roles and Status in the Antebellum South." *Journal of Family History* 8 (1993), pp. 314–22.

White, Richard: *The Middle Ground: Indians, Empires, and Republics in the Great Lakes Region, 1650–1815* (New York: Cambridge University Press, 1991).

Wilson, Joan Hoff: "The Illusion of Change: Women and the American Revolution." In Alfred Young, ed., *The American Revolution: Explorations in the History of American Radicalism* (DeKalb, IL: Northern Illinois University Press, 1976), pp. 383–445.

Wilson, Lisa: *Ye Heart of a Man: The Domestic Life of Men in Colonial New England* (New Haven, CT: Yale University Press, 1999).

Wood, Betty: *Women's Work, Men's Work: The Informal Slave Economies of Lowcountry Georgia* (Athens, GA: University of Georgia Press, 1995).

Wulf, Karin A.: *Not All Wives: Women of Colonial Philadelphia* (Ithaca, NY: Cornell University Press, 2000).

Zamora, Margarita: "Abreast of Columbus: Gender and Discovery." *Cultural Critique* 17 (1990–91), pp. 127–50.

CHAPTER TEN

Children and Parents

HOLLY BREWER

Children have been invisible in most historical narratives about early America except as their lives relate to those of adults. Even then, historians have tended to portray their lives as static across time, region, and rank. While scholars such as Alice Morse Earle, in *Child Life in Colonial Days*, took their lives seriously as early as 1899, her work was largely ignored by the mainstream historical profession. Dismissed as "antiquarian," interesting only to (perhaps) genealogists, it has remained outside the mainstream of our interpretation of early American history. Indeed, even today, despite the diligent work of the social historians of the 1970s, the lives of children are seen as essentially non-issues, or not interesting, by many older scholars, particularly those who are most interested in political history. Children are not actors, for them, and do not enter onto the political stage. Even in the audience to that stage, they sit mute, their lives unchanging and uninteresting.

When introduced to people at conferences, a common response to work on children has been to dismiss it as by definition irrelevant. When giving a paper at the Library of Congress in 1993, one senior historian, after hearing only the title of a talk that I was giving on Jefferson's policies towards children, responded: "Some people will write on anything." Indeed, some people will. Amazingly, children's histories during this period are of far more than "antiquarian" interest. This was a period, the "age of reason," where the status of children was at the center of a very big debate. Should your birth status determine your place in society or were all people born equal? To even speak about such issues as "English liberties" during this period, for example, begs the question: liberty for whom, and when?

Many children, in fact, were actors, even if they began their parts playing more passive roles. Without understanding children's lives and the ways that they transformed during this period, we cannot fully understand anything about it, whether social, intellectual, cultural, economic, or political. To shape children is to mold culture and identity. The opportunities open to children reveal much about the possibilities for everyone in this society. Children, to state a truism, are the future, and the colonists – richer, poorer, black, white, Indian, male, female – knew it.

In delineating children's lives in colonial America (and in England, to a lesser degree), this essay will survey the historiographical literature from a chronological perspective, which went through several phases in the past fifty years, with patches of interest first in the cultural history of childhood, and then in demography, psychology, and religion. The essay will then discuss education, opportunity, and changes in children's lives from a synthetic perspective, crossing issues and historiographical discussions to derive a more comprehensive analysis, and, at the same time, more questions.

Children have received more attention from European historians than from American, following the path opened by Philippe Ariès in his influential *Centuries of Childhood* (French, 1960, English, 1962). While focusing only on France, he saw his findings as representing broader changes in Western culture. He held that only in the early eighteenth century did French society "discover" childhood. In the early seventeenth century, children were seen as "little adults," often portrayed in portraits with solemn faces and bearing grave responsibility. He pointed to changing attitudes towards children in a variety of realms, including attitudes toward their sexuality (from "immodesty to innocence"), their dress and toys (increasing distinction of children), their labor, and especially their education, which he saw as becoming much more important. He speculated that the changes in attitudes were due largely to lower mortality rates. When children died so often and so young, then parents and society were afraid to love them. In support of this argument, he quoted such sources as Montaigne: "I have lost two or three children in their infancy, not without regret, but without great sorrow" (Ariès, 1962, p. 39). The practice of apprenticeship, which separated parents and children, also loosed the bonds of parental affection (Ariès, 1962, p. 411). As parents began to value children more, they also became more interested in raising them properly and more uniformly, especially in terms of their religious faith. The family assumed a more spiritual function, "it moulded bodies and souls" (Ariès, 1962, p. 412).

Lawrence Stone's *Family, Sex and Marriage*, which drew and expanded on Ariès and centered on England instead of France, has been especially influential. Stone was also drawing on older works by scholars of literature, who have long been interested in familial issues, and on a burgeoning interest in demography. The seventeenth and eighteenth centuries, according to Stone, were marked by a profound transition in parent–child relations, from "distance, difference, and patrimony" to "affective individualism" (Stone, 1977, p. 4). He focused on the family as the best way to analyze individual relations during this period, and had long sections on such issues as parental control over marriage and stories of the birth and death of children. Like Ariès, he examined the representation of children in paintings and their education. He agreed with Ariès that not until the eighteenth century could parents truly love their children because children died so frequently before then. While medieval scholars have sharply criticized Stone's arguments (see below), his book is still widely cited. Ariès, meanwhile, has entered our broader historical understanding, and his arguments about little adults and the discovery of childhood are a commonplace in textbooks of literature and history. Yet his arguments for a change in attitude towards children have fallen flat among scholars: demographic changes in mortality rates among children, when examined, do not fit chronologically with the changes in attitudes. Thus Stone and Ariès, while describing some sort of a shift in attitudes towards children, cannot explain why, or even exactly characterize that shift.

Perhaps because these changes were positioned during the time of the European settlement of the colonies in America, scholars of American history have largely ignored these debates, with a few exceptions such as Demos' borrowing of the phrase "little adults" in his discussion of family life in Plymouth Colony. Some of the work on parental consent to marriage, such as Daniel Blake Smith's *Inside the Great House*, has drawn deeply on Stone.

Demography

Demographic studies have paid a fair amount of attention to children, not, seemingly, because they were interested in children themselves, but because, following on international concerns about birth rates and fertility in the 1960s (and the publication of books like Paul Erlich's *The Population Bomb* in 1968), they sought to measure fertility rates in the American colonies. In the process, of course, they counted family size and calculated average age at marriage and average age at first birth. So these studies are a gold mine of information about children and families in many ways. One of the most important pieces of information is that the average age of the population was much younger than in America in the twenty-first century. According to the census of 1790, the average age of the population in America was sixteen (15.9 years), a statistic that is fairly representative of the preceding century and a half in the various colonies (see, e.g., Anderson, 1985, Table I). So half the population were children, at least if childhood is measured as under age sixteen, which was not far beyond puberty. Indeed, defining who were children proves to be part of the dilemma. Still, if we ignore children, then we ignore roughly half the population during this period.

Yet despite the rich statistics that have given us a better understanding of children and families, there are significant problems with these social-science-inspired demographic analyses for the colonial period. First, more data is missing than survives (and data was kept in ways that had systematic biases), so these numeric studies give a false certainty. Second, the researchers often incorporated twentieth-century assumptions (about the certainty of data, about the definition of childhood, about the law) into their collection and interpretation of data. Thus these studies tend to equate the colonial period more with the twentieth century than was probably the case. The Rutmans, for example, assumed that no one would marry under the age of fifteen (Rutman and Rutman, 1984, p. 65): yet some definitely did, such as Mary Hathaway, who married at age 9 in Stafford County, Virginia in 1689 and petitioned for a divorce at age 11 (Brewer, 2002, ch. 8). Her case is a symptom of broader problems in historians' assumptions that obscure our ability to see the differences in the past, particularly in the status of children.

Many scholars have examined family structure. Of these, one of the most important studies is Darrett and Anita Rutman's work on Virginia in the seventeenth century. They show, movingly, what the mortality statistics meant for families: most children grew up without both parents (Rutman and Rutman, 1979). Other studies have probed average family size and childhood mortality, often in quest of answers to economic questions, revealing, in the process, that families were much bigger then than comparable families in Europe and especially than in our own time.

Another problem with many of these studies is that, because of the questions they asked and the way they grouped their data, we end up with regionally differentiated but otherwise static pictures: The Puritans came over in families (e.g., Anderson, 1985). The Virginians did not (see Horn, 1994). There were seven to nine children on average in each family in Virginia in the eighteenth century, three or four of whom died before they reached adulthood. While families were approximately the same size in

New England, the demographers have found, fewer children died before adulthood, so that New Englanders ended up with larger families. (For summaries of these studies, see Beales, pp. 15–23; Schulz, 1985, pp. 75–80; Potter, 1984, p. 141). Yet these averages tend to blur the messy reality. Some, for example, had even larger families. While Increase Mather (his name was chosen from the biblical verse "Increase and Multiply") had only six children, his son Cotton Mather had fifteen children with three different wives, thirteen of whom preceded their father in death (Middlekauff, 1971, p. 365). In many cases, however, the majority of children survived. This led to tensions in New England, especially, because fathers divided their estates among surviving sons (daughters usually received dowries). After a certain number of generations, the plots became too small, pressuring some sons to look elsewhere for land (Greven, 1970). The studies on average numbers of children generally have not distinguished among richer and poorer families. Yet indications are that wealthier women, especially in the South, who did not breast-feed, were more likely to have larger families. Frances Anne Tasker Carter, the wife of Robert Carter III, bore seventeen children, only nine of whom lived to adulthood (Fithian, 1957, p. xxvii). (On elite wet nurses and fertility also see Stone, 1977, p. 64: "unlike today, the rich had more children than the poor".)

While there are major gaps in our demographic knowledge of white families (particularly those outside of New England, because New England churches kept much better birth and death records), the problems are acute for Native American and black families, for whom reconstruction of family statistics in demographic averages is impossible for the colonial period. The most we can hope to find is glimpses on particular plantations (where a master kept a good record of births and deaths among his enslaved population) or more occasionally, in a parish record book, where a slave happened to be baptized and brought in her children. For Native American families, we must rely on the (somewhat dubious) observations of explorers and traders such as John Lawson or others, who sometimes commented on such issues.

For black families who were enslaved, however, we can make a variety of conclusions despite the sparse demographic evidence. Almost necessarily, the experiences of black children tend to be telescoped over time and generalized across region even more acutely than for white children (e.g., Gutman, 1976). The laws did not recognize enslaved families as separate entities: the marriages of enslaved persons were not legally binding, and parents had no custodial rights to their children (Burnham, 1987). While on many plantations, young children lived with their mother, or even both parents, until at least age two (because of nursing) and perhaps significantly longer, it was not unusual to have children (and fathers) sold away. Indeed, fathers often did not live on the same plantation. These stark facts are essential to our understanding of what slavery was. As Philip Morgan summarized in his deep study of slavery in the colonial Chesapeake and Lowcountry, "No slave family was truly stable. All slave relations were contingent, held together by threads a master might cut at any time" (1998, p. 512). Some masters might make an effort to keep families together, but that effort often came to nought when they died, when their estates (and their slave families) were divided between their own children, their wife, and their creditors. In 1703, after William Fitzhugh's death, his estate went to six different claimants. Of nine slave families, four had at least two children separated from them (Morgan, 1998, p. 512).

Selling black children was normal: they were not yet as productive as an adult and were the easiest to do without, at least from the master's perspective. As one planter, Peter Randolph, advised another (William Byrd III, who was facing substantial debts) in 1757: it was better to sell "young Negroes, for it will by no means answer to sell the workers" (Morgan, 1998, p. 514). While masters rarely mentioned the ages of those sold, they were perhaps more likely to sell adolescents (although this clashes with Randoph's advice, above, Morgan, 518). The impact of such sales on children who were sold away is almost impossible to measure. One memoir by an ex-slave, Charles Ball, who was sold away from his mother and siblings at age four in 1785, recalled that "the horrors of that day sank deeply into my heart" (Ball, 1859, pp. 17–18).

Entail, a legal practice of inheritance which allowed slaves and their progeny, when it was invoked, to legally be attached to a piece of land (so that they and their progeny could not be sold or granted away from it), probably limited such sales, at least until it was abolished in 1776. Despite this legal restraint, however, such slaves could still be taken and sold to pay their master's debts (Brewer, 1997; Walsh, 1997, esp. pp. 44–5, 148, 211–13).

Biographies, Psychohistory, and Religion

Historians of biographies have long recounted their subjects' childhoods as ways of framing their adult characters. Perhaps influenced by Erik Erikson's *Young Man Luther* (1958), some historians have examined the childhoods of prominent figures to understand their later characters, using modern psychological theory, which assumes, to great degree, static notions of human psychology. So Kenneth Lockridge's *The Sources of Patriarchal Rage* attributes William Byrd's and Jefferson's misogyny to their relationships with their mothers when they were young and their feelings of inferiority. Nearly every person who has passed their high school history class knows something about the childhood of Ben Franklin, that tenth son, who, after being apprenticed to his brother, the printer, ran away. His childhood story signifies his lifelong search for independence.

During the 1970s, it was not only demographers who were interested in childhood, but also psycho-historians, who looked for child abuse in the past. A rash of books and articles re-examined such practices as "swaddling," whereby an infant was wrapped in cloths for up to a day or two at a time (that prevented walking or much movement), a practice that lasted until the end of the eighteenth century. These studies argued that these past practices were "cruel" to children and that abolishing them was a dramatic step forward for them. Likewise, they contended that parents cared less about their children and that infanticide was much more common, though with little evidence (see, e.g., Walzer, 1974; Radbill, 1987).

A few works have investigated how religion or politics or culture shaped child rearing. Edmund Morgan's *The Puritan Family* (1944, revised, 1966) painted a still-life portrait of the ways that their religion shaped their child rearing. Puritans were very concerned that their children experience saving grace and redemption in the same way as themselves. They argued that children were stained by Adam's sin, and prone to wickedness. Building on that story, John Demos' *A Little Commonwealth* mixed demographic techniques with more traditional primary sources to paint a richer picture (although still a portrait lacking both change over time and differentiation by wealth or race). In his far-reaching study of religion and discipline, Philip Greven has drawn the harshest picture of how Puritan theology, with its emphasis on children as the inheritors of original sin, led to harsh discipline and repression. By contrast, he finds Southerners, who have a more moderate faith, to be much more understanding of their children's inclinations. Barry Levy's *Quakers and the American Family* examined Quaker theology, particularly their belief that all children were born with an "inner light" from Christ within them, part of Christ that helped to guide them and made them naturally good. As a consequence of this belief, he argues, Quakers were gentler parents, less prone to punish or to assume wrongdoing. It is clear that religion was less important to child rearing in Virginia (Morgan, 1952).

Native Americans clearly had very different attitudes towards family organization and child rearing, as scholars have commented. Anthony F. C. Wallace's *Death and Rebirth of the Seneca* compared the child-rearing practices of Indians and colonists, arguing that the Senecas' gentle, responsive practices (and even their interpretation of dreams) led to well-adjusted adults, which he contrasted sharply with the Puritans' discipline, which led to, one presumes, repression. In surveying many of the colonists' comments about Native American family order, Carole Shammas tentatively invoked the word "anarchical." Still, her evidence was mostly about colonial reactions to Native American women's laboring in the fields, which they regarded as a form of slavery (Shammas, 1995, 109–115). A more systematic study of European comments about Native American families could be very revealing.

Economics

In England as well as in America, children were expected to labor from a young age. Exactly how young they began to labor, and how hard they were expected to work, is very difficult to measure. Some historians have tried to measure when children began to be paid (usually early teens, see, e.g., Kussmaul, 1981, p. 72), or when they began apprenticeship. Yet the latter, especially, is difficult, given that ages are often missing from the records of laboring contracts (Kussmaul, 1981, p. 14). Apprenticeship served multiple purposes, including, in a way, adoption, but certainly poor relief (children could legally enter an "apprenticeship" when only a few months old, usually as initiated by a churchwarden). So in Southampton, England, in the seventeenth century, 20 percent of apprentices were under age ten, in Frederick County, Virginia in the 1750s the average age of apprenticeship was under eight (7.9 years), and in Massachusetts in mid-century, poor illegitimate children, at least, were bound as soon as they stopped nursing, at ages of two or three (Brewer, 2002, ch. 7; Ben-Amos, 1994, p. 40, p. 260, n. 125; Herndon, 2001, ch. 1). Many historians have assumed that most apprenticeships began at the earliest at age fourteen, and that was certainly true for the most elite apprenticeships in London, for example, which had a tightly controlled market in producing skilled artisans. Indeed, those skilled apprenticeships were so sought after that many did not begin until age nineteen or twenty (Rappaport, 1989, p. 295).

Children's labor was important in all but the most elite levels of colonial society. Children helped on farms (where 90 percent of the population, North and South, lived) from about five and up, and were probably largely self-supporting not long after (Vickers, 1994, p. 65). Indeed, poorer and middle class children, including those enslaved, began their labor in earnest certainly by age ten, if not before. Daniel Vickers speculates that children played the role in New England that slaves did in the South, in that children in large families performed much of the labor on farms, just as slaves performed much of the labor on estates in the South (Vickers, 1994, p. 82). In some ways this is undoubtedly true: in a society where education was less important – indeed, where one's education was supposed to be largely about farming and housekeeping, having children working was training them for their future lives. They did much of the labor on Northern farms. And children, as enslaved children or as "indentured" servants, did much of the labor on Southern plantations, too. Many apprentices did not learn real "skills" (only "husbandry," "farming," or "huswifery" and perhaps some minimal reading and writing) but were more servants. Yet more adults, either enslaved or as tenant farmers or day laborers, worked for others in the South. And estates tended to be much bigger. One family could reasonably farm a 200- or 300-acre family farm in Massachusetts. But, to take the most extreme case, Robert "King" Carter and his sons were hardly going to be able to farm his 300,000 acres by themselves. As Vickers points out, even for Massachusetts, on the large estates, "servant labor did matter" (Vickers, 1994, p. 55).

While parallels exist between Massachusetts, for example, and Virginia, there are different balances: children were probably less likely to be bound in Massachusetts. Their system of poor relief was more likely to give money to poor families, who thus could stay together (thus the prominence in Massachusetts and other northern colonies of "warning out" non-residents who might rely on such relief). Children clearly learned a variety of useful skills, even if only destined to be farmers, fishermen, or housewives. But the extent of the binding of poor children in Virginia (some 8,000 cases in the scattered, remaining records for colonial Virginia), or about 7 percent of all children, in my survey of one county in the 1750s, along with the absence of "warning outs" suggests that it was a much more important practice there.

While taking account of the broad acceptance of children's labor is clearly key to understanding labor in general during this period, and the process of economic production, the children in the North who worked on their parents' farms, side by side with their parents, were clearly operating in a different system, one in which affection and interest played more of a role. Those white children, after all, were the ones who would inherit their parents' wealth (indeed, they would be given some of it at their marriages).

Education, Inheritance, and Opportunity

Education, which is universal for children in modern America, was not nearly as common in colonial America. The majority of children might learn a minimum of reading (to read the Bible, perhaps) but little else. Only the elite – and usually only boys – gained an education as we would think of it, and even then it was different: it was likely to focus much more on religion, morality, and classical languages. Elite girls and boys, by the eighteenth century, were also likely to learn dancing and other social skills. Girls, in particular, were also taught music and fine needlework. There were no law schools or medical schools in America, and even in England, legal and medical training often occurred outside of a university setting.

As a consequence, there was little demand for children's books. Children's literature was only beginning to emerge during the eighteenth century, in response to the Enlightenment. Aside from books like *Aesop's Fables*, very little was directed at children in the seventeenth century. By the early eighteenth century, the *New England Primer* and a *Token for Children* were two exceptions, but they were published only in New England (the latter, originally, in England). Both emphasized religious instruction and religious conversion. John Newbury, the first publisher of children's books in England, was influenced by John Locke's writings on education to publish a literature expressly for children that helped to develop their reason. He published books like *Little Polly Pocket*, that were for sale in the colonies and then republished there, finally, after the Revolution, especially by Isaiah Thomas in Worcester, Massachusetts (Pickering, 1981; Brown, 2001; Brewer, 2002).

In Massachusetts after 1647, all towns with more than 50 families had to provide a schoolteacher to educate the children. These schools were not always established (despite the law) and they tended to give more attention to male youths, and even then only gave minimal instruction in basic reading and to a lesser degree writing (Cremin, 1970; Lockridge, 1974, pp. 50–1). Their main purpose was to teach children to read the Bible, which Protestants (and Puritans in particular) regarded as fundamental to religious understanding. The preamble to the act creating grammar schools and assigning teachers began: "It being one chief project of that old deluder, Satan, to keep men from the knowledge of the scriptures." Still, they did give some instruction to youths and offer, in the process, some opportunity.

Offering education was not simply a religious, but a political act in the seventeenth century. Many believed that education itself would lead towards rebellion. Sir William Berkeley, governor of Virginia for much of the middle of the seventeenth century, was happy to report in 1671 that Virginia had no schools and no printing press: "I thanke God there is noe ffree schooles nor printing and I hope wee shall not have these hundred yeares, for learning has brought disobedience and heresaye [heresy] and [religious] sects into the world and printing has divulged them, and libells against the best Government: God keepe us from both" (Berkeley to the Lords of Trade and Plantations, as quoted by Wertenbaker, 1914, p. 144). While there were a few charity schools for children in the more southern colonies by the eighteenth century, they were sporadic. Some tended to focus on free black children or other special group (e.g. the Bray school in Williamsburg). This followed the pattern of so-called charity schools in England, whose main purpose was usually to teach reading the Bible. Children who were apprenticed were supposed to receive some education (reading and writing for girls, with cyphering (arithmetic) as well for boys), with the understanding that as tradesmen they would need such skills, but this provision was rarely enforced. In practice, it was mostly only the elite who had much education, and even then it varied significantly. Indeed, the increasing interest and prevalence of education was undoubtedly intertwined not only with religion, but with the invention of the printing press in the late fifteenth century and the spread in its use throughout the early modern period.

Colleges existed in most colonies by the early eighteenth century, but they were more like our high schools, at least in terms of the ages of most of those who attended them. This was likely to happen at younger ages, with college more comparable to a high school today, at least in terms of the ages of students: Robert Carter III, for example, began studying at William and Mary when he was only nine in the early eighteenth century (Fithian, 1957, intro.). Elite boys, in particular, from South Carolina and Virginia, were often sent to England for their education, at vast expense. They had mostly religious instruction, including moral philosophy, although in pursuit of religious understanding, the children learned Latin and Greek. Partly, it was because these were still early days, to some degree, in print culture.

The best work on colonial education is the first volume of Lawrence Cremin's extremely rich study, which draws deeply from both primary and secondary sources. His work was partly inspired by Bernard Bailyn's *Education in the Forming of American Society* (1960), which urged that education be seen from a broad perspective, not simply in terms of formal education, but also what was taught within the home, and not simply literacy, but other forms of education. Bailyn rightly criticized much of the earlier writing on the history of education in that it focused too much on the development of "civilization." Yet he also shortchanged the contributions of that literature in that formal education was important, and a political issue. After forty years of searching for this broader pattern of education within the home, it is clear that "education" such as it was then depended upon the literacy of the parents. If the parents could not read and write (not uncommon, especially in the South which emphasized Bible reading less), then how could they teach their children? Indeed, in thinking about Bailyn's critique, we must put it also in the perspective of consensus platitudes about opportunity in America. Berkeley's quote (above) underlines that education was about revolution and authority, and it was also about opportunity. Education, after all, provides hope for the next generation, particularly if they are born poor, that they might do better. If some segments of society never had that opportunity, it means that hope was not there. Bernard Mandeville's perspective in *Essay on Charity Schools* (1722) was not uncommon: Why educate poorer children above their status? If you teach them to read, they won't want to clean your stable. He argued forcefully that free schools were nothing more than "the great Nursery of Thieves and Pick-pockets" because the poorer sort became dissatisfied with their lowly occupations (Mandeville, 1988 [1722], p. 268).

Why should we assume that formal education in the form of free schools made no difference in education levels and opportunities? Everything, of course, depends on what is taught and for what purpose. But those who called for free education for children in the wake of the Revolution, such as Thomas Jefferson and Noah Webster, thought that education – learning to read and write and knowledge itself – was fundamental to what we would call democracy. They believed that the process of learning to read and interpret also teaches reason. It is this that the early writers on public education, such as Ellwood P. Cubberley, who focused on the changes in the wake of the Revolution, understood. Public education came much slower to the South, and the arguments over creating and funding it were about democracy and rank and opportunity (Rudolph, ed., 1965; Brewer, 2002, ch. 3; Cubberley, 1934, esp. ch. 4).

Likewise, on the question of apprenticeships and education, a consensus has emerged among historians that many children (especially sons) left their families' homes to serve apprenticeships elsewhere: one son would leave his father to apprentice in the shop of another master, and another son would begin an apprenticeship with the same father. This is repeated as a truism in books ranging from Peter Laslett's *The World We Have Lost* (1984 [1965]) to Demos to Rappaport. Rappaport's more systematic study of butchers and coopers and brewers in sixteenth-century London did find that most of those who were fifteen years beyond their apprenticeships in these trades and still living in London had become masters of shops (Rappaport, 1989, p. 340). So in these trades in sixteenth-century London there was some opportunity, and a child who was an apprentice might indeed become a master. But this does not consider which children were likely to become apprentices of various types.

In many other trades (and in other places) an apprenticeship did not necessarily signal mobility. Sharp distinctions in rank differentiated different types of apprenticeship opportunities from the beginning. Indeed, aside from skilled artisan families living in towns and cities (perhaps 10 percent of the population in England and colonial America), learning a "trade" was not the issue for apprentices: they were bound as "farmers" or "housewives" or simply "servants." Indeed, rank distinctions have been largely ignored by historians: yet much evidence indicates that these practices of sending children into other people's houses had sharp status distinctions, whether in the laws themselves or practice: boys and girls became servants in wealthier people's households, and their parents did not have the resources to have servants bound to them. Consider, for example, Martha Ballard in Laurel Ulrich's *The Midwife's Tale*: her children did not labor for others. Instead they helped in her household. But she did hire other young women to come and work in her house, as well. It was not a two-way street but a one-way exchange. It was thus status-linked and often status-appropriate education, education that taught basic tasks, but created only limited opportunities.

Inheritance is a key issue here. In a society where ownership of farmland was the key to earning a living, then access to that land helps to shape economic opportunity. Different colonies and England itself had different practices of inheritance, yet to a great degree, especially in England and the southern colonies, primogeniture was the norm, especially for land (and slaves). In New England, following religious beliefs about equality, they gave the older son only a double share of land, and divided the remainder among the other sons, with the daughters obtaining dowries, and the wife usually only a life interest in part of the estate (Shammas et al., 1987; Brewer, 1997). The consequences were that estates became smaller and smaller in New England, so that to obtain land, sons had to look elsewhere. Likewise in Virginia the pressure for westward expansion was even more intense.

So a key question in thinking about opportunities for children was whether land was freely available to all comers. The assumption used to be yes. Yet as studies like Alan Taylor's *Liberty Men and Great Proprietors* and the extensive studies on Native Americans and colonial warfare have made clear, the answer is not usually, or not without substantial costs. The opportunities for (white) children to obtain land ultimately raise Frederick Jackson Turner-type questions about democracy and the frontier: Could opportunity for poorer white children come only at the expense of taking land from the Native Americans? Did, indeed, poorer white children ever benefit from this expansion, or did it primarily benefit established, even wealthier families? We also need to return to questions of inheritance: how did the very different rules surrounding inheritance and lineage help to create societal structures in different colonies (e.g., entail, which enforced primogeniture in Virginia, meant that estates were not divided, unlike, in general, in New England; see Brewer, 1997).

Therefore, we need to pay more attention to differences in children's lives. If we project backwards from more substantial evidence in the nineteenth century, we can guess that enslaved children often began laboring in the fields of tobacco and rice and grain at the age of seven. Vickers may well be correct for Massachusetts in the eighteenth century when he says that apprenticeship was a two-way exchange between families, given that wealth distribution was more equitable there than in colonies like Virginia, where the evidence indicates otherwise. We need to be more careful about our assumptions and distinctions.

Coming of Age

What did it mean to "come of age"? When scholars have tried to measure it they focused on two transitions: when apprenticeships or labor contracts ended; and when people married. By this measure, it never happened for enslaved children: they never gained a full legal identity, though they often bore responsibility from young ages. It was thirty-one for mulatto children born to white mothers in Virginia: that was the age to which they were bound into service to a master. Other apprenticeships ended at ages ranging from 18 to 24. Status was a big factor here, in which race played an important part, especially by the early eighteenth century. The age at marriage, as discussed above could vary widely – children in service, for example, rarely married before the end of their service, because masters and mistresses could punish them severely for it (by extending the time of their service). Elite children could marry much younger.

Yet clearly these might not be the most important means to demarcate childhood from adulthood. For Martha Ballard in Ulrich's *Midwife's Tale*, setting up housekeeping was the key (a more important transition than the marriage itself was when the couple set up their own household). Status also played a key role.

When could one vote? Or hold office? Or make a will? Or be executor of an estate? Or sign a labor contract? Scholars have made a strong assumption that the age of "majority" has always been 21, but there were changing norms. In a wonderful article in 1976, Keith Thomas sketched out how norms for majority not only varied considerably across area of competency, but were changing dramatically in England from the sixteenth through the eighteenth centuries. Indeed, it turns out that competency was more linked to status (in terms of rank) than to age in England in the sixteenth and seventeenth centuries. Teenagers, for example, as young as twelve and thirteen, were routinely elected to the House of Commons in England during the seventeenth century: Christopher Monck, future second Duke of Albemarle, opened a debate in Parliament when he was only fourteen in 1667. Teenagers, likewise, at least as young as seventeen and eighteen were elected to the House of Burgesses in Virginia during the same period. All of these young men were heirs to property and power. Changes in norms about competency affected every area of the law, from criminal responsibility to the age of jurors (one had only to be fourteen years old – and male and own considerable property – to be a juror in Virginia until the Revolution). One only had to be four, for example, to make a will for goods and chattels. Only during the course of the eighteenth century, as a consequence of changes in the English common law that were linked to Enlightenment reforms and to two revolutions in England in the seventeenth century – and later to the American Revolution – did age assume the pivotal role that it plays in American society today in terms of measuring competency. These changes came first, however, to New England, because Puritans – religious reformers – played a critical role in making age more important. Puritans were the first, for example, to set an age of 21 for voting (in 1641). Age became an approximate measure of merit and virtue; by setting higher age standards, and making age more important to the law, it limited the authority of an inherited aristocracy (by excluding young heirs) (Brewer, 2002).

Changing Attitudes towards Children

In fact, there was nothing static about children's lives, neither on the individual level nor across time and between regions and between ranks. There were changes in nearly every aspect of children's lives, over time, between places, and between races. Some children were very much born to a status: slaves are only the most obvious example, at least after 1662 in Virginia (and later in all of the other colonies) when slavery was made hereditary.

Indeed, the issue of children's labor is only now being pieced together. While scholars have long acknowledged that many children worked, they have seen this as a natural part of the life process, through which most children, especially boys, passed. They labored, as teenagers, to learn the trade they would grow up to practice. Yet the closer we look, especially at practices outside of New England, the clearer it becomes that children's labor does not fit this pretty picture, especially in the seventeenth century. Wealthier children were of course never apprenticed, except, perhaps, to a merchant, and that under informal conditions.

While wealthier children were educated and some children of the middling sort, particularly boys, were apprenticed to learn a trade, the majority even of those boys did not: most boys did not grow up with a skilled trade, they became farmers. Indeed, the majority of children who worked did not do so to learn a particular skill. Poorer children, especially, were not apprenticed to learn a trade. These "apprenticeships," whereby poorer children received masters, were at best a kind of welfare policy (in many cases the only one), at worst gross exploitation.

The clearest way to see this is by pairing Virginia's and Barbados' laws about children who arrived in their colonies as "servants" who had no labor contracts with those children's origins in England. These children were what we would now call "kidnapped." Children were routinely "spirited" away during the seventeenth century in England, and kidnapping laws, even after they were written, were only sporadically enforced. Why were the English authorities essentially covering their eyes to widespread kidnapping of children between the ages of ten and fifteen throughout most of the seventeenth century, many of whom went to colonies like Barbados and Virginia, who welcomed these children "without contracts" with open arms? The issue of children's forced labor is fundamental, in fact, to how we see the whole of colonial history (see Johnson, 1970; Coldham 1975 & 1992; Brewer, 2001). In other words, we err in distinguishing so sharply between black children who are enslaved and clearly born to a status, and white children who have opportunity. If "consent" is forced, and poor children can be bound without their consent (or their parents') there are many more continuities about status in this society than historians usually acknowledge. To understand this, we must be acutely sensitive not only to changes over time in the status of black children, but to changes in the status of white children, in terms of both their labor and opportunities. Otherwise, we run the risk of obscuring fundamental transformations in the ordering of society.

Studies like Greven's which assumed static religious beliefs, likewise hide real transformations. Some of his evidence of greatest violence, although associated with

Puritans of the seventeenth century, turns out to come from early nineteenth-century evangelicals. As Linda Pollock has shown in her survey of more than 500 diaries in England and America, such harsh discipline was rare before the nineteenth century, and even then it was these evangelicals who most often invoked it. Indeed, the more that historians examine attitudes towards children, the clearer it is that religion is a key, that Puritans in particular helped to initiate the new attitudes towards childhood. In his analysis of children in seventeenth-century America, Ross Beales apologized for concentrating on the Puritans: they may be different from others, he admits, but they wrote so much more, so we can see their attitudes towards children. Beales used this Puritan evidence to challenge Demos and Ariès: clearly Puritan New England did have some ideas about children as distinctive (Beales, 1985, pp. 23–24; also see Beales, 1975). Likewise, in his insightful *The Discovery of Childhood in Puritan England* (1992), C. John Sommerville links the Puritans to this "discovery." Is the question simply that Puritans were more likely to write about issues related to childhood – or that because of something in their religious ideology, they were concerned with reshaping it? In many ways the answer is clearly that the Puritan theology (and Protestant theology more generally) has contributed to a reshaping of childhood and an increase in parental power. Reformation religious ideas, for example, magnified fathers' authority in Germany (Ozment, 1983). Two particular (and somewhat oppositional) elements of Protestant thought led in this direction: first, their focus on consent to religious membership; second, their focus on catechisms that emphasized the ten commandments, and particularly the fifth commandment about obedience to parents, which was not important to the earlier Catholic teachings. They recognized this dual focus, generally, by separating children who could not consent from adults who could (not only to religious questions but to political) and giving parents, particularly the father, dominion over the children (Brewer, 2002, ch. 2).

Patriarchal Authority: Separating the Powers of Fathers, Masters, and Husbands

The biggest blind spot that colonial American historians have had about the history of the family or household is that they have naturalized "patriarchal" authority. At the same time, they have blurred together various categories of patriarchal powers, blending the power of a father with that of master, husband, and guardian, under the category of "head of household" or "patriarch" (e.g., Laslett [1965], 1984, p. 4; Stone, 1977, p. 4; Wood, 1992, p. 147; Shammas, 1995, p. 105). Indeed, many women's historians have used the word "patriarchal" as if the word were primarily about the powers of husbands. They have done so on good authority: In his extremely influential *Commentaries on the Laws of England* (vol. 1, 1765), William Blackstone sketched out fundamental legal categories that circumscribed personal relations: Master and Servant, Husband and Wife, Parent and Child, and Guardian and Ward (in that order). Also, if examining the question from the perspective of the person in charge the categories might look the same: from the other side, they are very different. While one person might be master, husband, father, and guardian, one need only look at these parallels from the perspective of servant, wife, child, or ward to realize one person could not be all four, indeed: a child, a servant, a wife and a ward usually filled very different places in society: e.g., a child might be a servant or a ward, but not both. John

Demos (1970), for example, makes a critical error in his section on "masters and servants" when he calls the relative that a mother ("widow Ring") wants her son (Andrew) to live with after her death his "master." This young man did not have a master, and if he ever did, it would be at his choice, as is clear from the will. Widow Ring instead encouraged him to listen to the advice of the "overseers" of her estate (pp. 115–16). In creating a "master," Demos is putting Andrew into a structured relationship of obedience and control where none existed, not for him as an heir; he is blurring the statuses of servant, child, and ward. But while many children in this period might live with families other than their parents, the relationships of power and authority between the child and that other family varied substantially.

Blackstone's is the perspective of the late eighteenth century, one that both exaggerated and normalized these parallels, robbing them of any political character and of any history. Yet they had very different histories and the laws surrounding each were changing during the previous three centuries: the roles and powers of masters were becoming less important to the law, and those of husbands, fathers, and guardians (particularly the latter two) were becoming more central to the law, and increasing in strength. The extent to which these categories can be seen as similar – especially to the level of king (as highest "father" to his people) – was under fierce dispute throughout the seventeenth and eighteenth centuries.

Indeed, we can describe this period as the age of custody, as inventing the power of fathers. The word custody in the early seventeenth century applied only to the authority of guardians or "lords." Most children never had guardians, except if they were an heir, and then it was often only over their land (not their person) and only until they turned age fourteen. The first law giving fathers "custody" of their children was passed in England in 1660, part of the Restoration settlement, when Charles II agreed that fathers should be able to choose guardians for all of their children until they turned 21. Acceptance of this law was one of the conditions that Charles II had to agree to in order to assume the throne. Puritans in Massachusetts made earlier laws, as early as 1641, granting fathers, especially, significant authority. Indeed, the Long Parliament, while under the control of Puritans in England, passed an earlier law that became the model for the 1660 custody law mentioned above (it, along with all laws made during the Interregnum, when Charles I and II were out of power, was made void at the restoration of Charles II in 1660). This was one of the few separately ratified. The very notion of custody implies that they need someone to make decisions for them, which is what custodial power grants. Ideas about children's incapacity to consent developed during these two centuries in tandem with the very emphasis on consent in society.

With regard to parental authority, the debate has focused on parental consent to marriage, although it has also concerned discipline. Obviously, given the high mortality during the seventeenth century in the South, there was little parental control over marriage. But masters and mistresses did have extensive control over the marriages of their young servants. If a boy or girl (or young man or young woman) married without the master's consent, substantial time would be added to their contract. Indeed, comparing the laws about marriage between different colonies reveals increasing concern about parental control over time at the same time as masters' powers decreased. It seems clear that the Puritans were more concerned about influencing their children's marriages at the same time as they wanted them to marry later.

In a much discussed article, Daniel Scott Smith and Michael S. Hindus (1975) argued that in the wake of the Revolution, young couples evaded parental control (presumably inspired by the Revolution) by simply becoming pregnant before officially marrying. The problem with his analysis (which measures the time difference between official marriage and birth of first child) is that the private promises between spouses were binding in ways that we no longer recognize. The public marriage simply ratified the private, binding engagement. Otherwise, the discussion of parental control has been heavily influenced by Lawrence Stone's *Family, Sex, and Marriage* (1977), to which books like Daniel Blake Smith's *Inside the Great House: Planter Family Life in Eighteenth-Century Chesapeake Society* (1980) are heavily indebted. Stone described parental control over marriage as gradually decreasing over time, positing a strong patriarchal head of household in the early modern period that gave way to allowing children to choose their own romantic attachments because they loved their children more. Elsewhere, I have given a sustained critique of this argument, as have others. Medievalists, in particular, have fallen over themselves in their effort to show that parents loved their children during the Middle Ages. As David Herlihy summarized so beautifully after more than a decade of research by medieval historians: "The medieval family was never dead to sentiment; it is only poor in sources" (Herlihy, 1985, 158). Linda Pollock, who surveyed diaries over three centuries in England and America from 1600 to 1900, found little change in parental love (Pollock, 1983, pp. 267–8; Gies, 1987, pp. 295–9). Lawrence Stone and Edward Shorter, following on some hints in Ariès, were clearly mistaken to focus the issue on changes in parental love.

But perhaps parental roles and parental love became more idealized? Parental control also is a more complex issue than it might appear at face value. It does seem that marriage went from being more about status and property arrangements (in the late medieval and early modern period) to being more about love. But this does not necessarily mean that parents had more control in the earlier period. Indeed, the laws about parental control actually became stronger, rather than weaker, at least until the late eighteenth century. Puritan New England, the most studied area, is again an exception: their ideological emphasis on the power of the father had actually led them earlier to give him more control. This issue is complicated by evidence that elite children sometimes married very young (even pre-puberty) in order to give parents some control in the seventeenth century, when the laws did not support their authority.

Recent work on the material culture of childhood in America supports that attitudes towards children were changing. However, as Karin Calvert has argued, the changes were not about "whether parents loved their children but of how they treated the children they loved" (1992, p. 12). Swaddling, for example, was abandoned in the late eighteenth century in response to an idealization of the "natural child." She argues that before, it had been not been abusive, but used for safety reasons (it kept children, for example from crawling into open fireplaces) and kept their necks safe when tiny. It also accorded with medical ideas that held that children needed to be swaddled to grow up straight. While few toys existed for children before the eighteenth century, aside from an occasional top, by the late eighteenth and early nineteenth centuries, children were being given more and distinctive playthings. They were also beginning to have their own space in homes, particularly in wealthier houses. In paintings, they began to be portrayed less as "little adults" and more as part of nuclear families. Children's clothing also became more distinctive during the late eighteenth century (especially for boys) (Schulz, 1985, pp. 80–9; Calvert, 1992, pp. 21, 45, 47, 61, 70).

Fliegelman's *Prodigals and Pilgrims* (1982) and other studies have sketched a shift in thinking about mature children that accompanied the Revolution. Sons (especially) began to be seen as more independent from their fathers once they grew up. But the political changes were ongoing. Every issue we have discussed so far, from children's labor to slavery to education, is politically and legally constructed. Legislators had to sit and debate whether slavery would be hereditary. They had to decide what to do with little English children who arrived "without contracts." They had to decide whether to support some sort of public education. Religion, of course, influences those decisions, but so does political ideology: the Puritans supported public education because they wanted all people to learn to read and understand the Bible for themselves. But this was not unconnected to the political struggles of the seventeenth century, which in England led to two revolutions. They both relate to fundamental questions of authority. Who should consent, and when?

In fact, children could consent to a variety of legal contracts in the early modern period and were liable as early as age eight for crimes. What does one make of a girl of eleven seeking a divorce in Virginia in 1689? (She had married at age nine.) Why was a four-year-old girl, Dorcas Good, held in the Boston jail in chains for six months for the crime of witchcraft? Why was a two-year-old making her mark on a labor contract as late as 1811 in Chester County, Pennsylvania? (Brewer, 2002).

In considering the changes in the status as a whole, then, we must return to Philippe Ariès's influential thesis. He helped to demarcate a fundamental shift in thinking about children, particularly their education. Yet in transferring simplistic versions of his ideas to England and America: that children were "little adults" and that the eighteenth century witnessed the "discovery" of childhood, we misrepresent the character of the change. Children were not little adults. Clearly English and Euro-American society had some notions about child development prior to the eighteenth century, as poems such as Shakespeare's "The Stages of Life," about a wealthier boy (from *As You Like It)* make clear.

> . . . At first the Infant,
> Mewling, and puking in the Nurse's arms:
> And then the whining Schoole-boy with his Satchell
> And shining morning face, creeping like snaile
> Unwillingly to schoole.

It is not that children were not recognized as having distinct needs from adults – obviously a baby, to take the most obvious point, nurses and needs care that most adults do not, and there is no doubt that medieval society recognized this. It was more that the distinction between children and adults was less important. It is also a mistake to characterize this as a "discovery" of the true nature of children. It is more that society and the law were beginning to accept (and struggling over) different definitions of childhood, definitions that had everything to do with the structure and character of society.

Connecting the discussion of children to broad shifts in ideology not only explains origins but helps to delineate the nature of the changes more clearly. The fundamental change related to children was not a "recognition" of the innate nature of childhood. Rather, modern childhood is a by-product of the Age of Reason, which designated children as those without reason. It is also closely related to what we would now call democracy and to ideas about equality. But because we tend to naturalize our own powerful assumptions about children, we have been unable to understand the full scope of these changes in thought and practice.

Only when we differentiate children (as children) from adults can we fully see, for example, the impact of the Revolution. Freedom came to adult sons, and to some adult slaves, but children were different: even most of the plans for abolishing slavery did so gradually, leaving children born to slave women enslaved until they reached a particular age (e.g., 28? in Pennsylvania). The revolutionary arguments about equality applied only to adults (and exceptions could be made, as well for women and for blacks, if they could be compared with children in their ability to reason).

Suggestions for Further Research

Many fruitful questions about children remain to be answered. We are just beginning to take the lives of children seriously, to understand how central these issues about the treatment of children are to understanding the fundamental characters of these societies. We need to know more about children's labor. We need to think about slave law, especially as it relates to the status of children, in a more subtle manner. Clearly the slave codes in some ways kept the older norms about lordship (of masters), since the children of those who were enslaved belonged to the lord. But was it simply an extreme form of earlier norms? We need to do more with culture (particularly ethnographic comparisons). How does child-rearing and "education" itself relate to "civilization" and European ideas of superiority? How does it relate to so many other questions about the interaction of cultures, including, for example, what material goods children learn to take for granted (or forget how to make). Historians have now accepted Jim Merrell's argument in *The Indian's New World* that as a result of disease (like smallpox) wiping out the older generations, in a culture so reliant on oral histories for education, this erased those histories, and thus to some degree those identities. Can we take this generalization about Catawba and apply it to other groups, in more subtle ways? We need to do a lot more work in the legal history related to children. How did the concept of custody for children evolve? How often, for example, were children (as children) the "executors" of estates and not assigned guardians? How often were children liable for crime?

There are some good collections of primary documents related to childhood, including Abbot's now classic *Child and the State* and volume one of Bremner's collection (1970), which are good places to begin.

BIBLIOGRAPHY

Anderson, Virginia DeJohn: "Migrants and Motives: Religion and the Settlement of New England, 1630–1640." *New England Quarterly* 58 (1985), pp. 339–83, esp. Table 1.

Ariès, Philippe: *Centuries of Childhood: A Social History of Family Life* (1960), trans. Robert Baldick (New York: Vintage Books, 1962).

Bailyn, Bernard: *Education in the Forming of American Society: Needs and Opportunities for Study* (New York: W. W. Norton, 1960).

Ball, Charles: *Fifty Years in Chains* (New York: H. Dayton, 1859).

Beales, Ross, W.: "The Child in Seventeenth Century America." In Joseph M. Hawes and N. Ray Hiner, eds., *American Childhood* (Westport, CT: Greenwood Press, 1985).

Beales, Ross W., Jr.: "In Search of the Historical Child: Miniature Adulthood and Youth in Colonial New England." *American Quarterly* 27 (1975), pp. 379–98.

Ben-Amos, Ilana Krausman: *Adolescence and Youth in Early Modern England* (New Haven, CT: Yale University Press, 1994).

Blackstone, William: *Commentaries on the Laws of England* [1765], vol. 1 (repr. Chicago: University of Chicago Press, 1979).

Bremner, Robert H.: *Children and Youth in America: A Documentary History*, vol. 1, *1660–1865* (Cambridge, MA: Harvard University Press, 1970).

Brewer, Holly: "Entailing Aristocracy: Ancient Feudal Restraints and Revolutionary Reform." *WMQ* 3rd ser., 54 (1997), pp. 307–46.

Brewer, Holly: "Beyond Education: Thomas Jefferson's Republican Revision of the Laws Regarding Children." In James Gilreath, ed., *Thomas Jefferson and the Education of a Citizen: The Earth Belongs to the Living* (Washington, DC: Library of Congress, 1999), pp. 48–62.

Brewer, Holly: "Age of Reason? Children, Testimony, and Consent in Early America." In Christopher Tomlins and Bruce Mann, eds., *The Many Legalities of Early America* (Chapel Hill, NC: University of North Carolina Press, 2001).

Brewer, Holly: *By Birth or Consent: Children, Law, and Revolution in England and America, 1550–1820* (Chapel Hill, NC: University of North Carolina Press, 2002).

Brown, Gillian: *The Consent of the Governed: The Lockean Legacy in Early American Culture* (Cambridge, MA: Harvard University Press, 2001).

Britton, Edward: *The Community of the Vill: a Study in the History of the Family and Village Life in Fourteenth-Century England* (Toronto: Macmillan of Canada, 1977).

Burnham, Margaret A.: "An Impossible Marriage: Slave Law and Family Law." *Law and Inequality Journal* 5 (1987), pp. 187–225.

Cable, Mary: *The Little Darlings: A History of Child-Rearing in America* (New York: Scribner, 1972).

Calhoun, Arthur W.: *A Social History of the American Family*, vol. 1 (Cleveland, OH: Arthur H. Clark Co., 1917).

Calvert, Karin Fishbeck: "Children in American Family Portraiture, 1670 to 1810." *William and Mary Quarterly* 39 (1982), pp. 87–113.

Calvert, Karin Fishbeck: *Children in the House: The Material Culture of Early Childhood, 1600–1900* (Boston, MA: Northeastern University Press, 1992).

Carlton, Charles Hope: *The Court of Orphans* (Leicester: Leicester University Press, 1974).

Carr, Lois Green: "The Development of Maryland's Orphan Court, 1654–1715." In Aubrey C. Land, Lois Green Carr, and Edward C. Papenfuse, eds., *Law, Society, and Politics in Early Maryland: Proceedings of the First Conference on Maryland History, June 14–15, 1974* (Baltimore, MD: Johns Hopkins University Press, 1977).

Carson, Jane: *Colonial Virginians at Play* (Williamsburg, VA: Colonial Williamsburg Press, 1965).

Caulfield, Ernest: *The Infant Welfare Movement in the Eighteenth Century* (New York: P. B. Hoeber, 1931).

Coldham, Peter Wilson: "The 'Spiriting' of London Children to Virginia, 1648–1685." *VMHB* 83 (1975), pp. 280–87.

Coldham, Peter Wilson: *Emigrants in Chains* (Baltimore: Genealogical Publishing Co., 1992).

Coveny, Peter: *The Image of Childhood: The Individual and Society: A Study of the Theme in English Literature* (London: Penguin Books, 1967).

Cremin, Lawrence Arthur: *The American Common School* (New York: Columbia University Press, 1951).

Cremin, Lawrence Arthur: *The Wonderful World of Ellwood Patterson Cubberley: An Essay on the Historiography of American Education* (New York: Teachers College, Columbia University Press, 1965).

Cremin, Lawrence Arthur: *American Education: The Colonial Experience, 1607–1783* (New York: Harper and Row, 1970).

Cubberley, Ellwood: *Public Education in the United States: A Study and Interpretation of American Educational History* [1919], rev. and enl. ed. (Boston, MA: Houghton Mifflin Co., 1934).

Degler, Carl: *At Odds: Women and the Family in America from the Revolution to the Present* (New York: Oxford University Press, 1980).

Demos, John: *A Little Commonwealth: Family Life in Plymouth Colony* (Oxford, UK: Oxford University Press, 1970).

Dunlop, O. J. and Denham, Richard: *English Apprenticeship and Child Labor: A History* (New York: Macmillan Co., 1912).

Durston, Christopher: *The Family in the English Revolution* (Oxford: Basil Blackwell, 1989).

Earle, Alice M.: *Child Life in Colonial Days* (New York: Macmillan Co., 1899).

Ehrlich, Paul R.: *The Population Bomb* (New York, Ballantine Books, 1968).

Erikson, Erik H.: *Young Man Luther: A Study in Psychoanalysis and History* (New York: Norton, 1958).

Fithian, Philip Vickers: *Diary and Letters of Philip Vickers Fithian, 1773–1774: A Plantation Tutor of the Old Dominion* (Williamsburg, VA: Colonial Williamsburg Foundation, 1957).

Fleming, Sandford: *Children and Puritanism: The Place of Children in the Life and Thought of New England Churches, 1620–1847* (New Haven, CT: Yale University Press, 1933).

Fliegelman, Jay: *Prodigals and Pilgrims: The American Revolution against Patriarchal Authority, 1750–1800* (Cambridge, UK: Cambridge University Press, 1982).

Gies, Frances and Joseph: *Marriage and the Family in the Middle Ages* (New York: Harper & Row, 1987).

Goody, Jack: *The Development of the Family and Marriage in Europe* (Cambridge, UK: Cambridge University Press, 1983).

Green, Ian: *The Christian's ABC: Catechisms and Catechizing in England c. 1530–1740* (Oxford, UK: Clarendon Press, 1996).

Greven, Phillip, Jr.: *Four Generations: Population, Land and Family in Colonial Andover, Massachusetts* (Ithaca, NY: Cornell University Press, 1970).

Greven, Phillip, Jr.: *The Protestant Temperament: Patterns of Child-Rearing, Religious Experience and Self in Early America* (Chicago, IL: University of Chicago Press, 1977).

Griffiths, Paul: *Youth and Authority: Formative Experiences in England, 1560–1640* (Oxford: Clarendon Press, 1996).

Gutman, Herbert: *The Black Family in Slavery and Freedom, 1750–1825* (New York: Pantheon Books, 1976).

Hanawalt, Barbara A.: *The Ties that Bound: Peasant Families in Medieval England* (Oxford, UK: Oxford University Press, 1986).

Hanawalt, Barbara A.: *Growing up in Medieval London: The Experience of Childhood in History* (New York: Oxford University Press, 1993).

Hawes, Joseph M.: *The Children's Rights Movement: A History of Advocacy and Protection* (Boston: Twayne Publishers, 1991).

Hawes, Joseph M. and Hines, N. Ray, eds.: *American Childhood: A Research Guide and Historical Handbook* (Westport, CT: Greenwood Press, 1985).

Herlihy, David: *Medieval Households* (Cambridge, MA: Harvard UP, 1985).

Herndon, Ruth: *Unwelcome Americans: Living on the Margin in Early New England* (Philadelphia: University of Pennsylvania Press, 2001).

Hoffer, Peter Charles and Hull, N. E. H: *Murdering Mothers: Infanticide in England and New*

England, 1558–1803 (New York: New York University Press, 1981).

Horn, James: *Adapting to a New World: English Society in the Seventeenth Century Chesapeake* (Chapel Hill, NC: University of North Carolina Press, 1994).

Jernegan, Marcus W.: *Laboring and Dependent Classes in Colonial America 1607–1783: Studies of the Economic, Educational, and Social Significance of Slaves, Servants, Apprentices, and Poor Folk* [1931] (repr. Westport, CT: Greenwood Press, 1980).

Johnson, Robert: "The Transportation of Vagrant Children from London to Virginia, 1618–1622." In H. S. Reinmuth, ed., *Early Stuart Studies* (Minneapolis, MN: University of Minnesota Press, 1970), pp. 137–51.

Jones, Douglas Lamar: "The Transformation of the Law of Poverty in Eighteenth-Century Massachusetts." In *Law in Colonial Massachusetts, 1630–1800* (Boston, MA: The Colonial Society of Massachusetts, 1984).

Jones, M. G.: *The Charity School Movement* (Cambridge, UK: Cambridge University Press, 1938).

Kussmaul, Ann: *Servants in Husbandry in Early Modern England* (Cambridge: Cambridge University Press, 1981).

Lasch, Christopher: *Haven in a Heartless World: The Family Besieged* (New York: Basic Books, 1977).

Laslett, Peter: *Household and Family in Past Time: Comparative Studies in the Size and Structures of the Domestic Group Ovel A. Pike* (Cambridge, UK: Cambridge University Press, 1972).

Laslett, Peter: *The World We Have Lost Further Explored* [1965] (New York: Charles Scribner, 1984).

Lewis, Jan: *The Pursuit of Happiness: Family and Values in Jefferson's Virginia* (New York: Cambridge University Press, 1983).

Levy, Barry: *Quakers and the American Family: British Settlement in the Delaware Valley* (New York: Oxford University Press, 1988).

Lockridge, Kenneth A.: *Literacy in Colonial New England: An Inquiry into the Social Context of Literacy in the Early Modern West* (New York: W. W. Norton, 1974).

Lockridge, Kenneth A.: *On the Sources of Patriarchal Rage: The Commonplace Books of William Byrd and Thomas Jefferson and the Gendering of Power in the Eighteenth Century* (New York: New York University Press, 1992).

Mandeville, Bernard: "Essay on Charity Schools." In *The Fable of the Bees or Private Vices, Publick Benefits (1722)*, vol. 1 (repr. of 1924 Oxford ed.) (Indianapolis: Liberty Classics, 1988), pp. 253–322.

Middlekauff, Robert: *Ancients and Axioms: Secondary Education in Eighteenth Century New England* (New Haven, CT: Yale University Press, 1963).

Middlekauff, Robert: *The Mathers: Three Generations of Puritan Intellectuals, 1596–1728* (New York: Oxford University Press, 1971).

Morgan, Edmund S.: *The Puritan Family: Religion and Domestic Relations in Seventeenth-Century New England* (Boston, MA: Trustees of the Public Library, 1944).

Morgan, Edmund S.: *Virginians at Home: Family Life in the Eighteenth Century* (Williamsburg, VA: William Byrd Press, 1952).

Morgan, Philip D.: *Slave Counterpoint: Black Culture in the Eighteenth Century Chesapeake and Lowcountry* (Chapel Hill, NC: University of North Carolina Press, 1998).

Ozment, Steven: *When Fathers Ruled: Family Life in Reformation Europe* (Cambridge, MA: Harvard University Press, 1983).

Pickering, Samuel F.: *John Locke and Children's Books in Eighteenth Century England* (Knoxville, TN: University of Tennessee Press, 1981).

Pinchbeck, Ivy: "The State and the Child in Sixteenth Century England." *British Journal of Sociology* 7 (1956) and 8 (1957), pp. 59–74.

Pinchbeck, Ivy and Hewitt, Margaret: *Children in English Society*, vol. 1: *From Tudor Times to the Eighteenth Century* (London: Routledge & Kegan Paul, 1969).

Pleck, Elizabeth: *Domestic Tyranny: The Making of Social Policy Against Family Violence from Colonial Times to the Present* (New York: Oxford University Press, 1987).

Plumb, J. H.: "The First Flourishing of Children's Books." In Charles Ryskamp, comp., *Early Children's Books and their Illustration* (Boston, MA: Godine, 1975).

Pollock, Linda: *Forgotten Children: Parent–Child Relations from 1500 to 1900* (Cambridge, UK: Cambridge University Press, 1983).

Pollock, Linda: "Courtship and Marriage from the Middle Ages to the Twentieth Century." *Historical Journal* 30 (1987), pp. 483–98.

Pollock, Linda: *A Lasting Relationship: Parents and Children over Three Centuries* (London: Fourth Estate Ltd, 1987).

Potter, Jim: "Demographic Development and Family Structure." In Jack P. Greene and J. R. Pole, eds., *Colonial British America: Essays in the New History of the Modern Era* (Baltimore, MD: The Johns Hopkins University Press, 1984).

Radbill, Samuel X.: "Children in a World of Violence: A History of Child Abuse." In Ray Helfer and Ruth Kempe, eds., *The Battered Child* (Chicago, IL: University of Chicago Press, 1987).

Rappaport, Steve: *Worlds Within Worlds: Structures of Life in Sixteeenth-Century London* (Cambridge: Cambridge University Press, 1989).

Rorabaugh, William: *The Craft Apprentice: From Franklin to the Machine Age in America* (New York: Oxford University Press, 1986).

Rothman, David: "Documents in Search of a Historian: Toward a History of Childhood and Youth in America." In Theodore Rabb and Robert Rotberg, eds., *The Family in History: Interdisciplinary Essays* (New York: Harper & Row, 1971).

Rudolph, Frederick, ed.: *Essays on Education in the Early Republic* (Cambridge, MA: Harvard University Press, 1965).

Rutman, Darrett B. and Anita H.: "Now-Wives and Sons-in-law: Parental Death in a Seventeenth-Century Virginia County." In Thad W. Tate and David L. Ammerman, eds., *The Chesapeake in the Seventeenth Century: Essays on Anglo-American Society* (Chapel Hill, NC: University of North Carolina Press, 1979).

Rutman, Darrett B. and Anita H.: *A Place in Time: Explicatus* (New York: W. W. Norton, 1984).

Rutman, Darrett B. and Anita H.: *A Place in Time: Middlesex County, Virginia 1650–1750* (New York: W. W. Norton, 1984).

Schulz, Constance B.: "Children and Childhood in the Eighteenth Century." In Joseph M. Hawes and N. Ray Hines, eds., *American Childhood* (Westport, CT: Greenwood Press, 1985).

Seybolt, Robert Francis: *Apprenticeship and Apprenticeship Education in Colonial New England and New York* (New York: Teachers College, Columbia University Press, 1917).

Shahar, Shulamith: *Childhood in the Middle Ages*, trans. Chaya Galai (London: Routledge, 1990).

Shammas, Carole: "The Domestic Environment in Early Modern England and America." *Journal of Social History* 14 (Fall, 1980).

Shammas, Carole: "Anglo-American Household Government in Comparative Perspective." *William and Mary Quarterly* 3rd ser., 52 (1995), pp. 104–44.

Shammas, Carole, Salmon, Marylynn, and Dahlin, Michel: *Inheritance in America: From Colonial Times to the Present* (New Brunswick, NJ: Rutgers University Press, 1987).

Shorter, Edward: *The Making of the Modern Family* (New York: Basic Books, 1975).

Slack, Paul: *Poverty and Policy in Stuart England* (London: Longman, 1988).

Slater, Peter Gregg: *Children in the New England Mind in Death and in Life* (Hamden, CT: Archon Books, 1977).

Sloane, William: *Children's Books in England and America in the Seventeenth Century* (New York: Columbia University Press, 1955).

Smith, Abbot E.: *Colonists in Bondage: White Servitude and Convict Labor in America, 1607–1776* (Chapel Hill, NC: University of North Carolina Press, 1947).

Smith, Daniel Blake: *Inside the Great House: Planter Family Life in Eighteenth-Century Chesapeake Society* (Ithaca, NY: Cornell University Press, 1980).

Smith, Daniel Blake: "The Study of the Family in Early America: Trends, Problems and Prospects." *William and Mary Quarterly* 39 (1982), pp. 3–28.

Smith, Daniel Scott: "The Demographic History of Colonial New England." In Michael Gordon, ed., *The American Family in Social-Historical Perspective* (New York: St. Martin's Press, 1973).

Smith, Daniel Scott and Hindus, Michael S.: "Premarital Pregnancy in America, 1640–1971: An Overview and Interpretation." *Journal of Interdisciplinary History* 5 (1975), pp. 537–70.

Smith, Emerson: *Colonists in Bondage: White Servitude and Convict Labor in America, 1607–1776* (Chapel Hill, NC: University of North Carolina Press, 1947).

Smith, Steven Rau: "The Apprentices of London, 1640–1660: A Study of a Revolutionary Youth Subculture" (Ph.D. dissertation, Vanderbilt University, 1971).

Smith, Wilson, ed.: *Theories of Education in Early America* (New York: Bobbs-Merrill Co., 1973).

Snell, K. D. M.: *Annals of the Labouring Poor: Social Change and Agrarian England, 1660–1900* (Cambridge, UK: Cambridge University Press, 1985).

Sommerville, C. John: *The Discovery of Childhood in Puritan England* (Athens, GA: University of Georgia Press, 1992).

Spacks, Patricia Meyer: "'Always at Variance': Politics of Eighteenth-Century Adolescence." In *A Distant Prospect: Eighteenth-Century Views of Childhood* (Los Angeles, CA: William Andrews Clark Memorial Library, 1982).

Spring, Joel: *The American School, 1642–1985: Varieties of Historical Interpretation of the Foundations and Development of American Education* (New York: Longman, Inc., 1986).

Stone, Lawrence: *The Family, Sex and Marriage in England, 1500–1800* (London: Weidenfeld and Nicolson, 1977).

Sutton, John R.: *Stubborn Children: Controlling Delinquency in the United States, 1640–1981* (Berkeley, CA: University of California Press, 1988).

Taylor, Alan: *Liberty Men and Great Proprietors: The Revolutionary Settlement on the Maine Frontier, 1760–1820* (Chapel Hill, NC: UNC Press, 1990).

Thomas, Keith: "Age and Authority in Early Modern England." *Proceedings of the British Academy* 62 (1976), pp. 205–48.

Ulrich, Laurel: *A Midwife's Tale: The Life of Martha Ballard, Based on Her Diary, 1785–1812* (New York: Vintage Books, 1990).

Vickers, Daniel: *Farmers and Fishermen: Two Centuries of Work in Essex County, Massachusetts, 1630–1830* (Chapel Hill, NC: University of North Carolina Press, 1994).

Wallace, Anthony F. C.: *The Death and Rebirth of the Seneca* (New York, Knopf, 1970).

Walsh, Lorena: *From Calabar to Carter's Grove: The History of a Virginia Slave Community* (Charlottesville, VA: University of Virginia Press, 1997).

Walzer, John: "A Period of Ambivalence: Eighteenth Century American Childhood." In Lloyd de Mause, ed., *The History of Childhood* (New York: Psychohistory Press, 1974).

Wertenbaker, Thomas J.: *Virginia Under the Stuarts, 1607–1688* (Princeton, NJ: Princeton UP, 1914).

Wishy, Bernard: *The Child and the Republic: the Dawn of Modern American Child Nurture* (Philadelphia, PA: University of Pennsylvania Press, 1968).

Wood, Gordon S.: *The Radicalism of the American Revolution: How a Revolution Transformed a Monarchical Society into a Democratic One Unlike Any That Had Ever Existed* (New York: Alfred A. Knopf, 1992).

Wright, Bobby. "'For the Children of the Infidels': American Indian Education in the Colonial
    Colleges." *American Indian Culture and Research Journal* 12 (1988), pp. 1–14.
US Bureau of the Census: *Historical Statistics of the United States, Colonial Times to 1957* (Wash-
    ington, DC, 1960) (for average age in 1790).
Yazawa, Melvin: *From Colonies to Commonwealth: Familial Ideology and the Beginnings of the
    American Republic* (Baltimore, MD: Johns Hopkins University Press, 1985).

CHAPTER ELEVEN

Class

GREG NOBLES

Class is a concept that has often fit uncomfortably in the study of early American history. For one thing, the term itself did not appear often in contemporary accounts of colonial society, or certainly not with the same sort of meaning it carries today. As one historian has recently noted, most early Americans "did not use 'class' to describe social divisions, but rather spoke of 'ranks,' 'orders,' 'degrees,' or . . . 'interests, . . . using 'class' as a general term for any group" (Rosswurm, 1987, p. 18). Thus when the Rev. Timothy Dwight brought to a poetic conclusion his pastorate in rural Massachusetts ("Greenfield Hill," 1794), he used the term "class" to emphasize inclusion rather than division:

> Here every class (if classes those we call,
> Where one extended class embraces all,
> All mingling, as the rainbow's beauty blends,
> Unknown where every hue begins or ends)
> Each following each, with uninvidious strife,
> Wears every feature of improving life. . . .
> See the wide realm of equal shares possess'd!
> How few the rich, or poor! how many bless'd!
> (Dwight, 1794, pp. 36, 153)

But Dwight's poem also speaks to a more fundamental assumption underlying the study of class in early America. For over two centuries, the myth of America as a "classless society" lay rooted in the colonial era, and the early American rhetoric of equality and opportunity has often diverted academic analysis away from class relations. In one of the most famous passages from his *Letters from an American Farmer* (1782), Hector St. John de Crèvecoeur answered his own question, "What is an American?", by asserting the absence of strong social divisions, especially compared to the extreme stratification of European society: "Here are no aristocratical families, no courts, no kings, no bishops, no ecclesiastical dominion, no invisible power giving to a few a very visible one; no great manufacturers employing thousands, no great refinements of luxury." Instead, Crèvecoeur pointed to a "pleasing uniformity of decent competence" among the people; because of that, he declared, "we are the most perfect society now existing in the world" (Crèvecoeur, 1981 [1782], p. 67). This post-revolutionary perfection Crèvecoeur celebrated, like the "embrace" of "one extended class" that Dwight described, seemed to be the happy legacy of America's recent past, the gift of the colonial era to the new nation.

Throughout the twentieth century, American historians have differed greatly about whether or not to accept that "gift" as a given. No one, of course, could seriously describe an essentially "classless" colonial society and say, as Dwight did, "How few the rich, or poor!" The evidence of inequality has always been inescapable. Still, the historical implications of its existence have often been debated – and, in many cases, evaded. From the colonial period through the modern era, the apparent openness and opportunity inherent in American society have given the country a reputation of being all but devoid of class identity or class conflict. As the British historian Gareth Stedman Jones has observed from the comparative perspective of his side of the Atlantic, it has never been possible for American historians "simply to infer class as a political force from class as a structural position within productive relations" (Jones, 1983, p. 2). The task, of course, is to go beyond simple inference in order to explore the possible manifestations and meanings of class in a society so long noted for its supposed classlessness.

To be sure, in the early decades of the century, the Progressive historians – Charles Beard, Carl Becker, Arthur Schlesinger, and others – placed considerations of class at the center of scholarship, and they sought to develop an explanation of early American history that clarified the conflicting interests of different classes. The most famous and certainly most controversial of the works of the Progressive historians, Beard's *An Economic Interpretation of the Constitution of the United States* (1986 [1913]), argued that the creation of the American state clearly reflected the class interests of certain political and financial leaders who took control of the national constitution-making process in 1787. It was not wealth alone that determined their interests, Beard asserted, but wealth from particular sources – trade, manufacturing, and government securities, for instance, rather than land and slaves – that led them to push for a strong, centralized government that would ensure the stability of their investments. Thus the emergence of a small, self-interested elite at the end of the colonial era shaped, even determined, the transition to nationhood. In a similar vein, Schlesinger (1957 [1918]) argued that the coming of the American Revolution did not by any means stem simply from a transatlantic controversy about lofty political ideas, but was in large part the result of competing economic interests, both between the colonies and Great Britain and within the colonies themselves, that had developed in the late colonial era. In general, the Progressives opened the century by taking early American history out of the realm of ideas and disinterested statesmanship and locating it in the context of increasingly coherent economic concerns that suffused colonial society: the Revolution, as the critical event marking the end of the colonial era, both reflected and heightened class identities and tensions that had existed for years before.

But the Progressive interpretation was by no means the only school of historical analysis to address questions of class. By the middle of the century, a growing group of "consensus" historians offered a more conservative vision of American society that emphasized comparative social harmony, or certainly a lack of overt social conflict. Indeed, as Edmund Morgan has observed about his own early years in the historical profession in the late 1940s and 1950s, colonial American history was considered an especially "safe" subject because it seemed so distant from the ideological debates of the Cold War (and McCarthy) era. One of the most outspoken on the consensus historians, Daniel Boorstin, wrote about "the vagueness of American social classes" in his popular and prize-winning book, *The Americans: The Colonial Experience* (1958): echoing Crèvecoeur, Boorstin observed that "Distinctions which had been hallowed by custom, law, and language in Europe came to seem vague and artificial in America" (Boorstin, 1958, p. 185). Instead, Boorstin described a colonial context in which early Americans "had to look to their opportunities, to the unforeseen openings of the American situation . . . [and] everyone had to be prepared to become someone else" (Boorstin, 1958, pp. 194–5). Reflecting the post-war euphoria of mainstream America in the 1950s, this sense of optimism, openness, and opportunity provided a reassuring and seemingly less controversial alternative to the more unsettling emphasis on interest, inequality, and injustice that underlay the progressives' approach to the past. A decade later, in 1968, Jack P. Greene surveyed the scholarship of the pre-revolutionary era and pointed to several "tentative conclusions that flatly contradict earlier arguments of the Progressive historians" – among them a general agreement that "social and political opportunity was remarkably wide" and, perhaps as a result, "class struggle and the demand for democracy on the part of underprivileged groups were not widespread and not a primary causative factor in the coming of the Revolution" (Greene, 1968, p. 31). Writing at essentially the same time, the radical historian Barton Bernstein noted less happily that "the progressive synthesis had been under monographic attack before Pearl Harbor, and seemed to fall apart under the sustained assaults of the postwar years" (Bernstein, 1967, p. vii). In the realm of academic, if not class, conflict, there seemed to be a mid-century consensus not just about the nature of colonial society, but about the failure of progressive scholarship as well. Indeed, as late as 1991, Gordon Wood would still argue in his Pulitzer Prize-winning book, *The Radicalism of the American Revolution*, that most people in colonial American society "thought of themselves as connected vertically rather than horizontally . . . [and] few groups or occupations could as yet sustain any strong corporate or class consciousness, any sense of existing as a particular social stratum with long-term common interests that were antagonistic to the interests of another stratum" (Wood, 1991, pp. 23–4).

Yet this emphasis on the apparent absence of "long-term common interests" greatly understated the longer-term processes of change under way in early America – and likewise in early American scholarship. By the mid-1960s, the emphasis on consensus was beginning to face a serious challenge of its own, reflecting in the scholarly arena the more pervasive political and cultural challenges then taking place in American society as a whole. Two works – Jackson Turner Main's *The Social Structure of Revolutionary America* (1965) and Jesse Lemisch's "The American Revolution as Seen from the Bottom Up" (1967) – stand out as especially important, almost emblematic, in indicating both the growing concern with class and the ways historians would come to address the issue.

Main's book was an ambitious attempt to deal directly with the definition of class. Looking back at the major scholarly trends of the century, Main located himself in the aftermath of the clash between the progressive and consensus schools. The progressives, he noted, "took for granted the existence of economic classes, the conflict between which was assumed to be vitally significant" (Main, 1965, p. 3). On the other hand, the recently dominant consensus historians "minimize[d] social distinctions and class conflicts . . . [and] even denied that classes existed at all" (Main, 1965, p. 3). For his own part, Main took nothing for granted and neither assumed nor denied the existence of class: rather, he set out to demonstrate the dimensions of social and economic inequality in early America. And he succeeded – to a degree. As the title of his book indicates, Main described in some detail the social *structure* of pre-revolutionary America

– differing levels of wealth, position, prestige, and opportunity – but he ultimately
shied away from a more intensive investigation of social relations, much less social
conflict: "I had indeed originally planned to conclude this book with an essay on the
relationship between class and the structure of power," he admitted, "but the subject
proved much too large" (Main, 1965, p. viii). What he did conclude with was a distinction between class and class consciousness:

> If the word 'class' requires the presence of class consciousness, if it can be used only when
> men are aware of a hierarchical structure and of their own rank within it, then this study
> indicates that America during the period 1763–1788 was relatively classless. . . . If on the
> other hand the existence of classes does not depend on class consciousness but implies
> nothing more than a rank order within which an individual can move up or down without
> any insurmountable difficulty, then revolutionary America can and indeed must be de-
> scribed in terms of classes. (Main, 1965, p. 270)

He then invited other scholars to take his work as a point of departure for further
studies, both backward and forward in time, and ended his own analysis on a curious,
almost contradictory, note. After observing that at the end of the colonial era, "[t]he
long-term tendency seems to have been toward greater inequality, with more marked
class distinctions," he nevertheless suggested that someone living at the time might
have cause for "cautious optimism": "Classes remained, to be sure, and he might note
with alarm the growing concentration of wealth and the growing number of poor, but
the Revolution had made great changes, and westward the land was bright" (Main,
1965, p. 287). This final Turnerian twist, pointing to new opportunities inherent in
national expansion, might have been a necessary concession to the consensus historians, but it tended to undermine the impact of much that had come before.

Shortly after the appearance of Main's *Social Structure*, Jesse Lemisch took a more
combative stance toward the consensus historians by explicitly emphasizing class consciousness, or at least drawing attention to social *action* and historical *agency* among
the lower classes of early America. Beginning with his 1967 essay on "The American
Revolution Seen from the Bottom Up" and following that with "Jack Tar in the Streets:
Merchant Seamen and the Politics of Revolutionary America" (1968), Lemisch chided
historians for their willful denial of class in colonial history: "Our earliest history has
been seen as a period of consensus and classlessness, in part because our historians have
chosen to see it that way" (Lemisch, 1967, p. 4). By exploring the past from the
perspective of the poor, he argued, historians could "make the inarticulate speak" and
thus better understand that "the inarticulate could act on their own, and often for very
sound reasons" (Lemisch, 1967, pp. 6, 19).

In this regard Lemisch represented an American counterpart to the British Marxist
historian, Edward P. Thompson, whose important and influential new book, *The Making
of the English Working Class* (1963) was just beginning to have an impact on American
scholars. Unlike many scholars, Marxist and non-Marxist alike, Thompson did not rely
on traditional definitions of class that were limited to the distinct categories of "proletarian" and "bourgeoisie" that emerged with the rise of industrial capitalism. Class,
Thompson explained, could not properly be understood as a rigid social structure but
was, rather, "an historical phenomenon" that grew out of people's understanding of
their relationships with other people, when "as a result of common experiences (inher-

ited or shared), [they] feel and articulate the identity of their interests as between themselves, and as against other[s] . . . whose interests are different from (and usually opposed to) theirs" (Thompson, 1963, p. 9). The definition of class, then, depended on the awareness and actions of people "as they live their own history" and thus reflected a fluid process of becoming – or "making" to use Thompson's term – in different historical situations (Thompson, 1963, p. 11).

For Lemisch, the historical situation of early America provided excellent opportunities to examine the historical agency of the poorer sort in order to appreciate the making of class relations in colonial society. His pathbreaking investigation of the political values and behavior of common seamen, "Jack Tar in the Streets," provided an exciting invitation for other scholars, especially those in the early stages of their professional careers, to bring forth (or perhaps bring back) an historical emphasis on the roles of the many sorts of common people who both spoke and acted with self-directed agency in colonial society.

From the late 1960s on, the approaches suggested by Main's analysis of social structure and Lemisch's attention to social agency gained increasing importance in early American scholarship, though not always in equal measure. The "new" social history, with its emphasis on the close (and usually quantitative) study of the lives of common people, quickly became the most innovative and, to many, the most exciting development on the scholarly scene. Some established historians and, above all, junior scholars and graduate students eagerly embraced the almost-microscopic analysis of society with an academic passion that had been missing for decades, and the results of their research were especially impressive. That is not to say, however, that early American historians became, on the whole, an especially "class conscious" lot, at least not in comparison to some of their counterparts on both sides of the Atlantic who studied nineteenth- and twentieth-century history and the rise of industrial capitalism. More often, they have been content to make a brief bow to the theoretical discourse about class and then, apparently with pragmatic impatience, plunge into the evidence at hand to write about particular people, places, and events. More to the point, in many cases the most significant findings of the new social history among early Americanists remained located in a very localized context, safely isolated from larger social and political issues and too closely focused to offer a broader historical view; indeed, some studies became so obsessed with their own methodological sophistication that they made little effort to address larger historical or historiographical questions at all. Others considered only the experience of Anglo-American settlements in the eastern parts of North America, especially in New England and the Chesapeake region; to the extent that they explicitly invited a broader, comparative analysis, it was only to other Anglo-American communities or perhaps to rural villages in England. The economic distance between the hardscrabble inhabitants of colonial communities and the ruling classes of England seemed so immense as to be almost meaningless.

The face of early American historiography has changed dramatically in recent years, however, and scholars have challenged the earlier, and certainly easier, assumptions about what – or who – "American" means. Now the task is to develop a more inclusive yet still coherent analysis of early America that not only draws on the Anglo-American example but speaks to the experience of other European imperial powers, most notably the Spanish and French, not to mention the histories of the Native peoples of North America and the people of African descent, both enslaved and free. Admittedly, to approach these different peoples from the perspective of class carries some risks. Above all, we necessarily narrow our vision by making implicit yet important teleological assumptions about the emergence of capitalism and thus focusing attention on those societies that became, in a word, capitalist. We cannot lose sight of how those peoples who came into contact with (or as Edward Countryman [1996] has put it, collided with) Euro-American culture were marked, even scarred, by the experience in a variety of ways – including, in many cases, the imposition of class identity.

Yet taken together, the combined efforts of the past three decades of early American historiography – the almost inescapable emphasis on the lives of common people inherent in the new social history and the equally significant studies of the different cultures that encountered each other in North America – have created a picture of early American society that differed greatly from the harmonious images inspired by the consensus historians. Throughout the colonial era, and especially in the two or three decades leading up to the outbreak of the American Revolution, people repeatedly challenged the hierarchical structure of colonial society and, in so doing, often discovered and developed horizontal bonds of identity that would provide alternatives to the vertical. That recurring tension between horizontal and vertical relationships might not properly be called colonial-era class conflict, at least not in the more overt and enduring sense that scholars might find in later eras. Rather than enduring, class relations were emerging. With that notion in mind, the purpose of this essay is not to argue for imposing an ahistorical emphasis on class analysis on the pre-industrial era of American history, but instead to trace the origins of more explicit class relations back into the colonial era. In a sense, just as earlier historians found the roots of an allegedly unique American classlessness in the colonial era, I will argue the opposite – that the trajectory of increasingly explicit class divisions in the nineteenth and twentieth centuries stemmed, both economically and ideologically, from the evolution of early American society. Put simply, class in America did not begin with the birth of industrial capitalism; it had a history – a prehistory, as it were – in the various forms of inequality that suffused American society from the earliest days of European settlement.

* * * * *

Certainly, the most pervasive and persistent sort of social inequality in early America was unfree labor, especially slavery. Various forms of unfree labor had deep historical roots on both sides of the Atlantic, of course, and servitude was hardly unique to the colonial era. In the ancient Mediterranean world, for instance, early Greek and Roman cultures took slavery for granted as one of the common conditions of life, the unfortunate fate of people vanquished and captured in battle. By the same token, some indigenous peoples in Africa and the Americas also held other human beings in bondage, again usually as the result of war or captivity. But in those cases, unfree people did not always suffer a permanent loss of personal freedom, nor did their status extend to their offspring. More to the point, their bondage did not depend primarily on their racial or ethnic identity. Beginning in the fifteenth century, however, the European invasion of the Americas created an economic and social context in which unfree labor became the cornerstone of colonization and eventually evolved into a race-based system of perpetual slavery that had critical implications for the broader development of later class relations. Indeed, as Ira Berlin has observed, "if slavery made *race*, its larger purpose was to make *class*, and the fact that the two were made simultaneously by the same process has mystified both" (Berlin, 1998, p. 5). The task of Berlin and other historians, then, has been to demystify the process of class formation in the pre-industrial past by tracing it back to its early foundation in unfree labor.

The simultaneous making of race and class in early America began with the first moment of contact between Europeans and Native peoples. When Christopher Columbus encountered the Taino people in his initial island landfall in the Caribbean, he almost immediately projected their future social status. Although the Natives he saw were not as dark as he had expected and were, indeed, "very well-built people, with handsome bodies and very fine faces," he still concluded that they seemed different enough, physically and culturally, to be best suited for servitude: "They ought to make good and skilled servants," he reported to his Spanish superiors. "I think they can easily be made Christians, for they seem to have no religion. . . . With 50 men you could subject everyone and make them do what you wished" (Columbus, 1991 [1492], p. 47).

In the decades that followed, Spain sent many more men than that. In the early era of Spanish conquest, a combination of missionaries and the military made good the conquest Columbus had begun, and native people increasingly found themselves threatened with subservience and slavery. Officially the Spanish authorities in Madrid discouraged the enslavement of Indians, but as David Weber has observed, "The pragmatic Crown . . . often allowed appearances to mask harsh realities and did not look too closely into the ways in which its distant colonials circumvented laws intended to shield natives from compulsory labor" (Weber, 1992, p. 128). In Spain's North American colonies, Florida and New Mexico, Franciscan priests brought Indians into missions first for conversion, then for coercion, extracting forced labor from them on the assumption that hard work would cure them of their alleged indolence and make them better Christians. Soldiers and secular officials scarcely bothered with such rationalizations. They forced Indians to work for little or no pay under the *repartimiento* – a compulsory labor program instituted for public works deemed necessary by the Spanish – or simply enslaved them. In the North American colonies that did not yield the vast mineral riches of Central and South America, Spanish officials counted slaves as their most prized and profitable possessions; in New Mexico, in fact, slaves became a valuable export commodity and were shipped south to work in the mines of New Spain. While Spanish religious and secular leaders in the North American colonies both exploited Indian labor, they bickered about whose form of exploitation was best. Missionaries decried the enslavement of Indians, but government officials, soldiers, and frontier settlers pointed their fingers back at the friars for their own abuse of the Indians.

This conflict among the colonizers, Weber argues, undermined their authority and credibility in the eyes of the Native population, and Indians began to grow restive and even resistant. In both Florida and New Mexico, Indians engaged in small-scale rebellions against their Spanish oppressors, and in some cases they gained a measure of freedom from Spanish control. The most notable example of Indian revolt came in 1680, when a Pueblo leader named Pope led some 17,000 Indians in New Mexico in a widespread and well-organized attack against Spanish authority, both political and religious. The Pueblo Rebellion came remarkably close to succeeding, and as it spread to other native groups in the region, the Spanish conquest of New Mexico seemed on the verge of collapse. Ultimately, however, the revolt proved as disastrous to the Native peoples as it did to the Spanish, leaving everyone in the region exhausted and fearful. Still, in the wake of the various revolts, especially the Pueblo Rebellion, the Spanish began to modify their demands for Native labor, becoming less aggressive and certainly less confident in their practices of enslavement and oppression. Moreover, in addition to the resistance of Indians in the seventeenth century, the beginning of the eighteenth century brought a new worry to the Spanish – the increasing competition for land, power, and slaves from two other European imperial powers, England and France.

The Spanish may have taken the early lead in promoting slavery in early America, but it was the French and especially the English whose comparatively later embrace of slavery had the longest and most profound impact on race and class relations in America. That impact seems especially impressive because slavery had shallower cultural roots in northern Europe than it did in the Mediterranean region. Indeed, as Winthrop Jordan has argued in his classic study of early race relations, *White Over Black* (1968), slavery represented in many respects a significant departure from English law and custom. In the 1560s, for instance, an English explorer in western Africa turned down the offer of a slave with a rather huffy assertion of his country's commitment to higher standards: "I made answer, We were a people, who did not deale in any such commodities, neither did wee buy or sell one another, or any that had our owne shapes" (quoted in Jordan, 1968, pp. 60–1). That is not to say, however, that the English and French had no tradition of unfree labor. They had long accepted indentured servitude as a common form of employment, in which one person, usually a child or young adult, served a limited term of bondage to a master in exchange for food, clothing, shelter, and some measure of job training. Although there were laws that governed master–servant relations and prohibited excessively abusive behavior on the part of the master, actual practice often fell far below a modern measure of decency. As Peter Kolchin has observed, "In many ways the world from which the colonists came was a world of pre-modern values, one that lacked the concepts of 'cruel and unusual punishment,' equal rights, and exploitation; it was a world that instead took for granted natural human *in*equality and the routine use of force necessary to maintain it. In short, it was a world with few ideological constraints against the use of forced labor" (Kolchin, 1993, p. 7). When the English began to establish colonies in North America, they quite easily, even naturally, included indentured servitude in the process. In fact, indentured servants formed a significant segment of the colonizing population, especially in the southern settlements, where plantation agriculture quickly became the basis of the colonial economy.

In seventeenth-century Virginia, for instance, upwards of 85 percent of the English immigrants who came to the colony arrived as indentured servants, and the labor of unfree workers provided the basis for free men's success. Throughout at least the first half of the century, the curious combination of easy wealth and early death, of extremely profitable tobacco production and extremely inhospitable environmental conditions, created an almost unquenchable demand for bonded labor: landowners desperately wanted cheap agricultural workers to tend the tobacco fields and, not incidentally, to take the places of workers who had died of mistreatment and disease. In fact, as Edmund Morgan has shown in his impressive and persuasive *American Slavery, American Freedom* (1975), the exploitation of indentured labor proved to be one of the most prevalent, albeit least attractive, attributes of English settlement in the

Chesapeake region. From the beginning of Virginia's tobacco boom, masters were reported to "abuse their servantes there with intollerable oppression and hard usage" (Morgan, 1975, p. 126) – overwork, barbarous punishment, and even outright buying and selling of bonded labor. "Whether physically abused or not," Morgan observes, "Englishmen found servitude in Virginia more degrading than servitude in England" (Morgan, 1975, p. 127), and the terms of tobacco-boom bondage seemed to foreshadow the sort of exploitation that would become the more common fate of the laboring classes in subsequent centuries:

> In boom-time Virginia, then, we can see not only the fleeting ugliness of private enterprise operating temporarily without check, not only greed magnified by opportunity, producing fortunes for a few and misery for many. We may also see Virginians beginning to move toward a system of labor that treated men as things . . . . The boom produced, and in some measure depended upon, a tightening of labor discipline beyond what had been known in England and probably what had been formerly known in Virginia. (Morgan, 1975, p. 129)

At the same time, Morgan and other historians have indicated that this extreme exploitation of unfree labor in the colonial South was not initially race-based, or at least not exclusively so. In the very early stages of colonization, English and French settlers, like the Spanish, forced indigenous people into bondage, often obtaining their supply of Indian slaves among captives taken by other Indians. But in the long run, because they were both susceptible to European disease and capable of escape into a familiar landscape, Indians did not become as successful a source of unfree labor as people from the far side of the Atlantic, especially Africans. Still, despite the arrival in Virginia of twenty or so Africans on a Dutch ship in 1619, and despite the appearance in the English colonies of laws supporting the institution of slavery by the 1640s, the number of enslaved Africans remained comparatively small during most of the seventeenth century: as late as 1670, blacks in Virginia, the leading plantation colony, numbered only around 2,000, a little over 5 percent of the English colony's population. In fact, there is some evidence, or certainly sufficient historical ambiguity, to suggest that some people of African descent in early Virginia managed to gain their freedom – and with it, the freedom to buy the labor of others, both white and black. The point is that, in the early years of colonial settlement, the burdens of bondage apparently weighed almost equally on unfree people, no matter what their race or place of origin: the critical category of inequality seems not to have been white over black, but master over servant.

The balance between white and black began to shift significantly toward the end of the century, however, largely because of changing relations between masters and servants. For a combination of demographic and economic reasons – a drop in the birth rate and a rise in real wages in England – the supply of young people willing (or needing) to go to the English colonies as indentured servants began to decline: between 1680 and 1699, Allan Kulikoff has noted, the number of emigrant whites bound for Virginia, around 30,000, represented a decrease of about 20 percent over the preceding three decades (Kulikoff, 1986, p. 39). At the same time, changing demographic trends in the Chesapeake region – a modest but significant increase in life expectancy for both white and black workers in the second half of the century –

created new social and economic considerations for landowners employing unfree laborers. As indentured servants began to outlive their terms of service, they became an increasingly unsettling presence as freedmen, restless in their search for equal or even decent economic opportunity, resentful of the disadvantages they suffered in comparison to the wealthier, better established planters. Indeed, Kulikoff argues, "Class conflict therefore broke out between rulers and upwardly mobile freed servants in the third quarter of the seventeenth century" (Kulikoff, 1986, p. 261), coming to a head briefly but boldly in 1676, when a prosperous and politically ambitious newcomer named Nathaniel Bacon led an armed movement, first against Indians still living in Virginia's frontier regions and then against the governor and other wealthy whites who formed Virginia's ruling elite. In the midst of the racial and even personal hostility that suffused Bacon's Rebellion, there also ran a stream of social protest against the "grandees" who governed the colony to their own advantage but who, as Kulikoff points out, "inspired too little confidence to gain the respect of poorer whites and had too little power to suppress their demands" (Kulikoff, 1986, p. 261). Although short-lived and unsuccessful and not really a prelude to sustained class conflict in the longer historical run, Bacon's Rebellion did reveal the dangers of degrading workers who might one day become free. It made better sense, at least from the standpoint of masters, to inflict that sort of treatment on slaves, people who were offered very little prospect of ever gaining their freedom. Thus it was in the wake of – and, to some degree, because of – Bacon's Rebellion that masters in the Chesapeake region increasingly began to fill the demand for unfree labor by shifting from white servants to black slaves.

By 1700 the racialization of labor relations marked the emergence of a slave society not just in the Chesapeake, but in other southern colonies as well. In French Louisiana, for instance, the number of immigrant indentured servants (*engagés*) resident in the colony in 1721 slightly exceeded that of imported African slaves. Those *engagés* fortunate enough to survive the term of their indentures eventually joined the ranks of the free, however, while Africans continued to exist as slaves for life. By 1731, Louisiana had two thousand French settlers and four thousand slaves, and even with a slowing of slave imports over the next fifteen years, the colony's 4,100 slaves still outnumbered its 3,300 settlers and 600 soldiers in 1746. But as Daniel Usner (1992) points out, only a comparative few Frenchmen in Louisiana could afford to own slaves, and those wealthier settlers became increasingly worried as they saw poorer French settlers, African slaves, and Indians engage in economic exchange and other forms of intercultural interaction not sanctioned by colonial law or custom. Accordingly, French officials adopted a "divide and rule" policy to distinguish and separate the races and "improvised ways to impose a racially divided law and order upon peoples who crossed all kinds of boundaries whenever it suited their interests" (Usner, 1992, p. 76). Similarly, Peter Wood (1974) has noted both the emergence of a black majority in South Carolina's population by 1710 and, equally important, a growing emphasis on racial control. During the early stages of South Carolina's development as a slave society, Wood observes, "servants and masters shared the crude and egalitarian intimacies inevitable on a frontier," but increasing white anxiety about the growing black presence manifested itself in an increasing racial segregation of tasks: artisans of African origin found themselves "forced away from certain skilled trades . . . [and] receiving more exclusive custody of society's most menial tasks" (Wood, 1974, pp. 96, 229).

Although the social and economic distance between wealthy planters and poorer whites could be substantial when measured in its own right, the occupational and legal degradation of enslaved Africans created a racially distinct demarcation of the bottom of southern society, above which even the poorest white person could claim privileged status. Thus, race masked class in the eighteenth-century South. The power of that racial alliance seems especially striking in light of its economic and political imbalance. Even in the regions of the highest level of slaveholding, Tidewater Virginia and the South Carolina Lowcountry, most slaveowners held fewer than ten slaves; more to the point, in those regions around a third to half of all white landowners held no slaves at all. In the Piedmont and backcountry regions, the number of slaveowners (and slaves) was smaller still. Yet although the wealthy slaveowners always remained a small minority in the early American colonies, they retained an enormous degree of almost unchallenged authority over their poorer neighbors.

There is probably no colonial slaveholding elite that has been more carefully or creatively studied than the members of the Virginia gentry, men who clearly understood the connection between property and power. They reinforced their status through kinship ties, using marriage and inheritance strategies to create connections between families and thus both consolidate and extend their social and economic influence. The most prominent planter families acquired sizable holdings in several locations, which allowed them to pass property on to their offspring. More to the point, the geographical dispersion of planter families allowed them to send kinsmen from different counties to the colonial assembly. In Williamsburg, their common identity enabled them to direct political affairs to their own benefit, not the least of which was the acquisition of even greater property holdings by awarding themselves generous land grants. This mutually reinforcing relationship between property and political power also operated at the local level, where governors or the assembly appointed members of the gentry to other leadership positions of more immediate influence, especially in the vestry, militia, or county court. Control over such issues as taxation, military service, and legal matters – above all, credit and debt proceedings – gave them direct authority over critical concerns in the lives of the lesser landowners. Equally important, control over appointments to lower positions in the local political hierarchy gave them a patronage base that could enhance their prestige and gain them the loyalty of the grateful few they favored. In this sort of self-perpetuating and certainly self-serving system, a comparatively small number of wealthy kinsmen could hold enormous sway over a free but dependent population of their fellow white landowners.

But the system was never so enclosed as to insulate members of the gentry wholly from the people they governed, at least not those who could vote. As Kulikoff has rightly observed of Virginia, "Eighteenth-century elections were contests between representatives of gentry families rather than ideological battles" (Kulikoff, 1986, p. 285). Still, they were contests; there were local issues at stake; and two prominent men seeking the same seat in the assembly somehow had to convince the voters to choose one candidate over the other. To do so, they not only argued the merits of their respective stances on the issues, but they also, more subtly, reminded some men of earlier personal favors – a position conferred, a loan made and perhaps extended or even forgiven – and relied on personal largess to impress the rest. In many instances, free food and drink fueled the political process, providing both a real meal and a symbolic expression of respect to potential voters. Such patrician gestures of reciprocity seemingly loosened the grip the gentry had on political power, but in the longer run the two-way interplay of gentry–yeoman relationships reinforced a system of mutual support that defined a common identity for men of significantly different situations: those who owned enough land to be eligible to vote became, in a sense, partners with the more prominent planters, and together they dominated a society that gave no voice to the propertyless and politically impotent – poor white men, all women, and, of course, slaves. Based more on distinctions of gender and race than on class, this white men's alliance gave the colonial South a reputation for deferential social relations and comparative political stability that was not seriously challenged until the era of the American Revolution. But deference stems more from coercion than from persuasion, and behind the appearance of peaceful class relations always lay the reality of power that no man, rich or poor, could easily ignore.

* * * * *

In the North, slavery was not as prevalent nor were social distance and racial distinctions as pronounced as they were in the plantation South, but inequality nonetheless lay embedded in colonial culture. To a large degree, the religious traditions of the founding generations emphasized collective identity over individual interest and therefore mitigated against assumptions of social divisions. In one of the most emphatic, and certainly most famous, statements of initial intent, the English Puritan leader John Winthrop underscored the importance of mutuality, even while recognizing inequality. In 1630, even before the main Puritan migration reached the shores of North America, Winthrop preached a sermon aboard ship in which he told his followers that "God almighty . . . hath so disposed the condition of mankind, as in all times some must be rich, some poor, some high and eminent in power and dignity, others mean and in subjection." Still, since both rich and poor Puritans now found themselves bound together for a new beginning in the New World, "We must be knit together as one . . . We must delight in each other, make others' condition our own, rejoice together, mourn together, labor and suffer together, always having before our eyes . . . our community as members of the same body" (Winthrop, 1985 [1630], pp. 82, 91). This forceful repetition of the word "together" gave audible emphasis to the necessary acceptance of common concerns that would relegate the needs and desires of the individual to secondary status in favor of a covenanted community. In practice, early Puritan settlements sought to institutionalize this sentiment, especially when it came to distributing the community's most important resource, land: property was not a commodity to be bought and sold for profit, but a means of subsistence to be shared among households, giving everyone a stake in the community and thus reinforcing their communal commitment. Springfield, Massachusetts, for instance, which was established in 1636, just six years after the arrival of the main body of Puritans in Massachusetts Bay, spelled out the principles of property-holding in its initial articles of agreement: "We intend that our town shall be composed of forty families . . . rich and poor," in which "every inhabitant shall have a convenient proportion for a house lot, as we shall see meet for everyone's quality and estate" (Springfield, 1972 [1636], pp. 53–5). To be sure, the notation that some households would be (or already were) "rich and poor," and that land would be allocated according to the "quality and estate" of the male head of the household indicated that this early Puritan town was not exactly an experiment in strict Christian communism, but the initial distribution of land to all households did make clear the assumptions of social inclusiveness that defined the first religious settlements.

As Stephen Innes (1983) has shown, however, the degree of rough equality that existed in the early days of Springfield soon gave way to rising inequality and a pattern of economic dominance by one family and dependency for dozens of others. William Pynchon and his son John, prominent property-owners and entrepreneurs in seventeenth-century Springfield, extended their reach into a wide range of economic activities – farming, milling, commerce, land speculation, and loans – and became the most significant figures in the economy of western New England. In doing so, they exerted economic influence, if not outright control, over the lives of many of their fellow English settlers throughout the region, becoming generous patrons to some and perhaps a menacing presence to others. Whatever its intent or effect, the power of the Pynchons demonstrated quite strikingly that Springfield, not to mention other Puritan towns, would indeed be a community of "rich and poor" where the early emphasis on shared resources for all came to be replaced by a perhaps surprisingly early concentration of wealth in the hands of a few.

Springfield was perhaps the earliest, and probably the most extreme, example of a tension between mutuality and inequality that quietly underlay many other northern communities in the seventeenth century, and that tension became increasingly pronounced over the course of the colonial era. Certainly, the recognition of that tension emerged emphatically from the scholarly study of those communities in the late twentieth century. Beginning in the mid-1960s and taking its place as one of the most exciting areas of research in the 1970s, the "community study" became an important building block of scholarship in early American history. The earliest of these studies typically took a very local focus on Puritan villages, usually in Massachusetts, and tended to portray the New England town, to use Kenneth Lockridge's (1970) description of Dedham, as a "Christian Utopian Closed Corporate Community," in which the inhabitants defined themselves by inner-directed bonds of common commitment. While this sort of enclosed conceptual framework generally isolated the community from the rest of the region, much less the broader Atlantic world, it did allow for a close analysis of the internal transformations that would eventually expose conditions of increasing inequality and thereby undermine the intensity of initial commitment. Above all, by examining the interplay of patriarchy, property, and power in town after town, historians were able to discern patterns of change that proved common in many communities in the colonial North.

In 1970, Philip Greven's influential study of Andover, Massachusetts, first brought those three factors sharply into focus. As the title of Greven's book, *Four Generations* (1970), implied, the key to understanding the history of the community was the study of the family over time; more specifically, the critical issue was the passing of property through successive generations. Among the earliest English inhabitants of Andover, Greven discovered, the practice of partible inheritance – that is, dividing a father's land among his adult sons – offered important opportunities to both generations: it provided sons the prospect of being able to establish themselves as independent farmers in their own hometown and, as a result, it gave parents the assurance that their offspring would be around to care for them in their old age. But Greven also found that this system of inheritance was founded not so much on intergenerational generosity as on patriarchal authority. Fathers most often delayed giving their sons complete owner-ship of family lands until the young men were in their late twenties or early thirties, thus using the promise of inheritance as a form of familial leverage to maintain control of a son's labor and even dictate the timing of his marriage. "The psychological conse-quences of this prolonged dependence of sons are difficult to assess," Greven ob-served, "but they must have been significant" (Greven, 1970).

The social and economic consequences have been much easier to measure. As long as land remained reasonably abundant – or, more to the point, as long as some fathers could continue to amass adequate landholdings in the community – the system of inheritance seemed to promote both persistence and power for the more fortunate Andover families. However much they might quietly resent their fathers' continuing control over their adult lives, most sons stayed in town and eventually inherited not just their fathers' land but, in many cases, their fathers' local leadership positions as well: as Greven and other historians discovered, political office, like land, passed from father to son in these colonial communities, and a few leading families seemed to have a lock on local leadership year after year. But this practice of passing along property and political power from one generation to the next contained inherent, some would say even inevitable, flaws that became evident over time. Even the most successful intergenerational inheritance strategy eventually ran up against the demographic and geographical constraints of the community: after the first or second generation, as the growth of early settler families and the arrival of new ones increased the population of the community as a whole, fathers found it increasingly difficult to acquire enough land in the town to provide an adequate inheritance for all their offspring. The re-peated divisions of family land meant that successive generations of sons had to make do with smaller holdings or, increasingly, move on to other communities where land was more abundant and available. In Dedham, for instance, the average estate had shrunk from around 150 acres in the first generation to 100 acres in the third genera-tion, and it would continue to decline to around 50 acres by the middle of the eight-eenth century. In Andover, the near-universal practice of partible inheritance similarly declined after the first generation, so that by the third generation, just under 60 per-cent of all estates were divided among all of a father's sons. Indeed, in a study of colonial Concord, Massachusetts, Robert Gross (1976) wrote that the inhabitants of that community were coming increasingly to live in a "world of scarcity" in the middle of the eighteenth century, when opportunities for providing for family prosperity, and therefore posterity, had become severely constricted. "From mid-century onward," he wrote, "Concord was in the throes of a long, protracted decay to which [the inhabit-ants] adapted as best they could but which no one seemed able to stop. Signs of decline were everywhere . . . most of all, in the steady exodus of the young" (Gross, 1976, p. 105). Just as Greven speculated on the psychological implications of parental control among the young, Gross suggested that the members of the older generation in mid-eighteenth-century Concord paid "a heavy social and psychological price" for their understandable but nonetheless unstoppable failure to maintain the inheritance standards of the earlier generations (Gross, 1976, p. 106).

Many of these northern towns "failed" in another sense as well: among the "signs of decline" was the inescapable economic inequality among families in the community, a disturbing distance between those who maintained, even increased, their property holdings and those who had little or none. In Concord, for instance, the top 20 percent of property-owners held 55 percent of the town's land in 1749, while the bottom 40 percent owned only 3 percent; by 1771, both groups had experienced a slight shift in their shares of property, to 48 percent and 4 percent, respectively, but the meaning was essentially the same in Concord as it was in others: some families could be confident of living a reasonably comfortable existence and providing at least some of their offspring with a decent inheritance, but many households lived a hardscrabble life in which a "world of scarcity" was the only world they knew.

Evidence of economic and social stratification alone, however, cannot predict or explain human behavior, and inequality does not always lead to conflict. Several students of colonial-era tenancy have argued, for instance, that even those landless farmers who rented rural property from others generally seemed content with their condition. Daniel Vickers has observed that although tenancy arose from "the fact of economic inequality," it still served the needs of both landowner and tenant in the early years of English settlement in seventeenth-century Essex County, Massachusetts: not only was it "the most effective means of putting land under the plow and obtaining a revenue" for the landowner, but it offered the tenant a "measurable if qualified degree of independence" (Vickers, 1994, pp. 81–2). Likewise, in a study of eighteenth-century Chester County, Pennsylvania, Lucy Simler has concluded that tenancy "was, in general, a rational, efficient response to economic conditions, and both landowners and tenants . . . were able to use it to advantage. . . . Despite the rhetoric claiming that tenants were shiftless and landowners were tyrannical, in everyday life tenancy was widely seen as equitable and generally profitable" (Simler, 1986, p. 569).

Indeed, what is most striking about the many recent histories of rural society in the colonial North is the relative absence of sustained social unrest. To be sure, there occurred on occasion rather dramatic chapters in the histories of numerous communities, when the town erupted in conflict over some local issue – the location of the meeting house, the division of town lands, even the outbreak of suspected witchcraft – and those struggles have often been analyzed in economic terms, as contention between the community's "haves" and "have nots." In some cases, in fact, the level of conflict rose to remarkable intensity. During the middle decades of the eighteenth century, for instance, both New Jersey and the Hudson Valley of New York became the scene of recurring land riots. In both areas, vast tracts of land lay in the hands of wealthy proprietors and landlords, and common farmers, many of whom were tenants, resorted to collective violence when they felt a growing threat to their right to remain on the land. If historians agree on anything about the outbreak of violence in these regions, it is that the causes were complex – a combination of unclear and conflicting land titles, ethnic and cultural differences among the inhabitants, and potentially oppressive practices by the large landowners – and they are reluctant to oversimplify the roots of the unrest by ascribing it to economic inequality alone. On the whole, the picture that emerges of the rural North in the colonial era is that of a society in which inequality, even scarcity, clearly exists, but in which social conflict is stemmed by the traditions of communal cohesion and the comparatively open access to productive property.

Given the relative absence of anything that might reasonably be called sustained "class conflict" in colonial-era agrarian communities, then, the analysis of structural economic inequality in rural regions has created the context for a more intensive, albeit often elusive, investigation of cultural economic attitudes. Put simply, the question concerned the ways in which rural people understood the economic context in which they lived, and how that understanding manifested itself in behavior. More specifically, historians have explored the extent to which rural people pursued economic gain as a goal unto itself, or whether they restrained, even rejected, profit-seeking activities in favor of maintaining a comparatively moderate level of economic activity more in keeping with the traditions of family and community. Though difficult to answer, the question was important to ask. Like the long-standing assumption that America had been, from the beginning, a classless society, the notion that the American people were almost inherently eager profit-seekers had been often taken too easily for granted. In a study of rural southeastern Pennsylvania, *The Best Poor Man's Country* (1972), James Lemon had discovered a "'liberal' middle-class orientation" among the eighteenth-century inhabitants, people who produced for the market as much as for the family and who "planned for themselves much more than they did for their communities" (Lemon, 1972, p. xv). The implication, of course, was that such an individualistic, market-oriented attitude predicted the patterns of economic inequality that would become increasingly prevalent in early American society. Making the point in even more striking language, Charles Grant had found in colonial-era Kent, Connecticut, a "drive for profits" among the eighteenth-century settlers and "perhaps the embryo John D. Rockefeller" (Grant, 1961, pp. 53–4). Clearly, such assumptions made the eventual emergence of a much more complex capitalist society in the nineteenth century seem not only a logical extension of economic attitudes and behaviors in the seventeenth and eighteenth centuries, but a seemingly unquestioned one as well.

By the late 1970s, however, those assumptions suddenly defined the target of a sharp scholarly debate, which began with three pathbreaking articles by Michael Merrill (1977), James Henretta (1978), and Christopher Clark (1979), respectively. In an original and provocative essay rooted in Marxist theory, Merrill challenged the then-prevailing image of the liberal orientation of American rural society. While not denying that, as historians like Lemon and Grant had certainly demonstrated, many farm families did indeed engage in exchange relationships, Merrill nonetheless located those relationships within what he called a "household mode of production," in which economic exchange tended to be decentralized and horizontal, defined by patterns of localized reciprocity and "controlled by need rather than price." That is, when rural households engaged in economic relationships with each other (or, quite frequently, with a local merchant) they did not often use cash as the medium of exchange, Merrill observed; rather, they traded goods and services, often keeping track of debts that might run for years before balancing out. In this sense, indebtedness defined interdependence among rural households and "served not to separate the community into classes so much as bind it together" (Merrill, 1977, p. 63).

Following close on the heels of Merrill's important article, subsequent works by Henretta, Clark, and a host of other scholars made the rural (and usually New England) household a central issue of early American history. The goal, argued Henretta, was to go beyond the analysis of "the ever-growing mass of data that delineates the *structures* of social existence" that had been the signal contribution of the first generation of the 1970s community studies and inquire more deeply into "the *consciousness* of the inhabitants, the mental or emotional or ideological aspects of their lives" (Henretta, 1978, p. 3). In colonial Anglo-America, Henretta suggested, this cultural consciousness, or *mentalité*, of rural people was defined, first and foremost, not by the concerns of the economically energetic individual but by the needs of the lineal household – that is, the intergenerational welfare of the family over time. By pointing to a popular perspective that suggested widespread and deeply rooted skepticism about unfettered self-interest as the foundation of economic relations, historians challenged the primacy of the profit motive – and, by extension, the cultural acceptance of capitalism. The point was not to create a clear division between those rural people who were aggressively seeking after the main chance and those who were nostalgically clinging to their inherited traditions of farm and family; people's behaviors and beliefs are usually far too complex and inconsistent to lend credence to that sort of crude categorization. Instead, Henretta and other historians more often found a tension between immediate economic aspiration and long-term familial and communal cohesion that reflected creative adaptations among people in the colonial era. "Economic gain was important to these men and women," Henretta explained, "yet it was . . . subordinate to (or encompassed by) two other goals: the yearly subsistence and the long-run financial security of the family unit" (Henretta, 1978, p. 19). To describe better the desired balance between economic activity and security, Daniel Vickers put forward a term familiar to early American authors (among them Timothy Dwight, whose words introduce this essay) – competency. Competency, Vickers noted, "connoted the possession of sufficient property to absorb the labors of a given family while providing it with something more than a mere subsistence . . . in brief, a degree of comfortable independence" (Vickers, 1990, p. 3). To maintain this comfortable independence, rural households often produced a surplus for sale and engaged rather easily, if not eagerly, in market exchange: indeed, Vickers observes that the "distinction between production for use and production for sale was sometimes recognizable and sometimes not, but it was never a matter of significance." Market-oriented activities and profit *per se* were not a matter of cultural concern – as long as they helped promote the "propertied independence" of the household (Vickers, 1990, p. 7).

Had Merrill, Henretta, Vickers, and other historians not been decently clear-eyed in their description of this early American *mentalité*, the emphasis on the centrality of interlocking relationships within the rural community and in the rural household could well have contributed to the sort of romanticized rhetoric about the "self-sufficient" farm family that emerged later – not to mention the evocation "community values" and "family values" that often marked social and political discourse in the late twentieth century. It is one thing to analyze familial relationships, but quite another to sentimentalize them. In that regard, historians have been careful to distinguish between the independence of the property-owning rural family *as a unit* and the dependent status of its constituent members *as individuals*: indeed, the independence of the household essentially *required* conditions of dependency for most family members within it. For example, after arguing that the patterns of reciprocal indebtedness among rural households tended to mitigate against class divisions within the community, Merrill described the household mode of production in surprisingly stark terms, where "class relations are not market relations, but personal ones . . . [in which] the exploited class very likely consists of one's own family" (Merrill, 1977, p. 64). Vickers made the point more strongly still: "A rural economy that operated chiefly on child labor was to a significant degree responding to precisely the same pressures that created systems of slavery, servitude, and peonage elsewhere in the Americas" (Vickers, 1994, p. 82).

The depiction of family members as an "exploited class," even near-slaves, directs our attention to the inner workings of the household, which are discussed more extensively elsewhere in this volume. For the issue at hand, though, it is important to understand the ways familial relationships in rural society contributed to the development of class relationships in early American society more generally. Over time, the declining opportunities for dependent sons and daughters to gain the independent status of property-owners meant that a growing number of young people were available for alternative forms of labor. By the early years of the nineteenth century, many young men worked as hired hands on farms or as wage laborers in manufacturing or other forms of non-agricultural employment emerging in the North. Similarly, a sizable number of young women engaged in "outwork," making home-produced goods – hats, textiles, and the like – on a "putting-out" basis for local merchants; by the 1820s, others began to go one step further and, like many of their male counterparts, left home to work in the early textile mills. At the same time, their mothers began increasingly to take advantage of the greater availability of manufactured goods for the household, especially textiles, and bought from a local merchant the items they would formerly have made at home. As Christopher Clark has explained, "The altered household consumption patterns that saw many rural families purchasing essentials that even two decades before they would have acquired locally enhanced the local importance of merchants, storekeepers, and other traders . . . [and] this helped change the balance of power in rural society and brought rural households increasingly to the point where their 'independence' was compromised, not in this case by the need for interdependence with other rural households, but by essential connections with entrepreneurs" (Clark, 1990, p. 152). In turn, local merchants took advantage of the changing labor and consumption patterns to accumulate sufficient capital to develop, most often in partnership with other merchants, larger-scale enterprises (e.g., canal and turnpike projects, more fully integrated manufacturing concerns) that would form the infrastructure of early industrial capitalism in the United States – and thus the basis for the consequent creation of an increasingly self-conscious class identity among American workers. But such developments did not become commonplace until the era after the American Revolution, and especially in the second quarter of the nineteenth century. Keeping our focus on rural society in the colonial period, we can at best anticipate in the late eighteenth century the changing conditions that would contribute to a more fully elaborated set of class relations in the future.

* * * * *

To get a better view of class structure and class relations in early America, we can turn to the colonial cities, those emerging urban outposts of distant imperial systems. In looking at seventeenth- and eighteenth-century American cities, however, it is important to remember that they were hardly large by modern or even early modern standards. By 1690, for instance, Boston and New York, the leading Anglo-American cities were, as Gary Nash has put it, "really only overgrown villages," with populations of around 6,000 and 4,500, respectively; two more recently settled cities, Philadelphia, with around 2,200 inhabitants, and Charleston, with under 2,000, were still in their urban infancy (Nash, 1979, p. 3). Almost a century later, on the eve of the American Revolution, these seaport cities had grown considerably – Boston to just over 16,500 inhabitants, New York and Philadelphia to over 21,000, and Charleston to just under 10,000 – but they still remained much smaller than secondary cities in Europe, not to mention London, Paris, or Madrid. Similarly, New Orleans, which had been established by the French in 1718 and then had passed into Spanish hands at the end of the Seven Years' War in 1763, had only 3,000 inhabitants by 1777. Even the oldest North American city, St. Augustine, had a population of less than 2,000 by the second half of the eighteenth century; as David Weber notes, this provincial outpost on Spain's Florida frontier "could not boast of impressive cathedrals or public buildings, convents, seminaries, universities, libraries, theaters, newspapers, or presses – much less of the professors, nuns, lawyers, writers, and poets that such institutions supported elsewhere in Spanish America" (Weber, 1992, p. 322). In general, Nash's characterization of "overgrown villages" in the Anglo-American North could apply as well to all the European urban outposts in North America throughout the eighteenth century.

Yet despite their small size and the lack of institutional and social diversity, at least in comparison to larger contemporary cities, these emerging urban centers nonetheless contained the greatest concentration of population and the broadest continuum of social status one could find in colonial North America; from the mix of people and the range of social relations came the clearest expression of emerging class identity and activity. As Nash has argued at the outset of *The Urban Crucible* (1979) – still the most significant comparative study of colonial cities to date – the early American cities provided a preview of the future for society as a whole:

> Almost all the alterations that are associated with the advent of capitalist society happened first in the cities and radiated outward to the smaller towns, villages, and farms of the hinterland. In America, it was in the colonial cities that the transition first occurred from a barter to a commercial economy; where a competitive social order replaced an ascriptive one; where a hierarchical and deferential polity yielded to participatory and contentious civic life; where factory production began to replace small-scale artisanal production; where the first steps were taken to organize work by clock time rather than by sidereal cycles. (Nash, 1979, p. vii)

Similarly, Ronald Schultz – one of Nash's students and a historian of Philadelphia artisans – argues explicitly that "the roots of the American working class run deep into the eighteenth century and beyond" (Schultz, 1993, p. xi). Like Nash, Schultz finds these roots first taking hold in the urban environment.

Nash and other historians of social relations in early American cities have taken a page from Jackson Turner Main by beginning with a detailed description of the urban social structure. Though packed together in a relatively confined space, urban dwellers were separated by perceptible, yet to a degree permeable, boundaries of wealth and status. At the bottom of the urban population, as at the bottom of colonial society in general, stood several sorts of unfree people – European indentured servants and African and Indian slaves; indeed, Nash notes that the unfree population of the seventeenth-century northern cities was as significant as that of the Chesapeake tobacco colonies. At the other end of the urban social spectrum were men (and some widows) of wealth, people of modest fortunes made mostly in mercantile pursuits. In between these extremes lay people with a host of other occupations and social identities – common workers, mariners, journeymen and artisans of various sorts, lesser merchants, shopkeepers, clergymen, teachers, and government officials – all of whom interacted in the urban economy and shared, albeit unevenly, the wealth of the city. But in seven-teenth-century American cities, as Nash has argued, even the extremes were not espe-cially extreme, at least compared to conditions in contemporary European counterparts. "We need not be surprised," he notes, "that the top tenth of society controlled 40 percent of the community's wealth and the bottom half possessed only about 10 per-cent." The concentration of wealth at the top was even more pronounced in European cities, and the appalling poverty of those at the bottom had become a troubling social problem. In American cities, the poor "did not starve or go unclothed and unhoused . . . The incidence of poverty, in fact, was extremely low and was confined for the most part to the widowed, disabled, and orphaned, who were decently cared for" (Nash, 1979, pp. 20–1). On the whole, by the end of the seventeenth century the leading early American cities on the Atlantic coast could still be considered comparatively close communities, where social distinctions clearly existed, but where social distance did not involve the great gaps it did in Europe – or eventually would in America toward the end of the eighteenth century.

The long-traditional narrative of American history emphasizes upward social mobil-ity, and there is probably no more familiar story of such good fortune than that of young Ben Franklin, a printer's apprentice in Boston who would later rise to the posi-tion of elder statesman in Philadelphia. Throughout the eighteenth century, the path to improvement, or at least opportunity, could be as open to other early American urban dwellers. In times of prosperity – and especially in times of war, when the sud-den demand for military supplies pumped government money into seaport cities – some of the wealth trickled down to a broad pool of the urban population. But times of prosperity were not permanent, and even temporary economic upswings in the eighteenth century had a more enduring downside. As Nash notes, for instance, war profits for some were matched by privation for others. Common soldiers, most of whom were recruited from the lower ranks of society in the first place, often returned from military campaigns diseased, weakened, and maimed, frequently unfit to take up a productive life in the aftermath of war; those who did not return at all often left widows and children to fend for themselves in a community that had increasingly strained resources (and often equally strained tolerance) for poor relief. Throughout the eighteenth century, for a larger part of the population and for a large part of the time, the historical record tells a discouraging story: poverty became increasingly preva-lent, and the distance between those at the bottom of urban society and those at the top grew greater throughout the colonial era.

James Henretta's pathbreaking analysis of economic inequality in colonial Boston (which appeared in 1965, the same year as Main's *Social Structure*) offers detailed and compelling evidence of the increasing distance between the rich and the poor. In 1687, he notes, 14 percent of the adult males were listed on the city's tax rolls as propertyless; by 1771, the propertyless accounted for 29 percent of those listed. Dur-ing that same period, the concentration of wealth among the most prosperous prop-erty-holders increased substantially: in 1687, the top 15 percent owned 52 percent of taxable assets, and their portion rose to 65.9 percent by 1771; indeed, the top 5 per-cent raised their share from 25 percent to 44.1 percent. "Society had become more stratified and unequal," Henretta concluded, to the point that on the eve of the American Revolution, "'merchant princes' and 'proletarians' stood out as the salient characteris-tics of a new social order" (Henretta, 1965, p. 92). But perhaps most revealing about the implications of this growing economic divide was the situation of "well-to-do artisans, shopkeepers, and traders" who formed the middling group of property-holders: their collective hold on the city's wealth fell from 21 percent in 1687 to 12.5 percent in 1771. So it was elsewhere, at least in terms of the eighteenth-century trend if not the actual measure: those cities that have been documented all show an increasing level of social stratification, with a growing level of economic concentration among those at the top. Eighteenth-century urban dwellers did not have such statistical indicators available, of course, but they hardly needed them. The overfilled almshouses and the influx of the "strolling poor" gave ready evidence of the impact of poverty on city life, while the appearance of new mansions, liveried carriages, and elegantly dressed and bewigged residents in the city streets provided highly visible signs of the luxurious indulgence of the rich. More than a century before the nineteenth-century social critic Thorstein Veblen would coin the term, "conspicuous display" had come to the streets of colonial American cities.

The people with perhaps the best perspective on the growing distance between the rich and the poor were those of middling means, the small shopkeepers and artisans, who often associated with their wealthier neighbors in professional, if not social, relationships, but who more often worked and mingled with the common laborers and the poor. Whatever social aspirations they had to move upward in society were repeatedly offset by the prospect of falling downward, and they could seldom be assured of maintaining, much less improving, their status. Throughout the eighteenth century, their response to their uncertain situation provides the best historical insight into the nature of class relations and the emergence of class identity in colonial America.

Thanks to numerous and notable works by scholars in recent decades, Philadelphia, much more than Boston or New York, offers the best-documented case study of the economic and political lives of middling urban dwellers, especially artisans. To speak of "artisans," of course, is not to define a coherent, homogenous group, much less a consistently self-defined class. As Steven Rosswurm (1987) has noted in an important monograph on Philadelphia's "lower sort," the common tendency of historians to lump all laboring people into one class obscures the differences among them. Some occupations, such as baking, tanning, and bricklaying, required significant amounts of capital and were not readily open to anyone who wanted to enter the trade; others, such as goldsmithing, instrument-making, and clock-making, required specialized skills that only a few artisans possessed. Perhaps not surprisingly, the occupations requiring greater capital and skill also typically provided the best living, and practitioners of those trades ranked near the top of the artisanal social structure. At the other end of the artisanal spectrum, trades such as weaving, tailoring, and shoemaking offered easier access but lower income. Still, despite their occupational and economic differences, artisans did share a common sense of their place in society and, equally important, of the nature of a just society. Ronald Schultz writes of an "artisan moral tradition" in eighteenth-century Philadelphia, "encompassing an ethic of community, equality, competency, and the value of labor" (Schultz, 1993, p. xiii). Like the notion of competency that, as we have seen, suffused rural society, the ethic of competency among urban artisans went beyond income alone: as Schultz explains, it involved "an unwritten covenant between the artisan and his community . . . [whereby] the skilled artisan expected to receive the respect of his community and a life free from protracted want . . . an expectation of middling status in the community, and acknowledgment of economic independence that brought with it small comforts, a few luxuries, and an abiding sense of self-esteem" (Schultz, 1993, pp. 6–7). One Philadelphia artisan put it plainly: "Our professions rendered us useful and necessary members of the community; proud of that rank, we aspired no higher" (quoted in Rosswurm, 1987, p. 15).

Unfortunately, aspiring no higher did not protect them from falling lower. Like other Anglo-American cities involved in the Atlantic economy, Philadelphia suffered its share of economic downturn, disruption, and depression during the eighteenth century, and the artisan community saw its expectation of a decent competency repeatedly threatened. In the 1720s, for instance, the crisis of the Atlantic economy, most immediately occasioned by the collapse of the South Sea Bubble, a speculative investment scheme, but also by a longer-term decline in the West Indies trade, threw Philadelphia into a deep depression, sucking specie out of the city and leaving residents reeling from the loss of a readily available medium of exchange. Then, after three decades of comparative economic stability in the middle of the century, the effects of a postwar depression in the wake of the Seven Years' War once again shook the foundations of the artisanal order. Faced with declining wages and chronic unemployment, Schultz notes, "Philadelphia craftsmen now appeared to be witnessing the collapse of their small producer world" (Schultz, 1993, p. 39). Billy G. Smith has described the impact of that collapse in material terms, providing a detailed "analysis of the incomes and living costs of the lower sort in one city [that] paints a markedly darker portrait of their economic circumstances than that generally limned by historians." Where other scholars have emphasized good wages and regular employment, downplaying or denying the financial and occupational hardships facing working people, Smith concludes that in the late colonial period, the laboring poor of Philadelphia were as vulnerable as their counterparts in contemporary European cities, living "so near subsistence before the Revolutionary War that there appears to be no lower level from which they could have risen" (Smith, 1981, pp. 201–2).

Economic crisis occasionally caused the city's working people to take concerted action to protect their place in society – something they had not generally been accustomed to doing. Compared to the lower sort in eighteenth-century Boston and New York, who had a record and certainly a reputation for political volatility, the common people of Philadelphia had a much more placid appearance in politics. As was common throughout other parts of colonial America, deference defined the basic approach to Philadelphia's political life, and a combination of convenience and coercion kept the coalition of urban merchants, lawyers, and proprietary officials insulated from serious challenge in peaceful and prosperous times. The lower and middling classes usually accepted the city's elite leadership, "not because they believed others had a right to rule them," Rosswurm explains, "nor because they thought themselves inferior to those who stood over them, but rather because their social situation demanded that they display deference and accept powerlessness" (Rosswurm, 1987, p. 24). But when economic forces both within and beyond the city seemed to threaten their livelihood and legitimate place in society, artisans began to see themselves as an oppressed group greatly endangered by those in control.

During the currency crisis of the 1720s, for instance, when the lack of a circulating medium undermined their ability to pay or be paid, artisans took up the cry for paper money as an immediate source of relief. Doing so put them directly at odds with local leaders such as James Logan, a wealthy merchant who scorned the poor and unabashedly blamed the victims for their allegedly profligate habits and lack of industry and frugality. But they also found an ally in the colony's appointed governor, Sir William Keith, who for his own personal and political reasons had turned against the colony's ruling elite. The details of the alliance and its political successes need not be listed here: the important point is that the middling people of Philadelphia began to depart from their accustomed acceptance of deferential relations with the city's and colony's leaders and, indeed, to challenge their hold on power. "This antagonism grew in the course of the decade and became more pointed with each passing year, so that by 1729, Philadelphia's political rhetoric had begun to acquire the class-inflected voice that would distinguish it for more than a century," Schultz observes. Indeed, he concludes, "the entry of Philadelphia's laboring classes into the political arena during the 1720s marked the beginning of America's first working class" (Schultz, 1993, pp. 24, 26).

Throughout most of the era leading up to the American Revolution, however, that "class-inflected voice" remained relatively muted. Philadelphia's working people did not play an especially aggressive or altogether independent role in the political life of the city, and even in their occasional outbursts of extralegal activity, the "people out of doors" proved to be rather tame. Rosswurm points out that in the early stages of overt opposition against the policies of the British government, beginning with the Stamp Act struggle in 1765, the common people of Philadelphia engaged in a comparatively mild form of protest: "Crowds in Philadelphia, whether multi- or single class in composition, were neither as violent, as frequent, nor as significant as those in New York or Boston." They turned out, to be sure, but they still seemed to take their political cues from the established leadership of the city. "Though the laboring poor clearly had the capacity to organize themselves and act on their own," Rosswurm concludes, "none of this activity fundamentally challenged class relations in Philadelphia" (Rosswurm, 1987, p. 34).

But the increasing crisis of the early 1770s changed that, both quickly and dramatically. When local merchants proved reluctant to adhere to non-importation agreements designed to put economic pressure on Great Britain, Philadelphia's lower orders began to speak more forcefully with an independent voice and to take significant political action. Gary Nash describes how artisans began to run their own candidates for public office and, through them, to press for local as well as imperial reform. In Philadelphia as elsewhere, the agitation over British policy also provided an opportunity for common people to make demands for class-based changes, including, Nash notes, "curbing the individual accumulation of wealth, opening up opportunity, divorcing the franchise from property ownership, and driving the mercantile elite from power." Moreover, in Philadelphia, the outbreak of armed conflict in 1775 created an additional source of class identity for the city's artisans and their allies, the organization of a local militia that served, as Nash puts it, as a "school of political education" for the common people (Nash, 1979, pp. 378–79).

* * * * *

As it was in Philadelphia, so it was elsewhere in the British American colonies. In general, the American Revolution proved to be a time of accelerating awareness of class identity. Although a fuller consideration of the revolutionary era and its aftermath goes beyond the scope of this volume, the eighteenth-century trajectory of class relations had already become clear by the outbreak of war in 1775. The imperial crisis confronted people of all social strata with the need to evaluate their interests, to take a stance, and eventually to take action. As they did so, they brought into sharper focus not only the competing interests between the colonies and the mother country, but also the competing interests within American society itself. The point is not to reduce the Revolution to a crude caricature of a class conflict: if the recent historiography of the era has told us anything, it is that the War for Independence in all parts of America proved to be a struggle that revealed a complex pattern of economic, ethnic, racial, and regional conflicts and alliances. People defined and defended their interests for a variety of reasons, some quite personally pragmatic, some more loftily patriotic. But no matter what the particular cause of one's commitment, the more general call of the Revolution echoed long after the shooting was over: the rhetoric and spirit of the revolutionary era, the near-constant emphasis on liberty and equality, implied a promise of opportunity for all people. And for people in the lower ranks of American society, comprehending fully the possibilities of greater equality in the future could only come from understanding better the inequality they had experienced in the past.

Perhaps the best expression of this revolutionary-era awareness comes from Alfred Young, who has long been one of the leading students of the lower classes in colonial America. In his sensitive and engaging portrayal of George Robert Twelves Hewes, a poor cordwainer in pre-revolutionary Boston, Young describes the transformation Hewes experienced as he began to take part in the political protest of the 1760s and 1770s. Once awed by wealthy and powerful men like John Hancock, Hewes found himself suddenly assuming a new relationship with them as, to use his own term, "associates": no longer playing the deferential inferior because of his poverty and status, Hewes took on a decisive and self-directed role in the crisis facing Bostonians. He was no "leveler," to be sure, but neither was he a groveler. Along with his allies in the artisanal and laboring ranks, Hewes emerged as an increasingly independent actor: "His experiences transformed him," Young concludes, "giving him a sense of citizenship and personal worth" (Young, 1999, p. 55). Becoming a citizen meant more, of course, than simply taking part in the politics of protest. For Hewes and other members of the lower classes, it also meant embracing the ideal of equality that the Revolution offered, claiming legitimacy as actors in an unfolding democratic drama, and displaying a social identity, both personal and collective, that had been developing for decades.

To be sure, the American Revolution did not produce an immediate and dramatic social revolution for working people like Hewes: he remained barely a step above poverty for most of his life, as did many other people of the lower sort. But toward the end of his life, when he returned to Boston as a revolutionary-era relic and something of a working-class hero in the mid-1830s, he did so at a time when working people had begun to assert their rights quite forcefully and increasingly in direct opposition to the merchants and manufacturers who controlled the economy of the early republic. Young female factory workers in the nearby Lowell textile mills engaged in a "turn-out," or strike, singing defiantly that they were "too fond of liberty" to be enslaved by the emerging industrial system. Working-men likewise began to assert their place in society, proudly proclaiming their identity as "producers" of the new nation's wealth and clearly distinguishing themselves from the "parasites" who garnered the profits without doing the work. It was not until the early decades of the nineteenth century, a time history texts invariably call the era of the common man (and, increasingly, the common woman), that the language of class became openly spoken in American political and social discourse. But it was in the two centuries before that the structural and ideological roots of class became embedded in the soil of American society. Whether or not most people of the colonial era – and many historians writing of that era – felt comfortable in using the concept of class to describe the nature of their social relations, the legacy of inequality and its discontents in early America leads us inescapably to one point: the history of colonial period, no less than that of the more mature capitalist society that emerged later, not only connects but contributes to the larger analysis of class in America.

BIBLIOGRAPHY

Auwers, Linda: "Fathers, sons, and wealth in colonial Windsor, Connecticut." *Journal of Family History* 3 (1978), pp. 136–49.

Beard, Charles A.: *An Economic Interpretation of the Constitution of the United States* (New York, 1913; reprint, New York: Free Press, 1986).

Becker, Carl L.: *The History of Political Parties in the Province of New York, 1765–1776* (Madison, WI: University of Wisconsin Press: 1909).

Beeman, Richard R.: *The Evolution of the Southern Backcountry: A Case Study of Lunenburg County, Virginia, 1746–1832* (Philadelphia: University of Pennsylvania Press, 1984).

Berlin, Ira: *Many Thousands Gone: The First Two Centuries of Slavery in North America* (Cambridge, MA: Harvard University Press, 1998).

Bernstein, Barton J., ed.: *Towards a New Past: Dissenting Essays in American History* (New York: Random House, 1967).

Bissel, Linda Auwers: "From One Generation to Another: Mobility in Seventeenth-Century Windsor, Connecticut." *William and Mary Quarterly* 3rd ser., 1 (1974), pp. 79–110.

Boorstin, Daniel: *The Americans: The Colonial Experience* (New York: Vintage Books, 1958).

Breen, Timothy Hall: *Tobacco Culture: The Mentality of the Great Tidewater Planters on the Eve of Revolution* (Princeton, NJ: Princeton University Press, 1985).

Bridenbaugh, Carl: *Cities in Revolt: Urban Life in America, 1743–1776* (New York: Alfred A. Knopf, 1955).

Brown, Kathleen M.: *Good Wives, Nasty Wenches, and Anxious Patriarchs: Gender, Race, and Power in Colonial Virginia* (Chapel Hill, NC: University of North Carolina Press, 1996).

Brown, Robert E.: *Middle-Class Democracy and the Revolution in Massachusetts, 1691–1780* (Ithaca, NY: Cornell University Press, 1955).

Bushman, Richard Lyman: *From Puritan to Yankee: Character and the Social Order in Connecticut, 1690–1765* (Cambridge, MA: Harvard University Press, 1967).

Bushman, Richard Lyman: "Markets and Composite Farms in Early America." *William and Mary Quarterly* 3rd ser., 55 (1998), pp. 351–74.

Carr, Lois Green: "Inheritance in the Colonial Chesapeake." In Ronald Hoffman and Peter Albert, eds., *Women in the Age of the American Revolution* (Charlottesville, VA: University Press of Virginia, 1989), pp. 155–208.

Carr, Lois Green: "Emigration and the Standard of Living: The Seventeenth-Century Chesapeake." *Journal of Economic History* 52 (1992), pp. 271–92.

Carr, Lois Green and Walsh, Lorena S.: "The Planter's Wife: The Experience of White Women in Seventeenth-Century Maryland." *William and Mary Quarterly* 3rd ser., 24 (1977), pp. 542–71.

Carr, Lois Green, Menard, Russell R., and Walsh, Lorena S.: *Robert Cole's World: Agriculture and Society in Early Maryland* (Chapel Hill, NC: University of North Carolina Press, 1991).

Clark, Christopher: "The Household Economy, Market Exchange and the Rise of Capitalism in the Connecticut Valley, 1800–1860." *Journal of Social History* 13 (1979), pp. 169–90.

Clark, Christopher: *The Roots of Rural Capitalism: Western Massachusetts, 1780–1860* (Ithaca, NY: Cornell University Press, 1990).

Coclanis, Peter A.: *The Shadow of a Dream: Economic Life and Death in the South Carolina Low Country, 1670–1920* (Oxford and New York: Oxford University Press, 1989).

Columbus, Christopher: *The Diario of Christopher Columbus's First Voyage to America 1492–1493*, ed. Oliver Dunn and James E. Kelley, Jr. (Norman, OK: University of Oklahoma Press, 1991).

Cook, Edward M., Jr.: *The Fathers of the Towns: Leadership and Community Structure in Eighteenth-Century New England* (Baltimore, MD: Johns Hopkins University Press, 1976).

Countryman, Edward: *A People in Revolution: The American Revolution and Political Society in New York, 1760–1790* (Baltimore, MD: Johns Hopkins University Press, 1981).

Countryman, Edward: *Americans: A Collision of Histories* (New York: Hill & Wang, 1996).

Crèvecoeur, J. Hector St. John de: *Letters from an American Farmer and Sketches of Eighteenth-Century America* (1782), ed. Albert E. Stone (New York: Penguin, 1981).

Daniels, Bruce C.: *The Connecticut Town: Growth and Development, 1635–1790* (Middletown, CT: Wesleyan University Press, 1979).

Daniels, Bruce C.: *The Fragmentation of New England: Comparative Perspectives on Economic, Political, and Social Divisions in the Eighteenth Century* (New York: Greenwood Publishing Group, 1988).

Daniels, Christine: "From Father to Son: Economic Roots of Craft Dynasties in Eighteen-Century Maryland." In Howard B. Rock, Paul A. Gilje, and Robert Asher, eds., *American Artisans: Crafting Social Identity, 1750–1850* (Baltimore, MD: Johns Hopkins University Press, 1995), pp. 3–16, 201–9.

Doerflinger, Thomas M.: *A Vigorous Spirit of Enterprise: Merchants and Economic Development in Revolutionary Philadelphia* (Chapel Hill, NC: University of North Carolina Press, 1986).

Dwight, Timothy: *Greenfield Hill: A Poem in Seven Parts* (New York: Childs and Swaine, 1794).

Galenson, David W.: *White Servitude in Colonial America: An Economic Analysis* (Cambridge and New York: Cambridge University Press, 1981).

Grant, Charles S.: *Democracy in the Connecticut Frontier Town of Kent* (New York: Columbia University Press, 1961).

Greene, Jack P., ed.: *The Reinterpretation of the American Revolution: 1763–1789* (New York, Evanston, and London: Harper and Row, 1968).

Greene, Jack P.: *Pursuits of Happiness: The Social Development of Early Modern British Colonies and the Formation of American Culture* (Chapel Hill, NC: University of North Carolina Press, 1988).

Greene, Jack P. and Pole, J. R., eds.: *Colonial British America: Essays in the New History of the Early Modern Era* (Baltimore, MD: Johns Hopkins University Press, 1984).

Greven, Philip J.: *Four Generations: Population, Land, and Family in Colonial Andover, Massachusetts* (Ithaca, NY: Cornell University Press, 1970).

Gross, Robert A.: *The Minutemen and Their World* (New York: Hill & Wang, 1976).

Henretta, James A.: "Economic Development and Social Structure in Colonial Boston." *William and Mary Quarterly* 3rd ser., 22 (1965), pp. 75–92.

Henretta, James A.: "Families and Farms: *Mentalité* in Pre-industrial America." *William and Mary Quarterly* 3rd ser., 35 (1978), pp. 3–32.

Henretta, James A.: "Wealth and Social Structure." In Greene and Pole, eds., *Colonial British America*, pp. 262–89.

Hoerder, Dirk: *Crowd Action in Revolutionary Massachusetts, 1765–1781* (New York: Academic

Press, 1977).

Hoffman, Ronald, McCusker, John J., Menard, Russell R., and Albert, Peter J., eds.: *The Economy of Early America: The Revolutionary Period, 1763–1790* (Charlottesville, VA: University Press of Virginia, 1988).

Holton, Woody: *Forced Founders: Indians, Debtors, and Slaves in the Making of the American Revolution in Virginia* (Chapel Hill, NC: University of North Carolina Press, 1999).

Innes, Stephen: *Labor in a New Land: Economy and Society in Seventeenth-Century Springfield* (Princeton, NJ: Princeton University Press, 1983).

Innes, Stephen, ed.: *Work and Labor in Early America* (Chapel Hill, NC: University of North Carolina Press, 1988).

Isaac, Rhys: *The Transformation of Virginia, 1740–1790* (Chapel Hill, NC: University of North Carolina Press, 1982).

Jameson, J. Franklin: *The American Revolution Considered as a Social Movement* (Princeton, NJ: Princeton University Press, 1926).

Jones, Douglas Lamar: "The Strolling Poor: Transiency in Eighteenth-Century Massachusetts." *Journal of Social History* 8 (1975), pp. 28–54.

Jones, Gareth Stedman: *Languages of Class: Studies in English Working-Class History, 1832–1982* (Cambridge and New York: Cambridge University Press, 1983).

Jordan, Winthrop: *White Over Black: American Attitudes toward the Negro, 1559–1812* (Chapel Hill, NC: University of North Carolina Press, 1968).

Kim, Sung Bok: *Landlord and Tenant in Colonial New York: Manorial Society, 1664–1775* (Chapel Hill, NC: University of North Carolina Press, 1978).

Kolchin, Peter: *American Slavery, 1619–1877* (New York: Hill & Wang, 1993).

Kulikoff, Allan: "The Progress of Inequality in Revolutionary Boston." *William and Mary Quarterly* 3rd ser., 28 (1971), pp. 375–414.

Kulikoff, Allan: *Tobacco and Slaves: The Development of Southern Cultures in the Chesapeake, 1680–1800* (Chapel Hill, NC: University of North Carolina Press, 1986).

Kulikoff, Allan: *The Agrarian Origins of American Capitalism* (Charlottesville, VA: University Press of Virginia, 1992).

Kulikoff, Allan: "Households and Markets: Toward a New Synthesis of American Agrarian History." *William and Mary Quarterly* 3rd ser., 50 (1993), pp. 340–55.

Kulikoff, Allan: *From British Peasants to Colonial American Farmers* (Chapel Hill, NC: University of North Carolina Press, 2000).

Lemisch, Jesse: "The American Revolution Seen from the Bottom Up." In Bernstein, ed., *Towards a New Past*, pp. 3–45.

Lemisch, Jesse: "Jack Tar in the Streets: Merchant Seamen and the Politics of Revolutionary America." *William and Mary Quarterly* 3rd ser., 25 (1968), pp. 373–407.

Lemon, James T.: *The Best Poor Man's Country: A Geographical Study of Early Southeastern Pennsylvania* (Baltimore, MD: Johns Hopkins University Press, 1972).

Lemon, James T. and Nash, Gary B.: "The Distribution of Wealth in Eighteenth-Century America: A Century of Changes in Chester County, Pennsylvania." *Journal of Social History* 2 (1968), pp. 1–24.

Lockridge, Kenneth A.: "Land, Population, and the Evolution of New England Society." *Past & Present* 39 (1968), pp. 62–80.

Lockridge, Kenneth A.: *A New England Town: The First Hundred Years, Dedham, Massachusetts, 1636–1736* (New York: W. W. Norton, 1970).

Lockridge, Kenneth A.: "Social Change and the Meaning of the American Revolution." *Journal of Social History* 7 (1973), pp. 403–39.

Main, Jackson Turner: *The Social Structure of Revolutionary America* (Princeton, NJ: Princeton University Press, 1965).

Martin, John Frederick: *Profits in the Wilderness: Entrepreneurship and the Founding of New*

England Towns in the Seventeenth Century (Chapel Hill, NC: University of North Carolina Press, 1991).

Menard, Russell R. : "From Servants to Freeholder: Status Mobility and Property Accumulation in Seventeenth-Century Maryland." *William and Mary Quarterly* 3rd ser., 30 (1973), pp. 37–64.

Menard, Russell R., Harris, P. M. G., and Carr, Lois Green: "Opportunity and Inequality: The Distribution of Wealth on the Lower Western Shore of Maryland, 1638–1705." *Maryland History* 69 (1974), pp. 169–84.

Merrill, Michael: "Cash is Good to Eat: Self-Sufficiency and Exchange in the Rural Economy of the United States." *Radical History Review* 4 (1977), pp. 42–71.

Morgan, Edmund S.: *American Slavery, American Freedom: The Ordeal of Colonial Virginia* (New York: W. W. Norton, 1975).

Morgan, Philip D.: *Slave Counterpoint: Black Culture in the Eighteenth-Century Chesapeake and Lowcountry* (Chapel Hill, NC: University of North Carolina Press, 1998).

Nash, Gary B.: *The Urban Crucible: Social Change, Political Consciousness, and the Origins of the American Revolution* (Cambridge, MA: Harvard University Press, 1979).

Nash, Gary B.: *Race, Class, and Politics: Essays on American Colonial and Revolutionary Society* (Urbana, IL: University of Illinois Press, 1986).

Nobles, Gregory: "The Rise of Merchants in Rural Market Towns: A Case Study of Eighteenth-Century Northampton, Massachusetts." *Journal of Social History* 24 (1990), pp. 5–23.

Pruitt, Bettye Hobbs: "Self-Sufficiency and the Agricultural Economy of Eighteenth-Century Massachusetts." *William and Mary Quarterly* 3rd ser., 41 (1984), pp. 333–64.

Rosswurm, Steven: *Arms, Country, and Class: The Philadelphia Militia and the "Lower Sort" during the American Revolution* (New Brunswick, NJ and London: Rutgers University Press, 1987).

Rothenberg, Winifred: "The Market and Massachusetts Farmers 1750–1855." *Journal of Economic History* 41(1981), pp. 283–314.

Rothenberg, Winifred: "The Emergence of Farm Labor Markets and the Transformation of the Rural Economy." *Journal of Economic History* 45 (1985), pp. 537–66.

Rutman, Darrett B. and Rutman, Anita H.: *A Place in Time: Middlesex County, Virginia, 1650–1750* (New York: W. W. Norton, 1984).

Salinger, Sharon V.: *"To Serve Well and Faithfully": Labor and Indentured Servants in Pennsylvania, 1682–1800* (Cambridge and New York: Cambridge University Press, 1987).

Salmon, Marylynn: *Women and the Law of Property in Early America* (Chapel Hill, NC: University of North Carolina Press, 1986).

Shammas, Carole: "How Self-Sufficient Was Early America?" *Journal of Interdisciplinary History* 13 (1982), pp. 247–72.

Schlesinger, Arthur, Sr.: *The Colonial Merchants and the American Revolution* (New York: F. Unger, 1957 [1918]).

Schultz, Ronald: *The Republic of Labor: Philadelphia Artisans and the Politics of Class, 1720–1830* (Oxford and New York: Oxford University Press, 1993).

Simler, Lucy: "Tenancy in Colonial Pennsylvania: The Case of Chester County." *William and Mary Quarterly* 3rd ser., 43 (1986), pp. 542–69.

Smith, Billy G.: "The Material Lives of Laboring Philadelphians, 1750 to 1800." *William and Mary Quarterly* 3rd ser., 38 (1981), pp. 163–202.

Smith, Billy G.: *The "Lower Sort": Philadelphia's Laboring People, 1750–1800* (Ithaca, NY: Cornell University Press, 1990).

Springfield, Massachusetts: "Articles of Agreement." In John Demos, ed., *Remarkable Providences, 1600-1760* (New York: George Braziler, 1972), pp. 53–6.

Steinfeld, Robert J.: *The Invention of Free Labor: The Employment Relation in English and American Law and Culture, 1350–1870* (Chapel Hill, NC: University of North Carolina Press,

1991).

Stiverson, Gregory A.: *Poverty in a Land of Plenty: Tenancy in Eighteenth-Century Maryland* (Baltimore, MD: Johns Hopkins University Press, 1977).

Taylor, Alan: *Liberty Men and Great Proprietors: The Revolutionary Settlement on the Maine Frontier, 1760–1820* (Chapel Hill, NC: University of North Carolina Press, 1990).

Thompson, E. P.: *The Making of the English Working Class* (New York: Pantheon, 1963).

Thompson, E. P.: "Eighteenth-Century English Society: Class Struggle without Class?" *Social History* 3 (1978), pp. 133–65.

Ulrich, Laurel Thatcher: *Good Wives: Image and Reality in the Lives of Women in Northern New England, 1650–1750* (Oxford and New York: Oxford University Press, 1982).

Usner, Daniel: *Indians, Settlers, and Slaves in a Frontier Exchange Economy: The Lower Mississippi Valley before 1783* (Chapel Hill, NC: University of North Carolina Press, 1992).

Vickers, Daniel: "Competency and Competition: Economic Culture in Early America." *William and Mary Quarterly* 3rd ser., 47 (1990), pp. 3–29.

Vickers, Daniel: *Farmers and Fishermen: Two Centuries of Work in Essex County, Massachusetts, 1630–1830* (Chapel Hill, NC: University of North Carolina Press, 1994).

Waters, John J.: "Family, Inheritance, and Migration in New England: The Evidence from Guilford, Connecticut." *William and Mary Quarterly* 3rd ser., 39 (1982), pp. 64–86.

Weber, David J.: *The Spanish Frontier in North America* (New Haven, CT: Yale University Press, 1992).

Winthrop, John: "A Model of Christian Charity." In Alan Heimert and Andrew Delbanco, eds., *The Puritans in America: A Narrative Anthology* (Cambridge: Harvard University Press, 1985), pp. 81–91.

Wood, Gordon: *The Radicalism of the American Revolution* (New York: Vintage, 1991).

Wood, Peter: *Black Majority: Negroes in Colonial South Carolina from 1670 through the Stono Rebellion* (New York: W. W. Norton, 1974).

Young, Alfred F.: *The American Revolution: Explorations in American Radicalism* (DeKalb, IL: Northern Illinois University Press, 1976).

Young, Alfred F.: *The Shoemaker and the Tea Party: Memory and the American Revolution* (Boston, MA: Beacon Press, 1999).

Zuckerman, Michael: *Peaceable Kingdoms: New England Towns in the Eighteenth Century* (New York: Alfred A. Knopf, 1970).

CHAPTER TWELVE

Colonial Politics

ALAN TULLY

Any attempt to understand colonial politics must begin with recognition that the quest to do so has been of long duration. For over a century now, historians have been interpreting and reinterpreting the political behavior of early Americans. Frequently historiographic considerations – the framing of political activities in terms of a later democratic norm, the construing of colonial politics as a handmaiden to the American Revolution, and the more recent, postmodern-influenced, turning from politics – have inhibited our comprehension of the colonial political world. But despite that, the cumulative contributions of generations of writers, along with the strategic explorations of a handful of recent scholars have directed us to a broader, yet at the same time more focused, appreciation of the significance of colonial politics.

Excepting writers of the revolutionary generation, the first major historian of the United States was George Bancroft whose ten-volume chronicle has had a considerable impact on the American historical consciousness (Bancroft, 1834–74). Writing during the heyday of participatory politics among America's largely white, male electorate, Bancroft laid out a compelling version of Whig history: the relevant past consisted of a record of Liberty's progress, to which the colonial contributions were New Englanders' organization of town democracies and the successes all representative assemblies shared in striving for autonomy from Britain. This epic tale, which placed liberty, democracy, and attendant practices of politics at the heart and very beginning of an American identity, articulated nineteenth-century American romantic nationalism with such power and conferred on it such mystique that its legacy lived on in various permutations through many twentieth-century historical works.

Views of the New World order became more complicated in the late nineteenth and early twentieth centuries with the first wave of historical professionalism. Among the new academics were Charles M. Andrews (1924, 1934–8) and Herbert Levi Osgood (1904–7, 1924) at the head of a coterie of students, whose focus was more on the colonies than on the Revolution. Their perspective in some cases broadened to include all the North American, Atlantic, and West Indian colonies; their concerns were the institutional and administrative facets of the British empire that could be verified by "scientific" history; and their understanding of the political and social experiences of the colonists led them to deny the existence of colonial democracy but identify, through the conflict of legislatures with governors, the "rise of the assembly with its growth to self-conscious activity" (Andrews, 1944, p. 39). These so-called "imperial" historians added a breadth of vision, an identification of critical themes, a commitment to detail, and an ideal of precision to the study of colonial politics that inspired many who were to follow in their wake.

Other historians, fired by the excitement of the emerging social sciences and rejecting institutionalism in favor of a broader history, soon supplemented the ranks of the imperial-minded professionals. Their "progressive" story of America was informed by an often-simplified acquaintance with economic determinism and a reforming zeal against the apparent greed and duplicity of contemporary business interests. To them economic and social factors were the veins running through the hardrock of history and their tale was one of emerging American democracy fighting to free that valuable ore from the underground shadows that surrounded it. Although the eyes of the best progressive writers to work on the eighteenth century, Carl L. Becker and C. H. Lincoln, were firmly fixed on the Revolution, Becker and Lincoln did establish a theme for colonial politics. That theme was class conflict between "a landed and commercial aristocracy" and "the middle and lower classes" (Becker, 1909, p. 10; Lincoln, 1901, p. 77). The former held control of government, including the elected assemblies, by wielding economic power over tenants and mechanics, by disenfranchising most citizens, and by under-representing the backcountry areas. By mid-century, however, the "democratic ideal" had emerged among the middle and lower classes who, in New York at least, exploited the aristocracy's resort to the language of the "consent of the governed" and their quest for voter support in disputes with royal governors (Becker, 1909, pp. 14, 17).

While both imperial and progressive constructions of colonial politics continued to be represented in historical writings through the mid-twentieth century, others also appeared. The so-called "consensus" historians achieved the highest profile of those who initiated revisionism. To many mid-century observers, an America unscathed by fascism, victorious in war, resistant to class conflict, and affluent in the aggregate was exceptional – a principled liberal democracy with pragmatic flare. The historians who brought these views most directly to bear on colonial politics were Robert E. and B. Katherine Brown. In studies of Massachusetts and Virginia the Browns examined franchise laws, voter participation, and regional representation in the context of their interpretation of colonial property-holding patterns and economic opportunity. Their conclusions were striking. Colonial Massachusetts was an egalitarian, "middle-class society in which property was easily acquired," eligibility to vote approached 95 percent of adult white males, "sharp internal class conflicts" were non-existent, and representation was relatively equitable between agricultural and commercial areas (Brown, 1955, pp. 401, 403). In Virginia the situation was quite similar. Despite sharp retorts directed at the Browns' methodology and criticism of their embrace of that old straightjacketing binary, aristocracy and democracy, the Browns' work effectively blew apart the old progressive model based on class polarization, substantial disenfranchisement, and inequitable representation. The Browns may have minimized conflict in colonial politics but they contributed mightily to the opening up and consequent conflict of scholarly debate.

Independent of the Browns, scholarly engagement and argument escalated rapidly during the late 1950s, the 1960s, and the early 1970s. The commitment of huge amounts of federal funds to higher education as a response to the Cold War and the expansion of American universities to embrace the baby boom brought hundreds of eager students into graduate courses. Once enrolled, apprentice historians were part of an exciting world. The social sciences, such as sociology, economics, anthropology, and political science, were expanding as well and seemed to offer insights which historians felt they could put to good use. Non-American historiographical traditions, such as the Annales school, offered similar inspiration. Perhaps the most significant impact on new scholarship was not any constellation of ideas but a machine. The availability of computers made possible the organization of documentary evidence on a scale previously only imagined. The varied outcomes included the new social history, cliometrics, history from-the-bottom-up, and the new political history.

The cumulative impact of these developments on the study of colonial politics was substantial. Kenneth Lockridge (1970), Michael Zuckerman (1968, 1970), and Edward Cook (1976) all produced studies of New England towns that varied considerably in their stress on politics but together raised significant questions about how, and under what conditions, aristocratic, consensual, egalitarian, or elitist political practices took place in the presence of the Browns' relatively broad franchise. In his behaviorist-influenced study of Massachusetts provincial politics, Robert Zemsky (1971) also found a mix of elitist, insider political dominance along with a broader comity born of shared knowledge and shared standards of political morality. Others paid more attention to the political salience of colonial religious life. Richard Bushman (1967) located the break from traditional obedience to the magistracy to competitive politics in the dynamics of the Great Awakening. Building on Bushman's Connecticut and on studies of Pennsylvania that tied the character of provincial politics to inter- and intra-denominational relationships (Nash, 1968; Newcomb, 1972; Tully, 1977, 1983), Patricia Bonomi (1986) argued that during and after the Great Awakening the colonies shared in the development of a broadly based pattern of denominational politics.

At the same time as a number of the aforementioned historians indicated through their references to "democracy" how much Whig, consensus, and progressive approaches still influenced them, they and others who have explored such topics as the founding, dissemination, and development of representative governments and the connections between colonial and imperial government and politics, have encouraged a broad scholarly rejection of American exceptionalism. Cumulatively, along with those who have reflected more broadly on the texture of colonial society (Bailyn and Clive, 1954; Greene, [1970] 1992), they came to place heavy emphasis on the ways, and degree to which, colonial societies veered towards English norms in the eighteenth century. The individual most closely associated with the explicit identification with this process of "Anglicization" was John Murrin who, in his Ph.D. dissertation, demonstrated that Massachusetts lawyers built a powerful social and political presence on a professionalism that determinedly mimicked that of the English bar (Murrin, 1966). In the main, this and other potent scholarly statements of Anglicization were social, cultural, and intellectual – and not political. But they had a marked impact on the writing of colonial politics. No matter the divisions among colonial political elites, historians increasingly perceived them as sharing in the provincial urge to replicate metropolitan patterns that lent coherence to the myriad political studies appearing in the late 1960s and 1970s, which otherwise might seem to lose themselves in the minutia of local and provincial particularity.

If one feature of an emerging new conceptual focus in the study of colonial politics was Anglicization, a second was factionalism. The foundations for factionalism were laid in the 1930s and 1940s with some colonial historians' acceptance of the Namierite identification of interest, connection, and conflict as the substance of eighteenth-century politics and more recently in the profusion of 1960s and 1970s studies delineating the lives of prominent colonial leaders, examining the many forms of local government, explaining the changing relationships among groups of politicians, analyzing the bases of their power, and outlining the conflicts that took place within assemblies, between governors and legislators and among the different colonies. For many historians, factionalism seemed a way of making sense of colonial politics. Factional coalitions formed for any number of reasons but frequently they depended at any one moment on who was "in" favor (i.e., enjoying the benefits of power and patronage) or was "out" of favor. In some cases such as early Pennsylvania, the politics of the "ins" versus the "outs" constituted a volatile mix of economic, social, regional, and religious interests (Nash, 1968). In New York, for example, factious politics both reflected and encouraged the factiousness of society (Bonomi, 1971). When various crises such as Awakening revivalism unfolded, they simply intensified the volatility of political rivalries.

A third major characteristic of colonial politics that many colonial historians seemed to agree on was its apparent elitism. Popular politicians who vied for power and office were easily identifiable as the rich, the prominent, and the well-connected. In the light of the Browns' work establishing the breadth of the electorate and in that of subsequent studies detailing their success at attracting large numbers of supporting voters to the polls (Dinkin, 1977), this raised a problem that bedeviled a number of sensitive historians. Why were middle- and lower-class voters complicit in supporting an electoral system that, although it sporadically registered social, economic, and sectional discontents, excluded them from office? Among those who observed this phenomenon was J. R. Pole, whose interest in charting the development of representative government in both America and England made him aware of the complex ways in which eighteenth-century Whiggism encouraged, inhibited, and ordered the eventual establishment of democratic practices. In what is arguably the most important modern article written on early American politics, "Historians and the Problem of Early American Democracy," Pole explained the aforementioned conundrum of electoral politics by reference to Walter Bagehot's description of Victorian England as a deferential society. In early America, Pole suggested, lower-class and middling people voluntarily accorded deference to their upper-class leaders. For their part, members of the colonial elite, whose station, wealth, lifestyle, reputation, and connections were clothed in the language of political merit or capacity, *expected* support for their political aspirations (Pole, 1962). Compared to the heavy concrete of disenfranchisement and under-representation that had held the old progressive model together, deference was light and magical, able to stick to almost anything – a new scholarly superglue, capable of keeping modern interpretations intact. It immediately appeared in books as different as Bushman's and Zemsky's and it would bear far greater weight in more recent writings.

Of the three political touchstones, Anglicization, factionalism, and deference-based elitism, the issue of factionalism continued as the most bedeviling, challenging comprehension. This challenge was intensified by historians' awareness of the new concept, "political culture," that political scientists had begun to use effectively in trying to overcome a fragmentation of, and an overly mechanical approach to, political studies. To do this they focused on the substratum of attitudes, beliefs, and sentiments that imparted coherence and meaning to political systems and related processes. In the light of this conceptual breakthrough there seemed only two possible ways to treat the problem of factionalism: either to try to order the confusion or welcome it. In one of his well-known dramatic gestures Bernard Bailyn opted for the latter. He reached out to factionalism and embraced it with ardor. "The history of politics in eighteenth century America," Bailyn pronounced in his *Origins of American Politics*, "is the history of factionalism." The conditions that generated it were systemic. Governors were appointed with "swollen" prerogative claims but had only "shrunken" informal powers with which to effect their ends. Political rivalries and alliances among provincials – personal, regional, economic, social, and issue-related – produced a bewildering vista of "milling factionalism," an "almost unchartable chaos of competing groups." Overall, Bailyn concluded, the "political system [was] anomalous in its essence, lacking in what any objective observer would consider a minimal degree of functional integration" (Bailyn, 1968, pp. 64, 96, 124).

Bailyn's model of colonial politics proved enormously influential, partly because of its simplicity but also because of its logical relationship to his extraordinarily successful *Ideological Origins of the American Revolution*. According to Bailyn the chaotic factionalism of colonial politics predisposed Anglicized colonial minds – "steeped in the political culture of eighteenth century Britain" as he put it – to embrace a strand of British thought, created by a clearly identifiable "group of prolific opposition theorists, 'country' politicians and publicists" (Bailyn, 1968, p. 106; 1967, p. 34). Given their ongoing experiences, conceiving of the world in Walpolean opposition terms as a constant battleground between power-hungry officeholders and liberty-minded, independent freeholders made perfect sense to politically literate provincials. The colonists' embrace of this ideology not only increased the strife and contention that denoted factional politics; it also explained why some colonists were so quick to articulate their differences with Britain in these terms after 1763. Chaotic factionalism rode to fame, then, less on its merits as a mature synthesis of the complexities of colonial political behavior (in fact, it was reductionist and, prior to chaos theory, a denial of historians' ability to find meaningful systems of order) than as an essential part of what became known as the "republican" interpretation of the American Revolution.

Colonial politics, more often than not, have been held hostage to the American Revolution. Exuberant Whig histories, engaged progressive writings, and congratulatory consensus prose tended to treat colonial politics as revolutionary foreplay. In this respect Bailyn's work was similar. To Bailyn, Walpolean opposition thought, with its idealization of the British Constitution and balanced government, with its fear of power and attendant corruption through the machinations of government officers and placeholders, and with its shrill cries of warning to virtuous, independent men to banish self-interest and protect the people's liberties, constituted the "primary elements of American politics in its original eighteenth century form." Beginning at the turn of the seventeenth century this political language quickly came to "furnish . . . not only the vocabulary but the grammar of thought, the apparatus by which the world was perceived." Although Bailyn acknowledged the existence of other clusters of ideas in the public arena, the significance of colonial politics rested on this one strand of "latently revolutionary" thinking (Bailyn, 1968, pp. 53, 160).

The first individual of note to challenge Bailyn's synthesis was Jack P. Greene. Greene had already articulated assumptions about the colonies in his major study, *The Quest for Power*, that took him in different directions. That book's aim was first, to lend coherence to our understanding of colonial politics and second, to clarify our vision of the American Revolution. Greene's departure point was Charles Andrews' identification of "the rise of the colonial assembly" as "the most conspicuous feature" of colonial "political and institutional" development (Andrews, 1944, p. 39). Focusing on the four most southerly mainland colonies but with an eye also on the Revolution, Greene provided a much more American story than his imperial-minded predecessors had, yet within an "institutional and constitutional" framework consistent with their work. His investigations turned up a similarity of behavior and results in which the post-Glorious Revolution lower houses of assembly took control of public finances, carefully monitored the civil list, took over their own internal governance, and usurped what, by British standards, were executive powers. Befitting a body of practical politicians, they did so "spontane[ously]," "prosaic[ly]," and opportunistically as they felt specific slights, followed what they felt was the logic of English rights, and exploited some of the possibilities that gubernatorial weaknesses and various colonial wars brought their way. By 1763 the assemblies were practically, and psychologically, in a position to "react . . . violently" to changing British policies. But more importantly for our purposes, their pan-colonial pattern of development provided a common centerpiece for the discussion of colonial politics (Greene, 1963, pp. x, 9, 357).

In working through the political language expressive of the institutional and constitutional development he had posited, in broadening his comparisons to include all of the rebelling and non-rebelling, British mainland, West Indian, and Atlantic colonies with assemblies, and in thinking about the political sociology of elite leadership in the colonies, Greene repositioned himself to assess the political culture of the colonies. His highly persuasive article "Political Mimesis" took direct issue with Bailyn, arguing that the predominant "political tradition" in the colonies was the language of "seventeenth-century [English] opposition to the Crown" expressing engagement in "a continuing struggle between prerogative and liberty, between executive and legislative power." This tradition spoke to the colonists' situation, for "in the eighteenth century colonies . . . [were] the very conditions and circumstances that had initially spawned the conception in seventeenth-century England." Colonial governors, as Bailyn had recently observed, came with inflated prerogative claims and because of this they evoked "immoderate responses." The assemblies' success in "bridl[ing] the governors" because of the absence of various informal powers, which again Bailyn had noted, never quieted the assemblymen's anxieties. Always there were these powerful gubernatorial claims, and frightened of them, colonists invoked *both* arguments about the deserved similarities of their assemblies to the House of Commons *and* their special needs, given the dissimilarity of their situation with Britain, to justify their augmentation of legislative power. Although Greene gave a place to Bailyn's eighteenth-century "Walpolean opposition" thought and to a "mainstream" variant of Whiggism, he argued that these came into play in restricted circumstances. And even after 1763 when Walpolean opposition rhetoric was of greater salience, "the submersion of the older opposition tradition . . . was never total" (Greene, [1969] 1994, pp. 189, 190, 202, 205, 208, 209, 213).

The Bailyn and Greene models of colonial political thought were impressive constructs but in part that was because of their narrow profile. Each focused on what they considered to have been a key Anglo-American discourse and left much else out. One important omission from the debate was the factional character of colonial political behavior, an issue that Greene turned to in two other essays. In the first, he took the opposite tack than Bailyn, making an effort to order, rather than give in to, the confusion of factionalism. He suggested that political behavior in the mainland British North American colonies might be classified into four categories running from chaotic factionalism, through stable factionalism, to domination by a single group, and finally to freedom from faction altogether. Simple enough in theory, the model was somewhat cumbersome in application. Colonies that began in one mode in the seventeenth century might metamorphose into others at later dates. The "toing and froing" when classified and catalogued still seemed confusing. Nonetheless, Greene's analysis recognized that the diversity of the colonies was an essential component of any broad effort to comprehend the political cultures of colonial America (Greene, [1966] 1996).

In a second important article entitled "The Growth of Political Stability," Greene turned somewhat more obliquely to the issue of factionalism. This piece suggested that if we looked carefully at colonial political behavior we would see a developmental process at work that impelled the colonies from uncertain outposts to mature provincial societies. And the political component of that maturation was a rejection of factionalism and the creation of much more stable colonial regimes. "Development in leadership, institutions, political consciousness, the socialization of the electorate to their political systems, instruments of communication, and institutions of non-governmental political training," all contributed to this state (Greene, [1975] 1994, p. 161). To some extent Greene's argument had been inspired by J. H. Plumb's well-known book on late seventeenth- and early eighteenth-century England, but it also came from empirical work (Plumb, 1967). My study of Pennsylvania made the point that amid rapid growth and religious and ethnic diversity, and despite early decades of strife, the creation of a stable provincial polity was possible (Tully, 1977). Robert Weir's work on South Carolina (1969), and Robert Zemsky's on Massachusetts (1971), among others, pointed in the same direction. Greene himself added a quantitative study of the turnover rate of colonial legislators, the results of which supported the argument (Greene, [1981] 1994). Overall, Greene's "Stability" article reiterated the point of the aforementioned studies, that because colonies could never meet the test of stability Plumb had laid out for an autonomous Britain, such a test was inappropriate for political dependencies. What really mattered were the different ways in which Greene's five sample colonies each combined their unique social, economic, cultural, and political experiences to create something of a known and accepted political sphere within their respective provincial worlds.

Another voice suggesting a somewhat different way of ordering colonial politics arose from a more complicated background. In his early career John Murrin had criticized "Whiggish" emphasis on the rising power of the assemblies, arguing that the abilities of some eighteenth-century governors to mount offensives against the legislatures, the support they received from the Board of Trade, the psychological ramifications of Anglicization, and the growing socioeconomic stratification in market areas, laid the groundwork for a "feudal revival" (Murrin, 1965, 1966; Murrin and Berthoff, 1973). Murrin also reflected the influence of the other major contributor to the republican model (in addition to Bailyn and his student Gordon Wood), J. G. A. Pocock. In his various writings Pocock traced the republican tradition from fifteenth-century Florence to revolutionary America. Throughout its progress, the tradition expressed a substantial quarrel between corruption and civic virtue and in specific political terms between "court" factions of officeholders, officials, retainers, pensioners, and placemen and "country" opponents – independent, virtuous, and disinterested – who were very much like and included Bailyn's Walpolean opposition critics (Pocock, 1975). Finally, Murrin picked up on the impact of repeated warfare on colonial life around which Herbert Levi Osgood had structured his volumes on the post-1689 colonial experience (1924), on William Pencak's description of how Massachusetts politicians used wartime spending to create court parties (1981), and on Robert Zemsky's view of professional politicians as a provincial cadre of quiet courtiers (1971). Drawing on all these perspectives, Murrin suggested a loose typology of colonial political cultures. He classified the northern colonies of Massachusetts and New Hampshire as court worlds, shading into the "less successful" New York and New Jersey, the "troubled" politics of the proprietary Pennsylvania and Maryland followed by the country regimes of Virginia, South Carolina, and Georgia. Murrin drew back from any rigorous examination of the scheme, and probably just as well given his admission that, even at first glance, at least seven of the thirteen colonies displayed political dynamics not easily encompassed by the court–country model. Nonetheless, some effort to confront the court–country dichotomy was worthwhile, given its prominent place in the republican literature and its rhetorical presence in eighteenth-century colonial sources (Murrin, 1984, p. 440).

Throughout the 1960s and 1970s and into the 1980s, another major controversy centered on the kinds of questions colonial political historians were [or were not] asking. To some historians the harmonious melodies of consensus history, of the Browns' middle-class democracy, and of Jackson Turner Main's relatively egalitarian society (Main, 1965), seemed fanciful fairytales given prevalent socioeconomic conditions and the sharp, ongoing public battles to redefine justice and democracy in America. Jesse Lemisch was one of the first to expose the suspect reasoning of historians who used the words of upper-class colonists to speak for all of society. Lemisch argued that we needed a history "from the bottom up," built not only on the assumptions that lower-class members of street crowds could have their own minds and use them to express their views on politics, but also informed by the past accomplishments of leftist and progressive writers and perhaps, most importantly, instructed by the current work of British intellectual E. P. Thompson, who was singlehandedly reshaping Marxist history (Lemisch, 1967; Thompson, 1963). Much of the vigor of the resulting "neo-progressive" school (in its historical dimensions) went into social history. But they and their new left friends also demanded a broader definition of political activity. In his stirring article, "Jack Tar in the Streets," Jesse Lemisch pointed out how lower-class crowds would riot for causes that were important to them in a form of political action that was an expected part of colonial behavior (Lemisch, 1968). When E. P. Thompson turned to the eighteenth century with his famous article "The Moral Economy of the English Crowd," neo-progressives had what some critics argued could not be built on idiosyncratic seamen – a persuasive general model. According to Thompson "men and women in the crowd were informed by the belief that they were defending traditional rights or customs and that they were supported by the wider consensus of the community. On occasion the popular consensus was endorsed by some measure of license afforded by the authorities" (Thompson, 1971, p. 78). Thompson's views stood out but round them were a range of other influential opinions, agreeing and disagreeing with him. New leftists saw plebeian colonial crowds defending traditional rights (Young,

1976). Others saw crowds as "all-class" composites determined to strike out against official arbitrariness, and extra-institutional rather than anti-institutional in their focus (Maier, 1970). Still others recognized a variety of crowd behavior including somewhat less immaculately conceived categories of crowds such as election riots.

Although there were many contributors to a radical political history of early America one book stands out – Gary Nash's *Urban Crucible* (1979). In order to comprehend the direction Nash's account took it is helpful to understand that by the early to mid-1970s the republican view of the American Revolution and of pre-revolutionary America had carried the day. Bailyn's and Gordon Wood's work was reinforced by J. G. A. Pocock's *Machiavellian Moment* (1975) and by several articles, one of the most important of which, for colonial politics, was "The Classical Theory of Deference" (Pocock, 1976). The result was a political history of colonial America in which the "poorer sort" deferred to the "better sort," chaotic factionalism served the interests of the well-entrenched, and pamphlets written by the elite largely in the Anglicizing language of civic humanism or Walpolean opposition were the truly significant evidence of political discourse. It was this conceptual paramountcy grounded in ideology and deference that Nash attacked.

The foundations of Nash's book are a series of investigations he made of the growing maldistribution of wealth and the structure of poverty and mobility in Boston, New York, and Philadelphia between 1700 and 1775. As socioeconomic divisions grew so did class differences, and so did the political self-expression of mechanics. As early as the 1720s in Philadelphia factional leaders were "reflecting . . . [a] laboring-class view." When Awakening revivalism washed over Boston a little later it became a "class-specific movement," one facet of which expressed itself in the "class hostility" of "street politics." By the late colonial years "plebeian urban dwellers [had] forced their way into the political arena, not so much through the formal mechanisms of electoral politics as through street demonstrations, mass meetings, extralegal committees that assumed governmental powers, the intimidation of their enemies, and, in some cases, spirited defenses of traditional norms." But given the power of social discontent that Nash describes, the prevalence of self-interested, socioeconomic politics, the large numbers of city working men, and the relatively open voting system, why did the poorer sort not challenge elite political leadership more effectively? Obviously it was not deference. Rather than a world of upper-class condescension and reciprocal lower-class respect, Nash saw "the persuasive use of economic leverage from above." Colonial politics spun round a tempered hub of economic clientage and related intimidation, and ideologies built on class and interest (Nash, 1979, pp. 153, 208, 221, 227, 372, 384).

The tug between these various views of colonial politics continued into the 1980s but then soon abated. The juggernaut of republicanism rolled ahead from its revolutionary origins, through the self-defining era of the early republic and on into some odd far-flung fields. One related, major intellectual squabble that had implications for colonial politics was the republican–liberal debate (if America was born republican, where did liberal America come from?) and it was fought largely on late eighteenth- and early nineteenth-century ground (Rodgers, 1992). Occasionally someone would make the obvious point that liberalism was not just a product of the Revolution. John Brooke, for example, described the political culture of eighteenth- and early nineteenth-century Massachusetts as a binary yet evolving relationship between classical republicanism and liberalism (Brooke, 1989). My *Forming American Politics* makes the point that the underpinnings of liberal politics developed out of both the political practices and conceptual developments related to those practices in colonial New York and Pennsylvania (Tully, 1994).

With its slight participation in the republicanism–liberalism controversy, however, it became clear that colonial politics had lost much momentum. Partly that had been due to the explosive impact of Bailyn's two books which had sucked up much of the oxygen necessary to feed healthy alternative inquiries that did not subsume colonial politics to revolutionary explanations. But beyond that, social history, which had once enriched political studies, had gradually devolved away from politics towards a variety of specific interests touching on ethnic and racial minorities, class divisions, women's experiences, gender history – any of which might be interlocked with such themes as environmental history, Borderland studies, or decolonization. The desire to study history from below, to tell the story of ordinary people, similarly turned many historians away from a subject that was elitist, not to mention male, white, and exclusionary. Accompanying postmodern assumptions including the need to decenter studies, to broaden the notion of power, and to legitimize unheard voices encouraged potential historians to bypass colonial politics because of the difficulty of combining such interests with both the substance and sources of the eighteenth-century political world. Finally, disillusionment with contemporary American politics, combined with an increasing acceptance of the view that politics is in essence simply another entertainment arena or a form of theater, reinforced the conclusion that politics does not and, hence, did not matter very much.

This development was unfortunate because the multiplicity and diversity of colonial political studies had become its great strength. Unless there is vigorous debate about the character of colonial politics, survey course lecturers, specialists in later, allied fields, and textbook writers tend to look for a simple way to tell the story of colonial politics, to substitute for its decentralized complexities a backbone of "Pre-national history" which, of course, it doesn't have. The orthodoxy, which has emerged over the past ten to fifteen years, has come out of both old and odd conjunctions. The first of these was the repetition of the old scenario in which colonial politics are interpreted to most conveniently complement an interpretation of the American Revolution. The second is the rather odd historiographical occasion on which the views of right and left have converged sufficiently to create a somewhat similar framework for the discussion of colonial politics.

This story begins with the peculiar twist Richard Bushman gave to colonial society in his monograph *King and People in Provincial Massachusetts*. In this study, Bushman gave some play, in preparation for an explanation of the Revolution, to the Greene model of legal and legislative-based assembly aggressiveness and later to Bailyn's Walpolean opposition language. More important, however, was his emphasis on monarchy and what he called its attendant "protection-allegiance" formula. On the one hand, monarchy was built on "exalt[ation]," "awe," "ritual," "inequalities," "the exercise of power, the necessity for submission and even [a 'moral . . . and psychologically acceptable'] civil cruelty." With this went the promise and fulfillment of patronage. On the other hand, there was a popular expectation of protection, a sense of monarchical obligation, and a people's right to protest in the streets in extra-institutional fashion. Negotiating the terrain between were the politicians (Bushman, 1985, pp. 14, 20, 24).

The crucial element for Bushman was not the specific dynamics of negotiation and political change but the monarchical fact and the traditional aspects of social relationships that accompanied a monarchical order. And these were precisely the elements that Gordon Wood picked up on as distinguishing colonial society in his much noted revolutionary monograph *The Radicalism of the American Revolution*. According to Wood, "in some respects colonial society was more traditional than that of the mother country." In mid-century colonial America, monarchy was revered as never before, religion "bolster[ed] monarchical authority and order," and people thought of themselves as "connected vertically" in hierarchies of clientage. At the same time society was divided into a two-class world – the world of "patricians" (colonial gentry, the "better sort") who, "free and independent," were granted authority, honor, and respect. Patriarchs in their families, they became patrons in public constantly "reaffirm[ing] their hierarchical relationships," bringing tangible meaning to the "age-old distinction between rulers and ruled." The second class, the "plebeians," constituted the base of the hierarchical pyramid, but "they had no power, no connections, no social capacity for commanding public allegiance and deference." On the contrary, "a patrimonial conception of officeholding, . . . an identification between social and political authority, private and public leadership" created an "awesome" set of "obligations and dependencies that could be turned into political authority" (Wood, 1992, pp. 12, 17, 23, 33, 72, 73, 85, 86, 89).

This model of mid-eighteenth-century society owed something to Bernard Bailyn's earlier writings, something to the inspiration of J. C. D. Clark (1985) and his depiction of an *ancien régime*, eighteenth-century England as the object of colonial Anglicizing propensities, and something to certain congruencies with E. P. Thompson's work. Fifteen years earlier Thompson had described eighteenth-century English society as a patrician-plebeian world in which the tradition of paternalism, "clientage and dependency were so strong that, at least until the 1760s ['the professional and middle classes, and the substantial yeomanry'] . . . appear" not to have resisted that polarity (Thompson, 1974, p. 395). Thus, Thompson acolytes such as Edward Countryman could describe late colonial New York as a society different from Thompson's England in its diversity and commercialism, but still rife with "paternalism" and "hierarchy." Composed in the city of "artisans and laborers, [and] merchant and professional elite" and, in important parts of the countryside, by country tenants and landlords, with manorial rights becoming "more rather than less salient" in the minds of the latter, this was still a two-class society (Countryman, 1981, pp. 16, 30, 34). The differences between a Wood and a Countryman were significant, of course. Wood still had an important place for political factionalism within his patriarchal model and for him "popular rioting was ultimately evidence that politics remained essentially a preserve of the dominant gentlemanly elite" (Wood, 1992, p. 91). Countryman, on the other hand, saw a latent political dynamism in the betrayed "corporatist feeling[s]" of urban rioters, and in the "nostolgic communalism" of rural tenants because the upper-class regime of merchants and landowners were forswearing their traditional obligations in the service of increasing commercialization (Countryman, 1981, p. 60). Nonetheless, right and left converged enough to portray a colonial politics built on hierarchy, patriarchy, dependence, patronage, and deference either voluntary or coercive, with dissenting voices either co-opted or insufficiently assertive to break the mold, and with an economy not quite diverse enough to undercut the bifurcated world of patricians and plebeians, gentlemen and others.

Despite the immense influence of this model built on Anglicization, factionalism, and deference, some recent works on colonial politics offer worthwhile, alternative perspectives. The most traditional of these has roots in the quantification impulse of the 1960s' and 1970s' new political history which focused on the formation of mass political parties and the fault lines of ethnocultural voting behavior in the antebellum decades. Because of problems linking ethnocultural and political sources, colonial historians have either moved only tentatively onto that ground or come at the problem in different ways (Archdeacon, 1976; Tully, 1983; Murrin, 1988; Roeber, 1993). Alternatively, a number of writers influenced by the new political tradition have turned to legislative records in order to judge just how factional colonial politics were or to what degree the much noted anti-party rhetoric of the times was belied by politicians' behavior. We have two such studies of New Jersey, for example, both of which, while incorporating treatment of divisions over land titles, sectionalism, and paper money, present interpretations consonant with the aforementioned model of a developing political maturity and stability in the eighteenth century (Batinski, 1987; Purvis 1986). The most ambitious of recent quantitatively oriented studies, however, is Benjamin H. Newcomb's *Political Partisanship in the American Middle Colonies*. This is "an attempt," based on the New York, New Jersey, and Pennsylvania experiences, "to apply . . . [the new political history] to a portrayal of party politics in its earliest American stage." Newcomb adopts a well-known political science test for party (party in the legislature, party in the electorate, and party as organization) and argues that only in the third category did the colonial parties of the three colonies not quite meet nineteenth-century standards. He sees two-party systems active in all the colonies – a common, structured competition between "administration" and "opposition" parties. Overall, Newcomb's behavioral world looks very similar to the antebellum standard of mass, democratic parties with complex bases of partisanship, developed arts of electoral competition and persuasion, experience with party realignments and high voter turnout. By identifying middle colony politics in terms of the most tangible signifiers of nineteenth-century American "democracy," Newcomb raises the specter of the Browns' colonial democracy, foreshortens the cultural distance between eighteenth-century colonies and nineteenth-century national democracy, and suggests the existence of a political world that has virtually nothing in common with the aforementioned Bushman/Wood/Countryman framework for colonial political society. More than any other recent book, then, Newcomb forces us to confront again the issues of the distinctiveness of colonial politics (Newcomb, 1995, pp. 1, 18, 215).

Recent scholarship has given us three vantage points from which we can focus on the organizational side of colonial politics that Newcomb emphasizes. From Virginia John G. Kolp's *Gentlemen and Freeholders* most directly addresses the issue: "gentlemen (members of Virginia's House of Burgesses) ruled over common freeholders, while freeholders kept gentlemen in office. How did it work?" In presenting an exhaustive survey and quantitative analysis of eighteenth-century election materials throughout the colony and a detailed dissection of both political context and election polls in four sample counties, Kolp convincingly argues that there were great regional and diachronic variations in election behavior. In doing so he offers a rough typology ranging from non-competitive elections through various patterns of competitive activity. Thus, at any one time "gentry domination . . ., near hereditary seats . . ., uncontested elections, and voter apathy coexisted with highly competitive elections, long and costly campaigns . . ., and voter independence" (Kolp, 1998, pp. 2, 9). Virginia politics in this portrait was not some variation of the Browns' democracy or the deferential polity that Jack Greene had outlined in his characterization, but more an updated mixture of elements that had made Charles Sydnor's older, well-known study of the colony's "gentlemen freeholders" appear to critics as either a bundle of uneasy contradictions or a masterly evocation (Greene, [1976] 1994; Sydnor, 1952). To Kolp's mind, the freeholders gave the truly telling testimony: in Virginia's many non-competitive elections they passively endorsed gentry claims; but when active voters they seemed to take "into account a variety of factors, including deference, respect, familiarity, pride, as well as their own social, economic, and political well-being." Organizationally, however, the persistence of competitive, as opposed to non-competitive, elections had little effect. Virginia's provincial politics were "localized and personal," taking place within "intimate rural neighborhoods," only "rarely concerned or influenced" by "provincial and imperial" affairs, and giving no hint of inter-county coordination (Kolp, 1998, pp. 195, 197, 199).

The second vantage point is that of Massachusetts Bay and the book that exploits the opportunity is David W. Conroy's *The Public Houses*. Historians have long referred to the connection between taverns and politics but none with the thoroughness of Conroy. He identifies far more tavernkeeper-politicans than we have hitherto known and he ties them and the explosion in the number of taverns in the early eighteenth century to the emergence of "a critical reading public distinct from the social and political hierarchy." Critical polemical literature, growing numbers of public prints including newspapers, the interaction between oral and written cultures, growth in the number of taverns, and the development of a politics of opposition were synergistically hothoused in "tavern constituencies." Yet in their conscious development of tavern cultures as "mediums of communication," offering "an emerging egalitarian alternative to hierarchy," local, popular elites also worked to "control . . ., contain . . ., [yet] placate . . . the public they helped to invent." Beneath the focus on taverns, then, lie some familiar old themes. One is the social tension "popular" leaders generated as they spearheaded challenges to authority but expected deference to themselves. A second – fully dressed in the Habermasian idiom of the "public sphere" – is Conroy's emphasis on the political "mobilization" that has long been recognized as a fundamental feature of colonial political culture. A third is the underlying Gemeinschaft to Gesellschaft model so overused in New England history in which "consensus, harmony, and deference . . . weakened or dissolved into sometimes jarring conflict at both the local and provincial levels among groups competing to promote their interests." Organizationally, then, Conroy's tavern politics reaffirm known parameters. The bedrock of Massachusetts' politics was town and tavern localism. Although the appearance of "court" factions and such issues as gubernatorial patronage and the Land Bank proposal created periodic polarization among provincial politicians that transcended community boundaries, the determining feature of political relationships was their quintessential localism (Conroy, 1995, pp.158, 178, 186, 187, 218, 237, 240, 242).

The third vantage point is Newcomb's own, the middle colonies, but comes from my *Forming American Politics*. Certainly, one of "the outstanding feature[s] of political life in New York and Pennsylvania was . . . the partisan character of their respective political cultures." Yet that partisanship was distinguished by its diversity of expression rather than by the two-party symmetry that Newcomb finds. On the organizational level, for example, New York politicians never achieved more than "intermittent" "intercounty electoral cooperation" and popular government in Pennsylvania was largely a one-party suzerainty throughout the mid-eighteenth-century decades. Beyond that, the sociopolitical and intellectual texture of each colony's politics, including the way in which New Yorkers strove to legitimate contention, and Pennsylvanians a particular notion of party politics, was a more important component of the colonies' respective political cultures than any putative structural similarities to nineteenth-century American party systems (Tully, 1994, pp. 399, 401).

Although the Kolp, Conroy, and Tully volumes are very different in focus and intent, cumulatively they reinforce Newcomb's judgment that, notwithstanding considerations of patriarchy, patronage, hierarchy, clientage, and deference, colonial politics are better understood in terms of such systemic characteristics as regular elections, a significant incidence of voter choice, clustered experiences of electoral competition, various levels of informed (if sometimes ill-formed) public debate, the framing of competing policies and choices, and the ability of voters and constituents to register dissent and voice perceived dangers and needs without a paralyzing fear of retribution. In short, electoral politics did shape the conformation of the evolving colonial political systems. At the same time, there was considerable organizational asymmetry. Among the various mainland British colonies ranging from New England to the South, the most sophisticated in terms of party, or factional organization and identity, were those relatively heterogeneous polities of the mid-Atlantic area. Pennsylvania, New York, and New Jersey were fertile ground for the development of colony-specific intimations, if not expressions, of provincially organized, partisan politics. Further north in Massachusetts, the strength of town government and the community focus of town residents kept many of those provincial organizational tendencies at bay, despite the development of a public sphere consciousness that encouraged provincial mobilization and intermittent identification of common concerns. And in Virginia, a distinctive parochialism, expressed as community-mindedness, resulted in expressions of popular politics that, no matter if articulated in some common idioms of British American politics, sought little outlet in shared provincial rather than idiosyncratic local electoral relationships. Despite shared characteristics and heritage, political organization and the potential for different forms of organization varied considerably among these British North American colonial societies.

Other, more striking slants on the question of the distinctiveness of colonial politics come from the recent work of both Christine A. Desan and Alison Olson on the legislative–constituent relationship. With a fresh legal and constitutional eye, Desan has re-examined the familiar terrain of the colonial legislatures and presented her perspective in an extended essay on "Legislative Adjudication in the Early American Tradition." Based primarily on the test case of New York, but with some exploration of other colonies, Desan agrees with earlier scholars that the eighteenth-century colonial legislatures increasingly retreated from private legal matters. But in appraising the well-known growing financial powers of the assemblies, she spotted a pattern of behavior that others had barely noticed – the consolidation and growth of substantial adjudicative power over public rights and claims. When the assemblies laid hold of the power "to pay off" past debts and then "claimed the power over spending itself," they established much more than a sphere of fiscal competency. "The power to adjudicate the cases of constituents and rights that could not be enforced in courts" brought eighteenth-century assemblymen into close contact, and frequently on a large scale, with their constituents. "The legislatures, not the courts, received individuals with contract claims for services and materials, demands for military pay, salaries, and compensation for the impressment of property, petitions for disability pensions, and a wide range of other claims." Legislative adjudication, then, created a unique form of "political representation" unlike anything experienced in the seventeenth-century colonies, contemporary Britain, or post-revolutionary America (Desan, 1998, pp. 1383, 1384, 1382n).

It is at this point that the content of Olson's article "Eighteenth-Century Colonial Legislatures and their Constituents" becomes relevant. In this comparative study, Olson argues that colonial legislatures emerged as an unprecedented focus of government in the mid-eighteenth century. Whereas local and imperial governments had served the needs of colonials adequately during earlier times, "an array of new issues" unsuited for either arena, systemic change in the character of Anglo-American interest group representation, and the development of unprecedented institutional and leadership competency in the assemblies invited constituents to interact more directly in provincial political forums – not simply as voters in various elections but more regularly through petitions, memorials, and statements of interest. This higher incidence of constituent–legislator contact pushed the assemblies to become more organized. This, in turn, encouraged increased constituent contact. More contact resulted in demands for better means of political communication whether by means of assembly records, pamphlets, or newspapers. That, in turn, increased political awareness which fed political action depending on perceived situation and need (Olson, 1992, p. 550).

The Desan and Olson observations have another important implication for our understanding of colonial politics. One is to make us more aware (or aware again) of the extent to which, by the standards of the time, colonists participated in an expansive and vital political society. This is a theme which others writing on such subjects as petitioning (Tully, 1976; Bailey, 1979), information exchange (Brown, 1989, 1996), the public sphere (Conroy, 1995), and colonial sociability (Shields, 1997) have touched on, but none with the breadth and focus of Desan and Olson. Increasingly aware of the exclusionary features of colonial politics and of the brevity of political events such as election campaigns and legislative sittings, and conscious of the time and space colonists allotted to property, debt, religion, health, family relations, sociability, and a long list of other economic, social, and cultural concerns, many historians have tended to diminish politics. But Desan and Olson point out that politics did not simply accompany but was, indeed, deeply interrelated with social and cultural life. And social and cultural behavior was inextricably bound up with traditional definitions of government and politics. If we add to the Desan/Olson case for the importance of provincial politics some recognition of the ways in which local governmental activities, the services of JPs, sheriffs, various other court officials, poor relief overseers, and loan office commissioners, for example, were also woven onto the fabric of provincial politics at innumerable points, and if we recognize that government itself inhered in the actions, "labor, and goods" not of a bureaucracy but of "its citizens," then we can begin to capture some sense of the centrality of politics in colonial life (Desan, 1998, p. 1445). Translucent at many points, substantial and obvious at others, politics was a prominent part of the changing architecture of colonial society.

A second important feature of the Desan and Olson work consists of their independent testimony to the popular credibility of the colonial legislatures. Olson comes to this conclusion by highlighting the aforementioned systemic response to the increasingly intensive legislator–constituent demands. Despite differences among the colonies, Olson observes an overall tendency for the assemblies to "gather . . . power not only through their successful encounters with . . . colonial governors" but also by means of their "satisfaction of 'popular' demands" (Olson, 1992, pp. 566, 677). Conceptually, Desan moves the argument one step further. By taking on adjudicative powers, the colonial legislatures put themselves to the test of settling questions of right, justice, contract, debt, and public obligation. In so doing they made judgments, based on precepts of "common and commercial law, . . . custom, natural right and fundamental law . . . [and standards] of administrative practice" which were outside the political process yet fundamental to social cohesion. In other words the assemblies held themselves up to the standards of "public faith" "that bound . . . members of . . . [the] political community together." In doing so with reasonable success, in "plac[ing]" themselves "at the center of the province's daily life . . ., [in] mak[ing] . . . [the] determina[tion] . . . [of] rights in individual cases a matter of representation," "and [in] identif[ying] . . . themselves as critically preserving the very peace and integrity of the community," the legislatures generated systemic strength and resilience in the legislative–constituent relationship that factional and party disagreements were hard pressed to corrode (Desan, 1998, pp. 1462, 1463, 1481, 1495).

The third major strength of the Desan and Olson writings is their contribution to what might be called the taming of deference. An inspiration from the pen of J. R. Pole in 1962, deference became an integral part of the republican synthesis in 1976 when J. G. A. Pocock undertook to explain it. "Pure deference" occurred "spontaneously" in a "voluntary acceptance of a leadership elite by persons not belonging to that elite, but sufficiently free as political actors to render deference not only a voluntary but also a political act." Yet that purity was tough to find. In fact, the elites' "property and culture would be recognized by the *demos* as part of the superior natural capacities which the *demos* also recognized." And frequently integrated with time-sanctioned property and culture in the eighteenth century was the type of patronage, clientage, and economic dominance that shaded "pure deference" into "inducement and even coercion." This circumstance, along with both the fact that the "time sanctioned" attributes could not be too deeply rooted in colonies with such short pasts, and that many upper-class colonists (perhaps as a consequence) gave deferential obligations sustained emphasis, helps explain why new left historians could so easily turn to clientage to explain upper-class political dominance and why deference, tied to republicanism's influential version of early America, has had such a long run (Pocock, 1976, pp. 516, 517, 519).

The fundamental problem with deference is one that it shares with hegemony – it cannot be tested. In each case we have an ethereal concept, one which in practice only expresses itself through a series of complicated social, cultural, and political relationships that by their very nature are problematic. How do we isolate "pure deference" in a world of political hustle? Joy and Robert Gilsdorf have devised the best filter anyone has yet come up with to catch deference. And they conclude "that [in Connecticut] simple deference interpretations of elite–voter relations do not apply" (Gilsdorf and Gilsdorf, 1984, p. 242). Others have also expressed skepticism. Michael Zuckerman has recently resorted to life stories to indicate (some say without success) how little social deference there was in early America. The implications for politics are plain

(Zuckerman, 1998). In another recent piece, Richard R. Beeman has directly attacked political deference, demonstrating that in practice the "line between the voluntary and coercive aspects of the patron–client relationship becomes fuzzy." Rather, Beeman argues that "the direction in which the politics of all the colonies was moving was a popular one, . . . the dominant condition [of which was] diversity." While useful in drawing attention to the possible varieties of colonial politics, the designation "popular diversity" is much like Bailyn's chaotic factionalism in its reductionism. Nor does Beeman's emphasis on "interest" as the force behind "active advocacy and assertion by the many" offer us much as a means of understanding what prompted the different provincial systems to hold together (Beeman, 1992, pp. 411, 412, 430).

But Desan and Olson do. It is possible, for example, to ground Beeman's hypothesis of a variety of competitive, interest-driven, political forums on the responsiveness and reputation with regard to the public faith that these two authors suggest. The problem with this formulation, however, is that, if, as Beeman does, we leave out such descriptors as "democracy," "aristocracy," "oligarchy," and "deference," and leave only a ubiquitous "popular . . . diversity" based on constituent satisfaction and receptive leadership, we have not much more than a generalized pre-democratic politics – something akin to, but more varied and less specific than Newcomb's model (Beeman, 1992, p. 412).

A more plausible scenario is one that *Forming American Politics* offers. In both New York and Pennsylvania, despite the intermingling of highly competitive political conflicts, divisive issues, sporadic high voter turnout, the organization of interests, factions and parties, and the espousal of various popular causes, along with some apathy and intermittent quiescence, oligarchic patterns of politics held strong. The explanation of this is that a variety of circumstances in each colony placed the respective oligarchies in situations in which they could be "accessible" to expressed concerns. And given the evidence that Desan and Olson offer on the responsiveness of these provincial politicians and their ability through performance to bring credibility to their respective forums of legislative politics, the case for widespread citizen collusion in a system of oligarchic politics which excludes them from office is certainly strengthened (Tully, 1994).

Another recent example of this kind of reformulation of the underpinnings of colonial politics occurs in Rebecca Starr's recent book on South Carolina, *A School for Politics*. Starr depicts her late colonial legislative politicians as a "commercial, even bourgeois" "cousinage" "founded [on] a genuine social homogeneity" that monopolized all of the observable entitlements to elective office. Yet in her view "the gaps between rulers and ruled" were so "narrow . . . [that] deference [could] . . . not be relied on to legitimate power." The elite, then, had to interact with the broader political community in such a way as to build "unanimity" and "consent" (Starr, 1998, pp. 3, 14, 18, 87). For Starr this accomplishment came not out of the kind of considerations Desan and Olson have entertained but out of the political experience of Anglo-American lobbying. There are certainly those who would argue that Starr has it wrong, that deference played a large part in South Carolina politics. Yet, in his recent study of Virgina, John Kolp gives deference less prominence than one might expect in the kind of gentry-led, locally focused plantation politics that he describes. Perhaps in Massachusetts deference was particularly strong. Robert Zemsky's observation that most of those legislators who rated highly in their Harvard class simply stepped into leadership positions the moment they entered the Massachusetts House of Representatives could easily be construed as an example of Pocock's conjoining of "property and culture" with "capacity." And David Conroy gives a heavy emphasis to deference throughout the transformation he describes. But the point is that overall we now have available enough examples of the construction of credible alternatives to deferential politics that we may question it more closely and begin to develop clearer conceptual understandings of the various dynamics of constituent–representative relations.

If one way to answer the question, what distinguishes colonial politics, is to focus on the processes of government and politics and the structural patterns that define legislative–constituent relations, another is to look more clearly at the interstices of behavior and ideas. For much of the 1960s, 1970s, and 1980s efforts to do this were few and not particularly fruitful, largely because of the overwhelming impact of the major republican writings. Once Bailyn and Pocock's work had appeared the "country" tradition seemed to be everywhere and commanded immediate obeisance and sustained fealty. Even as late as 1992, for example, Richard Beeman's aforementioned article on the "emergence of popular politics" viewed this development as taking place within a generally shared framework of republican ideology. Critics of republicanism such as Joyce Appleby responded with an equally broad liberal ideology (Appleby, 1992). And neo-progressive Gary Nash was far more concerned with establishing the potential sharing of a working-class consciousness in Boston, New York, and Philadelphia in order to take issue with the historiographically ubiquitous upper-class republicanism, than with exploring potential variations in provincial political cultures. This trend was also strongly reinforced by a generation-long distaste for American exceptionalism and concurrent appreciation of the more subtle bouquets of Anglicization and, more recently, British American transatlanticism. Replication of intellectual strands and of the structure of traditional community and class consciousness was the orthodoxy of these decades.

The individual who, by the mid-1980s, best reminded us that there were other ways of approaching colonial politics was Jack P. Greene. In one book, *Pursuits of Happiness* (1988), he brought home something of the particularity of different regions and colonies. This was not a political history, but the richness of the social and cultural differences he pointed out suggested variations in political culture as well. In a second book, *Peripheries and Center* (1986), Greene went on to demonstrate that despite common transatlantic ties and powerful metropolitan paradigms there could be colonial innovation and significant deviation from the well-dredged channels of British thought. This book, too, was not political but rather a constitutional history. Nonetheless it had political implications. If the colonies were capable of such constitutional creativity, could provincial political cultures not take their own route, building of course on the multiple vocabularies and discourses that flourished within the empire and upon their own idiosyncrasies of first settlement and subsequent development?

Two recent monographs have taken this approach, arguing that in order to comprehend the variety of political dynamics within eighteenth-century Anglo-American politics we have to take seriously the interplay of political behavior and belief within specific colonies. *Forming American Politics* (Tully, 1994) does this by means of a comparison of Pennsylvania and New York. In the former case, the experience of Quaker settlement, continuing Quaker leadership, the proprietary form of government, the quest for legislative power, the organization of an accessible oligarchy, the consciousness of various British-generated public languages, and the acceptance of party as a legitimate form of political expression were developed into a discourse deserving the description "civil Quakerism." This cluster of ideas was founded on a deep appreciation of Pennsylvania's unique constitution, liberty of conscience, provincial prosperity, loosely defined pacifism, rejection of a militia, and resistance to the arbitrary powers of the province's proprietors. It is in relationship to the formulation and expression of "civil Quakerism," both in behavioral and linguistic terms, that we can best comprehend the shaping and movement of Pennsylvania's political culture. In New York, the peculiarities of conquest politics, the rivalries born of socioeconomic, geographical, familial, ethnic, and religious differences, the presence of a powerful drive for legislative authority, the existence of a small cadre of outspoken British placemen, the appearance of accessible oligarchs, the articulation of powerful Anglicizing discourses, and the positing of balance among political contenders as a desirable feature of local politics produced a provincial political culture revolving around popular and provincial Whig polarities. Two types of factions established their popular or provincial Whig identities in articulating different perspectives on colonial rights, the institutional and social context of such rights, their appraisal of the chief threats to public order, and their views of what constituted the relevant strands of English country discourses. In the interplay among these factors, we can see the crucial acceptance of balance amid a normalization of political contention which allows us to comprehend something of the tensions and confidences that New York politics brought to the eighteenth-century New World.

In her *School for Politics* (1998), Rebecca Starr proceeds not so much by comparison with other colonies as by a fresh look at provincial interest group lobbying in the empire. In her South Carolina, a united elite of "merchants . . . planters . . . and . . . professionals," understanding the common benefits they could derive from favorable imperial regulations of the rice and indigo trade, recognizing how much theirs was a mutual prosperity, and sharing in the values of "bourgeois sociability," determined the conformation of provincial political culture. To them, "trade and politics were inseparable" but given their commercial orientation they had a deep "aversion . . . [to] speculative . . . politics." The coincidence of "a non-ideological political culture maturing alongside a culture of commerce, inclined the strategy of lobbying to fall naturally, . . . into the context of both" and in politics it became a "familiar, accepted, available, and largely successful means of coping with . . . [public] problems." The ability of the South Carolina political elite to shut out competing interests fostered an "informality" that "ensured . . . [assembly] politics proceeded less competitively than in governments where open rivalry determined leadership and decision-making." The cumulative weight of these interlocking circumstances and experiences developed a "convention," "a behavioral language . . . a germ of constitutional thought in its arrangement, composition and practice" which became culturally internalized. It was colonial lobbying, then, that ultimately produced the "harmonious politics" that distinguished colonial South Carolina and that survived a later "transition . . . to a general politics with a representational character" (Starr, 1998, pp. 3, 14, 15, 19, 22, 25, 38, 41, 90).

Just as the recent writings of Newcomb, Kolp, Conroy, Tully, Desan, Olson, and others affirm the relevance of colonial politics for our comprehension of the dynamics of early American society, so do the aforementioned models of political behavior for New York, Pennsylvania, and South Carolina suggest future possibilities. Each colonial political universe was one of constant negotiation between the heritages of settlement origins, the influx of new peoples, the development of creole identities, the logic of provincial self-assertion, the structuring of electoral politics, the reconceptualing of political boundaries, the course of intercolonial ties, and the intellectual and practical imperatives of the imperial connection. If we take up the challenge to explore these circumstances in the different colonies, if we rethink the relationship between colonial political singularity and trans-colonial, transatlantic commonalities, we will certainly become more knowledgeable of what exactly constituted the early American political plurality. And with that, of course, we will gain a better understanding of the rich relationship of the politics of the colonies to their descendent societies.

BIBLIOGRAPHY

Andrews, Charles M.: *The Colonial Background of the American Revolution* (New Haven, CT: Yale University Press, 1924).

Andrews, Charles M.: *The Colonial Period of American History*, 4 vols (New Haven, CT: Yale University Press, 1934–1938).

Andrews, Charles M.: "On the Writing of Colonial History." *William and Mary Quarterly* 3rd ser., 1 (1944), pp. 27–48.

Appleby, Joyce: *Liberalism and Republicanism in the Historical Imagination* (Cambridge, MA: Harvard University Press, 1992).

Archdeacon, Thomas J.: *New York City, 1664–1710: Conquest and Change* (Ithaca, NY: Cornell University Press, 1976).

Bailey, Raymond C.: *Popular Influence upon Public Policy: Petitioning in Eighteenth Century Virginia* (Westport, CT: Greenwood Press, 1979).

Bailyn, Bernard: *The Ideological Origins of the American Revolution* (Cambridge, MA: Harvard University Press, 1967).

Bailyn, Bernard: *The Origins of American Politics* (New York: Random House, 1968).

Bailyn, Bernard and Clive, John: "England's Cultural Provinces: Scotland and America." *William and Mary Quarterly* 3rd ser., 11 (1954), pp. 200–13.

Bancroft, George: *History of the United States*, 10 vols (Boston, MA: Little, Brown and Company, 1834–74).

Batinski, Michael C.: *The New Jersey Assembly, 1738–1775: The Making of a Legislative Community* (Lanham, MD: University Press of America, 1987).

Becker, Carl L.: *The History of Political Parties in the Province of New York, 1760–1776* (Madison, WI: University of Wisconsin Press, 1909).

Beeman, Richard R.: "Deference, Republicanism, and the Emergence of Popular Politics in Eighteenth-Century America." *William and Mary Quarterly* 3rd ser., 49 (1992), pp. 401–30.

Bonomi, Patricia U.: *A Factious People: Politics and Society in Colonial New York* (New York: Columbia University Press, 1971).

Bonomi, Patricia U.: *Under the Cope of Heaven: Religion, Society, and Politics in Colonial America* (New York: Oxford University Press, 1986).

Brooke, John L.: *The Heart of the Commonwealth: Society and Political Culture in Worcester County, Massachusetts, 1713–1861* (New York: Cambridge University Press, 1989).

Brown, Richard D.: *Knowledge is Power: The Diffusion of Information in Early America, 1700–1865* (New York: Oxford University Press, 1989).

Brown, Richard D.: *The Strength of a People: The Idea of an Informed Citizenry in America, 1650–1870* (Chapel Hill, NC: University of North Carolina Press, 1996).

Brown, Robert E.: *Middle-Class Democracy and the Revolution in Massachusetts, 1691–1780* (Ithaca, NY: Cornell University Press, 1955).

Brown, Robert E. and B. Katherine: *Virginia 1705–1786: Democracy or Aristocracy?* (East Lansing, MI: Michigan State University Press, 1964).

Bushman, Richard L.: *From Puritan to Yankee: Character and Social Order in Connecticut, 1690–1765* (Cambridge, MA: Harvard University Press, 1967).

Bushman, Richard L.: *King and People in Provincial Massachusetts* (Chapel Hill, NC: University of North Carolina Press, 1985).

Clark, J. C. D.: *English Society, 1688–1832* (Cambridge: Cambridge University Press, 1985).

Conroy, David W.: *The Public Houses: Drink and the Revolution of Authority in Colonial Massachusetts* (Chapel Hill, NC: University of North Carolina Press, 1995).

Cook, Edward M., Jr.: *The Fathers of the Towns: Leadership and Community Structure in Eighteenth-Century New England* (Baltimore, MD: The Johns Hopkins University Press, 1976).

Countryman, Edward: *A People In Revolution: The American Revolution and Political Society in New York, 1760–1790* (Baltimore, MD: The Johns Hopkins University Press, 1981).

Desan, Christine A.: "The Constitutional Commitment to Legislative Adjudication in the Early American Tradition." *Harvard Law Review* 111 (1998), pp. 1381–503.

Dinkin, Robert J.: *Voting in Provincial America: A Study of Elections in the Thirteen Colonies, 1689–1776* (Westport, CT: Greenwood Press, 1977).

Gilsdorf, Joy B and Robert R.: "Elites and Electorates: Some Plain Truths for Historians of Colonial America." In David D. Hall, John M. Murrin, and Thad W. Tate, eds., *Saints and Revolutionaries: Essays on Early American History* (New York: W. W. Norton, 1984), pp. 207–44.

Greene, Jack P.: *The Quest for Power: The Lower Houses of Assembly in the Southern Royal Colonies, 1689–1776* (Chapel Hill, NC: University of North Carolina Press, 1963).

Greene, Jack P.: *Peripheries and Center: Constitutional Development in the Extended Polities of the British Empire and the United States, 1607–1788* (Athens, GA: University of Georgia Press, 1986).

Greene, Jack P.: *Pursuits of Happiness: The Social Development of Early Modern British Colonies and the Formation of American Culture* (Chapel Hill, NC: University of North Carolina Press, 1988).

Greene, Jack P.: *Imperatives, Behaviors, and Identities: Essays in Early American Cultural History* (Charlottesville, VA: University Press of Virginia, 1992).

Greene, Jack P.: *Negotiated Authorities: Essays in Colonial Political and Constitutional History* (Charlottesville, VA: University Press of Virginia, 1994).

Greene, Jack P.: *Interpreting Early America: Historiographical Essays* (Charlottesville, VA: University Press of Virginia, 1996).

Greene, Jack P. and Pole, J. R., eds.: *Colonial British America: Essays in the New History of the Early Modern Era* (Baltimore, MD: The Johns Hopkins University Press, 1984).

Kolp, John G.: *Gentlemen Freeholders: Electoral Politics in Colonial Virginia* (Baltimore, MD: The Johns Hopkins University Press, 1998).

Lemisch, Jesse: "The American Revolution Seen from the Bottom Up." In Barton J. Bernstein, ed., *Towards a New Past: Dissenting Essays in American History* (New York: Random House, 1967), pp. 3–45.

Lemisch, Jesse: "Jack Tar in the Streets: Merchant Seamen in the Politics of Revolutionary America." *William and Mary Quarterly* 3rd ser., 25 (1968), 371–407.

Lincoln, Charles H.: *The Revolutionary Movement in Pennsylvania, 1760–1776* (Philadelphia: University of Pennsylvania, 1901).

Lockridge, Kenneth A.: *A New England Town: The First Hundred Years* (New York: W. W. Norton, 1970).

Maier, Pauline, "Popular Uprisings and Civil Authority in Eighteenth-Century America." *William and Mary Quarterly* 3rd. ser., 27 (1970), pp. 3–35.

Main, Jackson Turner: *The Social Structure of Revolutionary America* (Princeton, NJ: Princeton University Press, 1965).

Murrin, John M.: "The Myths of Colonial Democracy and Royal Decline in Eighteenth Century America: A Review Essay." *Cithara* 5 (1965), pp. 53–69.

Murrin, John M.: "Anglicizing an American Colony: The Transformation of Provincial Massachusetts" (Ph.D. dissertation, Yale University, 1966).

Murrin, John M.: "Political Development." In Greene and Pole, eds., *Colonial British America* (1984), pp. 408–56.

Murrin, John M.: "English Rights as Ethnic Aggression: The English Conquest, the Charter of Liberties of 1683, and Leisler's Rebellion in New York." In William Pencak and Conrad Edick Wright, eds., *Authority and Resistance in Early New York* (New York: New York Historical Society, 1988), pp. 56–94.

Murrin, John M. and Berthoff, Rowland: "Feudalism, Communalism, and the Yeoman Freeholder: The American Revolution Considered as a Social Accident." In Stephen G. Kurtz and James H. Hutson, eds., *Essays on the American Revolution* (Chapel Hill, NC: University of North Carolina Press, 1973), pp. 256–288.

Namier, Sir Lewis: *The Structure of Politics at the Accession of George III* (London: Macmillan and Company, 1929).

Nash, Gary B.: *Quakers and Politics: Pennsylvania, 1691–1726* (Princeton, NJ: Princeton University Press, 1968).

Nash, Gary B.: *The Urban Crucible: Social Change, Political Consciousness, and the Origins of the American Revolution* (Cambridge, MA: Harvard University Press, 1979).

Newcomb, Benjamin H.: *Franklin and Galloway: A Political Partnership* (New Haven, CT: Yale University Press, 1972).

Newcomb, Benjamin H.: *Political Partisanship in the American Middle Colonies, 1700–1776* (Baton Rouge, LA: Louisiana State University Press, 1995).

Olson, Alison G.: "Eighteenth-Century Colonial Legislatures and their Constituents." *Journal of American History* 79 (1992), pp. 543–67.

Osgood, Herbert L.: *American Colonies in the Seventeenth Century*, 3 vols (New York: The Macmillan Company, 1904–7).

Osgood, Herbert L.: *The American Colonies in the Eighteenth Century*, 4 vols (New York: Columbia University Press, 1924).

Pencak, William: *War, Politics and Revolution in Provincial Massachusetts* (Boston, MA: Northeastern University Press, 1981).

Plumb, J. H.: *The Growth of Political Stability in England, 1675–1725* (London: Macmillan and Company, 1967).

Pocock, J. G. A.: *The Machiavellian Moment: Florentine Political Thought and the Atlantic Republican Tradition* (Princeton, NJ: Princeton University Press, 1975).

Pocock, J. G. A.: "The Classical Theory of Deference." *American Historical Review* 81 (1976), pp. 516–23.

Pole, J. R.: "Historians and the Problem of Early American Democracy." *American Historical Review* 67 (1962), pp. 626–46.

Pole, J. R.: *Political Representation in England and the Origins of the American Republic* (London: Macmillan and Company, 1966).

Purvis, Thomas L.: *Proprietors, Patronage, and Paper Money: Legislative Politics in New Jersey, 1703–1776* (New Brunswick: Rutgers University Press, 1986).

Rodgers, Daniel T.: "Republicanism: The Career of a Concept." *Journal of American History* 79 (1992), pp. 11–38.

Roeber, A. G.: *Palatines, Liberty, and Property: German Lutherans in Colonial British America* (Baltimore, MD: The Johns Hopkins University Press, 1993).

Shields, David S.: *Civil Tongues and Polite Letters in British America* (Chapel Hill, NC: University of North Carolina Press, 1997).

Starr, Rebecca: *A School for Politics: Commercial Lobbying and Political Culture in Early South Carolina* (Baltimore, MD: The Johns Hopkins University Press, 1998).

Sydnor, Charles S.: *Gentlemen Freeholders: Political Practices in Washington's Virginia* (Chapel Hill, NC: University of North Carolina Press, 1952).

Thompson, E. P.: *The Making of the English Working Class* (London: Victor Gollancz, 1963).

Thompson, E. P.: "The Moral Economy of the English Crowd in the Eighteenth Century." *Past and Present* 50 (1971), pp. 76–136.

Thompson, E. P.: "Patrician Society, Plebeian Culture." *Journal of Social History* 7 (1974), pp. 382–405.

Tully, Alan: "Constituent–Representative Relationships in Early America: The Case of Pre-Revolutionary Pennsylvania." *Canadian Journal of History* 11 (1976), pp. 139–54.

Tully, Alan: *William Penn's Legacy: Politics and Social Structure in Provincial Pennsylvania, 1726–1755* (Baltimore, MD: The Johns Hopkins University Press, 1977).

Tully, Alan: "Ethnicity, Religion, and Politics in Early America." *Pennsylvania Magazine of History and Biography* 107 (1983), pp. 491–536.

Tully, Alan: *Forming American Politics: Ideals, Interests, and Institutions in Colonial New York and Pennsylvania* (Baltimore, MD: The Johns Hopkins University Press, 1994).

Weir, Robert: "'The Harmony We Were Famous For': An Interpretation of Pre-Revolutionary South Carolina Politics." *William and Mary Quarterly* 3rd ser., 26 (1969), pp. 473–501.

Wood, Gordon S.: *The Radicalism of the American Revolution* (New York: Alfred A. Knopf, 1992).

Young, Alfred F.: *The American Revolution: Explorations in the History of American Radicalism* (DeKalb, IL: Northern Illinois University Press, 1976).

Zemsky, Robert: *Merchants, Farmers. and River Gods: An Essay on Eighteenth-Century American Politics* (Boston, MA: Gambit, 1971).

Zuckerman, Michael: "The Social Context of Democracy in Massachusetts." *William and Mary Quarterly* 3rd ser., 25 (1968), pp. 523–44.

Zuckerman, Michael: *Peaceable Kingdoms: New England Towns in the Eighteenth Century* (New York: Alfred A. Knopf, 1970).

Zuckerman, Michael: "Tocqueville, Turner, and Turds: Four Stories of Manners in Early America." *Journal of American History* 85 (1998), pp. 13–42.

Chapter Thirteen

Regionalism

Michael Zuckerman

Not so very long ago, scholars of early American history spoke with assurance of early America. They took for granted that they were engaged in an integrative enterprise. But now they do nothing of the sort. In recent years, the study of early America has been transformed from a unified endeavor to a fractured thing. A regional paradigm that scarcely existed when I was a student has acquired an absolute primacy in the past decade or two.

I have scarcely seen a graduate student reading list in the past fifteen years that was not organized by regions. Some lists acknowledge the backcountry; some do not. Some include the Caribbean; some do not. Some generalize the South; some particularize the Chesapeake and the Lower South. Some start with Europe, or with Native Americans. But all encompass the better part of the colonial epoch in three or four or five or six geographically defined units. None attempt anything integrative before the Revolution.

When I was a graduate student in the early 1960s, by contrast, everyone assumed that the colonial era could be conceived homogeneously. Without a qualm, we pronounced the inconsequential caveat "except the South" as a cover for getting on with studying America as an undifferentiated whole or as the North writ large.

Lest this invocation of olden days be dismissed as the figment of a fading memory, look at standard texts of the 1950s and 1960s. In Max Savelle's *Seeds of Liberty* (1948), for example, region plays no part at all in the design. Every chapter treats the colonists as men engaged in a common conversation, and the chapters on "Economic Thought," "Social Thought," and "Political Thought" all begin with sections on "The Old Way, in Europe and America" and on "The American Way." In Savelle's more sweeping survey, *Foundations of American Civilization* (1942), region is equally absent. A multitude of chapters discuss individual colonies, one by one, and these discussions are followed by integrative chapters on such subjects as "The Colonial Constitution," "The Expansion of the Colonial Economy," and "The Mind of Provincial America."

For that matter, look at the texts of the 1970s. In James Henretta's *Evolution of American Society* (1973), a young man schooled in the 1960s structured his work under headings such as "The Process of Economic Development," "The Social Synthesis," and "The Crisis of American Colonial Society." In Darrett Rutman's *Morning of America* (1971), the most ornery and iconoclastic of early Americanists organized his interpretation under titles such as "The Colonies in a Mercantile World," "The Colonial Milieu," and "Government and Politics," and under subtitles such as "The America of the Mind," "The Origins of Self-Government," and "The Political climate of the Eighteenth Century." Not a one of his eight chapters or twenty-eight subheadings differentiated the colonies regionally or in any other way.

In the past twenty years, all that has changed. Almost every one of the significant surveys of the country's colonial origins has abandoned the blithe assumption that scholars and students can speak undifferentiatedly of "the mind" of "Provincial America" or of "American Colonial Society." Almost all of them have embraced a regional perspective in their reconnaissances of early America.

Ironically, the earliest impetus to this transformation of historical reckoning came from the community studies of early New England. Almost without exception, those works of "new" social history perpetuated old presumptions of holism. Almost to a man, the "new social historians" of colonial New England took for granted that, in examining this locale or that, they were looking at specimens of America, much as nurses take for granted that, in drawing blood from this finger or that, they are securing a good sample on which technicians can run tests.

The colonial historians who came after the New Englanders made no such assumptions. On the contrary, they were often adamant about regional exceptionalism and sometimes touchy about regional primacy. A new generation of Chesapeake historians proudly proclaimed the inapplicability of the new New England social history to their own endeavor. The Philadelphia Center for Early American Studies explicitly confined its coveted fellowships to students working on the Philadelphia region or at least on the middle Atlantic. And after a period of a sort of shell-shock, students of New England resumed their researches, chastened, under the aegis of the new regionalism.

In the last dozen years, the transformation that turned up first in journal articles and graduate student reading lists made its way into books. Appearing almost year by year, one after another, a succession of synoptic works by senior scholars consolidated and legitimated regional ways of looking at early America.

Meinig's *Atlantic America* (1986) was probably the first major work to provide a partitioned model of colonial life. It was followed by Bailyn's *The Peopling of British North America* (1986), Greene's *Pursuits of Happiness* (1988), Fischer's *Albion's Seed* (1989), and then by Egnal's *Divergent Paths* (1996) and Engerman and Gallman's *Cambridge Economic History of the United States* (1996). It mattered less that each one of these integrative efforts drew its regional divisions differently than that every one of them gave up the older postulate of a solidary American people with a shared culture. It mattered most, perhaps, that the recourse to region as an organizing principle appeared not only in analyses like Fischer's, which evinced almost no concern for pervasive American themes, but also in accounts like Greene's and Bailyn's, which advanced larger hypotheses and did not have to depend on region as their central expository device.

The questions teem and tease and tantalize. Why has this seismic shift occurred, and what does it signify? What impels the rush to regional renderings of early America? What does this unprecedented pluralization of our past – indeed, of our very origins – tell us about the way life was in the seventeenth and eighteenth centuries and the way we think of that life today?

For much of the twentieth century, colonial history served as a refuge for old-stock Americans. It was studied and supported as an anglophilic foil for twentieth-century pluralism. In a nation increasingly contaminated, as the descendants of the earlier invaders believed, by invasion from the wrong parts of Europe, it enabled the children of the older immigrants to claim one part – one crucial part – of the country's history as uniquely their own. The story of American settlement would be an Anglo-Saxon story. The values of the founding would define the authentic ideals of the nation. And since those ideals affirmed national unity under the hegemony of the North, regional differentiation would have no real place in the story.

Since colonial history came to consequence in an era when elites sought to reconcile recently warring sections and to resist recently arriving newcomers, New England and Virginia would be set at the center of the narrative. New England, the one corner of the colonies that was in fact as English as the Yankee gentry fancied, would be celebrated as the purest distillation of genuine Americanism, especially in its Boston hearth where the Brahmins clung rabidly to their anti-Irish and anti-Catholic obsessions. New York and Pennsylvania would be extruded almost totally from the tale.

Since the 1960s, however, new idealizations of America have arisen. Nostalgic norms of a racially and ethnically homogeneous America no longer prevail unproblematically. And as the elites who crave an English imprimatur are increasingly challenged by others who cast about for more pluralistic ways of understanding our origins as a people, we reach for accounts that can accommodate regional variation.

Take the most recent comprehensive canvas of early American history, Greene and Pole's *Colonial British America* (1984). In their introduction to the volume, the editors admit the "paradoxical result" of the remarkable "reinvigoration" of early American history in the years since the 1960s. Impressive advances have produced "a severe case of intellectual indigestion." Recent research has rendered the traditional themes of colonial history "obsolete" but put nothing in their place. We have suffered a "signal loss of overall coherence." We are now "less clear than ever before about precisely what the central themes and the larger questions are in the field as a whole" (Greene and Pole, 1984, pp. 4, 7).

Worse, we have no inclination to come to clarity. Worried that the study of early American history both flourishes and flounders, Greene and Pole urged their fourteen contributors, senior scholars every one, to write about the "*general* themes" that "might help to structure studies [of] the field . . . in general." None did. None of these leading academic authorities were able to generalize across the colonies, even when they were explicitly instructed – or begged – to do so. Worse still, as Pole admitted, their failure even to attempt such generalization was "scarcely surprising" (1984, pp. 9, 10).

Despite the reluctance of their contributors to venture any synthesis at all, Greene and Pole did suggest that the "most essential features" of "a new, more inclusive framework" were already evident. It would, they said, "be based upon recognition that colonial British-America comprised several distinctive socioeconomic regions that transcended political boundaries." The editors seemed not to appreciate the paradox. Any "inclusive framework" would have to rest on the premise that there is *no* inclusive framework, only an unsettled number of "distinctive" regions. And yet they seemed not to doubt that they were right. Their premise was not just a matter of judgment or intuition. It was "indisputably clear." A conception of the colonies as congeries of disparate regional cultures was, and still is, the unchallenged orthodoxy of recent historical writing (1984, p. 11).

* * * * *

What are we to make of this extraordinary about-face? And of this odd if not incoherent consensus?

Certainly we could say that it is long overdue. As Justice Felix Frankfurter said half a century ago, regionalism is no abstruse academic affair. From the first, regional divergences in patterns of religion and residence, work and wealth, shaped the great conflicts that have come before the highest court in the land. Regionalism is, in that regard, "a recognition of the intractable diversities among men, diversities partly shaped by nature but no less derived from the different reactions of men to nature" (Frankfurter, 1951, p. xvi).

But exactly insofar as Frankfurter was right, his insistence on the rootedness of so many of our profoundest social contests in our "intractable diversities" of geography cannot explain the transformation of recent historiography. If regions have *always* mattered, the fact that they matter cannot account for our sudden discovery of their importance.

In any case, whether they matter mightily or not is quite beside a crucial part of the point. For, as Trevor Barnes and James Duncan remind us, the purpose of mapping is not mimetic. Our maps do not "mirror in summary form an objective world" beyond themselves. Rather, they "communicate ideas within a cultural and political context." Our new regional renderings of early American history speak of our present condition as well as of past conditions (Barnes and Duncan, 1992, p. xii).

What, then, does the emergence of this regional way of approaching our formative era tell us about contemporary American historians? If we take the turn to regional conceptualizations of our origins as a way of thinking about American life in our own time, what do we make of it? What forces are at work among us, politically and culturally, to propel this unprecedented pluralization of our past?

And, more poignantly, where does our acquiescence in such regional representations of our beginnings leave us? Does it preclude the recovery of a coherent America? Does it entail our acceptance of Humpty Dumpty as the inescapable emblem of early American history?

★ ★ ★ ★ ★

A paradox seems inescapable. Regions come to grander consequence in our historiography as they come to count less in our lives. We insist the more ardently on the distinctions between them in our first centuries as those distinctions diminish and even disappear in our own day.

Ineluctably, the tides of nationalization roll in. The transcontinental franchisers and fast food chains. The malls, the theme parks, and the convention centers. Each in its own way, they impose their unprecedented uniformity on the places we travel to and the very roads we travel on. The wonder of the American highway in the first half of the twentieth century was macadamization. In the second half of the century, it is homogenization. Do we dwell on regional differences, as Robin Winks once wryly suggested, because our infatuation with movement requires it? Do we deny what lies so plainly before our eyes, the vastness of our similarities, because our incessant movement would lose its meaning if we admitted to ourselves that there are no differences at our destinations (Winks, 1983, pp. 13–14)?

Ineluctably too, the tides of globalization roll in. Titanic transnational corporations reconfigure the landscape of international capitalism. "Role reversals of regions" become commonplace. Once-prosperous subnational regions such as the Northeast in the United States experience de-industrialization and economic decline. Once-poor peripheral regions such as the South take the lead in economic expansion. Can any region on the planet any longer determine its own destiny? Is any but a piece to be moved almost at will, by players from afar, in a game where traditional identities count for little, or for nothing at all (Soja, 1989, p. 172)?

But these nationalizing tides have been rolling for at least a century and a half, and the internationalizing ones at least since World War II. We have had national networks of transportation and communication, interstate commerce, mass production and mass consumption, and their attendant pressures toward the standardization of tastes and ideals for generations. We have had the multinationals and the havoc they wreak on established alignments for decades. There is nothing unique to very recent years, in these regards, that can explain the very recent turn to regional accounts of our antecedents as a people.

Or perhaps there is. Though the structures of modern life have not changed in any essential way in the past ten or twenty years, our attitude toward them has changed considerably. Even those who are not ardent adherents of the countercultural challenge of the 1960s have absorbed more of its outlook than they may know. Even those who are not passionate proponents of the epistemological challenge of postmodernism have imbibed more of its assumptions than they may be aware.

The past looks different now, to students of early America, because the present looks different now. As Irmina Wawrzyczek has argued, American historians have almost all accepted a "multiplication of subjects and stories" that dooms the old master narratives of nationalism. Indeed, by embracing such multiplicity, they have "aligned their discipline willy-nilly with postmodernism, with its philosophical postulate of openness and with its politics of the recognition of difference" (1997, p. 24).

No American historians took to these transformations as avidly as colonial historians did. Their period lent itself to a de-centered, multi-vocal view of the past as no other era did. The absence of political integration that had so long seemed a problem seemed, in the new perspective, an opportunity.

Colonialists seized that opportunity. Because they had never quite participated in the profession's nationalizing project, they had the least to lose in the turn from political to social history, and the most to gain in the shifts from the elite to the popular, from the white to the multiracial, and from the general to the local.

The recognition of regional heterogeneity that proved so corrosive for historians of the nation was actually integrative for chroniclers of the colonies. It carried them to the highest levels of generality they could credibly sustain. It afforded them at once an ideological vantage from which to challenge conventional wisdom and an aggregative conceptualization within which to challenge their own ingenuity.

★★★★★

If the regional readings that now shape our conception of the colonial experience are profoundly postmodern, another paradox besets us. For the recourse to region is also, and perhaps even more profoundly, anti-modern.

Regions are more than geographical realities. They are also, in David Lowenthal's evocative phrase, elements of our "geography of the mind." They afford us orientation. They enable us to compare our experience of the world with images of other and perhaps better worlds. In their inevitable duality, they provide us both a sense of the center of our existence and ideas of alternatives to that center (Lowenthal, 1976, p. 3).

In our own time, regions provide us alternatives to the imperious pressures of standardization that flatten our lives. By their very persistence in the face of vaster political, economic, and technological forces, regions nourish our yearning for reassurance that we may yet preserve our individuality against the totalizing logic of modern life.

Nationalism, the market, and technology all promote uniformity, in the facts of our lives and in the fictions by which we live. As D. W. Meinig says, they "pressure toward conformity and depress diversity." Regionalism implies a very different reality and a very different imaginary. Again as Meinig says, it is "grounded more directly in family and community life." It works routinely "to sustain local patterns of culture" and thus "to maintain diversity within the whole" (1986, pp. 452–53).

In that endeavor, regionalism is an extension of and framework for the old "new social history." It too seeks to get down to ground level. It too tries to touch real lives, as the lofty national histories never did. As Anthony Giddens observes, regional representations by their nature differentiate the whole, "counter-balancing the assumption that societies are always homogeneous, unified systems" (1984, p. 376).

It is no accident that, in Europe as well as in America, the deepest and most enduring regional formations were rooted in "resistance to the homogenization of cultural traditions" that is the hallmark of modernity. Nineteenth-century regionalism arose, as Edward Soja reminds us, to defend distinctive local lifeways against the impositions of "expansive market integration and the equally expansive national state" (1989, pp. 172–3, 165).

In Europe, areas such as Flanders, the Italian Mezzogiorno, Bavaria, Silesia, and a number of other "internal colonies" came to regional consciousness in their struggle to avoid absorption in the consolidating commercial capitalism of the age (Soja, 1989, pp. 164–5). In the United States, New England and the South also came to regional consciousness in the nineteenth century as they never had before, in an effort to preserve peculiar habits and institutions from the consolidating cultural imperialism of the age (Pierson, 1955).

Everywhere in the West, extra-local forces acted to subvert the cultural specificity of smaller communities. And everywhere in the West, regional reactions appeared. Their provincialism might be decried by those who presumed themselves responsible for the modernization of the realm, but their success was as palpable as it was implausible. Regional feelings did not in fact fade and vanish. Regional symbols, myths, and metaphors survived. More than that, they thrived, in societies shaped by the centralizing bureaucracies of European states and American corporations and even in societies shaped by the centralizing bureaucracy of the supranational government of the former Soviet Union (Reed, 1974).

Regional consciousness has waxed and waned over the course of the twentieth century. It was relatively strong in the 1920s and 1930s, relatively weak in the 1950s and 1960s. But despite incessant anticipations of its imminent demise, it has never disappeared. It has simply changed with the changing times, to serve shifting audiences and shifting ends.

Earlier in this century, its exponents sought reforms that would relieve the oppression of the provinces, especially in the South and the West. Now, its adherents evince minimal interest in structural reform. Their motives are more personal. They seek their own identity, and they sense that regions which can check the homogenizing power of the state and the market may be crucial to the defense of such individual identity (Brown, 1983, p. 61).

Indeed, in an era of expressive individuality, regionalism may become more than merely defensive. In very recent years, as Richard M. Brown points out, "the national myth of America is in decline, while the regional myths live on." Battalions of books drive home the discrepancies "between the national myth and the national reality," while few debunk the mythological pretensions of the regions (1983, p. 63).

Brown goes so far as to conjecture that "regionalism will not only rival but actually surpass nationalism" as a source of meaning in men's and women's lives (1983, pp. 63–4). That may be as may be, but it is certainly not preposterous. We are more diffident than we have been in generations about postulating an American essence and about finding our own finest qualities in it. The quest for national synthesis seems oddly old-fashioned. In truth, it has been by and large abandoned. In the waning days of an exhausted millennium, we seem incorrigibly chaotic, and we grow ever more implacably pluralistic and privatistic. We have no prospect of integration. Our regional representations suit us.

*****

If a regional perspective embodies our wistful quest for personal identity amid technological and economic forces that occlude it, another paradox appears. For the very regionalism that provides protection against the immense aggregations of modernity is necessarily expressive of imposed homogeneity.

By its nature, region is at once a de-centering idea and an integrating one. Relative to the nation, it affirms a persisting diversity. In itself, it inevitably denies such diversity.

To speak, say, of the South is to discount a myriad of differences between lowcountry and upcountry, white and black, and rich and poor that inscribe divergent and even antagonistic economies, ambitions, politics, and ideals on the landscape. To speak, similarly, of New England is to ignore the variations that led one scholar to distinguish fourteen "regions" in the English-speaking settlements of that area in the seventeenth century alone, each of them with its own "look and feel" and each with an agricultural praxis, a social system, or an ideological frame that set it apart from the others (Nissenbaum, 1996, pp. 41–2).

The notion of a region is every bit as essentializing or totalizing as the notion of a nation, even as the notion of a region riddles essentializing or totalizing notions of a nation.

We are always at liberty, logically, to lump or to split. Martyn Bowden (1994) argues with sophistication that, despite its Puritanism, early New England was never a coherent region. James Lemon (1972) insists with equal sophistication that, despite its ethnic and sectarian divisions and its topographic irregularities, early Pennsylvania was.

Even those who cling to a regional conception in one context show themselves ready to relinquish it in another. The colonial (or subsequent) South seems a region so long as it is compared with areas north of Mason and Dixon's line. It seems far less urgent to delineate its differences from New England or the middle Atlantic when the frame of reference is Russia, or Brazil, or even England.

In an intriguing analysis of early North America, Marc Egnal holds that the southern and the northern colonies of England and the Canadian colonies of France constituted three distinct regions. But the niceties of his tripartite interpretation soon prove unnecessary. Once past slavery, his distinctions between the English colonies dissolve. On his own account of their ownership and use of land, southern and northern colonists alike established freehold tenures very different from the "seigneurial system" of New France. On his account of their religiosity, all the English settlements instituted a pluralistic Protestantism utterly at odds with the hegemonic Catholicism of the French outposts (Egnal, 1996, chs. 3, 4). As Malcolm X said in another context, the South was "anywhere south of the Canadian border" (Egerton, 1974, epigraph).

Much depends on our frame of reference. And just as much depends on what we seek as on what we see, on how we start as on how we proceed.

If we would understand the assumptions that underlie current colonial history, we must understand the anthropological concept of culture. Or rather, we must understand the concept of culture that was prevalent when the historians who have shaped recent regional reckoning of that history were young. For that concept predicates an animating lifeway of a people – a set of "deep structures and durable patterns" – which resembles remarkably the notion of region by which we now map early America (Ayers and Onuf, 1996, p. 7).

Newer concepts of culture that are emerging among historians and anthropologists alike allow for more creativity, complexity, and contestation than the older one ever did. They accommodate more voices and more values than the older one could contain, and they assume more fragmentation and indeterminacy than it could even imagine.

The older concept was inherently holistic. It took for granted that the elements of a culture hung together – indeed, it defined them as a culture because they hung together – and it took for its task the discovery of the deep design of that unity. Its paradigm was the plural "patterns of culture" set forth so suggestively by Ruth Benedict, and its metaphors were generally organic and biological (Benedict, 1934).

The recent usage of region is analogous to the older usage of culture. Each region is driven by its own dynamic, bound by its own logic, organized by its own principles of connectedness. Each is set apart from each other by the very integrity of its own special impulsion.

This conflation of culture and region pervades present-day colonial history, but we can see it in its starkest, most adamant expression in David Hackett Fischer's *Albion's Seed* (1989). Fischer is as unabashed as he is ingenious in his insistence that his four regional configurations each had its own way of life, from its "foodways" to its "freedomways." Bearing the impress of its origins – its "seed" – each had its own distinctive dialect, its own vernacular architecture, its own attitudes toward gender and sexuality, its own ideas about raising children, its own beliefs about age and death, its own standards of work and play, and its own rituals of religion. Each was "a coherent and comprehensive whole."

Anthropologists never could put the cultures that they studied together. Those cultures shared the planet, to be sure. Some of them even traded with or borrowed from some others of them. But, by definition, they could not be assimilated into one overarching and inclusive analytic. In much the same way, Fischer cannot bring his four cultural constellations under any common theorization. They share the English corner of the continent, but that is all. They do not exhibit an American "mind" or constitute an American "tradition." In many ways they are, each in its own way, more like England than like each other.

And much of the most ambitious modern work in early American history is a lot like Fischer's. Kathleen Brown (1996) integrates race, class, and gender in Virginia. Joyce Chaplin (1993) weaves technology, economy, and ideas together in Carolina. Barry Levy (1988) links religion, family, and economy in Pennsylvania. All of them, and a multitude of others, find filaments that reveal their regions to us as none had managed to do before. All of them advance interpretations that make unprecedented sense of the Chesapeake, or the Lowcountry, or the Delaware Valley, but none of them advance interpretations that make sense of America. The very specificity of their syntheses makes more general synthesis the more difficult. The very particularity of their ethnographic rendering of their peculiar regions precludes all possibility of taking one or another of them as a touchstone for the nation.

Thus the triumph of the regional reconstruction of early American history turns out to be even more reactionary, even more resistant to modernity, than was obvious from the first. Because it is founded on a concept of culture very nearly as totalizing as the nationalism and internationalism against which it sets itself, it ends in ineluctable homogeneities of its own. It cannot, finally, embody the diversity that those who deploy it desire.

In truth, it can only produce new problems. Appreciation of regional disparities costs us our confidence in America as a coherent country. And appreciation of regions themselves as quasi-cultures deprives us of one of the means by which we once acquired such confidence. Our conception of regions as coherent cultures disallows the interpretive self-indulgence that enabled the imagination of a nation. A historiography that encouraged the plucking piecemeal of a court case here and a rebellion there, a charter provision here and a proclamation there, was wondrously convenient for those who sought by such *bricolage* to assemble an "American" tradition. A historiography that confines the significance of each attribute and episode within each self-contained region precludes the selectivity by which we created a heritage.

★ ★ ★ ★ ★

If our conception of regions is outmodedly anthropological – if it depends on deep consistencies and continuities that mark a coherent culture – then yet another paradox appears. For every effort to define a region on such terms entails the definitional dissolution of that region.

Holistic cultural definitions ascribe master patterns to entire populations. But no such patterns ever pertain to entire populations. The very predication of a cultural core or essence of a region excludes people who do not fit the predication, though they live within the geographical limits of the region. At the same time, the delineation of that cultural core blurs the very boundaries of the region, since others beyond those bounds always exhibit aspects of the imputed pattern.

The dilemmas of regional definition are, then, insoluble. Even today, with the vast resources of modern market research at our disposal, we cannot specify regions with the precision and sweep that the culture concept premises. As Joel Garreau notes, cultural geographers have mapped "the physical locations of vodka drinkers, Muslims,

Notre Dame football fans, long-distance telephone users, blue-grass-music enthusiasts, stock-car racers, high-rolling gamblers . . . anything you can imagine," but the maps do not map onto one another. The set of them, taken together, is "so complex and ambiguous" that it yields no real convergences at all. Indeed, it suggests that, "John Donne notwithstanding, every man *is* an island" (1981, p. xii).

In the seventeenth and eighteenth centuries, the variation was not nearly so vast, but it was daunting enough. No observer divided the British settlements as any other did. Commentators exhibited an intuitive awareness that colonies could be grouped in regional constellations. As soon as they advanced beyond such shared intuition, they exposed dramatic disagreements. In 1764–5, Fenning and Collyer put forth *A New System of Geography*. They divided Britain's possessions in America into northern, middle, and southern sectors, even as some scholars do to this day. But for them "the northern part" was confined to Hudson's Bay, Newfoundland, and Cape Breton. The middle part ran clear from the St. Lawrence to the Potomac, comprehending all the colonies from Canada and Nova Scotia through New England, New York, and Pennsylvania to Maryland. "The southern part" excluded half the Chesapeake but did encompass Virginia, the Carolinas, Georgia, and Florida (Mood, 1951, pp. 10–11).

Imperial administrators did not divide the colonies as imperial geographers did. Thomas Pownall, writing at the very same time as Fenning and Collyer, envisioned a system of appeals courts for the mainland colonies that also broke them into three parts. But Pownall's plan ignored Fenning and Collyer's northern part altogether. He divided their middle part into two separate circuits – one for Nova Scotia and New England, the other for New York, New Jersey, Pennsylvania, and Maryland – and took their southern part for his southern circuit (Mood, 1951, pp. 15–16).

Agriculturists did not reckon regions as either geographers or administrators did. In 1775 the anonymous author of *American Husbandry* proposed a scheme of five regions rather than three. He split Fenning and Collyer's northern part into two distinct regions, Hudson's Bay country and the Newfoundland fisheries. He crimped their middle part a little and denied it middling status altogether, aggregating the colonies that sprawled from Canada to Pennsylvania into a single region united by its lack of a staple crop, its pursuit of "common husbandry," and its "numerous and large" towns. He reserved the tag of middle, "medium," or "central" to "the tobacco colonies" of Maryland and Virginia, which had both a climate and a "situation" between the northern and southern spheres. And he called the remaining continental colonies, which subsequent scholars would sometimes call the Deep South, the "southern" region (Mood, 1951, pp. 11–13).

American political leaders did not embrace any of these regional schemes, but they did not concur on any other, either. In the Constitutional Convention of 1787, Alexander Hamilton and George Mason presumed that "distinctions of eastern, middle, and southern" would "come into view," but James Madison disdained their tripartite divisions. He held that the relevant regions were but two: "the great southern and northern interests of the continent" (Mood, 1951, p. 29).

The best representations of the maps of America in the minds of the new nation's Founding Fathers were the laws that created the early republic's circuit courts. But those enactments only testified to the instability of their apprehension of regions.

The Judiciary Act of 1789 established eastern, middle, and southern circuits. But those circuits were not the ones that we would expect today or indeed the ones to which contemporaries clung for long either. The eastern circuit included New York as well as New England. The middle circuit included Maryland and Virginia as well as New Jersey, Pennsylvania, and Delaware. The southern circuit included only the Carolinas and Georgia. The Act of 1789 provided for no western circuit at all (Mood, 1951, p. 35).

The revision of 1801 doubled the number of circuits. It divided the old eastern circuit on an east–west axis, placing Massachusetts, Rhode Island, New Hampshire, and Maine in one and New York, Connecticut and Vermont in the other. It split the old middle circuit on a north–south axis, allocating New Jersey, Pennsylvania, and Delaware to one and Maryland and Virginia to the other. It left the old southern district intact. And it acknowledged for the first time a backcountry district, comprised of the new trans-Appalachian states (and willfully oblivious to the slavery issue) (Mood, 1951, p. 35).

The revision of 1807, which remained in force for the next generation, rearranged the regions of the republic yet again. It preserved the placement of eastern New England in one circuit and of New York, Connecticut, and Vermont in another oddly distended one. It paired New Jersey and Pennsylvania in a third division, Delaware and Maryland in a fourth, Virginia and North Carolina in a fifth, and South Carolina and Georgia in a sixth. It retained the western entity – Ohio, Kentucky, Tennessee – that straddled the Mason–Dixon line (Mood, 1951, p. 36).

If men of the eighteenth century could not concur on the regional alignments that characterized the country, historians and geographers who have the help of hindsight have done no better. Even if we exclude the schemes that take in the entirety of England's American empire, its Canadian and Caribbean colonies as well as the thirteen that declared their independence in 1776, and even if we look only to the number of provincial regions that recent scholars have delineated, the disparities are striking. Egnal (1996), Engerman and Gallman (1996), McCusker and Menard (1985), and McWhiney (1988) all posit bipolar schemes. Jones (1980), Kniffen (1965), and Zelinsky (1970) advance tripartite divisions. Bailyn (1986), Fischer (1989), Glassie (1968), and Greene (1988) assert the precedence of four regions. Meinig (1986) maintains that there were five. As David Russo once remarked, "the question of what constitutes a region . . . is still a vexing one" (Russo, 1974, p. 104).

Even those who agree on the number of regions that divided early America do not agree on the areas that they assign to each region. Of those who postulate just two regions, most bifurcate south and north, slave and free, staple and non-staple; but McWhiney counterposes east and west, coast and backcountry, English and Celtic. Of those who predicate four, scarcely any predicate the same four. Bailyn identifies New England, a "middling circuit" on the Delaware and Hudson rivers, the Chesapeake, and two clusters in the Carolinas as the four "distinct zones" of the British mainland. Fischer makes greater Massachusetts, greater Pennsylvania, greater Virginia, and the backcountry his "seed" regions. Gastil has New England, "metropolitan" New York, Pennsylvania, and the South; Glassie, southern and eastern New England, southeastern Pennsylvania, the Chesapeake, and the Lower South; and Greene, New England, the middle colonies, the Chesapeake and the Lower South.

Even the extent of the apparent accord among these various versions is deceptive. To take just one example, Bailyn and Fischer seem to share three of their four regions. But Bailyn's regions, though all coastal, are also all backcountries, or "marchlands" as he calls them, far from civility (1986, pp. 87–131). Fischer's four "regional cultures" – even the backcountry – are all culturally continuous with the British places from which their settlers came (1989, pp. 783–898). Bailyn's zones are still "soft" and plastic into the eighteenth century, "emerging, unsurely, from a strange and unfamiliar past" (1986, p. 91). Fischer's cultures are coherent from the first, replicating Old World ways carried over from the regions of their origin.

Gastil's account is especially indicative of the difficulty that historians and geographers have had in specifying early American regions. At first, he maintains that "the story of the country lies to a large extent" in the struggle of two regions, New England and the South (1975, p. 5). Soon enough, he admits that there was a third region, the mid-Atlantic, though he hastens to add that the "differences among the middle colonies were more important than their similarities" (1975, pp. 8–9). Ultimately, he discloses his own scheme. It reveals neither two nor three but four colonial regions. His New England includes most of New York and the northern tier of Pennsylvania. His "New York metro" has the lower Hudson valley, Long Island, and the eastern half of New Jersey. His Pennsylvania extends east into New Jersey and south, below the Mason–Dixon line, into Delaware, Maryland, and West Virginia. And his South takes in the rest of Delaware and Maryland and everything else from Virginia southward (1975, pp. 28–30).

No consensus has ever obtained among historians or among geographers about where to put Pennsylvania, or Maryland, or New York, or the backcountry. Was Maryland to be counted among the middle colonies or the Chesapeake? Were the middle colonies a coherent region or, in reality, two quite divergent regions? Was New York a region in its own right, part of the middle colonies, or part of New England? Or were different parts of New York an autonomous region, a part of the middle colonies, *and* a part of New England? Was Pennsylvania to be defined by the boundaries of Penn's proprietary grant or was it to be conceived as a cultural hearth extending across a vast southern salient to the Carolinas and Georgia? Or was it itself fractured in sub-regional patterns decisive for the province's revolutionary experience? Was the Chesapeake a region in its own right or a part of a larger southern formation? Was the backcountry a region in its own right – or two regions in their own right – or just the westward extension of the seaboard regions?

These questions and quarrels, and their attendant answers and arguments, are not just idle issues of technical virtuosity or overactive ingenuity. They express the priorities and pragmatic purposes of their exponents. They make manifest in physical space the ideas and ideological emphases of their champions.

* * * * *

From the first, regional pride played a powerful part in the assertion of distinctive geographic entities. But at the first, only a few provincial intellectuals proclaimed such regional pride. The leading thinkers of the great intellectual centers of the young republic, Philadelphia and New York, mobilized for national life. As Meinig says, they evinced "relatively little concern for or consciousness of" regional interests. They took "middle" to refer to their geographic position rather than their cultural region. They translated "middle" as "central within a system," because the economic interests to which they attached themselves "commanded a nuclear area wherein . . . their region was itself the center of a truly *national* structure" (Meinig, 1986, pp. 400–1; see also Goldman, 1941).

By contrast, the spokesmen for Boston and Baltimore were "not centers of nation-building in quite the same way." Instead, they upheld more strongly the interests of their own New England and Chesapeake regions. In Meinig's words, they maintained a "strong dual allegiance committed to the building of a *federal* nation" (Meinig, 1986, p. 403).

Their devotion to their own distinctive regions was palpably defensive. In the aftermath of independence, in a new nation that honored neither puritans nor cavaliers, in a world in which slavery was suddenly under intellectual siege, New Englanders and southerners alike felt threatened as well as unappreciated. It was they and they alone who produced chauvinistic histories of an earlier America designed to deny their deviancy and sustain the authenticity of their Americanism. In the way of such defensive maneuvers, they often ended in overcompensations that asserted the superiority of their own regional peculiarities.

After the Civil War, southerners put forth regional versions of the American past with renewed fervor and urgency. They no longer sought to reconcile slavery with American freedom or to assert their own American ordinariness. On the contrary, they affirmed their aberrancy unabashedly and projected it proudly into the past. They appealed to the special trajectory of their history to rally the region to their tangled idealization of the Lost Cause and to steel the region to resist the authority of a central government they no longer took to be their own.

After the Civil War, old-stock New Englanders vindicated by military victory persisted in their smug identification of the ideals of the nation with those of their Puritan forebears. The identification was, by then, a regional reflex. And as the rest of the North experienced immigrant invasions at the turn of the century like those the Bostonians experienced in the Irish influx of the mid-nineteenth century, other old-stock elites embraced the myth of Puritan primacy. New Englanders eventually enjoyed a certain cultural authority that they had fantasized but never actually enjoyed before.

The New England myth appealed to northern elites because it afforded their robber baronies a patina of an older and nobler purpose. New York exposed America as it was. Boston emblemized America as its elites preferred to imagine it. The apotheosis of New England provided a reassuring paradigm of hierarchy preserved and piety persisting. Brahmins proposed and disposed. Others deferred (Zuckerman, 1982, pp. 3–25).

In keeping with their nationalizing enterprise and their assumptions of elite dispensation, colonial historians continued into the 1960s to think disproportionately of New England when they thought of regions at all. In keeping with their regional isolation and recalcitrance, southern colonial historians continued to stand apart from that cosmopolitan endeavor and to insist on southern distinctiveness. The impulsions that gave rise to regional self-consciousness in those two regions had long since dimmed or disappeared. But the self-consciousness itself had produced bodies of regional writing as distinguished as they were distorted.

If the traditions that confined early American historians to New England and the South augmented themselves almost despite themselves, the traditions that guided geographers and folklorists took them away from the regions to which historians attended so obsessively. Unlike historians, geographers and folklorists were less concerned with elites than with masses: land masses and popular masses.

Geographers and folklorists did not begin from regional defensiveness or unease. They began from simple, even crude, curiosity. They wanted to identify the formative hearths of American culture and to study their expansion across the continent. In that endeavor, they turned, almost ineluctably, to the first centuries of the English invasion of America. And in that turn, they found, almost unfailingly, that neither New England nor the South was as influential in the course of American civilization as the colonies of the middle Atlantic (Trewartha, 1946; Arensberg, 1955; Kniffen, 1965; Kniffen and Glassie, 1966; Glassie, 1968; Zelinsky, 1973; Harris, 1978; Mitchell, 1978; Meinig, 1986).

Tracing the dispersion of a remarkable variety of folkways, geographers always found the mark of New England lightest on the land and generally found the impress of Pennsylvania weightiest. Whether they studied architectural design or construction, house types or barn types, naming habits or rural settlement patterns, geographers never found New England influence beyond a narrow northern band that petered out in the upper Midwest. Though they did sometimes dispute the exact circuits of southern and mid-Atlantic jurisdiction, they usually discovered that the writ of the middle colonies ran farthest.

In recent years, historians have joined in this inquiry. They have done so, to be sure, with a chauvinistic edge. Jack Greene, of North Carolina and the Johns Hopkins University, maintains that the Chesapeake provided the model for American development (1988). Michael Zuckerman, of Philadelphia and the University of Pennsylvania, argues that the middle colonies did (1982). But more than mere chauvinism informs these differences of opinion. Our assertions of regional priority derive from the kind of country we think America is or ought to be. If we would stress the role of an old-stock ruling class, we assign pride of place to early New England. If we would make multiculturalism the core of our past or our future, we proclaim the primacy of the middle colonies. If we would affirm unbridled pursuit of individual interest, we find it first in the Chesapeake colonies.

Our very definitions and demarcations of regions derive from the kind of people we believe we are. If we think culture crucial to American life, we find at least three regions: the South, New England, the middle colonies (Bailyn, 1986; Greene, 1988; Fischer, 1989; though cf. McWhiney, 1988). If we believe economics more elemental, we see but two: slave and "free" labor, staple and yeoman agriculture (McCusker and Menard, 1985; Egnal, 1996; Engerman and Gallman, 1996; though cf. Egnal, 1996).

These variations are possible because, from the beginning, regions defined by culture were not congruent with those defined by market relations or by physiography. As Louis Wirth observes, "Nature does not always carve out neatly the lines that set off one area from another, nor does man in his works always obey the dictates of nature" (Wirth, 1951, p. 385).

These variations are also possible because, from the first, regions delineated by commentators have diverged from those recognized by contemporaries. In the eighteenth and nineteenth centuries, and increasingly in the twentieth, we have defined regional boundaries – physiographic, economic, or cultural – without asking if those borders were the ones of which Americans themselves were conscious.

In principle, it would certainly be possible to draw lines with a greater and even with a controlling regard for the ideas of the colonists. Meinig makes a distinction between approaching regions etically as "means of analysis and synthesis" and emically as entities "imbued with emotions" that can "influence our actions" (Meinig, 1978, p. 1202). We do adopt an etic posture. We could embrace an emic one. We could, to take an obvious example, treat regions as sociologists and historians increasingly treat ethnicities: as grounds of elective identity, significant only insofar as people in the group are aware of them and allow them to matter in their minds.

Humanistic geographers insist that a region must be more than a mere form of areal classification. An authentic regional affiliation must penetrate the private world of "feelings." The very reality of a region "is inseparable from the consciousness of those who inhabit it" (Daniels, 1985, pp. 145, 150-1).

Historians of early America do not demand evidence of conscious identification as a condition of regional reality. They do not because they cannot. Elective identities are, for the most part, luxuries of modern life and amenities of our own time. As Entrikin says, postmodernity puts "a greater burden on the individual to construct meaning in the world" (1991, p. 63). But elective regional identities were neither pervasive nor even present in colonial America outside a few Puritan precincts of New England.

If, with Wirth, we define region as a "state of mind" or a domain in which residents achieve "a sense of common belonging," then the early South cannot be considered a region (1951, pp. 386ff). Blassingame does not discover a single reference to the southern provinces as a coherent region in the entire era of imperial crisis (1968). Degler says the region did not come to self-consciousness before the 1820s (1977, pp. 27–33). Egerton maintains that it did not attain awareness of itself till even later. He insists on the embarrassing irony that "the Old South" was "created as a mental construct only a short time before it was historically eliminated as a material construct" (1974, p. 11).

If, with Meinig, we take regional culture to refer to the characteristics of "a group of people who are deep-rooted and dominant in a particular territory, who are conscious of their identity as deriving from a common heritage, and who share a common language and basic patterns of life" (1986, p. 80), then the middle colonies did not qualify on a single one of these counts. Their inhabitants had no deep roots, dominant class, consciousness of common identity, common heritage, or pervasive patterns of life.

To require self-consciousness as a criterion of authentic regions is to tangle interpretation in discomfiting quandaries. To the moment of independence, it compels a cartography more appropriate to the earliest seventeenth century: a map of British America as veritable *terre incognitae*, a land of vast blank spaces. At the same time, it invites a psychology more appropriate to the twentieth century: a mental geography replete with analytically irresponsible notions such as "subconscious regionalism" (Caughey, 1951, pp. 173–86).

Worst of all, the condition of self-consciousness invites a concept of regionalism at odds with one of the incentives to regional thinking. Precisely by privileging those areas aware of themselves as unified, this condition exaggerates the importance of the homogeneity from which we flee. Precisely by excluding places that speak in many voices, it precludes recognition of the multiplicities that modern men and women seek to affirm against the monolith of modernity (Barnes and Duncan, 1992, p. 252).

*****

Despite the demonstrable fatuousness of the criterion of self-consciousness, historians cling to it, as if unconsciously. To this day, efforts at "rethinking American regionalism" by otherwise sophisticated scholars elide the middle Atlantic (and the backcountry) entirely. To this day, such scholars take the South and New England for their sole subjects (Ayers, 1996).

More than that, they trace the trajectory of these regions not only *because* they came to awareness of themselves as no others did but also *when* they achieved such awareness. They discuss these regions on their own terms and, overweeningly, in the era in which they came to such terms. They are as obtuse to the past of the South and New England as they are slavishly devoted to each region's imagination of its past. Their diversion of attention from two centuries of early American history to two generations of nineteenth-century mythmaking would be an embarrassment no matter what its source. Coming as it does from historians, it is a humiliation.

Consider the treatment of the South in recent writing. In 1951, a standard reconnaissance of regionalism in America based southern distinctiveness on its semi-tropical climate and its poverty (Simkins, 1951, pp. 147–8). In the half-century since, a simple technological change, air-conditioning, has rendered the old climatic interpretations of the region irrelevant. But a complex economic alteration, the rise of the Sunbelt, has spurred no similar reconsideration of prosperity and dearth. Present-day historians still assert the perenniality of poverty in the South. Respected students of the region such as Edward Ayers and Carl Degler write as though the South scarcely existed before it endured the deprivations that came of losing the Civil War. Even in a book expressly dedicated to discovering the "continuity" of southern distinctiveness, Degler (1977) finds the hallmarks of the region's culture in an array of elements more appropriate to the past century and a half than to the first two centuries of southern life.

Prominent among the elements he claims characteristic of the culture are poverty, paucity of immigrants, pervasive Protestant religiosity, and conservatism (Degler, 1977, pp. 13–25). And every one of them is an emergent of the nineteenth century. So far from suffering poverty in the seventeenth or eighteenth century, the South was easily the richest region of mainland British America. So far from experiencing a paucity of immigrants, the South attracted more of them than all the northern colonies together in the seventeenth century and, if the forced migration of Africans is included, more even than the booming middle colonies in the eighteenth. So far from promoting a homogeneous Protestant religiosity, the South sustained a rich panoply of Protestant denominations, sometimes militant irreligiosity, and extensive religious indifference. So far from prizing conservatism, the South was, at its cultural core in the Virginia Tidewater, "the preeminent" province of America "in receiving fresh European ideas and disseminating them" (Zelinsky, 1973, p. 83).

Indeed, by Degler's own criteria, New England was much more "southern" than the South in the colonial era. It was far poorer, immeasurably more insular, a good deal more protective of its homogeneous Protestant religiosity, and markedly more conservative than any other region. Yet the clichés persist. Historians have as hard a time as anyone else recovering a region as it once was. Their view too is refracted through intervening developments and supervening assumptions. Ayers, who should know better, takes poverty and backwardness for hallmarks of the South (1996, pp. 62–82, esp. p. 80). And Stephen Nissenbaum, who should also know better, takes affluence and influence for the New England norm (1996, pp. 38–61, esp. p. 47).

The ironic truth is that, again and again, historians have treated regions ahistorically. They have taken regions as timeless and even teleological categories rather than as constellations and constructions that themselves have histories. They have treated regions as realities from the very first and as persistent into the present. They have scarcely thought to conceptualize them as dynamic social categories that form and fade with time (Meinig, 1978; Paasi, 1991, p. 243).

Dynamism is undeniable if we extend our temporal horizon. As Gastil observes, Boston was once the cultural core of greater New England. In the twentieth century, its influence has diminished if not dissipated. Mormon culture was once part of the periphery of the Boston core. In the late twentieth century, north central Utah is much more a cultural core than eastern Massachusetts (Gastil, 1975, p. 43).

But dynamism is not difficult to discern even if we confine our horizon to the colonial period. Take Marc Egnal's argument that "distinct, regional societies" did not even begin to form in North America before the middle of the eighteenth century. It is an argument that does appreciate change. It avers that a common yeoman culture prevailed across the colonies before 1750. Still, it does not go nearly as far as it might. It insists only that, after 1750, two regions of "sharply defined" identities appeared east of the Appalachians: a South that "emphasized hierarchy and social order" and a North that engaged in a "relentless drive for wealth" (Egnal, 1996, pp. vii, viii). It does not develop this divergence as tantalizingly as it might, for before 1750 New England emphasized hierarchy and social order while the South singlemindedly sought wealth.

Metaphorically, New England became more "southern" in the eighteenth century, and scholars such as Greene and Meinig have said so (Meinig, 1986; Greene, 1988). More than metaphorically, the South was "middle colonized" as Pennsylvanians poured into the Piedmont and the Shenandoah Valley of Virginia and on into the Carolinas and as wheat cultivation took over the tidewater. A multitude of historians, geographers, and idiosyncratic scholars in half a dozen other disciplines have described the diffusion of middle-colonial crops, land uses, settlement patterns, folk housing, and much more on a multitude of southern frontiers (Mitchell, 1978; Clemens, 1980; Ekirch, 1981; Lemon, 1984, pp. 88–9, 112–13).

But we do not dwell on these transformations. Even when we acknowledge them in passing, we recur soon enough to conventional divisions. It is not just that we are reluctant to historicize our mental maps. It is that our regional usages are essentially impervious to empirical evidence and beyond reconfiguration.

Our very language embeds those usages. Kniffen cannot speak of the upland South as middle colonial or Pennsylvanian in its deep culture without first calling it the upland South (Kniffen, 1965). Harris cannot remind us that New Englanders of the eighteenth century did not recognize their own regional culture without first calling them New Englanders (Harris, 1978). Our terminology concedes the very teleology we try to call into question.

If the evidence of deep culture mattered, we would long since have given up calling the colonies south of Pennsylvania the South. Anthropological, folkloric, linguistic, sociological, historical, and material cultural data all disclose the middle-colonial orientation of eighteenth-century southern settlers west of the fall line. But none of these disclosures offset our knowledge that the descendants of those settlers fought with the Confederacy in the Civil War.

Similarly, if the evidence of economics mattered, we would long since have recast our conceptions of early New England. Alice Jones's magisterial investigation of colonial wealth (1980) makes plain that the region was not only the poorest part of provincial America but also the least egalitarian. Eighteenth-century New England exhibited more extremity in the distribution of property than the South by a distinct margin and than the middle colonies by a more distinct margin still. But none of Jones's meticulous discoveries offset our conviction that the heirs of the Puritans were paragons of pioneer equality. Data are unavailing against the poetry of nineteenth-century nostalgia and our own yearning for yeoman simplicity.

We are wedded to definitions of colonial regions that do not derive from colonial experience. Both the South and New England came to see themselves as coherent regions after independence as they never had before. And they saw themselves so because they experienced a real need to do so and anticipated substantial benefits in doing so.

Ironically, there had been no incentive to think regionally before the Revolution. The birth of a nation brought into being a government that could distribute advantages and, consequently, impose penalties. At the same time, it created a forum in which to contest access to those advantages. Regional ideas arose as a response to this new government. They arose as instruments in the political struggles that inevitably attended it, especially for those who feared they were falling behind. They provided a prospect of mobilizing unity among people who were not in fact united.

Men and women in early America had multiple memberships. All of them had familial identities, and most had more than one. All of them had geographic attachments, almost all of them had work ties, and many of them had religious loyalties. Each of these affiliations and a multitude of others entailed conflict of interests and attenuation of allegiance.

Groups that sought to organize to promote singular interests knew all this. To overcome the diffusion of devotion that it entailed, they had to entice – or coerce – people's engagement in their own particular cause. In Wallerstein's words, they had to "persuade their 'members' to act . . . in some unified fashion." They had to convince those individuals that conduct that served the group's purpose was "normal, 'traditional,' hallowed by time and therefore expected in the present" (Wallerstein, 1988, p. 9).

In those endeavors, regions arose as rhetorical flags around which men and women might rally or be made to rally. They arose in New England and the South because influential leaders in those areas apprehended the perils of seeming peculiar in the eyes of the nascent nation. They did not arise in the middle Atlantic or middle West because the inhabitants of those areas took for granted that they were in the mainstream of national development (Goldman, 1941; Zuckerman, 1982).

To this day, students of southern culture cannot deal comfortably with the South in the colonial era because it does not serve their polemic project. In Bartley's recent collection on the evolution of southern culture, not a single one of the eight contributors to that putatively historical enterprise focuses on the South in the seventeenth or eighteenth century. Only two of them acknowledge those centuries – the first half of southern history – at all. In their effort to probe patterns of poverty and conservatism that they take to define the region, the pundits simply ignore an age when the South was neither poor nor conservative. They cannot encompass the southern colonies in their discourse of southern regionalism, because the south was not peculiar then (Bartley, 1988).

*****

Contemporary colonial history is not just disconnected from salient parts of the actual past. It is not just inattentive to the shifting borders of regions and the shifting significances of regional stories. It is not just oblivious to a transition from differentiations driven by divergent cultures to differentiations driven, in subsequent centuries, by a dynamic economy that has left people "rooted in place in the productive system rather than in place on the land" (Harris, 1978, p. 123).

Contemporary colonial history is also disconnected from the writing of the past. Where an older colonial history provided a prelude to the national narrative, the current conceptualization is powerless to offer such an overture.

The story of each individual region – of the backcountry every bit as much as of the South or New England – is distinctly different after independence than it was before. The tales of these regions in the provincial period are isolated from the passions and polemics that impel those tales in the national era and inform the very telling of those tales. And the story of early America itself, organized regionally, resists integration with the story of the nation, told as it must be from the center.

Rupert Vance once wrote that regions can have meaning only in a larger perspective, only as a relation of parts to a whole. The very notion of region necessarily implies an integrative entity: preeminently, the nation; alternatively, the market or even the world (Vance, 1951). But there was no such integrative entity in, or for, early America. Historians of the colonies have turned to regional orderings of provincial experience because they cannot find any overarching meanings in that experience or will not impose any overarching meanings on it.

Their histories may fit the de-centering endeavor of postmodern analysis. They may even fit the facts of colonial life. But they do not fit the histories being written of the Revolution, or of the early republic. They do not fit – and cannot even be connected to – the centered syntheses that still constitute the core of our national history.

These regional readings of the course of colonial history thus present one final paradox. They are at once antiquarian and avant-garde, indifferent to the pressures of presentism and exquisitely sensitive to the present temper. In their focus on multiple pasts regionally refracted, recent colonial historians sever their enterprise from histories that examine the making of modern America even as they attach themselves to the postmodern project and its rejection of hierarchy.

While early Americanists now prize pluralism, historians of the Revolution emphasize the overcoming of such particularism. While colonialists now stress the separate voices and separate cultures of the first settlements, students of the early republic focus on the forging of a nation and a national identity.

It does not have to be so. Historians of the colonies have not always dwelt on divergences and disjunctions. For a century and more, they bent their every effort to the evocation of continuity between pioneer beginnings and the advent of the new nation. Historians of the early republic have not always emphasized the consolidation of an imagined national community. For a half-century of progressive primacy, they focused on the emergence of the first party system and the deep ideological divisions they supposed it symbolized. Even now, students of the colonies could, if they wished, emphasize anticipations of national integration. Even now, students of the early republic could, if they wished, accentuate its incompleteness.

For the moment, however, there is a real rupture between the study of early America, predicated as it is on the priority of distinctive regions, and of the new nation, devoted as it is to charting the emergence of a new locus of loyalty at the center. Colonial historians now pose a problem which historians of the Revolution and the young republic currently do not deign even to see, let alone to solve.

And as long as they do, it is not clear how the history of American origins can ever be put together again. As regional syntheses consolidate themselves as our regnant interpretations of early American history, we are doomed to dismantle the very unity that the Founding Fathers so daringly declared.

BIBLIOGRAPHY

Arensberg, Conrad: "American Communities." *American Anthropologist* 57 (1955), pp. 1143–62.

Ayers, Edward, ed.: *All Over the Map: Rethinking American Regions* (Baltimore, MD: Johns Hopkins University Press, 1996).

Ayers, Edward: "What We Talk About When We Talk About the South." In Ayers (1996), 62–82.

Ayers, Edward and Onuf, Peter: "Introduction." In Ayers (1996), 1–10.

Bailyn, Bernard: *The Peopling of British North America: An Introduction* (New York: Alfred A. Knopf, 1996).

Barnes, Trevor and Duncan, James, eds.: *Writing Worlds: Discourse, Text, and Metaphor in the Representation of Landscape* (London: Routledge, 1992).

Bartley, Numan, ed.: *The Evolution of Southern Culture* (Athens, GA: University of Georgia Press, 1988).

Benedict, Ruth: *Patterns of Culture* (Boston, MA: Houghton Mifflin, 1934).

Blassingame, John: "American Nationalism and Other Loyalties in the Southern Colonies, 1763–1775." *Journal of Southern History* 34 (1968), pp. 50–75.

Bodle, Wayne: "The 'Myth of the Middle Colonies' Reconsidered: The Process of Regionalization in Early America." *Pennsylvania Magazine of History and Biography* 113 (1989), pp. 527–48.

Bogue, Donald and Beale, Calvin, eds.: *Economic Areas of the United States* (New York: Free Press of Glencoe, 1961).

Bowden, Martyn: "Culture and Place: English Sub-Cultural Regions in New England in the Seventeenth Century." *Connecticut History* 35 (1994), pp. 68–146.

Brown, Kathleen: *Good Wives, Nasty Wenches, and Anxious Patriarchs: Gender, Race, and Power in Colonial Virginia* (Chapel Hill, NC: University of North Carolina Press, 1996).

Brown, Richard M.: "The New Regionalism in America, 1970–1981." In Robbins (1983), pp. 37–96.

Caughey, John: "The Spanish Southwest: An Example of Subconscious Regionalism." In Jensen (1951), pp. 173–86.

Cayton, Andrew and Onuf, Peter, eds.: *The Midwest and the Nation: Rethinking the History of an American Region* (Bloomington, IN: Indiana University Press, 1990).

Chaplin, Joyce: *An Anxious Pursuit: Agricultural Innovation and Modernity in the Lower South, 1730–1815* (Chapel Hill, NC: University of North Carolina Press, 1993).

Clemens, Paul: *The Atlantic Economy and Colonial Maryland's Eastern Shore: From Tobacco to Grain* (Ithaca, NY: Cornell University Press, 1980).

Daniels, Stephen: "Arguments for a Humanistic Geography." In R. J. Johnston, ed., *The Future of Geography* (London: Methuen, 1985), pp. 143–58.

Daniels, Stephen: "Place and the Geographical Imagination." *Geography* 77 (1992), pp. 310–22.

Degler, Carl: *Place Over Time: The Continuity of Southern Distinctiveness* (Baton Rouge, LA: Louisiana State University Press, 1977).

Egerton, John: *The Americanization of Dixie: The Southernization of America* (New York: Harper's Magazine Press, 1974).

Egnal, Marc: *Divergent Paths: How Culture and Institutions Have Shaped North American Growth* (New York: Oxford University Press, 1996).

Ekirch, A. Roger: *"Poor Carolina": Politics and Society in Colonial North Carolina, 1729–1776* (Chapel Hill, NC: University of North Carolina Press, 1981).

Engerman, Stanley and Gallman, Robert, eds.: *The Cambridge Economic History of the United States* (New York: Cambridge University Press, 1996).

Entrikin, J. Nicholas: *The Betweenness of Place: Towards a Geography of Modernity* (Baltimore, MD: Johns Hopkins University Press, 1991).

Fischer, David: *Albion's Seed: Four British Folkways in America* (New York: Oxford University Press, 1989).

Frankfurter, Felix: "Foreword." In Jensen (1951), pp. xv–xvi.

Frantz, John and Pencak, William, eds.: *Beyond Philadelphia: The American Revolution in the Pennsylvania Hinterland* (University Park, PA: Pennsylvania State University Press, 1998).

Garreau, Joel: *The Nine Nations of North America* (Boston, MA: Houghton Mifflin, 1981).

Gastil, Raymond: *Cultural Regions of the United States* (Seattle, WA: University of Washington Press, 1975).

Gibson, James, ed.: *European Settlement and Development in North America: Essays on Geographical Change in Honour and Memory of Andrew Hill Clark* (Toronto: University of Toronto Press, 1978).

Giddens, Anthony: *The Constitution of Society: Outline of the Theory of Structuration* (Berkeley, CA: University of California Press, 1984).

Glassie, Henry: *Pattern in the Material Folk Culture of the Eastern United States* (Philadelphia: University of Pennsylvania Press, 1968).

Goldman, Eric: "Middle States regionalism and American historiography: a suggestion." In *Historiography and Urbanization: Essays in American History in Honor of W. Stull Holt* (Baltimore, MD: Johns Hopkins University Press, 1941), pp. 211–20.

Gough, Robert: "The Myth of the Middle Colonies: An Analysis of Regionalization in Early America." *Pennsylvania Magazine of History and Biography* 103 (1979), pp. 392–419.

Greene, Jack: *Peripheries and Center: Constitutional Development in the Extended Polities of the British Empire* (Athens, GA: University of Georgia Press, 1986).

Greene, Jack: *Pursuits of Happiness: The Social Development of Early Modern British Colonies and the Formation of American Culture* (Chapel Hill, NC: University of North Carolina Press, 1988).

Greene, Jack and Pole, J. R., eds.: *Colonial British America: Essays in the New History of the Early Modern Era* (Baltimore, MD: Johns Hopkins University Press, 1984).

Harris, R. Cole: "The Historical Geography of North American Regions." *American Behavioral Scientist* 22 (1978), pp. 115–30.

Harvey, David: *The Condition of Postmodernity: An Enquiry into the Origins of Cultural Change* (Oxford, England: Blackwell, 1989).

Henretta, James: *The Evolution of American Society* (Boston, MA: D. C. Heath, 1973).

Jensen, Merrill, ed.: *Regionalism in America* (Madison, WI: University of Wisconsin Press, 1951).

Johnston, R. J., ed: *The Future of Geography* (London: Methuen, 1985).

Jones, Alice: *Wealth of a Nation To Be: The American Colonies on the Eve of the Revolution* (New York: Columbia University Press, 1980).

Kniffen, Fred: "Folk Housing: Key to Diffusion." *Annals of the Association of American Geographers* 55 (1965), pp. 549–77.

Kniffen, Fred and Henry Glassie: "Building in Wood in the Eastern United States: A Time–Place Perspective." *Geographical Review* 56 (1966), pp. 40–66.

Koeniger, A. Cash: "Climate and Southern Distinctiveness." *Journal of Southern History* 54 (1988), pp. 21–44.

Lemon, James: *The Best Poor Man's Country: A Geographical Study of Early Southeastern Pennsylvania* (Baltimore, MD: Johns Hopkins Press, 1972).

Lemon, James: "Spatial Order: Households in Local Communities and Regions." In Greene and Pole (1984), pp. 86–122.

Levy, Barry: *Quakers and the American Family: British Settlement in the Delaware Valley* (New York: Oxford University Press, 1988).

Lowenthal, David: "Introduction." In Lowenthal and Bowden (1976), pp. 3–9.

Lowenthal, David and Martyn Bowden, eds.: *Geographies of the Mind: Essays in Historical Geosophy in Honor of John Kirtland Wright* (New York: Oxford University Press, 1976).

McCusker, John and Menard, Russell: *The Economy of British America, 1607–1789* (Chapel Hill, NC: University of North Carolina Press, 1985).

McWhiney, Grady: *Cracker Culture: Celtic Ways in the Old South* (Tuscaloosa, AL: University of Alabama Press, 1988).

Meinig, D. W.: "The Continuous Shaping of America: A Prospectus for Geographers and Historians." *American Historical Review* 83 (1978), pp. 1186–205.

Meinig, D. W.: *The Shaping of America: A Geographical Perspective on 500 Years of History*, vol. 1, *Atlantic America, 1492–1800* (New Haven, CT: Yale University Press, 1986).

Mitchell, Robert: "The Shenandoah Valley Frontier." *Annals of the Association of American Geographers* 62 (1972), pp. 461–86.

Mitchell, Robert: "The Formation of Early American Cultural Regions: An Interpretation." In Gibson (1978), pp. 66–90.

Mood, Fulmer: "The Origin, Evolution, and Application of the Sectional Concept, 1750–1900." In Jensen (1951), pp. 5–98.

Nissenbaum, Stephen: "New England as Region and Nation." In Ayers (1996), pp. 38–61.

Paasi, A.: Deconstructing Regions: Notes on the Scale of Spatial Life." *Environment and Planning A* 23 (1991), pp. 239–56.

Pierson, George: "The Obstinate Concept of New England: A Study in Denudation." *New England Quarterly* 28 (1955), pp. 3–17.

Reed, John: *The Enduring South: Subcultural Persistence in Mass Society* (Chapel Hill, NC: University of North Carolina Press, 1974).

Robbins, William et al., eds.: *Regionalism and the Pacific Northwest* (Corvallis, OR: Oregon State University Press, 1983).

Russo, David: *Families and Communities: A New View of American History* (Nashville, TN: The American Association for State and Local History, 1974).

Rutman, Darrett: *The Morning of America, 1603–1789* (Boston, MA: Houghton Mifflin, 1971).

Savelle, Max: *Foundations of American Civilization* (New York: Henry Holt, 1942).

Savelle, Max: *Seeds of Liberty: The Genesis of the American Mind* (New York: Alfred A. Knopf, 1948).

Scheiber, Harry, ed.: *The Old Northwest: Studies in Regional History, 1787–1910* (Lincoln, NE: University of Nebraska Press, 1969).

Simkins, Francis: "The South." In Jensen (1951), pp. 147–72.

Soja, Edward: *Postmodern Geographies: The Reassertion of Space in Critical Social Theory* (London: Verso, 1989).

Steiner, Michael and Mondale, Clarence, eds.: *Region and Regionalism in the United States: A Source Book for the Humanities and Social Sciences* (New York: Garland, 1988).

Trewartha, Glenn: "Types of rural settlement in colonial America." *Geographical Review* 36 (1946), pp. 368–96.

Tuan, Yi-Fu: *Space and Place: The Perspective of Experience* (Minneapolis, MN: University of Minnesota Press, 1977).

Tully, Alan: *Forming American Politics: Ideals, Interests, and Institutions in Colonial New York and Pennsylvania* (Baltimore, MD: Johns Hopkins University Press, 1994).

Vance, Rupert: "The Regional Concept as a Tool for Social Research." In Jensen (1951), pp. 119–40.

Wallerstein, Immanuel: "What Can One Mean by Southern Culture?" In Numan Bartley, ed., *The Evolution of Southern Culture* (Athens, GA: University of Georgia Press, 1988), pp. 1–13.

Wawrzyczek, Irmina: "Studying Early America amid the Extended Epistemological Crisis in American Historiography." *American Studies* (Warsaw) 15 (1997), pp. 23–30.

Winks, Robin: "Regionalism in Comparative Perspective." In Robbins (1983), pp. 13–36.

Wirth, Louis: "The Limitations of Regionalism." In Jensen (1951), pp. 381–93.

Zelinsky, Wilbur: "Cultural Variation in Personal Name Patterns in the Eastern United States." *Annals of the Association of American Geographers* 60 (1970), pp. 743–69.

Zelinsky, Wilbur: *The Cultural Geography of the United States* (Englewood Cliffs, NJ: Prentice-Hall, 1973).

Zuckerman, Michael: "Introduction: Puritans, Cavaliers, and the Motley Middle." In Zuckerman, ed., *Friends and Neighbors: Group Life in America's First Plural Society* (Philadelphia: Temple University Press, 1982), pp. 3–25.

CHAPTER FOURTEEN

Consumption

CARY CARSON

Why does the modern passion for getting and spending so excite the watchdogs of public morality, historians among them? Three centuries ago, when the "Torrent of Luxury" we take for granted was just beginning, preachers and pamphleteers thundered against the "baneful contagion" of extravagant consumption. Already it was spreading to "the very Dregs of the People" (Fielding, 1751, pp. 3–4). Today ours is another age of binge buying and mass consumption, and once again voices are raised to condemn and condone. This time historians have joined the clamor both as scolds and scholars. An avalanche of recent publications lays bare a topic that remained largely undiscussed, indeed, almost undiscovered, until twenty years ago. Sometimes termed the consumer revolution, the industrious revolution, or simply the birth of modern consumer society, the great transformation that turned a patchwork of ancient folkways into a tapestry of global culture now intrudes on historical debates as large and various as migration and settlement, economic growth and regional development, industrialization, class formation, women and children in the workforce, and even the causes and consequences of the American Revolution. The centuries have not softened the rhetoric. Arguments about America's first consumers often still end in squabbles about modern politics.

Americans are born consumers. They believe they are endowed by their Creator with an inalienable right to all the happiness money can buy to their maximum credit limit. Their creed spreads faster than e-commerce. To many the world around, triumphant materialism now proves that democratic capitalism is superior to all rival forms of political economy. Others draw a different lesson. As they see it, an international epidemic of "affluenza" degrades the environment, squanders resources, beggars poor nations, and everywhere leads to moral decline and spiritual emptiness. Historians on the political right are deeply suspicious that European and American history told as the march of material progress is old-fashioned Whig history resuscitated; left-leaning historians are equally skeptical because the subject elevates plenty over poverty and takes more notice of consumers than producers.

Such strongly held opinions are good for scholarship. They give urgency to the search for answers that can help historians and their audiences understand when and why we westerners first became addicted to consumer goods and services and how those habits have redrawn the line between haves and have-nots. A growing number of scholars from many different disciplines refuse to be warned off by the naysayers. They smell a big story behind the rebukes and polemics.

That story begins to sound something like this: Political and social stability in the

West has depended for the past 300 years on the success of national governments and national economies in helping people achieve "the good life" as measured by material goods and by the things that personal possessions enable them to do. Since the seventeenth century, Western nations have adopted policies and engaged in practices that enrich and empower men and women who are willing to participate in a consumer-driven economy as producers, middlemen, and, most of all, buyers and users. So doing, these nations have altered a fundamental connection between individuals and the groups to which they belong by making material things a universal language of social communications. Acquisition of status-bearing commodities opens access to social worlds and economic opportunities that former ages had controlled through mostly inherited (and therefore immutable) qualifications of race, gender, national identity, ethnic background, family bloodlines, and, by extension, property ownership and religious affiliation. Societies that have managed to lower those barriers and share the wealth of consumer goods widely and generously have mostly thrived. Those that haven't haven't, most recently and dramatically the former Soviet Union and its Iron Curtain satellites. Ample supplies of boom boxes and pantyhose today, or teapots and knitted hosiery two centuries ago, have had a remarkable cooling effect on people's ardor for butchering neighbors, beheading kings, and burning heretics.

How western European nations created this modern system of goods, how the industrial, marketing, and information revolutions have propelled it forward, and how a global economy now spreads its blessings and blights worldwide – surely here is a story that historians should be eager to call their own.

Those who study colonial North America have been among the first to respond. Colonies are particularly instructive places to make enquiries into the early history of consumption for two reasons. Almost as soon as it began, research on the subject sparked something resembling a nature-or-nurture controversy between economists and cultural historians, each convinced that they alone can explain the primal impulse to consume. Because newly settled colonies built economies and communities from the ground up, often simultaneously, they make excellent laboratories in which to observe both the economic and the cultural behavior of producers and consumers and to test theories about the genesis of such behavior in the seventeenth and eighteenth centuries.

There is a second reason why the colonial moment attracts special attention from students of consumption. Several theories advanced to explain the root cause of consumer demand postulate a historical link with overseas expansion, colonization, westward migration, and empire building up to and including cultural globalization at the turn of the twenty-first century. According to one argument, New World gold and silver put spending money in people's pockets, and New World commodities stocked stores with new products to spend it on (Mukerji, 1983; McCracken, 1988). Another hypothesis holds that portable, affordable, mass-produced consumer goods became the indispensable lingua franca of social communications for the vast numbers of people who began wandering the globe after 1600 (Carson, 1994; Wrightson, 2000). So, while no one denies that Europeans who stayed home became eager consumers too, colonies in general and North America and the West Indies in particular are accorded a leading role in inventing and spreading what has become our own modern consumer culture 400 years later.

This colonial version of the big story has emerged only recently. It was barely glimpsed even twenty years ago when consumption as a field of study began to take recognizable form. The history of material life does have a prehistory before that, before 1980, in a

Jurassic Age best remembered for four publications that loom large in the fossil record of consumption studies. While they have few modern ancestors, they serve as useful reminders that sustained scholarship flourishes in some intellectual climates better than in others.

Unsung Pioneers

Swiss sociologist Norbert Elias and French *annaliste* Fernand Braudel both wrote multi-volume books in which everyday objects and the rules and customs that governed their use supplied valuable evidence supporting their theses. Both authors addressed huge historical conundrums posed by the collapse of the old order in Europe at the end of the nineteenth century and the chaos following World War I. Elias wrote his highly eccentric *History of Manners* just as Hitler's National Socialists appeared to be reversing "the civilizing process" that Elias believed explained "the order underlying historical changes" going back to the Middle Ages. He chronicled that process by collecting and collating literary references to everything from table manners to toilet taboos. All, he believed, led in the "direction of a gradual 'civilization'" and illustrated "laws governing the formation of historical structures" (Elias, 1978 trans., pp. xii–xv).

Discovering structures was Fernand Braudel's passion too. In 1952 Lucien Febvre invited him to contribute a volume on European pre-industrial economies to the geographer-sociologist's great editorial project, *Destins du Monde* (*World Destinies*), a monograph series that capped Febvre's life work on race, environment, and human evolution – another career launched around the turn of the century. Braudel's own masterpiece in the series, *Civilization and Capitalism* (1981 trans.), begins, as he believed all economies do too, with *The Structures of Everyday Life*, volume one in a monumental trilogy not published until 1979. There he argues that the material limits to human existence – food supplies, housing stock, medical knowledge, energy sources, and other unalterable "limits of the possible" – were the basic economic building blocks that supported regional markets at the next level of complexity and ultimately transnational capitalism.

Consumption was not interesting to Braudel or Elias in and of itself. Nor were consumer goods *per se*, or rules of courtesy, or any other measures of consumer behavior except as they revealed evolutionary trends in Western civilization or the hidden structure underlying the world economy. All the same, both men amassed such a treasure-trove of unusual information in the course of their research that scholars who later took up the subject in earnest mined their tomes for the valuable nuggets they contained until their own hard work finally accumulated evidence better suited to their very different purposes. Since then, *The History of Manners* and *The Structures of Everyday Life* have become museum pieces.

Equally curious are two mid-century works by American authors. The Cold War challenged intellectuals in the United States to account for American exceptionalism. What happy providence had prepared such a young nation to "nobly save or meanly lose the last best hope of earth"? Two historians, David M. Potter and Daniel J. Boorstin, approached the question from very different directions, but arrived at a strikingly similar answer. They determined that the country owed its special destiny to its abundant resources and the aptitude of Americans to capitalize on this usable wealth. Abundance opened unparalleled economic opportunities, which a resourceful, ingenious, pragmatic, hardworking, freedom-loving people exploited to their own personal advantage and, so doing, redefined the concept of democracy by making "liberty" and "equality" nearly synonymous.

Potter's *People of Plenty* began as a systematic attempt to apply the science of human behavior to discovering Americans' national character. Nothing had shaped the country's distinctive personality so profoundly, he believed, as the influence of economic surplus on the ideal and practice of equality, American style. Europeans took that word to mean level status, uniform wealth, or shared power. Equality to Americans meant something different, namely, universal opportunity, parity in competition, or, as someone had put it 150 years earlier, the promise "that every man shall be free to become as unequal as he can." Alexis de Tocqueville had explained that "God Himself gave [Americans] the means of remaining equal and free by placing them on a boundless continent," an idea later expanded into Frederick Jackson Turner's "frontier thesis." Potter concurred, but added from his perspective as a historian with social science leanings that "upward mobility" fulfilled the American Dream too. "We often forget," he reminded readers in 1954, "that more Americans have changed their status by moving to the city than have done so by moving to the frontier" (Potter, 1954, pp. 92, 94).

Daniel Boorstin had not forgotten. For him, cities and the consumer culture that flourished there were wellsprings of the country's collective personality. Boorstin began writing and publishing *The Americans* in the late 1950s, but saved his fully developed argument for the third and final volume, *The Democratic Experience*, issued in 1973. As he saw it, descendants of New England Yankees, Pennsylvania Quakers, and southern planters were fast becoming a "new civilization" by the middle decades of the nineteenth century. Immigrants and their descendants had metamorphosed into a race of self-styled "go-getters" who classified themselves and one another "less by creed or belief" and more "by their wants, by what they made and what they bought" (Boorstin, 1973, p. 1). "Consumption communities," populated by people who shared lifestyles, brand names, income brackets, and many other statistical and market affinities, democratized luxury and homogenized "A Nation of Nations." That was the title Boorstin gave to an ambitious exhibition he mounted at the Museum of History and Technology when he became a director at the Smithsonian Institution in 1969 (Marzio, 1976). The title summed up his belief that there had always been a discernible flow to the broad river of American history, a movement toward assimilation and consensus that is solemnized and celebrated in the national motto, *E pluribus unum*. Not by coincidence that motto appears on the nation's money.

Boorstin's and Potter's books deserved a better reception than they got. Both made important breakthroughs by connecting consumption to equality and equality to mobility. Too bad the flaws in their scholarship waved such large red flags at a rising generation of social historians who came of age in the 1960s and early 1970s. These children of Sputnik, Little Rock, Kent State, Wounded Knee, and Seneca Falls had nothing but scorn for concepts like "American civilization" and "national character." Who could take seriously books that blithely ignored everybody who didn't conveniently figure in the national success story? Never mind Potter's honest concession that "the treatment of American Negroes" and others who were denied America's bounty were "conspicuous exceptions" to his thesis. No one was still listening when he added that the exceptions did not invalidate his generalizations.

The critics who damned these melting-pot historians for their sins against the new sacred doctrine of cultural pluralism also gave short shrift to the consumption issues that Potter and Boorstin were eager to raise. *People of Plenty* and *The Americans* were not easy books for younger historians to like in any case. Both glossed over other complex subjects besides the makeup of American society. Their failings were transparently obvious to scholars who repudiated the very existence of universal laws and cultural absolutes. Instead, the rising generation of historians held that any attempt to understand the larger forces at work in history had to build a synthesis piece by piece from the bottom up, preferably using quantitative evidence. And they were right. When students of consumption eventually ran the numbers, they proved that Potter and Boorstin had missed the consumer revolution by 200 years, thereby misunderstanding both its origins and its operation. Only very recently have these two pioneers enjoyed some belated recognition for their insights into the social consequences of consumer behavior, a contribution worth reassessing at the conclusion of this chapter.

Starting Fresh

The false starts had all played out by the late 1970s. Elsewhere, though, scholars working independently of one another began publishing research that quickly coalesced into the field of consumption studies that we know today. In the best tradition of multidisciplinary scholarship, the experimenters were usually working at the margins of their respective academic fields and often against the grain of received wisdom. Their surprise at discovering kindred spirits elsewhere and their eagerness to share ideas, borrow methodologies, and pool information have encouraged a collaborative endeavor that now invigorates studies of everything from history, anthropology, and archaeology to art, economics, and even policymaking.

Scholarship that ranks consumption alongside production as a competing explanation for historical change has implications that reach far beyond the place and period of England's seventeenth- and eighteenth-century American colonies. Likewise, outside influences from other disciplines and from historians who study the consumer habits of contemporary Americans have opened new vistas on consumption studies by students of the American colonies. Before taking a closer look at their work primarily, a summary review of the most important lines of investigation in the field as a whole will help explain why the topic has developed so rapidly and variously among historians who do write about consumer society in early America.

While the broader subject has its taproot deeply planted in economics, that fundament is sundered by a schism. Mainstream economists are baffled by students of consumption. For supply-siders, production is the problem to be solved, not the whys and wherefores of a consumer economy (Mokyr, 1977, 1985). As they see it, the Industrial Revolution raised standards of living in western Europe by churning out consumer goods in ever greater numbers at ever cheaper prices. Bigger, better, faster machines increased production; accelerated production multiplied goods and drove down prices; and a cornucopia of affordable goods excited demand. End of story, say most economists. Not so fast, answer a few maverick historians. How can the Industrial Revolution have set everything in motion when many observed that changes in demand actually preceded the rise of factories?

Elizabeth Gilboy proposed an alternative explanation seventy years ago that now bears her name. According to the Gilboy thesis, "the Industrial Revolution *presupposes* a concomitant development and extension of consumption" (1967, p. 122). Her cry in the wilderness went unheeded until Neil McKendrick (1974), Joan Thirsk (1978), Margaret Spufford (1984), and eventually other British historians began exploring how sixteenth-century cottage industries put underused labor to work earning extra pennies that were then spent on popular consumer sundries. Gradually and tentatively, a consensus has emerged that "economic growth began *earlier* . . . [and] the transforming power of industry was felt *later* than previously thought" (de Vries, 1993, p. 95).

Scholars of this persuasion pay close attention to standards of living, at first by doing research on the history of wages and prices (Fischer, 1996; Hoffman et al., 2000). Notable among those who have studied price movements in the American colonies are Winifred Rothenberg (1992) who collected farm prices in rural Massachusetts and Russell Menard (1977) who analyzed prices for tobacco and slaves in the Chesapeake colonies. Valuable as regional studies, their work proved even more useful by showing that standards of living could be turned into a quantifiable measure of consumption.

By itself the history of prices does not lead inevitably to the subject of consumption. A second group of influential scholars provided that connection. They were social historians, known famously as "new social historians" since the 1960s. They shared the *annalistes*' and Marxists' sympathetic interest in the lives of ordinary people, but not their obsession with typologies and not the notion that societies develop lockstep from one stage to another. Instead, they view the social order as a living organism – complex, protean, and dynamic. Their gaze focuses on the fuzzy margin that separates different groups in society, the contested no-man's-land they call "the middle ground." Here are waged the ongoing struggles for truth, wealth, power, and social acceptance that they see as the driving forces that make the world go round. Their practice of social history is therefore never a quest for universal states of being or natural laws or the essences of national character. Their work dissects and analyzes the messy real-life processes that make things work, get things done, and cause things to change. Their questions about the past often begin with "who" and "what;" they don't end until they have also asked "how" and "why."

It took a how question to point the way from price movements and growth rates toward a broader social history inquiry into living standards and consumer behavior. Alice Hanson Jones asked the question first: How well did the economic system in the thirteen colonies meet the needs of the "common man"? Her book, *Wealth of a Nation To Be* (1980), was the first major publication to apply modern statistical sampling techniques to eighteenth-century probate records (Jones had previously worked for the Bureau of Labor Statistics). Inventories of household goods and chattels are attached to English and American probate records by the tens of thousands. Jones, working with her thesis advisor Robert Fogel, discovered how to treat the appraised value of such goods as proxies for per capita wealth in an age before governments collected comprehensive income data. Furthermore, because wills and inventories carry information about individual decedents, they open the door to other questions that social historians want to ask about consumption, beginning with the basics: What commodities did consumers really acquire? How did they use them? And how have people's everyday lives been changed by their possession of up-market goods and the new things they can do with them? Better yet, large-scale inventory studies can raise questions that transcend individual households, and even local communities, to address society at large and to compare consumer cultures in different stages of development: Who exactly has shared in the wealth of material possessions? How evenly or unevenly have they been distributed? How have those differences upset the social order? How have advanced consumer societies worked their will on peoples and nations less developed?

Inventory research by Jones and her contemporaries – Lorna Weatherill (1988), Peter Earle (1989), James Horn (1994), and Carole Shammas (1990) working in British archives and Shammas, Horn, Gloria Main (1982; 1983; Main and Main, 1988), Lois Carr (Carr and Walsh, 1980, 1994), and Lorena Walsh (Walsh, Main, and Carr, 1988; Walsh in Schuurman and Walsh, 1994) in early American collections – soon branched out to other democratic sources and there made connections to other social history agendas. Like their politics, modern social historians are a loose assortment of special interest advocacy groups that make a few broad issues their common cause – race and gender principally, but now consumption as well, and, thus, inevitably, class consciousness too. Each has discovered that the spread of consumer culture left few groups untouched, but made a significantly different impact on not just rich and poor (Smith, 1981), but on families, women, and children (de Vries, 1993; Shammas, 1982; Calvert, 1992; Ulrich, 2001), Indians (Gilman, 1982; Axtell, 1992), and even slaves who were chattels themselves. Consumption studies have thus become another one of many lenses through which historians refract the lives of Everyman and Everywoman and their participation in a system of goods that was expanding rapidly by the eighteenth century. Social historians get credit for redrawing the figure of the consumer into someone much more complicated, more actively engaged in making choices, and more interesting historically than the highly rationalized supply-side automaton pictured by economists.

This emphasis on the cultural behavior of consumers has come from several directions, not just from history. Anthropologists and sociologists have been another influence on early American historians interested in colonists as consumers. They began writing books in the late 1970s and early 1980s that viewed consumption as a fundamental form of human communication and consumer goods as symbols that furnished a visually intelligible landscape. Two books by social scientists, *The World of Goods* (Douglas and Isherwood, 1979) and *The Meaning of Things* (Csikszentmihalyi and Rochberg-Halton, 1981), were perfectly timed to catch the second coming of consumption studies after 1980. Both made impressive debuts in academic circles where postmodernists were already preaching that all culture is socially constructed. Explaining how that process works became the highest calling for behavioral scientists and for cultural historians with a taste for semiotics, the study of symbolic language.

Little wonder that research soon focused on the history of marketing and advertising, those thoroughly modern arts of symbolic image-making (Ewen, 1976; Laird, 1998). A whole school of consumption scholarship sprang up in American Studies departments where students of popular culture have been busy ever since exploring American merchandizing in all its glitz and glory (Strasser, 1989; Harris, 1990; Leach, 1993). Their choice of subject matter harks back to David Potter and Daniel Boorstin, but the treatment they give it is entirely different. Jackson Lears, one of the earliest and most prolific writers in this vein, has suggested (1981) a postmodern explanation for Potter's observation that the national ethos shifted from production to consumption in the late nineteenth century. Lears argues that the Gilded Age packaged and promoted the lifestyles of the rich and famous as the new opium of the American masses. A ruling class of capitalists and financiers constructed their own self-aggrandizing "cultural hegemony" – their domination of society and politics – by literally selling everybody else a bill of consumer goods so irresistible that they happily surrendered to upper-class control in exchange for a piece of the American Dream. Critics have challenged this Vance Packard variation on the Marxist dialectic. Warren Susman, for example (1984), favors explanations based on developing technologies, and Daniel Horowitz has put forward a reciprocal model that takes into account "the ability of people, within limits, to shape the meaning of their [own] consumption patterns" (1985, p. 168). All start from a premise that is now accepted by everyone save only hardline economists, namely, that no Invisible Hand creates demand for consumer goods. People do.

Explaining why is the hard part. Answers differ depending on when scholars believe the consumer revolution happened. Not before the early twentieth century, say those who only study mass consumption as a modern phenomenon (Miller, 1987; Leach, 1993). Not much before 1880, according to the historians who want to make it a monster of Wall Street and Madison Avenue (Bronner, 1989). But these modernists have been ambushed from behind by another group of social scientists who take a longer historical perspective on the subject. Sociologist Chandra Mukerji (1983, p. 21) reads in the "patterns of modern materialism" an acquisitiveness that Europeans began learning when global trade delivered to their doors a flood of exotic novelties from Africa, Asia, and America beginning in the sixteenth century. These extraordinary goods "were so varied and so new" that they "created a crisis of meaning only solved by new attention to the material world." Similarly, anthropologist Grant McCracken (1988, pp. 10–22) has traced the first "consumer boom" to the court of Queen Elizabeth I. From her nobles, it trickled down to subordinates who, though uncomprehending, "nevertheless followed this behavior with care" and thus (a very big "thus") their descendants were "primed for a round of consumer excess" that began in the eighteenth century when competitive spending had become "a natural market force." Both arguments break down at the point where they take for granted that the consumer impulse was instinctive and its impact inescapable, a cultural variation on supply-side thinking. But McCracken's application of Mary Douglas's communications theory led him to the important insight that "role differentiation and anonymity" encouraged the use of goods to make "a cohesive society of perfect strangers," an idea full of implications that others have only recently begun to examine. So, while it is easy to poke holes in McCracken's and Mukerji's accounts of consumer behavior over the last 500 years, their long perspective served notice that modern consumption cannot be satisfactorily explained simply as the invention of department stores, world fairs, mail-order houses, and advertising agencies.

Pushing the genesis of consumer demand backwards in time, back before the nineteenth century, invited attention from still other investigators besides economists, social historians, and social scientists. These scholars have developed special skills for interpreting visual and artifactual evidence, often in circumstances where written records are missing or silent. By another happy coincidence of timing, an amphibious subject known as material culture was just emerging from the ooze of archaeology, social history, and museum curatorial studies when students of consumption began asking questions about material life in the centuries before 1800 (Quimby, 1978; Carson, 1997). Whether employed by universities or, notably, by history museums and historical societies, these material culture specialists all cast their eye on the extraordinary profusion of goods recorded in genre paintings, recovered by archaeologists, sought by collectors, and preserved in museums. The picture they see has not been easy to reconcile with the numbers compiled by economic historians that show a declining proportion of family incomes spent on consumer commodities precisely in the seventeenth and eighteenth centuries when material culture scholars insist that personal possessions and household furnishings multiplied dramatically. The quantifiers are vexed by such irrepressibly optimistic books as *The Embarrassment of Riches* (Schama, 1987) and *The Pursuit of Happiness* (Plumb, 1977), which interpret the proliferating abundance of worldly things as proof that people's standard of living was generally improving. These authors draw fire from the dismal science for trying "to make the study of commodities fun, liberating the material world of production and consumption from the dead positivist hand of the economic historian" (de Vries, 1993, p. 85).

The charge is that objects and artifacts lack the precision of prices and wages. Skeptics contend that the "direct evidence" of material culture is too impressionistic to be useful in dating significant changes in consumer behavior or demarcating its social and geographical limits (de Vries, 1993, p. 98). This is nonsense. Nothing could be more physically grounded than an archaeological site, and nothing more intrinsic to archaeological practice than determining the social and temporal contexts of excavated materials. Likewise, architectural historians and students of the decorative arts have been hugely successful in dating innovations in domestic living arrangements and the introduction (sometimes to the very year) of newfangled furnishings, tablewares, and fashionable clothing – all to the ultimate purpose of discovering the origins of the important social activities that these possessions made possible (Carson, 1994). Nor is there much mystery anymore to knowing how fast consumer goods spread through society or how far they traveled into the countryside and to faraway colonies. Students of material culture were among the first to perceive that comparative inventory studies could be used to map the diffusion of household goods from region to region, through time, and up and down the social pyramid (Cummings, 1964; Carr and Walsh, 1980; Main, 1982; Weatherill, 1988; Horn, 1994).

Best of all, because they study the use of objects and understand how they functioned as a consumer's personal tool kit in an ever more socially complex material world, scholars with material culture expertise are well qualified to address the question that remains unanswered even after others have satisfactorily explained how ordinary people eventually managed to afford so many store-bought amenities and luxuries. The ultimate question is one of motivation – again, the question why. Why did purchasers want these goods in the first place? What did they anticipate doing with them – things they absolutely couldn't do without them – that made their acquisition so desirable? In short, what special historical circumstances started our ancestors along the road to the shop on the corner first, the department store later, then the shopping mall, and nowadays Amazon.com?

Historians of colonial America have borrowed freely from all these players. Few topics in early American history have received such a thoroughly multidisciplinary treatment. Witness the many collaborators and contributors from history museums as well as history departments. Scholars working for Historic St. Mary's City (Maryland), the Smithsonian Institution, Colonial Williamsburg, Historic Deerfield (Massachusetts), and the Winterthur Museum have produced much of the basic research, written more than their usual share of key books and articles, and almost single-handedly introduced the general public to the notion of a pre-industrial consumer revolution in a number of major museum exhibitions. By now these shows have covered the entire colonial period and beyond, from "1699: When Virginia Was The Wild West!" at Colonial Williamsburg (Carson, Gilliam, Pittman, and Prown, 1999), through "Suiting Everyone: The Democratization of Clothing in America" (Cooper, Kidwell, and Kloster, 1974) and "New and Different: Home Interiors in Eighteenth-century America" at the Smithsonian (Golovin and Roth, 1986), to "Pursuing Refinement in Rural New England 1750–1850" at the Flynt Center of Early New England Life, Deerfield, Massachusetts (Zea, 1998).

These exhibitions have presented broad pictures of the past to the non-specialist visitors who attended them. But they have not been the only attempts by historians to construct a general narrative. In their published scholarship as well, those who study consumption in the thirteen colonies have gone as far as anyone in the field to define the major issues, debate points in contention, and strive for a synthesis that encompasses the whole Atlantic world. Maybe because the growth of consumer societies is easier to follow in settings where so much else was also new, Britain's mainland colonies in North America have become a center of intense investigation into the origins, operation, and consequences of consumer culture in the West.

Living Standards and Lifestyles

Historians have been easily persuaded that common folk enjoyed a rising standard of living in Elizabethan England because eyewitnesses said so. Old people alive in the 1570s told youngsters that many comforts they now took for granted had been "marveylously altered in Englande within their [elders'] remembraunce." Not until lately had farmers and tradesmen learned "to garnish their cubbords with plate, their beddes with tapistrie and silke hanginges [bed curtains], and their tables with fine naperie" (Harrison, 1577, p. 201). A few decades later, New Englanders expressed similar satisfaction in the progress of their fledging settlements: "The Lord hath been pleased to turn all the wigwams, huts, and hovels the English dwelt in at their first coming into orderly, fair, and well-built houses, well furnished many of them, together with Orchards . . . and gardens" (Jameson, 1910, p. 211). Recent research has not invalidated these observations, but it has revealed that they cannot be taken at face value.

For one thing, they gloss over a critical distinction that scholars now make between standards of living and standards of life (de Vries, 1993). Both measure people's well-being, but not the same way. Nutrition, fertility, disease resistance, life expectancy, and environmental conditions were matters over which pre-industrial peoples exerted little or no control. These were Braudel's "limits of the possible." By contrast, additions or improvements to dwellings, clothing, and household furnishings were real choices open to anyone who could afford them. The historical problems that most interest students of consumption usually concern those living standards that yielded to conscious decision-making, not to the hard realities of daily existence (Walsh, Main, and Carr, 1988). Diet – the consumption of food – figured somewhere between chance and choice. People had to eat whatever they could grow or get that also supplied them with the strength and energy to live and work. At the same time, dietary habits were heavily influenced by cultural preferences and taboos. These too had always responded to slowly changing tastes and, beginning in the seventeenth century, to the novelty of food fashions. In other words, foodstuffs perfectly illustrate the earlier point about social historians' special interest in understanding how things work. From one perspective, food is a source of life-giving caloric energy, quite literally a people's most basic living standard. From another, it is a profoundly habitual expression of their traditional culture. From a third, and this one is particularly pertinent to consumer studies, foodways sometimes deliberately break with tradition to signal fashionable diners' difference from or superiority to everybody else who eats some other way. Many other commodities serve multiple functions too, not just food. Historians, therefore, have to discover their particular uses in particular situations to fathom their true meaning.

That requires observing another distinction that is easily masked by eyewitness testimony to rising standards. This one is often overlooked by researchers who measure consumer behavior by "scoring" the presence or absence of commodities enumerated in probate inventories. Understanding the consumer revolution as a cultural phenomenon, over and above its part in transforming the early modern world economy, depends on appreciating the difference between living standards and lifestyles. Each was differently motivated. Standards refer to a people's level of welfare, their creature comforts, everything from their caloric intake to blankets on their beds and coats on their backs. People are motivated to seek a higher standard of living in order to feel warmer, drier, healthier, and better fed. Lifestyle means something else. It is a term that anthropologists define as a culture's characteristic manner of signaling its unique identity. Style is the outward sign of shared assumptions that pervade and invigorate everything a people does. Style uses a restricted vocabulary of words, forms, and actions to create a perceptible coherence in which self-acknowledged groups find consensus. The great differences in wealth and status that marked many traditional societies were reflected in the quantity and quality of material things, not in their different style. Style in folk cultures worked inclusively to bind all members of the group together by reaffirming everyone's similarities, be they kings or commoners.

A few style-setters began to change those rules in the seventeenth century for reasons that will soon bring my argument back to the question, why demand. Style was still used to signify belonging or not belonging. But its application and the motives behind it changed significantly. Increasingly after 1650, group membership was restricted to those men and women who demonstrated the skills of ladies and gentlemen and acquired clothing and other accouterments to match. Nowadays we call this lifestyle "fashionable"; to its earliest practitioners it was "genteel." Fashionable gentility showed off a look that accentuated divisions within cultural communities rather than between them. Eventually it made comrades of gentlefolk half a world away while leaving near but unequal neighbors worlds apart.

How are these different definitions of material life important to understanding consumption? Simply this: Economic historians who only count the volume and value of new consumer goods, but pay scant attention to their many different uses, have failed to grasp the big story outlined at the beginning of this chapter. Some even deny that a consumer revolution ever happened. By conflating standards and styles, they see only a long, gradual improvement in living conditions, not the transforming event avowed by cultural historians.

Early American Consumers

Migrating to North America was a journey back to basics for most colonists in the seventeenth century. By its very nature, planting colonies began by laying down social and economic foundations on which settlers endeavored to re-establish standards and styles of living that they hoped would eventually equal or better the lives they left behind. Nothing illustrates that ambition – and its frequent frustration – more clearly than their food consumption. English immigrants arrived in the colonies with a strong preference for a diet of grains, milk and cheese, salted fish, and meat from cattle, swine, and sheep when they could get it. The earliest settlers could not. So they substituted game, but not indiscriminately. Recent research by zooarchaeologists (animal bone specialists) reveals that the Virginia Company settlers at Jamestown ate only those species that were already familiar, however exotic, notably deer, rabbits, geese and ducks, snapping turtles, and various fish and fowl, some of which – gull, crow, cormorant, dolphin, and sturgeon – have disappeared from modern tables (Bowen and Andrews, 1999). Age-old rules restricted their choices to a few kosher foods despite a smorgasbord of wildlife just outside the gates. (Archaeologists further report that only once, during the desperate "starving time" in the winter of 1609–10, did Jamestowners violate ancient taboos against eating horse-flesh, dogs and cats, rats and mice, poisonous snakes, and even, infamously, each other.) Game and fish were lifesavers during the initial settlement years, wildlife accounting for half the colonists' meat diet c.1610. Yet, despite these abundant nearby food supplies, Englishmen eagerly reverted to the "solid sufficiency" of their customary cuisine as soon as they settled their own farms and plantations. Butchered livestock provided 90 percent of meat consumed after 1620 in the Chesapeake colonies and soon thereafter in New England as well (McMahon, 1985; Bowen, 1994). Restoring Old World standards was everybody's fondest hope if and when conditions in the New World allowed.

Besides the delays and compromises that frontier circumstances forced on colonists, there were other consumer choices they saw as trade-offs. Fieldwork by archaeologists and students of vernacular architecture has brought to light an investment strategy that was widely followed by beginning homesteaders (Carson et al., 1981). Most greenhorns could not afford to build or buy everything they needed all at once. So they deliberately denied themselves many comforts of home in order to invest their limited resources in income-producing assets, mainly land, labor, livestock, and capital improvements. It frequently took them three steps to regain the housing and furnishing standards they remembered from England. New arrivals on each frontier lodged temporarily in such makeshift "wigwams, huts, and hovels" as Edward Johnson said the Lord had later been pleased to replace in New England with well-built, well-furnished houses. Certainly "fair framed English houses" were the ultimate answer to many settlers' prayers and the third and final step toward achieving the living standard they had known at home. For most, though, getting there required an intermediate second step. Most homesteaders in every colony chose to build small, inexpensive houses and barns that were just good enough to see them through the critical start-up years. These structures were built by professional carpenters drawing partly on a repertoire of English impermanent building techniques and partly making free with America's prodigious timber resources. The hybrid was a building without foundations raised on structural posts that were set directly into holes in the ground, nailed together with as little expensive joinery as possible, and covered entirely with riven (split, not sawn) "clabbord-work" (Fig. 14.1). A timber chimney made it a dwelling; otherwise it was equally serviceable as a barn, stable, storehouse, or even courthouse.

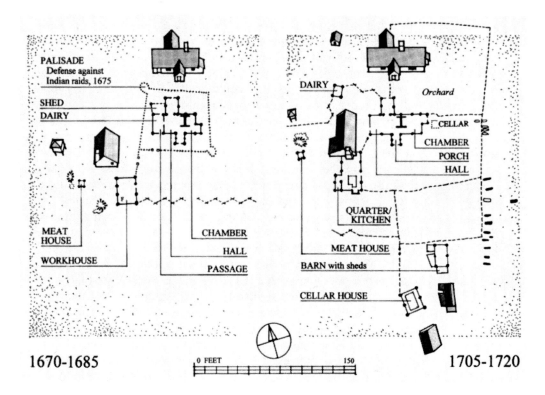

PALISADE
Defense against
Indian raids, 1675

SHED

DAIRY

MEAT HOUSE

WORKHOUSE

CHAMBER

HALL

PASSAGE

1670-1685

0 FEET   150

DAIRY

Orchard

CELLAR

CHAMBER

PORCH

HALL

QUARTER/ KITCHEN

MEAT HOUSE

BARN with sheds

CELLAR HOUSE

1705-1720

Figure 14.1 Different accommodations for race and class at Clifts Plantation, Westmoreland County, Virginia, c. 1670–1730. The substantial tenant who built the one-story, timber frame "manner house" on Thomas Pope's Northern Neck plantation chose a familiar three-part English plan that made the house a busy center of domestic activities and farm work. A through passage admitted indentured servants and slaves into a dairy and a work shed beyond and gave them direct access to the hall, which was kitchen and common mess hall for family and farmhands alike. Distribution analyses of ceramic shards and tobacco pipestem fragments show that masters and servants also labored side by side in a nearby workhouse used to process farm produce for bulk storage. Thirty years later Pope's son took up residence and altered the dwelling to restrict entry by farm workers who by then were mostly enslaved Africans and their descendents. The passage was closed, work shed pulled down, and dairy removed to an outbuilding. A quarter and kitchen replaced the workhouse. A very different pattern of ceramic and pipestem evidence indicates that whites and blacks were now cooking, eating, socializing, and sleeping separately. The hall, now entered exclusively through the porch tower, served principally as dining room for Pope's own family and friends; his bedchamber, enlarged twice before 1730, was turning into a sitting parlor. Even in death the races went their separate ways, whites to a graveyard adjoining the garden, blacks to a plot beyond the barn. (Drawing by Cary Carson and William Graham, Jr. after Fraser D. Neiman)

The point worth noting is that these starter houses resulted from colonists' calculated decisions to endure substandard accommodations temporarily so as to improve the odds of prospering over the long term. James Horn's comparative studies of English and Chesapeake probate records (1988, 1994) show that the strategy extended to household furnishings as well. Everyone hoped, of course, that success would restore the "English ways" to which they once had been accustomed or, at least, to which they aspired. Those expectations were soon fulfilled for many farmers in New England. By contrast, generations of small planters in Maryland and Virginia were trapped in a homesteader's limbo by the extortions of tobacco agriculture and a death rate that decimated many families prematurely.

Eventually – sooner for some, later for others – living conditions caught up with expectations. That meant a return to consumer lifestyles that were still profoundly traditional for almost everyone. Fashion – the exclusive style of gentility – appeared only here and there before the end of the seventeenth century and, then, mostly among officials and others with connections abroad. Material life for ordinary folk conformed to local custom, rich people often owning more and better things than their poorer neighbors, but more and better of the same things. All wore similar clothing, in spite of sumptuary laws and notwithstanding the privilege that wealth and rank conferred on those who could afford to wear quality fabrics and own clothing and accessories in quantity (Trautman, 1989). So too with foodways – the Englishman's diet, cookery, and table customs. Once established, farms and plantations were soon raising all the basic foodstuffs that transplanted Europeans hungered for: wheat for bread, cattle and hogs for meat, vegetables in season, and fruit for cider in the South and later in New England too when beer-making declined in the early eighteenth century. Rural households in the northern and middle colonies regularly produced two more English staples, butter and cheese, but dairying was rare in the South where the climate was too warm for good cheese-making and where planters usually let unfenced cattle fend for themselves. Imported grocery products such as sugar, tea, and coffee were not widely consumed until the eighteenth century and then first by fashionable folk before they became everyday staples after 1750 or so (McMahon, 1985; Shammas, 1990; Bowen, 1994).

Fashion was likewise mostly absent from the up-to-standard houses that successful colonists built and furnished to replace their homestead structures. Here too they clung to age-old customs that paid respect to social rank, not class, and expected deference from social inferiors, not invisibility. Halls, kitchens, and chambers were still rooms that combined numerous activities and accommodated everybody who performed them in spaces shared by all (Fig. 14.2). Even parlors, though increasingly reserved for householders and their guests, were frequently furnished for eating, sleeping, socializing, business and bookkeeping, and storing valuables – house habits that lasted well into the eighteenth century (Cummings, 1979; St. George, 1982). The idea of rooms set aside exclusively for dining or for otherwise entertaining class-conscious gentlefolk was utterly foreign to most tradition-minded colonists. Masters and servants generally entered through the same doorways and climbed the same staircases. Exceptions appeared earliest in the South when planters discovered that certain imported regional English house plans were easier than others to segregate against the indentured knaves and African slaves who worked around the house (Fig. 14.1) (Carson, 1976; Quimby, 1978, pp. 52–4; Neiman, 1980). Folk housing looked different in different regions, to be sure, but before the onset of fashion, few dwellings anywhere made distinctions between public and private living spaces.

The furniture and housewares that colonists acquired beyond a starter kit of "bare necessities" reveal something else about traditional lifestyles that the consumer revolution would sweep away. Before that modern age, domestic furnishings were either useful tools (tables, stools, and cooking utensils, for example) or the equipment needed to store and sometimes display the few household goods that did have real value, notably precious metals (plate and jewelry) and expensive textiles (table linens, blankets, and bed curtains). Probate inventories show that, as soon as Chesapeake planters could manage, they furnished themselves with extra cooking equipment first, then tables, chairs, and better beds, and, finally for the wealthy, cupboards, clothespresses, and the valuable things that were kept inside them or displayed on top (Horn, 1994). Many such improvements simply made life more comfortable and convenient and meals tastier and less monotonous. In other words, they raised basic standards. Additional luxurious furnishings seldom introduced new or alien lifestyles; on the contrary, they often supplied ancient and familiar accessories to social rank – special seating for the "chairman" of the "tableboard," "cup-boards" to show off his silver "plate," "dresser" sideboards for dressing his meat, and bedsteads draped with costly "tapestry" curtains. All were recognizable emblems of rank, befitting a yeoman in his own farmhouse no less than a king in his castle. Emblems are one thing; modern consumer goods would become something altogether different, namely, enabling instruments with the power to transform owners and users into whatever their hearts desired and their purses could afford.

The importance that Europeans had always attached to material things that identified kith and kin, measured social rank, and hoarded personal treasure was typical of other folk cultures, including the indigenous peoples that colonists encountered in North America. Although some ethnohistorians would give Native Americans credit for "the first consumer revolution" (Axtell, 1992), most Indians acquired European trade goods to improve their living standards and augment their Native traditions and customs. Excavated grave goods reveal exactly what Indians most desired. Durable, sharp-edged, iron tools performed traditional tasks faster and easier than stone and bone implements. Metal knives and scissors refashioned imported blankets into leggings, mantles, and other traditional articles of Indian clothing once hides and furs acquired a higher value as trade goods. Glass beads, silver coins, tinkling cones, and brass and copper ornaments became exotic jewelry worn in Native fashion. Most trade goods reinforced and elaborated Indians' customary standards and styles. Others – notably firearms and liquor – were enormously destructive. Later, when remnants of some Indian nations settled down in "praying towns" and individuals adopted the trappings of gentility, they were participating in the *European* consumer revolution, not a different one of their own making.

Africans were the bearers of another rich traditional culture, which the "Middle Passage" and the rigors of slavery put at extreme risk. Bondage stripped captives of almost all personal possessions, and servitude erased the social gradations that African status symbols had once calibrated. Yet, despite this deadly assault on their culture, survivors strove to rebuild sustainable standards of life and living that salvaged remnants of their former lifestyles. Recent research by Lorena Walsh (1992, 2001) has shown that regional slave-trading patterns along the Tobacco Coast landed newly arriving West Africans in locally concentrated ethnic groups, which greatly improved their chances of retaining common cultural traditions. A growing body of evidence suggests that enslaved newcomers often rejected European practices when they conflicted with their own. For example, Africans reserved the wearing of clothing to sexually mature adolescents, and even adults preferred fewer garments than Europeans considered decent. A taste for stewed vegetables prepared separately from starchy porridges may have encouraged traditional, African, two-pot cooking in slave quarters. Other remembered customs included eating with hands rather than spoons, living in small, earth-floored houses, and sleeping on floor mats, not bedsteads (Fig. 14.3). Eventually, a creole population of native-born African American slaves and free blacks grew sufficiently large and complex – and remote from any living experience of Africa – to begin making selective use of European-style goods as badges of personal identity within the black community.

In short, three venerable folk cultures collided in North America. None arrived or survived intact, so all required renewal, each in its own way. The first step, re-establishing livable standards, created demand for a bread basket and a shopping basket of basic consumables; restoring familiar lifestyles added other desirable goods for European settlers. Altogether they energized home production and quickened overseas trade. All by themselves, they fell well short of launching a consumer revolution.

Why Demand?

No one disagrees that the pace of consumption accelerated dramatically throughout the colonial period. But, so saying only brings up again the unreconciled perceptions of cultural historians and economists. "The world of goods," Jan de Vries observes (1993, p. 101), "seems oddly disconnected from the world of wealth." Ralph Waldo Emerson witnessed the one. In 1837 he recorded his astonishment at the "endless procession of wagons loaded with the wealth of all the regions of England, of China, of Turkey, of the Indies which from Boston creep by my gate to all the towns of New Hampshire and Vermont. The train goes forward at all hours, bearing this cargo of inexhaustible comfort and luxury to every cabin in the hills." By the 1830s consumerism was already far advanced. Yet, with few exceptions, each earlier generation, going back to the mid-seventeenth century, had left behind more and better possessions for inventory-takers to record.

Here is the paradox so puzzling to economists. These ever larger numbers of worldly goods assumed no commensurately larger proportion of the value of probated estates. Frequently, their relative value actually fell. Researchers find this contradiction almost everywhere they look in England, Holland, and North America from the late seventeenth century to and through the heyday of the Industrial Revolution. People everywhere acquired more and more consumer durables without reallocating their total wealth to pay for them. For some economists, this logical absurdity calls the whole notion of a consumer revolution into question. Others seek explanations in falling prices, rising wages, faster rates of depreciation when fashionable goods rapidly become old hat, or the substitution of new goods for old ones of equal value.

Jan de Vries, whose essay in *Consumption and the World of Goods* (1993) presents a closely reasoned analysis of early consumer behavior, works out which explanations were factors and which were not. In the end, he concludes that none fully explains the

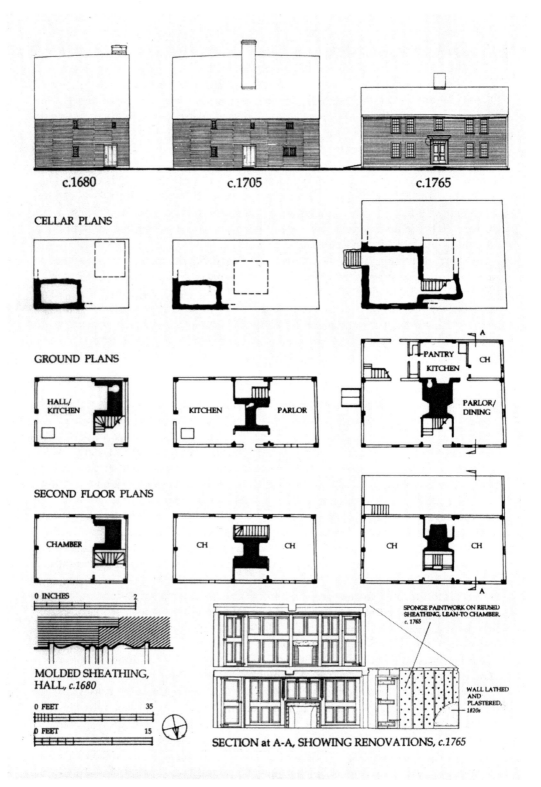

c.1680   c.1705   c.1765

CELLAR PLANS

GROUND PLANS

HALL/ KITCHEN

KITCHEN   PARLOR

PANTRY
KITCHEN   CH

PARLOR/ DINING

A

SECOND FLOOR PLANS

CHAMBER

CH   CH

CH   CH

A

0 INCHES   2

MOLDED SHEATHING, HALL, c.1680

0 FEET   35

0 FEET   15

SPONGE PAINTWORK ON REUSED SHEATHING, LEAN-TO CHAMBER, c. 1765

WALL LATHED AND PLASTERED, 1820s

SECTION at A-A, SHOWING RENOVATIONS, c.1765

Figure 14.2   Gentrification of the Thomas Lee House, Niantic, East Lyme, Connecticut. Built fourth quarter 17th century; enlarged c. 1705; sash windows replaced casements before 1760s; enlarged again c. 1765. The house that Thomas Lee (II) built new about 1680 provided accommodations that were considered sufficient by many prosperous farmers throughout the American colonies – a hall/kitchen and a bedchamber. New England farmhouses typically located the principal sleeping room upstairs. The hall below was still the traditional locus for all daytime activities from cooking and home production to eating and entertaining. Accordingly, Lee sheathed his one and only best room in shadow-molded vertical boards and stained them with red paint. But time was running out for such old-fashioned folkways, even in rural Connecticut. Either Lee himself shortly before his death in 1704, or his son soon after, doubled the size of the house by adding a parlor as a retreat from the hubbub of the kitchen and a superior bedchamber over the parlor for the master and mistress. The larger house thus made room for social distinctions among the inmates and social activities that needed separate spaces. The Lee House was still nowise fashionable. That concession to a genteel world beyond East Lyme was not made for another fifty years, not until the old casement windows were finally replaced by matched pairs of double-hung sash windows that faced passersby on the road outside. Fashion came indoors sometime in the 1760s. The working parts of the house – kitchen, pantry, another service room, and a small back chamber – withdrew into a lean-to at the rear and into a greatly enlarged cellar. That freed the front rooms for socializing. Now even farmers insisted on formal architectural settings to entertain family, friends, and a growing number of outsiders. The walls of grandfather's parlor and parlor chamber, still sheathed with planed and molded planks, lacked refinement. So Elisha Lee replaced them with raised panels in his two best rooms, perhaps taking the occasion to turn the parlor into a formal dining room. Archaeological excavations confirm the new front–back separation of household activities: shards from tea sets and refined table wares were swept out the front door, but no coarse wares; broken pots and pans were thrown out the back way. Although country customs were banished from the formal rooms, they still reigned in the lean-to, the domain of women, domestic servants, and farmhands. There second-hand sheathing from the front rooms was reused to build partitions. Whitewash took the place of paint, and traditional spongework decoration still delighted unsophisticated eyes. Refinements such as plastered walls and ceilings spread gradually through the whole house only after 1820. (Drawing by Cary Carson)

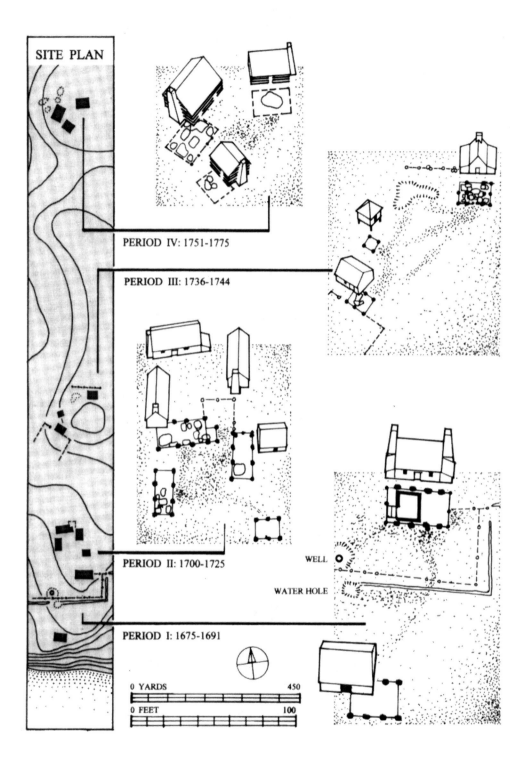

SITE PLAN

PERIOD IV: 1751-1775

PERIOD III: 1736-1744

PERIOD II: 1700-1725

PERIOD I: 1675-1691

WELL

WATER HOLE

0 YARDS   450

0 FEET   100

Figure 14.3 Four generations of housing for indentured servants and enslaved Africans at Utopia Quarter, Pettus-Bray-Burwell Plantation, James City County, Virginia, *c.*1675–1775. Owners and the occupants themselves built a variety of accommodations for a changing labor force on the plantation. Period I, *c.*1675–1691: Thomas Pettus II employed both English servants and transported Africans to grow tobacco and raise livestock. The quarter, overlooking the James River, consisted of a drying barn for the crop, stock pond, fenced yard, well, and a dwelling. Although smaller, the timber-framed cottage resembled Pettus's own house with glazed windows, wooden floor, and timber chimneys heating the principal rooms, a hall and bedchamber. Possibly built by a tenant, the house had become a quarter for servants or slaves when Pettus later installed a brick-lined cellar for dry storage of plantation supplies or produce. Period II, 1700–1725: By the time James Bray II acquired the property by marriage to Pettus's widow, the slave trade was fast replacing the traffic in indentured servants. Bray owned 75 slaves by 1725. Their number enabled many to live together in an African-like compound of three dwellings, a barn, and fences arranged around a common yard. Covered pits in the earthen floors near the hearths in all three buildings protected root vegetables from frost; numerous smaller pits in two houses were personal cubby holes that belonged to unrelated inmates typical of newly arrived Africans. Bray's black overseer may have been a woman, Debb, who exercised a traditional African matriarch's authority over this heterogeneous community. Period III, 1736–1744: Young James Bray III inherited his grandfather's plantation in 1736 and began raising wheat in addition to tobacco and cattle. He rebuilt Utopia Quarter farther inland to accommodate his field hands, 27 slaves in all by 1744. Some had lived on the plantation long enough to form families; others were newcomers judging from their African names. The new quarter housed both groups. A 12 by 16 ft cottage was probably a dwelling for a second generation African-Virginian family, or alternatively for Bray's overseer, now a white man. Single farmhands, probably including Africans fresh off the boat, bunked together in a barracks some distance away. Sheds on both sides and a doorway in the gable suggest that this dormitory was a reused tobacco or hay barn. Its earth floor was studded with root cellars and personal storage pits. Period IV, 1751–1775: Before 1750, all buildings at Utopia Quarter employed the cheapest technology known to Chesapeake carpenters – earthfast timber frames covered with riven clapboards. When Nathaniel Burwell acquired the plantation and moved the quarter again, he lodged his slaves in another form of low cost housing, log houses. One was a duplex for two families. The quarter was abandoned after the American Revolution, by which time Burwell owned almost 100 slaves, probably not all housed here. (Unpublished research courtesy of Garrett Fesler; drawing by Cary Carson and William Graham, Jr.)

evidence for growth in consumer demand. Instead, he argues that consumption of marketed goods grew because large numbers of households reallocated their productive resources. Underemployed labor, especially women's and children's, was put to harder, more constant, market-oriented work earning the money income needed to purchase store-bought foodstuffs, manufactured goods, and commercial services. Those commodities were often imported into the colonies too. By the 1770s average Americans spent over a quarter of their household budgets on consumer goods imported from outside their own colony (Shammas, 1982). Women, servants, and slaves produced much of the income-earning surplus needed to buy into this expanding commercial world. So both in England and her colonies, what de Vries calls an "industrious revolution" preceded and prepared the way for the technology-driven Industrial Revolution by concentrating household labor on market production. As a result, households could increase their yearly money earnings relative to individual daily wage rates, and this growth in purchasing power could occur independently of technological advances or the growth of capital wealth. Busy hands account for rising demand. De Vries offers a complementary explanation for the fact that the stock of new goods purchased with this extra pin money failed to show up in probate inventories as an enlarged share of householders' total wealth. The reason, he theorizes, is because fashionable goods, often less durable, were not only cheaper, but more quickly depreciated and replaced, in effect, coming and going many times over before the consumer's death finally occasioned the making of an inventory. Thus can de Vries rest easy at last that "the resolution to the contradiction between the wage and probate inventory data is at hand" (1993, p. 114).

His work does finally explain how the consumer revolution was made affordable. It does not answer the question of motivation. If anything, it begs that question more urgently because now we know that tens of thousands of ordinary men, women, and even children willingly sacrificed leisure for labor to become (in the words of one eighteenth-century political economist) "slaves to their own wants." So, what explains their shifting expectations? Even de Vries concedes that wanting material things over and above "a physiological minimum," that is, over and above basic living standards, is a "social decision," a choice defined by the chooser's cultural values (de Vries, 1993, pp. 112, 117).

To discover what those values were, and how they were changing, social historians who study material culture have asked what choices people actually made. It stands to reason that the function of the material things they acquired and learned to use is a strong indicator of their motives for making those choices in the first place and, therefore, also a clue to the meanings they attached to the goods themselves and to the benefits they expected them to bring.

In reality, demand for almost everything skyrocketed over the whole colonial period. Benjamin Franklin, testifying before the House of Commons in 1766, grouped the goods that colonists consumed into "necessities, mere conveniences, [and] superfluities." By Franklin's time, the luxuries he termed "articles of fashion" accounted for "much the greatest part" of Britain's import trade to the colonies. Even so, the market for basic commodities had grown rapidly too, partly in step with America's burgeoning population and partly because mere conveniences had become essential necessities for everyone, even for people at the margins of society. At first, almost everything needed to settle colonies and improve basic living standards had been imported from abroad. One hundred and fifty years later, the mix of merchandise included many American manufactures, but an even greater spur to galloping materialism was the abundance of store-bought goods that had become indispensable necessities to a universe of consumers, including poor whites and even slaves by 1790 (Walsh, 1992; Martin, 1992). Purchases by the millions began making a significant dent in the eighteenth-century economy. All the same, most commodities still only fulfilled people's everyday wants; they were choices people still made for convenience, comfort, and conceit. Far fewer acquisitions were the sort that fundamentally changed their culture, their lifestyle.

Those few that did – "the right stuff" we call such things today – assumed a social significance disproportionate to their numbers initially. Paying close attention to the function of these special, fashion-laden goods shows how newfangled class-consciousness invaded old-style culture-consciousness. It calls attention to social behavior that subdivided cultural communities differently than folk cultures had been rank ordered in the past. The difference is a reminder that English society was undergoing a realignment in the seventeenth and eighteenth centuries, one that not so much overturned the traditional social order as it imbued the leisured squirearchy with cultural attributes that set them apart from the laboring classes below them. The qualities that distinguished and differentiated them were embodied in a code of conduct that people at the time called gentility (Bushman, 1992). Its refinement of mind and manners was something gentlemen and ladies had to take time to learn, time that working people could not spare. It required the mastery of prescribed social skills and practice in the use of objects that were made and bought specially for those purposes. When well rehearsed and correctly presented, gentility transformed activities of everyday life into the art of fashionable living. Fashion became a badge of membership (or a bid for membership) in newly class-conscious social groups. As the outward signs of gentry superiority, consumer goods and the social arts they were used to perform served, first, as shared symbols of group identity and, second, as instruments and opportunities that social climbers mimicked in their haste to scramble up the social ladder.

Is emulation then the common-sense explanation for "the frenzy of Fashion"? Is it the ultimate answer to the enigma of demand? Certainly, many eighteenth-century observers thought so. A refrain heard repeatedly in the British press – "While the Nobleman will emulate the Grandeur of a Prince; and the Gentleman will aspire to the proper State of the Nobleman; the Tradesman steps from behind his counter into the vacant place of the Gentleman" – was sounded in the colonies as well: "The wife of the laboring man wishes to vie in dress with the wife of the merchant, and the latter does not wish to be inferior to the wealthy woman of Europe." Many believed that mass-produced luxuries would lead inevitably to social mischief. A gloomy Samuel Adams foresaw the day when they would erase "every Distinction between the Poor and the Rich" (Carson, 1994, pp. 519–21).

Many modern historians share the assumption that keeping up with the Joneses comes as naturally to humankind as getting fat and turning gray and has always waited only on the right conditions to take effect. "The novel feature of the eighteenth century," says Neil McKendrick, for example (1974, p. 198), "was not its desire to pursue fashion, but its ability to do so." Consequently, students of consumption have seldom bothered to explain why ordinary people chose to spend their discretionary income on very different things than those that their forefathers desired. Instead they prefer to investigate the social and economic conditions that released a universal impulse to consume. British historians argue that the dense layering of English society fostered competition, excited emulation, encouraged upward mobility, and gave manufacturers and shopkeepers price points for every pocketbook (McKendrick, Brewer, and Plumb, 1982; Brewer and Porter, 1993). They take account of other factors as well: the size and magnetism of London, a growing population, easy access to cheap money, rapidly expanding markets, improved food supplies, the division of labor for mass production, and a happy combination of other circumstances that came together in the eighteenth century to create an ideal breeding ground for England's embryonic consumer society.

Those who study consumer behavior in North America have tried equally hard to identify and isolate the prerequisites to emulative spending in the colonies. Using a microscope rather than the telescope favored by English historians, they have scrutinized New England, Maryland, and Virginia region by region. Their work shows that, within the broad time limits that bracket the advent of consumerism everywhere, close attention to the timing of its appearance from one place to another can help historians distinguish primary pre-conditions from those that were only contributing factors. The key determinants in the upper South turn out to have been the density of settlement necessary to sustain local stores and the spread of mixed agriculture needed to stabilize local economies by smoothing out the market ups and downs endemic to the tobacco trade. Many localities in the Chesapeake region achieved both conditions in the first decades of the eighteenth century. In New England and the middle colonies, regional economies built on the sale of agricultural commodities not only pumped up consumer spending among farmers, the profits provided venture capital to invest in shipping, shipbuilding, coopering, chandlering, milling, and manufacturing. Such enterprises in turn gave work to thousands of sailors, clerks, artisans, and laborers. These wage earners eagerly consumed additional goods and services, which further expanded the market for English and American manufactures (Carr and Walsh, 1994; McCusker and Menard, 1985, chs. 5, 9, 13; Shammas, 1982; Breen, 1986; Main and Main, 1988).

Regional studies go a long way to explain a people's readiness to participate in an international consumer culture. In the last analysis though, neither the closely argued American approach nor the broad-brush treatment that the subject has received from British scholars tells us why so many ordinary people in the eighteenth century put aside the tradition-rich lifestyles of their forebears to become avid seekers after fashion – not unless historians swallow the notion that people's passion for frock coats and sugar tongs is encoded in their genes and had only lain dormant and frustrated until events after 1700 finally set it free.

Another explanation requires no leap of faith. Not only is it grounded in circumstances peculiar to the decades when modern consumerism first appeared, but it applies to all those regions and countries where fashion flourished, regardless of their different stages of economic development. Best of all, it explains how fashion-bearing consumer goods solved specific social problems better than anything else. It accounts for demand in terms of the things demanded.

To note all the special furniture forms and tablewares that were created brand-new or entered mainstream popular culture between approximately 1650 and 1750 is to demonstrate with astonishing clarity when and where the modern consumer environment originated. Its birthplace was the domestic parlor, the social center of the gentleman's and gentlewoman's house; and it made its first appearance at their dinner table, the prime household setting for genteel social interactions. Parlors have a history even older than England's American colonies. They began as best bedrooms in medieval times. Gradually they acquired additional uses as sitting rooms, dressing rooms, and private withdrawing chambers where family, friends, and guests took meals separately from the farmhands and servants who were left behind in the "mess" hall. These developments varied from place to place, but everywhere to the same effect: to partition houses according to the inmates' social rank, to direct traffic along social lines, and to reserve special places for gatherings of social equals (Fig. 14.2). This architectural evolution took a couple of centuries to spread to ordinary houses almost everywhere. Before it was done, the fashionable dwelling had become a precision machine for receiving newcomers in a central entryway, admitting peers into salons and drawing rooms, entertaining guests in parlors and dining rooms, giving family members private bedchambers, and keeping servants, slaves, and tradesmen hidden away in kitchens and pantries and their movements channeled along back passages and up and down concealed staircases. By the end of the eighteenth century even prosperous farmhouses were zoned into public entertaining rooms, private rooms for family activities, and work spaces and staff quarters located "below stairs," in back rooms, or outside in separate service buildings. Household furnishings further refined the functions of these specialized interiors. They also show how gentlefolks put them to use every day coping with social situations that were increasingly governed by a new set of rules called etiquette. Telltale innovations appeared first at the dining table. For long ages past, mealtimes had been daily occasions when household members were seated around the table according to their rank, a time William Cobbett remembered when the typical English farmer used "to sit at the head of the oak table along with his men, say grace to them, and cut up the meat and the pudding." Gradually, master and mistress excused themselves from those communal tableboards and withdrew from the hall into the nearby parlor, often still serving as their bedchamber as well. There they took private meals at a smaller table in the more exclusive company of family and friends.

Fashion transformed the dining event. No longer was it the everyday occasion where the householder acted out his seigniory. Instead formal dining gave each and every person at the table numerous scripted opportunities to demonstrate his or her table manners, culinary sophistication, and mastery of the specialized tools that set each place. Identical place settings with matching sets of plates, drinking vessels, and utensils replaced ancient tablewares whose different forms and materials had signified the different status of the users. Gone too was the hierarchy of seating furniture from the master's wainscot great chair to the benches, stools, and miscellaneous chests and boxes for everybody else. Their places around a fashionable table were taken by sets of matching, upholstered, "turkeywork" back-stools or highbacked chairs covered with cane or leather. Chairs by the dozen flooded the American market in the second half of the seventeenth century; in 1688 it was estimated that "above Two thousand Dozens [were] yearly Transported into almost all the Hot Parts of the World." That number did not include thousands more made by chair-frame makers in Boston and Philadelphia by 1700 and shipped south to port cities all along the seaboard.

The advent of fashionable dining even changed the shape of four-sided tables. They became round or oval. Tables without corners made a closed circle of men and women whose shared commitment to the arts of civility outweighed any meaningful differences in their rank. Master and mistress were replaced by host and hostess, and so thorough was the revolution in manners that husbands and wives actually traded places. The meat and pudding duties were reassigned to the hostess, who took up the place of honor. The host, seated opposite at the foot, was responsible for the guests' "entertainment," that is, the company's exchange of pleasantries. Companions seated at an oval table enjoyed greater informality, what an English hostess called "this French fashion of perfect ease."

Gentility and good manners made their first public appearance in the parlor. Behind the scenes they also refurnished the dressing chamber where parlor-users made their careful preparations, and they re-equipped the kitchen where housewives, cooks, and slaves produced a nouvelle cuisine served now in formal courses. Eventually these parlor and dining room activities were enlarged on and elaborated until tea tables, looking glasses, daybeds, and easy chairs ruled over a fashionable gentleman's entire house as completely as they ruled his whole life.

What benefit did this fashionable lifestyle confer on men and women whose ancestors had in their own way, of course, never lacked material and visual indicators of social standing? Theirs had simply been status symbols of a different kind. Understanding that difference is the secret to understanding the utility of fashion and the demand for its products. Reputation in those older English and European folk communities had always been measured in terms of a man's land, labor, livestock, expensive textiles, precious plate, and capital improvements among his property, estimable kinfolk among his relations, and the offices he held and the largess he dispensed in the exercise of his authority. All but plate and textiles were rooted in their locality, and linens, gold, and silver were always safest locked away. Reputation was indivisible from place in the small worlds that dotted medieval and Tudor England. A farmer's renown was his only letter of credit beyond the village boundaries. And while his network of acquaintances might extend some miles around – country folk were not as homebound as scholars once believed – he usually did not travel very far afield. Most yeomen, husbandmen, and farm laborers placed the village of their birth at the center of their universe. So it had been for centuries.

This patchwork quilt of commonplaces began to come unraveled, and the local colors run together, as economic pressures accelerated the movement of people and as new ideas expanded their horizons in the sixteenth century. The colonization of North America was a spillover from these local and regional migrations across the British Isles and eventually across large parts of northern Europe as well. Likewise, the restless populations of Spain and Portugal supplied soldiers and settlers to Central and South America during the same period. The westward transoceanic movement of Europeans and enslaved Africans not only forms the foundation of New World history, it is the key event in understanding the origins of modern consumer behavior and the development of visual literacy since the Middle Ages. It holds the answer to the question, why demand.

A world in motion was a world full of strangers. Accidental tourists and neighbors by happenstance spoke unintelligible languages and practiced unfamiliar customs. They were necessarily unacquainted with each other's social standing back home since the traditional and continuing measures of reputation – property, family, and offices – were unavoidably left behind. Immigrants and long-distance travelers therefore had need to invent a brand-new system of status identification, one that was portable and affordable and one that would be understood and acknowledged wherever they went. Wayfarers required a set of universal conventions, a code of manners, a repertory of performances, a wardrobe of look-alike costumes, and a prop box of standardized accessories that could be recognized by anyone who knew the rules. Etiquette and fashion substituted for the reputations that people abroad had been accorded (or claimed they had) back where they came from. The new system of genteel behavior was borrowed ultimately from courtly protocol, then wedded to an esthetic developed in Italy and France, and finally disseminated through Amsterdam and London to the rest of Europe and its far-flung colonies. Gentility – the lifestyle of fashion – became the premier passport carried by anyone who fancied himself a citizen of the world at large.

The immediate beneficiaries were the travelers themselves, the merchants, sea captains, immigrants, colonists, army officers, crown officials, churchmen, tourists, scientists, sportsmen, convalescents, and a host of other footloose men and women whose journeys carried them far outside the effective range of their home-grown reputations. In their need to make themselves known in strange places they adopted a new mode of social communications. For it to work, the information they transmitted had to be received, understood, and heeded by fellow travelers and new acquaintances alike. Increasingly it was. The frequent appearance of strangers abroad altered the chemistry of everyday life in the established communities into which they and their affairs intruded. Their traffic, whether for business or pleasure, brought advantage to the settled individuals with whom they dealt. Thus local yokels too soon discovered that they could advance their own fame and fortune by welcoming outsiders into their social circles on these new terms. Little by little, a value system prized initially for its portability spread far and wide among peoples who were less traveled and appeared in many ways scarcely different from medieval villagers except that now some of their affairs and some of their friends had long-distance connections.

Thus the new system of manners that spurred the consumption of fashionable goods solved a major problem of social communications in an age of rapid expansion. To people on the move it offered a universal code of behavior to smooth their reception in faraway places. To homebodies, who often had their own reasons to make themselves presentable to outsiders, the new international language of gentility supplemented the traditional measures of rank and reputation, especially in North America where, it was said, the "pride of wealth is as ostentatious as ever the pride of birth has been elsewhere."

Economists, fixated for so long on producers and suppliers, have been slow to recognize that far larger numbers of buyers and consumers created an interconnected empire of goods in the century between 1650 and 1750 (Breen, 1986). Even that is not the whole story. The information system that the trade in consumer goods pushed to the outer limits of that empire also became the modern world's first common language, a non-verbal Esperanto understood by peoples whose cultures were otherwise profoundly dissimilar in almost every other respect.

Once in place, such a system could broadcast a band of information much wider than the messages that signified only social status and identity. Not unlike the Internet today, the language of standardized consumer products was quickly turned to other extraordinary applications. Timothy Breen has written several essays that explore how politics in the era of the American Revolution began making adjustments to consumer behavior. He believes (1988) that Americans' avid participation in consumer culture provoked the taxation crises of the 1760s and '70s. He argues further (1993) that the patriots' shared experience of consumption gave a unified voice to the thirteen colonies' common cause against British tyranny. British officers, returning home from the Seven Years' War, widely reported that the colonies were "wallowing in wealth and luxury." Americans' "insatiable itch for merchandizing; and the folly and extravagance of the people in imitating the customs and dress of foreigners" were turned into a justification for parliamentary taxation. Some Americans blamed "this fatal effect" on their own fickleness. Others suspected a British plot to keep the colonies poor. Again, the medium – goods (or their threatened interruption) – conveyed the substance of the political message. As one pamphleteer warned his countrymen, "How much soever we may possess the ability of acquiring wealth and independence," crushing taxes imposed by Parliament "will most effectively prevent our enjoying such invaluable acquisitions." The accouterments to gentility, and the pursuit of happiness they made possible, had already begun to acquire the sanctity of a right no less precious than life and liberty. Buying and using the "baubles of Britain" had become so widespread in the decades before the Revolution that consumption, Breen says, was the principal common denominator that overcame the colonies' sectional differences. It was the rallying cry that made co-conspirators of merchants, planters, farmers, and artisans when the call went out to boycott British manufactures. The conflict with Britain was not essentially a dispute over imports, but consumer goods became the language of protest that mobilized a populace and linked abstract ideas to everyday experiences that already were shared by a multitude of men and women throughout the colonies.

The connection Breen draws between ideology and creature comforts brings the subject of consumption partway back to the point where David Potter and Daniel Boorstin left it more than thirty years ago. They were saying then that the promise of plenty has always been central to Americans' experience of democracy. The country's abundant resources give dimension and definition to the idea of equal opportunity for all. That certainly was not the Founders' understanding of the words they enshrined in the Declaration of Independence. Far from it. But, as Gordon Wood demonstrates in the concluding chapters of *The Radicalism of the American Revolution*, the new-born republic delivered a prosperous free society into the hands of obscure people who were absorbed in "their workaday concerns and their pecuniary pursuits of happiness" (1992, p. 369). They quickly set about translating that preoccupation with "making money and getting ahead" into a dollars-and-cents meritocracy that, ever since, has challenged the presumption that caste, race, gender, and other hereditary entitlements should determine who gets the largest slice of the American Dream.

And so back again to modern politics and the alarm that many intellectuals still register regarding Americans' love affair with material things. Thirty years ago, before the serious study of consumption got under way, it was easy, even right, to criticize any telling of American history that left out the many millions who conspicuously were not "people of plenty" and, worse, had been systematically denied the education, the vote, the breaks, and ultimately their constitutional right to compete alongside everybody else in the grand national scramble for the country's wealth. Students of colonial America numbered in the vanguard of academic historians who learned to write another kind of history, one that recognized and celebrated people's separate but equally worthy differences, usually ascribed to their race, gender, or ethnic background. Those historians have strenuously resisted the temptation to integrate (and thereby risk losing) this multitude of separate stories in a sweeping, synthesizing, national narrative.

But a curious thing has happened to American history as a consequence. The good intentions of leftist social historians and much of their excellent scholarship have been misappropriated by politicians and voters who perceive that their own interest might be threatened if the country's dispossessed citizens recognized their common plight and made common cause for reform. History writing that dwells on the "otherness" of victimized groups in American society has played into the hands of those who welcome a divided, distracted, and disenfranchised underclass. Historians cannot now unlearn the cultural diversity they have taken such pains to discover in the American past. Nor should they. An appreciation for the country's rich and complex legacy is essential to understanding how it continues to be a "nation of nations" to this day.

The commitment to telling everybody's history must not, however, be allowed to obscure the rest of the story, the follow-on story of making a nation. However much pride individuals and groups take in their ethnic heritage, most also want to feel that they belong to the nation at large. They demand its constitutional guarantees; they seek the protection of its laws; they learn to speak its language; and, most tangibly of all, they expect to earn their fair share of its wealth and enjoy the material things that money can buy. The attention that scholars have given to women, blacks, gays, Indians, and Americans of every stripe has helped them win their rights. It is also fair to say that this important historical enterprise looks backwards to a time – a time before the founding of America even – when blood and heredity ruled everything. By contrast, the history of consumption is a modern history for modern times. Its subject is the bigger, still unfolding, forward-looking story about the achievement of political and social stability in the West and the influence of materialism on the ideal and practice of equality.

BIBLIOGRAPHY

Axtell, James: "The First Consumer Revolution." In James Axtell, ed., *Beyond 1492: Encounters in Colonial North America* (New York and Oxford: Oxford University Press, 1992), pp. 125–51.

Boorstin, Daniel J.: *The Americans*, 3 vols, vol. 3, *The Democratic Experience* (New York: Random House, 1973).

Bowen, Joanne: "A Comparative Analysis of New England and Chesapeake Herding Systems." In Paul A. Shackel and Barbara J. Little, eds., *Historical Archaeology of the Chesapeake* (Washington and London: Smithsonian Institution Press, 1994), pp. 155–67.

Bowen, Joanne and Andrews, Susan Trevarthen: "The Starving Time at Jamestown." Report (Jamestown, VA: Association for the Preservation of Virginia Antiquities, 1999).

Braudel, Fernand: *Les Structures du Quotidien: Le Possible et L'Impossible* (Paris: Librairie Armand Colin, 1979); trans. Sian Reynolds, *Civilization and Capitalism, 15th–18th Century*, 3 vols, vol. 1, *The Structures of Everyday Life* (New York: Harper & Row, 1981).

Breen, T. H.: "An Empire of Goods: The Anglicization of Colonial America, 1660–1776." *Journal of British Studies* 25 (1986), pp. 467–99.

Breen, T. H.: "'Baubles of Britain': The American Revolution and Consumer Revolution of the Eighteenth Century." *Past and Present* 119 (1988), pp. 73–104.

Breen, T. H.: "Narratives of Commercial Life: Consumption, Ideology, and Community on the Eve of the American Revolution." *William and Mary Quarterly* 3rd ser., 50 (1993), pp. 471–

501.

Brewer, John and Porter, Roy, eds.: *Consumption and the World of Goods* (London and New York: Routledge, 1993).

Bronner, Simon J., ed.: *Consuming Visions. Accumulation and Display of Goods in America, 1880–1920* (New York and London: W. W. Norton & Co., 1989).

Bushman, Richard L.: *The Refinement of America: Persons, Houses, Cities* (New York: Alfred A. Knopf, 1992).

Calvert, Karin: *Children in the House: The Material Culture of Early Childhood, 1600–1900* (Boston, MA: Northeastern University Press, 1992).

Carr, Lois G. and Walsh, Lorena S.: "Inventories and the Analysis of Wealth and Consumption Patterns in St. Mary's County, Maryland, 1658–1777." *Historical Methods* 13 (1980), pp. 81–104.

Carr, Lois G. and Walsh, Lorena S.: "Changing Lifestyles and Consumer Behavior in the Colonial Chesapeake." In Cary Carson, Ronald Hoffman, and Peter J. Albert, eds., *Of Consuming Interests: The Style of Life in the Eighteenth Century* (Charlottesville, VA: University Press of Virginia, 1994), pp. 59–166.

Carson, Barbara G.: *Ambitious Appetites, Dining, Behavior, and Patterns of Consumption in Federal Washington* (Washington, DC: American Institute of Architects Press, 1990).

Carson, Cary: "Segregation in Vernacular Buildings." *Vernacular Architecture* 7 (1976), pp. 24–9.

Carson, Cary: "The Consumer Revolution in Colonial British America: Why Demand?" In Cary Carson, Ronald Hoffman, and Peter J. Albert, eds., *Of Consuming Interests: The Style of Life in the Eighteenth Century* (Charlottesville, VA: University Press of Virginia, 1994), pp. 483–697.

Carson, Cary: "Material Culture History: The Scholarship Nobody Knows." In Ann Smart Martin and J. Ritchie Garrison, eds., *American Material Culture: The Shape of the Field* (Winterthur, DE: Henry Francis du Pont Winterthur Museum, 1997), pp. 401–28.

Carson, Cary, Barka, Norman F., Kelso, William M., Stone, Garry Wheeler, and Upton, Dell: "Impermanent Architecture in the Southern American Colonies." *Winterthur Portfolio* 16 (1981), pp. 135–96.

Carson, Cary, Gilliam, Jan, Pittman, William, and Prown, Jonathan, exhibition curators: "1699: When Virginia Was The Wild West!" DeWitt Wallace Museum, Colonial Williamsburg Foundation (1999–2000), Rick Hadley, designer. Gallery guide by Martha Hill: *1607–1699: When Virginia Was The Wild West* (Williamsburg, VA: Colonial Williamsburg, 1999). Exhibition reviewed in *American Quarterly* 53 (June 2001), *Journal of American History* 88 (March 2002), *Journal of Southern History* 66 (February 2000), *The Public Historian* 22 (Fall 2000), *Vernacular Architecture Newsletter* 80 (Summer 1999), *William and Mary Quarterly* 3rd ser., 57 (July 2000), and *Winterthur Portfolio* 35 (Winter 2000).

Cooper, Grace R., Kidwell, Claudia B., and Kloster, Donald E., exhibition curators: "Suiting Everyone: The Democratization of Clothing in America." Museum of History and Technology, Smithsonian Institution (1974–8), James P. Baughanan, consulting historian; Nadya Makovenyi, designer. Kidwell and Margaret C. Christmas wrote a catalogue-monograph by the same title (Washington, DC: Smithsonian Institution Press, 1974). Exhibition reviewed in *Newsweek* (September 30, 1974).

Csikszentmihalyi, Mihaly and Rochberg-Halton, Eugene: *The Meaning of Things: Domestic Symbols and the Self* (Cambridge: Cambridge University Press, 1981).

Cummings, Abbott Lowell, ed.: *Rural Household Inventories [Suffolk County, Massachusetts], 1675–1775* (Boston, MA: Society for the Preservation of New England Antiquities, 1964).

Cummings, Abbott Lowell: *The Framed Houses of Massachusetts Bay, 1625–1725* (Cambridge, MA and London: The Belknap Press, 1979).

de Vries, Jan: "Between Purchasing Power and the World of Goods: Understanding the Household Economy in Early Modern Europe." In John Brewer and Roy Porter, eds., *Consumption and the World of Goods* (London and New York: Routledge, 1993), pp. 85–132.

Douglas, Mary and Isherwood, Baron: *The World of Goods: Towards an Anthropology of Consumption* (New York: Basic Books, 1979).

Earle, Peter: *The Making of the English Middle Class. Business, Society, and Family Life in London, 1660–1730* (Berkeley and Los Angeles, CA: University of California Press, 1989).

Elias, Norbert: *Uber den Prozess der Zivilisation* (Switzerland, 1939); trans. Edmund Jephcott, *The History of Manners*, vol. 1, *The Civilizing Process* (New York: Urizen Books, 1978).

Ewen, Stuart: *Captains of Consciousness: Advertising and the Social Roots of the Consumer Culture* (New York: McGraw-Hill, 1976).

Fielding, Henry: *An Enquiry into the Causes of the Late Increase in Robbers* (London, 1751).

Fischer, David Hackett: *The Great Wave: Price Revolutions and the Rhythm of History* (New York and Oxford: Oxford University Press, 1996).

Gilboy, Elizabeth Waterman: "Demand as a Factor in the Industrial Revolution." In R. M. Hartwell, ed., *The Causes of the Industrial Revolution in England* (1932; London: Methuen & Co., 1967), pp. 121–38.

Gilman, Carolyn: *Where Two Worlds Meet: The Great Lakes Fur Trade* (St. Paul, MN: Minnesota Historical Society, 1982).

Golovin, Ann and Roth, Rodris, exhibition curators: "New and Different: Home Interiors in Eighteenth-Century America." National Museum of American History, Smithsonian Institution (1986–87), Dru Colbert, designer. No catalogue. Reviewed in the *Baltimore Sun* (August 24, 1986) and *Technology and Culture* 29 (July 1988).

Harris, Neil: *Cultural Excursions: Marketing Appetites and Cultural Tastes in Modern America* (Chicago: University of Chicago Press, 1990).

Harrison, William: *The Description of England* (London, 1577), ed. George Edelen (Ithaca, NY: Cornell University Press, 1968).

Hoffman, Philip T., Jacks, David, Levin, Patricia A., and Lindert, Peter A.: "Prices and Real Inequality in Europe since 1500." Working paper series no 102, 2000 (Agricultural History Center, University of California, Davis, California).

Horn, James P. P.: "'The Bare Necessities': Standards of Living in England and the Chesapeake, 1650–1700." *Historical Archaeology* 22 (1988), pp. 74–91.

Horn, James P. P.: *Adapting to a New World: English Society in the Seventeenth-Century Chesapeake* (Chapel Hill, NC: University of North Carolina Press, 1994).

Horowitz, Daniel: *The Morality of Spending: Attitudes Toward the Consumer Society in America, 1875–1940* (Baltimore: Johns Hopkins University Press, 1985).

Jameson, John Franklin, ed.: *Johnson's Wonder-Working Providence, 1628–1651* (New York: C. Scribner & Sons, 1910).

Jones, Alice Hanson: *Wealth of a Nation To Be: The American Colonies on the Eve of the Revolution* (New York: Columbia University Press, 1980).

Laird, Pamela Walker: *Advertising Progress: American Business and the Rise of Consumer Marketing* (Baltimore, MD: Johns Hopkins University Press, 1998).

Leach, William: *Land of Desire: Merchants, Power, and the Rise of a New American Culture* (New York: Pantheon Books, 1993).

Lears, T. J. Jackson: *No Place of Grace: Antimodernism and the Transformation of American Culture, 1880–1920* (New York: Pantheon Books, 1981).

Main, Gloria L.: *Tobacco Colony: Life in Early Maryland, 1650–1720* (Princeton, NJ: Princeton University Press, 1982).

Main, Gloria L.: "The Standard of Living in Colonial Massachusetts." *Journal of Economic History* 43 (1983), pp. 101–8.

Main, Gloria L. and Main, Jackson T.: "Economic Growth and the Standard of Living in Southern New England, 1640–1774." *Journal of Economic History* 48 (1988), pp. 27–46.

Martin, Ann Smart: "Consumerism and the Retail Trade in the Eighteenth-Century Backcountry." Paper presented to the Shenandoah Regional Studies Seminar, 1992 (MS copy, Rockefeller Library, Colonial Williamsburg Foundation, Williamsburg, Virginia).

Marzio, Peter C., ed.: *A Nation of Nations* (New York: Harper & Row, 1976).

McCracken, Grant: *Culture and Consumption: New Approaches to the Symbolic Character of Consumer Goods and Activities* (Bloomington and Indianapolis, IN: Indiana University Press, 1988).

McCusker, John J. and Menard, Russell R.: *The Economy of British America, 1607–1789* (Chapel Hill, NC: University of North Carolina Press, 1985).

McKendrick, Neil: "Home Demand and Economic Growth: A New View of the Role of Women and Children in the Industrial Revolution." In McKendrick, ed., *Historical Perspectives: Studies in English Thought and Society* (London: Europa, 1974), pp. 152–210.

McKendrick, Neil, Brewer, John, and Plumb, J. H.: *The Birth of a Consumer Society. The Commercialization of Eighteenth-Century England* (Bloomington, IN: Indiana University Press, 1982).

McMahon, Sarah F.: "A Comfortable Subsistence: The Changing Composition of Diet in Rural New England, 1620–1840." *William and Mary Quarterly* 3rd ser., 42 (1985), pp. 25–65.

Menard, Russell R.: "From Servants to Slaves: The Transformation of the Chesapeake Labor System." *Southern Studies* 16 (1977), pp. 355–90.

Miller, Daniel: *Material Culture and Mass Consumption* (Oxford and New York: Basil Blackwell, 1987).

Mokyr, Joel: "Demand v. Supply in the Industrial Revolution." *Journal of Economic History* 37 (1977), pp. 981–1008.

Mokyr, Joel: "The Industrial Revolution and the New Economic History." In Joel Mokyr, ed., *The Economics of the Industrial Revolution* (Totowa, NJ: Rowman & Allanheld, 1985), pp. 1–51.

Mukerji, Chandra: *From Graven Images: Patterns of Modern Materialism* (New York: Columbia University Press, 1983).

Neiman, Fraser D.: *The "Manner House" Before Stratford* (Stratford, VA: Robert E. Lee Memorial Association, 1980).

Plumb, J. H.: *The Pursuit of Happiness: A View of Life in Georgian England* (New Haven, CT: Yale University Press, 1977).

Pogue, Dennis J.: "The Transformation of America: Georgian Sensibility, Capitalist Conspiracy, or Consumer Revolution?" *Historical Archaeology* 35 (2001), pp. 41–57.

Potter, David M.: *People of Plenty: Economic Abundance and the American Character* (Chicago and London: University of Chicago Press, 1954).

Quimby, Ian M. G., ed.: *Material Culture and the Study of American Life* (New York: W. W. Norton & Co., 1978).

Rothenberg, Winifred B.: *From Market Places to a Market Economy: The Transformation of Rural Massachusetts, 1750–1850* (Chicago: University of Chicago Press, 1992).

Schama, Simon: *The Embarrassment of Riches: An Interpretation of Dutch Culture in the Golden Age* (New York: Alfred A. Knopf, 1987).

Schuurman, A. J.: *Materiele Cultuur en Levensstijl* (Wageningen: A. A. G. Bijdragen no. 30, 1989).

Shammas, Carole: "The Domestic Environment in Early Modern England and America." *Journal of Social History* 14 (1980), pp. 3–24.

Shammas, Carole: "Consumer Behavior in Colonial America." *Social Science History* 6 (1982), pp. 67–86.

Shammas, Carole: "How Self-Sufficient Was Early America?" *Journal of Interdisciplinary History* 13 (1982), pp. 247–72.

Shammas, Carole: *Pre-industrial Consumer in England and America* (Oxford: Clarendon Press,

1990).

Smith, Billy G.: "The Material Lives of Laboring Philadelphians, 1750–1800." *William and Mary Quarterly* 3rd ser., 38 (1981), pp. 163–202.

Spufford, Margaret: *The Great Reclothing of Rural England: Petty Chapmen and their Wares in the Seventeenth Century* (London: Hambledon Press, 1984).

St. George, Robert B.: "'Set Thine House in Order': The Domestication of the Yeomanry in Seventeenth-Century New England." In Jonathan L. Fairbanks and Robert F. Trent, eds., *New England Begins: The Seventeenth Century*, 3 vols (Boston, MA: Museum of Fine Arts, 1982), vol. 2, 159–88.

Strasser, Susan: *Satisfaction Guaranteed: The Making of the American Mass Market* (New York: Pantheon, 1989).

Susman, Warren I.: *Culture as History: The Transformation of American Society in the Twentieth Century* (New York: Pantheon Books, 1984).

Thirsk, Joan: *Economic Policy and Projects: The Development of a Consumer Society in Early Modern England* (Oxford: Clarendon Press, 1978).

Trautman, Patricia: "Dress in Seventeenth-Century Cambridge, Massachusetts: An Inventory-Based Reconstruction." In Peter Benes, ed., *Early American Probate Inventories* (Boston, MA: Northeastern University Press, 1989), pp. 51–73.

Ulrich, Laurel: *Age of Homespun* (New York: Alfred Knopf, 2001).

Walsh, Lorena S.: "Fettered Consumers: Slaves and the Anglo-American 'Consumer Revolution'." Paper presented to the annual meeting of the Economic History Association, 1992 (MS copy, Rockefeller Library, Colonial Williamsburg Foundation, Williamsburg, Virginia).

Walsh, Lorena: *"Material Culture: Consumption, Life-style, Standard of Living, 1500–1900."* In Anton J. Schuurman and Lorena S. Walsh, eds., *Proceedings of the Eleventh International Economic History Congress* (Milan: Universita Bocconi, 1994).

Walsh, Lorena S.: "The Chesapeake Slave Trade: Regional Patterns, African Origins, and Some Implications." *William and Mary Quarterly* 3rd ser., 58 (2001), pp. 139–70.

Walsh, Lorena S., Main, Gloria L., and Carr, Lois G.: "Toward a History of the Standard of Living in British North America." *William and Mary Quarterly* 3rd ser., 45 (1988), pp. 116–66.

Weatherill, Lorna: *Consumer Behaviour and the Material Culture of Britain, 1660–1760* (London and New York: Routledge, 1988).

Wood, Gordon S.: *The Radicalism of the American Revolution* (New York: Alfred A. Knopf, 1992).

Wrightson, Keith: *Earthly Necessities: Economic Lives in Early Modern Britain* (New Haven, CT: Yale University Press, 2000).

Zea, Philip, exhibition curator: "Pursuing Refinement in Rural New England, 1750–1850." Flynt Center of Early New England Life, Historic Deerfield (1998–2001), Richard L. Bushman, Barbara G. Carson, and Kevin M. Sweeney, consulting historians; Jim Sims, designer. Zea wrote a catalogue-monograph by the same title (Deerfield, MA: Historic Deerfield, Inc., 1998). Exhibition reviewed in *New York Times* (September 25, 1998) and *Winterthur Portfolio* [forthcoming].

CHAPTER FIFTEEN

Religion

MARILYN WESTERKAMP

When the history of early North America was transformed by the "new" social history of the 1970s, the history of religion came to the table with both advantages and disadvantages. Up to this point, American religious history had been a poor stepchild to historical scholarship, replete with apologetical positions that began with the truth of religion, usually Christianity, and often a particular brand. With the exception of some works exploring the writings of Protestant reformers as a sort of theological history of ideas, the books and articles tended toward anecdotal, often uncritical celebrations. And yet, unlike other colonialists, who never seemed to get much beyond the New England mind, the Virginia House of Burgesses, and the economics of empire, historians of religion explored an extraordinary diversity of people and communities. They were fascinated with the idiosyncratic as well as committed to understanding hegemonic institutions, and they foolishly, or perhaps insightfully, resisted the need to distinguish between the two.

During the first six decades of the twentieth century, while colonialists were exploring seventeenth- and eighteenth-century America, church historians were crafting their own interpretive narratives of religious developments in the colonial era and beyond. And while colonialists anticipated the Revolution and founding of the republic, church historians looked forward to evangelicalism, reform, disestablishment, and the development of an American culture that has remained pluralistic yet deeply religious. Few colonialists know these early histories. Some were descriptive, narrow denominational studies; others were works of ambitious synthesis; and most traversed several centuries at a time with the colonial period covered in a "background" chapter or two. Among the many historians working in this period, Nathan Glazer (1957) crafted a brief study of American Judaism; Abdel R. Wentz (1955) wrote of the Lutherans; Arthur J. Lewis (1962) treated the Moravians; and Elizabeth Davidson (1936), William Manross (1950), and Raymond Albright (1964) all examined the Anglican Church. Because these were not focused historical monographs, they have remained mostly unread except by seminarians, educated churchmen and women, and the odd graduate student seeking background. Yet because colonial historians hesitated to approach denominational histories, significant early American scholarship was missed. For example, Leonard Trinterud's *Forming of an American Tradition* (1949), a transformative study of the Presbyterian Church, remained relatively unknown as late as twenty-five years after its publication in 1949. As an historian of religion, Trinterud directly engaged a historiography that contextualized specific research projects within the overarching counterpoint of religious pluralism working against the rise of a Protestant national culture. He charted the development of an intercolonial institution, with multiple points of origin, in a community afflicted by competing ethnic agendas and regional conflicts. Informed by a particular set of questions concerning conflict, schism, and compromise, Trinterud plunged into areas that social historians would rediscover twenty years later unaware that a historian of Presbyterianism had gotten there first.

About thirty years ago, the history of religion began to move from the periphery to one center of early American historical scholarship, a movement that was brought about in part by the parallel engagement of both colonialists and religious historians with interdisciplinary methods. In the 1970s, early Native American historians, following the lead of colonial Latin Americanists, turned to ethnohistory, an explicitly interdisciplinary endeavor combining anthropological frameworks and strategies with historical research techniques. At the same time, historians of religion expanded their own research beyond great men and institutions, approaching the people in the pews through the methods of anthropology and the tools of folklore. Similarly, in the 1990s historians of religion and colonial society accepted the challenges of cultural studies and postmodern language analysis. In other words, over the past thirty years, religious historians became leaders within certain historiographic developments. In terms of theoretical and methodological positions, historians of religion have been active proponents of both cultural anthropology, further extending the ability of social historians to research and interpret their subjects, and postmodern analysis, pushing colonialists to deeply engage the structure and power of colonial languages, many of which were explicitly religious in vocabulary, syntax, content, and metaphor. Yet even prior to these methodological changes, historians of religion had, within their own parochial world, heralded such new contextual frameworks as popular behavior, missionary activities, social diversity, and transatlantic analysis.

Before the 1970s colonialists had not been unaware of religious history, although they suffered from a myopia created, in part, by the breathtaking intellectual histories of Perry Miller. When Miller published his *Orthodoxy in Massachusetts* (1936) followed by the two volumes of *The New England Mind* (1939, 1956) he charted the course for Puritan studies and, in the process, transformed the place of New England in the historical understanding of British colonial history. Before Miller, New England had been seen as an exceptional, unpleasant place characterized by intolerance, theocracy, hypocrisy, and witch hunts: the New England of Nathaniel Hawthorne's *Scarlet Letter*. Miller redeemed the Puritans and their colonies, reconstructing their worldview and their theology, and recognizing their complexity, dedication, and focus upon the divine. Encountering anxious people seemingly plagued with ideological contradictions, Miller untangled the contradictions and argued that the Puritans' intellectual system was a logically constructed network of scientific, theological, and philosophical views. Miller's Puritan founders were men of high principle and commitment who strove to create a godly community in the New World. The nature of their failure is chronicled in Miller's second volume and has become so much a part of the historiography that Miller's "declension" paradigm with its accompanying discovery of the "jeremiad" has become part and parcel of arguments about New England. For those who found Miller too dense and obscure, the crystalline writings of Edmund S. Morgan (1958, 1963) clarified Puritans' theological and social ideology, Sacvan Bercovitch (1978) explained the genre of the jeremiad, and Kenneth Lockridge (1970) applied the "declension" analysis to the social history of the New England town of Dedham. Not all historians accepted Miller's interpretation: Robert Pope's dissection of the Half-Way Covenant (1969) as well as Darrett Rutman's social and political history of Boston (1965), while utilizing intellectual tools and narrative pieces uncovered by Miller, directly challenged declension.

In the 1960s and 1970s, early Americanists wrote New England into the center of the colonial narrative. Much of what the Puritans wrote had been saved; many graduate students lived near the archives where these writings were stored; and historians still privileged complex intellectual endeavor above the mundane behaviors of migration, settlement, farming, trade, and negotiating/fighting with indigenous peoples. Thus, New England came to stand for America as a whole. The Chesapeake and the Deep South became exceptional because of slavery, despite the historical reality of slavery in every colony and despite New England's deep involvement in the slave trade and the still oppressive legacy of racial slavery in the United States. The mid-Atlantic colonies were judged exceptional due to their heterogeneity – the presence of Dutch settlers, German dissenters, and Quakers – despite the historical development of the United States as a heterogeneous nation.

Considering this focus upon New England and Puritans, it is not surprising that the religious piece of the eighteenth-century master narrative was concentrated upon the upheavals of the Great Awakening. Initially understood as a religious phenomenon indigenous to the colonies, the brilliant New England philosopher/theologian/pastor Jonathan Edwards was placed at the center of the movement. The Great Awakening provided all that intellectual historians could desire, particularly a hefty polemical battle providing texts and countertexts for analysis. Theologians supporting the Awakening articulated a new, intricate vision of conversion and spirituality that was denounced with equal critical skill and linguistic elegance by its detractors. Key clerics, particularly Edwards, reformulated and returned to a primitive version of Puritan Calvinism; Edwards lost his pastorate as a consequence (Gaustad, 1965; Tracy, 1980). Puritanists also found in the Awakening a logical Weberian phase within the declension model as religiosity spiraled downward until a revitalized piety, led by a charismatic leader, swept through the countryside (Weber, 1963). Many were entranced by Anthony Wallace's model of revitalization (1956). And if this were not enough, Alan Heimert (1966) proceeded to reconfigure the Great Awakening as a precursor to the American Revolution in terms of political ideology and structure. In key ways Heimert's impressive analysis did much to place the Great Awakening at the center of early eighteenth-century history. Within a historiography that, until twenty years ago, founded colony after colony and then jumped to the Revolution, the Great Awakening became a pivot around which disparate narratives gathered together and spun off the early threads of a united colonial, proto-national social and political identity (Cowing, 1971).

But what of the English colonists who were not Puritans? Or those who were not English? Flashes of attention highlighted the peculiar Quakers of Pennsylvania, and works reconstructing the state's Quaker heritage received the esteem of many who honored William Penn and the Quakers for their early espousal of the core American political values of fair play and religious freedom (Jones, 1911; Bronner, 1962). Students of Pennsylvania argued that the colony's development, like that of Massachusetts, was inseparable from its religious principles. Frederick Tolles' *Meeting House and Counting House* (1948), a foundational work of political and economic history, persuasively drew connections among religious, economic, and political ideologies and structures within Weber's model of *Protestant Ethic and the Spirit of Capitalism* (1976). Fifteen years later, Gary Nash titled his explicitly political history of Pennsylvania *Quaker Politics* (1968). Yet stories of the diverse religious communities that came to Pennsylvania, New York, and New Jersey seeking toleration were scarcely noted. Historians frequently said that the Great Awakening, for example, had swept through the colonies, and the evidence certainly revealed the outbreak of enthusiastic religion throughout the mid-Atlantic and Chesapeake regions. Yet with the exception of unpublished dissertations (Lodge, 1964), the scholarship blithely worked around the non-New England origin of itinerants George Whitefield and Gilbert Tennent, seeing only the vitality of New England while consigning other regions to the unremarkable.

Compared with historians of religion, other colonialists wrote little about the extraordinarily diverse cultures of early America. The low esteem that Protestant America had always held for Catholicism may have led them to avoid the French and Spanish North American enterprises; or a national narrative that privileged the thirteen British colonies may have been responsible. In any case, the Catholic missionary endeavors pursued in New France, including the Great Lakes region, and in Spanish Florida and the Southwest were barely considered, except by Catholic historians (Ellis, 1965; Hennesey, 1981; Dolan, 1985). Even among the thirteen, Maryland's early history as a sanctuary for English Catholics was noted but rarely explored, and again only by Catholic historians.

Of course, the majority of the English colonists would have counted themselves Anglicans; yet historians' knowledge of that central institution was also minimal. By the 1960s, all that had been written about the established church, outside of denominational histories, was directly tied to colonial politics. Charles Sydnor (1962) recognized the importance of the vestry as a body through which elite men acted out their status. Carl Bridenbaugh (1962) explored disputes that heralded (or, perhaps, reflected) the coming of the Revolution. The parson's cause of Virginia demonstrated the ultimate power that vestrymen held over ministers and, incidentally, revealed strains of anticlericalism. The intercolonial battle over the establishment of a bishop in the British colonies, a *cause célèbre* during the revolutionary era, revealed not only the determination of southern laymen to maintain their authority over the clergy but also the siege-like mentality of both clerical and lay Anglicans in the mid-Atlantic and, especially, New England colonies where they disliked their minority status.

In moving colonial historiography towards a wider geographical coverage, social and cultural diversity, and transatlantic frameworks, historians of religion led the way. Sydney E. Ahlstrom's *Religious History of the American People* (1971) reflects well the arena in transition. As late as 1970, this sub-field may have been lodged in institutions, great men, and transformative moments, but Ahlstrom's coverage was geographically and denominationally inclusive, with forays into the worlds of religious believers. In this remarkable work of synthesis Ahlstrom crafted a thousand-page tome that reconstructed the history of religion in the United States from its colonial roots to the 1960s. While his traditional embrace of pluralism required an emphasis upon the nineteenth century (fully half the pages) as the onset of the cultural diversity feast, the colonial chapters reflect a respect for the multiple traditions forming the roots of American religious culture even as they wallow a bit in Puritanism.

Religious historians of the United States generally held a transatlantic mindset, if only because their origin stories began in Reformation Europe. Ahlstrom, however, opened with a seven-chapter prologue examining the European roots of Catholicism and Catholic colonization as well as the continental Reformation and the progress of reform in England. He then dedicated a fair space to Puritanism but followed this with descriptions of the range of religions available to colonists. In 1700, claimed Ahlstrom, a traveler going from Boston to Carolina would meet Congregationalists, Baptists, Presbyterians, and Quakers; "Dutch, German, and French Reformed; Swedish, Finnish, and German Lutherans; Mennonites and radical pietists, Anglicans, Roman Catholics; here and there a Jewish congregation, a few Rosicrucians; and, of course, a vast number of the unchurched – some of them powerfully alienated from any form of institutional religion" (1974, p. 4). When he plunged into the Great Awakening century, he, again, began in New England, but moved southward, then left evangelical religion for Roman Catholicism and Judaism, and finished up with the Enlightenment and the Revolution.

As the heir of traditional religious history, Ahlstrom's work echoed the centrality of Puritanism and New England in his master narrative. Moreover, he continued to emphasize great men and movements, devoting chapters to the Mathers, Jonathan Edwards, the Great Awakening, and the Enlightenment. Institutionalized church organizations constituted the list of subjects examined, but Ahlstrom reiterated a desire (and the need) to explore the beliefs and behaviors of ordinary believers. He also foreshadowed the geographic and cultural expansion of later scholarship in dedicating chapters to Catholicism, New Spain, and New France, as well as German, Scottish, and Scots-Irish settlers. Highly significant was a preface articulating an agenda that church historians had been moving toward for the previous two decades. In addition to challenges to consider the social context and the diversity of American religious cultures, Ahlstrom demanded that religious historians work by the same rules of "evidence and plausibility" accepted by other historians. No longer should they perform as historical theologians, reconstructing narratives of divine truth, but as scholars working with sources and arguments in an ethically neutral interpretive space (1974, p. xiv). Not all historians of religion were apologists, but by 1970 there was little space for such history outside of explicit works of theology. Like social and political historians who had begun to question the national myths of dauntless colonists and idealistic revolutionaries, religious historians sacrificed their faith in unselfish Christians committed to godly virtues and the betterment of the New World.

As historians of the 1970s turned their attention to the common man and community studies flourished, colonialists, particularly those working outside New England, paid little attention to religion. In the heady climate of the Marxist paradigm, ideological forces, especially religion, took second place to material circumstances as factors worthy of study. Churches were recognized as institutions of social, sometimes hegemonic control, but since the focus was upon the non-elites, and the analysis privileged the material realities of their lives, social historians frequently bypassed religion. James Lemon (1972), one of the few working outside of New England who did consider religion as a factor, argued against the significance of religiosity and church identification as a factor determining the settlement patterns and lifestyles of the eighteenth-century Pennsylvanians. Gary Nash (1979), on the other hand, acknowledged the importance of the Great Awakening for its participants in Boston and Philadelphia, seeing in the religious revivals signifiers of discontent and pathways to transformation. Puritan studies continued, though by the 1970s historians had concluded that the Puritan colonies were idiosyncratic, and even in the new social histories of New England, Puritanism, if not absent, faded from the center of the argument (Rutman, 1965; Greven, 1970).

Some religious historians have responded to the new social history by training their scrutiny beyond Euro-Americans and their faiths. The rise of African American Studies turned historians of religion toward the question of slave religion. Most monographs have been firmly placed within the antebellum era, but Albert Raboteau's definitive *Slave Religion* (1978) begins with the colonial period and a serious consideration of the analytical problems laid out by historians of slavery in Latin American and the Caribbean. His initial discussion grapples with the problem of African cultural continuities first articulated by Melville Herskovits, *The Myth of the Negro Past* (1941). Raboteau places his analysis within a comparative framework, building upon the foundational questions and structures laid out in Sidney Mintz's and Richard Price's anthropological study of African American culture in the Caribbean (1976). For African Americanists such as Raboteau, religion provides an ideal point of departure from which to explore the larger question of syncretic cultural development: how Christianity, a spiritual system largely imported from Europe, impacted upon and was transformed by enslaved African Americans. More recent works have examined African American religion as a significant piece of eighteenth-century societal development, including Mechal Sobel's *The World They Made Together* on the Chesapeake (1987), and Gary Nash's *Forging Freedom* on the African American community, slave and free, in Philadelphia (1988). In both cases, the conversion of many African Americans to Christianity and the efforts of blacks to claim respect and control over their own spirituality, communities, and institutions stand as a significant segment of the larger story.

European settlers who were not English have also become prominent in recent publications. Richard Pointer, *Protestant Pluralism and the New York Experience* (1988), directly confronts the impact of ethnic diversity and toleration policies (whether official or not) upon the colony's culture and society as a whole. Sally Schwartz, *Mixed Multitude* (1988), takes up the same questions for Pennsylvania, but chooses instead to describe in great detail the enormous array of religious organizations in Pennsylvania and the effect that toleration and diversity had upon the individual groups. Other historians have chosen to focus upon a single group and, in more traditional church history fashion, provide enlightenment upon the lesser known. Among the best is Beverly Smaby's study (1988) of the Moravians, a small German Pietist group whose remarkable enthusiasm had a surprising impact upon surrounding colonists, German and otherwise. Because of Moravians' involvement in the Great Awakening and their extremist reputation, historians have often been engaged by this tale of Count von Zinzendorf and his enthusiastic followers. Smaby, however, looks beyond those limited episodes and explores the church's history from within. There she finds a self-conscious religious community initially established along communitarian principles but embracing private property relatively quickly in order to ensure continuity and prosperity. A story of utopians whose zeal for perfection conflicted with the drive (and need) for material success, Smaby's research provides a perceptive portrait of the rise and fall of an experiment. But she also illuminates the religious climate of the era in her discussion of other religionists lured by the peculiar attractions of the Moravians.

In superlative examples of this new religious history of ethnic communities growing within and working against English hegemony, Jon Butler, *The Huguenots in America* (1983), and Randall Balmer, *A Perfect Babel of Confusion* (1989), explore the experiences of French and Dutch Calvinists. Butler focuses upon the Huguenots who emigrated to British America during the late seventeenth century, asking questions about identity, community construction, and the process of a seemingly inevitable assimilation of individuals that necessarily marked the end of a separate, ethnically identified community. Analyzing Huguenots within a diasporic framework, Butler finds that the extensive, but varied, colonial opportunities available in Boston, New York, and South Carolina opened British society to the emigrants and brought them quickly into the center of each region's economy and culture.

The story Balmer works to explain is more complicated, involving the Dutch Reformed Church, headquartered in New York, within the world of a Dutch colony suddenly gone English. Balmer traces the structure of the early Dutch church and the trajectory that it followed across the century after the English takeover. He also examines, in broader terms, the relationships between the Dutch and British churches and the impact that these relationships had upon the colony itself. In his analysis, the Reformed Church attempted to maintain its Dutch integrity by working with and through its Anglican equivalent. Of course, the paradox could not be maintained, and the steady deterioration of a separate Dutch religious culture was reflected in the inability of the Reformed Church to serve or maintain the loyalty of its own members. Not only is the church's complicity in its own cultural disintegration notable in and of itself, but, Balmer argues, those who rejected what they judged a betrayal of Dutch ethnic interests to English money followed an evangelical pathway to the same space of Anglicization. Like Butler, Balmer navigates the complexities of the early colonies with clarity and insight, effectively demonstrating the connections among religious, ethnic, regional, and economic identities.

As must also be clear from the works cited, historians have not only moved outward across communities and regions, but also across the Atlantic. Smaby, Butler, and Balmer all begin with European institutions, not merely in terms of origin stories, but as a dialogic process of cross-oceanic communication and influence. Several works on the Great Awakening have also been centered within a transatlantic framework, including Leigh Eric Schmidt's *Holy Fairs* (1989), Michael Crawford's *Seasons of Grace* (1991), and my own *Triumph of the Laity* (1988), all of which trace connections between Scotland or Ireland and the colonies. Historians of African American religion have continued exploring West Africa as a source of New World spiritual systems and tracing the continuities of African patterns and beliefs among slaves and free blacks. Debates on African cultural continuities that began decades before are still actively engaged through the application of comparative mainland/Caribbean frameworks. Mechal Sobel (1987) maintains that African beliefs and ritual patterns account for the appeal of evangelical religion to African Americans, while Jon Butler, referring to an "African Spiritual Holocaust," identifies African continuities but argues that slave holders "destroyed traditional African religious systems as *systems* in North America" opening the way for Africans' conversion to Christianity (Butler, 1990, pp. 129, 130). In spite of the absence of consensus concerning the transference of African religion to America, no historian writes about the religion of African Americans without discussing Africa. This move across the Atlantic has even infiltrated northwards to New England, where Puritanists have not only returned to their English religious roots, but argue for a cultural exchange, back and forth between England and the colonies (Foster, 1991; Bremer, ed., 1993).

The most obvious impact of social history has been a growing emphasis upon the people in the pews. The best indicator of this development lies in the two major works of synthesis published in the past twenty years. In *Under the Cope of Heaven* (1986), Patricia Bonomi asks directly questions about church membership and displays a refreshing recognition of the vast numbers of the unchurched. She does not see the growth and multiplication of congregations as inevitable, but instead notes (and explains) a relatively brief, but intense, period of institution building. Her interpretation automatically engages gender, ethnicity, class, and region as she answers questions of who joined which churches; when and why they were willing to commit money to clerical salaries and a church building; and whether one institution was affected by another. Jon Butler's *Awash in a Sea of Faith* (1990) also deals in ordinary believers and strives for inclusivity. In particular, Butler calls upon historians to note that most colonists were members of no church. Moreover, while both Bonomi and Butler find it important to include the smaller communities, they incorporate extensive discussions of Anglicans into their work. Both recognize the size and importance of the Anglican Church in the colonies; both use the rich archives of the Anglican Society for the Propagation of the Gospel; and both take seriously the impact of the Anglican Church and its ministers upon the lives of the unchurched. Butler, in particular, pays attention to the role of the Anglican Church in the initial missionizing among Africans, activities largely ignored by historians of African American Christianity who focus upon the evangelical Presbyterians, Baptists, and Methodists.

Of course, approaching people in the pews to uncover their religious beliefs and commitments required students of religion not only to borrow new methods and strategies, but to rethink the nature of religion itself. Moving away from institutional and theological definitions of religion brings its own epistemological challenge. Can scholars identify some ideological, social, or cultural characteristics that transcend time and place and practitioner? Does a religion exist apart from its practitioners? The scholars' conviction that belief systems, in some pure form, exist is a fast declining conviction. However, although few would argue that there could be a pure form of theology apart from its systematizers, many historians nevertheless spend years of analysis and pages of text recovering theological fragments and ritual celebrations in order to evaluate them against a plumb line of a system's true essence.

Until the last fifteen years, investigations of practitioners have moved in one of two directions. Practitioners could be understood either as a de facto synonym for an intellectual elite or as an institutional church of members that accepted the beliefs promulgated by the elite in an institutionalized creed, complete with prescribed services and hierarchical structures. Although the institutions and ministers examined lived in times past, such an approach often works against historical study, since it posits theologies and institutions as if they were timeless, static entities to be understood in and of themselves. In addition, this interpretation of religion risks losing touch with the people who, in their devotions and participation, created, maintained, and promulgated these cultural systems. Now, following the lead of cultural theorists, some historians question the validity of efforts to reconstruct the true theological or sociological essence. To employ the oft-cited onion metaphor, in peeling off layers of language, rituals, systems of relationship, and meanings, analysts find, at the end, a core of

nothing. The historical religious system, in all its ideological, social, cultural, and political complexities, comprises not some illusive center, but all of the layers.

In no sub-field is the structure of this debate more apparent than in Puritan studies,
where historians have traditionally asserted that real Puritans embraced a particular
composite of beliefs or congregational polities. While this model of homogeneity was
set in motion by early, anti-Puritan writers such as Benjamin Franklin and Nathaniel
Hawthorne, and owes far more to Perry Miller's *The New England Mind*, I fear this
position actually represents a victory for Puritan historians themselves. The histories
penned by Edward Johnson (1654), William Hubbard (1677), and, especially, Cotton Mather (1702) all present portraits of Massachusetts that envision the colony's
history as the struggle of an idealistic, united community of believers against the frontier environment, the indigenous people, a few heretics, and their own inability to
maintain godliness. And while modern students of Puritanism have not accepted everything at face value, too often they have allowed their objects of study to set the
boundaries of their research and analysis.

Historians argue about the role of the clergy, the relation of the church to the state,
the education required of clergymen and lay believers, and the relative importance of
divine grace vs. human effort in Puritan theology. But behind all of these debates lies
an assumption of a single, unified hegemonic theology and sociology widely accepted
among the populace: historians have not so much worked to track development and
change as to get the system right. Any individual or group whose theology or practice
dissented from Miller's model of Puritan orthodoxy was understood as a deviant. Even
the work of sociologist Kai Erikson, whose *Wayward Puritans* (1966) persuasively
argued that only with the identification of deviance can orthodoxy be established,
could not change the historiographic trajectory. For example, the scholarship on Anne
Hutchinson and the Antinomian crisis has been largely a discussion of the nature of
her heresies, the sources of those odd beliefs, and the threat that this movement represented to orthodoxy and order (Hall, 1968; Pettit, 1966; Maclear, 1975; Stoever,
1975). Few have considered the possibility that Hutchinson represented one among
many branches of Puritan theology, one among many styles of Puritan religiosity (Foster, 1981; Gura, 1984; Westerkamp, 1990).

Qualifying portraits of Puritans with the distinction between English Puritanism
and New England Puritanism does little to resolve the interpretive problem. Without
even daring the complicated question of describing English Puritanism, can one know
at what point real, pure, 'true' New England Puritanism existed? Upon arrival in 1630?
In 1638, after Roger Williams, Anne Hutchinson, and their followers had been cast
out and New Englanders became choosier about church membership? (Morgan, 1963;
Rutman, 1965) Yet these are only the most famous of the dissenters. Baptists caused
multiple problems in the 1640s, and a Quaker contingent arose in the midst of Massachusetts in the 1650s (Pestana, 1991; Chu, 1985). Massachusetts residents dismissed
Rhode Island as a sink hole filled with heretics and anarchists; yet most early Rhode
Islanders migrated as Puritans to New England and followed spiritual trajectories first
imagined by various English Puritan communities.

No, as Philip Gura has so astutely outlined in his *A Glimpse of Sion's Glory* (1984),
an amazing variety of English Protestant theologies and polities coexisted in old and
New England – multiple ideologies all descended from "Puritan" dissidence. Puritans
did share some basic commonalities that set them apart from other British Protestants,

including an unwavering theological commitment to predestination, a strong faith in the efficacy of divine grace, a deep, focused devotional life, and an experiential hope in an emotionally intense spiritual conversion (Hambrick-Stowe, 1982; Cohen, 1986). However, even among the relatively small number of the New England elite, one finds disagreement about the application of predestination and grace to the believer's spiritual journey as well as the core nature of the conversion experience (Foster, 1991). Concentrating explicitly upon the various practitioners leads one towards Erikson's conclusion: namely, that orthodoxy was a creation of the magisterium in response to the pressures brought by this very diversity. And, as more recent scholars have noted, even this orthodoxy changed over time (Foster, 1991; Knight, 1994).

Anthropologists have taught historians much about how religion is promulgated, maintained, and transformed through its believers – ordinary practitioners as well as ministers and shamans. Historians have been greatly influenced by the work of Anthony Wallace (1966), Clifford Geertz (1966), Victor Turner (1967), and Mary Douglas (1966, 1970) in their efforts to interpret religions as cultural and social systems. Responding to a functionalist model that interpreted religion as a social system that fulfilled specific needs within a society, such as providing meaning for the intellectually meaningless or reinforcing community identity or nationalist unity, Geertz, Turner, and Douglas have emphasized the symbolic quality of these systems. They have portrayed religions as ideological systems in which beliefs about God, the cosmos, humanity, and the relationship among these three are encoded in language and acted out in rituals that are characterized by the use of symbols of extraordinary complexity and multiplicity of meanings. While granting the centrality of an explicit language of words and phrases understood commonly by the group in ways not shared by outsiders, anthropologists pointed to ritual performances as a kind of behavioral, sacralized language to be deconstructed as keys to understanding religious systems. In other words, a scholar's ability to understand a religious system depends upon the ability to decode the linguistic and ritual systems that constructed it. What historians have added to these analytical possibilities is the understanding that theologies and rituals are historically situated, and that they change over time and among different communities and sites of practice. Moreover, even when the beliefs and rituals remained the same, that is, the same language was used or the ritual was performed in the same pattern, the meanings could change over time and vary among different participants.

Some important contributions of anthropology can be traced within the arena of ethnohistorians, where anthropological theory has been combined with historical methods to recover lost or hidden histories of indigenous American peoples at the time of European contact. Inspired by transformative work in colonial Latin American history, students of British North America began in the 1970s to take on the challenge of Native American cultural systems. In this project historians discovered the analytical absurdity of compartmentalizing religion, politics, and society, as if any of those could exist and be understood apart from the other pieces. Historical anthropologist Anthony Wallace led the way in *Death and Rebirth of the Seneca* (1972). There he provided an illuminating portrait of a revitalization movement among the Senecas and argued for a pattern of cultural change – decline, transformation through individual charisma, then growth – that was repeated among several Native American communities. This hypothesis has been further tested and expounded by Gregory Dowd (1992), who has located and traced revitalization movements among several nations east of the Mississippi River.

Among ethnohistorians, European/Amerindian contact has provided a range of questions to explore as well as opportunities for serious and therefore revealing comparative work. In his *Manitou and Providence* (1982), Neal Salisbury has reconstructed the cultures of New England Natives before European contact and considered indigenous and English colonizers' culture as they responded to the new land and its residents. Taking this approach further, James Axtell's voluminous scholarship has explored Native American communities, French traders and missionaries, and English colonizers in cultural exchange with one another across this landscape (1985; 1992). By taking each community seriously as both receptor and promulgator of cultural systems, his work not only describes pre-contact societies but argues for the mutuality of cultural exchange itself. Because all three communities were transformed by contact with the others, understanding Puritans or Jesuits requires understanding Native American communities and Euro-American developments that grew out of that contact. Axtell's research on Europeans who have chosen to join or remain among specific indigenous communities provides an especially enlightening window into this process of cultural exchange. More recently, Richard White (1991) has built upon anthropological theories of liminality and argued that colonizers and Native Americans moved together into social and cultural spaces opened by the instability inherent in the process of colonization and contact to create new economic, political, and ideological systems.

In their examination of behavior as keys to deconstructing popular culture and cosmology, anthropologists have pointed to the performance of religion through ritual. In the explorations of Anglo-American culture, Rhys Isaac broke new ground in his "Evangelical Revolt" (1974) and his *Transformation of Virginia* (1982). Putting aside the historian's traditional interest in curious phenomena, unique people, and moments of transformative significance, Isaac's scholarship reveals a fascination with the small, seemingly inessential actions performed repeatedly by colonists within the public arena. From oath-taking to dancing to drinking and toasting to entering church late, Virginia behavior patterns not only revealed but constructed the deferential nature of the developing plantation society. Isaac's discovery of the mid-century Baptist culture as a community that acted out its difference from and antagonism toward the gentry through the performance of oppositional rituals drives a class-conflict interpretation of the Great Awakening with as much force as the meticulous social data provided by Gary Nash (1979). And his conclusions are buttressed by a second non-traditional work, Dell Upton's *Holy Things and Profane (1986)*, an illuminating analysis of the buildings and furnishings of Virginia's Anglican churches.

Historians of the Great Awakening have also followed the lead of cultural historians in their exploration of a religious movement through the economics of cultural production and consumption. Fifteen years ago, Harry S. Stout (1986) completed a remarkable study upon a key piece of the promulgation of religion, preaching, tracking across 150 years the changing structure, content, and impact of sermons. Nathan Hatch (1989) in his examination of the relationship between popular religion and popular politics followed a secondary theme, tracing the ways in which evangelical religion was promoted in the years following the Revolution. He demonstrated a connection between popular politics and popular religion, but in the process he also provided fascinating insights into the role of itinerant clerics, lay preachers, print culture, and hymnology in the expansion of Methodist and Baptist culture. By the mid-1990s, several historians had moved their focus to the tools themselves. R. Laurence Moore

(1994) and Colleen McDannel (1995), for example, both examined the promulgation of religion in the cultural emporium of the nineteenth century. While McDannel's *Material Christianity* focused upon the objects that people purchased and displayed in order to reinforce and promote their own faith or denominations, Moore's *Selling God* examined the myriad of ways and means through which professional religionists marketed religion within an increasingly pluralistic society.

For several decades, the Great Awakening, an event that occurred in the 1740s and served to gather the colonies together into a single British American culture, stood as a fact of history. In 1982, Jon Butler challenged this assumption, labeling the Great Awakening an interpretive fiction, the creation of historians, and in the same year Ned Landsman's excellent essay on revivalism among the Scottish community in New Jersey demonstrated that the canonical mold did not fit the experiences of mid-Atlantic colonists (1982). To a certain extent, historians were already moving toward this argument, questioning the chronological and geographical dimensions of the movement as well as its ultimate impact. Moreover, as in the debates concerning the nature of Puritanism, historians sought for those features that best defined the character of the new phenomenon. Alan Heimert (1966) argued for a growing spirit of anticlericalism as a defining characteristic of the Awakening and saw this development as the beginning of the fragmentation of deference necessary to the resistance movement of the 1760s and 1770s. Butler and others have challenged this conclusion, noting that many ministers came through the battles and revivals of the mid-eighteenth century with enhanced influence and authority. Others have turned to the community revivalism as the primary descriptor of this movement (Westerkamp, 1988; Schmidt, 1989), demonstrating that in some colonies the Awakening was less an American religious innovation than the transference from Europe of ritual patterns that developed new meanings in the colonial environment.

In the 1990s, however, it was within the paradigmatic construction of religion as a competitor for adherents and audience that Frank Lambert (1994) and Timothy Hall (1994) crafted alternative portraits of this phenomenon. Like Moore and McDannel, they focus upon the means by which theology and religiosity were promulgated; but like Hatch, they are engaged with the strategies and tools of the eighteenth, not the nineteenth, century. Both Hall and Lambert explore these tools to provide insights that account for the transition from the institutionalized denominations of the seventeenth and early eighteenth centuries to the popular religion that Hatch described. Hall's *Contested Boundaries* focuses upon one specific tool of the revivalists, namely the use of itinerancy as a means of spreading the movement. Lambert's study of one particular itinerant, George Whitefield, pursues more deeply the problems of promoting the new religiosity to increasingly anxious cultural consumers. In this study, Whitefield becomes the master vendor and public relations expert, joining the old methods of clerical correspondence with new advertising techniques of pamphlets, broadsides, newspapers, even the publication of his journal to get the word out and attract people to his lectures. Even his activity on both sides of the Atlantic was publicized to buttress the truth inherent in his message and, in the process, demonstrate and thus further increase Whitefield's effectiveness. Although the traveling preacher was not an entirely new character, the significant number of itinerants, the size of their audiences, their ultimate effectiveness as religious recruiters, and the predictably hostile response from settled pastors served to reshape the American religious landscape.

As both Hall and Lambert argue, the remarkable transformation of American Christianity was not only about ideology and ritual; it also concerned the forms of verbal expressions, the publication of those expressions, and the methods by which these messages were spread. In other words, evangelicalism was characterized, not only by beliefs and rituals, but also by the employment of innovative, outwardly directed practices whose purpose was to create audiences for preachers who would then pull people into the network.

As historians of religion have developed an appreciation of the complexities of indigenous American cultural systems, and as they have moved toward a more sophisticated understanding of the workings of Protestant Christianities of the eighteenth century, they have also realized that colonizing Europeans were not modernist practitioners of institutionalized denominations. Keith Thomas (1971), pursuing research in early modern English religion and culture, has broken away from institutional constructions of religion and reframed the interpretive question in terms of popular conceptions of the supernatural, the natural world, humanity, and the relationships among them. By placing magical thinking at the core of his analysis, Thomas has built upon the anthropological work of a previous generation, especially Evans-Pritchard (1937; 1965). Here, the term magic refers to the manipulation of the natural world through the use of specific tools and substances, the utterance of key verbal expressions, and the performance of detailed rituals; together these efforts unfailingly engaged supernatural means to effect the material change desired. This is not an unpredictable but hope-filled system such as prayer, where God might be entreated, though not forced, to respond positively. A magical cosmology is one of certainty: accurate performance always achieves the expected result. Within a community that shares a commitment to magical thinking, the failure of a particular practice does not undermine the overall faith in magic itself. Like Tom Sawyer, who never questioned magical methods, even when all his lost marbles did not appear in the hole alongside the marble that he ritualistically buried, believers blame the failure of a particular effort upon either the lack of skill or knowledge of the individual practitioner or the active, magical interference of another individual. Tom Sawyer muttered a chant at a ladybug and discovered that, yes indeed, a witch had interfered.

Thomas examines a range of magic systems, including magical healing, witchcraft, astrology, and beliefs in ancient prophecies, ghosts, and omens. He argues persuasively for the persistence of magical beliefs long after Christianity, even Reformation Christianity, had taken hold in England and challenges the arguments of European historians that the Reformation represented an immediate turning away from traditional folk beliefs toward a rationalist systematization of theology and scriptural interpretation. For Thomas, the ultimate establishment of rational Protestant systems and the corresponding transformation of religiosity from one of mystery and magic to one of language and learning represented a fairly late development. Brought about as much by the development of capitalist economics as by the scientific revolution and the ensuing Enlightenment, the dismissal of magical alternatives as reasonable solutions heralded the beginning of modernity.

Within this same framework, Jon Butler (1979; 1990) stands against the assumption that European colonizers arrived in North America accompanied only by rational, credal structures of belief, practice, and polity. He has located across the British colonies indications of the continued practice of magic and the occult. Much of the evidence can be found in the literature and legal records that surround witchcraft, although Butler devotes space to astrology as well as to an interesting commentary upon almanacs. Like Thomas, Butler is tracking the changing role that magic plays in the cosmology of colonizers, though Butler uses the analytical paradigm of "folklorization of magic" to describe the transformation that occurred in the eighteenth century. He opens his discussion by outlining the efforts of Christians to discourage magical practices, charting various laws and manuals. Yet it would be mistaken to see Christianity and belief in magical thinking as antitheses. As Thomas notes, the medieval church was among the most prominent purveyors of magical thought, incorporating many traditional beliefs and practices into Catholic rituals. Moreover, although English Protestants, particularly Puritan dissenters, claimed to reject the "superstitious" trappings of formal rituals and celebrations, that is, Catholic rituals, believers did embrace several practices and beliefs that qualify as magical, including astrology and prophecy readings. That institutionalized Christianities at this time were opposed to magic should not be confused with a dismissal of magical practices as nonsense. During the eighteenth century, Christianity may have moved toward a system that held less and less ideological space for magical thinking. Before 1700, however, the response of religious leaders to such practices, particularly witchcraft, was designed not to correct misguided or superstitious believers but to control dangerous criminals.

For both Thomas and Butler, beliefs in witchcraft as recorded in official records and unofficial correspondence and diaries, along with literary observations about practical applications of charms, incantations, and herbal remedies stand as primary evidence of the continuity of folk religion in the seventeenth and eighteenth centuries. New England witchcraft accusations and trials have themselves inspired a scholarship industry, beginning with Paul Boyer's and Stephen Nissenbaum's *Salem Possessed* (1974), which incorporates almost no discussion of religion, focusing instead upon the local social and political instability in which such accusations flourished. John Demos' *Entertaining Satan* (1982), considering all cases except those of Salem, pursues a variety of explanations for the rise and fall of accusations. Interestingly, both Demos and Boyer and Nissenbaum are more interested in the accusations than the practices themselves.

Richard Weisman (1984) and Richard Godbeer (1992) are both interested in the discourse and practice of magic and witchcraft. Weisman sees magical practices in New England as efforts on the part of ordinary people to hurt their neighbors or, more importantly, to protect themselves against their neighbors. His understanding of magic is placed within an elite/popular dichotomy that sees a divergence between the elite and the laity not only in terms of the practice of magic, but in definitions of witchcraft itself. Godbeer's work benefits from more recent scholarship in popular religion as he lays out the complexity of practices that could be found in New England. Plagued by a scarcity of evidence, Godbeer nonetheless makes an excellent, if speculative, case for the widespread use of witchcraft by people in all social strata. While many historians, including Thomas and Weisman, see an opposition between Puritanism and magic, Godbeer argues that Puritan cosmology, with its willingness to blame Satan for individual sin, actually nurtured fears of evil magic. Moreover, in their very opposition to magic and witchery, Puritan leaders revealed themselves as believers in magic. In other words, Godbeer works against previous analytical efforts to dichotomize folk religion and institutional Christianity, ordinary folks and the elite.

In these efforts, Godbeer is in good company. David Hall's exploration of religious culture through elite and popular texts, including the more sensational publications, illustrates the difficulties of distinguishing between elite theology and popular beliefs (1990). If the intellectual elite embraced a theological system largely beyond the comprehension of the ordinary congregant, they shared key cosmological assumptions with the populace, often reinforcing those convictions with their own writings. As Hall notes, the sensationalist literature about storms at sea, fires, lightning strikes, and monster births (the language used to describe infants with severe birth defects) were produced by the intellectual elites and, despite the often lurid details and graphic illustrations, generally approved for popular reading because of the strength of the moral lessons taught within.

Despite the strength of all of these studies of magic and witchery in the New World, it is unfortunate that discourses engaging indigenous Americans rarely appear. Many Amerindian communities believed in witchcraft, and many colonizers described the Native peoples as practitioners of magic and "followers of Satan." Surely casual interactions as well as long-term friendly and hostile relationships between colonizers and Natives had an impact upon Europeans' constructions of goodness and evil. Fernando Cervantes' enlightening *The Devil in the New World* (1994) provides a model of what could come from such efforts. Because Spanish missionaries were deeply committed to missionizing and converting the Native population, interactions between the two were continuously characterized by constructions and reconceptualizations of spirituality and theology. Products of the hyper-theologized world of Catholic Spain, where heretics and blasphemers constantly threatened the sanctified purity of the religious community, the missionaries proved vigilant seekers of error. In Spanish America, they actively challenged indigenous religious practices through accusations of witchcraft, suggestions that indigenous people appeared to find completely plausible. What Cervantes discovers is not only a tale of inquisitorial oppression but a dialogic cultural process through which missionaries and Natives were both impacted socially and ideologically through official religious confrontations that employed the language of witchery, magic, and Satan.

Any discussion of witchcraft opens up the conversation to gender, one of the most fruitful new areas of research and analysis. Among the first, Carol Karlsen's study of the witch trials demonstrates that the demographic and psychological profile of accused witches fits not the powerless old women of legend but the empowered middle-aged women with aspirations to property and authority (1987). Her methodology is social analysis, and yet here one sees the analysis of witchcraft as a crime that was perceived to naturally devolve upon women. Taking up issues of both possession and witchcraft accusations, Karlsen asks questions of the ideas surrounding witchcraft and the relationship between gender politics and gender ideology. Elizabeth Reis (1997) takes this even further, when she asks not why society embraced the satanic criminality of women, but why many women embraced this argument, even in applying it to themselves. Heavily influenced by the "new cultural history," Reis examines the confessions of witches alongside the conversion narratives of female saints, identifying engaging gendered patterns of the construction of self, society, and salvation.

While the witch trials have attracted particular attention, some historians of women and gender have pursued Puritanism in other directions. Laurel Thatcher Ulrich's social history of New England women was among the first, incorporating into her analysis Puritans' construction of womanhood and motherhood as impacted by English custom, the common law, and Puritans' own peculiar religious culture (1985). Amanda Porterfield's *Female Piety in Puritan New England* (1992) addresses the spirituality question directly. Building upon the extensive scholarship on the Puritan conversion (Morgan, 1963; Hambrick-Stowe, 1982; Cohen, 1986), she argues that Puritan spirituality was in its nature feminine, and then discusses the impact of that conclusion, namely that this religiosity granted women greater authority and power within the society. In my own work, I have joined many historians of mid-seventeenth-century English sectarianism and argued that Puritan religiosity opened the way for all individuals, regardless of status, education, or gender, thus making space for the spiritual authority of the disfranchised (Westerkamp, 1997; Hill, 1972; Mack, 1992; Warnicke, 1983). Further, I agree with Porterfield's assessment of the feminine nature of Puritan spirituality – feminine within the Puritans' own understanding of masculinity, femininity, and gender difference. Rather than directly empowering women, however, this open-ended, feminine spirituality, in the cultural context of sharply drawn biblically patriarchal lines of authority, created a liminal space characterized by gender confusion. While Puritan religious culture certainly opened to women pathways of spiritual authority, Puritan leaders, disconcerted by this challenge to order, responded sharply to these movements, curtailing any power that women may have pursued.

The application of the anthropological paradigm of liminality is also used by Susan Juster in her study of New England Baptist women in the eighteenth and early nineteenth centuries (1994). The Great Awakening brought to the eighteenth-century colonies the same sort of cultural instability and liminal space produced by colonization and Civil War in seventeenth-century New and Old England. Juster argues that Baptist women experienced even greater authority and influence than Puritan women had, including some authority in disciplinary procedures. She, too, finds these avenues closed off with the efforts of Baptist male leaders to establish order within the church and accommodate to the surrounding society of the new nation. What is particularly interesting about Juster's work is her focus upon the intricacies of language as the creator, sustainer, and disturber of ideological and social structures. In their efforts to articulate their experience of the Holy Spirit, men and women ended up outlining the spiritual pathways that believers would follow, and the distinctions among descriptions, prescriptions, and predictions became difficult to maintain. Through an analysis of the language of testimonies, sermons, and even disciplinary records Juster tracks a change in the religiosity and polity of the New England Baptists from a position of openness and equity in the 1740s and 1750s to one of closed structures and hierarchy after 1800. The promise of deep language exploration has been picked up by two historians of gender, Elizabeth Reis, whose work is discussed above, and Jane Kamensky. While Kamensky's *Governing the Tongue* (1997) does not explicitly focus upon religion, the materials she investigates include texts produced by ministers, believers, and churches. Kamensky analyzes language through the lenses of seventeenth-century philosophy and speech and twentieth-century theories of language production and consumption, and she can therefore further an understanding of the Puritan ethos and the relationship between the sacred and profane as constructed through words.

With the current fascination with cultural theory, language, and gender, the historiography of religion in British North America has embraced the theories and methodologies that currently preoccupy cultural historians of other times, places, and systems. The impact of social history in the late 1960s and 1970s pushed scholars' attention toward the ordinary believers. The growing interest in cultural history has not only influenced the approaches taken toward religion, but it has served to move religion from the periphery toward the center of colonial historiography, for, as colonialists know, the cultural worlds of the sixteenth, seventeenth, and eighteenth centuries were permeated with constructions that could be classified as religious. As questions of race, class, and gender have made their way through the scholarship, they have been pursued by historians of religion as well.

However, religious history has not merely followed trends. What historians of religion brought to the table in the twentieth century was an early interest in diversity and pluralism along with the need to understand multiple communities internally as well as intersectionally. Drawn by an interest in religious systems, they were among the first to examine German, Scots-Irish, even Pennsylvania Quaker colonists. These scholars also provided early pressures to maintain an analytical paradigm that incorporated a transatlantic framework, brought from their own peculiar interpretation of church history as institutional systems that originated in Reformation Europe. Yet, despite this push towards new and diverse topics, the historiography of religion has traveled the well-known path of colonial American scholarship. New England still dominates the scholarship; the Great Awakening still holds second place.

Not surprisingly, all of the outstanding studies of language mentioned above focus upon colonial New England, the ultimate producer (and accumulator) of written language. At some point soon, this level of scrutiny needs to be fixed upon other arenas. While some have researched the mid-Atlantic colonies, much more needs to be done. This region is filled with the ethnic, class, and religious conflicts for which historians yearn, and the records are there for the finding. The South has received even less attention, although here one might suspect a scarcity of evidence. Still, Rhys Isaac (1982) and Mechal Sobel (1987) have managed to locate significant sources and to craft intriguing, illuminating portraits of the evangelical culture of the mid-eighteenth century.

In spite of the new breadth to which historians currently aspire, there still remains a remarkable absence of research on Catholic and Jewish settlers. Both communities were admittedly small, but research on each of them is essential to piecing together the portrait of the colonial world, particularly as it moved toward a nation that would break with tradition by refusing to disfranchise both groups. Like the stories of the Dutch Calvinists and the Huguenots, the history of Jewish immigrants provides an excellent opportunity to explore the dynamics of assimilation and acculturation, intriguing because of the community's twofold determination to remain Jewish and yet fully participate within the surrounding society. On the other hand, the difficulties that Catholic settlers encountered within the colonies along with the era's conflation of political and religious identities make the Catholic population an excellent point from which to explore the intersection of religious identity and political structures. Colonizing Catholics and their relationships with their neighbors can provide a prime opportunity for defining the nature of religious identity, its connection with ethnicity and nationalism, and, significantly, the rise and fall (at least temporarily) of religious intolerance.

Ironically, one of the primary gaps is the absence of developed study of the Anglican establishment in the colonies. Until the 1750s, the Anglican Church was almost the only church available to colonists in the South; and in the mid-Atlantic region, Anglicans often comprised the majority of English settlers. Patricia Bonomi (1986) and, later, Jon Butler (1990) have both emphasized the importance of this denomination, and each has incorporated into their more general histories an exceptionally fine introduction to the Anglican church network. Years earlier, Carl Bridenbaugh (1962) had noted the importance of the Anglican Church to disentangling the murky problem of establishment, dissent, and politics. Except in Puritan New England, as Butler has explained, Anglicans, until the 1750s, were the primary English missionaries among African Americans and Native Americans. The Society for the Propagation of the Gospel that funded so many missionary and ministerial efforts was in fact an organization sponsored by the Church of England, channeling funds to the work of Christianization in the North American colonies. Yet with the exception of John Woolverton's fine, general history of the colonial Anglican network (1984), historians have not taken up the challenge of exploring the established church.

Perhaps it is in the nature of American historians to be more interested in dissent than in the forces of order. Anglicans often appear only as repressors or counterpoints for the more interesting groups, as in the case of Balmer's exploration of New York (1988) or Isaac's study of Virginia (1982), yet this approach sidesteps the promise of the subject. Anglicans in the South may have held unquestioned sway; nonetheless, they often acted (almost as if they were Congregationalists) in opposition to the policies of the Bishop of London, under whose authority they were placed. In the mid-Atlantic, the presence of so many different ethnic and English dissenter communities, some far better prepared to deal with the lack of state support for the church, rendered the experience of Anglicans as one of struggle to maintain an institution that in England had always been taken for granted. And in New England, Anglicans were the dissenters who finally in 1691 were granted official toleration and permission to build their own churches by the new king although they were left, again, to support those churches voluntarily. The failure to study Anglicans probably reflects religious historians' forward focus upon the rise of evangelicalism, which in the colonies grew from other roots. Until more work is done on this central church network, however, early Americanists will not have a sound foundation from which to reconstruct the religious landscape of the colonies.

In the past thirty years, social history has enhanced and expanded the research and writing of religious history. During these decades scholars have pushed themselves beyond clergy, institutions, and theology to examine popular beliefs and spiritual identity, while social and anthropological theory and methods have provided strategies for approaching the new subjects. The rise of cultural studies has destabilized the field productively and provocatively, challenging in difficult ways assumptions that have always formed the foundations of research and analysis. Historians can no longer identify timeless systems without comment; there is no more security in a master narrative; and the methods and agents of cultural production are no longer obvious. Yet this dissonance and lack of certainty has been and will continue to be a positive force in the development of historical scholarship. The search for multiple visions and spaces will continue to push historians to research horizons beyond English colonists and the thirteen colonies. Historians may even go beyond the Caribbean and converse in earnest with those who concentrate on Spanish and French colonization. As this volume demonstrates, some colonialists now write with enthusiasm of an Atlantic world and the colonial Americas.

As historians of religion accept an ever expanding macrohistorical vision, they must engage the same interpretive challenge confronting all world historians: removing Europeans/Euro-American religions from the center of the Atlantic world. As scholars grapple instead with the reality of multiple communities, cosmologies, and epistemologies of indigenous Americans, Europeans, and Africans in comparative colonial American systems, they will discover the varied ways that contact not only affects economics and demography but also transforms the ideological worlds of all participants in relation to the others. Explorations of specific religious networks and regions will continue to stand at the core of new scholarship, but more and more these studies will be forced beyond parochial boundaries toward an extended framework of world systems and cultural pluralism. This broader understanding of interlocked religious systems will serve as a significant, perhaps essential interpretive pathway for building a macro-understanding of the Atlantic world and the processes of early modern colonialism.

BIBLIOGRAPHY

Ahlstrom, S. E.: *A Religious History of the American People* (New Haven, CT: Yale University Press, 1972).
Albright, R. W.: *History of the Protestant Episcopal Church* (New York: Macmillan Co., 1964).
Axtell, J.: *The Invasion Within: The Contest of Cultures in Colonial North America* (New York: Oxford University Press, 1985).
Axtell, J.: *Beyond 1492: Encounters in Colonial North America* (New York: Oxford University Press, 1992).
Balmer, R. H.: *A Perfect Babel of Confusion: Dutch Religion and English Culture in the Middle Colonies* (New York: Oxford University Press, 1989).
Bercovitch, S.: *The American Jeremiad* (Madison, WI: University of Wisconsin Press, 1978).
Bonomi, P.: *Under the Cope of Heaven: Religion, Society, and Politics in Colonial America* (New York: Oxford University Press, 1986).
Boyer, P. and Nissenbaum, S.: *Salem Possessed: The Social Origins of Witchcraft* (Boston, MA: Harvard University Press, 1974).
Bremer, F. J., ed.: *Puritanism: Transatlantic Perspectives on a Seventeenth-Century Anglo-American Faith* (Boston, MA: Massachusetts Historical Society, 1993).
Bridenbaugh, C.: *Mitre and Sceptre: Transatlantic Faiths, Ideas, Personalities, and Politics, 1689–1775* (New York: Oxford University Press, 1962).
Bronner, E.: *William Penn's Holy Experiment: The Founding of Pennsylvania* (Philadelphia: Temple University Press, 1962).
Butler, J.: "Magic, Astrology, and the Early American Religious Heritage, 1600–1760." *American Historical Review* 84 (1979), pp. 317–46.
Butler, J.: "Enthusiasm Described and Decried: The Great Awakening as Interpretive Fiction." *Journal of American History* 69 (1982), pp. 305–25.
Butler, J.: *The Huguenots in America: A Refugee People in New World Society* (Cambridge, MA: Harvard University Press, 1983).
Butler, J.: *Awash in a Sea of Faith: Christianizing the American People* (Cambridge: Harvard University Press, 1990).
Cervantes, F.: *The Devil in the New World: The Impact of Diabolism in New Spain* (New Haven, CT: Yale University Press, 1994).
Chu, J. M.: *Neighbors, Friends, or Madmen: The Puritan Adjustment to Quakerism in Seventeenth-Century Massachusetts Bay* (Westport, CT: Greenwood Press, 1985).

Cohen, C. L.: *God's Caress: The Psychology of Puritan Religious Experience* (New York: Oxford University Press, 1986).

Cowing, C. B.: *The Great Awakening and the American Revolution: Colonial Thought in the 19th Century* (Chicago: Rand McNally, 1971).

Crawford, M. J.: *Seasons of Grace: Colonial New England's Revival Tradition in its British Context* (New York: Oxford University Press, 1991).

Davidson, E. H.: *The Establishment of the English Church in the Continental American Colonies* (Durham, NC: Duke University Press, 1936).

Demos, J. P.: *Entertaining Satan: Witchcraft and the Culture of Early New England* (New York: Oxford University Press, 1982).

Dolan, J. P.: *The American Catholic Experience: A History from Colonial Times to the Present* (Garden City, NY: Doubleday, 1985).

Douglas, M.: *Purity and Danger: An Analysis of Concepts of Pollution and Taboo* (London: Routledge and Kegan Paul, 1966).

Douglas, M.: *Natural Symbols: Explorations in Cosmology* (New York: Pantheon Books, 1970).

Dowd, G.: *A Spirited Resistance: The North American Indian Struggle for Unity, 1745–1815* (Baltimore, MD: Johns Hopkins University Press, 1992).

Ellis, J. T.: *Catholics in Colonial America* (Baltimore, MD: Helicon, 1965).

Erikson, K.T.: *Wayward Puritans: A Study in the Sociology of Deviance* (New York: John Wiley and Sons, 1966).

Evans-Pritchard, E. E.: *Witchcraft, Oracles, and Magic Among the Azande* (Oxford: Clarendon Press, 1937).

Evans-Pritchard, E. E.: *Theories of Primitive Religion* (Oxford: Clarendon Press, 1965).

Foster, S.: "New England and the Challenge of Heresy, 1630 to 1660: The Puritan Crisis in Transatlantic Perspective." *William and Mary Quarterly* 3rd ser., 38 (1981), pp. 624–60.

Foster, S.: The *Long Argument: English Puritanism and the Shaping of New England Culture, 1570–1700* (Chapel Hill, NC: University of North Carolina Press, 1991).

Gaustad, E. S.: *The Great Awakening in New England* (Gloucester, MA: P. Smith Press, 1965).

Geertz, C.: "Religion as a Cultural System." In M. Banton, ed., *Anthropological Approaches to the Study of Religion* (Edinburgh: Tavistock Publications, 1966), pp. 1–46.

Glazer, N.: *American Judaism* (Chicago: University of Chicago Press, 1957).

Godbeer, R.: *The Devil's Dominion: Magic and Religion in Early New England* (New York: Cambridge University Press, 1992).

Greven, P. J.: *Four Generations: Population, Land, and Family in Colonial Andover* (Ithaca, NY: Cornell University Press, 1970).

Gura, P. F.: *A Glimpse of Sion's Glory: Puritan Radicalism in New England, 1620–1660* (Middletown, CT: Wesleyan University Press, 1984).

Hall, D. D.: "Introduction." In Hall, ed., *The Antinomian Controversy, 1636–1638: A Documentary History* (Middletown, CT: Wesleyan University Press, 1968), pp. 3–23.

Hall, D. D.: *Worlds of Wonder, Days of Judgment: Popular Religious Belief in Early New England* (Cambridge: Harvard University Press, 1990).

Hall, T. D.: *Contested Boundaries: Itinerancy and the Reshaping of the Colonial American Religious World* (Durham, NC: Duke University Press, 1994).

Hambrick-Stowe, C. E.: *The Practice of Piety: Puritan Devotional Disciplines in Seventeenth-Century New England* (Chapel Hill, NC: University of North Carolina Press, 1982).

Hatch, N.: *The Democratization of American Christianity* (New Haven, CT: Yale University Press, 1989).

Heimert, A.: *Religion and the American Mind: From the Great Awakening to the Revolution* (Cambridge, MA: Harvard University Press, 1966).

Hennesey, J. J.: *American Catholics: A History of the Roman Catholic Community in the United States* (New York: Oxford University Press, 1981).

Herskovits, M. J.: *The Myth of the Negro Past* (1941; Boston, MA: Beacon Press, 1990).

Heyrman, C. L.: *Southern Cross: The Beginnings of the Bible Belt* (New York: Alfred A. Knopf, 1997).

Hill, C.: *The World Turned Upside-Down: Radicalism and Religion during the English Revolution* (New York: Viking Press, 1972).

Hubbard, W.: *A Narrative of the Indian Wars in New-England, from the First Planting thereof in the year 1607, to the year 1677* (Boston, 1677).

Isaac, R.: "Evangelical Revolt: The Nature of the Baptists' Challenge to the Traditional Order in Virginia, 1765–1775." *William and Mary Quarterly* 3rd ser., 31 (1974), pp. 345–68.

Isaac, R.: *The Transformation of Virginia, 1740–1790* (Chapel Hill, NC: University of North Carolina Press, 1982).

Johnson, E.: *Wonder-Working Providence of Sion's Saviour in New England* (London, 1654).

Jones, R. M.: *The Quakers in the American Colonies*, assisted by I. Sharpless and A. M. Gummere (London: Macmillan and Co., 1911).

Juster, S.: *Disorderly Women: Sexual Politics & Evangelicalism in Revolutionary New England* (New York: Cornell University Press, 1994).

Kamensky, J.: *Governing the Tongue: The Politics of Speech in Early New England* (New York: Oxford University Press, 1997).

Karlsen, C.: *The Devil in the Shape of a Woman: Witchcraft in Colonial New England* (New York: Norton, 1987).

Knight, J.: *Orthodoxies in Massachusetts: Rereading American Puritanism* (Cambridge, MA: Harvard University Press, 1994).

Lambert, F.: *Pedlar in Divinity: George Whitefield and the Transatlantic Revivals, 1737–1770* (Princeton, NJ: Princeton University Press, 1994).

Landsman, N.: "Revivalism and Nativism in the Middle Colonies: The Great Awakening and the Scots Community in East New Jersey." *American Quarterly* 34 (1982), pp. 149–64.

Lemon, J.: *The Best Poor Man's Country; A Geographical Study of Early Southeastern Pennsylvania* (Baltimore, MD: Johns Hopkins University Press, 1972).

Lewis, A. J.: *Zinzendorf, The Ecumenical Pioneer: A Study in the Moravian Contribution to Christian Mission and Unity* (London: SCM Press, 1962).

Lockridge, K.: *A New England Town: The First One Hundred Years, Dedham, Massachusetts, 1636–1736* (New York: W. W. Norton, 1970).

Lodge, M. E.: "The Great Awakening in the Middle Colonies" (Ph.D. dissertation, University of California, Berkeley, 1964).

Mack, P.: *Visionary Women: Ecstatic Prophecy in Seventeenth-Century England* (Berkeley, CA: University of California Press, 1992).

Maclear, J. F.: "New England and the Fifth Monarchy: The Quest for the Millennium in Early American Puritanism." *William and Mary Quarterly* 3rd ser., 32 (1975), pp. 223–60.

Manross, W. W.: *A History of the American Episcopal Church*, 2nd ed. (New York: Morehouse-Gorham, 1950).

Mather, C.: *Magnalia Christi Americana* (Boston, 1702).

McDannel, C.: *Material Christianity: Religion and Popular Culture* (New Haven, CT: Yale University Press, 1995).

Miller, P.: *Orthodoxy in Massachusetts, 1630–1650* (Cambridge, MA: Harvard University Press, 1933).

Miller, P.: *The New England Mind*, 2 vols (Cambridge: Harvard University Press, 1939; 1956).

Mintz, S. W. and Price, P.: *An Anthropological Approach to the Afro-American Past: A Caribbean Perspective* (Philadelphia: Institute for the Study of Human Issues, 1976).

Moore, R. L.: *Selling God: American Religion in the Marketplace* (New York: Oxford University Press, 1994).

Morgan, E. S.: *The Puritan Dilemma: The Story of John Winthrop* (Boston, MA: Little, Brown and Co., 1958).

Morgan, E. S.: *Visible Saints: The History of Puritan Idea* (1963; Ithaca, NY: Cornell University Press, 1965).

Nash, G. B.: *Quakers and Politics: Pennsylvania, 1681–1726* (Princeton, NJ: Princeton University Press, 1968).

Nash, G. B.: *The Urban Crucible: Social Change, Political Consciousness, and the Origins of the American Revolution* (Cambridge, MA: Harvard University Press, 1979).

Nash, G. B.: *Forging Freedom: The Formation of Philadelphia's Black Community, 1720–1840* (Cambridge, MA: Harvard University Press, 1988).

Pestana, C. G.: *Baptists and Quakers in Colonial Massachusetts* (New York: Cambridge University Press, 1991).

Pettit, N.: *The Heart Prepared: Grace and Conversion in Puritan Spiritual Life* (New Haven, CT: Yale University Press, 1966).

Pointer, R. W.: *Protestant Pluralism and the New York Experience: A Study of Eighteenth-Century Religious Diversity* (Bloomington, IN: University of Indiana, 1988).

Pope, R.: *The Half-Way Covenant: Church Membership in Puritan New England* (Princeton, NJ: Princeton University Press, 1969).

Porterfield, A.: *Female Piety in Puritan New England: The Emergence of Religious Humanism* (New York: Oxford University Press, 1992).

Raboteau, A. J.: *Slave Religion: The "Invisible Institution" in the Antebellum South* (New York: Oxford University Press, 1978).

Reis, E.: *Damned Women: Sinners and Witches in Puritan New England* (Ithaca, NY: Cornell University Press, 1997).

Rutman, D. B.: *Winthrop's Boston: Portrait of a Puritan Town* (Chapel Hill, NC: University of North Carolina Press, 1965).

Salisbury, N.: *Manitou and Providence: Indians, Europeans, and the Making of New England, 1500–1643* (New York: Oxford University Press, 1982).

Schmidt, L. E.: *Holy Fairs: Scottish Communions and American Revivals in the Early Modern Period* (Princeton, NJ: Princeton University Press, 1989).

Schwartz, S.: *"A Mixed Multitude": The Struggle for Toleration in Colonial Pennsylvania* (New York: New York University Press, 1988).

Smaby, B. P.: *The Transformation of Moravian Bethlehem: From Communal Mission to Family Economy* (Philadelphia: University of Pennsylvania Press, 1988).

Sobel, M.: The *World They Made Together: Black and White Values in Eighteenth-Century Virginia* (Princeton, NJ: Princeton University Press, 1987).

Stoever, W. K.: "Nature, Grace and John Cotton: The Theological Dimension in the New England Antinomian Controversy." *Church History* 44 (1975), pp. 22–33.

Stout, H. S.: *The New England Soul: Preaching and Religious Culture in Colonial New England* (New York: Oxford University Press, 1986).

Sydnor, C. S.: *American Revolutionaries in the Making: Political Practices in Washington's Virginia* (New York: Collier Books, 1962).

Thomas, K.: *Religion and the Decline of Magic* (New York: Scribner, 1971).

Tolles, F. B.: *Meeting House and Counting House: The Quaker Merchants of Colonial Philadelphia, 1682–1763* (Chapel Hill, NC: University of North Carolina Press, 1948).

Tracy, P.: *Jonathan Edwards, Pastor: Religion and Society in Eighteenth Century Northampton* (New York: Hill and Wang, 1980).

Trinterud, L. J.: *The Forming of an American Tradition: A Re-Examination of Colonial Presbyterianism* (Philadelphia: Westminster Press, 1949).

Turner, V.: *The Forest of Symbols: Aspects of Ndembu Ritual* (Ithaca, NY: Cornell University Press, 1967).

Ulrich, L. T.: *Good Wives: Image and Reality in the Lives of Women in Northern New England*

1650–1750 (New York: Oxford University Press, 1985).

Upton, D.: *Holy Things and Profane: Anglican Parish Churches in Colonial Virginia* (Cambridge, MA: MIT Press, 1986).

Wallace, A. F. C.: "Revitalization Movements: Some Theoretical Considerations for their Comparative Study." *American Anthropologist* 58 (1956), pp. 264–81.

Wallace, A. F. C.: *Religion: An Anthropological View* (New York: Random House, 1966).

Wallace, A. F. C.: *Death and Rebirth of the Seneca* (New York: Vintage, 1972).

Warnicke, R.: *Women of the English Renaissance and Reformation* (Westport, CT: Greenwood Press, 1983).

Weber, M.: *The Sociology of Religion*, trans. E. Fischoff, introd. Talcott Parsons (Boston, MA: Beacon Press, 1963).

Weber, M.: *The Protestant Ethic and the Spirit of Capitalism*, trans. T. Parsons (New York: Scribner, 1976).

Weisman, R.: *Witchcraft, Magic, and Religion in 17th-Century Massachusetts* (Amherst, MA: University of Massachusetts Press, 1984).

Wentz, A. R.: *A Basic History of Lutheranism in America* (Philadelphia: Muhlenberg Press, 1955).

Westerkamp, M. J.: *Triumph of the Laity: Scots-Irish Piety and the Great Awakening 1625–1760* (New York: Oxford University Press, 1988).

Westerkamp, M. J.: "Anne Hutchinson, Sectarian Mysticism, and the Puritan Order." *Church History* 59 (1990), pp. 482–96.

Westerkamp, M. J.: "Engendering Puritan Religious Culture in Old and New England." *Pennsylvania History* 64 (1997), pp. 105–22.

White, R.: *The Middle Ground: Indians, Empires, and Republics in the Great Lakes Region, 1650–1815* (New York: Cambridge University Press, 1991).

Woolverton, J. F.: *Colonial Anglicanism in North America* (Detroit: Wayne State University Press, 1984).

CHAPTER SIXTEEN

Secular Culture in Search of an Early American Enlightenment

DARREN STALOFF

There is a curious irony about the historiographic treatment of the Enlightenment in America. On the one hand, no nation bears as profound a relationship to the Age of Reason as the United States. American national identity emerged from the forge of the Enlightenment, the source of our much-vaunted secular humanism and pluralism. Its slogans and maxims are embedded in our political culture and institutions. Its phrases resound in such cherished founding documents as the Constitution, the Declaration of Independence, and the *Federalist*. Europeans were not alone when they saw in the new republic, in Peter Gay's words, "the program of the philosophies in practice, and found themselves convinced that the Enlightenment had been a success" (Gay, 1969, p. 568). Americans then and now have seen in their Revolution and subsequent political development the Enlightenment in action, and the rise of American hegemony has been interpreted as a testament to the high-minded rationality of its Founding Fathers. On the other hand, the historical literature on the American Enlightenment is remarkably slender. Dwarfed in comparison to the historiography associated with far more temporally and geographically limited fields like Puritan New England or the Great Awakening of the mid-eighteenth century, what little scholarship there is does not precede the middle of the 1970s.

Part of the reticence historians have shown toward grappling with the American Enlightenment can be attributed to the elusive nature of the topic itself. Analysis of the Enlightenment and its doctrines has proven remarkably protean. Where Ernst Cassirer saw a rejection of systematic thought and the quest for apodeictic certainty, Carl Becker found a utopian mentality fraught with logical contradictions and enthusiastic delusions. More recently, Peter Gay has described the Enlightenment as the birth of modern paganism, when the Age of Reason came to understand itself in contrast to the superstitious "dark age" of Christian devotion it sought to displace and supersede (Gay, 1966, 1969). By far the more cogent explanation, however, was the apparent irrelevance of studying the course of enlightened thought in early America. Particularly in its revolutionary and early national epochs, America simply was the Enlightenment put in practice. Once the actions and intentions of those years were understood, there was little need to say anything else about the role of reason and political science in early America. American political institutions and practices were so deeply immersed in enlightened thought that an analysis of the former exhausted the latter. To the extent that those institutions and practices continue to constitute the parameters of American political culture, its public life still lives under the shadow of the eighteenth-century Enlightenment.

All this began to change in the mid-1960s with the emergence of the ideological interpretation of the American Revolution. Bernard Bailyn and Gordon Wood saw the intellectual roots of resistance in the "country" or real Whig rhetoric of the Walpolean opposition. But whereas for Bailyn the country rhetoric was part and parcel of the Lockean Enlightenment, for Wood writers like John Trenchard, Thomas Gordon, and Henry St. John, Viscount Bolingbroke, both dialectically opposed and displaced Montesquieu, Hume, and (especially) Locke as the guiding lights of the American resistance. Hardly dispassionate rationality, country rhetoric was emotionally volatile, rejecting the skeptical postures of the liberal *philosophes* and embracing in its stead the ardent and virtuous patriotism of the commonwealthmen. Inspired by this rhetoric, Wood found revolutionary Americans in the throes of an almost paranoiac conspiratorial worldview (Wood, 1982), while in the early 1970s Bernard Bailyn described a disturbingly irrational, indeed almost maniacal, patriotic mob that terrorized the last sane man in Boston, loyalist Thomas Hutchinson (Bailyn, 1974). The coup de grace was applied the next year with J. G. A. Pocock's stunning *The Machiavellian Moment* (1975). Pocock traced country ideology back through such seventeenth-century republicans as Algernon Sidney and James Harrington and the mid-century Commonwealthmen, all the way to the Florentine Renaissance of Machiavelli. This extended Machiavellian moment entailed the utter irrelevance of Lockean liberalism and other strains of Enlightenment political theory to the American revolutionary and republican movements. Indeed, only Rousseau remained relevant in Pocock's telling, and his relationship to the republic of letters has always been strained and complicated to say the least. With Pocock's extended synthesis of the ideological roots of the American Revolution, the American political tradition and the Age of Reason appeared to part company. This in turn stimulated historians to examine anew what evidence there was for the impact of enlightened doctrines on early America.

The historiography of the Enlightenment in America that finally emerged in the 1970s understandably took the form of the history of ideas. Capping a small flurry of scholarship were two grand syntheses, Donald H. Meyer's *The Democratic Enlightenment* and Henry F. May's *The Enlightenment in America*. Like all good historians of ideas, May and Meyer sought traces of the Enlightenment in early American habits of reading, writing, and citation. Despite subtle differences in accent, the overall interpretations offered in these works were strikingly similar. Both saw the Enlightenment as essentially an attempt to assimilate the ethos and methods of the scientific revolution to all aspects of culture, an attempt which produced a basic, if often unacknowledged, tension between the latitudinarianism, humanism, and rationalism of "natural" religion and the dogmatic "enthusiastic" piety of bibliocentric Calvinism. Fundamentally elitist and conservative, the Enlightenment had little impact beyond the urban seaports and upper classes in the countryside. May and Meyer also agree that, although enlightened ideas had little influence in the struggle leading to independence, they veritably dominated the thinking of the Federalist movement of the 1780s. Most notable of all, however, is their common periodization of the American Enlightenment into four distinct stages. While the exact configuration of some of the phases differs, both offer a model of the progress of the Enlightenment in America that begins moderately, builds momentum, explodes in revolutionary ardor, and then recedes into "didactic" conservatism. This common periodization, with its implied model of dynamic development, was the most important contribution of the first wave of scholarship on the Enlightenment in early America. It offered a sophisticated and nuanced interpretive scheme or "conceptual grid" that every subsequent work on the subject has had to come to terms with.

For both May and Meyer, the first phase of the Enlightenment was far and away the most important. Covering roughly the first half of the eighteenth century, this cultural movement was profoundly influenced by the contemporary English republic of letters. The central issue of that discourse was the relation between religion and reason, or science, and its tone was decidedly moderate if not conservative. Both Newton and Locke, the leading luminaries of the early Enlightenment, had adopted moderate stances on the religion question, seeing a fundamental harmony between theological and scientific truth while rejecting the emotional excesses of evangelical piety and the dogmatic, abstract rationalism of seventeenth-century reformed scholasticism. This tone of moderate compromise was best exemplified in the late seventeenth century by John Tillotson, Archbishop of Canterbury, whose latitudinarianism downplayed doctrinal differences while stressing the fundamental reasonableness of Christianity. In the eighteenth century, latitudinarianism created a discursive "big tent" covering a wide range of religious thinkers from moderate Presbyterians like William Robertson and Francis Hutcheson to Anglican Arians like Samuel Clarke and such Deists as John Toland and Anthony Collins. What united these men in their defense of the rationality of Christian religion were both an implicit acknowledgment that such a defense was necessary and an utter eschewal of biblical revelation as a source of dialectical support. Instead, the religious thinkers of the moderate Enlightenment defended Christianity on natural religious grounds by invoking the famed "argument from design" (from the elaborate structure and mechanism of the universe to the existence of a divine craftsman) and thus "made the eternal relations of things, the character of the universe, and the nature of rights and wrong prior to the will of God himself" (May, 1976, p. 12).

There were two critical features of this attempt to strike a moderate compromise between religion and reason. The first was its implicit conservatism. What made the rational defense of Christianity conservative was precisely its reliance on the argument from design, an argument that resulted in a deity whose most salient feature was perfect rationality. Assuming the benevolence of such a deity, it was a short inferential leap to optimistically conclude that such a God was only capable of creating a universe that rationally maximized the good, or in Leibniz's famous phrase (as vulgarized by Voltaire), "the best of all possible worlds." Such metaphysical optimism, central to the philosophical musings of Shaftesbury and Hutcheson and redolent in the belletristic writing of the ever popular Addison and Pope, has been described by historians, following Basil Willey, as Cosmic Toryism. This is because a perfect world order implies a perfect social order within that world, and a perfect social order is hardly in need of reform, much less radical reconstruction. Characteristic of this complacent optimism was the early Enlightenment celebration of cosmic harmony and order in contrast to the seventeenth-century commonwealthmen's valorization of social criticism and just political struggle.

The other critical feature of the early Enlightenment's compromise between religion and science, one not sufficiently explored by May and Meyer, was its inherent instability. Natural religious arguments had a tendency to ineluctably support natural, as opposed to revealed, religious conviction, a tendency that Peter Gay has characterized as the rise of Christian paganism (Gay, 1966). And while the religious writers of the early Enlightenment always identified themselves as Protestants rather than pagans, they did broach a broad range of heretical tenets, from Arminianism and Arianism to Socinianism and full-blown Deism. What made such thinkers nominally orthodox Christians was their willingness to identify themselves as such as well as the willingness of their more Calvinistically inclined co-religionists to respect that identification. When that identification was denied, either by the thinkers themselves or by more evangelically minded Protestants, moderation and compromise gave way to conflict and controversy.

Both of these features of the early Enlightenment, the instability of its religious compromises and its complacent optimism, can be found in early America in the first half of the eighteenth century. Harvard had successfully absorbed the new Cartesian "Port Royal" logic into its curriculum in the closing decades of the seventeenth century, using its axiomatic approach and revised faculty psychology (a view of the mind that analyzed it into distinct operational powers or "faculties," e.g., will, understanding, affection, etc.) to buttress Puritan orthodoxy (Fiering, 1981a; Kennedy, 1993). The injection of Locke, Newton, Bacon, Boyle, and other exponents of the new learning into Yale in 1714, however, resulted in the public defection of seven promising scholars led by college rector Timothy Cutler to the Anglican Church at the commencement exercises of 1722. While such eruptions could be contained by ostracizing the apostates, the controversy and name-calling surrounding the Great Awakening in New England raged out of control. Itinerant revivalists like Whitefield and Tennent refused to acknowledge the orthodox and "saving" credentials of their "unconverted" Arminian Old Light foes, who in turn denounced the evangelists as irrational "enthusiasts." It was in the heat of this conflict that "the Moderate Enlightenment was both defined and limited" (May, 1976, p. 42). The unbridled Calvinism and experiential piety of the New Lights evoked the latent Arminianism of such Old Lights as Charles Chauncy, who was openly defending free will and denying the existence of hell by the 1750s. Caught in the middle were the Old Calvinists, "men who were trying to reconcile the doctrines of Calvinism with the spirit of the Moderate Enlightenment," a task that proved increasingly unworkable (May, 1976, p. 60).

The classic exposition of American Cosmic Toryism was undoubtedly Benjamin Franklin's *Dissertation on Liberty and Necessity, Pleasure and Pain* (1725). Influenced by the deistic writings of William Wollaston, Franklin optimistically concluded that the creation of a rational God could not possibly include any real evil or, more controversially, free will. Despite his disavowal of a central Arminian tenet, Franklin's complacent reassurance that "God is in His heaven and all is right with the world" exemplifies the early Enlightenment's celebration of a rational order that was presumably as evident at the social as at the celestial level (Meyer, 1976, p. 12). Indeed, it was this very concern with order that inclined Samuel Johnson of Connecticut (one of the seven Yale defectors of 1722 and first president of King's College in New York) to join the Anglican Church and, almost half a century later, sympathize with the British authorities in the years of colonial protest before independence (Ellis, 1973).

Assuredly, the most problematic figure of the first phase of the American Enlightenment was Jonathan Edwards. A revivalist preacher of fire and brimstone sermons as well as a cogent student of the new learning in physics and philosophy, Edwards poses a fundamental challenge to any chronicler of enlightened ideas in early America. Following Perry Miller, Meyer finds Edwards' deployment of Lockean epistemology and Shaftesburean ethics and aesthetics representative of the moderate American attempt "to reconcile pietism and the Enlightenment" (Meyer, 1976, p. 32; Miller, 1949). In contrast, May, more sensitive to the ends to which Edwards invoked such philosophic vocabularies, sees Edwards' overall position as hostile to the Enlightenment. The inadequacy of merely human knowledge and volition to achieve true virtue without divine grace meant for Edwards that "the Arminian, compromising, complacent spirit of the age was the worst enemy" (May, 1976, p. 49). In either case, Edwards' thought reveals the tenuousness of the early Enlightenment's alliance between faith and reason, just as his dismissal from his pulpit in Northampton over issues of parochial discipline and church government evidence the pursuit of an elusive order and harmony.

Beginning in the 1740s, May and Meyer detect the emergence of a second wave of Enlightenment issuing from Scotland and France. The presiding genii of this phase were Hume and Voltaire, followed by the *encyclopédistes*, Diderot and d'Alembert, and the Scottish moralists, Hutcheson and Ferguson. The authors differ in their assessment of this literature, Meyer detecting a turn from religious to moral issues while May sees a rise of epistemological skepticism and metaphysical materialism. Yet this difference should not be exaggerated, for the skepticism of Hume, Voltaire, and the *encyclopédistes* was never thoroughgoing Pyrrhonism. Instead, it was intended to serve as a critique of dogmatic intolerance and unthinking traditionalism. Their moral and political writings, on the other hand, just like those of Hutcheson and Ferguson, were based on empirical/historical observation rather than on *a priori* systematic reasoning, and thus eschewed any claims to apodeictic certainty. In any case, both authors agree that this second phase of the Enlightenment had little impact on early America, particularly before the Revolution. Dwarfed in impact by the earlier moderate phase, the second Enlightenment enjoyed a brief florescence in the South (particularly Virginia) in the 1780s only to be subsumed once again under a third revolutionary wave of Enlightenment.

Inspired by revolutionary events in America and France, authors like Jacob Priestley, Joseph Price, James Burgh, Condorcet, Raynal, and Volney injected a new-found radicalism into the discursive tradition of enlightened thought at the end of the eighteenth century. This third phase of the Enlightenment was characterized by its revolutionary ardor, as the primitivism of Rousseau combined with the implicit faith in the inevitability of human progress most famously expressed by Condorcet to produce a veritable secular chiliasm. Equally radical was the critical spirit of the time, exemplified by such thinkers as William Godwin, Thomas Paine, and Mary Wollestonecraft, who ruthlessly exposed social, political, and religious institutions to the harsh judgment of reason and utility. Militant Deism, feminism, democratic egalitarianism, and economic liberalism were all championed by these partisans of the "rights of man" in the struggle against the monarchic, aristocratic *ancien régime* and its "moderate" intellectual supporters. A heady mixture of enthusiasm and scientific rationalism, the revolutionary Enlightenment was deeply divisive wherever its presence was felt. Early America was no exception, as devotees of the earlier moderate Enlightenment bitterly resisted the intrusion of more radical doctrines that threatened to undermine the very intellectual foundations of order and harmony.

Both May and Meyer acknowledge that the reception of this enlightened radicalism in America in the years after the commencement of the French Revolution varied widely between regions. This largely reflected the partisan division of the 1790s, when Jeffersonian Republicans eagerly embraced the new wave of thought, along with the revolutionary cause it vitiated, while Federalists continued to defend the more conservative convictions of the earliest phase of the Enlightenment. Not surprisingly, the third Enlightenment achieved its greatest success in the republican South, where freethinking Deism and militant pro-French sentiment became fashionable among the educated planter elite, although it never reached the scurrilous and salacious pitch that Robert Darnton has chronicled in *The Forbidden Best-Sellers of Pre-Revolutionary France*. Equally unsurprising was its frosty, if not utterly hostile, reception in solidly Federalist New England. The new American literature of Joel Barlow, Timothy Dwight, and the other Connecticut Wits was ultimately a recapitulation of the belletristic convention of the moderate Enlightenment; "Both in their ideas and in their style, the Wits were a survival in an odd environment of the early eighteenth century" (May, 1976, p. 187). Even Noah Webster, who had appreciatively absorbed much of the writing of the revolutionary Enlightenment, adopted a more conservative stance by the end of the 1780s, stressing the need for order over the struggle for democracy. With the colleges and the clergy of the region as implacable foes, the radicalism of the third phase of the Enlightenment was unable to make any inroads in the northeastern states. Only in the hotly contested mid-Atlantic states was there something like an even match between the devotees of the new radicalism and its moderate opponents. On the side of progress and the rights of man stood David Rittenhouse, Timothy Matlack, James Cannon, and the Democratic clubs, a curious combination of freethinking Deists and New Light commonwealthmen. Opposed to them were some of the greatest champions of the early Enlightenment values of moderation and order like James Wilson, John Jay, and Alexander Hamilton (although the last named drew heavily on the moral and political writings of the skeptical Hume). Both a political and high cultural conflict, the fight was fairly even until the end of the century, which brought the revolutionary Enlightenment to an abrupt close.

Ironically, the victory of the Republicans in the "Revolution of 1800" coincided with the demise of the revolutionary Enlightenment they had defended. Beginning with the Quasi-War with France in 1798, American colleges (with the notable exception of William and Mary) pledged patriotic fealty to the Adams administration in its struggle against the radical atheist foe. The New England clergy followed suit, most famously in Jedidiah Morse's fulminations about a vast conspiracy by the Bavarian Illuminati against order and religion. Such themes were recapitulated in pulpits across the nation in the "century sermons" of 1799, in which a variety of Protestant clergymen sought "to distinguish between true and false progress in the age that was coming to an end" (May, 1976, p. 138). The result was the emergence of a fourth, didactic phase of the Enlightenment in America that, according to Meyer and May, covered almost the first half of the nineteenth century. The rising popularity of the earnest Scottish moral realism of Thomas Reid, James Beattie, and Dugald Stewart, and their growing domination of the nation's college curricula, signaled a retreat on the part of America's educated elite from the radicalism and divisiveness that had plagued them in the previous decade. Henceforth enlightened scientism would be invoked in exclusively hortatory fashion "to defend and declare, rather than criticize, fundamental truths, by giving scholarly support to the basic tenets of the American public faith" (Meyer, 1976, p. 182). Even freethinking Virginia got swept up in the new intellectual conservatism: early nineteenth-century revivalism made converts of many previously deistic planters, particularly after the evangelicals quashed their qualms about the righteousness of slavery (May, 1976, pp. 327–32). Defanged of its critical and skeptical edge, didacticism domesticated the Enlightenment, turning it into a docile source of support and boosterism for the boisterous young democracy. Fittingly, the conservatism of this final phase exemplifies the overall thrust of the Enlightenment in early America. The ideals of the early moderate Enlightenment cast a long shadow over the eighteenth century, and would dominate both the federal Constitution and the writings of Publius, its most articulate defender. The basic imperative of early American secular high culture was the defense of rational order, not the pursuit of rational critique.

There have been no fresh efforts since the 1970s to synthesize the history of enlightened ideas in early America. There has, however, been a spate of significant if more narrowly specialized research. Although some of this work has confirmed the findings of May and Meyer, much of it has not. The result, while hardly a refutation of their overall interpretations, has been a thoroughgoing revision of central themes and issues. Although May and Meyer have established the rough parameters of American Enlightenment, its implications have become problematic. One important revision has come in the relationship between reason and religion in the early Enlightenment, particularly in Puritan New England. The claim that the Puritan educated elite had successfully assimilated the new learning of the first Enlightenment, using it as a support for learned orthodoxy, was confirmed in the ensuing years by Norman Fiering (1981a) and Rick Kennedy (1990). As recently as 1991, John Corrigan substantiated and further extended this claim in his study of Boston's "Catholick Congregational Clergy." Puritan ministers like Benjamin Colman, Thomas Foxcroft, and Nathaniel Appleton used the rationalist writings of Anglican Latitudinarians to create a more emotionally evocative religious discourse. It was by reinvigorating the "religious affections" – particularly Christian love – that Boston's "liberal" clergy sought to revitalize the lapsed communitarianism of the Puritan religious community. The enlightened use of reason not only supported orthodoxy, it also promoted piety and vital heart religion (Corrigan, 1991).

This felicitous alliance between reason and religion has been undermined by Michael Winship's cogent study of Puritan providentialism in the early Enlightenment (1994). Winship has confirmed Pocock's claim in *Virtue, Commerce, and History* that "rational religion aimed at repressing, moderating, or replacing the 'enthusiasm' now thought of as the essential characteristic of Puritanism" (Pocock, 1985). By rejecting Calvinism and Reformed scholasticism in the name of reason, claims Winship, Anglican Latitudinarians explicitly proscribed the providential interpretation of nature and history that underlay Puritan homiletics as a species of irrational enthusiasm that threatened social and political order. The natural religion of the early Enlightenment was thus a fundamental challenge to the Puritan worldview, one which led Increase Mather to defend the providential tradition of New England despite its growing disfavor among educated gentlemen. Increase's son Cotton, like most of his generation of New England divines, sought to reach an accommodation with the new learning, but it came at a high price. Rational religion not only undermined the "world of wonders" that epitomized the Puritan sense of the ever present supernatural, it also debunked "the experimental edge of Reformed piety, specifically the idea that the Deity communicated directly with the faithful" (Winship, 1996, p. 33). What kept Cotton Mather within the fold of Puritan orthodoxy was the limited use he made of the new enlightened mode of discourse, as well as his refusal to utterly discard the providentialism and experimental Calvinism of his father's faith. His more logically consistent brethren, however, followed the road of intellectual respectability all the way to its Arminian end. Shorn of its moorings in Calvinism, human depravity, and providential dispensation, the religion of liberal Old Lights can hardly be seen as Puritan in any but a most attenuated sense.

A similar reappraisal has occurred in the treatment of Jonathan Edwards. Following Miller, Meyer and Fiering had depicted Edwards as a thinker who, while deeply committed to vital piety, was nonetheless fully immersed in the world of enlightened thought, pushing its conceptual vocabularies to their logical limits. This view has been challenged, however, by a growing chorus of dissenters. More than thirty years ago Wallace E. Anderson noted that, although Edwards did invoke enlightened modes of disputation, the end to which they were invoked was a spiritualist metaphysic that was remarkably similar to Berkeleian immaterialism (Anderson, 1964). Stephen R. Yarbrough's discussion of Edwards' understanding of conversion and its relation to discourse suggests that, for Edwards, "Grace is a seat of Rhetorical Authority in exactly the same way as, to the rationalists whom Edwards opposed, such as the Earl of Shaftesbury, taste would be a seat of rhetorical authority" (Yarbrough, 1993, p. 55). Stephen H. Daniel has further pursued the implication of Edwards' semiotic musings, finding that conversion figured in Edwards' thought as means of undermining the representational model of language and thought that underlay Enlightenment epistemology. In its stead, Edwards embraced the older Renaissance/Ramist episteme based on resemblance and analogy (Daniel, 1994). What emerges from this revisionism as central to Edwards' position is not his absorption of Newton and Locke, but rather his "reassertion of the structure and authority of the Puritan saint" (Yarbrough, 1993, p. 57). Although an avid student, Edwards was hardly a disciple of the new learning. He was, in fact, the last relic of the spiritual and intellectual world of the seventeenth-century Puritan founders of New England.

The presumed conservatism of the early Enlightenment has also been questioned in recent years. Critical to this effort has been John Andrew Bernstein's denial of the identification of early enlightened optimism as Cosmic Toryism. Bernstein claims that the supposedly conservative "analogy between the cosmos and society" was hardly a staple of early enlightened thought. Instead, it was occasionally offered as "a mere imaginative expression," and largely devoid of "a serious political meaning" (Bernstein, 1987, pp. 89–90). More pointedly, he notes that the optimism of Pope, Bolingbroke, and Shaftesbury all rejected the doctrine of innate depravity and original sin. This in turn had distinctly progressive implications. If there was no inherent human depravity to cause evil, then its source could be sought in flawed institutions. This in turn implied that "more equitable government, like more tolerant religion, could then emerge as a means for the improvement of human behavior" (Bernstein, 1987, pp. 93–4). While this discursive tradition was still decidedly moderate in its tone, the impact of Bernstein's work is to cast it in a more reformist than conservative light. This finding has been echoed in Douglas Anderson's recent work on Benjamin Franklin, America's Cosmic Tory. Anderson describes the impact of enlightened doctrines on Franklin's thought and career as "radical." Franklin's immersion in London's coffeehouse culture, as well as his reading of Addison, Mandeville, and Hutcheson, resulted in a secular and civic humanist outlook. Committed to promoting virtue, harmony, and progress, the Franklin that emerges from Anderson's treatment is a far cry from the pragmatic, smug, *homo economicus* Max Weber described. The junto and the party for virtue as well as the Albany Plan of 1754 are all expressive of a reformist optimism rather than a complacent conservatism (Anderson, 1997).

Even the presumed irrelevance of Enlightenment theory for the American Revolution has been challenged. Not long after May's and Meyer's books first appeared, Morton White pointed out the heavy reliance of the revolutionaries on the natural law tradition of argument, especially as found in the work of the Swiss jurist Jean Jacques Burlamaqui (White, 1978). Far more important has been a growing debate over the influence and interpretation of Locke's work in the revolutionary and constitutional eras. This debate has become one of the most critical (and uncivil) in early American intellectual historiography. On the one hand, scholars like John Dunne and J. G. A. Pocock have argued that Locke's influence was slight. Pocock in particular has argued that the juristic nature of Locke's thought tended to undermine the *via activa* that underlay republican civic humanism and virtue in favor of the stark and largely apolitical individualism of an emerging Augustan *homo economicus*. In Pocock's telling, Lockean liberalism was part of a larger English Enlightenment that served as a philosophically conservative defense of the dominant Whig oligarchy (Pocock, 1985). Similarly, Roy Porter has argued that, at least prior to the Wilkesite enthusiasm of the 1760s, the Enlightenment in England was pragmatic rather than oppositional. He has even suggested that "Sir Robert Walpole's self-presentation as 'no saint, no Spartan, no reformer' has a distinctly Enlightenment tinge" (Porter, 1981, p. 9). Given the conservative, indeed almost "court Whig," nature of the English Enlightenment, Pocock has plausibly argued that radical opposition on both sides of the Atlantic had to draw instead on the resources of republican humanism as found in the country (and, ironically, largely Tory) Old Whig tradition (Pocock, 1985, p. 264).

On the other hand, Joyce Appleby and Isaac Kramnick have argued for the centrality of the early enlightened tradition of Lockean liberalism that, in John Diggins' apt phrase, "spearheaded the Revolution through the writings of Jefferson and Thomas Paine" (Diggins, 1984, pp. 4–5). Far from a conservative defense of the Whig oligarchy, Kramnick has seen the Lockean liberal tradition as the bearer of bourgeois radicalism that reached its apex in the writings of Burgh, Paine, and Priestley. This view has received confirmation from Richard Ashcraft's *Revolutionary Politics and Locke's Two Treatises of Government* (1986). Ashcraft has shown that, in close association with the first Earl of Shaftesbury and other leaders of the Whig opposition during the Exclusion Crisis, Locke constructed a revolutionary political doctrine to appeal to dissenters, artisans, tradesmen, and other middling sorts excluded from the political nation. Locke and his fellow Whig propagandists did this by stressing themes that echoed older leveling and commonwealth traditions. Indeed, a recent editor of *Cato's Letters* has gone so far as to argue that Thomas Gordon was actually a Lockean himself, and his assaults on financial miscreancy were only intended to castigate the corrupt "insider trading" that produced the South Sea Bubble (Hamowy, 1990). On another front, Jay Fliegelman has argued that Lockean psychology, epistemology, and pedagogical theory served as the philosophical foundation for a critique of patriarchal domination (in the family as well as the state) that found expression in a trajectory of "familial" fiction running from *Robinson Crusoe* through *Clarissa* and *Tristram Shandy*. "Just as the American Revolution was commencing, a turning point had been reached in the history of sentimental fiction," Fliegelman notes, one where passive resistance to patriarchal power "had given way to active resistance" (Fliegelman, 1982, p. 151). The political impact of enlightened thought, and Locke in particular, seems to have been a bit more transformative than previously conceived.

If there have been no grand syntheses of enlightened ideas in recent years, this has in part been because scholars have begun to search for the Enlightenment in other quarters. The most important example of this quest is Michael Warner's *The Letters of the Republic: Publication and the Public Sphere in Eighteenth-Century America* (1990). A study of the impact and meaning of printed textuality in the American Enlightenment, Warner draws heavily on the Marxist critical theory of Jurgen Habermas. More than merely bourgeois ideology, Habermas sees the Enlightenment (particularly in its early English phase) as central to the emergence of a "public sphere" or realm of public opinion. Organized in admittedly private settings of educated sociability like salons, coffeehouses, and Masonic lodges, what made this new discourse public was its immersion in the new world of print culture and journalism. Interceding between the civil society of economic individuals on the one hand and political institutions on the other, Habermas sees this Enlightenment print culture as creating a "transformation of the public sphere" from, in Warner's pithy expression, "a world in which power embodied in special persons is represented before the people to one in which power is constituted by a discourse in which the people are represented" (1990, pp. 38–9). Once this new public sphere emerged as a result of new habits of reading enlightened essays, no political authority could retain its legitimacy without the sanction of public opinion.

What made this new "publicity" so transformative were the radical implications of print textuality itself, principally its anti-hierarchical and critical tendencies. Enlightened textuality was anti-hierarchical precisely because the radical de-contextuality of print precluded any epistemic appeal by writers to their social status or "authority." Warner refers to this republicanization of the discursive field as the principle of negativity: "Persons who enter this discourse do so on the condition that the validity of their utterance will bear a negative relation to their persons" (1990, p. 38). While such "self-negation" was obviously limited to white, male property-owners, it nonetheless represented a significant leveling of social distinctions, as evidenced by the polite complaisance that characterized the cheek-by-jowl sociability of aristocrats, merchants, and educated men of letters in London's clubs and coffeehouses and Parisian salons.

Enlightened print textuality was critical because its publicity presupposed what Warner calls the principle of supervision. No longer representative of distinct social orders, the new ideal of statesmanship that emerged in enlightened discourse demanded that legislators embody a virtuous concern for the general good, a demand that was enforced by intrusive journalism that exposed all "corruption" to the censure of public opinion. Legislators now had to speak for the general will or face the criticism of an informed political nation. At the same time, this critical principle of supervision transformed the nature of politics itself and dramatically increased the authority of elected legislators because it "empowered representatives by raising them from being parties in an Aristotelian alliance of orders to being the embodiment of the basic principle of the political" (1990, p. 58).

In Warner's treatment, the American Revolution emerges as dependent on the spread of critical print textuality. Not only did this new development create a discursive space for the critique of metropolitan policy, but printed texts also served as the principal means of spreading the message of protest and resistance. Indeed, beginning with the Stamp Act crisis, the growing imperial conflict "had the effect of strengthening the identification of print culture and republicanism" (1990, p. 71). American Whig journalists and essayists "engineered a newspaper and pamphlet war in a way that was arguably more integral to the American resistance than to any other struggle" (Warner, p. 3). This in turn had two palpable consequences. First, print culture served as the principal medium uniting the revolutionary American public, as "newspaper readerships" quickly became "among the most important forms of political organization in the colonies" (1990, p. 68). Secondly, the centrality of this medium catapulted its educated purveyors into positions of prominence and power; "Those who organized the revolutionary struggle and were placed in power by it were men of letters" (1990, p. 3). Warner's analysis allows us to see the fundamental affinity of the American Revolution with other insurrections of the time, led as they often were by radicalized journalists and intellectuals disaffected toward an irrational *ancien régime*. Thus the new bourgeois public sphere, comprised of consumers of printed texts, emerges as the sine qua non not only of American republicanism, but all the democratic revolutions of the late eighteenth century and their resultant nation-states. Only in the years after the Revolution, as its "overdetermined unity" with religion and surface affinity with polite belletrism broke down, was the new print-based public sphere challenged by alternate cultural imperatives (1990, p. 58). The new medium may not have been the message, but its transformative effect on political institutions and modes of legitimation can hardly be denied.

Only recently has Warner's analysis found its dialectical "other" and complement in David S. Shields's *Civil Tongues & Polite Letters in British America* (1996). Like a Gadamer to Warner's Habermas, Shields seeks traces of the Enlightenment in America in the realm of belletrism. Drawing on Richard Bushman's insightful study of modes of gentility in early America (1992), Shields chronicles the rise of polite sociability in such loci as colonial clubs, salons, taverns, and private dancing and dining assemblies. More than an "Anglicizing" imitation of London's bon ton, Shields sees the playing of poetic games like crambo as the early American cultural and social elite's participation in a cosmopolitan beau monde situated between Habermas's public sphere and the Renaissance court culture of Restoration England. What unified such discursive and "clubbical" practices was not the public criticism that Warner heralds, but rather a private pursuit of esthetic pleasure. Indeed, aside from its remarkable heterosociability, it is the privacy of this beau monde that is its most striking feature, exemplified by the imperative to withhold its circulating manuscripts from the publicity of print. It was this privacy, and attendant snobbish exclusivity, that allowed prominent political leaders to pursue literary and gustatory pleasures and sociability in a setting dominated by precise rules and norms of civility. Indeed, the values of polite belletrism were espoused in no small part as a challenge to the growing pugnacity of public print and journalism; "the cultural struggles between politeness and Grub Street incivility, resort heterosociability and libertinism, and salon conversation and print polemic must be situated in a context of institutional contestation (thus the libertine extravagances of the Tory tavern oppose the polite conversation of the Whig coffeehouse)" (Shields,

1996, p. xviii). Shields's analysis uncovers far more than the elite pursuit of literary pleasure. Polite belletrism not only helped early America's elite identify themselves in an exclusive way, it also served as means of improving social status and visibility for those who might otherwise be excluded from the discourse of colonial high society. *Salonnières* like Boston's Elizabeth Magawley and female wits like Elizabeth Graeme of the Delaware Valley deployed the conventions of polite letters to fashion a new semi-public role as censors of taste, sociability, and refined manners. Equally significant was the authority it gave them as arbiters of heterosociable mores and upper-class gender relations. After a triumphant tour in England, culminated by her recognition by the popular novelist Laurence Sterne, Graeme's wit emerged as a "vehicle of judgment useful in gaining perspective on the foibles of the world and deflecting the claims of passion" (Shields, 1996, pp. 138–9). While such poetic authority was challenged by the homosociable criticism of coffeehouse and Masonic wits, it nonetheless represented a powerful expansion of female rhetorical authority beyond the seventeenth-century realm of gossip.

Polite belletrism also served as a source of cultural capital for educated men of letters lacking the financial resources requisite for inclusion in the colonial elite. Such cultural capital could be parlayed into social status and wealth as Shields illustrates in the case of Dr. Thomas Dale. A medical botanist, Dale arrived in Charleston, South Carolina in 1732 with little to his name save his degree from the University of Leiden, his reputation as an author of medical texts, and his outstanding debts. In short order, Dale was mixing with much of the colony's elite, including the royal governor himself. Within a few months of his arrival, thanks to the marriage brokerage of no less a figure than Attorney General Charles Pinckney, Dale found himself engaged to Mary Brewton, the daughter of the wealthiest merchant in the province. Pinckney's patronage also resulted in Dale's admission to the Carolina bar despite an utter lack of any legal training. By 1734 he had been appointed a provincial judge and justice of the peace by the governor and council, and would ultimately serve as an assistant justice on the colony's Court of General Sessions. With the right kind of clientele, Dale's medical practice boomed, supplemented as it was by a pharmaceutical manufactory (the largest in the colony) and a distillery.

According to Shields, what made Dale's meteoric ascent possible was his mastery of polite learning. No sooner had he arrived in Charleston than he began offering essays and letters to the newly founded *South-Carolina Gazette*. Two years later his poetic "Prologue" was read before a dramatic performance in Charleston, and in the following year he offered a poetic epilogue for Farquhar's *The Recruiting Officer* that was read at the city's new playhouse that he had helped to establish. When George Whitefield dared critique the joviality of the planter elite, Dale could be counted on to lampoon the Great Itinerant in the newspapers. A founder of the Charleston Library Society, Dale served a variety of civic and cultural roles which located him within the charmed circle of the provincial beau monde. It was his ability to create esthetic pleasures for the social elite that facilitated Dale's rise to social and economic prominence. His "elevation to civic employments had been enabled by one talent that few in the colony possessed to a supreme degree: Dale was a master of words, an expert reader as well as writer. Mastery over texts was one of the warrants to rule in the eyes of the ruling oligarchy" (Shields, 1996, p. 196). This exchange economy between esthetic pleasure and the prestigious glow of high cultural activity on the one hand and political and economic patronage on the other is equally evident in Shields's incisive reading of hospitality in the plantation societies of Virginia and Barbados.

Admittedly, Shields's polite pleasures stand in obvious tension with the republican virtue of Warner's print publicity. Not surprisingly, Shields notes how republican critics, despite their own Democratic clubbing, denounced the private assemblies and levies of their Federalist opponents as aristocratic and effeminate pursuits of luxury. In turn, Warner is struck by the fact that, while the vast majority of printers and publicists were Whigs, "a vastly disproportionate number of colonial belletrists" expressed "loyalist sympathies during the imperial crisis" (Warner, 1990, p. 133). Yet this is not a contradiction within enlightened modes of discourse, but rather an index of historical progression. The polite practices Shields chronicles arose from the early Enlightenment and only grudgingly gave way to the moral imperatives of the later public sphere. In the years after the Revolution the latter displaced the former from the public stage but did not entirely vanquish them. Instead, as Richard Bushman has suggested, the conventions of the beau monde became both privatized and diluted; the markers of elite gentility in the eighteenth century became the guideposts of middle-class respectability in antebellum America.

The implications of Shields's and Warner's work for future study of the American Enlightenment are profound. Conjointly, they offer the prospect of a new grand synthesis of the field, one which unites the history of ideas with the polite and print conventions of the new learning. The ground of this synthesis can be located in a careful attentiveness to the politics of the Enlightenment. A history of such a politics would have to work at two levels. On the one hand it would have to chronicle the relationship between enlightened communities of discourse and constituted political authorities. Scholars of the European Enlightenment have been far ahead of their American colleagues on this question. Nicholas Phillipson, for example, has shown that the Scottish Enlightenment's celebrated "science of man" was a response to the loss of autonomy and power occasioned by the Act of Union, a loss that led them to seek civic virtue in cultivation, commerce, and criticism rather than in active political participation (1981). Daniel Roche has argued that the French Enlightenment emerged from within the notability and bureaucracy of the old regime (1998), a claim that Robert Wuthnow has recently extended to the entire European scene (1999). On the other hand, there must be a thorough examination of the shifting social constituencies that comprised those communities, an examination that is sensitive to distinct historical needs and desires of different participants. In Hume's brief piece "On Essay Writing," he argued that what characterized the Enlightenment of his age was the discursive and social "League betwixt the learned and conversible Worlds" (Hume, 1985, p. 535). Any politics of the Enlightenment must identify the changing demands and imperatives of the learned intellectuals as well as the apparent growth and broadening of their allies in the world of educated conversation, as enlightened ideas seeped lower into the social structure toward the end of the eighteenth century.

The broad outlines of such a synthesis might take the following form. As Winship has argued (1996), the early English Enlightenment emerged from the Restoration reaction against the religious enthusiasm that had racked the continent with doctrinal wars and precipitated a revolution within England itself. Intellectuals who used reason to ridicule the dogmatism of "precise" Protestantism were rewarded with patronage by the court and later by the high-minded aristocrats of the Whig oligarchy. By the early eighteenth century, the circle of London's conversible world had expanded to include the great and near-great merchants of London. The patronage of educated elites like Shaftesbury gave way to the growing market for printed texts, particularly the newspapers and journals that the merchants consumed in their coffeehouses and clubs. In exchange for the possibility of a financially rewarding private literary career (one that conferred honorary gentry status), men of letters gave their increasingly bourgeois readers a new principle of association as the older communities of conscience gave way to the new club culture based on polite pleasures. The moderation of the early Enlightenment is as much a function of its social basis as of the internal logic of its ideas.

This same trajectory can be seen in the early years of the Enlightenment in America. The principal consumers of rational religion in New England were, after all, the merchant elite of eastern Massachusetts. Not surprisingly, all of Corrigan's "catholick congregational clergy" ministered to wealthy mercantile congregations, just like the bulk of later Arminian opponents of the Great Awakening. In return for pleasantly edifying discourses and the prestige of participation in high cultural pursuits, the ministers received handsome pecuniary compensation and high social status. The same relation between men of letters and socially prominent patrons can be seen in the previously mentioned career of Thomas Dale as well as the rise of that great autodidact, Benjamin Franklin. Unlike the simple hortatory didacticism of Franklin's public journalism, his more recondite essays were pitched to an elite audience. Nor is it coincidental that it is mainly in such recondite writings that we find traces of enlightened thought, for the readers of his almanac were clearly not yet part of the conversible world.

Beginning about the middle of the century, enlightened doctrines and principles of association began to seep down lower into the social structure, a development that would ultimately have radical implications. Margaret C. Jacob has shown how the English purveyors of the new science in the early eighteenth century pitched their message to an elite audience of merchants and refined gentlemen, who "were repeatedly told that what they were learning sanctioned the existing social and constitutional order" (Jacob, 1987, pp. 136–7). As new philosophical societies sprang up in the latter half of the century, however, they often contained the rising new industrialists, often from dissenting backgrounds, who had little affinity with the court Whig oligarchy. The results of this new constituency were striking, as "the whole burden of scientific culture" moved "in a politically and socially radical direction by the addition of two ideological ingredients: philosophical materialism and republicanism" (Jacob, 1987, p. 154). Drawing on Jacob's insights, Stephen Bullock has recently shown how early American upper-class urban speculative Freemasonry centered on a pseudo-mysterious celebration of orderly cosmic mechanism, gave way to the blander and more strictly associational Ancient Masonry of those directly below the elite during these very years. By the time of the Revolution, "aspiring urban artisans like Paul Revere elbowed their way into lodges, claiming a fraternal standing that paralleled their new political position" (Bullock, 1996, p. 4). More than twenty years ago, Eric Foner demonstrated that Thomas Paine found in revolutionary Philadelphia an artisanal community fully initiated in the mores of enlightened thought and eagerly receptive to initiatives which extended those mores in a more liberal and egalitarian direction (1976). Nor was such popular Enlightenment limited to Philadelphia. Pauline Meier's subtle reading of Dr. Thomas Young, a largely autodidactic radical Deist and Democrat, shows how in the years surrounding the Revolution economically disadvantaged "commoners" could appropriate the language of Enlightenment to both further their own political careers and champion scientific literacy as a means of liberation from hierarchy and a basis for a new republican meritocracy (1976).

Such an account of the politics of the American Enlightenment must be sensitive to three critical issues. First, it must be attentive to the shifting public role of intellectuals in the spread of the new learning. Initially purveyors of pleasure and refinement, men of letters found themselves thrust into positions of political prominence by the Revolution and its aftermath. Did they perceive themselves as disinterested spokesmen of the general will actually representing the desires of their constituencies, or was their self-conception tied in with the ideal of natural aristocracy whereby their superior knowledge and rationality required them to lead, rather than follow, public opinion? And how did such conceptions relate to their intellectual and political constituencies? Jefferson championed the cause of rural America because he saw in the social condition of the sturdy yeomen the independence and virtue necessary to support republicanism and its civic humanism. In stark contrast, Hamilton viewed the urban grand bourgeoisie as the most enlightened social class in the new nation, whose interests were inextricably bound to the quest for prosperity, progress, and national growth. Did this difference merely reflect different temperaments and judgments, or was it the result of the contrasting social conditions under which such intellectual statesmen formulated and expressed their beliefs?

The second issue that a politics of the American Enlightenment must consider is the social environment under which high culture was produced and disseminated. Who mediated conflicts and controversies within the commonwealth of learning? Who arbitrated high cultural taste? Speaking for the intellectuals, Hume thought that role was best served by educated women; "were not my Countrymen, the Learned, a stubborn independent Race of Mortals, extremely jealous of their Liberty, and unaccustom'd to Subjection, I shou'd resign into their fair Hands the sovereign Authority over the Republic of Letters" (Hume, 1985, pp. 535–6). Recent work on the French Enlightenment has demonstrated that just such an authority was held by the *salonnières* who presided over the republic of letters during the age of the *encyclopédistes*. When, in response to Rousseau's critique of such female sovereignty, the *philosophes* rejected that authority in the 1770s, the result was a breakdown of comity within the republic of letters, as the turn to print polemic unmediated by the polite intercession of female *philosophes* shortly produced deep partisan, speculative, and personal disputes within the community of the enlightened (Goodman, 1994). What impact did the decline of heterosociability in the revolutionary and early national epochs have on the American commonwealth of learning? Was the disappearance of American female wits and *salonnières* a result of the republican rejection of luxury and effeminacy, or did it signal the emergence of a more bitterly divided intellectual community whose discursive efforts became increasingly colored by a masculine agonism that characterized the bitter partisan division of the 1780s and 1790s? Any future synthesis of the American Enlightenment must grapple with these issues.

Finally, the politics of Enlightenment must be sensitive to regional and temporal variation. The timing in which the Enlightenment reached various constituencies and regions obviously varied widely. Initially a northern urban phenomenon, the early Enlightenment did not uniformly permeate the countryside. The southern planter elite clearly embraced its codes long before it reached into the rural North. When and how did it reach the backcountry? Can traces of enlightened thought be found among Jefferson's virtuous southern yeomanry, and if so of what variety? Why did southern planters embrace the radical thought of post-*salonnière* France while northern optimates eschewed it? Similarly, any new synthesis must recognize that the various coalitions of the learned and the conversible that characterized the Enlightenment stood in competition to each other. The struggle between northern Federalists and southern Republicans was also a struggle over the appropriation of the legacy of Enlightenment, pitting its early moderate maxims against the later, more radical positions associated with the revolutionary Enlightenment. Nor did the ultimate victory of one on the political stage entail the end of the other. As Peter S. Field has demonstrated in his incisive study of the origins of Boston's Brahmins, the alliance of "liberal" clergymen and urban bourgeois elites in Massachusetts easily survived the political demise of Federalism on a national level. The great merchants continued to avidly patronize the new learning and its belletrism, seeing in it a source of distinction and a code of class gentility. For their part, enlightened clerical intellectuals did not retreat into didacticism so much as buttress their cultural authority by appropriating the role of the last defenders of cultivation, learning, and civilization amid the growing "mediocrity" of democratic culture. The coalition of these interests, often cemented by marriage, created the Brahmin elite against which the later American Renaissance and Transcendentalist movements would rebel (Field, 1998). Earlier phases of the Enlightenment lived on after their rejection in the public sphere, casting a long shadow over the nineteenth century.

The prospects for such a synthesis (or syntheses) are indeed exciting. Although the groundwork has been laid, the field is still open and inviting. The relevance of the Enlightenment can now be seen in politics, society, and culture. Forms of sociability commingle with philosophical speculation, as chroniclers of America's age of reason are forced to combine the disciplines of social, political, and intellectual history while remaining sensitive to the gendered and class-specific implications of enlightened criticism and discourse. The search for an early American Enlightenment has just begun.

BIBLIOGRAPHY

Anderson, Douglas: *The Radical Enlightenments of Benjamin Franklin* (Baltimore, MD: Johns Hopkins University Press, 1997).

Anderson, Wallace E.: "Immaterialism in Jonathan Edwards' Early Philosophical Notes." *Journal of the History of Ideas* 25 (1964); reprinted in Frank Shuffelton, ed., *The American Enlightenment* (Rochester: University of Rochester Press, 1993), pp. 27–46.

Appleby, Joyce: *Capitalism and a New Social Order: The Republican Vision of the 1790s* (New York: NYU Press, 1984).

Ashcraft, Richard: *Revolutionary Politics and Locke's Two Treatises of Government* (Princeton, NJ: Princeton University Press, 1986).

Bailyn, Bernard: *The Ideological Origins of the American Revolution* (Cambridge, MA: Harvard University Press, 1967).

Bailyn, Bernard: *The Ordeal of Thomas Hutchinson* (Cambridge, MA: Harvard University Press, 1974).

Becker, Carl L.: *The Heavenly City of the Eighteenth-Century Philosophers* (New Haven, CT: Yale

University Press, 1932).

Bernstein, John Andrew: "Shaftesbury's Optimism and Eighteenth Century Social Thought." In Alan Charles Kors and Paul J. Korshin, eds., *Anticipations of the Enlightenment in England, France, and Germany* (Philadelphia: University of Pennsylvania Press, 1987), pp. 86–101.

Brown, Richard D.: *Knowledge is Power: The Diffusion of Information in Early America, 1700–1865* (New York: Oxford University Press, 1989).

Bullock, Stephen C.: *Revolutionary Brotherhood: Freemasonry and the Transformation of the American Social Order, 1730–1840* (Chapel Hill, NC: University of North Carolina Press, 1996).

Bushman, Richard L.: *The Refinement of America: Persons, Houses, Cities* (New York: Alfred A. Knopf, 1992).

Cassara, Ernest: *The Enlightenment in America* (New York: Twayne, 1975).

Cassirer, Ernst: *The Philosophy of the Enlightenment*, trans. Fritz C. A. Koellin and James P. Pettegrove (Boston, MA: Beacon Press, 1966).

Chai, Leon: *Jonathan Edwards and the Limits of Enlightenment Philosophy* (New York: Oxford University Press, 1998).

Conkin, Paul K.: *Puritans and Pragmatists: Eight Eminent American Thinkers* (New York: Dodd, Mead, 1968).

Corrigan, John: *The Prism of Piety: Catholick Congregational Clergy at the Beginning of the Enlightenment* (New York: Oxford University Press, 1991).

Daniel, Stephen H.: *The Philosophy of Jonathan Edwards: A Study in Divine Semiotics* (Indianapolis, IN: Indiana University Press, 1994).

Darnton, Robert: *The Forbidden Best-Sellers of Pre-Revolutionary France* (New York: W. W. Norton, 1995).

Diggins, John Patrick: *The Lost Soul of American Politics: Virtue, Self-Interest, and the Foundations of Liberalism* (New York: Basic Books, 1984).

Dunn, John: *The Political Thought of John Locke: An Historical Account of the Argument of the 'Two Treatises of Government'* (Cambridge: Cambridge University Press, 1969).

Ellis, Joseph: *The New England Mind in Transition: Samuel Johnson of Connecticut, 1696–1772* (New Haven, CT: Yale University Press, 1973).

Ellis, Joseph: "Habits of Mind and an American Enlightenment." *American Quarterly* 28 (1976), pp. 150–64.

Field, Peter S.: *The Crisis of the Standing Order: Clerical Intellectuals and Cultural Authority in Massachusetts, 1780–1833* (Amherst, MA: University of Massachusetts Press, 1998).

Fiering, Norman: *Moral Philosophy at Seventeenth Century Harvard: A Discipline in Transition* (Chapel Hill, NC: University of North Carolina Press, 1981a).

Fiering, Norman: *Jonathan Edwards's Moral Thought and Its British Context* (Chapel Hill, NC: University of North Carolina Press, 1981b).

Fiering, Norman S.: "Irresistible Compassion: An Aspect of Eighteenth-Century Sympathy and Humanitarianism." *Journal of the History of Ideas* 37 (1976); reprinted in Shuffelton (1993), pp. 73–96.

Fliegelman, Jay: *Prodigals and Pilgrims: The American Revolution Against Patriarchal Authority, 1750–1800* (New York: Cambridge University Press, 1982).

Foner, Eric: *Tom Paine and Revolutionary America* (New York: Oxford University Press, 1976).

Gay, Peter: *The Enlightenment: An Interpretation*, vol. 1, *The Rise of Modern Paganism* (New York: W. W. Norton, 1966).

Gay, Peter: *The Enlightenment: An Interpretation*, vol. 2, *The Science of Freedom* (New York: W. W. Norton, 1969).

Goodman, Dena: *The Republic of Letters: A Cultural History of the French Enlightenment* (Ithaca, NY: Cornell University Press, 1994).

Haakonssen, Knud: "Natural Law and Moral Realism: The Scottish Synthesis." In Stewart (1990), pp. 61–85.

Habermas, Jurgen: *The Structural Transformation of the Public Sphere: An Inquiry into a Category of Bourgeois Society*, trans. Thomas Burger (Cambridge, MA: M.I.T. Press, 1991).

Hamowy, Ronald: "Cato's Letters, John Locke, and the Republican Paradigm." *The History of Political Thought* 11 (1990), pp. 273–94.

Hume, David: "Of Essay-Writing." In David Hume: *Essays Moral, Political and Literary*, ed. Eugene F. Miller (Indianapolis, IN: Liberty Fund, Inc., 1985), pp. 533–7.

Jacob, Margaret C.: "Scientific Culture in the Early English Enlightenment: Mechanisms, Industry, and Gentlemanly Facts." In Kors and Korshin (1987), pp. 134–64.

Jeske, Jeffrey: "Cotton Mather: Physico-Theologian." *Journal of the History of Ideas* 47 (1986); reprinted in Shuffelton (1993), pp. 61–72.

Kennedy, Rick: "The Alliance Between Puritanism and Cartesian Logic at Harvard, 1687–1735." *Journal of the History of Ideas* 51 (1990); reprinted in Shuffelton (1993), pp. 3–26.

Kors, Alan Charles and Korshin, Paul J.: *Anticipations of the Enlightenment in England, France, and Germany* (Philadelphia: University of Pennsylvania Press, 1987).

Kramnick, Isaac: *Republicanism and Bourgeois Radicalism: Political Ideology in Late Eighteenth-Century England and America* (Ithaca, NY: Cornell University Press, 1990).

Lunenberg, David and May, Henry F.: "The Enlightened Reader in America." *American Quarterly* 28 (1976), pp. 262–93.

May, Henry F.: *The Enlightenment in America* (New York: Oxford University Press, 1976).

Meier, Pauline: "Reason and Revolution: The Radicalism of Dr. Thomas Young." *American Quarterly* 28 (1976), pp. 229–49.

Meyer, Donald H.: *The Democratic Enlightenment* (New York: Putnam, 1976).

Miller, Perry: *Jonathan Edwards* (New York: Meridian Books, 1949).

Moore, James: "The Two Systems of Francis Hutcheson: On the Origins of the Scottish Enlightenment." In Stewart (1990), pp. 37–59.

Phillipson, Nicholas: "The Scottish Enlightenment." In Roy Porter and Mikulas Teich, eds., *The Enlightenment in National Context* (New York: Cambridge University Press, 1981), pp. 19–40.

Pocock, J. G. A.: *The Machiavellian Moment: Florentine Political Thought and the Atlantic Revolution* (Princeton, NJ: Princeton University Press, 1975).

Pocock, J. G. A.: *Virtue, Commerce, and History: Essays on Political Thought and History, Chiefly in the Eighteenth Century* (New York: Cambridge University Press, 1985).

Pole, J. R.: "Enlightenment and the Politics of American Nature." In Porter and Teich (1981), pp. 192–217.

Porter, Roy: "The Enlightenment in England." In Porter and Teich (1981), pp. 1–18.

Porter, Roy and Teich, Mikulas, eds.: *The Enlightenment in National Context* (New York: Cambridge University Press, 1981).

Roche, Daniel: *France in the Enlightenment*, trans. Arthur Goldhammer (Cambridge, MA: Harvard University Press, 1998).

Shields, David S.: *Civil Tongues & Polite Letters in British America* (Chapel Hill, NC: University of North Carolina Press, 1996).

Shuffelton, Frank: *The American Enlightenment* (Rochester: University of Rochester Press, 1993).

Spurlin, Paul Merrill: *The French Enlightenment in America: Essays on the Times of the Founding Fathers* (Athens, GA: University of Georgia Press, 1984).

Stewart, M. A., ed.: *Studies in the Philosophy of the Scottish Enlightenment* (Oxford: Oxford University Press, 1990).

Warner, Michael: *The Letters of the Republic: Publication and the Public Sphere in Eighteenth-Century America* (Cambridge, MA: Harvard University Press, 1990).

White, Morton: *Science and Sentiment in America: Philosophical Thought from Jonathan Edwards to John Dewey* (New York: Oxford University Press, 1972).

White, Morton: *The Philosophy of the American Revolution* (New York: Oxford University Press, 1978).

Winship, Michael P.: *Seers of God: Puritan Providentialism in the Restoration and Early Enlightenment* (Baltimore, MD: Johns Hopkins University Press, 1996).

Wood, Gordon S.: *The Creation of the American Republic, 1776–1787* (Chapel Hill, NC: University of North Carolina Press, 1969).

Wood, Gordon S.: "Conspiracy and the Paranoid Style: Causality and Deceit in the Eighteenth Century." *William and Mary Quarterly* 3rd ser., 39 (1982), pp. 401–41.

Wuthnow, Robert: *Communities of Discourse: Ideology and Social Structure in the Reformation, the Enlightenment, and European Socialism* (Cambridge, MA: Harvard University Press, 1999).

Yarbrough, Stephen R.: "Jonathan Edwards on Rhetorical Authority." *Journal of the History of Ideas* 47 (1986); reprinted in Shuffelton (1993), pp. 47–60.

CHAPTER SEVENTEEN

Borderlands

DANIEL H. USNER, JR.

Although the study of non-English colonial societies in North America and their relations with Native American societies has improved significantly over the past quarter-century, ideological and methodological burdens inherited from the past have not been easy to overcome. For most of the last two hundred years, histories of New France, Florida, Louisiana, Texas, New Mexico, California, and Alaska were written in the shadow of a nationalist history of the United States that privileged its founding English colonies. Malign neglect might best characterize American historians' particular treatment of those Spanish and French colonial regions that became part of the United States over the first half of the nineteenth century. Representation of life in places like seventeenth-century New Mexico and eighteenth-century Louisiana was selectively shaped to contrast with that along the Atlantic seaboard of North America. Cultural differences between European nations were essentialized in order to explain why England's colonies grew and expanded "more successfully" than others. This construction of the otherness of non-English colonial regions can be traced back to the processes of European imperial conflict, but should also be understood as an evolving discourse over American identity. Different stories of empire across North America were scripted into another imperial story, that of American territorial expansion.

Except for Frederick Jackson Turner and American Frontier studies, there is no comparable association between a single scholar and field of American history as that between Herbert Eugene Bolton and Spanish Borderlands. Indeed, Bolton himself was directly influenced by Turner, as an undergraduate and master's student at the University of Wisconsin during the mid-1890s. Published in 1921, *The Spanish Borderlands: A Chronicle of Old Florida and the Southwest* was an influential synthesis, and for a long time to come, Bolton shaped Borderlands historiography through his more specialized studies and the many students that he directed at Berkeley. Yet, the fundamental dilemmas and issues faced by the field's founder have persisted long after his death in 1953. Defining the Spanish Borderlands as the "southern fringe of the United States . . . once . . . lightly sprinkled with Spanish outposts and criss-crossed with Spanish trails," Bolton wanted to capture the important as well the picturesque history of this vast region (Bolton, 1939, p. 55). The potential dissonance between historical significance and historical romance was only one of several incongruent objectives that affected the work of Borderlands scholars since his day. Bolton worried that fellow citizens in the United States were deriving false inferences about Spanish America from their narrow exposure to the borderlands. "With a vision limited by the Rio

Grande, and noting that Spain's outposts within the area now embraced in the United States were slender, and that these fringes eventually fell into the hands of the Anglo-Americans, writers concluded that Spain did not really colonize, and that, after all, she failed" (Bolton, 1939, p. 57). In a 1929 address at the Boulder Conference on the History of the Trans-Mississippi West, Bolton captured this fallacy in the metaphor of "mistaking the tail for the dog, and then leaving the dog out of the picture" (Bolton, 1939, p. 57). So he advocated the need for Americans to learn more about the dog, that is, Spanish America that lay south of the Rio Grande.

Given Bolton's concern over American ignorance about the core areas of Spain's American empire, it is somewhat ironic that he devoted his own highly productive career to studying the dog's tail. But he also believed that Spanish America's northern frontier had been an important international borderland, "the meeting place of two streams of European civilization" (Bolton, 1939, p. 55), holding vital lessons about Anglo-American expansionism that might benefit United States relations with Latin America in the twentieth century. The eventual conquest of the Spanish Borderlands by Anglo-America did not reflect the superiority of one civilization over another, but revealed instead "the advantage of an expanding economic frontier working from an immediate base, over a defensive frontier operating a long distance from the centers of resources and population" (Bolton, 1939, p. 87). Understanding this geographical circumstance, Bolton hoped, would help Americans realize and respect their historical bonds with their Latin American neighbors. Lasting traces of Spanish colonization in the American Southwest – language, architecture, customs, laws, and folklore – also served as contemporary reminders of a shared past in Bolton's view of the Borderlands.

While wishing to rescue Spanish America from the nationalistic treatment it suffered in United States textbooks and classrooms, Bolton unnecessarily contained the Spanish Borderlands within the nationalist narrative of American westward expansion. In his 1932 presidential address before the American Historical Association, he looked forward to "The Epic of Greater America" in which hemispheric comparisons and connections among all European colonial endeavors would be explored (Bolton, 1939, pp. 1–54). Yet his own treatment of the Spanish empire's northern fringe tended to isolate the Borderlands from the rest of Latin America's colonial history and to hinge their importance on American national development.

Bolton should not be faulted too much for this seeming contradiction. After all, he was boldly confronting some deep biases in American culture and history. The belief that Spain and France failed to colonize America – as represented through images of conquistadors and *coureurs de bois* – was widespread in the United States. Rooted early in the rivalry between European empires and cultivated later by New England-centered writers, the diminution of non-English colonies was built into national histories of the United States. Spanish and French adventurers usually appeared briefly at the beginning of the story, before attention focused on English settlers along the Atlantic seaboard. Florida, Louisiana, and the Southwest reappeared only when they were being incorporated into the expanding nation. Derogatory glances at the colonial background of these places were used to minimize the extent of non-English settlement north of the Rio Grande and to display the righteousness of United States expansion across North America. Herbert Bolton and his students worked hard at disproving these fundamental notions, delving into the colonial archives of Spain's North American provinces to uncover two centuries of colonization that predated the birth of the United

States. Spanish Borderlands historians, though, also had to wrestle with the rising inclination in American culture to imagine that the Southwest under Spain had been a romantic and pastoral world, whose cultural legacy now served tourism and escapism. Anthropological and archaeological work already played an instrumental role in representing Hispanic and Indian cultures as enchanting features on the western landscape. Now Borderlands historians began to participate in conflicting ways, with some of their work contesting the romance and others contributing to it.

Much of the scholarship practiced by the Bolton School tended to make the Spanish Borderlands seem marginal and anomalous in ways that actually undermined fruitful comparison and connection with British North American studies, while also detaching them from the rest of Spanish America. Emphasis on political and diplomatic forces, along with neglect of social and economic conditions, exaggerated the contrast between Spanish and English colonies. "Instead of promoting the integration of the Spanish Borderlands into United States history," observed Gerald Poyo and Gilberto Hinojosa, "the comparative framework apparently led most historians to believe that the Spanish era was a failure and could thus be dismissed as an integral part of this nation's history" (Poyo and Hinojosa, 1988, p. 397). Meanwhile, the Borderlands scholars' preoccupation with the defensive character of New Spain's northern provinces – particularly directed toward Anglo-American imperialism – also marginalized the region in the developing field of Latin American history. Perceived as "an exotic subset of United States history that has risen to treat the pre-Anglo, yet European, past of the United States Southwest and Southeast," in the words of José Cuello, Borderlands history remained "peculiar and mystifying to Latin Americanists" (Weber, 1991, p. 279).

So essential questions about the role of Spanish Borderlands studies in early American history lingered for most of the twentieth century. How should Florida, Louisiana, Texas, New Mexico, Arizona, and California be related to other colonies in North America? Are there comparisons and connections worth pursuing that would result in a wider understanding of American colonial history? Can the history of Spanish colonization north of the Rio Grande and Gulf of Mexico be raised from its subordinate role in United States national narratives and understood on its own terms, while still providing grist for the comparative mill? Is it better for historical study of the Borderlands to be attached more firmly to Latin American scholarship?

The compromising position of Borderlands scholarship – caught between Latin American and Early American historiographies – has left these and other questions largely unanswered. But in no way did it deter the production of abundant studies by outstanding historians. Mainly under the influence of Bolton's own example, Spanish Borderlands scholars explored – in great detail – missions, presidios, administration, law, and Indian relations from California to Florida. In 1966 the eminent Latin Americanist Charles Gibson apologized for merely skimming the many known facts about the Spanish Borderlands in his final chapter of *Spain in America*, "for it is probable that no other part of colonial Spanish America has stimulated so extensive a program of research" (Gibson, 1966, pp. 189–90). The historiography on Spain's colonial possessions in the present-day United States did indeed grow into a vibrant field of study over the middle decades of the twentieth century. In addition to writing many books and articles himself, Herbert Bolton supervised 104 doctoral dissertations and more than 320 master's theses. Many of his students became university professors and directed their own students into the field. Among the most influential of Bolton's former students were Charles Wilson Hackett at the University of Texas, John Bannon at St. Louis University, Abraham Nasatir at San Diego State University, and Lawrence Kinnaird as Bolton's colleague and successor at Berkeley (Bannon, 1978).

Borderlands scholarship followed Bolton's lead on a number of methodological fronts. Spanish exploration of the coasts and interior of North America was naturally an important area of study. Early attention focused on the military and clerical agents of Spanish expansion, but eventually the American Indian populace would be considered for impacts suffered and interactions engendered from the expeditions. Although this scholarship received minimal notice from historians of English America, it did in the long run force them to recognize that North America experienced a long period of European contact and conflict before the founding of Jamestown and Plymouth. Other Borderlands historians concentrated their research on colonial institutions created by the Spanish, first in Florida and New Mexico and later in Texas, Louisiana, and California. Missions and presidios were the foci of much scholarship, while biographies of provincial officials and histories of colonial administration also proliferated in the historiography. Trade, diplomacy, and war developed into significant themes, as Borderlands scholars closely examined Spanish relations with Indian nations and with other European powers. The historians engaging these lines of inquiry comprised a diverse group, and the label "Borderlands" can too easily conceal the various paths that they followed to reach different points of expertise across such a vast region. Some contemporaries of Herbert Bolton launched parallel and intersecting projects on their own. Isaac Cox (1918) and Arthur Whitaker (1927, 1934), for example, were distinguished Latin Americanists who concentrated on diplomatic relations between Spain and the United States in the Gulf South region. During the 1960s a new generation of scholars researched the Spanish Borderlands with a strong sense of association and collaboration. These included Jack Holmes (1965), William Coker (1986), Helen Hornbeck Tanner (1963), Gilbert Din (1993, 1999), Eugene Lyon (1976), Max Moorehead (1968, 1975), and David Weber (1971, 1982). Some Latin Americanists specializing in other regions of Spanish America turned to the Borderlands at different phases of their careers. Works by John TePaske (1964), John Preston Moore (1976), and Paul E. Hoffman (1990) represent this path. Other scholars approached the Borderlands soil with a primary interest in American Indians inhabiting regions once included in the Spanish empire. Edward Spicer (1962), Jack Forbes (1960), Charles Hudson (1990, 1994, 1997), and Elizabeth A. H. John (1975) are among this group. Anthropologists and historians studying Indian–colonial relations in both the Southeast and Southwest also contributed to the development of ethnohistory and thereby traveled the busiest bridge between the Borderlands and Anglo-American colonies. In a book that had a profound impact on Atlantic seaboard studies, *The Invasion of America*, Francis Jennings acknowledged Edward Spicer's *Cycles of Conquest*, a comprehensive study of Indian–colonial relations in the Southwest, as "perhaps the finest example of ethnohistorical method in a large-scale study" (Jennings, 1975, p. 13, n. 30).

In 1970 John Francis Bannon published *The Spanish Borderlands Frontier, 1513–1821*, a landmark synthesis based on the work of three generations of Borderlands scholarship. Bannon offered his comprehensive overview of the Spanish frontier in North America to "show that the Anglo-American experience, magnificent and thrilling though it was, actually was not quite as unique as it is sometimes pictured and chauvinistically thought to be." The Anglo-American frontier, he argued, was not the only "advance of civilization into the wilderness" and ought to be compared with the northward movement of Spanish pioneers (Bannon, 1970, p. 3). Unfortunately applying Frederick Jackson Turner's narrow definition of frontier to his subject, Bannon then proceeded to amplify what he thought was distinctive about the Spanish Borderlands in a way that familiarly undermined the comparative value of his project. Missions, ranching and mining, absolutism, regimentation, and a mestizo population were listed as major features that sharply distinguished Spanish North America from English North America. Bannon's *Spanish Borderlands Frontier* nonetheless proved to be a valuable contribution to the historiography of the American West. But not surprisingly, it made little impression on students of early American history.

Since 1970 much of the isolation and cohesion of scholarship on the Borderlands have diminished because of disparate changes inside and outside the field. First of all, new students of Spanish and French colonies of North America have diversified their methods and approaches. With the sense of common identity previously held by Borderlands scholars weakening from expansion and specialization, the label itself began to lose its clear meaning as a sub-field of either United States or Latin American colonial history. Now it is likely that "Borderlands," as a particular space on maps of North America, will become more commonly applied to the cultural and geographical area that strictly spans the present-day boundary between Mexico and the United States. Social scientists, historians, cultural critics, and artists have already appropriated the upper-case spelling of "Borderlands" in order to address post-colonial identity and experience along the international border (Saldívar, 1997). Meanwhile, a less geographically specific usage of the lower-case term "borderlands" by early American historians – referring here to all zones contested by rival empires – is actually facilitating stronger interest in the Spanish colonies of Florida, Louisiana, Texas, New Mexico, and California. As connections and comparisons across imperial boundaries become more systematically explored, North American places once viewed with indifference by most colonial scholars will receive greater attention.

The best way to survey recent advances inside Spanish Borderlands scholarship is to summarize the literature colony by colony. Because of its proximity to English colonies along the Atlantic seaboard, we might expect Spanish Florida to have received plenty of attention from early American historians. But this was not the case until the 1970s, when archaeologists and historians began to bring the full scale of Spanish colonization in that province into sharper view. Among the Borderlands scholars themselves, Florida was relatively neglected – especially for the seventeenth and early eighteenth centuries. For a long time, Bolton's own *The Debatable Land*, co-authored with his student Mary Ross (Bolton and Ross, 1925), and John Lanning's *Spanish Missions of Georgia* (1935) stood as the only reminders that even the coast of Georgia had once been occupied by Spanish missionaries and soldiers. The long-held view of Florida in American colonial history was captured in fleeting references to Juan Ponce de León, Hernando de Soto, and other Spanish explorers and in the obligatory observation that St. Augustine was founded in 1565 to become the oldest continuous town in European America. The sense that not much happened, except for the maintenance of a Spanish garrison, conveniently catered to the premise that Spain was a feeble competitor with England for the settlement of North America.

A long but forgotten period of missionary activity among Florida's large Indian population, punctuated by some of Native America's earliest and most dramatic rebellions against colonialism, has finally been recovered. In the middle of the seventeenth century, while New Englanders were attempting their own reorganization of American Indian communities into praying towns, Spanish Florida included nearly forty missions inhabited by some twenty-five thousand Indians – mostly Timucuans and Apalachees. By the beginning of the eighteenth century, most of the mission towns were abandoned because of disease and rebelliousness among the proselytes or because of English-led attacks from Carolina. Unlike New Mexico and California, the Florida landscape showed no architectural signs of the mostly wooden buildings that constituted so many Indian missions. More evidence of this forgotten past began to surface with the 1951 publication of *Here They Once Stood: The Tragic End of the Apalachee Missions* by Mark F. Boyd, Hale G. Smith, and John W. Griffin.

Not until archaeologists began systematic excavation, in conjunction with archival research by historians, did Indian missions and colonial settlements in Florida become visible again. Increasingly, fieldwork by Kathleen Deagan (1991), David Hurst Thomas (1987), Jerald Milanich (1993, 1999), Bonnie McEwan (1992), and other archaeologists has uncovered evidence of Indian adaptation and agency as well as of colonial plans and policies. Analysis of written records by historians like Eugene Lyon (1976), Amy Turner Bushnell (1981, 1994), and John Hann (1988, 1996) has captured the crucial role that Indian labor played in early Florida, while also demonstrating how the missions were integrally related to the lives of colonial settlers and soldiers. Although relatively sparse in its non-Indian population throughout the colonial period, society in Spanish Florida was no less diverse and dynamic than that in the English provinces to its north. Hann and McEwan's overview of Mission San Luis (1998), Jane Landers' work on African Americans (1999), and Claudio Saunt's study of Creek Indians (1999) have recently added much to our understanding of this complexity.

Louisiana began as a French colony in 1699 and did not become a Spanish province until 1763. But the history of both French and Spanish Louisiana shared an unusually long lapse between romantic narratives written during the nineteenth century and scholarship produced after World War II. Historians of French North America familiar to the United States audience – particularly Francis Parkman and Reuben Thwaites – had paid much greater attention to Canada and the Great Lakes than to Louisiana. Important works produced over the early twentieth century by Jean Delanglez, Nancy Miller Surrey, Verner Crane, and others examined archival sources from the Mississippi Valley much more closely but were too few and far between to accelerate professional scholarship on colonial Louisiana. Substantial improvement in the study of French Louisiana occurred only with the five volumes published by French historian Marcel Giraud between 1953 and 1974. Meanwhile in the United States, specialized studies by Charles O'Neill (1966) on early church–government relations, Jay Higginbotham (1977) on early Mobile, and John Clark (1970) on New Orleans commerce began to awaken readers to what French Louisiana held in store for future scholars.

Largely because of Herbert Eugene Bolton's influence, the Spanish regime in the Mississippi Valley received more sustained attention over much of the twentieth century than did the French regime. Bolton himself contributed only a single important work on Spanish Louisiana, a compilation of documents with a long introduction centering on the border town of Natchitoches (Bolton, 1914). But several of his students, including John Caughey (1934, 1938), Abraham Nasatir (1976), and

Lawrence Kinnaird (1946–49), chose to concentrate on Louisiana's Spanish era. A larger number of works on Louisiana and West Florida came from subsequent generations of Spanish Borderlands historians, especially Jack Holmes (1965), Gilbert Din (1983, 1993, 1996, 1999), John Preston Moore (1976), Light Cummins (1991), and William Coker and Thomas Watson (1986). Joining them were Barton Starr, J. Leitch Wright, Robert Rea, Robert Haynes, and other historians with an interest in West Florida during the English regime and the American Revolution.

The study of colonial Louisiana lagged behind the new social history and ethnohistory that were being applied to other regions of colonial North America by the early 1970s. Contemporaneous work on the eighteenth-century lower Mississippi Valley focused instead on such areas as exploration, immigration policy, commercial organization, provincial leadership, European diplomacy, and imperial conflict. Very little attention was paid to the general population of colonists, slaves, and Indians or to long-term patterns of social and economic change. While historians of English North America began to closely examine community life, slavery, Indian relations, and other neglected dimensions of colonial society, students of French and Spanish Louisiana as well as English and Spanish West Florida were apparently trying to make up for lost time by producing basic biographical and institutional histories. The most significant impetus behind an eventual interest in ordinary inhabitants of the lower Mississippi Valley came from historians of Acadian descent, whose ethnic and linguistic identity went through a revitalization during the 1960s. Based at the University of Southwestern Louisiana in Lafayette, a small but devoted group of scholars began to promote the importance of learning about the origins and evolution of French Louisiana. In 1968 Glenn Conrad launched a project to microfilm archival materials in France and assemble a comprehensive collection of colonial records. This Colonial Records Collection steadily expanded to include microfilmed documents from Spanish archives, and USL created the Center for Louisiana Studies in order to publish essential primary sources and to encourage new historical research. State and university archives in both Louisiana and Mississippi, meanwhile, purchased their own microfilmed copies of colonial records.

With colonial records more readily available in the United States, the past quarter-century has witnessed a significant growth in the number of historians becoming interested in the eighteenth-century Mississippi Valley. Many of the scholars venturing into this relatively unexplored region were strongly influenced by abundant studies of migration, slavery, and intercultural relations in other colonial settings. They attempted to apply social history, anthropology, and other approaches to groups of people usually left out of studies that confined their coverage of early America to Great Britain's Atlantic seaboard colonies. Works by Morris Arnold (1985, 1991, 2000), Carl Brasseaux (1987), Carl Ekberg (1985, 1998), Patricia Galloway (1982, 1995), Gwendolyn Hall (1992), Kimberly Hangar (1997), Thomas Ingersoll (1998), Tanis Thorne (1996), Daniel Usner (1992), and Joseph Zitomersky (1994) helped underscore the fact that the Mississippi Valley is fertile ground for innovative, and even comparative, approaches to eighteenth-century life. Current research on settlement patterns and population growth, economic and environmental change, Indian–colonial relations, the African slave trade and slavery, religion, gender, and family life will uncover a complexity in colonial Louisiana that resembles what historians of other North American colonial regions have recently found.

The history of early Texas has lagged even farther behind than Florida and Louisiana in the volume of scholarship undertaken, but current work is rapidly expanding our knowledge of its colonial origins and evolution. Although one of Bolton's most important monographs was *Texas in the Middle Eighteenth Century: Studies in Spanish Colonial History and Administration*, this 1915 publication did little to spread interest in this part of the Borderlands. With presidios and missions portrayed mainly as Spanish institutions scattered in a vast wilderness, it took a long time for historians to examine how a provincial society developed across southern and eastern Texas. Odie Faulk (1964) brought attention to the closing years of Spain's rule over Texas. But neglected mission buildings in the San Antonio area have been better known for the role that just one – the Alamo – played in the Americanization of Texas than for the generations of Coahuiltecan Indians who had prayed, worked, and lived in them since the early eighteenth century.

Following an initial advance and retreat of Spanish activity in response to French possession of Louisiana, a steady process of Spanish colonization got under way in Texas by 1716. Studies by Jack Jackson (1986), Donald Chipman (1992), and Armando Alonzo (1998) have begun to capture the extent of colonial settlement and military occupation in Spanish Texas between San Antonio and Los Adaes. Elizabeth John (1975) and Todd Smith (1995) have contributed significantly to a fuller understanding of Caddo relations with both Texas and Louisiana, while Gilberto Hinojosa (1983), Gerald Poyo (1991), and Jesús de la Teja (1995) have brought community formation among settlers into sharper focus. As in all of the Spanish Borderlands from Florida to California, relations between Indian communities and neighboring colonial towns in Texas involved complicated patterns of socioeconomic exchange and jurisdictional conflict. And the ethnic composition of colonial society was heterogeneous.

The longer and stronger continuity of Hispanic communities in New Mexico, along with the persistence of Pueblo Indians in their midst, gave this colony's history a notable edge over other parts of the Borderlands. Strong anthropological as well as historical interest in the origins and traditions of northern New Mexico's Indian and non-Indian inhabitants meant that local archives and archaeological sites would be explored by many scholars both inside and outside the Bolton school. The all-important Pueblo Revolt of 1680 drew much attention, causing most students of colonial New Mexico to focus on the seventeenth century. France Scholes (1942a), a close associate of Bolton, and Charles Hackett (1941), one of Bolton's students, mined church and state records to lay the groundwork for later investigations of the causes and consequences of the Pueblo Indians' successful war against New Mexico colonists. Major contributions to the study of seventeenth-century New Mexico appeared in books by Marc Simmons (1968, 1991) on the colony's founder Juan de Oñate and the Spanish provincial government and a more recent examination of the Pueblo Revolt written by Andrew Knaut (1995). The reconquest of Pueblo Indians by Spanish military forces was included in some studies, but the eighteenth century remained largely neglected. Important works by Oakah Jones (1966, 1979) and John Kessell (1979) helped correct this mistake.

The most ambitious and innovative books on colonial New Mexico, however, have been Thomas Hall's *Social Change in the Southwest, 1350–1880* (1989) and Ramón Gutiérrez's *When Jesus Came, the Corn Mothers Went Away* (1991). A sociologist, Hall applied a world-system analysis to the Southwest. He provocatively explored on a grand regional scale how New Mexico and its surrounding Indian societies were invaded by a series of overwhelming economic forces. The land and labor of indigenous and colonial inhabitants were transformed to serve outside interests, while traditional and adaptive strategies were pursued by local communities. Hall's work provided a useful framework for re-examining the wider world of colonialism and resistance in which New Mexico evolved over the Spanish, Mexican, and American periods. In sharp contrast, Ramón Gutiérrez drew attention to intimate forces at work inside Indian and colonial communities. *When Jesus Came, the Corn Mothers Went Away* boldly examined the role of gender and marriage in intercultural relations. Missionary and Pueblo concepts of sexuality, Gutiérrez argued, deeply affected the conversion process. This line of inquiry shed some new light on the 1680 revolt but also extended into the development of colonial society during the eighteenth and early nineteenth centuries. Gutiérrez's approach to family and community life in early New Mexico has sparked a surge of interest in neglected aspects of Borderlands history, while also demonstrating the benefits and opportunities of comparative history.

The historiography of early California has likewise gone through major change over recent years. More than any other Borderlands region, California's Hispanic past was trapped inside an exoticization of mission and ranch life. The survival of mission buildings and their place in tourism played a major role in reducing Spanish California to a one-dimensional image. The tendency to romanticize life in and around missions not only downplayed the plight suffered by Indian neophytes beginning in 1769, but also concealed the extent and importance of Spanish colonization along the Pacific coast. The groundbreaking demographic work of Sherburne Cook (1976) finally exposed Indian hardship and suffering in California, and the commercial and diplomatic role of the colony in international affairs was thoroughly explored by Warren Cook (1973).

Newer books by Albert Hurtado (1988), Robert Jackson and Edward Castillo (1995), and George Phillips (1993) have significantly improved our understanding of early California. Their work reflects an effort to scrutinize how imperial designs influenced daily life, while resistance and adaptation by California Indians are captured more effectively than ever. Essays recently compiled by Ramón Gutiérrez and Richard Orsi in *Contested Eden* (1998) further represent current directions in the study of California before1848. The socioeconomic and political functions of Indian missions are analyzed in relationship to their religious role, while complex social networks and diverse colonial communities are brought to the foreground.

Between 1989 and 1991 David Hurst Thomas edited a three-volume collection of essays, *Columbian Consequences*, which provides a valuable overview of ongoing analysis of the Spanish Borderlands. Work by social scientists overshadowed that of historians in this survey, but as Light Cummins observed in his review of the book, "a quiet revolution in borderlands scholarship outside the discipline of history has been occurring during the last several decades" (Cummins, 1995, p. 204). The historiographical foundation of Borderlands study will consequently take a new shape. In 1992 David J. Weber produced a timely and prize-winning synthesis of Spanish Borderlands history, *The Spanish Frontier in North America*. Weber brought to his own survey a keen awareness of how borderlands history had been marginalized. Excluded from an early American historiography that concentrates on English colonies, ignored by Latin Americanists who focus on more central places in the Spanish empire, and treated as background to a Chicano history more interested in the nineteenth and twentieth centuries, the Spanish Borderlands warranted scrutiny on its own terms more than ever. And this is exactly what Weber provided. He pulled together all of the latest scholarship on the individual colonies from Florida to California by featuring current findings and approaches and, moreover, steered the field into a new comparative direction by emphasizing the agency of American Indians in their relations with Spanish colonists.

The historical study of the Borderlands now stands at an exciting threshold. Scholars are paying greater attention to social and economic conditions inside the Spanish provinces north of Mexico. Preliminary works altogether demonstrate how much will be learned by examining local communities and intercultural relations more closely. As long-neglected topics move to the forefront of discussion, it will no longer be possible for historians to downplay the extent of Spanish colonization. Migration and settlement patterns, labor and land systems, gender and race – deeply mined subjects in the history of English North America – are also important themes in Spanish and French colonies of North America, and their comparative value crosses imperial boundaries and transcends national categories. As Gerald Poyo and Gilberto Hinojosa declared about current literature on Texas, "paradoxically, it is the regional and local framework, and the consequent focus on socioeconomic development, that will prompt scholars to reconsider the colonial Borderlands' significance to the United States" (Poyo and Hinojosa, 1988, p. 415).

Another advance in Spanish Borderlands scholarship is the stronger consideration being given to their Caribbean and Mexican contexts. Peter Gerhard (1993) has systematically examined all of the provinces on the northern frontier of New Spain, thereby linking New Mexico, Texas, and California to general patterns and processes on this edge of the Spanish empire. Essays edited by Donna Guy and Thomas Sheridan in *Contested Ground* (1998) further demonstrate how a fuller appreciation of the Mexican framework can allow historians to compare the Greater Southwest of the present-day United States with other frontier regions in Spanish America. Amy Turner Bushnell (1994) has contributed significantly to a new understanding of Florida by explaining much of its development in terms of Spain's wider colonial designs and networks. Proposing that a model of maritime peripheries replace Bolton's borderlands paradigm, Bushnell fixes Spanish Florida within a Caribbean web of administrative and commercial interaction. Explaining the importance of these wider continental and oceanic connections is the surest way to integrate the study of Spain's northernmost American colonies more centrally into the larger field of Latin American history.

While specialists on Spanish North America scrutinize colonial societies more closely and survey their external linkages more thoroughly, a general shift in thinking among early American historians promises to have a great influence on the changing role of Spanish Borderlands studies. Scholars of English North America have begun to use the term "borderlands" in a more comparative and generic way to explore any region where two or more European empires face each other amidst autonomous Indian societies. As this new direction in scholarship has been delineated by Jeremy Adelman and Stephen Aron (1999), "contested boundaries between colonial domains" might serve as a more durable and versatile definition of borderlands. Conflict over imperial boundaries shaped "the peculiar and contingent character of frontier relations." But as colonial borderlands gave way to national borders, "fluid and 'inclusive' intercultural frontiers yielded to hardened and more 'exclusive' hierarchies" (Adelman and Aron, 1999, pp. 815–16). Partly influenced by Herbert Bolton's understanding of interethnic and international relations, Adelman and Aron advocate a new line of inquiry that just might advance his dream of a more comparative and common early American history. Other students of colonial America have called for greater inclusion of non-English provinces in the field (Hijiya, 1994; Wall, 1997), and important works forthcoming from the Omohundro Institute of Early American History and Culture signal steady progress (Brooks, 2002; Clark, forthcoming; and Hackel, forthcoming).

As boundaries and borders of all kinds receive closer attention, vaguely defined national characteristics will carry less weight in a comparative analysis of North American colonies. Different types of development resulted as much from what happened to colonial policies on the ground as from what colonial rulers intended. Whether comparing provinces within a single empire or comparing provinces from different empires, historians need to consider an array of factors: the scale, composition, and timing of migration; the means of adaptation and resistance deployed by Indians; local environmental and economic circumstances; and even a colony's location in its particular empire and its proximity to a rival empire. As we learn more about both Spanish and French colonies in North American, similarities as well as differences across the divide with British America will become apparent. Jaime E. Rodríguez O. (2000) has extended this point further than anyone else, arguing that autonomy and self-governance practiced by colonists differed in degrees and that all three monarchies lacked power to control development in their New World provinces. Negotiation between metropolis and colony occurred in French, Spanish, and English America, but played out in different ways because of different demographic, environmental, and economic circumstances. Struggles for independence also varied in complex ways.

As a result of widening and deepening interest in Spanish colonial regions, historians are asking new questions about how they were actually incorporated into the United States. The old assumption that feeble Latin provinces inevitably gave way to a vigorous Anglo-American nation cannot prevail against systematic analysis of United States territorial expansion. Contemporary students of Spanish Borderlands are finding much variation and nuance in the ways that their diverse inhabitants faced processes of conquest or annexation over the early nineteenth century (Hinojosa, 1983; Haas, 1995; Landers, 2000; Clark, forthcoming). Recent essays on the Southwest by Andrés Reséndez (1999), Ross Frank (2000), and James Brooks (1999), for example, forcefully demonstrate that local communities responded in complex ways, driven by objectives different from the designs of both Mexico and the United States. Class and ethnic divisions within territories being annexed, as well as economic alliances crossing international boundaries, presented countervailing and complicating challenges to the construction of nationalist borders and narratives.

With scholarship on the Borderlands accelerating and early American history widening its gaze, we now face an opportunity to re-conceptualize our understanding of boundaries in eighteenth-century North America. First of all, the lines putatively dividing English, French, and Spanish empires on maps of the continent should no longer separate the different regional historiographies from each other. The borders between colonial regions were flexible and permeable, yet historians have been slow in attending to important movement and interaction across them. But now that we are more closely examining Indian societies' multifaceted relations with two or more different European empires, networks of interaction that transgressed or spanned imperial boundaries begin to come into sharper focus. This form of border crossing, therefore, promises to become a serious subject for students willing to read sources in more than a single national and linguistic category. Secondly, as historians read more widely across the international boundaries of early American historiography, we will enhance our ability to compare different colonial regions in innovative ways. How diverse peoples within these distinct colonial regions demarcated borders between themselves and how groups and individuals attempted to cross them might become a major comparative theme in the colonial history of North America. The iconic differentiation of early North America – into England's robust settlements along the Atlantic coast, France's extended string of trading posts from the Gulf of St. Lawrence to the Gulf of Mexico, and Spain's weakly held borderlands north of Mexico – is finally breaking down, so we should no longer be discouraged from exploring similarities as well as differences across imperial lines.

BIBLIOGRAPHY

Adelman, Jeremy and Aron, Stephen: "From Borderlands to Borders: Empires, Nation-States, and the Peoples in Between in North American History." *American Historical Review* 104 (1999), pp. 814–41.

Alonzo, Armando C.: *Tejano Legacy: Rancheros and Settlers in South Texas, 1734–1900* (Albuquerque, NM: University of New Mexico Press, 1998).

Arnold, Morris S.: *Unequal Laws unto a Savage Race: European Legal Traditions in Arkansas, 1686–1836* (Fayetteville, AR: University of Arkansas Press, 1985).

Arnold, Morris S.: *Colonial Arkansas, 1686–1804: A Social and Cultural History* (Fayetteville, AR: University of Arkansas Press, 1991).

Arnold, Morris S.: *The Rumble of a Distant Drum: The Quapaw and Old World Newcomers, 1673–1804* (Fayetteville, AR: University of Arkansas Press, 2000).

Bannon, John Francis: *The Spanish Borderlands Frontier, 1513–1821* (New York: Holt, Rinehart and Winston, 1970).

Bannon, John Francis: *Herbert Eugene Bolton: The Historian and the Man, 1870–1953* (Tucson, AZ: University of Arizona Press, 1978).

Bolton, Herbert E., ed. and trans.: *Athanase de Mézières and the Louisiana–Texas Frontier, 1768–1780*, 2 vols (Cleveland, OH: Arthur H. Clark Co., 1914).

Bolton, Herbert E.: *Texas in the Middle Eighteenth Century: Studies in Spanish Colonial History and Administration* (Berkeley, CA: University of California Press, 1915).

Bolton, Herbert E.: *The Spanish Borderlands: A Chronicle of Old Florida and the Southwest* (New Haven, CT: Yale University Press, 1921).

Bolton, Herbert E.: *Wider Horizons of American History* (New York: D. Appleton-Century Company, 1939).

Bolton, Herbert E. and Ross, Mary: *The Debatable Land: A Sketch of Anglo-Spanish Contest for the Georgia Country* (Berkeley, CA: University of California Press, 1925).

Boyd, Mark F., Smith, Hale G., and Griffin, John W.: *Here They Once Stood: The Tragic End of the Apalachee Missions* (Gainesville, FL: University Press of Florida, 1951).

Brasseaux, Carl A.: *The Founding of New Acadia: The Beginnings of Acadian Life in Louisiana, 1765–1803* (Baton Rouge, LA: Louisiana State University Press, 1987).

Brooks, James F.: "Violence, Justice, and State Power in the New Mexican Borderlands, 1780–1880." In Richard White and John M. Findlay, eds., *Power and Place in the North American West* (Seattle, WA: University of Washington Press, 1999), 23–60.

Brooks, James F.: *Captives and Cousins: Slavery, Kinship, and Community in the Southwest Borderlands* (Chapel Hill, NC: University of North Carolina Press, 2002).

Bushnell, Amy Turner: *The King's Coffer: Proprietors of the Spanish Florida Treasury, 1565–1702*

(Gainesville, FL: University Presses of Florida, 1981).

Bushnell, Amy Turner: *Situado and Sabana: Spain's Support System for the Presidio and Mission Provinces of Florida* (New York: American Museum of Natural History, 1994).

Caughey, John Walton: *Bernardo de Gálvez in Louisiana, 1776–1783* (Berkeley, CA: University of California Press, 1934).

Caughey, John Walton: *McGillivray of the Creeks* (Norman, OK: University of Oklahoma Press, 1938).

Chipman, Donald E.: *Spanish Texas, 1519–1821* (Austin, TX: University of Texas Press, 1992).

Clark, Emily: *Masterless Mistresses: The New Orleans Ursulines and the Development of a New World Society, 1727–1834* (Chapel Hill, NC: University of North Carolina Press, forthcoming).

Clark, John G.: *New Orleans, 1718–1812: An Economic History* (Baton Rouge, LA: Louisiana State University Press, 1970).

Coker, William S. and Watson, Thomas D.: *Indian Traders of the Southeastern Spanish Borderlands: Panton, Leslie and Company and John Forbes and Company, 1783–1847* (Pensacola, FL: University of West Florida Press, 1986).

Conrad, Glenn R., ed.: *The Louisiana Purchase Bicentennial Series in Louisiana History*, vol. 1, *The French Presence in Louisiana* (Lafayette, LA: Center for Louisiana Studies, 1995).

Cook, Sherburne F.: *The Conflict Between the California Indian and White Civilization* (Berkeley, CA: University of California Press, 1976).

Cook, Warren L.: *Flood Tide of Empire: Spain and the Pacific Northwest, 1543–1819* (New Haven, CT: Yale University Press, 1973).

Cox, Isaac J.: *The West Florida Controversy, 1798–1813: A Study in American Diplomacy* (Baltimore, MD: Johns Hopkins University Press, 1918).

Cummins, Light T.: *Spanish Observers and the American Revolution, 1775–1783* (Baton Rouge, LA: Louisiana State University Press, 1991).

Cummins, Light T.: "Getting Beyond Bolton: Columbian Consequences and the Spanish Borderlands: A Review Essay." *New Mexico Historical Review* 70 (1995), pp. 201–15.

Deagan, Kathleen, ed.: *America's Ancient City: Spanish St. Augustine, 1565–1763* (New York: Garland, 1991).

Din, Gilbert C.: *Francisco Bouligny: A Bourbon Soldier in Spanish Louisiana* (Baton Rouge, LA: Louisiana State University Press, 1993).

Din, Gilbert C., ed.: *The Louisiana Purchase Bicentennial Series in Louisiana History*, vol. 2, *The Spanish Presence in Louisiana 1763–1803* (Lafayette, LA: Center for Louisiana Studies, 1996).

Din, Gilbert C.: *Spaniards, Planters, and Slaves: The Spanish Regulation of Slavery in Louisiana, 1763–1803* (College Station, TX: Texas A&M University Press, 1999).

Din, Gilbert C. and Harkins, John E.: *The New Orleans Cabildo: Colonial Louisiana's First City Government, 1769–1803* (Baton Rouge, LA: Louisiana State University Press, 1996).

Din, Gilbert C. and Nasatir, A. P.: *The Imperial Osages: Spanish–Indian Diplomacy in the Mississippi Valley* (Norman, OK: University of Oklahoma Press, 1983).

Ekberg, Carl J.: *Colonial Ste. Genevieve: An Adventure on the Mississippi Frontier* (Gerald, MO: Patrice Press, 1985).

Ekberg, Carl J.: *French Roots in the Illinois Country: The Mississippi Frontier in Colonial Times* (Champaign: University of Illinois Press, 1998).

Faulk, Odie B.: *Last Years of Spanish Texas, 1778–1821* (The Hague: Mouton & Co., 1964).

Forbes, Jack D.: *Apache, Navaho, and Spaniard* (Norman, OK: University of Oklahoma Press, 1960).

Frank, Ross: *From Settler to Citizen: New Mexican Economic Development and the Creation of Vecino Society, 1750–1820* (Berkeley, CA: University of California Press, 2000).

Galloway, Patricia K., ed.: *La Salle and His Legacy: Frenchmen and Indians in the Lower Mississippi Valley* (Jackson, MS: University Press of Mississippi, 1982).

Galloway, Patricia K.: *Choctaw Genesis 1500–1700* (Lincoln, NE: University of Nebraska Press, 1995).

Galloway, Patricia K., ed.: *The Hernando de Soto Expedition: History, Historiography, and "Discovery" in the Southeast* (Lincoln, NE: University of Nebraska Press, 1997).

Gerhard, Peter: *The North Frontier of New Spain*, rev. ed. (Norman, OK: University of Oklahoma Press, 1993).

Gibson, Charles: *Spain in America* (New York: Harper & Row, 1966).

Giraud, Marcel: *A History of French Louisiana*, vols 1–2, 5, trans. Joseph C. Lambert (Baton Rouge, LA: Louisiana State University Press, 1974–1993).

Gutiérrez, Ramón A.: *When Jesus Came, the Corn Mothers Went Away: Marriage, Sexuality, and Power in New Mexico, 1500–1846* (Stanford, CA: Stanford University Press, 1991).

Gutiérrez, Ramón A. and Orsi, Richard J., eds.: *Contested Eden: California before the Gold Rush* (Berkeley, CA: University of California Press, 1998).

Guy, Donna J. and Sheridan, Thomas E., eds.: *Contested Ground: Comparative Frontiers on the Northern and Southern Edges of the Spanish Empire* (Tucson, AZ: University of Arizona Press, 1998).

Haas, Lisbeth: *Conquests and Historical Identities in California, 1769–1936* (Berkeley, CA: University of California Press, 1995).

Hackel, Steven W.: *Indian–Spanish Relations in Colonial California, 1769–1845* (Chapel Hill, NC: University of North Carolina Press, forthcoming).

Hackett, Charles Wilson, ed.: *Revolt of the Pueblo Indians and Otermín's Attempted Reconquest, 1680–1682*, 2 vols, trans. Charmion Clair Shelby (Albuquerque, NM: University of New Mexico Press, 1941).

Hall, Gwendolyn Midlo: *Africans in Colonial Louisiana: The Development of Afro-Creole Culture in the Eighteenth Century* (Baton Rouge, LA: Louisiana State University Press, 1992).

Hall, Thomas D.: *Social Change in the Southwest, 1350–1880* (Lawrence, KS: University Press of Kansas, 1989).

Hanger, Kimberly S.: *Bounded Lives, Bounded Places: Free Black Society in Colonial New Orleans, 1769–1803* (Durham, NC: Duke University Press, 1997).

Hann, John H.: *Apalachee: The Land between the Rivers* (Gainesville, FL: University Presses of Florida, 1988).

Hann, John H.: *A History of the Timucua Indians and Missions* (Gainesville, FL: University Press of Florida, 1996).

Hann, John H. and McEwan, Bonnie G.: *The Apalachee Indians and Mission San Luis* (Gainesville, FL: University Press of Florida, 1998).

Higginbotham, Jay: *Old Mobile* (Mobile, AL: Museum of Mobile, 1977).

Hijiya, James A.: "Why the West Is Lost." *William and Mary Quarterly* 3rd ser., 51 (1994), pp. 276–92.

Hinojosa, Gilberto Miguel: *A Borderlands Town in Transition: Laredo, 1755–1870* (College Station, TX: Texas A&M University Press, 1983).

Hoffman, Paul E.: *A New Andalucia and a Way to the Orient: The American Southeast during the Sixteenth Century* (Baton Rouge, LA: Louisiana State University Press, 1990).

Holmes, Jack D. L.: *Gayoso: The Life of a Spanish Governor in the Mississippi Valley, 1789–1799* (Baton Rouge, LA: Louisiana State University Press, 1965).

Hudson, Charles M.: *The Juan Pardo Expeditions: Exploration of the Carolinas and Tennessee, 1566–1568*, with documents relating to the Pardo expeditions, transcribed, translated, and annotated by Paul E. Hoffman (Washington, DC: Smithsonian Institution Press, 1990).

Hudson, Charles M.: *Knights of Spain, Warriors of the Sun: Hernando De Soto and the South's Ancient Chiefdoms* (Athens, GA: University of Georgia Press, 1997).

Hudson, Charles M. and Tesser, Carmen Chaves, eds.: *The Forgotten Centuries: Indians and Europeans in the American South, 1521–1704* (Athens, GA: University of Georgia Press, 1994).

Hurtado, Albert L.: *Indian Survival on the California Frontier* (New Haven, CT: Yale University Press, 1988).

Ingersoll, Thomas N.: *Mammon and Manon: The First Slave Society in the Deep South, 1718–1819* (Knoxville, TN: University of Tennessee Press, 1998).

Jackson, Jack: *Los Mesteños: Spanish Ranching in Texas, 1721–1821* (College Station, TX: Texas A&M University Press, 1986).

Jackson, Robert H., ed.: *New Views of Borderlands History* (Albuquerque, NM: University of New Mexico Press, 1998).

Jackson Robert H. and Castillo, Edward: *Indians, Franciscans, and Spanish Colonization: The Impact of the Mission System on California Indians* (Albuquerque, NM: University of New Mexico Press, 1995).

Jennings, Francis: *The Invasion of America: Indians, Colonialism, and the Cant of Conquest* (Chapel Hill, NC: University of North Carolina Press, 1975).

John, Elizabeth A. H.: *Storms Brewed in Other Men's Worlds: The Confrontation of Indians, Spanish, and French in the Southwest, 1540–1795* (College Station, TX: Texas A&M University Press, 1975).

Jones, Oakah L.: *Pueblo Warriors and Spanish Conquest* (Norman, OK: University of Oklahoma Press, 1966).

Jones, Oakah L.: *Los Paisanos: Spanish Settlers on the Northern Frontier* (Norman, OK: University of Oklahoma Press, 1979).

Kessell, John L.: *Kiva, Cross, and Crown: The Pecos Indians and New Mexico, 1540–1840* (Washington, DC: National Park Service, 1979).

Kinnaird, Lawrence, ed.: *Spain in the Mississippi Valley, 1765–1794*. In *Annual Report of the American Historical Association for the Year 1945*, 3 vols (Washington, DC: American Historical Association, 1946–49).

Knaut, Andrew L.: *The Pueblo Revolt of 1680* (Albuquerque, NM: University of New Mexico Press, 1995).

Landers, Jane G.: *Black Society in Spanish Florida* (Urbana, IL: University of Illinois Press, 1999).

Landers, Jane G., ed.: *Colonial Plantations and Economy in Florida* (Gainesville, FL: University Press of Florida, 2000).

Lanning, John Tate: *The Spanish Missions of Georgia* (Chapel Hill, NC: The University of North Carolina Press, 1935).

Loomis, Noel M. and Nasatir, Abraham P.: *Pedro Vial and the Roads to Santa Fe* (Norman, OK: University of Oklahoma Press, 1967).

Lyon, Eugene: *The Enterprise of Florida: Pedro Menéndez de Avilés and the Spanish Conquest of 1565–1568* (Gainesville, FL: University Presses of Florida, 1976).

McDermott, John Francis, ed.: *The Spanish in the Mississippi Valley, 1762–1804* (Urbana, IL: University of Illinois Press, 1974).

McEwan, Bonnie G.: *Archaeology of the Apalachee Village at San Luis de Talimali* (Tallahassee, FL: Florida Bureau of Archaeological Research, 1992).

Milanich, Jerald T.: *Laboring in the Fields of the Lord: Spanish Missions and Southeastern Indians* (Washington, DC: Smithsonian Institution Press, 1999).

Milanich, Jerald T. and Hudson, Charles M.: *Hernando de Soto and the Indians of Florida* (Gainesville, FL: University Press of Florida, 1993).

Moore, John Preston: *Revolt in Louisiana: The Spanish Occupation, 1766–1770* (Baton Rouge, LA: Louisiana State University Press, 1976).

Moorehead, Max L.: *The Apache Frontier: Jacobo de Ugarte and Spanish–Indian Relations in Northern New Spain, 1769–1791* (Norman, OK: University of Oklahoma Press, 1968).

Moorehead, Max L.: *The Presidio: Bastion of the Spanish Borderlands* (Norman, OK: University of Oklahoma Press, 1975).

Nasatir, Abraham P.: *Borderland in Retreat: From Spanish Louisiana to the Far Southwest*. (Albuquerque, NM: University of New Mexico Press, 1976).

O'Neill, Edward: *Church and State in French Colonial Louisiana* (New Haven, CT: Yale University Press, 1966).

Phillips, George: *Indians and Intruders in Central California, 1769–1849* (Norman, OK: University of Oklahoma Press, 1993).

Poyo, Gerald E. and Hinojosa, Gilberto M.: "Spanish Texas and Borderlands Historiography in Transition: Implications for United States History." *Journal of American History* 75 (1988), pp. 393–416.

Poyo, Gerald E. and Hinojosa, Gilberto M., eds.: *Tejano Origins in Eighteenth-Century San Antonio* (Austin, TX: University of Texas Press, 1991).

Rabasa, José: *Writing Violence on the Northern Frontier: The Historiography of Sixteenth-Century New Mexico and Florida and the Legacy of Conquest* (Durham, NC: Duke University Press, 2000).

Reséndez, Andrés: "National Identity on a Shifting Border: Texas and New Mexico in the Age of Transition, 1821–1848." *Journal of American History* 86 (1999), pp. 668–88.

Rodríguez O., Jaime E.: "The Emancipation of America" [AHR Forum]. *American Historical Review* 105 (2000), pp. 131–52.

Saldívar, José David: *Border Matters: Remapping American Cultural Studies* (Berkeley, CA: University of California Press, 1997).

Sandos, James A.: "From 'Boltonlands' to 'Weberlands': The Borderlands Enter American History." *American Quarterly* 46 (1994), pp. 595–604.

Saunt, Claudio: *A New Order of Things: Property, Power, and the Transformation of the Creek Indians, 1733–1816* (New York: Cambridge University Press, 1999).

Scholes, France V.: *Church and State in New Mexico, 1610–1650* (Albuquerque. NM: University of New Mexico Press, 1942a).

Scholes, France V.: *Troublous Times in New Mexico, 1659–1670* (Albuquerque, NM: University of New Mexico Press, 1942b).

Simmons, Marc: *Spanish Government in New Mexico* (Albuquerque, NM: University of New Mexico Press, 1968).

Simmons, Marc: *The Last Conquistador: Juan de Oñate and the Settling of the Far Southwest* (Norman, OK: University of Oklahoma Press, 1991).

Smith, F. Todd: *The Caddo Indians: Tribes at the Convergence of Empires, 1542–1854* (College Station, TX: Texas A&M University Press, 1995).

Spicer, Edward H.: *Cycles of Conquest: The Impact of Spain, Mexico, and the United States on the Indians of the Southwest, 1533–1960* (Tucson, AZ: University of Arizona Press, 1962).

Tanner, Helen Hornbeck: *Zéspedes in East Florida, 1784–1790* (Coral Gables, FL: University of Miami Press, 1963).

Teja, Jesús F. de la: *San Antonio de Béxar: A Community on New Spain's Northern Frontier* (Albuquerque, NM: University of New Mexico Press, 1995).

TePaske, John J.: *The Governorship of Spanish Florida, 1700–1763* (Durham, NC: Duke University Press, 1964).

Thomas, David Hurst: "The Archaeology of Mission Santa Catalina de Guale: 1. Search and Discovery." *Anthropological Papers of the American Museum of Natural History* 63, pt. 2 (1987), pp. 47–161.

Thomas, David Hurst, ed.: *Columbian Consequences*, vol. 1, *Archaeological and Historical Perspectives on the Spanish Borderlands West*; vol. 2, *Archaeological and Historical Perspectives on the Spanish Borderlands East*; vol. 3, *The Spanish Borderlands in Pan-American Perspective* (Washington, DC: Smithsonian Institution Press, 1989–91).

Thorne, Tanis C.: *The Many Hands of My Relations: French and Indians on the Lower Missouri* (Columbia, MO: University of Missouri Press, 1996).

Usner, Daniel H., Jr.: *Indians, Settlers, and Slaves in a Frontier Exchange Economy: The Lower Mississippi Valley before 1783* (Chapel Hill, NC: University of North Carolina Press, 1992).

Wall, Helena M.: "Confessions of a British North Americanist: Borderlands Historiography and Early American History." *Reviews in American History* 25 (1997), pp. 1–12.

Weber, David J.: *The Taos Trappers: The Fur Trade in the Far Southwest, 1540–1846* (Norman, OK: University of Oklahoma Press, 1971).

Weber, David J., ed.: *New Spain's Far Northern Frontier: Essays on Spain in the American West* (Albuquerque, NM: University of New Mexico Press, 1979).

Weber, David J.: *The Mexican Frontier, 1821–1846: The American Southwest under Mexico* (Albuquerque, NM: University of New Mexico Press, 1982).

Weber, David J., ed.: *The Idea of the Spanish Borderlands* (New York: Garland Publishing, Inc., 1991).

Weber, David J.: *The Spanish Frontier in North America* (New Haven, CT: Yale University Press, 1992).

Weddle, Robert S.: *The San Sabá Mission: Spanish Pivot in Texas* (Austin, TX: University of Texas Press, 1964).

Weddle, Robert S.: *San Juan Bautista: Gateway to Spanish Texas* (Austin, TX: University of Texas Press, 1968).

Weddle, Robert S.: *Wilderness Manhunt: The Spanish Search for La Salle* (Austin, TX: University of Texas Press, 1973).

Weddle, Robert S.: *Spanish Sea: The Gulf of Mexico in North American Discovery, 1500–1685* (College Station, TX: Texas A&M University Press, 1985).

Whitaker, Arthur Preston: *The Spanish–American Frontier, 1783–1795: The Westward Movement and the Spanish Retreat in the Mississippi Valley* (Boston, MA: Houghton Mifflin, 1927).

Whitaker, Arthur Preston: *The Mississippi Question, 1795–1803: A Study in Trade, Politics, and Diplomacy* (New York: D. Appleton-Century, 1934).

Wright, J. Leitch: *Anglo-Spanish Rivalry in North America* (Athens, GA: University of Georgia Press, 1971).

Zitomersky, Joseph: *French Americans–Native Americans in Eighteenth-Century French Colonial Louisiana: The Population Geography of the Illinois Indians, 1670s–1760s* (Lund, Sweden: Lund University Press).

CHAPTER EIGHTEEN

Comparisons: The Caribbean

VERENE SHEPHERD AND CARLEEN PAYNE

Writing the Caribbean

The project of writing the Caribbean has a long history dating back to the period of European conquest and colonization in the late fifteenth century. The early accounts, focused primarily on the Spanish-colonized Caribbean, were not produced by professional historians but by conquistadores, government officials, and missionaries from whom the ideology of the conquest emerged. Christopher Columbus and his crew provided some of the earliest accounts which informed the narratives of subsequent writers. The inherently conquistadorial accounts were followed in the sixteenth and seventeenth centuries by more detailed descriptions of Spanish colonization and the consequences of the encounter with the indigenous peoples (Casas, 1520–61; Oveido, 1535; Martyr, 1530).

Interest in the colonies intensified as exclusive Spanish hegemony gave way to the incursion of other European colonizers and as English, Dutch, and French writers generated their own literature. The seventeenth and eighteenth centuries saw the emergence of texts by many resident planters and missionaries with first-hand knowledge of the Caribbean (Richard Ligon, 1657; Charles Leslie, 1739; Jean Baptiste du Tertre, 1667–71). These contemporary works focused on the settlement history of particular territories, with some attention to flora and fauna, economic resources, trade, the diverse experiences of the buccaneers, settlers, and indigenous peoples, and law and liberty. Other historical works appeared in the eighteenth century dealing with the colonies' general development and social evolution, including several local histories and special studies, for example, on the maroons. Arguably the three most influential works of this period were written by Guillaume [Abbé] Raynal ([1770] 1779), Edward Long (1774), and Bryan Edwards (1793). Since the eighteenth century was also the height of slavery and the slave trade, as well as wars for empire, these themes are amply reflected in the works of the period.

The nineteenth century was the age of the classical school of British historians, some of whom targeted the Caribbean for their discourses. Most supported the idea of the British empire and Britain's continued domination of so-called "inferior" races. Thomas Carlyle (1849), for example, vituperated the emancipated black. Most of the writers of the late nineteenth century, like Carlyle, Anthony Trollope (1860), and James Anthony Froude (1888), inveighed against emancipation and the liberty restored to the Africans/African-Caribbeans. They were decidedly imperialist in their view of post-slavery resistance, particularly the Morant Bay Rebellion.

The nineteenth century also saw the proliferation of local histories that provided various perspectives on post-slavery society in individual territories. Pan-Caribbean or regional histories and micro-studies of special themes such as migration and population growth, labor conditions and the condition of the sugar planters, also emerged. The dominant note in the still largely amateur writings from around 1880 to 1900 was imperialism: the justification, encouragement, defense, and apology for colonies. Even in the early twentieth century, authors like Charles Lucas (1902) and Rhodes Chair of Imperial History at London, A. P. Newton (1933), were still writing in the imperialist mode, and few challenges were forthcoming.

A change only became noticeable in the post-World War II period. The escalation of decolonization movements and the re-empowerment of non-Western states signaled a more democratic intellectual age. One decisive trend after 1945 was that the Euro-centric tendencies of the earlier works were increasingly overtaken by the revisionist approaches of a new generation of scholars such as Eric Williams (1944) and C. L. R. James (1963), who grounded their work in solid archival research. These Caribbean-born writers questioned the essentialism of the traditional historiography and master narrative imposed on former colonized peoples, and they introduced their own discursive practices. In the post-1970s in particular, there were renewed attempts – though not always successful – to dethrone the old intellectual absolutisms and introduce new interpretations of Caribbean history.

The history of the Caribbean continues to attract the attention of modern scholars on both sides of the Atlantic, and the historiography is now not only vast, but on the whole empirically rich, intellectually gripping, and conceptually contentious. The perspectives have not been unified; rather two distinct trends are still observable in the writings on the colonial Caribbean: one imperial/colonialist, the other distinctly revisionist and located firmly in the "creole"/black nationalist genre.

This chapter, drawing upon only a *sample* of the rich historical accounts (mostly the modern accounts) of the region, attempts to set out the main trends in the historiography of the British-colonized Caribbean since the seventeenth century when Britain joined Spain and other powers in the overseas colonization project. It begins with the writings about the indigenous peoples and ends with an engagement with historical developments up to 1865, including analyses of post-slavery labor migration and the momentous Morant Bay Rebellion. The events at Morant Bay did not, of course, signal the demise of colonialism in the region, though, because of the chronological focus of this anthology, our analysis necessarily stops long before the end of the colonial period. If anything, by eliminating the elective principle in the majority of colonies after 1865, Britain tightened her colonial grip on the region even further. The events at Morant Bay, nevertheless, represented a watershed period in the history of the colonized British Caribbean. By expanding Crown Colony government, Britain unleashed another spate of resistance activities that escalated into a full-scale decolonization movement by the 1930s, and ended in independence for some territories by the 1960s. The activism of the post-1865 period continued the pre-emancipation trend of violent and non-violent resistance that has so defined Caribbean history.

Writing the Indigenous Caribbeans

Before modern historians, conscious of the need to avoid the conceptual trap that the history of the Caribbean began with the arrival of Columbus, began to revisit and reinterpret the history of the indigenous peoples, the available accounts were those of the conquistadores, government officials, and missionaries. Accounts by Père Labat (1722) and Sir William Young (1795), who advocated the banishment of the "Black Caribs" from St. Vincent to Honduras, were particularly influential. For the most part, the seventeenth- and eighteenth-century works engaged in the project of mis/representation of the indigenes, dichotomizing Taino (Arawak) and Kalinago (Carib) into peaceful/docile and cannibalistic respectively. Their objective was to demonize the people of the eastern Caribbean and project them as uncivilized and barbaric in order to justify their military and spiritual subjugation. Post-conquest works exhibited a tendency to negate or minimize the role of the indigenous peoples in the advance of Caribbean modernity, presenting both text and sub-text that projected perceptions of the indigenous Caribbeans as a "problem" for colonial development and an obstacle to the European march to progress.

A few of the newer works have tried to destabilize many of the assumptions of the colonial historiography by highlighting the role of the indigenous people in the economic development of the region, in colonization and in resistance to the land appropriation designs of the colonizers. Philip Boucher (1992), for example, has cast great doubts on the accuracy of the term "cannibal" traditionally used by writers such as du Tertre and Labat to describe the Kalinago (Caribs), and he has focused readers' attention on the misinformation which had been previously used to construct the history of the indigenous people. Bernard Marshall (1973) and Hilary Beckles (1987) also remind us that the indigenes did not accept European colonization unproblematically but rather must be credited with pioneering the tradition of resistance that was carried on by enslaved and indentured peoples thereafter. Yet, there are very few studies that seek to theorize or specify their significant role in the social history of colonial and post-colonial societies. As Helen Seaman (1999) has stressed, most works continue to confine the indigenous people within conquistadorial perceptions and models, grounded in an uncritical acceptance of European Enlightenment agendas.

Thus, despite the revisionist deposits of the post-1992 period, myths of Taino (Arawak) docility remain; and the image of Kalinago (Carib) cannibalism continues to be a powerful conceptual construct that shapes opinions and attitudes. Philip Sherlock and Hazel Bennett's recent book, *The Story of the Jamaican People* (1997), for example, testifies to how historical representations of elites about subject people can find their way into texts of domination. This book, while setting out to tell the story of the Jamaican people from a well-needed Afro-centric perspective, falls short of its objectives, repeating old stereotypes about the indigenous and enslaved peoples.

Conquest and Colonization

All European colonists arriving in the region after the Columbus mission of 1492 considered it necessary to use their more developed military technology to subjugate the indigenous populations as a prerequisite to successful colonization. The results were tragic demographically; but the European social design of Atlantic modernity was centered around notions of military conquest, slavery, and cultural domination. Historians such as David Henige (1978) and Alvin Thompson (1987) have not only recounted the quantitative dimensions of the genocidal consequences of colonization, but also the complex commercial, political, and social relations established between

Amerindians and Europeans. Debates over precisely how many indigenous peoples were in the region and over the hierarchy of factors responsible for their decimation continue to rage, with Alfred Crosby (1972) giving primacy to the disastrous role of epidemic diseases. While the impact of diseases was catastrophic, however, the role of European cruelty and military designs should not be underestimated.

A fundamental aspect of European colonization was the "othering" of the indigenous peoples as justification for atrocities committed in the name of "civilization." Instead of looking positively at their agency, particularly their success in preventing Europeans from completely establishing their monopolistic economic system in the region when they introduced structural discontinuity, scholars such as Donald Akenson (1997) have written about the indigenous peoples as "problems" and "disasters" for European colonization. Emphases on European military superiority have resulted in the construction of the Caribbean as a colonized space and have effectively marginalized indigenous people's continuing social dynamism and command over the engine of development and creation.

Richard Ligon, Dalby Thomas (1690), and other seventeenth-century writers detailed ways in which colonization was made effective through military conquests, and settlements made permanent through economic development following the European mercantilist rather than the indigenous people's model. Professional historians provided more engaging studies by the 1970s, among them Richard Pares (1960), Richard Dunn (1972), and Richard Sheridan (1974). David Watts' monumental 1987 study facilitated an even greater comparative look at the region's early colonial history, while Jurgen Osterhammel (1996) interjected a refreshing theoretical analysis of the phenomenon of colonialism. Writers on conquest and colonization have also pointed to different dimensions of imperial warfare, especially the attempts of rival European powers to displace the Iberians and establish their own hegemony, the role of the buccaneers in facilitating the project of northwest Europeans, and the formation of resistant maroon enclaves. All concur that the Dutch were essential to the creation of the Atlantic systems and played a key role in reducing Spanish influence in the Caribbean.

Various authors have examined several levels of engagement with the financial system of colonialism. All agree that the planters' aim in the global mobilization of productive resources was to realize a surplus from the transfer of money into the purchase of land, laborers, and machinery. Tensions have been evident among economic historians, however, over the source of capital for investment in the colonial economy. The traditional view had been that it was external capital from the Dutch and from the various imperial centers that financed colonization and the establishment of sugar plantations. The debate over the capitalization of colonial enterprises has advanced somewhat over the years with assertions that local capital was much more fundamental than previously thought in the capitalization of the sugar industry. Arguing counter to Dunn, Robert Batie (1976), Nuala Zahedieh (1988), and Verene Shepherd (1988) have demonstrated that the pre-sugar era was much more profitable than traditionally argued and that the production of various staples, livestock, and buccaneering proceeds generated local income to plough into sugar plantations.

Establishing Slavery and the Plantation System

All European colonizing nations – with significant variation between them – were committed to slavery as the institution that determined social relations within colonial society. The northern Europeans, coming to the region at a time when the Spanish had settled the dispute between competing forms of social subjection, made a head-long rush into the chattel enslavement of Africans whenever and wherever it was finan-cially viable and socially necessary. As David Galenson (1984), Hilary Beckles (1989a), and others have shown, white servitude was tried for varying periods in most places, but with the development of the productive activities throughout the Caribbean, the enslavement of Africans was deemed critical to economic accumulation and the cul-tural imperatives of white supremacy.

It is the subject of slavery, perhaps more than any other, that has dominated histori-cal writing on the British-colonized Caribbean in the post-colonial period. Modern scholars such as Orlando Patterson (1969), Elsa Goveia (1965), Kamau Brathwaite (1971), and Barry Higman (1976, 1984) have built on the contemporary works of Ligon, Long, and Edwards, who provided detailed accounts of the structure of slavery and the sugar plantation system in the Caribbean. As the most overtly racist of the three, Long has, understandably, been subjected to intense criticism by historians, even as they continue to use his work for its wealth of empirical data on Jamaica. Elsa Goveia (1956) and Brathwaite (1971) problematized its essential racism and scholars, such as Lucille Mathurin-Mair (1986) and Veronica Gregg (1995), have exposed Long's sexism.

The modern works on slavery illustrate the dynamic relations between modes of production and social life. The slave superstructure has fascinated scholars perhaps to a greater degree than their economic substructures. Thus, debates on race and color relations, health and mortality, religion, recreational culture, women, family organiza-tion and kinship patterns, as well as the endemic problems of social reproduction, are represented in many different works. The transformation of the ideology of a multi-ethnic slavery to one fixed on black Africans has attracted considerable attention, with arguments over whether racism or economic imperatives should be accorded primacy. As part of this debate, Beckles and Andrew Downes (1987) have shown that planta-tion agriculture in the Caribbean had not always been associated with enslaved Afri-cans, and that, in fact, early Africans, like working-class whites, were at one time classified as indentured servants. Thus, the historical dichotomization of blacks as slaves and whites as indentured laborers seems inaccurate. The role of enslaved indigenous peo-ples in the development of the economic resources of the Caribbean after 1492 has also been emphasized.

This begs the question: if slavery was multi-ethnic originally, why did it attach itself so parasitically and exclusively to black Africans, and how did it become linked to racism? Early explanations rooted in the climatic theory that, unlike whites, blacks were more suitable to labor on tropical plantations have been long discounted. Eric Williams' (1944) explanation for the rise of large-scale slavery points to the transition to large-scale sugar cane cultivation, the decline of the indigenous population, and the increasing scarcity and high cost of white servants at a time when enslaved Africans were becoming more affordable for planters. Thus, slavery did not have its origins in Eurocentric racist ideology but in the specific circumstances of the development of a global market economy. Williams' materialist thesis, however, has not been received with enthusiasm by those who insist that chattel enslavement for blacks was rooted in far more than rational economic choice to maximize profits.

The success of the colonization project depended on the export of agricultural commodities to provide raw material for Europe's industries. The plantation was considered the most efficient basis of the agrarian export economy and large-scale slavery the most efficient means of labor exploitation on the large plantation. Researchers such as Dunn (1972), Sheridan (1974), and Beckles and Downes (1987) have offered explanations for the uneven pace of development in the use of enslaved labor throughout the region and for the relations between differential growth and patterns of economic activity. The usual explanations for the uneven pace of development have been imperial policies, the decline of the settler populations, indigenous resistance, and the slow availability of capital for investment. Scholars have also looked at the internal characteristics of the sugar plantation, including the organization of slave labor, demographic features of the laboring population, the production process, and aspects of sugar technology. Barry Higman (1976, 1984), in particular, has looked at the occupational distribution of the British Caribbean slave population, demonstrating that there was no homogeneous slave experience. Rather, the enslaved worked in a variety of physical environments and were engaged in a wide range of economic activities. Higman's analysis of plantation maps and plans has also shown quite clearly that while social control was an important variable in the spatial organization of units, movement minimization seems to have been uppermost in the location of fields, factories, and other estate buildings (1988).

As the creation of the Atlantic world as an integrated economy rested heavily on the enormous movement of Africans into the Americas, studies on sources, prices, traders, and the demographic profile of captives have proliferated. The quantitative aspects of the transatlantic trade in African captives have continued to generate an enormous body of scholarship, and the debates have grown more contentious and racialized over the years. Nineteenth-century abolitionists had estimated that between 15 and 25 million Africans were exported over the whole period of the trade. Philip Curtin (1969), believing this to be an exaggeration, came up with an estimate of 9.6 million, 6 million of whom were exported in the period 1701–1810. Another 15 percent, he argued, died before reaching the Americas. Most other scholars believe that Curtin's figure is too low and have accepted a figure of around 11–12 million. Joseph Inikori (1982, 1992) has gone even further, estimating that over the entire period of the transatlantic trade (1492–1870), 15.4 million were traded globally, with 13.3 million being traded to the Americas, and 10–20 percent probably dying before arrival. Although his estimates have been regarded as inflated by some, the Nigerian scholar maintains that a more accurate figure than Curtin's is possible and has increased Curtin's figures by 49.2 percent on the British trade from 1701 to 1807.

Less contentious than the numbers game between Curtin, Inikori, and others has been the debate over the origins of the enslaved Africans. There is still a lingering discussion over whether or not planters requested specific ethnicities for different Caribbean territories and whether those imported to Jamaica were more innately rebellious than those shipped to Barbados. Most accept that there was more multi-ethnic mixture in individual territories than previously thought. Ever increasing attention has been paid to the resistance on the Middle Passage and the sexual disparity of the trade, since an average of 38 percent of the total numbers shipped to the Americas comprised females. Explanations for the sexual disparity in the trade continue to fuel debates among feminist and other scholars and there is still an absence of consensus. What is clear from the works of Janet Momsen (1988), Barbara Bush (1960), and Hilary McD.

Beckles (1999), however, is that the disparity was not linked to any male sensitivity about women's capability with respect to arduous agricultural labor. Rather, planters' initial preference for men and high cost and demand for females within Africa have been offered as more convincing explanations.

While historians like Herbert Klein (1978) have produced studies of the Middle Passage, accounts from those who made the horrendous journey from Africa remain comparatively few. A few slave narratives, most notably those of Mary Prince and Olaudah Equiano – which expose the experience of slavery in the Americas – have been unearthed by scholars such as Moira Ferguson (1987) and Paul Edwards (1988). UNESCO's *Slave Voices* (Beckles and Shepherd, 1999) and Shepherd and Beckles' edited collection, *Caribbean Slavery in the Atlantic World* (2000), have reintroduced the subaltern's voices into the Caribbean discourse of anti-slavery.

Slave Demography

The quantitative study of the trade in African captives has predictably created an explosion of scholarship in the demographic history of slavery, in particular, problems of fertility, mortality, and population growth/decline. Enslavers in the Caribbean were caught in the web of a major dilemma. As rational entrepreneurs they sought to maximize profits by reducing the cost of productive inputs, and expenditures on those enslaved were suppressed to subsistence levels. At the same time, however, the protection of property rights in chattel was a top priority that required carefully policy formulation and implementation. The effective social maintenance of the enslaved meant that the daily management of subsistence and health care could not be left to chance. Those enslaved had to be properly nourished and medically assisted if they were to be productive workers. At the same time the impact of class and race prejudice upon economic thinking oftentimes led to subsistence levels being located below what was required to maintain general health and population growth.

The 1970s and 1980s saw the emergence of an impressive array of demographic bio-histories which have widened the empirical base of knowledge on the internal demographic characteristics of Caribbean enslaved populations. Much of this was generated in response to the need to explain the differential demographic experiences of Caribbean and North American slaves; for while the slave population in the USA grew by natural means, that of much of the Caribbean was not self-sustaining. North American explanations have centered around treatment of the enslaved population, but Higman (1976), Kenneth Kiple (1984), and Sheridan (1985), among others, have demonstrated that the origins of those enslaved (creole vs. African-born), poor health and nutrition, color, sex ratio, work regime, age, family structure, and the anti-natalist strategies of women contributed to the general inability of Caribbean enslaved populations, in particular those engaged in the sugar culture, to reproduce themselves naturally until the closing years of the slavery system. Scholars have also shown that the pro-natalist policies of the post-1807 ameliorative period were doomed to fail as long as the majority of enslaved women labored in the field. And some practiced gynecological resistance. Planter strategies required that women's productive capacity not be sacrificed for reproduction; between the two there was a clear incompatibility. While the demographic historians are mostly agreed on the differential roles of diet, other material conditions, and the work environment on the fertility and mortality experiences, skepticism still abounds over the feminist claim of gynecological resistance. But the references to abortion and women's reluctance to reproduce in the 1750–83 journals of Thomas Thistlewood (Hall, 1989), and the writings of the planter Matthew Gregory Lewis (1834) respectively cannot be ignored. More empirical data are needed, however, before this question can be settled satisfactorily.

The cultural life of the enslaved – their ability to re-create and maintain family within the restrictions of chattel enslavement, their relationship with owners, and their attempt to become autonomous economic agents – have all been major concerns for historians and social scientists. Orlando Patterson (1969), Brathwaite (1971), Sidney Mintz and Douglas Hall (1970) showed that the culture of marketing emerged among blacks as a common expression, and material and social conditions on the plantations as well as in the towns made it particularly attractive. Such own-account activities allowed the enslaved to improve the quality of their diets in a context of general malnutrition as well as to possess property in a system that also defined them as property, and it offered them time to travel and to attempt to normalize their social lives under generally restrictive circumstances. These "benefits," however, had to be militantly pursued; and it is here that women in particular displayed great tenacity. The right to possession and open engagement in the market as autonomous buyers and sellers was aggressively demanded, and forms of collective bargaining, usually associated with industrial wage workers, emerged among the enslaved as O. Nigel Bolland (1995), Mary Turner (1995), and others demonstrate. Not surprisingly, some owners acquiesced to the enslaved's demand rather than always relying on the coercive power of the whip.

Research into the structure and life of the family of the enslaved has also expanded since the 1960s, with differences in interpretations emerging between structuralists, who claim that slavery constrained cultural expression including family formation, and class theorists whose view is that slavery allowed the enslaved some autonomy in constructing kinship and other forms of culture. Contemporary observations denying the ability of enslaved women to establish and maintain families on account of their so-called "pathological promiscuity" carried over into later works. Anthropologist M. G. Smith (1953), for example, suggested that it would have been impossible for the enslaved to establish stable marriages because they lacked the kinship and lineage groups to sanction and give permanence to unions. Patterson's work similarly suggested that the symbolic estrangement from kin and the corresponding social illegitimacy of the enslaveds' natal ties precluded family formation (1982). The references to promiscuity in the works of some scholars, however, (e.g. Patterson, 1969), are deeply offensive to African-Caribbean women who continue to be painted with that particular brush of slavery. Happily, Higman (1991) and Michael Craton (1979), basing their conclusions on solid quantitative analysis rather than on racist and sexist notions, argued that family, even the nuclear type, was prevalent in the later years of slavery in the British-colonized Caribbean. In keeping with the need for a reorientation of perspectives and redefinition of terms, Beckles (1989b) and Bush (1990) stress the multidimensionality of the family types among the enslaved and discount early perceptions of their inability to sustain lasting unions.

Slavery Outside of the Sugar Estates

Recent research reveals the pitfalls of the wholesale application of the plantation economy model, by economists, sociologists, and historians, to the Caribbean. The plantation economy model negates the fact that diversification is the real Caribbean experience. During the period of enslavement, those without the capital to invest in sugar turned to other ways of making a living. Despite the desire of colonizers to plant sugar all over the region, the physical environment did not always cooperate. Thus, crops like coffee and cotton thrived; as did livestock farming. The pre-conquest economic model that Europeans tried to exterminate and reconfigure upon conquest, therefore continued in many places like Jamaica and the Windward Islands. The implications were internal capital generation, internal trade, and a low rate of absenteeism among non-sugar producers not engaged in the export trade. Higman (1976, 1984) and Shepherd (1988, 1998b) are among those seeking to pluralize the study of slave work and ownership to incorporate research on non-sugar properties (devoted to coffee, cotton, forest products, livestock, food), which employed enslaved labor and gave small capital investors an alternative to sugar estate ownership. Indeed, *Slavery without Sugar* (Shepherd, 1998b) – which secured contributors such as Pedro Welch and Simon Smith – is one attempt to challenge the fact that Caribbean socioeconomic history has displayed a totalizing tendency, focusing on the sugar sector and ignoring other sectors regarded as less important.

While not attempting to downplay the overall brutality of the system, these scholars conclude that slavery was less regimented on non-sugar properties, though the work was no less hard. Gang labor was less marked, and tasks were more individualized, with many of those who labored on non-sugar properties working unsupervised. On Caribbean non-sugar properties, those enslaved tended to live in smaller units. The criteria for allocating tasks to enslaved labor seemed similar to those on sugar plantations. Gender was the determinant in all occupations except field work, where age and color were more important. It does not appear that the attitudes of the enslavers towards bondsmen and women varied much from those of sugar planters. Whether the enslaved served their bondage on sugar or non-sugar properties, or whether their enslavers were male or female, white or colored, made little difference to the brutalizing conditions of enslavement that resulted from the existence of a pro-slavery ideology among the slaveholding elite. The journals of the Lincolnshire slave manager, Thomas Thistlewood, and the narrative of Mary Prince provide ample evidence, from both sides of slavery, of the brutalizing regimes and attitudes of those who were not always engaged in sugar production. Furthermore, the values of those property-owners who were involved in diversified production, even those born in the Caribbean (creoles), paralleled those of the sugar planters. Thus, exploiting the resources of the Caribbean and exporting profits if possible to facilitate an elite lifestyle in the metropole were unifying ideals of sugar and non-sugar proprietors. There was no dichotomy, in other words, between colonial and creole.

Slavery has been most closely associated with agricultural labor in the Caribbean. But beyond the farms and plantations there was a minority who functioned in urban regimes. Higman (1976, 1984), Beckles (1998b), and Welch (1998) have shown that the urban enslaved men worked as skilled laborers, sellers, transport and wharf workers, fishermen, and general laborers. The even larger group of enslaved females had a narrower range of occupations, working as domestic servants, washerwomen, seamstresses, and sellers. Interestingly, as Hilary Beckles demonstrated (1993), the majority of urban enslavers also tended to be female.

Women, Gender Analysis, and Slavery

Recent scholarship, attempting to compensate for past discursive short-sightedness, has emphasized that there was no homogeneous slave experience and that analyses of slave conditions, and, indeed, of slave society, must take gender differentiation into consideration. Pioneering researchers Brathwaite (1971), Mathurin (1974), Mathurin-Mair (1975), along with Higman (1976, 1984), Beckles (1989b, 1999), and Bush (1990) emphasize that women did not live the way men did, and slavery as a social system of oppression impacted on them differently. Enslaved women, for example, despite being under-represented in the transatlantic slave trade, formed the majority of the field gangs and worked as hard as men did. As Mathurin-Mair points out, there was a sharp differentiation in the lives of women of different ethnic, class, and color groups and little solidarity existed across these lines, particularly because some white women as well as some black and colored women themselves owned chattel.

As Beckles (1999) and Brereton (1994) show, white women were active contributors to the development of a pro-slavery ideology in the Caribbean and were assigned special roles within the slave system, which in turn determined their experiences as free persons within the gender order. European racism dictated that the progeny of these women could not be enslaved because although white women could reproduce the slavery ideology in order to protect the myth of white supremacy, their bodies were not allowed to reproduce slaves. Black women – both free and enslaved, field-hands and domestics – also experienced society in fundamentally different ways, though categories were not always clear, and edges invariably blurred. Brereton's exploration of the nineteenth-century diaries and writings of white women like Maria Nugent and A. C. Carmichael reveals that they displayed little solidarity with black women, and were just as likely to be racist and sexist as their male counterparts.

Social Aspects of Slavery and Slave Society

The social and political organization of slave society continues to be studied, though apparently it is no longer considered fashionable to write political/constitutional history. There are no recent works to compare with political histories like Hume Wrong's (1969), although Moore and Wilmot's edited collection *Before and After 1865: Education, Politics, and Regionalism in the Caribbean* (1998) may serve to re-energize that field. Since the 1960s, however, interest has shifted to politics at the grassroots level, manifested more in slave resistance studies than in centers of government. A feature of the research of the 1960s and 1970s was its attempt to understand the internal dynamics of Caribbean society of the eighteenth and nineteenth centuries – in particular, the role of "creolization" and cultural change on that society. Kamau Brathwaite's (1971) view was that after years of colonization and settlement of different culture groups in Caribbean society, a "creole" society had emerged, one that was neither purely African nor purely European, but a blend of the two. Over the years, vigorous polemics have developed over this theory. Bolland (1998) is among those who have subjected Brathwaite's "creole society" model to intense debate, his main criticism being that the model is too dichotomous. Yet the inherent idea that Caribbean society was not held together totally by force is more appealing to many than alternatives like the "plantation society" model advanced by George Beckford (1972), which gives a greater role to coercion than consensus.

The dynamics of color, gender, race, and class within the Caribbean have traditionally been popular foci of historical research. This interest is due, in part, to the fact that wherever blacks were slaves and whites were masters, a prominent feature of society was the existence of people of mixed racial ancestry, their numbers and rate of growth varying according to situational demographic, ideological, and economic factors. Researchers like Brathwaite (1971), Edward Cox (1984), and Carl Campbell (1992a) have unearthed quantitative and qualitative data respecting the size of the free colored population, the restrictions placed upon them, their economic and social roles, and their attitude to the chattel enslavement of their kin. Beckles (1999) and Boa (1993), among others, have interjected a greater gender perspective into the study of free people of color, showing the ways in which their economic and social world departed from those of their male counterparts. Their ownership of enslaved blacks and their participation in the suppression of slave rebellions continue to be complicated aspects of their history.

In the complex and dynamic order that constituted slave society, marginality necessarily extended to other groups beside the enslaved. Small farmers, women, free non-sugar producers, and landless whites felt in varying ways the effects of economic alienation and social oppression. Gender, cultural, and racial domination also underpinned the white supremacy ideology of elite slaveholders. Not much new insight has been shed on these issues, especially on race relations, since authors like Goveia (1965), Brathwaite (1971), and Beckford (1972), to name a few, studied the racial dynamics of the slave/creole/plantation society. However, attention to the role of gender has gone a long way to reveal the ways in which racism combined with sexism to determine the relations between white men and black women on the one hand, and white women and black/colored women on the other. Nowhere is this relationship more evident than in Douglas Hall's 1989 edited version of the Thistlewood Journals. We also now know that sexual contacts between black men and white women were not unheard of, and that, as Beckles' 1993 work has revealed, Caribbean racist society during slavery ensured that white women reproduced free, instead of slave, offspring. In general, historians still concur that there was a racial and authoritarian hierarchy and that racism helped to keep this firmly in place long after slavery was abolished.

The matter of slaveholding is now being revisited, with scholars like Beckles (1993), Trevor Burnard (1991), and Kathleen Butler (1995) stressing that slaveholding was not an exclusive white, male project, though it was overwhelmingly so. Women – freed black, free colored, whites – were slaveholders and managers; and they were not necessarily kinder slave managers than men. Free colored women were described as harsh slaveowners and they were among the first to lose their laborers in 1838. The narrative of Mary Prince demonstrates unambiguously the cruelty of white women who were slaveholders or managers. Butler's pathbreaking research also indicates that while, on the whole, women tended to own smaller properties than men, there were some very large female landowners in the Caribbean who acquired and managed properties in their own right.

The final two issues which have attracted the energies of historians of the slavery period are resistance and emancipation processes. Resistance effectively indicates how most Africans felt about their entrapment and enslavement. The evidence of resistance

– from marronage (land and sea) to armed revolts – is compelling and speaks to the
existence of the slave trade and slavery as existing within a context of endemic mass
opposition (Mathurin-Mair, 1975; Barry Gaspar, 1985; Craton, 1982; Beckles, 1989b/
1999; Bush, 1990; Shepherd, 2000). The enslaved (Africans and creoles), free colored,
poor whites, and indigenous peoples constantly opposed internal sociopolitical arrangements. Indeed, historians are now in agreement that in the Caribbean anti-slavery revolt was endemic; it has even been suggested by Beckles (1982) that the period
of slavery was characterized primarily by one protracted war launched by those enslaved against their enslavers.

Three new trends in the study of slave resistance include: firstly, the incorporation of
women's resistant behavior into the discourse of anti-slavery; secondly, the attempt to
identify texts written/narrated by the enslaved which would provide more accurate
versions of resistance; and thirdly, a broadening of the discussion of resistance to include those enslaved on non-sugar properties such as livestock farms. The focus on
women and resistance is based on the belief that the ideology of anti-slavery was not
gender-free. While the struggles of the slavery period were inherently collective in that
they were conceived in the consciousness of the communities inhabited by the enslaved, the gender relations of slavery determined actions in many ways. The system of
slavery sought to degrade women and womanhood in ways that forced aspects of their
resistance to assume specific forms. The use of rape as a brutal form of control and
punishment, for example, targeted women more than men as far we know. Certainly
most of those like Shepherd (1988), Hall (1989), and Beckles (1999) who have studied the Thistlewood Journals cannot help but be confronted by the violence of this
slaveholder towards women, though Sherlock and Bennett (1997) manage to ignore
this aspect, choosing instead to project what they seem to believe was the benevolent
side of Thistlewood.

Maternity and fertility were also placed at the core of strategies for plantation survival, and so women's resistance to these policies, as Mathurin-Mair (1975), Gaspar
(1985), Beckles (1989b), and Bush (1990) have shown, meant that their opposition
to slavery was probably more broadly based than previously believed. Furthermore, it
can be argued that women's leadership of the resistance to the enslavers' attempts to
disintegrate the slave communities culturally and morally provided much of the organizational strength necessary for ideological and armed resistance. Resistance was
not confined to sugar estates. Urban enslaved people and those enslaved on non-sugar
properties also used various strategies to undermine slavery. Interestingly, as Shepherd
(1988, 2000) has shown for Jamaica, sugar planters, conscious of the potential of pen
slaves to foment rebellions, tried to insulate their own bondspeople from contact with
those slaves – an impossibility given the symbiotic relations between pens and plantations.

Many Caribbean scholars promote slave agency and capitalist forces above the traditional religious/humanitarian explanations of the Reginald Coupland school (1933)
in the study of emancipation. Those who link capitalism with anti-slavery argue that
capitalism promoted slavery as part of its primitive accumulation and removed it subsequently as part of a systemic rationalization in search of efficiency gains. Eric Williams
(1944) and C. L. R. James (1963) have been in the forefront of this thesis. First, they
stated that both the slave and sugar trades were lucrative and that Caribbean economies provided a significant amount of the critical surplus capital that propelled Eng-

land and France into self-sustained economic growth in the eighteenth and nineteenth centuries. Second, they argue that with the ability of European capitalism to reproduce internally its own surplus capital, largely associated with the ascendancy of industrial capital over merchant finance in the late eighteenth and early nineteenth centuries, came the economic context for the reduced economic significance of the British-colonized Caribbean. Declining importance and adverse market forces led to a long-term crisis in the Caribbean economy and hence the movement towards abolition. Not all have accepted this materialist explanation of emancipation. Over these theses, rigorous polemics with transatlantic dimensions have developed, with scholars like Seymour Drescher (1977) opposing the thesis which links economic decline (especially decreased profit from Caribbean agricultural regimes) with the abolition of slavery. The economic historians do not now seem to dispute the issue of profitability as scholars like A. P. Thomas did in the late 1960s, and the focus has shifted to the length of the period of profitability, the level of profits, the use of profits, and the chronology of declining profitability. The view that it was the abolition of slavery that created economic decline, and thus this was the fault of the freed African Caribbeans, has not found favor with cultural/nationalist historians like Selwyn Carrington (1991), Beckles (1984, 1990), and Inikori (1992).

Whatever the explanations, it was clear by 1831, when a major slave revolt erupted in Jamaica, that if emancipation did not come from above through British legislation, it would come from below through slave resistance. In 1833 the Emancipation Act was passed, and in 1834 freedom (albeit partial) became a reality for those enslaved in the British-colonized Caribbean.

Post-Slavery British Caribbean Historiography: Continuity or Change?

The passing of the Abolition Act in 1833 and the introduction of the apprenticeship system in 1834 provided new areas for historical research. The wealth of ideological viewpoints that Gordon Lewis (1983) attributes to the region has ensured that the historiography is continually being revised to reflect the changing perspectives of the burgeoning group of historians concerned with this crucial aspect of Caribbean history. Contemporary observers, for instance, were largely concerned with the great event of emancipation and particularly its economic outcomes for the planter class. But with the escalation of nationalism in the region in the twentieth century, histories written in what William Green (1993) describes (and opposes) as the creole genre have gained currency.

The nature of emancipation has received considerable attention, not surprisingly, since interpretations of contemporary society and economy rest to a great extent upon perceptions of what actually transpired at the onset of freedom. The current trend is to question idealistic concepts of freedom endorsed by earlier historians and to demonstrate that it was not actualized in the same way for all people. Contributors to Beckles and Shepherd's *Caribbean Freedom* (1993) take the view that emancipation was a protracted process that had to be negotiated by descendants of ex-slaves well into the twentieth century.

No matter how freedom is conceived, dichotomous models based upon variables of fundamental continuity and change emerge, seeking to problematize the idea that emancipation was in the final analysis a revolutionary measure. While few historians would deny that legal freedom opened up opportunities for pursuing a life independent of the plantation, some have questioned the time-honored divide between slavery and emancipation. An anthology edited by Turner (1995) demonstrates that the wage slaves were faced with the continuance of exploitation and oppression in the post-slavery era. Freedmen and women were enmeshed in a dialectical struggle with the large landholders and resorted to traditional and innovative methods of resistance, including industrial bargaining and violent confrontation (Craton, 1988; Wilmot, 1986, 1995).

Despite this perspective there is a general consensus that emancipation did transform the nature of their lives in such drastic ways that altogether it constituted a revolutionary experience. After all, the legislation that ended slavery substituted a wage labor system for unpaid labor, and removed the legal authority that had enabled a minority to exercise arbitrary power over the lives and activities of the majority.

Although specialized studies on apprenticeship – the transitional work regime that preceded full freedom – would await the development of more stringent academic standards in the twentieth century, several sources by contemporary observers have proven to be invaluable to researchers. Abolitionists Joseph Sturge and Thomas Harvey, who toured the region in 1837, published a candid account of what they considered a little more than mitigated slavery largely based on coercion and corrupt administration. Sturge and Harvey's shrewd onsite observation and unprecedented interviews with the apprentices provided ammunition for more modern studies on the free order, which conclude that apprenticeship was a failed experiment.

The apprenticeship process (1834–8) has also engaged the attention of professional historians, with most debating its necessity and failure. While W. L. Mathieson's treatment of the character and working of apprenticeship (1926) was spoiled by his unbridled racism, W. L. Burn's *Emancipation and Apprenticeship* (1937) provided an exhaustive and still useful coverage of the role of the stipendiary magistrates – the architects of freedom under the free order. However, the preoccupation of the two British academics with imperial policymaking and its repercussions allowed for only a top-down look at a system which is increasingly exposed from the bottom up as little more than a cosmetic modification of slavery. Wilmot (1984) and Thomas Holt (1992) have been among those who have shown the ways in which apprenticed women brought the system into disrepute, showcasing, for example, the conditions on the treadmills in the prisons. Apprenticeship, conceived in an unreflectively masculine gender, was doomed to fail, particularly since apprenticed women's conditions gave much ammunition to the anti-slavery and anti-apprenticeship forces.

The florescence of social history over the past few decades has been amenable to an exploration of the implications of freedom for the black majority and has served to destabilize some of the early assumptions of Mathieson and Burn. And while there are no post-slavery narratives comparable to those for the slavery era, several accounts have surfaced which allow a glimpse into the motivations and behavior of the working population both before and just after full emancipation. Revisionist historians Woodville Marshall (1993) and Wilmot (1986) managed to mine sources that facilitate a recovery of workers' voices and experiences and have framed the discourse on apprenticeship and anti-apprenticeship within the articulated hopes and expectations of the freed people. Although both writers conclude that the anticipated revolution did not mate-rialize, their overwhelming concern is with the black strategists who possessed their own aspirations toward a new way of life and acted – whether through wage bargain-ing, absenteeism, or political struggle – to secure their goals.

The post-slavery period – which represented something of a watershed in Caribbean history – has been subjected to even greater academic scrutiny. Colonialist concerns with "free society" have been largely espoused by a continuing white male stream of nineteenth-century history-writers or British sojourners who shared the values and concerns of the traditional land-holding class. William Gardner's (1874) and Edward Underhill's (1970) optimistic assessment of post-slavery society was based on the con-viction that blacks now faced the prospect of liberation from what Gardner suggests was their "degraded heathenism." Not surprisingly, pro-planter historians embraced a racialized project of acculturation that included concessions to the patriarchal ideol-ogy of men as breadwinners and women as dependent housewives. Ironically, they were inclined to blame post-slavery misfortunes on the alleged inefficiency of the newly de-feminized workforce.

The nineteenth-century works concerned with the immediate socioeconomic im-pact of emancipation expressed sympathy for an elite class ruined by the actions and new mobility of the emancipated. Thomas Carlyle drew a picture of the once-flourish-ing sugar industry lying idle while the freed people happily consumed pumpkins (1849). This myth of the lazy Negro otherwise referred to as "Quashie" was subsequently propagated by Anthony Trollope who similarly asserted that blacks' idea of emancipa-tion was freedom to lie in the sun and imbibe breadfruit and yams (1860). But perhaps the most controversial exhibition came from traveling writer Froude who predicted the demise of the colonies should the British adopt a hands-off policy, and he sup-ported this conclusion by repeating the reactionary opinions of his planter hosts (1897). This hegemonic discourse that tended towards the denigration of blacks provoked an equally impassioned counter-discourse by pioneers of the black intellectual tradition in the anglophone Caribbean.

In an 1889 work satirically titled *Froudacity*, Trinidadian schoolmaster J. J. Thomas challenged and summarily dismissed charges that black acquisition of land in the post-emancipation era signified nothing more than a relapse into "barbarism." The in-tensely analytical Thomas drew attention to the Oxford professor's ignorance of the region and reminded his then largely British audience of the Caribbean people's ac-complishments both during and beyond the post-slavery period. Half a century later, another Oxford graduate, Eric Williams (1966), exposed the pseudo-scientific racism of Carlyle, Froude, and others of their ilk. The tendency of the first black professional historian of the anglophone Caribbean to use his scholarship to castigate British Caribbeanists for their biased historical interpretations represented a turning point from the previously dominant imperial perspective to a more democratic approach.

But William Green (1986) – the most outspoken critic of this creolization of Carib-bean history – has since provided an interpretation of emancipation in the imperial mold. In keeping with the title of his work, *British Slave Emancipation* (1976) is primarily concerned with the evolution of political and economic relations between Britain and the colonies in the post-slavery era. Although this popular text purports to include an examination of salient aspects of anglophone Caribbean life, black agency is subordinated to his empathetic portrayal of the planter class whom he identifies as the victims of emancipation. Like the intransigent planters, he upholds the conviction that the sugar plantation was absolutely necessary for the welfare of the post-slavery Caribbean.

An explosion of historical research has further expanded and pluralized the post-slavery historiography particularly as it pertains to blacks' response to emancipation. An issue that has received much scholarly attention is the controversial exodus of formerly enslaved from the plantations after 1838. The pioneering works of Hugh Paget (1945) and Rawle Farley (1953) had laid to rest stereotypical ideas of the free village settlements as escape hatches, with forecasts of freed people's desire for personal liberty and their own economic advantage. However, in a rare instance of auto-criticism, Douglas Hall articulated the modified view (1978) that freed people had initially preferred to stay close to the estates where they could exercise choice but later withdrew in protest against the inequities of early freedom. Woodville Marshall's reconsideration of the issue (1991) postulated that neither the conventional pull considerations nor Hall's push explanation is entirely adequate to characterize this post-slavery adaptation. Michel-Rolph Trouillot's case study on Dominica (1984) supports the need for exploration of post-slavery rural society which reveal that freed people were more likely to maintain an active (though part-time) role in estate production, even while they pursued their own-account activities.

While the study of land in post-slavery society continues to occupy a prominent place in the revisionist literature, there is a greater tendency towards detailed examinations of the lives of the laboring majority. This historiographical shift was already evident in William Sewell's *Ordeal of Free Labor* (1861, repr. 1968), which portrayed the newly freed as an industrious people whose independent farming activities would be the salvation of the post-slavery economy. Sidney Mintz (1974) has also revolutionized our understanding of a proto-peasantry nurtured in the crevices of the slave plantation and reconstituted in the post-slavery era. Hall (1959, 1978), Marshall (1993), Eisner (1961), and Curtin (1955) provided compelling portraits of a resilient peasantry in competition with their former enslavers, and have concluded that black landholders' engagement in export crop production led to the further diversification of the original plantation economy after 1838.

The historiography heralding the triumph of the peasantry and focusing on land as a contested terrain has been tempered in recent years by increased sensitivity to changing patterns of land tenure. Shepherd's research on livestock farms (1988) as well as Marshall's (1965) and Howard Johnson's (1991) work on varieties of sharecropping in the Windward Islands and Bahamas all point to the fact that workers engaged in a broader process of land exploitation than the peasantry studies reveal. A budding concern with arbitrary typology has informed Richard Frucht's (1967) argument that in small territories like Nevis, Dominica, and Tobago, shareholders were "part-peasants, part proletarians" since they combined peasant-like means of production with proletarian relations of production. Fraser's "fictive peasantry" essay (1981) argues that while independent farming sectors existed in patches throughout the Anglophone Caribbean, the term "peasant" can only best be applied to Haiti.

One virtual casualty of the emphasis on empirical data and social science techniques has been Merivale's (1841) and Green's (1976) classificatory paradigm linking land availability and population density to settlement patterns after emancipation. Bolland

(1981) took issue with Green's high, medium, and low density categories and demonstrated (with reference to Belize) that availability of land did not always translate into economic independence for the formerly enslaved. According to Bolland, an often overlooked but key determinant was institutional rigidity, particularly as the elite continued to resort to a continued control of land and economic power in order to secure control over both the land and the working population. While William Green's (1984, 1986) predictable response has been to warn against the perils of looking at proprietor/labor relations through the lens of dialectical analysis, Bolland's thesis is more consistent with increasing scholarly recognition of conflict as one of the most pressing challenges of emancipation.

Another issue that is increasingly receiving scholarly attention is the nature of proprietors' responses to what they perceived as a "labor problem." Some of the leading historians of multi-ethnic labor migration from places such as India, China, and Madeira, beginning in the late 1830s, illustrate with the greatest clarity how everywhere freedom meant the reproduction of the class struggle within the nexus of a new legal status for the freed (Laurence, 1971, 1994; Look Lai, 1993; Shepherd, 1994). Indeed, after studying recruitment, the conditions aboard ships, the mortality rates on estates, the poor repatriation policies, the transformation of indentured labor migration into a form of settler colonization, and the gender discriminatory policies and abuses of women, many scholars of Indian immigration have been forced to agree with Hugh Tinker's conclusion (1974) that the adoption of Indian indentureship was a new form of slavery.

To be sure, revisionists like David Northrup (1995) and Pieter Emmer (1985) have challenged the neo-slavery thesis, focusing on the economic rationale of emigrants and their material gains in the colonies. The lack of focus on gender differences in the early works on migration has now largely been corrected with scholars like Reddock (1993) and Shepherd (1993, 1999) detailing the experiences of female immigrants. While not dismissing the accounts of women suffering spousal abuse, studies are now becoming available that reveal that few were confined to a strictly domestic life. Reddock (1993) has pointed out that the wage-earning ability of the predominantly single Indian women in Trinidad allowed them to take control of their own lives. Emmer (1985) argues that a majority of Indian women in Suriname used contract labor to increase their status, though Hoefte (1998), Reddock (1993), and Shepherd (1993) have questioned Emmer's optimistic conclusion.

Whatever the outcome for immigrants, few writers would deny that the plantation system in Trinidad & Tobago and colonial Guyana survived and expanded as a result of the large-scale importation of laborers. In fact, some researchers like Jay Mandle (1973), using the methods and theoretical framework of economics, have attempted to show that post-slavery economic adjustments can best be understood in light of the plantation legacy. Veront Satchell's statistical analysis of land transactions in Jamaica (1990) reveals that despite the initial proliferation of "free villages," a significant shift in ownership patterns resulted in the consolidation of large-holdings in the latter part of the nineteenth century. Adamson's Guyana study (1972) emphasizes the ability of the planter class to employ fiscal, technological, and political strategies to frustrate the development of the peasantry. Still there is resistance to attempts by modern Caribbean political economists, Beckford and Lloyd Best (1968), to popularize the overarching (if contested) plantation economy/society model for the post-slavery period. Planter resistance to technological changes and international competition brought on by the passing of the 1846 Sugar Duties Act prevented the plantation sector from maintaining dominance in all but a few territories after 1838.

Benefits did not only accrue to enterprising indentured workers and planters in the post-slavery agricultural economy. A recent essay by Brereton (1999) on the under-explored phenomenon of the post-slavery withdrawal of female labor from estates al-ludes to women's involvement in domestic food production and marketing, as well as child rearing. Jean Besson's (1984) fieldwork on the minuscule hereditary plots of family land cultivated by women similarly identifies the phenomenon as both a way of strengthening family ties and a mechanism of resistance to the plantation. The increas-ing body of literature on freed women reflects the influence of sociological theories on the gender division of labor and has gone a long way in replacing notions of familial patriarchy with the view that Caribbean women outside the upper and middle strata constructed their own way of life.

Although there are few studies devoted entirely to society and culture in the post-slavery era, there is increasing consensus that the post-slavery attempts of the black underclass to retain a separate ethnic identity have often been conducted along cul-tural as well as political lines. Shirley Gordon (1963) and Carl Campbell (1992b), for example, interpret the educational activity of church missions as a double-edged sword that provided for upward social mobility even as it propagated the values of the colonizers and restrained the black struggle for cultural space. Monica Schuler (1980) and Robert Stewart (1992) show how, despite the cultural intolerance of the mainline churches, blacks increasingly resorted to their African-derived cosmology as a vehicle of cultural resistance. Brian Moore's pathbreaking cultural history (1995) gives even greater at-tention to the attempted integration of both immigrants and blacks into the dominant Victorian culture of colonial Guyana. His entertainment of the triple dynamics of cul-tural power, cultural resistance, and pluralism goes beyond concession to either plural-ist or creole society perspectives.

Broader analyses have begun to delineate the implications of race and class for social interaction. Although Hall's Jamaica study (1959/69) records some cooperation be-tween both planters and laborers with interests in the sugar industry, this is set against the backdrop of a broader society polarized along class and cultural lines. Even more significantly, Phillip Curtin's engagement with the dichotomous attitudes of blacks and whites in post-emancipation Jamaica (1955) concludes that this failure to adjust placed the society on a confrontational path epitomized by the Morant Bay Rebellion of 1865. As Holt (1992) and Heuman (1994) have pointed out, the scale of repres-sion and fallout from Morant Bay was linked to perceptions of it as a race war.

Some of the most interesting aspects of the literature on the Morant Bay revolt are the competing perspectives on its origin, nature, and ultimate significance. Hall (1959/69) identified it as a "notorious riot" caused by a series of unhappy coincidences. Curtin (1955) similarly dismissed the events at Morant Bay as "another in the succes-sion of riots since emancipation." With the exception of Underhill's engagement with the plight of the masses (1895), contemporaries on both sides of the Atlantic were more concerned with the brutality of the suppression rather than with the rebellion itself. But traditional notions of a spontaneous "disturbance" have given way to claims by Heuman (1994) and Holt (1992) of a bona fide rebellion based on a great deal of premeditation and organization on the part of the rebels. And while its instigation was blamed on religious "demagogues" (most notably Baptist deacon Paul Bogle and brown landowner George William Gordon), the prevailing consensus expressed most volubly by Don Robotham (1981) is that it emerged out of the undesirable material conditions of the working population.

The radical reorientation of the literature, "a reflection, no doubt, of the increased interest in popular agency," is prominently reflected in the attitude of revisionist writers towards the key individuals involved in the crisis. Since Lord Olivier's indictment of Governor Eyre in the suppression controversy (1933) and Geoffrey Dutton's attempt to vindicate his Australian hero (1967), attention has shifted towards the grassroots participants. Wilmot (1995) highlighted the striking role played by women during the actual confrontation. And in keeping with a modern tendency towards the elevation of heroes in the national interest, Robotham argues for the recognition of the previously marginalized Bogle as undisputed leader of the revolt. The question of Gordon's complicity in the rebellion remains the subject of discussion, but Heuman's micro-study (1994) places him on the side of the people.

Since Caribbean historians have seldom been drawn to constitutional history, revisionist works have not been as forthcoming on the political implications of the Morant Bay crisis. Robotham read the dissolution of the local Assembly in 1865 and the institution of Crown Colony government as a clear-cut suppression of all democratic tendencies in the polity. Gad Heuman (1981) suggested that the gradual emergence since emancipation of a brown middle class with political connections was severely stifled. Roy Augier's perceptive assessment of Jamaica "before and after 1865" (1966) views the loss of political authority by Jamaicans as the most significant outcome, with watershed implications for the protracted fight for political autonomy in the future.

Indeed, the abrogation of the elective principle was the prelude to another century of colonial rule in which descendants of the enslaved and indentured immigrants continued to struggle for the realization of freedom in all its dimensions. Although the protracted struggle against British colonial rule up to the de-colonization of the 1960s is beyond the scope of this essay, signature events such as the 1930s labor revolts have encouraged modern historians to continue questioning and replacing the Eurocentric discourse and master narrative initially imposed on the region. In the process, they have asserted a distinct historical approach that treats colonial outcomes in a decidedly anti-colonial manner. Thus, the project of writing the British Caribbean has provided an educational foundation for Caribbean nationhood.

BIBLIOGRAPHY

Adamson, D.: *Sugar Without Slaves: The Political Economy of British Guiana, 1838–1900* (New Haven, CT: Yale University Press, 1972).

Akenson, D. H.: *If the Irish Ran the World: Montserrat, 1630–1730* (Mona: The Press, 1997).

Augier, F. R.: "Before and After 1865." *New World Quarterly* 2 (1966), pp. 21–40.

Batie, R. C.: "Why Sugar?: Economic Cycles and the Changing of Staples on the English and French Antilles, 1624–1654." *Journal of Caribbean History* 8 & 9 (1976), pp. 1–41.

Beckford, G.: *Persistent Poverty: Underdevelopment in Plantations Societies of the Third World* (New York: Oxford University Press, 1972).

Beckles, H. McD.: "The 200 Years War: Slave Resistance on the BWI: An Overview of the Historiography." *Jamaican Historical Review* 13 (1982), pp. 1–10.

Beckles, H. McD.: "Capitalism and Slavery: The Debate Over Eric Williams." *Social and Economic Studies* 33 (1984), pp. 171–90.

Beckles, H. McD.: "Kalinago (Carib) Resistance to European Colonization of the Caribbean." *Caribbean Quarterly* 21 (1987), pp. 55–77.

Beckles, H. McD.: *White Servitude and Black Slavery in Barbados, 1687–1715* (Knoxville, TN: University of Tennessee Press, 1989a).

Beckles, H. McD.: *Natural Rebels: A Social History of Enslaved Black Women in Barbados* (New Brunswick, NJ: Rutgers University Press, 1989b).

Beckles, H. McD.: "A Riotous and Unruly Lot: Irish Indentured Servants and Freemen in the English West Indies, 1644–1713". *William and Mary Quarterly* 3rd ser., 47 (1990), pp. 503–22.

Beckles, H. McD.: "Caribbean Anti-Slavery: the Self-Liberation Ethos of Enslaved Blacks." In Beckles and Shepherd (1991), pp. 363–72.

Beckles, H. McD.: "White Women and Slavery in the Caribbean." *History Workshop Journal* 36 (1993), pp. 65–82.

Beckles, H. McD.: "Freedom Without Liberty: Free Blacks and Slavery in Barbados." In Shepherd (1998b), pp. 255–80.

Beckles, H. McD.: *Centering Woman: Gender Discourses in Caribbean Slave Society* (Kingston: Ian Randle Publishers, 1999).

Beckles, H. McD. and Downes, A.: "The Economics of Transition to the Black Labour System in Barbados, 1630–1680." *Journal of Interdisciplinary History* 18 (1987), pp. 225–47.

Beckles, H. McD. and Shepherd, V. A., eds.: *Caribbean Slave Society and Economy: a Student Reader* (Kingston: Ian Randle Publishers, 1991), revised as *Caribbean Slavery in the Atlantic World* (1999).

Beckles, H. McD. and Shepherd, V. A., eds.: *Caribbean Freedom: Society and Economy from Emancipation to the Present* (Kingston: Ian Randle Publishers, 1993).

Beckles, H. McD. and Shepherd, V. A., eds.: *Slave Voices: The Sounds of Freedom* (Paris: UNESCO, 1999).

Besson, J.: "Land Tenure in the Free Villages of Trelawny, Jamaica: A Case Study in the Peasant Caribbean Response to Emancipation." *Slavery and Abolition* 5 (1984), pp. 3–23.

Best, L.: "Outlines of a Model of a Pure Plantation Economy." *Social and Economic Studies* 17 (1968), pp. 283–326.

Boa, S. M.: "Urban Free Black and Coloured Women: Jamaica, 1764–1834." *Jamaica Historical Review* 18 (1993), pp. 1–6.

Bolland, O. N.: "Systems of Domination After Slavery: The Control of Land and Labour in the British West Indies after 1838." *Comparative Studies in Society and History* 23 (1981), pp. 591–619.

Bolland, O. N.: "Reply to William A. Green's 'The Perils of Comparative History'." *Comparative Studies in Society and History* 26 (1984), pp. 120–5.

Bolland, O. N.: "Proto-Proletarians: Slave Wages in the Americas." In M. Turner, ed., *From Chattel Slaves to Wage Slaves: The Dynamics of Labour Bargaining in the Americas* (Kingston & London: Ian Randle & James Currey, 1995), pp. 123–47.

Bolland, O. N.: "Creolization and Creole Societies: A Cultural Nationalist View of Caribbean Social History." In V. A. Shepherd & G. Richards, eds., *Konversations in Kreole. Caribbean Quarterly* 44 (1998), pp. 1–32.

Boucher, P.: *Cannibal Encounters: Europeans and Island Caribs, 1492–1763* (Baltimore, MD: Johns Hopkins University Press, 1992).

Brathwaite, E. K.: "Women of the Caribbean during Slavery." Elsa Goveia Memorial Lecture. UWI, Cave Hill, 1984.

Brathwaite, K.: *The Development of Creole Society in Jamaica, 1770–1820* (Oxford: The Clarendon Press, 1971).

Brereton, B.: *Gendered Testimony: Autobiographies, Diaries and Letters by Women as Sources for Caribbean History* (Mona: Department of History, University of the West Indies, 1994).

Brereton, B.: "Family Strategies, Gender and the Shift to Wage Labour in the British Caribbean." In B. Brereton and K. Yelvington, eds., *The Colonial Caribbean in Transition: Essays on Postemancipation Social and Cultural History* (Kingston: The Press University of the West Indies, 1999), pp. 77–107.

Burn, W. L.: *Emancipation and Apprenticeship in the British West Indies* (London, 1937; New York: Johnson Reprint Corp., 1970).

Burnard, T.: "Inheritance and Independence: Women's Status in Early Colonial Jamaica." *William and Mary Quarterly* 3rd ser., 48 (1991), pp. 93–116.

Bush, B.: *Slave Women in Caribbean Society, 1650–1838* (Kingston: Heinemann, 1990).

Butler, K. M.: *The Economies of Emancipation: Jamaica and Barbados, 1823–1943* (Chapel Hill, NC: University of North Carolina Press, 1995).

Campbell, C.: *Cedulants and Capitulants: The Politics of the Coloured Opposition in the Slave Society of Trinidad, 1783–1838* (Port of Spain: Paria Pub. Co., 1992a).

Campbell, C.: *Colony and Nation: A Short History of Education in Trinidad and Tobago* (Kingston: Ian Randle Publishers, 1992b).

Carlyle, T.: *The Occasional Discourse on the Nigger Question* (London: Fraser's Magazine, 1849).

Carrington, S.: "The State of the Debate on the Role of Capitalism in the Ending of the Slave System." In Beckles & Shepherd (1991), pp. 435–45.

Casas, B. de las: *Historia de las Indias*, 5 vols, 1520–61 (Madrid: Impr. De M. Ginesta).

Coupland, R.: *The British Anti-Slavery Movement*, 1933 (2nd ed., London: Frank Cass, 1964).

Cox, E.: *Free Coloureds in the Slave Societies of St Kitts and Grenada, 1763–1833* (Knoxville, TN: University of Tennessee Press, 1984).

Craton, Michael: "Changing Patterns of Slave Families in the British West Indies." *Journal of Interdisciplinary History* 10 (1979), pp. 1–36.

Craton, M.: *Testing the Chains: Resistance to Slavery in the British West Indies* (Ithaca, NY: Cornell University Press, 1982).

Craton, M.: "Continuity Not Change: Late Slavery and Post-Emancipation Resistance in the British West Indies." *Slavery and Abolition* 7 (1988), pp. 144–70.

Craton, M.: "Changing Patterns of Slave Families in the British West Indies." In Beckles & Shepherd (1991), pp. 228–49.

Crosby, A. W., Jr.: *The Columbian Exchange: Biological Consequences of 1492* (Westport, CT: Greenwood Press, 1972).

Curtin, P. D.: *The Atlantic Slave Trade: A Census* (Madison, WI: University of Wisconsin Press, 1969).

Curtin, P. D.: *Two Jamaicas: The Role of Ideas in a Tropical Colony* (Cambridge, MA: Harvard University Press, 1955; New York: Atheneum, 1970).

Drescher, S.: *Econocide: British Slavery in the Era of Abolition* (Pittsburgh: University of Pittsburgh Press, 1977).

du Tertre, J. B.: *Histoire Général des Antilles Habitées par les Francais*, 3 vols, 1667–71 (Fort de France: Edition des Horizons Caraibes, 1973).

Dunn, R. S.: *Sugar and Slaves: The Rise of the Planter-Class in the English West Indies, 1624–1713* (Chapel Hill, NC: University of North Carolina Press, 1972).

Dutton, G.: *The Hero as Murderer: The Life of Edward John Eyre* (Sydney: William Collins, 1967).

Edwards, B.: *The History, Civil and Commercial of the British Colonies in the West Indies* (London: J. Stockdale, 1793).

Edwards, P., ed.: *The Life of Olaudah Equiano, or Gustavus Vassa, the African: written by himself*, 1789 (London: Longman, 1988).

Eisner, G.: *Jamaica, 1830–1930: A Study in Economic Growth* (Manchester: Manchester University Press, 1961; Westport, CT: Greenwood Press Publishers, 1974).

Emmer, P. C.: "The Great Escape: The Migration of Female Indentured Servants From British India to Suriname." In D. Richardson, ed., *Abolition and its Aftermath: The Historical Context, 1790–1916* (London: Frank Cass, 1985), p. 245–66.

Engerman, S. L.: "The Slave Trade and British Capital Formation in the 18th Century: A Comment on the Williams Thesis." *Business History Review* 46 (1972), pp. 430–43.

Farley, R.: "The Rise of the Free Village Settlements of British Guiana." *Caribbean Quarterly* 2 (1953), pp. 101–9.

Ferguson, M. ed.: *The History of Mary Prince, a West Indian Slave Related by Herself,* 1831 (London: Pandora, 1987).

Fraser, P. D.: "The Immigration Issue in British Guiana, 1903–1913." *Journal of Caribbean History* 14 (1981), pp. 18–46.

Froude, J. A.: *The English in the West Indies, or the Bow of Ulysses* (London: Longman, Green & Co., 1888; New York: Charles Schribner's Sons, 1897).

Frucht, R.: "A Caribbean Social Type: Neither Peasant nor Proletarian." *Social and Economic Studies* 13 (1967), pp. 295–300.

Galenson, D. W.: "The Rise and Fall of Indentured Servitude in the Americas." *Journal of Economic History* 44 (1984), pp. 1–25.

Gardener, W. J.: *A History of Jamaica* [1873] (London: Frank Cass, 1971).

Gaspar, D. B.: *Bondmen and Rebels: A Study of Master–Slave Relations in Antigua, with implications for Colonial British America* (Baltimore, MD: The Johns Hopkins University Press, 1985).

Gordon, S.: *A Century of West Indian Education: A Source Book* (London: Longman, 1963).

Goveia, E.: *Slave Society in the British Leewards Islands at the End of the Eighteenth Century* (New Haven, CT: Yale University Press, 1965).

Goveia, E.: *A Study on the Historiography of the British West Indies to the end of the 18th century* [1956] (Washington: Howard University Press, 1980).

Green, W. A.: "The Perils of Comparative History: Belize and the British Sugar Colonies after Slavery." *Comparative Studies in Studies in Society and History* 26 (1984), pp. 112–19.

Green, W. A.: "The Creolization of Caribbean History: The Emancipation Era and the Critique of Dialectical Analysis." *Journal of Imperial and Commonwealth History* 14 (1986), pp. 149–69.

Green, W. A.: *British Slave Emancipation: The Sugar Colonies and the Great Experiment 1830–1865* [1976] (Oxford: Clarendon Press, 1991).

Green, William: "The Creolization of Caribbean History: The Emancipation Era and a Critique of Dialectical Analysis." In Beckles and Shepherd (1993), pp. 28–40.

Gregg, V. M.: *Jean Rhys's Historical Imagination: Reading and Writing the Creole* (Chapel Hill, NC: North Carolina Press, 1995).

Hall, D. G.: *Free Jamaica, 1838–1865: An Economic History* [1959] (London: Caribbean University Press, 1969).

Hall, D. G.: "The Flight from the Estate Reconsidered: The British West Indies, 1838–1842." *The Journal of Caribbean History* 10 & 11 (1978), pp. 7–24.

Hall, D. G.: *In Miserable Slavery: Thomas Thistlewood in Jamaica, 1750–1786* (London: Macmillan, 1989).

Henige, David: "On the Contact Population of Hispaniola: History as Higher Mathematics." *Hispanic American Historical Review* 58, no. 2 (1978), pp. 217–37.

Henige, D.: "On the Contact Population of Hispaniola: History as Higher Mathematics." In Beckles & Shepherd (1991), pp. 2–12.

Heuman, G.: *Between Black and White: Race, Politics, and the Free Coloureds in Jamaica, 1792–1865* (Westport, CT: Greenwood Press, 1981).

Heuman, G.: *The Killing Time: The Morant Bay Rebellion in Jamaica* (London: Macmillan,

1994).

Higman, B. W.: *Slave Population and Economy in Jamaica, 1807–1834* (Cambridge: Cambridge University Press, 1976).

Higman, B. W.: *Slave Populations of the British Caribbean, 1807–1832* (Baltimore, MD: The Johns Hopkins University Press, 1984).

Higman, B. W.: *Jamaica Surveyed: Plantation Maps and Plans of the Eighteenth and Nineteenth Centuries* (Jamaica: Institute of Jamaica, 1988).

Higman, B. W.: "Slave Populations of the British Caribbean: Some Nineteenth Century Variations." In Beckles and Shepherd (1991), pp. 221–7.

Hoefte, R.: *In Place of Slavery: A Social History of British Indian and Javanese Laborers in Suriname* (Gainesville, FL: University Press of Florida, 1998).

Holt, T.: *The Problem of Freedom, Race, Labour and Politics in Jamaica and Britain, 1832–1938* (Baltimore, MD: Johns Hopkins University Press, 1992).

Inikori, J., ed.: *Forced Migration: The Impact of the Export Slave Trade on African Societies* (London: Hutchinson University Library, 1982).

Inikori, J.: *The Chaining of a Continent* (Kingston: ISER, 1992).

James, C. L. R.: *The Black Jacobins* (London: Allison and Busby, 1963).

Johnson, H.: "The Share System in the Nineteenth and early Twentieth Centuries." In Howard Johnson, *The Bahamas in Slavery and Freedom* (Kingston: Ian Randle Publishers, 1991), pp. 55–68.

Kiple, K.: *The Caribbean Slave: A Biological History* (Cambridge: Cambridge University Press, 1984).

Klein, H.: *The Middle Passage: Comparative Studies in the Atlantic Slave Trade* (Princeton, NJ: Princeton University Press, 1978).

Labat, J. P.: *The Memoirs of Père Labat, 1693–1705* [1722], trans. J. Eaden (London: Constable & Co., 1931).

Laurence, K. O.: *Immigration into the West Indies in the 19th Century* (Bridgetown: Caribbean Universities Press, 1971).

Laurence, K. O.: *A Question of Labour* (Kingston: Ian Randle, 1994).

Leslie, C.: *A New and Exact History of Jamaica* (London [1739], 1740).

Lewis, G.: *Main Currents in Caribbean Thought: The Historical Evolution of Caribbean Society in its Ideological Aspects, 1492–1900* (Baltimore, MD: The Johns Hopkins University Press, 1983).

Lewis, M. G.: *Journal of a West India Proprietor* (London: John Murray, 1834).

Ligon, R.: *A True and Exact History of the Island of Barbados* [1657] (London: Frank Cass: 1970).

Long, E.: *The History of Jamaica*, 3 vols (London, 1774).

Look Lai, W.: *Indentured Labour, Caribbean Sugar: Chinese and Indian Migrants to the British West Indies, 1838–1918* (Baltimore, MD: Johns Hopkins University Press, 1993).

Lucas, C.: *A Historical Geography of the British Colonies*, vol. 2 (Oxford: The Clarendon Press, 1902).

Mandle, J. R.: *The Plantation Economy: Population and Economic Change in Guyana, 1838–1960* (Philadelphia: Temple University Press, 1973).

Marshall, B.: "The Black-Carib Native Resistance to British Penetration into the Windward Side of St. Vincent, 1763–1773." *Caribbean Quarterly* 19 (1973), pp. 4–27.

Marshall, W.: "Notes on Peasant Development in the West Indies Since 1838." *Social and Economic Studies* 17 (1968), pp. 252–63.

Marshall, W.: *The Post-Slavery Labour Problem Revisited* (Mona: Department of History, University of the West Indies, 1991).

Marshall, W.: "Metayage in the Sugar Industry of the British Windward Islands, 1838–65." In Beckles and Shepherd (1993), 64–79.

Marshall, W.: "We Be Wise to Many More Things: Blacks; Hopes and Expectations of Emancipation." In Beckles and Shepherd (1993), pp. 12–20.

Marshall, Woodville: "Metayage in the Sugar Industry of the British Windward Islands, 1838–1865." *Jamaica Historical Review* 5 (1965). Also pub. in Beckles and Shepherd (1993), pp. 64–79.

Martyr, P. (Pietro Martire D'Angheiri): *Historie of the West Indies* [1530] (London, 1612).

Mathieson, W. L.: *British Slavery and its Abolition 1823–1838* (London: Longman, Green & Co. Ltd, 1926).

Mathieson, W. L.: *British Slave Emancipation, 1838–1849* [London, 1932] (New York: Octagon Books Inc., 1967).

Mathurin, L.: "A Historical Study of Women in Jamaica, 1807–1834" (Ph.D. dissertation, University of the West Indies, Mona, 1974).

Mathurin-Mair, L.: *The Rebel Woman in the British West Indies During Slavery* (Kingston: Institute of Jamaica, for African Caribbean Institute of Jamaica, 1975).

Mathurin-Mair, L.: *Women Field Workers in Jamaica During Slavery*. Elsa Goveia Memorial Lecture, Mona, 1986.

Merivale, H.: *Lectures on Colonization and Colonies* [London, 1841] (London: Longman, Green and Roberts, 1861).

Mintz, Sidney: *Caribbean Transformations* (Chicago: Aldine, 1974).

Mintz, S. W.: "The Origin of Reconstituted Peasantry." In S. Mintz, *Caribbean Transformations* (Baltimore: Johns Hopkins University Press, 1984), pp. 146–56.

Mintz, S. W. and Hall, D.: "The Origins of the Jamaican Internal Market System." In Beckles and Shepherd (1991), pp. 319–34.

Momsen, J.: "Gender Roles in Caribbean Agriculture Labour." In M. Cross and G. Heuman, eds., *Labour in the Caribbean* (London: Macmillan Publishers, 1988), pp. 141–58.

Moore, B.: *Cultural Power, Resistance and Pluralism: Colonial Guyana, 1838–1900* (Jamaica: The University Press of the West Indies, 1995).

Moore, B. and Wilmot, S.: *Before and After 1865: Education, Politics, and Regionalism in the Caribbean* (Kingston: Ian Randle, 1998).

Newton, A. P.: *The European Nations in the West Indies, 1493–1688* (London: A. and C. Black, 1933).

Northrup, D.: *Indentured Labour in the Age of Imperialism, 1834–1922* (Cambridge: Cambridge University Press, 1995).

Olivier, S.: *The Myth of Governor Eyre* (London: Hogarth Press, 1933).

Osterhammel, J.: *Colonialism: A Theoretical Overview* (Princeton, NJ: Marcus Weiner, 1996).

Oveido y Valdés, G.: *Historia general y natural de las Indias* (Seville, 1535).

Paget, H.: "The Free Village System in Jamaica." *Caribbean Quarterly* 1 (1954), *Jamaican Historical Review* 1 (1945), pp. 31–48.

Pares, R.: *Merchants and Planters. Economic History Review: Supplement #4* (Cambridge: Economic History Society, 1960).

Patterson, O.: *The Sociology of Slavery* (Rutherford, NJ: Fairleigh Dickinson University Press, 1969).

Patterson, O.: *Slavery and Social Death* (Cambridge, MA: Harvard University Press, 1982).

Raynal, G. (Abbé Raynal): *A Philosophical and Political History of the Settlements and Trade of the Europeans in the East and West Indies*, 4 vols, trans. J. Justamond ([1770]; Dublin: J. Exshaw, 1779).

Reddock, R.: "Indian Women and Indentureship in Trinidad and Tobago, 1845–1917: Freedom Denied." In Beckles and Shepherd (1993), pp. 225–37.

Robotham, W.: *"The Notorious Riot": The Socio-Economic and Political Basis of Paul Bogle's Revolt* (Mona: Institute of Social and Economic Research, 1981).

Satchell, V.: *From Plots to Plantations: Land Transactions in Jamaica, 1866–1900* (Mona: Institute for Social and Economic Research, 1990).

Schuler, M.: *"Alas, Alas, Kongo": A Social History of Indentured African Immigration into Jamaica 1841–1865* (Baltimore, MD: Johns Hopkins University Press, 1980).

Seaman, H.: "Territoriality and Nationhood: Colonial Dispossessions and the Resurgent Identity of the Native (Carib) Caribbean" (Ph.D. dissertation, University of the West Indies, Cave Hill Campus, 1999).

Sewell, W. G.: *The Ordeal of Free Labour in the British West Indies* [New York: 1861] (London: Frank Cass, 1968).

Shepherd, V. A.: "Pens and Penkeepers in a Plantation Society" (Ph.D. dissertation, University of Cambridge, 1988).

Shepherd, V. A..: "The Apprenticeship Experience on Jamaica Livestock Farms." *Jamaica Journal* 22:1 (1989), pp. 48–55.

Shepherd, V. A.: "Marginality and Livestock Farmers in Jamaica." *Social and Economic Studies* (1991), pp. 189–201.

Shepherd, V. A.: "Emancipation through Servitude: Aspects of the Condition of Indian Women in Jamaica, 1845–1945." In Beckles and Shepherd (1993), pp. 245–50.

Shepherd, V. A.: *Transients to Settlers: The Experience of Indians in Jamaica 1945–1950* (Leeds/Warwick: Peepal Tree & University of Warwick, 1994).

Shepherd, V. A.: "Questioning Creole: Domestic Producers in Jamaica's Plantation Economy." In V. A. Shepherd and G. Richards, eds., *Konversations in Kreole. Caribbean Quarterly* 44 (1998a), pp. 93–107.

Shepherd, V. A., ed.: *Slavery Without Sugar. Plantation Society in the Americas*, 5 (1998b).

Shepherd, V. A.: "Diversity in Caribbean Economy and Society from the 17th to the 19th Century." In Shepherd (1998b), pp. 175–88.

Shepherd, V. A., ed.: *Women in Caribbean History* (Kingston: Ian Randle Publishers, 1999).

Shepherd, V. A.: "Liberation Struggles on Livestock Farms in Jamaica". In Shepherd and Beckles (2000), pp. 896–904.

Shepherd, V. A.: "Journey Interrupted: Maharani's Misery on the *Allanshaw* to Colonial Guyana." Paper presented at the Social History Projects' Symposium, University of the West Indies, Mona, April 15, 2000.

Shepherd, V. A. and Beckles, H. McD., eds.: *Caribbean Slavery in the Atlantic World* (Kingston: Ian Randle Publishers, 2000).

Shepherd, V. A., Brereton, B., and Bailey, B., eds.: *Engendering History: Caribbean Women in Historical Perspective* (Kingston: Ian Randle, 1995).

Sheridan, R. B.: *Sugar and Slavery: An Economic History of the British West Indies, 1623–1775* (Barbados: Caribbean University Press, 1974).

Sheridan, R. B.: *Doctors and Slaves: A Medical and Demographic History of Slavery in the British West Indies, 1680–1834* (Cambridge: Cambridge University Press, 1985).

Sherlock, H. and Bennett, H.: *The Story of the Jamaican People* (Kingston: Ian Randle Publishers, 1997).

Smith, M. G.: "Some Aspects of Social Structure in the British Caribbean about 1820." *Social and Economic Structures* 1 (1953), pp. 55–80.

Smith, M. G.: *The Plural Society of the British West Indies* (Berkeley: University of California Press, 1962).

Smith, S.: "Coffee and the 'Poorer Sort of People' in Jamaica During the Period of Slavery." In Shepherd (1998b), pp. 227–254.

Stewart, R.: *Religion and Society in Post-Emancipation Jamaica* (Knoxville, TN: University of Tennessee Press, 1992).

Sturge, J. and Harvey, T.: *The West Indies in 1837* (London, 1838).

Thomas, A. P.: "The Sugar Colonies and the Old Empire: Profit or Loss for Gt. Britain." *Economic History Review* 2nd ser., 21 (1968), pp. 30–45.

Thomas, D.: *An Historical Account of the Rise and Growth of the West India Colonies* [1690] (New York: Arno Press, 1972).

Thomas, J. J.: *Froudacity: West Indian Fables Explained* [London, 1889] (Port of Spain: New Bacon Books, 1969).

Thompson, A.: *Colonialism and Underdevelopment in Guyana, 1580–1803* (Barbados: Carib Research and Publications, 1987).

Tinker, H.: *A New System of Slavery: The Export of Indian Workers Overseas, 1830–1920* (London: Oxford University Press, 1974).

Trollope, A.: *The West Indies and the Spanish Main* [1860] (London: Dawsons of Pall Mall, 1968).

Trouillot, M.-R.: "Labour in Emancipation in Dominica: Contribution to a Debate." *Caribbean Quarterly* 30 (1984), pp. 73–84.

Turner, M., ed.: *From Chattel Slaves to Wage Slaves: The Dynamics of Labour Bargaining in the Americas* (Kingston: Ian Randle Publishers, 1995).

Underhill, E.: *The Tragedy of Morant Bay* (London: Alexander and Shepherd, 1895).

Underhill, E.: *The West Indies: Their Social and Religious Conditions* (Westport, CT: Negro University Press, 1970).

Watts, D.: *The West Indies: Patterns of Development, Culture and Environmental Change Since 1492* (Cambridge: Cambridge University Press, 1987).

Welch, P.: "The Urban Context of Slave Life: Views from Bridgetown, Barbados in the 18th and 19th Centuries." In Shepherd (1998b), pp. 281–97.

Williams, E.: *Capitalism and Slavery* (Chapel Hill, NC: University of North Carolina Press, 1944).

Williams, E.: *British Historians and the West Indies* [1964] (London: Andre Deutsch, 1966).

Wilmot, S.: "Not 'Full Free': The Ex-Slaves and the Apprenticeship System in Jamaica, 1834–1838." *Jamaica Journal* 17 (1984), pp. 2–10.

Wilmot, S.: "Emancipation in Action: Workers and Wage Conflict in Jamaica, 1838–40." *Jamaica Journal* 19 (1986), pp. 55–62.

Wilmot, S.: "Females of Abandoned Character: Women and Protest in Jamaica, 1838–65." *Engendering History* (1995), pp. 233–57.

Wrong, H.: *Government of the West Indies* (New York: Negro Universities Press, 1969).

Young, Sir W.: *An Account of the Black Charaibs in the Island of St Vincent* [London, 1795] (London: Frank Cass, 1971).

Zahadieh, N.: "Trade, Plunder and Economic Development in Early English Jamaica, 1655–1689." *Economic History Review* 39 (1988), pp. 205–22.

CHAPTER NINETEEN

Comparisons: New Spain

ROBERT FERRY

New Spain was arguably the most richly complex of the American colonial societies that were constructed after 1492. Two primary factors – a dense, sedentary, remarkably sophisticated indigenous population numbering in the many millions at the time of conquest, and the discovery of extraordinary deposits of silver soon after the Europeans arrived – converged to create this complexity. There is no surprise, therefore, that the twin topics (broadly considered) of Indians and mineral wealth have always been at the center of interest in colonial Mexico, from the time of Cortés and Moctezuma, through the centuries of Spanish administration, and on to the historical scholarship of more recent times. In recent decades a very broad range of social and cultural features of New Spain have attracted historians, as historical interest now increasingly reflects the complexities that characterized early Mexico. But even as the scholarship has widened, much of the most recent historiography – including some of the best work – continues to research time-honored, mainline themes: the initial Spanish–Indian encounters and the interaction that continued for centuries, the nature of ethnicity and identity, and the role of silver mining and silver-driven economies.

Until rather recently the history of the native people of early New Spain was based almost exclusively on what was imagined to be the essential natures of Indians and Spaniards at the time of contact, followed by an assessment of the displacement of things indigenous by the Europeans. This pattern was set out clearly by William H. Prescott in his enormously popular epic *History of the Conquest of Mexico* (1843). Drawing from Spanish chronicles, Prescott wrote a narrative history that followed a simple interpretive framework of conflict and some resistance followed by significant European changes made at the core of the pre-conquest indigenous world. Almost a century later essentially the same paradigm was still easily visible in the work of the French historian Robert Ricard, *La "Conquête spirituelle" du Mexique* (1933). Working directly from Spanish ecclesiastical sources, Ricard believed that in the realm of ideas and beliefs, especially Christianity and conversion, indigenous cultural elements either gave way under pressure to European replacements, or novel European elements were introduced into a vacuum and took hold without opposition.

These two classic studies viewed the conquest in an essentially favorable light, and in that sense they are not at all typical of much that has been written recently about the conquest and its aftermath. But Prescott and Ricard do represent, if in rather extreme form, what could be called the "opposite poles" or "oppositionalist" view. This perspective also underlies the work of many scholars, determinedly opposed to imperialism or colonialism, whose research examines Indian resistance to conquest and rebellion against colonial rule. It is also the underlying view of histories that emphasize instances of indigenous non-change, isolation, and the continuity of Native cultural elements. The opposition model (in whatever of its various forms – European displacement, indigenous resistance, or isolation and stasis) has in recent decades given ground to a different paradigm that sees the European and Native American encounter as an ongoing, interactive, in a word – historical – process. Basing their research mostly on Native language sources, and focusing on the central regions of pre-conquest and colonial Mexico, historians of the "Nahuatl school" as it has been labeled (MacLeod, 2000) have created a substantial body of innovative scholarship that explores this encounter history primarily from an indigenous perspective. The Nahuatl school historiography, because it has substantially altered the way historians must approach the traditional theme of the conquest of Mexico, occupies a central place in this essay.

Iberian and Native Peoples

Spanish institutions, administrative policies, and the activities of the administrators themselves were once seen as defining the viceroyalty of New Spain in the sixteenth century, creating its physical parameters and its skeletal structure. Much of the history of New Spain until at least the late 1950s was written from a formalist perspective, which used institutionally generated sources to create histories that took Spanish administration, broadly defined, as a fundamental frame of reference. Examples of this scholarship include Arthur Scott Aiton's classic biography *Antonio de Mendoza: First Viceroy of New Spain* (1927), Ricard's *La "Conquête spirituelle" du Mexique* (1933), and Clarence Haring's sweeping study – described by Lockhart (1999) as "that massive monument to institutionalism" – *The Spanish Empire in America* (1947). More recent scholarship has moved away from the formal and generalized to an understanding of the inner workings of colonial institutions, to collective biographies of the functionaries who comprised them, and to comparisons between bureaucrats and other colonial elites. Perhaps the most interesting recent work on the early administration of New Spain is found in the synthetic treatment offered by James Lockhart (1984). Characterizing broadly, Lockhart observes that colonial administrators, whether they were in royal service or were ecclesiastics, by and large followed similar career patterns, and that these patterns also resembled those of large-scale, transatlantic merchants. The administrators and the transatlantic merchants of New Spain both functioned in networks that reached into the viceroyalty from a primary center located in Spain or, in the case of the Church, in Rome (although by papal–royal concordant the high-ranking ecclesiastical appointments were made by the Castilian monarch). The lowest rung in the career ladders of both administrators and merchants – the place occupied by young men new to their professions – was almost always a post in a rural district or provincial town. In New Spain professional success meant an upward move in rank and a physical move from the countryside to Mexico City, the viceregal center of administration, both royal and ecclesiastic, and the center of commercial activity. The final step, made by the most successful merchants and royal administrators, was the return to Spain to fill high-ranking posts in colonial government and as directors of the family-based, transatlantic business enterprises.

These patterns persisted for the almost three centuries of colonial New Spain, with several important consequences. Since individuals' institutional mobility was linked to movement from countryside to city, as friars and rural-parish priests and bottom-rung royal officials improved their career status, they brought with them to the centers of power information about the circumstances and conditions in the rural reaches of the viceroyalty. This pattern was very similar to that of merchants, who were sent out from Spain to begin their careers in the Indian hinterland or in rough-and-tumble mining towns and insalubrious seaports. As the merchant factors rose to management positions, moving to regional primary towns or to Mexico City, and finally in some cases returning home to Seville to take the reins of family-run Atlantic enterprises as a whole, they carried with them first-hand knowledge of the business as it was done at every step from Mexican mining town and Native village to Spanish metropolis. Thus, in the commercial arena as well as the administrative realm, there was a steady, constantly updated flow of information toward the center, carried by career-minded individuals on their way up. At the highest levels of administration there were usually to be found experienced veterans (whether in service to Church, Crown, or commerce) who knew their territory well.

From a place of great wealth like New Spain, thorough and up-to-date information flowed constantly to Spain: to the king and to the commercial centers. The news arriving from Mexico was as diverse as we might imagine, everything from official reports about Native people to the Mexico City price for imported cloth. While such information certainly facilitated the orderly, top-down administration of the empire, the order that was actually created in the Americas was almost always at least somewhat different from what the centers of power and economy intended it to be. For example, royal policy with regard to the Indians of New Spain was developed by the king's counselors who received considerable input from first-hand reports of European and Native encounters. But delivery of the royal will always depended on the will of the local elite, and this was particularly true in the indigenous countryside. The country-side held little attraction for town-oriented Iberians, and royal salaries, which were not intended to be more than subsidies, could not command to-the-letter loyalty from frontier-province-level royal bureaucrats. Ambitious profiteering, and activities that a modern eye would see only as corruption, seem to have frequently driven the actual practice of authority as it was carried out by the king's officers in Indian New Spain. As the sixteenth century continued, in an increasingly sophisticated economy driven by the export of silver, the pressures for Native labor were so great that, with both royal officials and churchmen also greatly interested in the profits of indigenous labor, the potential for profound destruction of Indian society and culture was constantly present.

Yet this destruction did not occur. In the last several years scholars have come to recognize that a broad range of indigenous cultural and social systems continued to function effectively through the course of the sixteenth century, with such systems experiencing only a slow and variable alteration or Hispanization well into the seventeenth century. The history of this process changes dramatically the "oppositionalist" view that had predominated in the colonial Mexican historiography since Prescott: the view that in the most important areas of indigenous life – religion, economy, social organization – Native culture had been virtually eliminated by the force of conquest. The importance of this new scholarship is difficult to overestimate.

The most comprehensive work in this innovative indigenous-centered scholarship –

labeled the "Nahuatl school" (MacLeod, 2000) – is James Lockhart's masterful *The Nahuas after the Conquest* (1992). However, as Lockhart and many others have acknowledged, the pioneer in the effort to know the indigenous history of the conquest and the colonial society that followed was Charles Gibson. In *The Aztecs Under Spanish Rule* (1964), Gibson sought to trace from conquest to independence the major patterns of the response of indigenous people to conquering and colonizing Europeans. While the book is formally a study of the institutions that reshaped the lives of New Spain's Indians: the *encomienda*, the Indian municipal councils, and the rural agricultural and ranching estates known as the *hacienda*, it is hardly an institutional history of the traditional sort. In one remarkable chapter after another and in comprehensive detail, Gibson explained the implementation and evolution – the inner workings – of these colonial social forms. The extraordinary, lasting significance of *The Aztecs Under Spanish Rule* stems from Gibson's recognition that pre-conquest Native forms (social, spatial, cultural) continued to be significant for generations in the context of these European intrusions. In scholarship that was meticulous, sweeping in scope, and imaginative, Gibson demonstrated how in central Mexico the three primary Spanish enterprises involving indigenous people – the systematic exploitation of their labor, the Christian proselytization project, and the implementation of royal and municipal legal systems – were laid over a base of Native structures that were in place at the time of first contact. Frequently overlapping one another, the *encomienda*, the parish, and the Indian town, the primary features of the Spanish conquest, were themselves all established in the context of a resilient indigenous entity that Gibson labeled the tribe. He recognized that indigenous elites, the *caciques*, continued to exercise power (circumscribed as it was by their obligation to work as middlemen to both *encomendero* and clergy), and that the continuing presence of the *caciques*' traditional authority served to buffer, mediate, and even to some degree define the impact of European colonial rule. It was a pathbreaking call to view Mexico's Native people as ongoingly active in shaping the history of which they were a part, a history which, prior to Gibson, had for the most part seen them only as victims.

Comprehensive indigenous history along Gibsonian lines did not follow immediately after *The Aztecs Under Spanish Rule*. Much of the historical scholarship written from the 1950s to the 1970s continued to view the catastrophic decline in Native population in the sixteenth century as the defining fact of colonial Mexico, and it is likely that from the perspective of this overwhelming demographic disaster it probably seemed unimportant to study what were believed to be the mere remnants of pre-conquest indigenous society. The French scholar François Chevalier (1952, 1963) and, in his early work, Woodrow Borah (1951) advanced the idea that the vertiginous collapse of the Indian population was an instrumental cause of the economic decline of the seventeenth century, as the ongoing destruction of the Native labor force resulted in reduced output from silver mines, the motor force of the economy. Chevalier argued further that without silver Spaniards were obliged to withdraw from the transatlantic market, and that they retreated to the countryside, where they formed manor-like, mostly isolated, micro-economic agriculture and ranching estates – the earliest Mexican haciendas.

By the early 1970s, there were successful scholarly challenges to the Chevalier–Borah argument that assumed links between the demographic history of Mexico's Native people, the silver-based economy, and the formation of the hacienda. The important study of the beginnings and early development of silver mining by Peter Bakewell (1971) demonstrated that the production of silver at Zacatecas reached a peak in the early seventeenth century – at precisely the same time that the Indian population was at its lowest point. In addition, Bakewell's detailed analysis indicated that through the middle years of the seventeenth century, as the Indian population began to recover, silver output continued to decline. Bakewell's argument was simple and clear: there had always been more than enough indigenous laborers to work the mines; the collapse of the Native population was not a factor in mining production. Bakewell also made it clear that, far from coming into existence in reaction to a precipitously declining Indian population and a declining silver-driven market economy, the early Mexican hacienda had from its inception flourished as an integral part of that market. Created to meet the material demands – draft animals, fuel, construction materials, food – associated with mining and urban growth, as Bakewell demonstrated, the hacienda had never been anything like the isolated, self-contained, medieval manor that Chevalier had depicted.

Even though after Bakewell the decline of Indian labor could no longer be used to explain waning silver production, historians' interest in the Native demographic collapse continued unabated. Of course, as the scholarship showed with increasing clarity, this was a human disaster of extraordinary dimension. During the 1970s, in a series of remarkably creative and rigorous studies, Woodrow Borah and his University of California Berkeley colleague Sherburne F. Cook wrote the population history of New Spain's Indians (1971–79). This research generated what many regard as the best estimates of the Native population of central Mexico at several intervals from the time of conquest – in 1519 there were perhaps as many as twenty-five million people – through the course of the sixteenth century to the nadir point – in 1622 there remained in Mexico only an estimated three-quarters of a million Indians. This "Berkeley school" of demographic history did little to alter the long-standing Black Legend vision of defeat and destruction as the defining features of post-conquest Indian Mexico. The methodological exactness of the demographers confirmed in a straightforward, mathematical-scientific way the standard view that the Spanish conquest had left in its wake only widespread death and profound social and cultural disintegration.

Despite the Gibsonian insights, which proclaimed the importance of indigenous continuities and called for their close examination, historians were slow to begin to ask questions about the actual nature of the lives of the Native people in the decades following European conquest and settlement. One of the first to do so was William Taylor, not surprisingly a student of Gibson's, who opted to explore varieties of Indian behavior in limited, precisely defined regional contexts. First in his *Landlord and Peasant in Colonial Oaxaca* (1972) and then in *Drinking, Homicide and Rebellion in Colonial Mexican Villages* (1979) Taylor made the indigenous communities of south-central New Spain his focus, and he examined these corporate entities in detail, as land-holding entities, as political agencies, and in general as forces for cultural and social cohesion. Like Taylor's, most of the research on Indian history that followed would be done at the corporate or community level. However, once the turn to indigenous ethnohistory had been made, there proved to be a variety of ways to get at the rich features of Native life in early colonial Mexico. To cite just one of the more interesting examples, Woodrow Borah, whose sophisticated scholarship was not limited to historical demography, found in his institutional study of the establishment of Spanish law in New Spain, *Justice by Insurance: The General Indian Court of Colonial Mexico* (1983), that the creation of courts and the application of the procedures of Spanish justice provided Native people with a context and the instruments for social action that were used to reinforce the integrity of indigenous society and culture as much as they modified it.

Certainly no one has taken Charles Gibson's appreciation of the ongoing vitality of Native social life in colonial Mexico more to heart than James Lockhart. With remarkable creativity and industry, using diverse sources, especially Nahuatl and other Native language materials, Lockhart and others – in particular the students he has taught and inspired – have sought to understand the history of early New Spain from the perspective of indigenous culture. This spring tide of scholarship is sophisticated and complex, but several main currents can be identified within it. Perhaps the most fundamental discovery, the Native social units identified by Gibson as the surviving detritus of the ruined Aztec empire, are now known to have been social and cultural entities (*altepetl* in Nahuatl), ethnic states in fact, that were basic to indigenous life before conquest and remarkably resilient to European changes thereafter. Understanding the internal workings of the post-conquest *altepetl* has been a primary objective of the Lockhart school.

The centerpiece of this research is Lockhart, *The Nahuas after the Conquest* (1992), which offers as a central argument that the post-conquest *altepetl* demonstrates a history of European and indigenous society in central colonial Mexico that can be best described as a convergence of social and cultural elements. The two societies, Lockhart argues, were in basic ways either similar to one another or appeared to be. Both were sedentary agriculture societies with comparable sociopolitical systems, including tax collection policies and the relationship between rulers and those who were ruled; both recognized spatial distinctions between primary towns and satellite settlements; both gave considerable importance to the physical location and function of community structures and to the ritual observances that took place in the context of those structures. What matters in the Lockhart view is not that these elements were equal, but rather that they were decidedly *not* in conflict with one another. Each side of the cultural exchange presumed that its customary forms and concepts continued to function in ways "familiar within its own tradition . . . and unaware or unimpressed by the other side's interpretation" (Lockhart, 1999, p. 99).

Most of the recent ethnographic histories have a doubly circumscribed focus: they are limited to a specific region – often a single town and its hinterland – and they are restricted to a comprehensive examination of that region for a limited period of time. S. L. Cline, for example, studied the Indian town of Culhuacan for a twenty-year period, 1580 to 1600 (1986), and Rebecca Horn's history of Spanish and indigenous interaction in the town of Coyoacan covered the period from the conquest to 1650 (1997). Others explore particular features of social life, such as rulership, in a singular setting (Haskett, 1991), while still others have a wider geographical and temporal scope similar to the earlier perspectives of Gibson and Taylor (Restall, 1997; Kellogg, 1995). The Lockhartian ethnohistory of convergence is obviously very different from the sharp distinctions and destructions of the traditional Black Legend or "oppositional" scholarship. With it, the burgeoning indigenous history of colonial Mexico has become the study of a complex process of ongoing cultural interaction.

Society

In his excellent essay on the economy of colonial Spanish-America, Arnold J. Bauer (1996) describes the two distinct, but closely connected, economic worlds that characterized New Spain. Beginning with the fabulous wealth generated by the conquistadors' division among themselves of the labor of thousands of conquered indigenous people, the Spaniards' buying power made Mexico a market center for goods brought from Europe. Once the exchange system was in place, New Spain remained a significant market for Atlantic commerce for several centuries. The trade for European cloth, wine, iron products, and luxury goods boomed after the middle of the sixteenth century as the great Sierra Madre silver deposits began to yield their fortunes. The flow of merchandise was sustained by abundant bullion, money, and credit, and the towns and portions of New Spain's vast countryside – cochineal dye, beef and hides, wheat and wool – were quickly knit together in an extensive economic network. By the 1570s the last part of this system was in place as other, opulent, Asian products entered New Spain at the Pacific port of Acapulco. Moving on muleback through the established market space, some of theses silks and spices went on to Europe, but much of what left the Spanish port of Manila remained in Mexico.

Alongside this dynamic world of cash and credit was another powerful and important economy, one of subsistence and local markets. Sustained by the Holy Trinity of Mesoamerican food – beans, maize, squash – supplemented by indigenous chiles, the chicken (a marvelous gift of the Europeans), and such humble commodities as homespun cottons, this other economy existed underneath the monetarized and integrated layers of global and regional markets. Bauer cautions us not to see this characterization as a simple-minded "dual economy," or to see economic New Spain as sharply divided in "modern" and "traditional" or much less "capitalist" in contrast to "feudal" sectors. Distinctive as they certainly were, the Hispanic and the Native worlds were always, to a certain degree, interdependent. The nature of this interdependence is still not fully understood, not the least because the subsistence-based world of the colonial Mexican villages and micro-regions – removed as it was from tax collectors and other record-keeping officials – is itself not fully understood. There is no doubt, however, that lives lived to the rhythms of subsistence were increasingly pressured by the steadily rising tide of a more Hispanicized or Europeanized economy. Although some enterprising self-sufficient producers voluntarily took their modest surpluses to market for cash sales, in the sixteenth and well into the seventeenth centuries it was primarily compulsion (tribute and tithe) that forced the labor and products of the subsistence sector into the world of cash and credit markets. In the eighteenth century rapidly increasing rural population, unemployment, and land pressures forced unprecedented numbers of people into the market economy.

The distinction – and intersection or overlap – that Bauer sees in the economic worlds of New Spain can be seen in other aspects of colonial Mexican life. Material culture followed this difference. According to Woodrow Borah (1992), in the sixteenth century there were two distinct populations with different patterns of consumption in the areas of food, dress, dwellings, and household furnishings. This European–Indian polarity, of course basic in the generations after conquest and constantly important thereafter, was also subject to constant interaction between the poles. This process created a steadily expanding, culturally braided, mestizo and plebeian society in the middle. Much of the best recent scholarship on New Spain examines this process and its consequences. R. Douglas Cope (1994) examines the elite-Spanish ideology of a hierarchically racially stratified society and finds that urban plebeian people – middling and poor people, both Iberian immigrants and people of color (*castas*) – did not accept domination based on their assigned status as racially inferior. Both Cope and Richard Boyer, *Lives of the Bigamists* (1995), demonstrate how non-elites used the legal system to their advantage, depended on the personal relationships they formed with elite patrons, and most of all worked with one another to secure their individual and collective well-being. These important studies open windows on the inner workings of the largely unexplored middle areas of colonial Mexican society. The plebeians' sense of justice and social order led them to protest and riot when their expectations were violated, as Cope's analysis of the 1692 Mexico City riot demonstrates.

In recent work Richard Boyer and others have recognized the central importance of honor in the lives of ordinary people in early Mexico. Traditionally historians have tended to follow colonial elites who claimed honor as their exclusive prerogative, denying it to others on the basis of the assumed inferiority that was part of the poverty, illegitimacy, and racially admixed ancestry that characterized the lower orders. But it is increasingly evident that the importance of reputation and character was not limited to elites. Patricia Seed, in *To Love, Honor and Obey in Colonial Mexico* (1988), explains that until the first decades of the eighteenth century the Church worked to enforce respect for honor in marriage cases regardless of the ethnicity or social status of the individuals involved. Using its own power of excommunication and its influence with royal authority, the Church obliged men to fulfill their word of honor in promises to marry (failure to do so could result in exile and extended service in the royal galleys in the Philippines). Similarly, in very un-Romeo and Juliet fashion, the Church successfully defended the honor of young couples that wanted to marry against the opposition of their parents or any other third party.

Honor, complex and subtle, has become a topic of considerable interest to historians of early Ibero-America. According to Ann Twinam (1999), honor was a pervasive "mental matrix" that defined and shaped the identity of everyone in colonial society. While there was often ample opportunity for elites to adjust or manage their social reputations, the private lives of non-elites were significantly more public and consequently their honor was more often a social matter (Boyer, 1998). New Spain's plebeian society and culture, and the nature of class conflict in late colonial Mexico, is explored in Juan Pedro Viqueira Albán, *Propriety and Permissiveness in Bourbon Mexico* (1987). During the second half of the eighteenth (Bourbon) century, New Spain authorities sought to regulate a variety of private customs and public entertainments, including the bullfight, the theater, gambling, and ball games. Viqueira Albán asks whether this reforming effort was a shift in the state's attitude toward no longer acceptable traditional social practices, or whether it was an authoritarian reaction to a changing urban popular class. Viqueira Albán emphasizes that understanding the state–society tension in New Spain is made particularly difficult, compared to France for example, by the extraordinary complexity of urban plebeian society (the ethnic diversity of its people and the varieties of their social provenance – European immigrants and rural migrants). The universalizing, enlightened despotism of the Bourbon Spanish state found the Mexican popular class disorderly and no doubt especially troubling because of its very diversity; and Viqueira Albán makes it clear why the members of that class found the state's administrators to be autocratic and threatening to their traditions and life patterns. A complementary but very different kind of study is that of Silvia Marina Arrom, *Containing the Poor* (2000), which focuses on the effort to control the urban poor of Mexico City during the late colonial period and most of the nineteenth century. Arrom believes that the purpose of the Mexico City Poor House – to control the poor by criminalizing begging and isolating beggars in order to convert them into productive workers – was unique in Spanish America. As it turned out, the plan was a resounding failure. Poverty and paupers, as deeply embedded in society as the moral economy of begging, continued on a large scale in late colonial and national Mexico. Arrom concludes that the failure of the Bourbon Poor House project in fact reveals the resilience of popular culture to preserve social and cultural traditions in the face of state efforts to change society.

In their studies of the complex ways in which the popular sectors of Mexico City reacted to elite-sponsored, state-building projects, Viqueira Albán and Arrom address important questions about the nature and resiliency of popular culture and popular political resistance, and the changing argument over what was public and what was private, in late New Spain. Popular opposition to what Eric Van Young (1994) has called "the state as vampire" was a fundamental feature of social life during the second half of the eighteenth century, was central to popular participation in the wars of independence beginning in 1810, and would continue to be a primary aspect of popular politics in Mexico through the revolution of 1910 and beyond.

Economy

Several million pesos of silver were taken every year from Mexican mines, and, with periodic downturns, the quantity of silver mined increased steadily over time (Sluiter, 1998; Klein and TePaske, 1981; TePaske, 1983). This mineral wealth was of enormous importance in the evolving world economy during the sixteenth to the eighteenth centuries, and, as the motor force of New Spain's market economy, the flow of silver structured social relations in the viceroyalty, set the parameters of material culture, and determined the very meaning of Mexican wealth. Silver greatly stimulated economic activity of all kinds in all contexts – transatlantic, transpacific, and domestic-viceregal – and, not surprisingly, this activity was channeled and diligently taxed by the Spanish state. As important as silver was in its own right and as a stimulus to every other economic activity, in the eighteenth century the direct contribution of mining to the royal treasury was never more than a quarter of the total receipts taken by the Mexican exchequer. Taxes on trade and commerce, on royal monopolies (on such standard European monopoly items as playing cards, official stamped paper, gunpowder, and on American items such as tobacco), and the obligatory head tax on indigenous people comprised the rest of royal revenues. Given the abundance of royal taxing mechanisms (there were twenty-three treasury offices in eighteenth-century New Spain) and the efficiency with which they were applied, there exists an extraordinary volume of highly detailed tax records for New Spain. In addition, these data record the expenditures of the royal treasuries as well as their revenues. While they have proved often difficult to decipher and challenging to analyze, these records form the basis of several important studies of the fiscal and economic history of the viceroyalty.

The classic tax-based historiography, in which the role of New Spain was only a part of the broader economic history of the Spanish Atlantic, began with Earl J. Hamilton's classic study of prices (1934) and continued through the equally classic multi-volume Atlantic trade project of Pierre and Hughette Chaunu (1955–60). The broad sweep of New Spain's trade with Asia by way of the Philippines was also analyzed by Pierre Chaunu (1960), and the wide-ranging interests of Woodrow Borah led him to explore the intercolonial Pacific trade with Peru (1954). In the 1970s the macro-level study of Spain's transatlantic commerce was extended to cover the late seventeenth and eighteenth centuries (García Fuentes, 1978; García-Baquero González, 1976). And it was at the same time that historians interested in the economic history of New Spain began to consider the regional impact of these broader trade patterns. For example, the question of whether there had been an economic crisis in the seventeenth century was explored in a series of well-known essays by Herbert Klein and John TePaske (1981, 1982), J. I. Israel (1982), and Henry Kamen (1982).

The most recent research into New Spain's economic history continues both the careful analysis of fiscal records and the effort to construct a synthesis from tax data and other sources. An example of the fiscal record research is the remarkable and not well-known work of Engel Sluiter, *The Gold and Silver of Spanish America* (1998). This book, essentially a series of tables representing mining income and royal expenditures accompanied by detailed annotations, is the product of twenty years of truly extraordinary research. An excellent, sophisticated analysis of tax data is Herbert S. Klein, *The American Finances of the Spanish Empire* (1998). Klein's comprehensive review of the different categories of taxes and tax revenue flows illuminates general trends in the viceregal economy and allows for a precise measure of the fiscal dimension of New Spain as the jewel in the crown of Spain's American empire. At least two-thirds of Spain's net imperial income came from New Spain by the eighteenth century, and Klein's study of taxes allows him to determine this income both by economic sector – mining, agriculture, Indian head taxes, monopoly taxes on tobacco, gunpowder, and mercury – and by geographical region within the viceroyalty. In the late eighteenth century Crown expenditures for salaries and colonial administration generally amounted to no more than 20 percent of collections. More than 25 percent of revenue income was remitted to Spain, and a similar portion was spent in defense of the empire – military salaries, fort construction, and armaments – in New Spain proper and throughout the Caribbean and the Pacific. The best effort to form a synthesis of New Spain's economic history in the eighteenth century, using tax records and other sources, is Richard L. Garner (1993).

There was a long and pervasive tradition, stretching from the sixteenth to the late twentieth century, which claimed that the perduring, martial mindset of the conquistadors and the persistence of seigniorial values militated against the development of business acumen and entrepreneurship in colonial Spanish America. Numerous studies now exist that put this myth to rest. Those who managed businesses and sought to profit from New Spain's often dynamic economy are the subject of two classics: David Brading's *Miners and Merchants* (1970) and Bakewell's book on Zacatecas silver mining (1971) discussed earlier. Also important are John Kicza's survey (1983) of elite businessmen in the eighteenth century, and the marvelous history of a critical early period, Louisa Schell Hoberman, *Mexico's Merchant Elite* (1991). Among the excellent studies of particular sectors of economic production are Richard J. Salvucci on textile manufacturing (1987), Susan Deans-Smith on tobacco, the business and the royal monopoly (1992), and the unsurpassed study by the geographer Ward Barrett on New Spain's most important sugar estate (1970).

The economic history of rural New Spain, meaning agriculture and ranching and including the nature and control of labor on the land, has followed the general pattern of increasingly close examination of particular segments of the social reality. Regional studies predominate, and in this, as in much else, William Taylor was a pioneer. His study of Oaxaca (1972) was followed by Brading's work on the important north-central region, the Bajío, colonial New Spain's breadbasket (1978); Van Young on the haciendas and markets of Guadalajara (1981); and Cheryl Martin on rural society in south-central Morelos (1985). Research on the seventeenth century lags behind in economic history as it does in every other aspect of colonial Mexican history, and for this reason Lolita Gutiérrez Brockington's study of labor during the seventeenth century on the Cortés estates in the isthmus of Tehuantepec (1989) is especially welcome. More recent work continues to be characterized by a finite geographical focus, but considers the economy more broadly, often including its environmental and ecological dimensions. Elinor Melville's book on the Spaniards' introduction of ranching and the environmental consequences of the conquest (1994) is a landmark study. Also important are Arij Ouweneel's comprehensive analysis of the economy and ecology of eighteenth-century central New Spain (1996), Cheryl Martin's careful reconstruction of governance and society on the northern frontier – Chihuahua – in the eighteenth century (1996), and Cynthia Radding's remarkable work on ethnicity, the environment, and colonialism on late colonial and early national Mexico's northwestern frontier (1997).

One product of the ongoing close examination of New Spain's complex and varied economy is a reconsideration of the leading role of silver mining in late colonial New Spain. Its importance has been questioned by Eric Van Young (1986) and Richard Garner (1990) who point out that much of the silver produced during the last decades of the eighteenth century was appropriated by the Crown and shipped to Spain, and that mining had a limited linkage effect on agriculture, textiles, and production generally, and little impact on consumer power. Others suggest that the real value of silver mining actually declined during the last quarter of the century, even in spite of increased production (Coatsworth, 1986). Recent scholarship (an excellent summary is in Garner, 1993, pp. 246–58) attributes the nominal growth in production in the New Spain economy more to population expansion than to silver mining. Dramatic increases in taxation, especially after the 1770s, coupled with a stagnant or declining agricultural economy, led to a proportionately greater drain of silver from the viceroyalty. As per capita income dropped, and pressure on the land increased, people moved from the countryside to the mining centers and cities in search of work, and the price of staples increased generally. This economic context formed a part of that extraordinary conjuncture of events that would give rise to the wars of Mexican independence.

Late Colonial Crisis and Independence

The connections between these declining material conditions and the social and political events of the late eighteenth and early nineteenth centuries, including the struggle for independence beginning in 1810, have long been a subject of interest to historians.

Two remarkable recent books, which are certain to be ranked with the most important histories of colonial history ever written, address these themes.

William B. Taylor has long held a place of privilege among historians of New Spain. His monumental study, *Magistrates of the Sacred* (1996), is a far-reaching study that explores first and foremost the complex, fascinating nature and practice of religion in New Spain. Taylor here builds his analysis on an extensive comparison of the two most important ecclesiastical jurisdictions in New Spain: the archdiocese of Mexico and the diocese of Guadalajara. These were the richest and most populous of the ten dioceses in eighteenth-century New Spain, and Taylor's focus on religion is firmly tied to the social and economic histories of these regions. *Magistrates of the Sacred* is theoretically sophisticated, especially with regard to the fundamental issues of Native belief and religious behavior. Drawing together the results of years of innovative scholarship and study, Taylor addresses the broad questions relating to the encounter between Christianity and Native worldviews. He points out that most modern interpreters of Mesoamerican Indian religion view the process of the indigenous transition to pre-conquest to colonial as following one of three distinct paths: acceptance and transformation to Christianity, resistance to that process, or syncretism. He finds that although syncretism has been the most favored interpretive framework, many of those who have used the concept have employed a variety of mechanical and organic metaphors ("welding, blending, fusion, synthesis, amalgamation and hybridization") which have not allowed them to go much beyond invoking the idea that Catholic and Native elements did combine to create a new, by and large stable, religion which is most often labeled "syncretic." However, for Taylor the process in Mexico was not one of a synthesis of religions or the assimilation of one religion by another, nor was it a process that had been mostly completed sometime during the first centuries after conquest. To the contrary, he finds that local religion in Mexico in the eighteenth century was still fluid and frequently contested, as conflicts over religious practices, symbols, and the role and authority of the priest in indigenous villages were commonplace. Taylor argues that Indians' identification as Christians continued late into the colonial period to be a process of interpreting and adjusting to the expectations of their priests, without simply being directed by them. Priests provided the framework for Catholic practice and often had considerable influence in other areas of social and cultural life, but they were not able to actually determine the religious aspects of Indians' everyday lives. In its most general formulation, Taylor's understanding of the significance for Native people of religious encounter in colonial Mexico is that the changes that took place in Indian religions had less to do with specific practices and doctrine than with habit and concepts regarding ultimate concerns; that is, faith was more important than belief. The changes that occurred cannot be understood by adding up substituted behaviors, or by regarding apparent substitutions as assimilated. Indians sought access to Spaniards' spiritual knowledge and power in order to fortify the connection between the sacred and the profane in ways that were meaningful to them. This was as true in the eighteenth century as it was in the sixteenth.

Magistrates of the Sacred combines a sweeping appreciation of the priesthood in late colonial New Spain – the recruitment and formation of priests, the nature of their careers, their roles as judges, teachers, and as clergymen in parish service – with an equally comprehensive understanding of the religious lives and the roles of religion in the lives of their parishioners. The dynamics of these priest–parishioner encounters were shaped significantly in the eighteenth century by a third element: a resurgent royal effort to reform local society. This "triangle of authority" (priests, parishioners, and district governors) constituted the structure of politics in late colonial parishes. Tensions between provincial royal governors and parish priests became endemic as the government sought to gain greater control over the public life of villagers. The jurisdictional crisis that formed between secular and ecclesiastical officials focused on several specific issues, most of which involved a diminution of traditional priest authority. Some of these issues, such as the government innovation of a schedule of fees that could be charged for clerical services, led to direct conflicts between priests and governors. Other reform issues presented a challenge to the traditional, if always tenuous, balance between priests and parishioners. The government's insistent interest in social order and decorum brought governors to blame priests for the large number of village-based fiestas and disorderly behavior that they contained. Priests, whose sponsorship of these events was embedded in local community life (and who benefited financially from their celebration), suffered a tangible loss of traditional authority as they were increasingly relegated by the governors to a role of honored spectators. Such issues as control of fiestas led to much deeper conflicts over power in the community.

The eighteenth-century Bourbon monarchy's desire to institute a modernized, standardized, and more absolutist authority, and to increase the royal patrimony, pulled New Spain's parish priests in several different directions as they felt the threat that these reforms presented to their traditional roles of judge and pastor. When the empire began to unravel in 1810, having been moved by these royal initiatives to a more marginal place in what had long been understood as a full partnership with the Crown in the colonial enterprise, many priests in the archdiocese of Mexico and the diocese of Puebla, the heartland of the viceroyalty, found themselves divided in their loyalties. Still tied closely to the empire, and the systems of patronage and authority that had been in place since the conquests, many parish priests were nevertheless considerably less loyal in 1810 than others of their social class. Some priests, perhaps one in twelve according to Taylor's calculations, became insurgents, but, more importantly, many more, a substantial majority, followed a course of determined neutrality in the war for independence. The choice of neutrality was more damaging to the Crown than it was to the insurgency, for in as much as parish priests had been essential features of the royal administration for three centuries, neutrality was in effect a form of defection.

The twenty-first century begins with a second extraordinary book of great significance. Eric Van Young's *The Other Rebellion* (2001), like Taylor's *Magistrates of the Sacred*, is a profound exploration of the political actions and mindsets of ordinary people in the tumultuous contexts of late New Spain. Although ostensibly more limited chronologically (to the war for Mexican independence) than Taylor, both historians are primarily concerned with popular reactions to the broad range of changing circumstances in eighteenth-century New Spain. Both see the village or the rural parish as the fundamental unit of popular identity and the locus of social life and political action. Like Taylor, Van Young finds the interaction between priest and parish to be a critical axis of political life in the late colonial countryside, but *The Other Rebellion* is a sweepingly broad inquiry that moves magnificently in many directions. The general argument of the book is that, to the extent that it can be considered a single entity, the popular insurgency in New Spain during the years 1810 to 1821 was most of all an effort by rural communities to reach an end of a prolonged period of resistance against a panoply of forces that threatened change – imperial policies, economic shifts, population growth, ideological and cultural innovations. This was "the other rebellion" in as much as popular participation in the violence that resulted did not have independence from Spain as a goal.

Van Young argues that the hundreds of towns and villages that were still predominantly indigenous in sociocultural makeup at the end of the eighteenth century mobilized to reach "some sort of standoff" in the long-standing struggle against eighteenth-century change. Along the way to this conclusion, Van Young develops a remarkable understanding of the politics of late colonial Mexico's rural people. His methods, which are as passionate and artistic as they are rigorously intellectual, lead him to find that these people entered the insurrection for reasons that cannot be reduced to structural factors, either political or economic. He finds that participation depended on identification with home communities, and that the variety of motivations leading to insurgency was tied closely to leadership patterns, whether those leaders were indigenous notables, priests, or local firebrands. The broad question of how people passed from personal circumstances to collective action lies at the root of *The Other Rebellion*. Van Young demonstrates that people were not "whipped up" into artificial frenzy by such leaders, nor were they "swept away" by ideological or moral arguments that tied them to the cause of independence. The role of leaders was definitely not one of articulating an ideology of incipient nationalism to the rural masses. Rural people had their own political and cultural agendas, and, more than simply led by charismatic strongmen, insurrectionary countryfolk can be seen to have used these leaders to focus their own, often inchoate, energies as often as they were themselves directed.

This argument is built on a careful study of the patterns of village riots in the decades before the insurgency. The goals and forms of collective expression characteristic of these local uprisings, which were an enduring aspect of the political culture of New Spain, carried over into the insurrection of 1810–1821. In particular, rural rebellion remained largely communitarian in origin and localist in goals. The most widely shared attitude among rural rebels was a continued loyalty to the king, and the fact that the popular insurgent ideology had room for this loyalty (Van Young describes it as "naïve monarchism conflated with messianic expectation") while simultaneously supporting with enthusiasm the murder of individual Spaniards, indicates that something very different from a proto-nationalist attack on the Spanish colonial regime was at work in the Mexican countryside.

Van Young's understanding of the rural rebellion that occurred as part of the crisis of Mexican anti-colonialism lies with issues of community and group identity – ethnic identity for the most part – more than with struggles for land or between classes. Very early in *The Other Rebellion* he addresses the marginal attention that has been given to the independence conflict in Mexico by scholars of the Europe-Atlantic and ex-colonial worlds. He offers several reasons for this, but to him the most important is the great analytical difficulties that are associated with understanding the deep ethnic and cultural divisions characteristic of Mexican society. The ethnocultural conflict engendered by these divisions, an understanding of which is at the core of *The Other Rebellion*, is the chief element that distinguishes the Mexican independence movement from the great revolutions of that era. Van Young argues that the insurgency of 1810–1821 has much broader historical significance than has been recognized. It was, he writes, arguably the first great war of national liberation in which the ethnic difference between colonizers and colonized became a major political issue. It was the first mass rebellion of the nineteenth century to combine, within an incipient national context, elements of ethnic confrontation among colonial dominated indigenous peoples, the descendants of settler colonists, and the colonial regime. (p. 7)

The Other Rebellion may be thought of as bringing the history of New Spain full circle, marking as it does the end, or rather the beginning of the end, of what was begun in 1519 as the first full-scale European project of colonizing Native people. While the history of New Spain is, from start to end, most importantly the history of indigenous people, colonialism, and finally decolonization, as this essay hopefully makes clear, it is also the history of the many other people: mestizos, Afro-Mexican, plebeian Iberians among them.

BIBLIOGRAPHY

Aiton, Arthur Scott: *Antonio de Mendoza: First Viceroy of New Spain* (Durham, NC: University of North Carolina Press, 1927).

Arrom, Silvia Marina: *Containing the Poor: The Mexico City Poor House, 1774–1871* (Durham, NC: Duke University Press, 2000).

Bakewell, Peter: *Silver Mining and Society in Colonial Mexico: Zacatecas 1546–1700* (Cambridge: Cambridge University Press, 1971).

Barrett, Ward: *The Sugar Hacienda of the Marqueses del Valle* (Minneapolis, MN: University of Minnesota Press, 1970).

Bauer, Arnold J.: "The Colonial Economy." In Louisa Schell Hoberman and Susan Migden Socolow, eds., *The Countryside in Colonial Latin America* (Albuquerque, NM: University of New Mexico Press, 1996), 22–34.

Borah, Woodrow W.: *New Spain's Century of Depression* (Berkeley, CA: University of California Press, 1951).

Borah, Woodrow W.: *Early Colonial Trade and Navigation between Mexico and Peru* (Berkeley: University of California Press, 1954).

Borah, Woodrow W.: *Justice by Insurance: The General Indian Court of Colonial Mexico and the Legal Aides of the Half-Real* (Berkeley, CA: University of California Press, 1983).

Borah, Woodrow W.: *Price Trends of Royal Tribute Commodities in Nueva Galicia, 1557–1598* (Berkeley, CA: University of California Press, 1992).

Borah, Woodrow W. and Cook, Sherburne F.: *Essays in Population History*, 3 vols (Berkeley, CA: University of California Press, 1971–79).

Boyer, Richard: *Lives of the Bigamists: Marriage, Family, and Community in Colonial Mexico* (Albuquerque, NM: University of New Mexico Press, 1995).

Boyer, Richard: "Honor Among Plebians: *Mala Sangre* and Social Reputation." In Lyman Johnson and Sonya Lipsett-Rivera, eds., *The Faces of Honor: Sex, Shame and Violence in Colonial Latin America* (Albuquerque, NM: University of New Mexico Press, 1998).

Brading, David: *Miners and Merchants in Bourbon Mexico* (Cambridge: Cambridge University Press, 1970).

Brading, David: *Haciendas and Ranchos in the Mexican Bajío, León, 1700–1860* (Cambridge: Cambridge University Press, 1978).

Chaunu, Pierre: *Les Philippines et le Pacifique des Ibériques. xvi, xvii, xviii siècles* (Paris: SEVPEN, 1960).

Chaunu, Pierre and Chaunu, Hughette: *Seville et l'Atlantique (1504–1650)*, 9 vols (Paris: Librairie

Armand Colin, 1955–60).

Chevalier, François: *La formation des grands domaines au Mexique: terre et société aux XVIe–XVIIe siècles* (Paris: Université de Paris, 1952); English edition, *Land and Society in Colonial Mexico: The Great Hacienda* (Berkeley, CA: University of California Press, 1963).

Cline, S. L.: *Colonial Culhuacan, 1580–1600: A Social History of an Aztec Town* (Albuquerque, NM: University of New Mexico Press, 1986).

Cline, Sarah L.: "Native Peoples of Colonial Central Mexico." In MacLeod and Adams (2000), pp. 187–222.

Coatsworth, John H.: "The Mexican Mining Industry in the Eighteenth Century." In Nils Jacobsen and Hans-Jürgen Puhle, eds., *The Economies of Mexico and Peru During the Late Colonial Period, 1760–1810* (Berlin: Colloquium Verlag, 1986), 26–45.

Cope, R. Douglas: *The Limits of Racial Domination: Plebeian Society in Colonial Mexico, 1660–1720* (Madison, WI: University of Wisconsin Press, 1994).

Deans-Smith, Susan: *Bureaucrats, Planters and Workers: The Making of the Tobacco Monopoly in Bourbon Mexico* (Austin, TX: University of Texas Press, 1992).

Deans-Smith, Susan: "Native Peoples of the Gulf Coast from the Colonial Period to the Present." In MacLeod and Adams (2000), pp. 274–301.

Deeds, Susan M.: "Legacies of Resistance, Adaptation and Tenacity: History of the Native Peoples of Northwest Mexico." In MacLeod and Adams (2000), pp. 44–88.

Frye, David: "The Native Peoples of Northeastern Mexico." In MacLeod and Adams (2000), pp. 89–135.

García Fuentes, Lutgardo: *El comercio español con América (1650–1700)* (Seville: Escuela de Estudios Hispano-Americanos, C.S.I.C., 1978).

García-Baquero González, Antonio: *Cádiz y el Atlántico (1717–1778)*, 2 vols (Seville: Escuela de Estudios Hispano-Americanos, C.S.I.C., 1976).

Garner, Richard: "Prices and wages in eighteenth-century Mexico." In Lyman L. Johnson and Enrique Tandeter, eds., *Essays on the Price History of Eighteenth-Century Latin America* (Albuquerque, NM: University of New Mexico Press, 1990), 74–108.

Garner, Richard L.: *Economic Growth and Change in Bourbon Mexico* (Gainesville, FL: University Presses of Florida, 1993).

Gibson, Charles: *The Aztecs Under Spanish Rule: A History of the Indians of the Valley of Mexico, 1519–1810* (Stanford, CA: Stanford University Press, 1964).

Gutiérrez Brockington, Lolita: *The Leverage of Labor: Managing the Cortés Haciendas in Tehuantepec, 1588–1688* (Durham, NC: Duke University Press, 1989).

Hamilton, Earl J.: *American Treasure and the Price Revolution in Spain, 1501–1650* (Cambridge, MA: Harvard University Press, 1934).

Haring, Clarence Henry: *The Spanish Empire in America* (New York: Oxford University Press, 1947).

Haskett, Robert: *Indigenous Rulers: An Ethnohistory of Town Government in Colonial Cuernavaca* (Albuquerque, NM: University of New Mexico Press, 1991).

Hoberman, Louisa Schell: *Mexico's Merchant Elite, 1590–1660: Silver, State, and Society* (Durham, NC: Duke University Press, 1991).

Horn, Rebecca: *Postconquest Coyoacan: Nahua–Spanish Relations in Central Mexico, 1519–1650* (Stanford, CA: Stanford University Press, 1997).

Israel, J. I.: "Mexico and the 'General Crisis' of the Seventeenth Century." *Past and Present* 97 (November 1982), pp. 144–50.

Jones, Grant D.: "The Lowland Maya, from the Conquest to the Present." In MacLeod and Adams (2000), pp. 346–91.

Kamen, Henry: "Debate: The Seventeenth-Century Crisis in New Spain: Myth or Reality?" *Past and Present* 97 (1982), pp. 144–50.

Kellogg, Susan: *Law and the Transformation of Aztec Culture, 1500–1700* (Norman, OK: University of Oklahoma Press, 1995).

Kicza, John: *Colonial Entrepreneurs; Families and Business in Bourbon Mexico City* (Albuquerque, NM: University of New Mexico, 1983).

Klein, Herbert S.: *The American Finances of the Spanish Empire; Royal Income and Expenditures in Colonial Mexico, Peru, and Bolivia, 1680–1809* (Albuquerque, NM: University of New Mexico, 1998).

Klein, Herbert and TePaske John: "The Seventeenth-Century Crisis in New Spain: Myth or Reality?" *Past and Present* 90 (1981), pp. 116–35.

Klein, Herbert and TePaske, John: "Rejoinder [to the critiques of Israel and Kamen]." *Past and Present* 97 (1982), pp. 157–62.

Lockhart, James: "Social Organization and Social Change in Colonial Spanish America." In Leslie Bethell, ed., *The Cambridge History of Latin America*, 11 vols. Vol. 2 (Cambridge: Cambridge University Press, 1984), pp. 265–319.

Lockhart, James: "Charles Gibson and the Ethnohistory of Postconquest Central Mexico." In James Lockhart, ed., *Nahuas and Spaniards: Postconquest Central Mexican History and Philology* (Stanford, CA: Stanford University Press, 1991), pp. 65–82.

Lockhart, James: "Views of Corporate Self and History in Some Valley of Mexico Towns, Seventeenth and Eighteenth Centuries." In James Lockhart, ed., *Nahuas and Spaniards: Postconquest Central Mexican History and Philology* (Stanford, CA: Stanford University Press, 1991), pp. 39–64.

Lockhart, James: *The Nahuas after the Conquest: a Social and Cultural history of the Indians of Central Mexico, Sixteenth through Eighteenth Centuries* (Stanford: Stanford University Press, 1992).

Lockhart, James: *Of Things of the Indies; Essays Old and New in Early Latin American History* (Stanford, CA: Stanford University Press, 1999).

Lockhart, James: "Double Mistaken Identity: Some Nahua Concepts in Postconquest Guise." In Lockhart (1999), pp. 98–119.

Lovell, W. George: "The Highland Maya." In MacLeod and Adams (2000), pp. 392–444.

MacLeod, Murdo J.: "Mesoamerica since the Spanish Invasion: An Overview." In MacLeod and Adams (2000), pp. 1–43.

MacLeod, Murdo J. and Adams, Richard E. W., eds.: *The Cambridge History of the Native Peoples of the Americas*, 3 vols, vol. 2, *Mesoamerica* (Cambridge: Cambridge University Press, 2000).

Martin, Cheryl: *Rural Society in Colonial Morelos* (Albuquerque, NM: University of New Mexico Press, 1985).

Martin, Cheryl: *Governance and Society in Colonial Mexico: Chihuahua in the Eighteenth Century* (Stanford, CA: Stanford University Press, 1996).

Melville, Elinor: *A Plague of Sheep: Environmental Consequences of the Conquest of Mexico* (Cambridge: Cambridge University Press, 1994).

Ouweneel, Arij: *Shadows over Anahuac: An Ecological Interpretation of Crisis and Development in Central Mexico, 1730–1800* (Albuquerque, NM: University of New Mexico Press, 1996).

Prescott, William: *History of the Conquest of Mexico* (New York: Harper and Brothers, 1843).

Radding, Cynthia: *Wandering Peoples: Colonialism, Ethnic Spaces, and Ecological Frontiers in Northwestern Mexico, 1700–1850* (Durham, NC: Duke University Press, 1997).

Restall, Matthew: *The Maya World: Yucatec Culture and Society, 1550–1850* (Stanford, CA: Stanford University Press, 1997).

Ricard, Robert: *La "Conquête spirituelle" du Mexique* (Paris, 1933); Eng. trans. *The Spiritual Conquest of Mexico* (Berkeley, CA: University of California Press, 1966).

Romero Frizzi, María de los Angeles: "The Indigenous Population of Oaxaca from the Sixteenth Century to the Present." In MacLeod and Adams (2000), pp. 302–45.

Salvucci, Richard J.: *Textiles and Capitalism in Mexico: An Economic History of the Obrajes,*

1539–1840 (Princeton, NJ: Princeton University Press, 1987).

Seed, Patricia: *To Love, Honor and Obey in Colonial Mexico: Conflicts over Marriage Choice, 1574–1821* (Stanford, CA: Stanford University Press, 1988).

Sluiter, Engel: *The Gold and Silver of Spanish America c. 1572–1648* (Berkeley, CA: The Bancroft Library, 1998).

Taylor, William B.: *Landlord and Peasant in Colonial Oaxaca* (Stanford, CA: Stanford University Press, 1972).

Taylor, William B.: *Drinking, Homicide and Rebellion in Colonial Mexican Villages* (Stanford, CA: Stanford University Press, 1979).

Taylor, William B.: *Magistrates of the Sacred: Priests and Parishioners in Eighteenth-Century Mexico* (Stanford, CA: Stanford University Press, 1996).

TePaske, John: "Economic Cycles in New Spain: The View from the Public Sector." *Bibliotheca Americana* 1:3 (1983), pp. 169–203.

Twinam, Ann: *Public Lives, Private Secrets: Gender, Honor, Sexuality and Illegitimacy in Colonial Spanish America* (Stanford, CA: Stanford University Press, 1999).

Van Young, Eric: *Hacienda and Market in Eighteenth-Century Mexico: The Rural Economy of the Guadalajara Region* (Berkeley, CA: University of California Press, 1981).

Van Young, Eric: "The Age of Paradox: Mexican Agriculture at the End of the Colonial Period." In Nils Jacobsen and Hans-Jürgen Puhle, eds., *The Economies of Mexico and Peru During the Late Colonial Period, 1760–1810* (Berlin: Colloquium Verlag, 1986), pp. 64–90.

Van Young, Eric: "Agrarian Rebellion and Defense of Community: Meaning and Violence in Late Colonial and Independence-Era Mexico." *Journal of Social History* 27 (1993), pp. 245–69.

Van Young, Eric: "Conclusion: The State as Vampire – Hegemonic Projects, Public Ritual, and Popular Culture in Mexico, 1600–1990." In William H. Beezley, Cheryl E. Martin, and William French, eds., *Rituals of Rule, Rituals of Resistance: Public Celebrations and Popular Culture in Mexico* (Wilmington, DE.: Scholarly Resources, 1994) pp. 343–74.

Van Young, Eric: "The Indigenous People of Western Mexico from the Spanish Invasion to the Present." In MacLeod and Adams (2000), pp. 136–86.

Van Young, Eric: *The Other Rebellion: Popular Violence, Ideology, and the Mexican Struggle for Independence, 1810–1821* (Stanford, CA: Stanford University Press, 2001).

Viqueira Albán, Juan Pedro: *Propriety and Permissiveness in Bourbon Mexico* (Mexico, 1987), trans. Sonya Lipsett-Rivera (Wilmington, DE.: Scholarly Resources, 1999).

CHAPTER TWENTY

Comparisons: New France

ALLAN GREER

Overviews

New France has never possessed a single, integrated historiography. Instead, scholarship in French and English has generally followed separate tracks, with the English-language stream tending, at times, to subdivide into distinct American and Canadian components. The walls of national and linguistic isolation are by no means impermeable – cross-fertilization does occur and, indeed, a dialectical exchange is essential to the development of the different schools – but the various historiographical traditions have developed largely separately. Incompatible nationalisms – Canadian, Québécois, and American – have long been at work constructing their different versions of the history of New France.

Actually, the earliest histories of New France often tended to stress religious, rather than national, identities. The Jesuits led the field in the seventeenth century by virtue of their substantial works. François Du Creux published a Latin *History of Canada* (1664), centered on the exploits of French missionaries. However, a later Jesuit author, P.-F.-X. Charlevoix (1744), wrote a multi-volume history with a broader scope, encompassing secular as well as ecclesiastical subjects, and displaying a definite proto-nationalist outlook. In some respects a representative eighteenth-century figure, Charlevoix tended to regard New France from the viewpoint of a mercantilist-minded servant of the Bourbons, defending French territorial claims, assessing the revenue potential of the colony's resources, and evaluating the colonists as economic producers and potential soldiers.

After the British conquest of 1759–60, historical writing went into hibernation for the better part of a century, only to reawaken to the clamour of liberal nationalism. Like their counterparts around the Atlantic world, the young radicals of the *patriote* movement began in the 1830s to reinvent a history for the "peuple canadien." François-Xavier Garneau devoted the first three volumes of his *History of Canada* (1845–52) to New France, emphasizing the colony's heroic exploits in war and exploration and reflecting occasionally on the unfortunate effects of royal absolutism and clerical ascendancy. The hero of his work was the French-Canadian people, struggling against Indians and foreign invaders before the conquest and against British tyranny thereafter. In the conservative atmosphere which increasingly enveloped Quebec following the defeat of the abortive revolution of 1837–8, however, this liberal view fell out of favor. Clerical historians such as J.-B.-A. Ferland and Lionel Groulx came to the fore with an idealized vision of New France as an orderly, hierarchical, Catholic utopia of pious settlers, brave soldiers, and heroic mystics. After the conquest, the vigilance of the Catholic Church saved French Canada from the potential disasters threatened by foreign rule, but the French regime remained as a golden age when the nation's Christian, royalist, and conservative essence was fully manifest (Gagnon, 1982, pp. 44–66, 111–21).

Meanwhile, New France was being discovered by the great romantic American historian, Francis Parkman. Searching for an epic story in the colonial history of North America, Parkman settled upon the century-long duel of France and Britain, a conflict with as conclusive and as satisfactory an outcome as any Victorian novelist could desire. Published between 1865 and 1892, his multi-volume series, *France and England in North America* (1865, new ed., 1983), was a life's work, still awe-inspiring in its scope and magnitude. Parkman's books were dramatic, but also saturated in meaning, largely because of the way the author succeeded in making the two colonial antagonists the embodiment of fundamentally opposed principles (pp. 565, 607, 860–3). Whereas New England represented liberty, industry, and civic virtue, French Canada was marked by absolutist despotism and Catholic obscurantism. "Overweening authority" produced a character type among the settlers of New France which vacillated between blind obedience and, when released into the wilderness, wild freedom. These contradictory traits gave the French a great advantage in exploring the continent and in overcoming their numerical disadvantage in time of war to the extent that they could usually carry the fight to the English settlements. Alongside the main confrontation between French and English, Parkman's works hinged on the opposition of European civilization and depraved Indian "savagery"; the French were all too susceptible to the allurements of savage existence. Thus, New France, with its dedicated missionaries, its swashbuckling adventurers, and its hardy pioneers, was fated to fall in the end. Eventually, peaceable Anglo-Americans would rouse themselves, bring their steadier, more restrained powers to bear, and then finally, inevitably, providentially, they would prevail. Though Parkman devoted far more space to the history of French Canada than to that of its Anglo-American antagonists, there is a sense in which New England provided the implicit yardstick by which everything pertaining to New France was measured. To that degree, New England – as the United States in embryo – remained the central subject of *France and England in North America*.

Parkman's influence among later American and English-Canadian historians was enormous. In the late nineteenth and early twentieth century, when enthusiasm for the British empire ran high, Canadians such as G. M. Wrong (1928; Berger, 1986, pp. 8–21) could relish stories of daring Canadian *coureurs de bois*, all the while secure in the knowledge that England would ultimately prevail and that that brave but rather backward people would then be placed in the protective custody of a truly civilized empire. Ultimately, a British Canada with a quaint French element would arise as the happy result of the conquest. Attitudes towards New France changed over the course of the twentieth century as English-speaking Canadians came to feel less British and more Canadian. W. J. Eccles, who wrote several general works on the French regime in the 1960s and 1970s, including *France in America* (1972; see also Eccles, 1987), exemplifies the changed attitude. In his chronicles of war, politics, and exploration, the author's sympathies were all with France and the French Canadians. More wholeheartedly than that of earlier English-Canadian historians, Eccles's nationalism encompassed the French, and reserved all its antipathy for the colonists who would one day form the United States. At a time when Canadian nationalism often took the form of anti-Americanism, Eccles made Francis Parkman, the quintessence of Yankee arrogance, the target of his most stinging polemics (Eccles, 1987, pp. 16–25).

For more than a century, a profusion of nationalisms infused historical overviews of New France: Garneau's radical patriotism, Ferland's Catholic nationalism, Parkman's Americanism, Wrong's British-Canadian loyalty, and Eccles's pan-Canadian nationalism. In more recent decades, historians have been much more wary of the grand generalizations and essentialist conceptions of national character that underlie nationalist historiography. Instead, the accent has been on rigorous empirical research on particular subjects; for Quebec historians, the influence of the Annales school was decisive in this reorientation. The publication of Louise Dechêne's meticulous monograph, *Habitants and Merchants in Seventeenth-Century Montreal* (1974; trans. ed., 1992), marked the turning point in this respect. From then on, quantitative research on the social and economic structures of settler society was the dominant mode in Quebec historiography (Wien, 1998). Historical geographers such as Cole Harris also played a major part in this shift, a contribution epitomized by the *Historical Atlas of Canada* (Harris, 1987), a synthesis and a work of original scholarship, which presents systematic data on a wide range of topics including the fur trade, migrations of aboriginal peoples, the development of French settlements, and patterns of domestic architecture. My book, *The People of New France*, is a brief survey of recent developments in the social history of the French regime (Greer, 1997).

And did nationalism disappear as historians moved away from the drums and trumpets of "traditional" historiography and into the realms of science? Not really. Traces of Parkman, alloyed with a kind of "Orientalism," still pervade much of the English-language literature on New France. One still encounters the language of quaintness, not to mention attempts to diagnose the various "problems" and "weaknesses" inherent in pre-conquest Canada. Various customs, social formations, and economic practices are treated as symptomatic of some essential inadequacy that makes French Canada, by implication, an incomplete entity needing to be integrated into something larger. This is the approach characteristic of Canadian nationalism. The nationalist strain in Quebec historiography usually takes the form, not of blatant flag-waving, but of a reaction to anglophone othering. If "outsiders" treat early French Canada as the aggregate of various deviations from a norm, then the nationalism of the "insiders" naturally tends to manifest itself in an insistence on the "normality" of New France. Ironically though, "normal" is an outsider's concept, in this case an updated version of Parkman's view of the spirit of New England: enterprising, individualistic, resolutely non-feudal.

While nationalism continues to condition much that is written about New France, nationality has been at work carving it into territorial spheres. With a few notable exceptions, French-Canadian historians limit their studies of the French regime to the St. Lawrence settlements now within the borders of the province of Quebec. English-Canadian historians generally avoid the pre-conquest period altogether, but when they do venture back beyond 1760, they are more likely to include the Atlantic colonies of Acadia and Ile Royale. Louisiana, Illinois, and much of the *pays d'en haut* remain the province of Americanists. Even as intrepid and as wide-ranging a historian as Richard White rarely ventures north of the Great Lakes in tracing his portrait of the *Middle Ground* (1991). Americans study the Iroquois, Canadians look at the Huron. There is something quite irrational about the way Canadians and Americans divide New France along an anachronistic boundary line, confining their research each to their own side and rarely even reading the work of their opposite numbers in any systematic way.

There are auspicious signs, however, of a general broadening of horizons as American historians in increasing numbers take an interest in the northern French colonies (Axtell, 1985; Egnal, 1996; Sayre, 1997) and as Canadianists demonstrate a greater inclination to situate their research in a North American and North Atlantic framework. Perhaps the ghost of Francis Parkman can take some comfort from this development; after denigrating his work for its prejudice, we may now be better able to appreciate it for its breadth of vision.

French Exploration

As Eurocentric stories of heroic exploration have fallen from favor, attention has shifted to the effects of the growing French presence on the aboriginal peoples of northeastern America. Bruce Trigger's *Natives and Newcomers* (1985) provides a good overview of the subject, beginning with a review of the situation of the Iroquoians of the St. Lawrence and lower Great Lakes in the late prehistoric period. Trigger draws on archaeological evidence to show that Natives living far inland procured European goods long before the French established a year-round settlement at Quebec in 1608. As fishermen, whalers, and fur traders, the French were frequenting the coasts of Canada through most of the sixteenth century, but until recently knowledge of their contact with the land and its inhabitants remained quite sketchy. Laurier Turgeon's research in the notarial archives of Bordeaux has shed considerable light on this early transatlantic world (Turgeon, 1986). Taking up the archaeologist's trowel, Turgeon has supplemented this European research with exploration of a Basque whaling station on the St. Lawrence. It is evident now that Europeans and local Natives lived and worked together on intimate terms as early as 1580 (Turgeon, 1998).

Traditionally, discussions of French–Indian contact in the sixteenth century were confined to Jacques Cartier's three expeditions to the Gulf and River St. Lawrence between 1534 and 1541. A new English edition of the first-hand accounts of the voyages is now available, edited and with an illuminating introductory essay by Ramsay Cook (Cook, 1993). Cook's discussion of the explorer's colonialist gaze and of his notoriously high-handed treatment of the Iroquoian people of Stadacona and Hochelaga nicely complements Trigger's ethnohistorical treatment of this momentous encounter.

The supply of narrative source material increases tremendously for the seventeenth century when the French came to stay and explorers, missionaries, and settlers wrote of their experiences in the nascent St. Lawrence settlements and beyond. Several of these, including texts by Champlain (Biggar, 1922–36) and Gabriel Sagard (Wrong, 1939), were translated into English and published by the Champlain Society in the first half of the twentieth century. For researchers interested in reading these works in the original language, the Bibliothèque du Nouveau Monde offers a more rigorously edited series of exploration texts featuring extensive introductions by experts in French literature. For some time now, historians of New France have tended to neglect such material, too closely associated perhaps with the older cult of white colonizers, leaving analysis of these rich sources almost entirely to literary scholars and anthropologists.

Gordon Sayre's *Les Sauvages Américains* (1997), to take one recent example of the literary approach, an English-language work in spite of its title, has a great deal to teach historians. Sayre systematically compares English and French travel writing from the colonial period, showing how these texts were structured according to the conventions of the ancient genre traditions of ethnographic description and travel narrative. In examining the work of Samuel de Champlain, the "Father of New France," alongside that of his English contemporary and counterpart, John Smith, Sayre provides a model of comparative analysis that historians might well emulate.

After establishing their colony on the St. Lawrence in the early seventeenth century, the French quickly penetrated the Great Lakes region and then moved on in the second half of the century to the Mississippi, the northern waterways leading up to Hudson Bay, and after 1730 on to the northern prairies. The main economic basis for these expansionist movements and one of the prime motives for exploration was the fur trade. The *Historical Atlas of Canada* (Harris, 1987, Plates 33–41) contains a series of plates that are the best place to begin tracing these initial probes and the ramifying network of canoe routes and outposts that spread out from Montreal. Another reference work, the first three volumes of the *Dictionary of Canadian Biography* (1966–74) provides authoritative information on all the major explorers, such as Louis Jolliet, René-Robert Cavelier de la Salle, and Pierre Gaultier de Varennes et de la Vérendrye.

On the fur trade, Harold Innis's classic work, *The Fur Trade in Canada* (1929), is still cited but seldom read, for Innis, notwithstanding his brilliance, was no stylist. This book was the occasion on which Innis enunciated his "staple thesis" of colonial development. Overseas settlements, he maintained, tended to specialize in a single, semi-raw product of nature, produced for export, and this staple trade shaped the colony's society, politics, and metropolitan relations. In the case of New France, dependence on the trade in beaver pelts conditioned relations between French and Natives, drove the French to penetrate into the interior of North America, fostered the development of economic monopoly and authoritarian politics, and fomented commercial conflict with the British that led in turn to war and conquest. Since Harold Innis's death, his view of the early Canadian fur trade has been challenged in almost every particular. W. J. Eccles (1987, pp. 61–95) is among those who have denounced Innis's dogmatic commercial determinism, noting that the French often had non-economic motives for exploring the interior and opposing the British; often the fur trade was pursued at a loss in order to bind Natives more closely to the French interest.

There is no modern synthesis on the fur trade to match Innis's, perhaps because "the fur trade" no longer seems a self-contained topic. New research proceeds apace on several of the issues initially raised in *The Fur Trade in Canada*, but the results are appearing in widely dispersed publications. Ethnohistory monographs, such as those of Trigger (1976) and White (1991), discuss cross-cultural commerce in the context of broader patterns of interaction between Europeans and Indians. The old notion that the fur trade rapidly reduced Natives to a state of abject dependence on imported goods has been replaced by more complex treatments of the integration of new objects into existing patterns of material culture. Other historians have concentrated on the French-Canadian side of the trade, examining the merchants and outfitters of Montreal, as well as the *voyageurs* who freighted the bales of merchandise across the canoe portages of the distant West (Dechêne, 1974, pp. 50–77, 140–50, 217–29). Thomas Wien (1994) has extended the reach of Canadian fur-trade studies back across the Atlantic, as he follows the trail of pelts through the countries of eighteenth-century Europe.

Colonial Encounters

Although Natives played a crucial role in all the narratives of New France, they were until recently treated as a *condition* affecting the establishment and development of the colony, not as a part of the story. In Canada as in other sites of colonial history, the tendency over recent decades has been to move from a one-way story of European exploration and settlement to a focus on the interaction of "Natives and Newcomers." The complex, reciprocal relationship between French and Indians now appears as the obvious central theme of the history of New France. New research in this vein is fueled partly by extraordinary sources such as the *Jesuit Relations* (Thwaites, 1896–1900; Greer, 1999), a series of detailed reports from the mission field published in France between 1632 and 1673. Some researchers have drawn on these primary texts to help construct an Indian-centered account of early Canadian history, while others have taken a new look at the French themselves, treating the colonizer's outlook as a historical problem rather than an unexamined given.

The landmark work in this historiographic reorientation was Bruce Trigger's *The Children of Aataentsic* (1976). Trigger was not the first to employ the ethnohistoric approach, but his study of the history of the Huron people was so full and authoritative – and, notwithstanding the author's credentials as an anthropologist, so resolutely historical – that it transformed the field. Combining historical sources with ethnographic theory and archaeological evidence, Trigger set out to trace the history of the Huron, the Iroquoian peoples who inhabited what is now central Ontario until their society was shattered in 1649 by attacks emanating from the Five Nations of the Iroquois Confederacy. "My aim," he announced in the Preface, "has been to write a history of the Huron, not of New France or of French–Indian relations in the seventeenth century" (Trigger, 1976, p. xxi), but historical and historiographic circumstances forced him to undertake a thorough re-examination of the early decades of French colonization. As traders, missionaries, and chroniclers, the French cast too long a shadow over the seventeenth-century Huron country for Trigger to ignore them. They, and especially the Jesuits among them, do emerge in his account as exceptionally obtuse observers of the aboriginal scene, but then that is probably how they appeared to the Hurons. In focusing on the Natives themselves, their experience of epidemics, wars, and economic upheaval, and their attempts to come to grips with the disruptions associated with colonization, Trigger provided the perfect antidote to a tradition of interpretation which took seriously only the aims and outlook of the Europeans. His interpretation lays stress on material factors in shaping the fate of the Huron, though he avoids any universalizing economism in favor of a culturally specific understanding of economic advantage.

Though the lessons of *The Children of Aataentsic* were not universally accepted, Trigger's work did open up possibilities in several disciplines, while paving the way for further Native-centered research. Books by Denys Delâge and Georges Sioui are particularly notable in this connection. Delâge's *Bitter Feast: Amerindians and Europeans in Northeast North America, 1600–64* (1985) examines the colonization process on a broad canvas that includes New Netherland and New England as well as New France.

Emphatically economic, Delâge's interpretation situates French–Indian relations within the emerging capitalist world system as delineated by Immanuel Wallerstein and others. Unequal exchange in the fur trade between the European core and the North American periphery structured this relationship to the immense disadvantage of the Native trappers. Sioui (1988) shows more interest in an Amerindian cultural essence; he finds this identity, fundamentally opposed to European hegemony, among Algonquins, Hurons, Iroquois, and others as early as the seventeenth century. Huron–Iroquois conflict, in Sioui's account, stemmed mainly from the Hurons' delusional belief that a mutually beneficial alliance with the French was possible. Heavily dependent on Bruce Trigger's work for empirical information, Sioui's work takes the form of philosophical reflections on the history of Native–European relations.

More specialized studies have looked at the military-diplomatic and missionary aspects of French–Amerindian relations. The Beaver Wars, which in the seventeenth century pitted the Iroquois against a northern alliance of French, Huron, Algonquin, and Montagnais, forms one focus of inquiry. Long ago, George Hunt (1940) analyzed this struggle as a straightforward commercial competition with control over the fur trade as the prize. While agreeing that a desire to gain access to fur supplies lay behind Iroquois aggression, Trigger (1976) demonstrated the inadequacy of Hunt's Eurocentric assumptions about the workings of commercial diplomacy in an aboriginal context. Iroquoians, he argued, had recourse to force and negotiation in pursuit of material advantage in a specifically Iroquoian version of economic rationality. In an excellent study of the Five Nations in the colonial period, Daniel Richter (1992) illuminates the Beaver Wars through a close examination of the Iroquoian culture of warfare. Richter introduces the concept of the "mourning war complex" as the key to understanding the Iroquois (and presumably Huron) tendency to attack enemies as a way of grieving over the death of a loved one. Iroquois warriors always concentrated on seizing prisoners who could be taken home to be tortured and then either killed or adopted by the bereaved family. In a more recent study of Iroquois warfare, Roland Viau (1997) takes a broadly similar view.

In the history of French–Indian relations, alliance is generally a more prominent feature than war and so many historians, Richter among them, have examined the various diplomatic, commercial, and personal strands that tied the French into aboriginal networks. Richard White's justly influential *Middle Ground* (1991) examines the French–Indian alliance in the Great Lakes region as an extended exercise in creative misunderstanding. Though they never erased basic cultural differences, French and Algonquians did work out a mutually beneficial modus vivendi in the wake of the devastating Beaver Wars. Central to the connection was the governor of New France – known as "Onontio" to the Indians – who acted, personally and through subordinate officers, as "father" of the anti-Iroquois (later anti-English) alliance. But whereas the French saw their paternal role as one of command, the Natives never accepted dictation; for them, a father was a provider and a mediator of conflicts and so they expected presents from the French and assistance in settling intertribal disputes. The fur trade, sexual liaisons, and military cooperation were all aspects of the constantly renegotiated relationship that was the "middle ground."

White focused on the period beginning in the late seventeenth century and on one crucial area of French–Indian interaction, but it seems that many aspects of the middle ground system operated earlier in the seventeenth century in regions further to the east. In a wide-ranging essay on the overall Native–French alliance of the seventeenth century Denys Delâge anticipated many of White's points (Delâge, 1989). It seems probable that future research will add further flesh to the White interpretation through closer study of particular episodes (the Second Iroquois War of the 1680s and 1690s, for example), individuals (middle ground creatures such as the *coureur de bois* Nicolas Perrot or the Huron chief Kondiaronk), and locales (alliance gathering points such as Green Bay and Detroit).

One well-documented aspect of intercultural relations was the effort by French Catholic missionaries to convert Natives to Christianity. This campaign generated a rich trove of source material since the missionaries – the Jesuits more than the rest – tended to be tireless letter writers and publishers. Mission history was long dominated by apologetic writing, with a Catholic version in which the historian accepted and identified with the religious program of conversion, and a Protestant or secular version in which the civilizing thrust of the missions was taken as self-evidently good. Proving that the Catholic apologetic tradition remains alive and well, Father Lucien Campeau continues to edit documents and to produce some of the most careful and thoroughly researched studies in the field (Campeau, 1987). Reactions against the apologists' ethnocentric treatment of Indians led to the growth of an anti-missionary historiography which blamed the missionaries for damaging Native cultures or dismissed them for failing to secure more than the most superficial "conversions" (Ronda, 1979). This critical current, though impelled by a concern to do justice to Natives, still left the focus on the Europeans; indeed, it tended to operate through a negative identification with the missionary whose aims and actions were evaluated morally rather than historically.

Missions, Protestant English missions as well as French Catholic ones, loom large in James Axtell's expansive study of "acculturation" in colonial North America, *The Invasion Within* (1985). Axtell is particularly sympathetic to the Jesuits of New France who strike him as comparatively tolerant and enlightened agents of Europeanization. Throughout this elegantly written work, the author displays sensitivity to the diversity of French, English, and Indian actors involved and to the complexity of their interaction. And yet, there is a Hegelian quality to his analysis, a tendency to incorporate the messy details of a history that included episodes of violence, trade, misunderstanding, love, and adaptation into one unified narrative of conflict between antithetical principles. "The Contest of Cultures in Colonial North America," Axtell's subtitle and his theme, appears to be a "contest" pitting an Indian cultural essence against a French (or an English) one.

Frequently in the past, historians, whether religious, secular, or critical, have tended to assume that the outlook of the Christian missionaries was, if not transparent, at least comprehensible to researchers who had done their homework on Thomist philosophy; only the Natives were truly inscrutable. Of late, historians have been coming increasingly to the realization that the Jesuits, Ursulines, and Recollets of the seventeenth century are as remote from today's world as are their Huron and Algonquin contemporaries. Hence the growing interest in using the rich missionary sources to conduct ethnohistorical investigations which treat both the Europeans and the Indians as mysteries to be probed. Studies along these lines require textual as well as *con*textual research and so historians are bringing to their analysis of the *Jesuit Relations* backgrounds in the European Counter-Reformation and/or a knowledge of aboriginal culture and spirituality. The ongoing work of Dominique Deslandres (1990) and

Peter Goddard (1997) on the Canadian missions is informed and enriched by the authors' work on internal Catholic missions in France. And the European historian Natalie Davis brings new dimensions to our understanding of missionary women through her examination of the Canadian career of Marie de l'Incarnation (Davis, 1995).

The work of French literature specialists such as Réal Ouellet, Jack Warwick, and Gilles Thérien (1988) deserves a wider audience among historians. To take one recent example of the literary approach, Marie-Christine Pioffet examines the *Jesuit Relations* as a text shaped in important ways to conform to the conventions of the epic genre (Pioffet, 1997). Linguists too have much to teach us about the documents we rely on as sources. Though everyone knows that Europeans and Natives found it difficult to communicate any but the most basic, concrete information across the language barrier, John Steckley (1992) analyses Jesuit texts in the Huron language to see just how the missionaries opted to convey essentially untranslatable religious concepts. In spite of themselves, he discovers, the Jesuits had to present Jesus as a Huron war chief and the Holy Spirit as a version of *oki*. Adopting a different approach, other scholars from Egon Hanzeli (1969) to Margaret Leahy (1995) have looked at the Jesuits as historians of language and linguistic theorists.

Some scholars, coming at the topic of christianization from an initial interest in Native history, have been looking more closely at the Native converts. Many Catholic Iroquois, Huron, and Abenaki settled on reserves near the French settlements of the St. Lawrence. In striking contrast to the rigidly controlled *reducciones* of colonial Latin America, however, these "Amerindian enclaves" – to borrow Marc Jetten's phrase (1994) – retained a high degree of Native autonomy. Whereas historians once argued over whether conversions were "genuine" or merely tactical, researchers are now more inclined to wonder what a ritual such as baptism might mean for the Indians who accepted it (Morrison, 1990; Koppedrayer, 1993). Conversion, then, is being seen not as the endpoint of a story of European triumph, but as one event in a story of cultural interpenetration through which Indians were christianized and Christianity was Indianized.

Beyond the theme of religion, the historiography of French–Indian relations generally seems to be evolving away from a preoccupation with the assimilation/resistance polarity to a post-colonialist-inspired interest in instances of exchange, *métissage*, and hybridity (Davis, forthcoming). Men and women who made their lives in the border zones of colonization – and New France produced more than its share of individuals of that sort – increasingly fascinate scholars in the field. Eunice Williams, the Puritan girl and later Catholic Mohawk matron, has found her biographer (Demos, 1994), while her Native counterpart, the saintly Christian virgin Catherine Tekakwitha, continues to attract researchers (Koppedreyer, 1993). Most French-Canadian *coureurs de bois* appear in the record quite anonymously, but two of them left rich memoirs recounting their experiences as Indianized Europeans: Pierre-Esprit Radisson and Nicolas Perrot (Warkentin, 1996; Perrot, 1996).

Social History

The notoriously vague rubric "social history" provides ample space to accommodate the bulk of the past three decades of New France scholarship, but it is invoked here with something more specific in mind: a discussion of research on population growth, agrarian class relations, and the commercial bourgeoisie, three topics that have been particularly attractive to French-Canadian historians.

Blessed with exceptionally complete and reliable registers of births, deaths, and marriages, New France has long been the favored laboratory for the emergent science of historical demography. Jacques Henripin's (1954) monograph pioneered the technique of family reconstitution as a means of measuring fertility with a high degree of precision. Henripin found that the early settlers of Canada, though highly fecund, were not outside the normal range of pre-industrial variation. Whereas Henripin's early probe relied on sample data assembled by genealogists, a team of demographers led by Hubert Charbonneau and Jacques Légaré of the University of Montreal has since succeeded in reconstituting the entire French-Canadian population from the founding of Quebec to the end of the eighteenth century. From parish register data, supplemented by information from other sources, the Montreal demographers have assembled a database that is proving itself invaluable to social historians as well as to population experts (Légaré, 1980–90). Most of their research has been published in French journals, but Charbonneau's book, *The First French Canadians* (1993), is available in English. When historians read these works, they tend to be impressed with the technical rigor of the demographers' analyses, but disappointed by the rather unhistorical framework of many of the inquiries. The focus tends to alternate between strictly biological processes and frankly antiquarian, or even filio-pietistic, research agendas.

Like other North American settler populations, the French grew rapidly in numbers, thanks mainly to almost universal marriage and the prompt remarriage of widows and widowers. Immigration played a part, of course, but the numbers coming from Europe were quite small compared with the transatlantic movement to the English colonies. (Estimates vary between 10,000 and 20,000 for the 150-year period.) In the virtual absence of passenger lists and other, similar sources, social historians such as Peter Moogk (1989) and Leslie Choquette (1997) have had to reconstruct patterns of migration and profiles of immigrants as best they can from uncooperative documents. Their research confirms the impression that the trickle of French migrants crossing the Atlantic was composed primarily of poor young men from the cities. In order to balance the sexes and give a boost to the procreative process, the government of Louis XIV sponsored the transport of unattached women, known as the "king's daughters," a topic examined by the demographic historian, Yves Landry (1992).

Though they came mostly from the towns of western France, the majority of immigrants and their offspring ended up settling on the land in Canada, forming a New World peasantry known as the "habitants." Taking their cue from France where agrarian studies long dominated *ancien régime* historiography, the social historians of New France have made the habitants and the social and economic patterns of colonial life a favored object of study. Discussion has revolved around several questions. Was habitant agriculture subsistence oriented or did it respond to the demands of the market? Should Canada's rural social formation be seen as essentially European and "feudal," or was it fundamentally individualistic, acquisitive, and American? How significant a role did the institution of seigneurial land tenure play in shaping agrarian class relations?

Certainly Francis Parkman saw rural French Canada as a quaint and archaic social formation, peopled by medieval peasants and feudal landlords. Similarly, though with a different value judgement, Catholic French-Canadian historians of the nineteenth century tended to idealize the seigneurie as a happy, conservative family presided over by an aristocratic father-figure. A break came in 1966 when the geographer R. C. Harris (1966) presented evidence indicating that early Canadian seigneurialism was little more than an empty shell. Seigneurs exercised only minimal influence over the process of settlement and they were powerless to oppose the liberating forces inherent in the New World environment. Consequently, the habitants, as described by Harris, were typical North American settlers enjoying freedom of action and paying only small token rents to their landlords.

A few years later, Louise Dechêne (1974) published a monograph on Montreal and the surrounding countryside that reinforced some of Harris's points, even as it challenged others. Like the geographer, she found no support for the traditional notion that the seigneurie provided a framework for community life in rural New France, but she did not go along with his suggestion that rents were light and seigneurial tenure a negligible institution. Though they did not act as local leaders to any important extent, seigneurs did impose a substantial economic burden on the habitants. Much more than Harris, Dechêne detected basic similarities in the situation of the habitants and that of the French peasantry of the period.

Since the publication of *Habitants et marchands de Montréal*, other historians have followed Dechêne's lead in examining rural society and economy through local studies based primarily on the notarial archives, with their marriage contracts, estate inventories, and inheritance papers. Closer acquaintance with the agrarian history literature on *ancien régime* France has dampened enthusiasm for extreme versions of a North-American-uniqueness argument. Still, discussion tends to revolve around questions about the self-sufficiency of the household economy and the degree to which "capitalist" outlooks and behavior penetrated the rural world (Desbarats, 1992). The debates tend to parallel discussions on "individualism" and "household economies" in early United States historiography, with somewhat similar ideological forces at play. Whereas earlier generations of French-Canadian nationalist historians emphasized the ordered, hierarchical character of rural New France, modern nationalists tend to celebrate evidence of a liberal atmosphere and a striving, entrepreneurial quality among the settler population. In spite of the historiographic parallels, and the apparent opportunities for comparative analysis, US and Canadian historians have generally pursued debates in mutual isolation.

The cities of Canada – really there were only two, Quebec, the capital and seaport, and Montreal, the gateway to the western interior – have attracted less attention from social historians than has the countryside. And yet the towns concentrated colonial political power, ecclesiastical life, and business activity to a remarkable degree. In the 1970s, there was a heated debate over the merchants of New France – their mentality, business techniques, and influence – which did focus attention on that aspect of urban life. This was a time of intense confrontation between nationalists and federalists in Quebec, and historiography tended to function as a major ideological battleground. Generally, the tendency was for historians sympathetic to the independence of Quebec to portray the merchants of New France as up-to-date, forward-looking entrepreneurs who set the tone for the entire colony before the British conquest ruined everything. Federalist historians denigrated the merchants and emphasized their marginality, implying that the English domination of post-conquest business was the product of superior enterprise, not political power. Several contributions to this debate are available in English translation in Dale Miquelon's collection, *Society and Conquest* (1977). The ideological blasts and counter-blasts of the sixties had the valuable effect of stimulating the curiosity of more careful researchers such as Louise Dechêne (1974) and Dale Miquelon (1978) who succeed in situating the merchants of Montreal and Quebec in their early modern setting. More recently, John Bosher (for example, 1987) has produced a series of studies situating the merchants and the trade of New France as part of the French Atlantic commercial network. Bosher emphasizes the role of the Huguenot diaspora in colonial and international trade.

Gender

Gender as a major "category of historical analysis" has been rather slow to catch on in French-Canadian historiography. Over the years, there have been several studies of women in New France, but most of these were in the "contributionist" mode. Books and articles gave due recognition to the role of hospital nuns and religious lay women such as Jeanne Mance in furthering the French colonial project by caring for the sick and destitute; Madeleine de Verchères's exploits leading the defense of her family fort against Iroquois attackers was commemorated; and the vital contribution of generations of habitant women to family livelihoods was not forgotten. In all this traditional literature, there was little sense of any divergence of interest between the sexes, nor was the essentially male-centered conception of the colony and its interests ever questioned. Nevertheless, in the context of a historiography inclined to treat New France as an exclusively male entity, there was real value in attempts to balance the record by drawing attention to heroines and helpmates.

Jan Noel (1986) began to reorient the discussion by asking not only what women did for New France, but what New France did for women. Canada, she concluded, was on the whole a good place for women. There was no shortage of potential husbands, and married women retained a degree of economic independence thanks to the egalitarian property regime of French civil law. With men frequently called from home for service in the fur trade or the military, wives were commonly left in charge of family and business affairs for long periods of time. Noel's thesis, though not universally accepted, did set the agenda for discussion.

Meanwhile, feminist scholars working in the area of contact and colonization were beginning to insist that a history that was serious about including women had to reconsider historical processes in more fundamental ways. Taking gender as a central dimension of the colonial relation between Europeans and natives, Eleanor Leacock and Karen Anderson set out to re-examine the seventeenth-century Jesuit sources. The anthropologist Leacock (1986) looked particularly at the missionaries' attempts to impose a European version of patriarchy on Montagnais women, while Anderson's monograph, *Chain her by one Foot* (1991) amplified and extended her predecessor's analysis. Anderson's rather sweeping conclusions about the subjugation of women generally, on the basis of a limited number of missionary accounts, seem overblown to some critics. The Jesuits, she implies, not only tried to subjugate converted native women, they succeeded. In pointing out that Native gender systems were not entirely egalitarian and in noting the uncertain and variable outcomes of conversion, more recent work (Davis, 1994) suggests the need for more nuanced conclusions in this area. Certainly there is room for further research on the interplay of European and

Indian gender systems in New France to follow up on the bold initial essays of Leacock and Anderson. The growing literature on Latin America and the United States should provide fruitful points of comparison.

For the later stages of colonial history, when the French predominated in the St. Lawrence valley, researchers interested in women and gender face different challenges, largely to do with sources. Source limitations, especially the paucity of documents written by women, is a problem historians of the early modern period have become accustomed to, but the situation of post-contact New France is special in certain respects. After the 1660s, missionary writings become less helpful and, at the same time, the lack of surviving diaries and collections of private correspondence (nuns excepted: see below) makes it difficult to undertake the kind of studies of women and gender favoured by American colonialists. By way of compensation, however, the judicial records and the notarial archives of New France contain masses of material bearing on the situation of women and on the construction of colonial gender systems. Documents of this sort have been subjected to quantitative analysis in the past, but more is likely to be learned in the future through a more "ethnographic" examination of carefully selected cases drawn from the records of criminal trials or of inheritance settlements.

Unlike other categories of colonial women, whose voices have to be sought in court documents, nuns wrote extensively and their letters and chronicles have survived in substantial numbers. The all-time champion correspondent was Marie de l'Incarnation, the first Mother Superior of the Ursulines of Quebec. A mystic visionary, self-taught intellectual, and dynamic ecclesiastical administrator, Marie sent literally thousands of letters to colleagues, benefactors, and relatives back in France. The fascinating story of her efforts to come to terms with Canada and its Native inhabitants forms one-third of Natalie Davis's *Women on the Margins* (1995). Other French *religieuses* such as the hospital nun, Catherine de St-Augustin (Ragueneau, 1671), await modern biographers. In the meantime, Dominique Deslandres (1991) provides a good, brief overview of women missionaries.

The Colonial State

French historians of the *ancien régime* have never shown much interest in the overseas dimension of the Bourbon monarchy. The subject of American empire arises in studies of Louis XIV's commercially minded minister, Jean-Baptiste Colbert (Cole, 1939), but there is only the thinnest literature on imperial France, one of the major players in seventeenth- and eighteenth-century North America and the Caribbean. The contrast with British imperial historiography is quite striking and the results unfortunate for historians of the colonial state who have had little help in constructing a Euro-Atlantic background for their studies of the administration of New France.

Source materials are by no means lacking for research into the workings of the highly bureaucratized Bourbon empire. A voluminous collection of dispatches (the "*correspondence générale*") from the major colonial officials – especially the governor and intendant of New France – to the Minister of Marine, the minister in charge of trade, the navy, and colonies, has been preserved in France, with microfilm copies available in North America and a detailed guide on CD-ROM available from the National Archives of Canada. With its reports and attached documents treating trade, administration, justice, Indian affairs, and all manner of other subjects, the *correspondence générale* has long been a prime resource for researchers. Private papers, on the other hand, are quite rare. Researchers also have at their disposal an invaluable reference work, the *Dictionary of Canadian Biography* (1966–74), whose profiles of French-regime officials constitute a storehouse of raw data for any study of the colonial administration.

The most important recent contributions in this area have focused on finance, criminal justice, and the military. John Bosher, a specialist in French finances on the eve of the Revolution, published an influential essay on the colonial state and finance in New France (1967). In it, he argued that the financial integrity of the colony, like that of the mother country, was undermined by the failure to draw a clear line separating government funds from those of the king's officials and tax farmers. "Public" and "private" were not distinct categories, according to Bosher, and as a consequence, corruption could not even be understood, much less eliminated. This thesis has been challenged by many scholars, including Louise Dechêne (1994, pp. 137–39), who finds that, for all their failings, the administrators of New France recognized the difference between their private wealth and that of the king. Corruption only reached serious levels, she adds, in wartime when massive government spending provided irresistible temptations to privileged insiders. Colonial finances are coming into clearer focus as Catherine Desbarats (1995) continues to publish her ongoing research on the subject.

The courts and criminals of New France form the focus of several monographs, most of which tend to use judicial records to construct statistical profiles on the people who came before the courts (e.g., Lachance, 1978 and Dickinson, 1982). The courts and their professional legal personnel, far more removed from local communities and more fully integrated into the state than were their English colonial counterparts, have been thoroughly anatomized in these studies. In a suggestive article, Douglas Hay (1981) looks at the decades following the British conquest to see what happened when English and French approaches to criminal justice confronted one another. Comparative approaches come naturally in this sort of historical laboratory situation, and Hay takes advantage of the opportunity to discuss some essential differences – inquisitorial vs. adversarial procedures, the use of torture, closed vs. public trials – between French and British justice in the eighteenth century.

Military forces formed an important element of the French state in Canada, especially after the formation of the *troupes de la marine* in 1683. Some historians, such as Parkman and Eccles (1987, pp. 110–24), have indeed suggested that New France was essentially a military colony, its bellicose character shaped by the difficulties of competing with the much more populous and developed British colonies. Current research, while not inclined to reject this view entirely, tends to insert more distinctions into the image of New France as armed camp. In wartime, the king could call on the services of Native allies, French-Canadian militia, and professional *troupes de la marine*, and though they fought under similar conditions, these categories of men stood in quite different political relations to the sovereign. Only the *troupes de la marine* could be considered as purely a branch of the state, occupying the armed retainer role that was so essential a feature of continental European monarchies in the age of absolutism. The militia was something quite different: a mechanism for projecting state power into the midst of civilian communities. And Indian warriors – the men who undertook the lion's share of fighting in most colonial wars – were only loosely and problematically connected to the king of France. Thus, "the military in New France" is anything but a simple category when considered from a political point of view. We await Louise Dechêne's forthcoming study to renew our understanding of this important topic.

Many aspects of the political history of New France have generated empirical research and lively debate, but the opportunities for new departures remain numerous. Alexis de Tocqueville long ago proposed seventeenth-century Canada as the prototype absolutist polity, a political New World upon which Louis XIV could put his centralizing principles into practice without traditional privileges to hinder him ([1856] 1955, pp. 253–4). Historians might well test this hypothesis by re-examining the colonial state as a system, and not simply in its constituent parts. Christophe Horguelin (1997) has initiated the process of re-evaluation with a vigorously argued study of the advent of royal rule in New France. According to Horguelin, it was the office of intendant, instituted in 1665, which brought the colonial oligarchy to heel and placed Canada firmly under Bourbon control.

War

War, W. J. Eccles asserted, was the main industry of New France (1987, p. 110). First the French faced the formidable Iroquois Confederacy in the mid-seventeenth century and then, after 1689, they fought with Britain and the British colonies in the course of recurrent conflicts that made Canada the most important base of operations in America. These imperial struggles were at the center of Francis Parkman's view of the history of New France, and for many years after Parkman's death the historiography remained wedded to military themes. But in the 1960s, social and economic history began to crowd out military history. French-Canadian historians, in particular, tended to be interested in soldiers only to the extent that they stayed away from the battlefield and entered the colonial workforce. After a long period of neglect, however, military history seems to be staging a comeback, though now in a socially informed, multicultural form, with Indians, habitant militiamen and rank-and-file regulars now receiving their due.

For those seeking an outline of the events of the French–English wars of the 1689–1760 period, Ian Steele's *Guerillas and Grenadiers* (1969) still provides the best overview. As his title implies, Steele concentrates on the respective roles of irregular units waging *la petite guerre* after the Native fashion and regular European forces following conventional tactics. He argues that, although Canada specialized in the "guerilla" style through most of the early conflicts with Britain, the formal European version of warfare came to predominate in the Seven Years' War (1754–60), the struggle which brought the downfall of the French empire in North America. Guy Frégault tells the story of the Seven Years' War (known in the United States as the "French and Indian War") in *Canada: The War of the Conquest* (1955). Though attentive to events in Europe, the West Indies, and other theaters of this global struggle, Frégault's French-Canadian nationalist interpretation revolves around the cataclysm that tore Canada away from its natural home in the French empire and subjected it to permanent foreign occupation. France, represented at Quebec by the defensively minded General Montcalm, is the main villain of this piece, its lacklustre and defeatist pursuit of the war amounting to a virtual "abandonment" of the colony. Though colonial opinion, led by the Canadian-born governor, Pierre de Rigaud de Vaudreuil, favored an aggressive policy of taking the war to the enemy through frontier raids over a broad front. Whereas other historians tended to personify the war's climax as a duel between Montcalm and

General James Wolfe, Frégault dramatized the confrontation between the French general and the Canadian governor.

The 1759 siege of Quebec and the Battle of the Plains of Abraham, with its risky tactics, decisive outcome, and death of both commanders, has always provided material for romantically inclined historians. Reacting to the sentimental excesses of the existing historiography, the military historian C. P. Stacey (1959) undertook a coolly technical examination of Wolfe's victorious campaign, publishing his study in time to celebrate the two-hundredth anniversary. W. J. Eccles (1987, pp. 125–33) complained that Stacey, like Parkman before him, was too quick to take British superiority for granted, failing to appreciate the strength and competence of the French who, but for one unfortunate blunder on Montcalm's part, might well have won the day. Reverting to a neo-Parkman perspective, Simon Schama (1991) tells the story of the capture of Quebec as the triumph of Jack Tar and other sturdy British types over an army of cartoon-caricature French fops.

Conclusion

Nationalism has not disappeared from the historiography of New France, and though horizons have broadened and national parochialism has receded, French-Canadian, English-Canadian, and American historians still tend to view the subject from their own respective vantage points. Without fetishizing these national/linguistic distinctions, it is fair to recognize the general tendency for French-Canadian historians to focus on the settlements of the St. Lawrence Valley and to favor socioeconomic analysis, while English Canadians have gravitated more to political and military topics, and Americans have been drawn more to the study of Indian–European contact.

It should also be said that New France remains an uncrowded field with far fewer historians to the square kilometer than "Early American" (i.e., United States) history. The result is an uneven historiography with large areas and important topics still rather neglected. Thus, while the existing monographic literature offers Early Americanists opportunities to gain a comparative perspective on agrarian systems, demography, Native–European relations, and law, it has less to say on many other topics – theology, gender, and ecology, to name a few – that have been fairly thoroughly examined in relation to the British colonies. Clearly there is no shortage of research opportunities in the history of New France.

Earlier in this essay, I mentioned the growing tendency for colonialists to follow the lead of Axtell, White, and Sayre in casting their work in a North American framework that encompasses Indians, French, and English. A different approach, but equally promising in my opinion, would undertake genuinely comparative studies of the French and English studies. There have been some syntheses along these lines based on secondary works, but few attempts to examine a theme through primary research in the archives of New France and the English colonies. It is surprising that no one has looked, for example, at the utopianism of the New England Puritans alongside that of their Catholic counterparts, the Counter-Reformation idealists who founded that other "city upon a hill," Montreal. Marital relations under the contrasting family property regimes of French and English law seems another obvious candidate for comparative study. And finally there is the question of self-sufficiency and commercial orientation in settler households, and whether the situation of habitants under seigneurial tenure differed significantly from that of New England farm families.

New France may not have been New England's Other in quite the way Francis Parkman imagined, but it did represent an alternative version of European colonization, one that shaped the destiny of half a continent, from Hudson Bay to the Gulf of Mexico. What sort of colonial history can afford to ignore it?

BIBLIOGRAPHY

Anderson, Karen: *Chain her by one Foot: The Subjugation of Women in Seventeenth-Century New France* (London: Routledge, 1991).

Axtell, James: *The Invasion Within: The Contest of Cultures in Colonial North America* (New York: Oxford University Press, 1985).

Berger, Carl: *The Writing of Canadian History: Aspects of English-Canadian Historical Writing since 1900*, second edition (Toronto: University of Toronto Press, 1986).

Biggar, H. P., ed.: *The Works of Samuel de Champlain*, 6 vols (Toronto: Champlain Society, 1922–36).

Bosher, J. F.: "Government and Private Interests in New France." *Canadian Public Administration* (June 1967), pp. 244–57.

Bosher, J. F.: *The Canada Merchants, 1713–1763* (New York: Oxford University Press, 1987).

Campeau, Lucien: *La Mission des Jésuites chez les Hurons 1634–1650* [*The Jesuit Mission to the Hurons, 1634–50*] (Montreal: Bellarmin, 1987).

Charbonneau, Hubert: *The First French Canadians: Pioneers in the St. Lawrence Valley* (Newark, NJ: University of Delaware Press, 1993).

Charlevoix, Pierre-François-Xavier: *Histoire et description générale de la Nouvelle-France avec le journal historique d'un voyage fait par ordre du roi dans L'Amérique septentrionale*, 6 vols (Paris, 1744); trans., ed., J. G. Shea, *History and General Description of New France*, 6 vols (New York: J. G. Shea, 1866–72).

Choquette, Leslie: *Frenchmen into Peasants: Modernity and Tradition in the Peopling of French Canada* (Cambridge, MA: Harvard University Press, 1997).

Cole, Charles Woolsey: *Colbert and a Century of French Mercantilism* (New York: Columbia University Press, 1939).

Cook, Ramsay, ed.: *The Voyages of Jacques Cartier* (Toronto: University of Toronto Press, 1993).

Davis, Natalie Z.: "Iroquois Women, European Women." In Margo Hendricks and Patricia Parker, eds., *Women, Race, and Writing in the Early Modern Period* (London: Routledge, 1994), pp. 243–58.

Davis, Natalie Z.: *Women on the Margins: Three Seventeenth-Century Lives* (Cambridge, MA: Harvard University Press, 1995).

Davis, Natalie Z.: "Polarities, Hybridities: What Strategies for De-centring?" In Germaine Warkentin and Carolyn Podruchny, eds., *De-Centring the Renaissance: Canada and Europe in Multi-disciplinary Perspective, 1500–1700* (Toronto: University of Toronto Press, forthcoming).

Dechêne, Louise: *Habitants et marchands de Montréal au XVIIe siècle* (Paris and Montreal: Plon, 1974); trans. L. Vardi, *Habitants and Merchants in Seventeenth-Century Montreal* (Montreal: McGill-Queen's University Press, 1992).

Dechêne, Louise: *Le partage des subsistences au Canada sous le régime français* (Montreal: Boréal, 1994).

Delâge, Denys: "L'alliance franco-amérindienne, 1660–1701" ["The French–Indian Alliance, 1660–1701"]. *Recherches amérindiennes au Québec* 19 (1989), 3–15.

Delâge, Denys: *Le pays renversé: Amérindiens et européens en Amérique du nord-est, 1600–1664*

(Montreal: Boréal, 1985); *Bitter Feast: Amerindians and Europeans in Northeast North America, 1600–64* (Vancouver: UBC Press, 1993).

Demos, John: *The Unredeemed Captive: A Family Story from Early America* (New York: Norton, 1994).

Desbarats, Catherine: "Agriculture within the Seigneurial Regime of Eighteenth-Century Canada: Some Thoughts on the Recent Literature." *Canadian Historical Review* 73 (1992), pp. 1–29.

Desbarats, Catherine: "The Cost of Early Canada's Native Alliances: Reality and Scarcity's Rhetoric." *William and Mary Quarterly* 3rd ser., 52 (1995) pp. 609–30.

Deslandres, Dominique: "Le modèle français d'intégration socio-religieuse, 1600–1650: missions intérieures et premières missions canadiennes" ["The French Model of Social and Religious Assimilation, 1600–1650: Internal Missions and Early Canadian Missions"] (Ph.D. dissertation, Université de Montréal, 1990).

Deslandres, Dominique: "Le role missionaire des femmes en Nouvelle-France" ["The Role of Women in the Missions of New France"]. In J. Delumeau, ed., *La religion de ma mère: la femme et la transmission de la foi* (Paris: Cerf, 1991).

Dickinson, J. A.: *Justice et justiciables: la procédure civile à la Prévoté de Québec, 1667–1759* [*Justice and Society: Civil Procedure in the Prevote [court] of Quebec, 1667–1759*] (Quebec: Presses de l'Université Laval, 1982).

Dictionary of Canadian Biography, vols 1–3 (1000–1770) (Toronto: University of Toronto Press, 1966–74).

Du Creux, François: *Historiae Canadensis, sev Novae-Franciae libri decem, ad Annum usque Christi MDCLVI* (Paris: Sebastianus Cramoisy, 1664); trans. P. J. Robinson, ed. James B. Conacher, *The History of Canada or New France*, 2 vols (Toronto: The Champlain Society, 1951).

Eccles, W. J.: *Essays on New France* (Toronto: Oxford University Press, 1987).

Eccles, W. J.: *France in America* (Markham: Fitzhenry & Whiteside, 1972); rev. ed., *The French in North America, 1500–1783* (Markham, Ontario: Fitzhenry and Whiteside, 1998).

Egnal, Marc: *Divergent Paths: How Culture and Institutions Have Shaped North American Growth* (New York: Oxford University Press, 1996).

Frégault, Guy: *La Guerre de la conquête* (Montreal: Fides, 1955); trans. M. Cameron, *Canada: The War of the Conquest* (Toronto: Oxford University Press, 1969).

Gagnon, Serge: *Quebec and its Historians, 1840 to 1920* (Montreal: Harvest House, 1982).

Garneau, François-Xavier: *Histoire du Canada depuis sa découverte jusqu'à nos jours*, 4 vols (Quebec: Imprimerie Fréchette et Frère, 1845–1852); *History of Canada from the Time of its Discovery till the Union Years* (Montreal: J. Lovell, 1860).

Goddard, Peter: "The Devil in New France: Jesuit Demonology, 1611–50." *Canadian Historical Review* 78 (1997), pp. 40–62.

Greer, Allan: *The People of New France* (Toronto: University of Toronto Press, 1997).

Greer, Allan, ed.: *The Jesuit Relations: Natives and Missionaries in Seventeenth-Century North America* (Boston, MA: Bedford Books, 2000).

Hanzeli, Victor Egon: *Missionary Linguistics in New France* (The Hague and Paris: Mouton, 1969).

Harris, R. C.: *The Seigneurial System in Early Canada: A Geographical Study* (Madison, WI: University of Wisconsin Press, 1966).

Harris, R. C. ed.: *Historical Atlas of Canada*, 3 vols, vol. 1, *From the Beginning to 1800* (Toronto: University of Toronto Press, 1987).

Hay, Douglas: "The Meanings of the Criminal Law in Quebec, 1764–1774." In Louis A. Knafla, ed., *Crime and Criminal Justice in Europe and Canada* (Waterloo: Wilfrid Laurier University Press, 1981), pp. 77–110.

Henripin, Jacques: *La population du Canada au début du XVIIIe siècle: nuptialité, fécondité, mortalité infantile* [*The Population of Canada at the Beginning of the 18th Century: Marriage,*

Fertility and Infant Mortality] (Paris: Presses universitaires de France, 1954).

Horguelin, Christophe: *La Prétendue République: Pouvoir et société au Canada (1645–1675)* [*The Would-be Republic: State and Society in Canada, 1645–75*] (Quebec: Septentrion, 1997).

Hunt, George: *The Wars of the Iroquois: A Study in Intertribal Trade Relations* (Madison, WI: University of Wisconsin Press, 1940).

Innis, Harold A.: *The Fur Trade in Canada: An Introduction to Canadian Economic History* (Toronto: University of Toronto Press, 1929).

Jetten, Marc: *Enclaves amérindiennes: les "réductions" du Canada 1637–1701* [*Amerindian Enclaves: the "Reductions" of Canada, 1637–1701*] (Sillery: Septentrion, 1994).

Koppedrayer, K. I.: "The Making of the First Iroquois Virgin: Early Jesuit Biographies of the Blessed Kateri Tekakwitha." *Ethnohistory* 40 (1993), pp. 277–306.

Lachance, André: *La justice criminelle du roi au Canada au XVIIIe siècle: tribunaux et officiers* [*Criminal Justice in the royal Courts of Canada in the 18th Century: Courts and Legal Officers*] (Quebec: Presses de l'Université Laval, 1978).

Landry, Yves: *Orphelines en France, pionnières au Canada: les filles du roi au XVIIe siècle* [*Orphans in France, Pioneers in Canada: The King's Daughters of the 17th Century*] (Montreal: Lémeác, 1992).

Leacock, Eleanor: "Montagnais Women and the Jesuit Program for Colonization." In V. Strong-Boag and A. Fellman, eds., *Rethinking Canada: The Promise of Women's History* (Toronto: Copp Clark, 1986), pp. 7–22.

Leahey, Margaret J.: "'Comment peut un muet prescher l'évangile?' Jesuit missionaries and the native languages of New France." *French Historical Studies* 19 (1995), pp. 105–31.

Légaré, Jacques, ed.: *Répertoire des actes de baptême, mariage, sépulture et des recensements du Québec ancien* [*Catalog of the records of Baptism, Marriage, and Burial and of the Censuses of Old Quebec*], 47 vols (Montreal: les Presses de l'Université de Montréal, 1980–1990).

Miquelon, Dale, ed.: *Society and Conquest: The Debate on the Bourgeoisie and Social Change in French Canada, 1700–1850* (Toronto: Copp Clark, 1977).

Miquelon, Dale: *Dugard of Rouen: French Trade to Canada and the West Indies, 1729–1770* (Montreal: McGill-Queen's University Press, 1978).

Miquelon, Dale: *New France 1701–1744: A Supplement to Europe* (Toronto: McClelland and Stewart, 1987).

Moogk, Peter N.: "Reluctant exiles: emigrants from France in Canada before 1760." *William and Mary Quarterly* 3rd ser., 46 (1989), pp. 463–505.

Morrison, Kenneth: "Baptism and Alliance: The Symbolic Mediations of Religious Syncretism." *Ethnohistory* 37 (1990), pp. 416–37.

Noel, Jan: "New France: Les femmes favorisées." In V. Strong-Boag and A. Fellman, eds., *Rethinking Canada: The Promise of Women's History* (Toronto: Copp Clark, 1986), pp. 23–44.

Parkman, Francis: *France and England in North America*, 7 vols (Boston, MA: Little, Brown, 1865–92); new ed., 2 vols (New York: Library of America, 1983).

Perrot, Nicolas: "Memoir on the Manners, Customs, and Religion of the Savages of North America." In E. H. Blair, ed., *The Indian Tribes of the Upper Mississippi Valley and Region of the Great Lakes* (Cleveland, 1911), vol. 1 (Lincoln, NE: University of Nebraska Press, 1996), pp. 23–272.

Pioffet, Marie-Christine: *La tentation de l'épopée dans les Relations des Jésuites* (Sillery: Septentrion, 1997).

Ragueneau, Paul: *La Vie de la mère Catherine de Saint Augustin, religieuse hospitalière de la miséricorde de Québec en la Nouvelle-France* [*The Life of Mother Catherine de Saint Augustin, Sister of the Hospital Order of Mercy at Quebec in New France*] (Paris: Florentin Lambert, 1671).

Richter, Daniel K.: *The Ordeal of the Longhouse: The Peoples of the Iroquois League in the Era of European Colonization* (Chapel Hill, NC: University of North Carolina Press, 1992).

Ronda, James P.: "The Sillery Experiment: A Jesuit-Indian Village in New France, 1637–1663." *American Indian Culture and Research Journal* 3 (1979), pp. 1–18.

Sayre, Gordon M.: *Les Sauvages Américains: Representations of Native Americans in French and English Colonial Literature* (Chapel Hill, NC: University of North Carolina Press, 1997).

Schama, Simon: *Dead Certainties: Unwarranted Speculations* (New York: Knopf, 1991).

Sioui, Georges: *Pour une autohistoire amérindienne* (Montreal: McGill-Queen's University Press, 1988); trans. Sheila Fischman, *For an Amerindian Autohistory: An Essay on the Foundations of a Social Ethic* (Montreal: McGill-Queen's University Press, 1992).

Stacey, C. P.: *Quebec, 1759: The Siege and the Battle* (Toronto: Macmillan, 1959).

Steckley, John: "The warrior and the lineage: Jesuit use of Iroquoian images to communicate Christianity." *Ethnohistory* 39 (1992), pp. 478–509.

Steele, Ian K.: *Guerillas and Grenadiers: The Struggle for Canada, 1689–1760* (Toronto: Ryerson Press, 1969).

Thérien, Gilles, ed.: *Figures de l'Indien* [*Figures of the Indian*] (Montreal: Université du Québec à Montréal, 1988).

Thwaites, Reuben, ed.: *The Jesuit Relations and Allied Documents*, 73 vols (Cleveland: Burrows Brothers, 1896–1900).

Tocqueville, Alexis de: *L'ancien régime et la révolution* (Paris, 1856), trans. S. Gilbert, *The Old Régime and the French Revolution* (New York: Doubleday, 1955).

Trigger, Bruce: *The Children of Aataentsic: A History of the Huron People to 1660* (Montreal: McGill-Queen's University Press, 1976).

Trigger, Bruce: *Natives and Newcomers: Canada's "Heroic Age" Reconsidered* (Montréal: McGill-Queen's University Press, 1985).

Turgeon, Laurier: "Pour redécouvrir notre 16e siècle: les pêches à Terre-Neuve d'après les archives notariales de Bordeaux" ["Pour redécouvrir notre 16e siècle: les pêches à Terre-Neuve d'après les archives notariales de Bordeaux"]. *Revue d'histoire de l'Amérique française* 39 (1986), pp. 523–49.

Turgeon, Laurier: "French fishers, fur traders, and Amerindians during the sixteenth century: history and archaeology." *William and Mary Quarterly* 3rd ser., 55 (1998), pp. 584–610.

Viau, Roland: *Enfants du néant et mangeurs d'âmes: guerre, culture et société en Iroquoisie ancienne* [*Children of Darkness, Hungering for Souls: War, Culture and Society among the Iroquois of Old*] (Montreal: Boréal, 1997).

Warkentin, Germaine: "Discovering Radisson: a Renaissance adventurer between two worlds." In J. S. H. Brown and E. Vibert, eds., *Reading Beyond Words: Contexts for Native History* (Peterborough, Ont.: Broadview Press, 1996), pp. 43–70.

White, Richard: *The Middle Ground: Indians, Empires and Republics in the Great Lakes Region, 1650–1815* (New York: Cambridge University Press, 1991).

Wien, Thomas: "Exchange patterns in the European market for North American fur and skins, 1720–1760." In J. S. H. Brown, W. J. Eccles, et al., eds., *The Fur Trade Revisited: Selected Papers of the Sixth North American Fur Trade Conference* (Lansing, MI: Michigan State University Press, 1994), pp. 19–37.

Wien, Thomas: "Introduction: habitants, marchands, historiens" ["Introduction: Settlers, Merchants and Historians"]. In Sylvie Dépatie, Catherine Desbarats, et al., eds., *Vingt ans après Habitants et marchands: lectures de l'histoire des XVIIe et XVIIIe siècles canadiens* [*Twenty Years On: Readings on 17th and 18th Century Canada*] (Montreal: McGill-Queen's University Press, 1998), pp. 3–27.

Wrong, George M.: *The Rise and Fall of New France*, 2 vols (Toronto: Macmillan, 1928).

Wrong, George, ed.: *Sagard's Long Journey to the Country of the Hurons* (Toronto: Champlain Society, 1939).

CHAPTER TWENTY-ONE

Comparisons: Atlantic Canada

PETER POPE

Introduction

If a single issue pervades the early history of Atlantic Canada it is the question of who ought to be here. This question resonates differently in Newfoundland than it does in Nova Scotia or Acadia. The latter toponyms are ambiguous and imply mutually exclusive claims about what are now the Canadian maritime provinces of Nova Scotia, New Brunswick, Prince Edward Island, and even parts of Maine and Quebec's Gaspésie. These competing claims are part of a complex demographic and political history involving Native Mi'kmaqs and Maliseets, as well as the Acadians, the non-Acadian French of Louisbourg, neighboring New Englanders, the English, a few Scots, and a late cohort of German immigrants. French and British military forces sometimes enacted parallel territorial battles in Newfoundland, but the question of who ought to inhabit this sub-arctic island has often been posed as an existential challenge to settlement itself. Historians of Atlantic Canada have also tended to worry about underdevelopment, often by implicit contrast to New England. This is bound to raise the existential issue again – to the extent that advisers to governments have for centuries recommended re-emigration as an appropriate cure for underemployment. "Failure," supposed or otherwise, is a *leitmotif* of Atlantic regional history, whether in accounts of early Newfoundland colonies or in analysis of the administration of eighteenth-century Nova Scotia (Cell, 1982, pp. 1–59; Barnes, 1990). There are, of course, many strands in the historiography of any region; but historians of Atlantic Canada have tugged at the loose ends of the existential questions often enough to have affected the shape of the fabric as a whole.

The older literature, even when written by denizens, usually adopted a point of view external to the region and focused on questions of imperial policy and trade. Recent research adopts a different paradigm. Harold Innis' work on the cod fishery (1940, rev. 1954) looks less momentous than it once did and Arthur Bailey's study of the conflict between European and eastern Algonquian cultures (1937) more seminal. Bailey initiated the study of North American ethnohistory, and his influence has been widespread, not merely on Native history but also on studies of European settlement in the region. Important monographs by historical geographers have likewise centered on the successful adaptation of small-scale societies to their environment, rather than on their failure to match economic or political milestones elsewhere (Clark, 1968; Head, 1976). The regional visibility of historical archaeology has also encouraged a turn to social history. The development of a National Historic Park at Louisbourg is one example, but recent excavations of Basque Labrador, Newfoundland outports, and Acadian farmsteads are having similar influence (Moody, 1994, pp. 84–8; Pope and Tuck, 1996).

Atlantic Canada in the early modern period is best understood within four intersecting contexts: the development of a migratory European cod fishery, the rapid evolution of post-contact Native societies, gradual European settlement, and, eventually, the conflicting imperial ambitions of France and Great Britain. Following English and Portuguese explorations at the dawn of the sixteenth century, a cross-section of western Europeans intruded into the maritime domain of Canada's eastern Algonquian peoples, although we may remember better those who came to settle in the seventeenth century, most of whom arrived from western France and western England. Ties with New England and New France date from this original European settlement; ties to Ireland and the Caribbean grew in the eighteenth century.

European "Discovery" and Native Peoples

The Gulf of Mexico and Gulf of St. Lawrence were the American regions first exploited by Europeans. Atlantic Canada has its own early history of "discovery," distinct from the one Americans have borrowed from the Caribbean. The obscure Venetian, Zuan Caboto, explored the eastern coast of Newfoundland in 1497, as far north as the Strait of Belle Isle between Newfoundland and Labrador. At the close of the nineteenth century, the limited and ambiguous documentation of this voyage encouraged a nationalist debate between Newfoundland and mainland Canadian historians over his landfall (Pope, 1997). While these debates had their echoes in the twentieth century, scholars today are more concerned with the background and the results of his voyage. Cabot was not the first European to visit the region, for archaeologists have uncovered the turf houses of Norse Greenlanders in northern Newfoundland (Ingstad and Ingstad, 1985; Wallace, 1986). Verification that the Norse actually reached North America raises the issue of the "failure" of eleventh-century colonization. The archaeological evidence suggests that the expeditions celebrated in the sagas were not, in fact, colonizing ventures but that the Greenlanders used northern Newfoundland as a temporary base camp for ship repair and exploration in the Gulf of St. Lawrence (Wallace, 1991). A key issue in the history of European expansion is whether Cabot's visit to this Norse gateway was coincidence or an application of the geographical tradition of Vinland, mediated perhaps by late medieval fishermen. The question is complicated, by debates over the authenticity of the only surviving medieval Vinland map and by indications that Bristol fishermen reached the region before Cabot's voyage.

The elder Cabot rediscovered North America, at least in the sense that he made it known to his contemporaries. Within a decade this had three results. First, he was followed northwards in a series of expeditions mounted by Bristol merchants and Azorean Portuguese captains, sometimes in cooperation. These included voyages to Newfoundland, Labrador, and Greenland, as well as early attempts at a northwest passage, perhaps under the command of Cabot's son Sebastian, though some doubt his claim to have reached northernmost Labrador (Morison, 1971, pp. 218–25). Europeans did not penetrate the Nearctic farther until the voyages of John Davis and Martin Frobisher in the 1570s and 80s. The earlier voyages are significant conceptually, as an indication that by 1500 or so Europeans had realized that they had not found Tartary, to be coasted southwards to Japan, but something else between Europe and Asia (Quinn, 1977, pp. 60–67). The second great result of the Cabot voyage was the publicity it gave the marine resources of the northwest Atlantic. The first recorded cargo of North American cod reached Bristol in 1502 and within a decade European crews were fishing the waters of Atlantic Canada, then known indiscriminately as "the new found land," "*terre neuve*," or "*terra de bacalhao*" – land of the cod. Migratory Breton, Norman, and Basque fishers were already exploiting Newfoundland, Cape Breton, and even the Gulf of St. Lawrence itself, before Cartier's explorations in the "River of Canada" between 1534 and 1541. This new industry in turn provoked the third major result of Cabot's expedition. Although he himself avoided encounters with Native people, Cabot opened a long period of seasonal contact between European mariners and Natives, of which Cartier's experiences are only the best documented (Hoffman, 1961).

Although some early encounters were brutal, Europeans and Amerindians in Atlantic Canada entered into an increasingly complex relationship of mutual dependence, which lasted for several centuries. At first, neither the English, Portuguese, nor French had moral or even tactical qualms about taking individuals back to Europe, as specimens, slaves, hostages, or future translators; but this did not become a pattern. Violence could be a two-way street, as the Azorean settlers of an abortive Portuguese colony in Cape Breton appear to have discovered in the 1520s. Until the 1750s the concept of conquest is less relevant in Atlantic Canada than the rubrics of economic exploitation and dependence. Ethnohistorians have not always been able to identify Native peoples described in early reports. These difficulties arise not only from the vagueness of European itineraries but also from the impact of contact itself on ethnic boundaries. Changes in subsistence patterns, economic crisis, and, particularly, demographic disaster in the face of introduced Old World disease caused shifts in identity and social organization. In any case, European mariners interacted with the ancestors of the historic Maliseet and Mi'kmaq in Acadia, Iroquoians in the Gulf of St. Lawrence, Beothuk in Newfoundland, and the Montagnais-Naskapi (now Innu) of Quebec-Labrador, not to mention the Inuit from farther northwards on the Labrador coast (Hoffman, 1961; Trigger, 1978). Ethnohistorical and archaeological research suggests that contact exacerbated existing ethnic tensions and accelerated territorial shifts (Pastore, 1990).

At first, trade with Native peoples was casual, involving unspecialized goods typical of sailors' inventories (knives, clothing, kettles, etc.) and depending on the right of European mariners in this period to carry goods for private trade. As early as 1550 European goods traded informally in Atlantic Canada reached Native peoples of the Great Lakes. Trade became increasingly commercialized after 1575, especially by Basque merchants, who developed seasonal *comptoirs* to trade specially produced goods for furs, farther up the St. Lawrence (Turgeon, 1998). The archaeological record makes it clear that the Mi'kmaq, a maritime people long before contact, adapted rapidly to these new economic possibilities, becoming middlemen who supplied the woodland Algonquian peoples south of the Gulf of Maine (Bourque and Whitehead, 1985; Martijn, 1986). Ethnohistorians are only beginning to work out the sociocultural implications of these developments. Surely one of the most interesting was a Basque-Algonquian pidgin used for cross-cultural trade in the St. Lawrence region, *c*. 1540 to

1640 (Bakker, 1989). While the commercialized fur trade gradually penetrated the continent, casual trade between fishermen and Native peoples continued on the Atlantic coast into the seventeenth century. Fishing crews traded informally with Newfoundland Beothuk, as did Basque whalers in Labrador with the Montagnais, although emphatically not the generally hostile Inuit.

The greatest impact Europeans had on North American peoples was to precipitate a population crash. Although decline is not itself in question, the timing and extent of demographic change in Atlantic Canada are contested issues (Pastore, 1990). The Mi'kmaq, for example, who eventually numbered perhaps 3,000, originally numbered at least 12,000; some give much higher figures. The issue here is, in part, chronology: some ethnohistorians assume that epidemics of European disease swept across sixteenth-century North America; others note the lack of archaeological evidence for early demographic collapse in Acadia. They see epidemics as a later problem, since European settlements were more likely to harbor disease than ships' crews, following the involuntary quarantine of an Atlantic crossing. Diet was another demographic factor, as the growing trade in furs upset subsistence patterns and Natives began to depend on Europeans for grains, pulses, and alcohol – conditions for decline which were in place by 1580. The Beothuk avoided such dependence and a pre-contact population in the order of 1,000 likely did not come under serious pressure until the later seventeenth century, when English settlement began to reach the northeast coast of Newfoundland (Marshall, 1996). The cultural impact of epidemic disease is another much-debated issue. Calvin Martin's (1978) thesis that Native peoples, blaming spiritual "keepers of the game," essentially declared war on animal life has been rejected by most researchers (Pastore, 1990). Yet, his summary of the stresses on Native societies occasioned first by the growth and later by the decline of the fur trade remains a provocative attempt to put cultural change, including the developing market for alcohol and the ideological warfare of Christian missionaries, within an environmental perspective (Bumsted, 1993, pp. 85–107). The engine of European contact was not government, intermittent official expeditions apart. Even when England and France revived these late in the sixteenth century, they were less significant for Native peoples than the seasonal presence of migratory fishing crews, for the seventeenth-century commercial fur trade in Acadia and the Gulf of St. Lawrence had its origins in the evolving sixteenth-century fishery.

The Fisheries

Until the collapse of cod stocks in the early 1990s and the subsequent moratorium on the pursuit of northern cod, this species remained critical to the northwest Atlantic fishery. Early European mariners did, however, bring other species to market, beginning in the sixteenth century with walrus and whales. The salmon fishery and the seal hunt have seventeenth-century origins but became commercially significant only after 1750. For five centuries cod drew ships and boats to sea. Only whaling remotely approached the cod fishery in significance and did so for less than a century.

Basque mariners were pursuing right and bowhead whales in the Strait of Belle Isle by 1540. This early and once very important industry was never completely forgotten, but the actual Labrador ports used seasonally as tryworks for the land-based hunt were identified only relatively recently. Archaeological investigations at the largest station, Red Bay, including work on a Basque shipwreck of 1565, have clarified industrial methods and emphasized the large scale of the trade (Tuck and Grenier, 1989; Proulx, 1993). Whaling has a long history in northern Spain and the hunt at Labrador was a keystone of the Basque economy until 1600 (Huxley, 1987). Given the economic integration of the Bay of Biscay, the trade involved France too, through provisioning of voyages at Bordeaux (Turgeon, 1997). By 1610 the Labrador industry had failed, although French Basque crews pursued the smaller beluga whales up the St. Lawrence. Eco-archaeological considerations suggest the Labrador industry declined following depletion of whale stocks; Huxley and other text-oriented scholars emphasize Armada losses and a contemporary reorientation of Iberian trade.

Breton, Norman, and French Basque crews dominated the nascent cod fishery and their efforts grew dramatically in the 1540s. Crews from the Basque coast of Spain had joined this fishery by 1550, albeit in limited numbers; recent work suggests neither Portuguese nor English interests committed themselves seriously before this time (Abreu-Ferreira, 1998). The Portuguese had other fish to fry; it is less obvious why intermittent English efforts expanded only after 1565. By 1610, West Countrymen had displaced continental Europeans from their preferred fishing grounds along the east coast of Newfoundland's Avalon Peninsula. The French had other stations on the south and northeast coasts of Newfoundland, nearby Labrador, and the Gulf, particularly on Cape Breton; furthermore, they had developed a new high-seas fishery on the Grand Banks. Spanish Basque and Portuguese interests, on the other hand, essentially abandoned an industry to which they were not heavily committed. For Innis (1956), the inflationary inflow of American gold and silver precipitated the decline of the Spanish fishery. The contemporary realignment of European geopolitics strengthened neither Spain nor Portugal, the latter now politically incorporated into the former, and both became key English markets for dried cod.

After 1600 then, this was a French and British industry, in which France predominated by a factor of two until the later eighteenth century. The eclipse of a few Iberian ports was part of a general trend that saw an initially locally organized trade spread over many European ports, increasingly concentrated in a few. Non-specialists curious about these fisheries still defer to the substantial monographs of de la Morandière (1962) and Innis (1940, rev. 1954); specialists find these overdue for revision (Turgeon, 1997). Both are syntheses of published sources: the former a repetitive compendium of data, raising its gaze beyond France's interests only enough to decry British imperialism; the latter an international economic history with a wider view, drawing sweeping conclusions about loosely defined abstractions like "commercialism." Earlier works on the British fishery are even less persuasive analytically and are, indeed, often the source of Innis' preconceptions, particularly the *idée fixe* of perennial conflict between settlers and fishers (Lounsbury, 1934). Grant Head's historical geography of eighteenth-century Newfoundland (1976) clarifies this relationship; the only other substantial work on the British fishery to do so remains unpublished (Matthews, 1968). The French fishery has been better served (Turgeon, 1987; Brière, 1990).

Doubts about these monuments of fisheries history have returned scholars to some basic questions. Ecological concern over the cod moratorium has raised questions about the chronology of human impact on fish stocks and recent estimates revise upwards the scale of the early industry. Such revision hints at human impact long before eighteenth-century effects, already noticed. Recent research has exposed some other intriguing long-term continuities in the fishery: catch per man has remained roughly

constant, as has the wholesale price relative to agricultural products. Historians of the
French fishery conclude that cod was never cheap: it was a luxury rather than the staple
Innis supposed (Turgeon, 1987). This does not, however, detract from the importance of the trade. By 1580, about 500 ships returned annually from Atlantic Canada
to Europe with the cured product of a catch of something like 200,000 metric tonnes
of fish, others with burgeoning cargoes of fur – a level of activity which challenged the
status of the Gulf of Mexico as the center of gravity of European commerce in the New
World (Turgeon, 1998).

It is increasingly clear that markets are also a key to understanding the complex
relationship of the wet and dry fisheries; the former salt-intensive and often carried on
far offshore; the latter requiring shore stations, more labor, and less salt. The precedence Innis and others accord the wet fishery now appears mistaken: the French did
not develop an offshore banks fishery until the later sixteenth century and the English
confined themselves to a shore fishery until 1713 (Head, 1976; Turgeon, 1987). Nor
was the dry fishery essentially English: the Basques and Bretons also excelled in this
cure while the Normans developed the high-seas industry on the Grand Banks. Scholars continue to parrot Innis' pronouncement that the English preferred the dry cure
because they lacked their own supplies of salt, thereby ignoring both the international
market in salt and the demand for dry fish in Britain's Mediterranean markets. De la
Morandière's suggestion, that ports with the cheap labor pool of a pastoral hinterland
could afford to engage in the labor-intensive dry fishery, merits attention (1962, pp.
96–7).

The turn of the seventeenth century saw the entry of Dutch "sack" or cargo ships
into the emerging triangular trade linking Newfoundland, the Mediterranean, and
northern Europe (Kupp, 1974). Cell (1969) has emphasized English efforts to compete at this time, although it appears London interests, at least, were not very successful until the 1630s (Pope, 1996). These trading ventures further reduced the limited
capital requirement to enter the cod fishery to an inshore fishing boat and gear, since
marketing could be handled by the sacks. This made resident fisheries possible, hence
facilitating coastal settlement: by 1680 the Newfoundland planters shipped about a
third of the British catch. Inhabitants of the French military establishment at Placentia
on Newfoundland's south coast in the 1660s played a similar, if smaller, role
(Humphreys, 1970). Important as the fishery was to Acadia's early settlers, over time
it became more a subsistence strategy, although New England fishermen developed
their own seasonal industries on the east coasts of Newfoundland and Nova Scotia.
Innis (1954) tended to interpret commercial conflict among emerging sectors of the
fishery in a Smithian way, as an index of the maturation of merchant capitalism; recent
scholarship stresses the growing interdependence of these sectors. After 1670 France
and Britain systematically collected data about their fisheries, statistics which have invited questions about fluctuations in eighteenth-century catch and participation rates.
Price levels and war are obvious factors; but recent research on French data indicates
that climate fluctuation and secular shifts in market demand also affected the location
and extent of fishing effort (Head, 1976; Turgeon, 1987; Brière, 1990). The relative
importance of these factors remains in question; the increasing diversification of the
fishery is not, for by 1700 seal and salmon were becoming significant commercial
species.

In 1713, the Treaty of Utrecht marked a turning point in the fisheries of Atlantic

Canada. France removed its military and fishing establishment from Placentia in New-foundland and established Louisbourg on "Ile Royale," as Cape Breton Island was renamed. While France abandoned her traditional fishing grounds along the south coast of Newfoundland, Britain guaranteed continued French access to the northeast coast and Great Northern Peninsula or "Petit Nord." An English resident fishery in Newfoundland spread gradually along the south coast, and up the northeast coast, at the expense of migratory French crews, who were pushed towards the Petit Nord and the west coast, a redefinition of the French Shore eventually recognized by treaty in 1783. France gave up Ile Royale and much else, in 1763, to retain access to the banks fishery and the coastal fishing rights it would enjoy until 1904 (Hiller, 1996). Brière's contention that Paris traded New France at the negotiating table for continued access to the Newfoundland fishery merits serious consideration (1990, pp. 219–46).

The Atlantic cod fishery of the early modern period represented a dispersed indus-trialism, before its time (Candow and Corbin, 1997, pp. 45–64). Although techniques evolved slowly, the industry was not static. In the early eighteenth century, fishers in Ile Royale and Newfoundland added to their repertoires a new processing technology, already used in New England – a combination cure permitting small schooners to make voyages of several days to offshore banks, wet salting their catch, then drying it on return to a shore station. Limited inshore stocks forced Ile Royale fishers offshore; in Newfoundland, planters used the technique to expand their catches by entering the Grand Banks fishery for the first time. Inevitably this produced an inferior product – but one cheap enough to compete in the expanding Caribbean market. The general pattern of trade in the seventeenth century was a triangular exchange of fish for wine or specie in southern Europe, returned to northern Europe; increasingly the trade exchanged fish for rum and molasses, returned to New England from the slave-based sugar plantations of the Caribbean (Head, 1976).

In the last few decades, archaeological finds and documents from Britain, France, and Spain have provided a fresh look at Atlantic Canada in the sixteenth century. The ample documentation of the eighteenth-century industry has made this period a labo-ratory for an *annaliste* reimagining of the fishery, in order to see beyond "an interna-tional economy" to social interaction and culture. Further work on the seventeenth century will doubtless follow.

History and Myth in Acadia and Newfoundland

In 1749, when Britain began the systematic colonization of Nova Scotia, there were three small European societies in Atlantic Canada. About 8,000 Acadian farm folk flourished on the Bay of Fundy tidelands, enjoying commercial relations not only with their own English garrison government but also with New England, the Mi'kmaq, and the French establishment at Louisbourg. In Newfoundland, about 6,000 fisherfolk over-wintered in hamlets dispersed around the rocky bays of the English Shore. St. John's and the outports had commercial and demographic ties to England's West Country ports, to New England, and increasingly to southeast Ireland. They also endured a kind of military administration, the seasonal governor being the senior Royal Navy officer at the Newfoundland station. A similar, if more nucleated, society of French fisherfolk had taken root on Cape Breton Island, around the military-com-mercial complex of Louisbourg, after transplantation from Newfoundland in 1713, numbering with the garrison about 6,000. The military governors of Ile Royale were generally unsuccessful in attracting Acadians to their rocky territory, although by the early 1750s several thousand farmers and fishers were established on the administrative outlier of Ile St. Jean, today Prince Edward Island (Clark, 1959). A few French fishing families crossed to southwestern Newfoundland to found illegal coastal settlements there (Janzen, 1992). After 1758 Louisbourg went the way of Carthage, although some French fisherfolk returned to Newfoundland waters to occupy St. Pierre and Miquelon, Britain's sole North American territorial concession to France in 1763. In Atlantic Canada today, only the Acadians and the West Country folk of Newfoundland have seventeenth-century roots in the region.

Acadia and Newfoundland are rarely compared, regional specialists preferring the New England yardstick. Yet these communities have much in common, not least because the history of each is structured by a myth and each myth begins with an account of failure. The Acadian myth is factually based in the expulsion of 1755–58, which became the organizing principal of Acadian history after publication of Longfellow's poem "Evangeline" in 1847. An extensive historical literature on Acadia attempts to recast the narrative, to explain or condemn the terrible fact (Barnes, 1988; Daigle, 1995). In J. B. Brebner's venerable interpretation of regional colonial history (1927), Acadia's intimate relationship with New England, "*nos amis les ennemis*," was a prelude to violation: New England's expanding energies having led "naturally" to Acadian expulsion. A serious challenge to this thesis finds no cumulative Massachusetts policy of deportation, which was after all the work of the British military (Rawlyk, 1973). *Le grand dérangement* remains a central issue: even recent studies which purposefully evade nationalist debate are inevitably structured by the expulsion, attempting as they do to account for success, that is, the formation of an ethnos strong enough to regroup and to reclaim part of its patrimony after 1763 (Griffiths, 1973, 1992).

The myth that has dominated early Newfoundland history has a weaker factual basis but is nevertheless remarkably persistent, perhaps because it also nominates ancestral tragic heroes. The supposed illegality of settlement in Newfoundland is part of a traditional historiography, popularized a century ago by Judge Prowse (1895), in which powerful West Country commercial interests were accused of impeding settlement. In a key article, oft-cited if less often digested, Matthews (1978) observed that settlers and merchants were mutually dependent and that the only attempt to ban the planters, in 1675, was ineffective. Nevertheless, the mythology remains influential and scholars have only begun the task of exposing the extent to which paper regulation of the fishery has been over-interpreted as a practical attempt to eliminate settlement (Bannister, 1998a). In a larger sense, what is in question is the traditional assumption of Newfoundland exceptionalism. Seen with other peripheral regions in a comparative context, Newfoundland looks less unusual, with respect to population mobility and the weakness of the state, than is traditionally assumed (Pope, forthcoming). Revisionism is a tall order here: the myth of impeded settlement is so pervasive that presumed failure remains a datum requiring explanation (Story, 1982, pp. 97–114).

Acadia and Newfoundland share comparable early histories. As elsewhere in North America, first-generation proprietary colonies failed as commercial ventures, even while they succeeded in settling the nucleus of a European population by 1640. Relatively well documented and mythically eligible as "origins," these proprietary colonies are the subjects of meticulous study (Cell, 1969; Reid, 1982). Native peoples helped the early Acadians and early friendly contacts are attested in Newfoundland as well. Neither the Fundy marshes nor Newfoundland's Avalon Peninsula was crucial to Native subsistence. The Atlantic colonial experience benefited first-wave colonists like Champlain, Calvert, Mason, Squanto, and others – and hence the grander colonies to which they graduated, although such success has been conceptualized as failure too.

In both Newfoundland and Acadia, early colonists had to deal with divisive religious issues (Story, 1982, pp. 115–38; Jones, 1986). For a few brief years in the 1620s William Alexander's New Scotland challenged the Acadian proprietorships of French merchants like Charles de la Tour. In the same period, French privateers attacked George Calvert's colony of Avalon, in Newfoundland. The treaty of 1632 put an end to this phase of the Anglo-French duel, but not to open violence over proprietary rights. In Acadia, the subsequent struggle between la Tour and Charles d'Aulnay amounted to a protracted civil war (MacDonald, 1983). This was, perhaps, not so different from the situation in Newfoundland, where the English Civil War of the 1640s had a serious impact on David Kirke, who had enforced his proprietary privileges with organized violence. The survivors of these struggles among the second wave of proprietors (or their kin) would dominate their respective communities through the rest of the century.

In mid-century, commercial warfare impeded development of both societies. Metropolitan governments groped towards workable regional administration, albeit so clumsily that settler populations were considered ungovernable. New England merchants administered Newfoundland between 1651 and 1660, Acadia between 1654 and 1670, in each case promoting close commercial relations with Massachusetts which flourished, even when they later became illicit (Lounsbury, 1934; Rawlyk, 1973). While both communities grew through informal settlement, gender imbalance limited natural growth, although continued friendly relations with the Mi'kmaq gave Acadian men a better chance of marriage. By the end of the century, over-wintering European populations in each region had reached about 2,000. Migratory fishermen still greatly outnumbered the Newfoundland planters every summer, while nomadic Native people and seasonal fishermen outnumbered the Acadians. After the outbreak of hostilities in 1689, both communities would suffer the traumas of war. At this point the histories of Acadia and Newfoundland diverge, despite some painful parallels. The Acadians of 1751 were not the first colonial population to suffer mass deportation: even before Britain moved the French population of Newfoundland in 1713, France had expelled the settlers of Newfoundland's English Shore in 1697 (Williams, 1987). Lack of a Longfellow is only part of the reason that the first of the Atlantic deportations remains an historical footnote. According to the myth of illegal settlement, this is what planters might expect anyway. That prejudice aside, the English Shore was repopulated almost immediately – a nice indication of Britain's effective settlement policy. The Newfoundland deportation, in other words, had far less impact on population geography than the Acadian expulsion, although the economic toll was equally severe. The rapid resettlement of Newfoundland after 1697 marks the extent to which these were different societies, despite the parallels sketched above. Newfoundland's repopulation reflected resilience; but this resilience was based less on ethnic solidarity in the face of oppression than on local and continuing ties between peripheral fishing stations and West Country ports, whose prosperity depended on the reinvigoration of specific transatlantic communities.

Newfoundland Settlement to 1763

The English settlement of Newfoundland occurred within the matrix of the seasonal migratory fishery, that is, the fishery served as both support and conduit for settlement (Handcock, 1989). The open-access nature of the fishery promoted competition among crews, particularly in times of resource depletion. Planters and migratory men competed for shore space, as did all crews in the dry fishery, but for practical reasons a migratory crew's best strategy was cooperation with a planter. Meanwhile, planters depended on ships for supplies and servants (Matthews, 1978). The time-worn premise that the interests of planters, ship fishermen, and sack ships were somehow irreconcilable makes little economic sense, whatever its appeal to an earlier generation of scholars (Innis, 1954; Cell, 1969). As in Acadia, commercial competition over proprietorships erupted into physical struggle in the 1640s. The decline of proprietorship after the Restoration of 1660 meant that responsibility for law and order devolved on certain migratory masters, the "fishing admirals," under the re-proclaimed "Western Charter." Social and economic relations in Newfoundland continued to be governed less by administrative fiat than by custom, although by 1675 the Royal Navy had begun to take on some administrative responsibilities.

Intermittent conflicts among settlers and migratory crews underscore the real difficulties faced by the planters because Newfoundland lacked effective or permanent local administration. This raises interesting issues about the class, or at least status, of Newfoundland planters. Matthews (1988, pp. 83–8) reads the naval commodores' "Replies to Inquiries" to suggest that planters were impoverished and powerless. Yet in 1697 Abbé Beaudoin thought some planters rich, and a study of the Kirke family, who displaced the Calverts at the well-established settlement of Ferryland, suggests they functioned as a merchant "gentry" (Pope, forthcoming). As in other isolated regions dependent on a single staple, patron–client relations became a substitute for politics, insofar as ordinary folk relied on the patronage of a literate gentry to put contracts or administrative issues on the table in the metropolis. This was not a reliable means of representation, and, despite their oft-expressed fears of French attack, the planters of Newfoundland's English Shore were not influential enough to get landward military protection until after the sack of Newfoundland in 1697. What they failed to overcome was the absence of coherent metropolitan policy rather than considered imperial opposition to their interests. The challenge of dealing with a distant imperial government continued to affect Newfoundland, although after 1713 the settlers did not suffer another invasion until the short-lived French capture of St. John's in 1762.

As already noted, the seasonal conveyor-belt of the West Country fishery rapidly repopulated English Newfoundland after each of the setbacks associated with the destructive wars of 1689–1713. Genealogical continuity across the expulsion of 1697/1698 remains an unresolved issue, of special interest to Newfoundlanders: it is not clear to what degree the island was repopulated by its own refugees. The issue is instructive because of its complications, notably long-term kin ties between particular Newfoundland and West Country ports in the context of continuing population flows. A key desideratum here is the distinction between permanence and transience in the Newfoundland context. In the past, most scholars considered fishing servants as transients, even when they over-wintered; recently scholars have identified different kinds of permanence within the context of circum-Atlantic population mobility (Mannion, 1977; Handcock, 1989; Pope, forthcoming). Paradoxically, transhumant "winter-housing" in the eighteenth century was one of the factors that facilitated permanent settlement (Smith, 1987).

Irish immigration had begun as a trickle in the late seventeenth century, but after 1720 southwest Ireland became an increasingly important labor pool for the fishery. Irish fishing servants often settled themselves in Newfoundland, so that this ethnic fraction grew rapidly, particularly in St. John's and south (Harris, 1988). Governor Palliser made this an imperial issue between 1764 and 1768, when he attempted to restrict Irish Catholic settlement. Despite this policy, such immigrants formed a large proportion of a rapidly growing population that reached 12,000 by 1776 – a flow facilitated by the entry of Irish merchants, particularly from Waterford, into the New-foundland trade after 1750 (Mannion, 1986). Irish settlement was most significant in precisely the period in which serious attempts were made to control it. Rapid popula-tion growth and the historical mythology of impeded settlement may thus have their roots in the same period.

The development of local institutions in the eighteenth century is clear enough in outline (Rogers, 1911; Matthews, 1988). There is, however, no consensus on how to read the pertinent regulations, for example King William's Act of 1699, which explic-itly permitted settlement but which is often read otherwise (English, 1990). (Such is the power of myth.) A recent interpretation emphasizes the crucial role of custom in the maintenance of civil order in Newfoundland (Bannister, 1998a). This principle could shed light on the seventeenth century as well, particularly regarding the inter-mittent governance of the "fishing admirals," about whom generalization is common and documentation rare. Lately, scholars have been squeezing more out of the evi-dence we do have. The censorious attitude of transient administrators to the flow of wine into the fishing periphery raises interesting cultural questions (Pope, 1994). Records of the local courts, established in the eighteenth century, underscore the key role played by medical men in local governance (Bannister, 1998b). The local admin-istrative and economic customs which had evolved in Newfoundland over most of two centuries constituted a cultural adaptation to a specific environment, economic and natural. This was not simply a failed New England.

The peace of 1763 affected Native peoples, directly or indirectly. On one hand, British administrators became more solicitous of the harassed and increasingly fragile Beothuk population; on the other hand, Palliser's anti-Catholic policy became a ra-tionale to exclude Mi'kmaq refugees from Nova Scotia. While it is clear bands did remove to western Newfoundland from Cape Breton at this time, debate continues as to whether they were joining an existing and long-established population on the south coast (Martijn, 1986; Bartels and Janzen, 1990). How this territorial expansion relates to the demise of the Beothuk is another contested issue. A recent monograph makes the Mi'kmaq complicit in a ruthless European policy of elimination (Marshall, 1996). Other studies propose a more complex explanation of Beothuk decline, emphasizing their avoidance of Europeans and the consequent exclusion from traditional coastal resources by the late eighteenth-century expansion of English settlement up the north-east coast (Pastore, 1987, 1989).

Acadia

Acadia and Newfoundland were doomed to become war zones in the eighteenth century because they were borderlands between the developing empires of Britain and France. Yet, neither was simply an imperial bastion, and Acadia was an even more complex terrain than Newfoundland. The history of Canada's mainland littoral in this period can be articulated from at least four regional points of view: those of Native peoples, the Acadians, Louisbourg, and the New Englanders who poured into Nova Scotia after 1749.

Even after 1670, when the Acadians began to find their feet economically under a renewed French regime, the intricate interplay with New England and Native peoples continued. By the time war ended in 1713, the fundamentals of Acadian realpolitik were clear. The Mi'kmaq and Maliseet had allied themselves with France and the new military establishment at Louisbourg supported them with weapons and supplies in their maritime and riverine hinterlands; hence Native peoples remained a threat to those who chose to be their enemies. Meanwhile, New England had conquered mainland Nova Scotia, so that the Acadians had become British subjects. After fervent explanation by Acadian leaders of these pressures to remain neutral, the small British garrison government at Annapolis eventually accepted an Acadian oath of allegiance that did not require service against France or its Native allies. This postponed the imperial struggle for several decades, although the ambiguity of the compromise arguably laid the groundwork for the expulsion of 1755 (Griffiths, 1973).

If that event is, necessarily, the great turning point in Acadian history, the central issue must surely be the nature of Acadian neutrality. Was it calculated, considered, and therefore genuine, or was it feigned or forced? Francophones have often assumed that neutrality was a tactic, imposed by circumstance, and that the Acadians' "natural" alliance was with other francophones (Barnes, 1988; Daigle, 1995, p. 37). These were, in fact, the working assumptions of the Quebec-based *agent provocateur* Abbé Jean-Louis Le Loutre, who tried to use the Acadians to contain Nova Scotia in the 1740s. The issue intersects with another cultural question: were these simple peasants, easily swayed, as Brebner (1927) argued? Or were they a self-conscious ethnos with an acute sense of their own self-interest, perfectly capable of discerning "natural" regional alliances with New England? From this point of view, "the neutral French" were genuinely so: neutrality was not merely a tactical expedient but a strategy of cultural survival against outside threats, including France and Louisbourg as well as Britain and New England (Griffiths, 1992). Acadian culture has thus become an increasingly central topic, in various guises. Demographic analysis suggests that available land and low taxation promoted early marriage and large families. Acadians were well fed and relatively healthy, hence there were few checks on rapid population growth. Archaeological research has provided concrete evidence of Acadian prosperity in this period and has validated, in some senses, the tradition of a "golden age." It is thus questionable whether the Acadians were really a peasantry, since by this time neither ostensible proprietors nor the weak British administration were able to extract much of their surplus. In theory land tenure depended on an oath of loyalty, hence tenure in practice remained largely informal. There are parallels here with the ambiguous status of the Acadian elders, who were excluded from office by their Catholicism, yet who actually functioned as representatives of local clans or clientages. Arguably, both the tactical successes and the administrative failures of the British regime between 1713 and 1749 can be explained by its weakness and acceptance of such ambiguities (Barnes, 1990).

This perspective returns us to the deportation and debates about whether this was a contingent result of the acts of individuals like the British lieutenant-governor Charles Lawrence or Abbé Le Loutre, or whether the Acadians were "unhappy pawns" of some policy hatched elsewhere, or whether their own policy of neutrality was tragically untenable (Barnes, 1988). Economic factors made neutrality increasingly elusive, for the French at Louisbourg and their Native allies in the hinterland consumed Acadia's agricultural surplus, a strategic economic dependence which the British became increasingly serious about undermining in the 1740s. Exile itself has also proved a fertile topic for research: the Acadians were scattered across the colonies of the eastern seaboard, England and France, some eventually reaching the Caribbean and Louisiana (Griffiths, 1992). Many returned after 1763 to Atlantic Canada, if not to their original farmlands, and return itself is another significant historical theme, laden with ethnic significance (Wade, 1975). The Seven Years' War dramatically changed the human geography of Atlantic Canada, not only through expulsion and resettlement, but also through the arrival of thousands of English and German-speaking settlers and by the destruction of Louisbourg.

Louisbourg is probably the best-researched early eighteenth-century topic in the Atlantic region, if not Canada (Moody, 1994, pp. 88–93). For thirty years, development of a National Historic Park at the site has supported archaeological and archival research. The historiographic results go beyond the original aims, perhaps because the topic is nicely defined in both space and time. Developed as a fortified harbor by the French after the negotiated withdrawal from Placentia in 1713, it was obliterated by the British after its fall in 1758 (McLennan, 1918). Extensive archaeological research has undercut Louisbourg's "appearance of strength" (Fry, 1984) but has also brought the community behind the walls to life. Accounts of New England's successful siege in 1745 underscore Louisbourg's dependence on imported provisions and its commercial ties to Massachusetts (Rawlyk, 1973; Godfrey, 1982). An analysis of the mutiny of 1744 has exposed the grimy realities of life of ordinary soldiers under the *ancien régime* and social historians have returned to this period as a focus for intimate portraits of a surprisingly complex community (Greer, 1977; Moore, 1982).

Louisbourg was much more than a fortress. The arrival of French fisherfolk from Newfoundland in 1713 encouraged the growth of both migratory and resident fisheries in the region and by mid-century the value of cod exported from Ile Royale exceeded the value of furs exported from New France (Balcom, 1984). The Atlantic fishery was a key desideratum in the diplomacy of the period, for both economic and military reasons, and perhaps the varied threads of the Louisbourg tapestry can be reassembled only as part of a grander imperial design (McNeill, 1985). In part, France did value Louisbourg as it had Placentia, and as New England valued Canso, for its support of the fishery; but Louisbourg also became an entrepôt, serving New England, Quebec, France, and the Antilles (Moore, 1979). A commercial community came to life here, serving what soon became much more than a garrison, while in its hinterland Native people became key players in the regional power struggle.

Traditionally, the Mi'kmaq depended on maritime resources, by this time including the adjacent coasts of Newfoundland; the Maliseet inhabited the St. John River valley. In 1725, Britain sought Native treaty acceptance of British sovereignty over Acadia, including what is now New Brunswick. Most Mi'kmaq, however, did not interpret the French diplomatic capitulation of 1713 as binding them to accept British sovereignty and they remained allies of France until the fall of Louisbourg in 1758, waging an intermittent naval war against New England shipping. In accord with their own diplomatic traditions, Native people expected treaty presents from Europeans and their strengthened bargaining position after 1713 meant they could now demand these. The relationship of the Mi'kmaq with France was thus transformed from a trade to a military alliance, cemented not only with words of friendship but with annual presents of weapons, clothing, and food (Dickason, 1986; Martijn, 1986, pp. 233–248).

Although the major belligerents did not sign the Peace of Paris until 1763, the British administration in Nova Scotia negotiated peace with the Mi'kmaq in 1761. The Halifax treaty marked a decisive defeat for Native peoples. From the Mi'kmaq perspective those with power expressed their status by distributing available goods to those in need and they accepted British terms in part because they were endorsed with provisions. The British budgeted for annual presents when they made their first Mi'kmaq treaties, but after 1763 policy changed. Native peoples might have patched together an alternative subsistence, if they had obtained secure access to their traditional maritime resources. The 1761 treaty protected such rights, and in 1762 the local administration proclaimed free Mi'kmaq access to the resources of the coast. However, the appointed government was not the real power in Nova Scotia, and planter interests in the person of the powerful merchant Joshua Mauger soon blocked Native coastal access, driving the Mi'kmaq into poverty or Newfoundland or both. The newly arrived New England planters continued to regard Native people with suspicion in the decades that followed until, as Leslie Upton (1979) puts it, they gradually ceased to pay any regard at all. The scholarly consensus in the Atlantic region follows Bailey (1937) in emphasizing the autonomous character of Native decision-making until the late eighteenth century. These chapters in the histories of the Beothuk and the Mi'kmaq also shed a great deal of light on the European occupation of Atlantic Canada.

In 1749 the British founded Halifax, as a base to protect the fishery and to mollify the New England interests who had taken Louisbourg in 1745 only to see it restored by treaty to France. What began as a military establishment grew rapidly into a seaport. This marked the beginning of serious British settlement of Nova Scotia, for the earlier Annapolis regime was only a garrison. The wave of rapid settlement in the early 1750s is best thought of as Protestant rather than British: over half the arrivals were "foreign" German-speaking immigrants from Hanoverian principalities, many of whom settled in the Lunenburg area south of Halifax (Bell, 1961). The occupation of the vacated Acadian lands by New England immigrants followed the end of hostilities in 1761. They are sometimes remembered as the first English settlers of Canada (e.g., Brebner, 1969, pp. xi–xiv). Perhaps they were, but only in a sense that discounts a century and a half of anglophone settlement in Newfoundland. The arrival of these "planters" remains a key topic in Nova Scotia history. From the American point of view, this was part of the New England expansion – which raises a difficult political issue, since the Nova Scotia planters became "Neutral Yankees" who took little part in the subsequent American revolutionary war (Brebner, 1937; Rawlyk, 1973). Did they fail to remain Americans by force of geography or were they loyalists before their time? (Rawlyk, 1988, pp. 97–119). The last few years have seen a great interest in planter studies, in effect paralleling recent work on Acadian social history (Conrad, 1988,

1991). Two topics are particularly well explored. The Great Awakening as a movement and, in particular, the career of the Nova Scotian Henry Alline overlap American colonial history. The land question is a more distinctively regional issue, dealing as it does with the emergence of legal tenure (Moody, 1994, pp. 102–11). Those interested in governance and politics of the period can turn to Brebner (1937).

Conclusion

Some present-minded historians have implied that we can ignore the early modern settlement of Atlantic Canada, seeing this as essentially a region of later occupation (e.g., Alexander, 1980). It is, perhaps, conceivable that the experiences of the earlier inhabitants of Newfoundland and Acadia are somehow irrelevant to later developments, but one must wonder how scholars could know this without analysis of the earlier period. For too long it has been assumed that anything significant on this periphery is explicable in terms of metropolitan policy or the requirements of the economic core. This is, perhaps, the last vestige of the colonial mindset. Of course, colonial history must strike a balance between the imperial policy context and the regional practicalities of social history but in Atlantic Canada only Louisbourg is ready for such a synthesis. Acadian colonial history is well developed, but so many-faceted that we can expect to see much further work. The social history of early Newfoundland has only begun to see the light.

A general survey of Atlantic Canada in the early modern period is an improbable creature: this was not a colony, nor even a region, in the sense that New England was. Atlantic Canada is, in a sense, a chimera given coherent identity only by the faint scent of cod. This is not to say that Acadia and Newfoundland had nothing to do with one another. Their histories intersect, as they do with the histories of Maine and Massachusetts and New France. We might also concede that Acadia and Newfoundland have been subject to similar misunderstanding: underdevelopment is a poor conceptual framework for the early history of Atlantic Canada. Acadia proper, Cape Breton, and Newfoundland were productive enough to attract various Amerindian and European peoples, who then fought to hold these territories. The intensity of competition, evidenced in war and deportation, is itself a testament to the value of what was put at risk. Atlantic Natives and newcomers made their own history in this period (within the framework of inconsistent and evolving imperial policies, to be sure). Underdevelopment theory presupposes victimhood. There are other, more instructive, ways to understand Atlantic Canada in the early modern period.

BIBLIOGRAPHY

Abreu-Ferreira, D.: "Terra Nova through the Iberian Looking Glass: The Portuguese-Newfoundland Cod Fishery in the Sixteenth Century." *Canadian Historical Review* 79 (1998), pp. 100–115.

Alexander, D.: "Newfoundland's Traditional Economy and Development to 1934." In J. K. Hiller and P. Neary, eds., *Newfoundland in the Nineteenth and Twentieth Centuries: Essays in Interpretation* (Toronto: University of Toronto Press, 1980), pp. 17–39.

Bailey, A. G.: *The Conflict of European and Eastern Algonkian Cultures 1504–1700* (Toronto, 1937; rev. ed., Toronto: University of Toronto Press, 1937).

Bakker, P.: "'The Language of the Coast Tribes is Half Basque': A Basque-American Indian Pidgin in Use between Europeans and Native Americans in North America, ca. 1540–ca. 1640." *Anthropological Linguistics* 31 (3–4) (1989), pp. 117–47.

Balcom, B. A.: *The Cod Fishery of Isle Royale, 1713–58* (Ottawa: Parks Canada, 1984).

Bannister, J.: "Convict Transportation and the Colonial State in Newfoundland, 1789." *Acadiensis* 27 (2) (1998a), pp. 95–123.

Bannister, J.: "Surgeons and Criminal Justice in Eighteenth-Century Newfoundland." In G. T. Smith, A. N. May, and S. Devereaux, eds., *Criminal Justice in the Old World and the New* (Toronto: Centre of Criminology, 1998b), pp. 104–134.

Barnes, T. G.: "Historiography of the Acadians' *grand dérangement*, 1755." *Québec Studies* 7 (1988), 74–86.

Barnes, T. G.: "'The Dayly Cry for Justice': The Juridical Failure of the Annapolis Royal Regime, 1713–1749." In P. Girard and J. Philips, eds., *Essays in the History of Canadian Law*, vol. 3, *Nova Scotia* (Toronto: University of Toronto Press, 1990), pp. 10–41.

Bartels, D. A. and Janzen, O. U.: "Micmac Migration to Western Newfoundland." *Canadian Journal of Native Studies* 10 (1990), pp. 69–94.

Bell, W. P.: *The Foreign Protestants and the Settlement of Nova Scotia: The History of a Piece of Arrested British Colonial Policy in the Eighteenth Century* (Toronto: University of Toronto Press, 1961).

Bourque, B. J. and Whitehead R. H.: "Tarrantines and the Introduction of European Trade Goods in the Gulf of Maine." *Ethnohistory* 32 (1985), pp. 327–41.

Brebner, J. B.: *The Neutral Yankees of Nova Scotia: A Marginal Colony During the Revolutionary Years* (New York, 1937; repr. ed., Toronto: McClelland and Stewart, 1969).

Brebner, J. B.: *New England's Outpost: Acadia Before the Conquest of Canada* (New York, 1927; repr. ed., New York: B. Franklin, 1973).

Brière, J. F.: *La pêche francaise en amérique du nord au xviiie siècle* [*The French fishery in North America in the eighteenth century*] (Quebec: Editions Fides, 1990).

Buckner, P. A. and Reid, J. G.: *The Atlantic Region to Confederation: A History* (Toronto: University of Toronto Press, 1994).

Bumsted, J. M., ed.: *Interpreting Canada's Past* (Toronto: Oxford University Press, 1993).

Candow, J. E. and Corbin, C., eds.: *How Deep is the Ocean? Historical Essays on Canada's Atlantic Fishery* (Sidney: University College of Cape Breton Press, 1997).

Cell, G. T.: *English Enterprise in Newfoundland, 1577–1660* (Toronto: University of Toronto Press, 1969).

Cell, G. T., ed.: *Newfoundland Discovered, English Attempts at Colonization, 1610–1630.* Hakluyt Society, 2nd ser., 160 (London, 1982).

Clark, A. H.: *Three Centuries and the Island: A Historical Geography of Settlement and Agriculture in Prince Edward Island, Canada* (Toronto: University of Toronto Press, 1959).

Clark, A. H.: *Acadia: The Geography of Early Nova Scotia to 1760* (Madison, WI: University of Wisconsin Press, 1968).

Conrad, M., ed.: *They Planted Well: New England Planters in Maritime Canada* (Fredericton: Acadiensis Press, 1988).

Conrad, M., ed.: *Making Adjustments: Change and Continuity in Planter Nova Scotia, 1759–1800* (Fredericton: Acadiensis Press, 1991).

Daigle, J.: "Acadia from 1604 to 1763: An Historical Synthesis." In J. Daigle, ed., *Acadians of the Maritimes: Thematic Studies* (Moncton: Université de Moncton, 1995), 1–43.

de la Morandière, C.: *Histoire de la pêche française de la morue dans l'Amérique septentrionale (des origines à 1789)* [*History of the French cod fishery in North America (from the origins to 1789)*] (Paris: Maisonneuve et Larose, 1962).

Dickason, O. P.: "Amerindians between French and English in Nova Scotia, 1713–1763." *American Indian Culture and Research Journal* 10 (4) (1986), pp. 31–56.

English, C.: "The Development of the Newfoundland Legal System to 1815." *Acadiensis* 20 (1) (1990), pp. 89–119.

Fry, B. W.: *"An Appearance of Strength": The Fortifications of Louisbourg* (Ottawa: Parks Canada, 1984).

Godfrey, W. G.: *Pursuit of Profit and Preferment in Colonial North America, John Bradstreet's Quest* (Waterloo: Wilfrid Laurier University Press, 1982).

Greer, A.: "Mutiny at Louisbourg, December 1744." *Histoire Sociale/Social History* 10 (1977), pp. 305–36.

Griffiths, N. E. S.: *The Acadians, Creation of a People* (Toronto: McGraw-Hill Ryerson, 1973).

Griffiths, N. E. S.: *The Contexts of Acadian History, 1686–1784* (Montreal and Kingston: McGill-Queen's University Press, 1992).

Handcock, W. G.: *Soe Longe as There Comes Noe Women: Origins of English Settlement in Newfoundland* (St. John's: Breakwater, 1989).

Harris, R. Cole, ed.: *Historical Atlas of Canada*, vol. 1, *From the Beginning to 1800* (Toronto: University of Toronto Press, 1987).

Head, C. G.: *Eighteenth Century Newfoundland: A Geographer's Perspective* (Toronto: McClelland and Stewart, 1976).

Hiller, J. K.: "The Newfoundland Fisheries Issue in Anglo-French Treaties, 1712–1904." *Journal of Imperial and Commonwealth History* 24 (1996), pp. 1–23.

Hoffman, B. G.: *Cabot to Cartier: Sources for an Historical Ethnography of Northeastern North America 1497–1550* (Toronto: University of Toronto Press, 1961).

Humphreys, John: *Plaisance: Problems of Settlement at This Newfoundland Outpost of New France, 1660–1690* (Ottawa: National Museums of Canada, 1970).

Huxley, S. B., ed.: *Los vascos en el marco Atlántico Norte. Siglos XVI y XVII* [*The Basques in the North Atlantic. 16th and 17th Centuries*] (Spain: Eusko Kultur Eragintza Etor, n.d. [*c.* 1987]).

Ingstad, A. Stine and Ingstad, H.: *The Norse Discovery of America*, 2 vols (Oslo: Norwegian University Press, 1985).

Innis, H. A.: *The Cod Fisheries: The History of an International Economy* (New Haven, CT: 1940; rev. ed., Toronto: University of Toronto Press, 1954).

Innis, H. A.: "The Rise and Fall of the Spanish Fishery in Newfoundland." In M. Innis, ed., *Essays in Canadian Economic History* (Toronto: University of Toronto Press, 1956), 43–61.

Janzen, O. U.: "'Une Petite Republique' in Southwestern Newfoundland: The Limits of Imperial Authority in a Remote Maritime Environment." In L. R. Fischer and W. Minchinton, eds., *People of the Northern Seas* (St. John's: International Maritime Economic History Association, 1992), pp. 1–33.

Jones, E.: *Gentlemen and Jesuits: Quests for Glory and Adventure in the Early Days of New France* (Toronto: University of Toronto Press, 1986).

Kupp, J.: "Le développement de l'intérêt hollandais dans la pécherie de la morue de Terre-Neuve" ["The development of Dutch interest in the cod fishery of Newfoundland"]. *Revue d'histoire de l'Amérique francaise* 27 (1974), pp. 565–69.

Lounsbury, R. G.: *The British Fishery at Newfoundland 1634–1763* (New Haven, CT, 1934; repr. ed., Hamden, CT: Archon, 1969).

MacDonald, M. A.: *Fortune & La Tour: The Civil War in Acadia* (Toronto: Methuen, 1983).

Mannion, J. J., ed.: *The Peopling of Newfoundland* (St. John's: ISER, 1977).

Mannion, J. J.: "Irish Merchants Abroad: The Newfoundland Experience, 1750–1850." *Newfoundland Studies* 2 (1986), pp. 127–90.

Marshall, I.: *A History and Ethnography of the Beothuk* (Montreal and Kingston: McGill-Queen's University Press, 1996).

Martijn, C. A.: *Les Micmacs et la mer* [*The Mi'kmaqs and the Sea*] (Montreal: Recherches Amérindienne au Québec, 1986).

Martin, C.: *Keepers of the Game: Indian–Animal Relationships and the Fur Trade* (Berkeley,

CA: University of California Press, 1978).

Matthews, K.: "A History of the West of England–Newfoundland Fisheries" (D.Phil. dissertation, University of Oxford, 1968).

Matthews, K.: "Historical fence building: a critique of the historiography of Newfoundland." *Newfoundland Quarterly* 74 (1978), pp. 21–30.

Matthews, K.: *Lectures on the History of Newfoundland* (St. John's: Breakwater, 1988).

McLennan, J. S.: *Louisbourg, from Its Foundation to Its Fall, 1713–1758* (London, 1918; Halifax: Book Room, 1979).

McNeill, J. R.: *Atlantic Empires of France and Spain: Louisbourg and Havana, 1700–1763* (Chapel Hill, NC: University of North Carolina Press, 1985).

Moody, B.: "Acadia and Old Nova Scotia to 1784." In M. B. Taylor, ed., *Canadian History: A Reader's Guide*, 2 vols, vol. 1, *Beginnings to Confederation* (Toronto: University of Toronto Press, 1994), pp. 76–111.

Moore, C.: "The Other Louisbourg: Trade and Merchant Enterprise in Ile Royale, 1713–58." *Histoire Sociale/Social History* 12 (1979), pp. 79–96.

Moore, C.: *Louisbourg Portraits: Life in an Eighteenth-Century Garrison Town* (Toronto: Macmillan, 1982).

Morison, S. E.: *The European Discovery of America*, vol. 1, *The Northern Voyages* (New York: Oxford University Press, 1971).

Pastore, R. T.: "Fishermen, Furriers, and Beothuks: The Economy of Extinction." *Man In the Northeast* 33 (1987), pp. 47–62.

Pastore, R. T.: "The Collapse of the Beothuk World." *Acadiensis* 19 (1) (1989), pp. 52–71.

Pastore, R. T.: "Native History in the Atlantic Region during the Colonial Period." *Acadiensis* 20 (1) (1990), pp. 200–25.

Pope, P. E.: "Fish into Wine: The Historical Anthropology of the Demand for Alcohol in 17th-Century Newfoundland." *Histoire Sociale/Social History* 27 (1994), pp. 261–78.

Pope, P. E.: "Adventures in the Sack Trade: London Merchants in the Canada and Newfoundland Trades, 1627–1648." *Northern Mariner* 6 (1) (1996), pp. 1–19.

Pope, P. E.: *The Many Landfalls of John Cabot* (Toronto: University of Toronto Press, 1997).

Pope, P. E.: *Fish into Wine: The Newfoundland Plantation in the Seventeenth Century* (Chapel Hill, NC: University of North Carolina Press, forthcoming).

Pope, P. E. and Tuck, J. A.: "British Colonial Archaeology of Canada to 1700." In H. M. Miller et al., eds., *The Archaeology of Sixteenth- and Seventeenth-Century British Colonization in the Caribbean, United States, and Canada*. Society for Historical Archaeology, Guides to Historical Archaeological Literature, no. 4 (1996), pp. 101–21.

Proulx, J. P.: *Basque Whaling in Labrador in the 16th Century* (Ottawa: Parks Canada, 1993).

Prowse, D. W.: *A History of Newfoundland from the English, Colonial and Foreign Records* (London, 1895; repr. ed., Belleville, Ont: Mika, 1972).

Quinn, D. B.: *North America from Earliest Discovery to First Settlements: The Norse Voyages to 1612* (New York: Harper and Row, 1977).

Rawlyk, G. A.: *Nova Scotia's Massachusetts: A Study of Massachusetts–Nova Scotia Relations, 1630 to 1784* (Montreal: McGill-Queen's University Press, 1973).

Rawlyk, G. A.: "J. B. Brebner and Some Recent Trends in Eighteenth-Century Maritime historiography." In Conrad (1988), pp. 97–119.

Reid, J. G.: *Acadia, Maine and New Scotland: Marginal Colonies in the Seventeenth Century* (Toronto: University of Toronto Press, 1982).

Rogers, J. D.: *A Historical Geography of the British Colonies*, vol. 5, part 4, *Newfoundland* (Oxford: Clarendon Press, 1911).

Smith, P. E. L.: "In winter quarters." *Newfoundland Studies* 3 (1) (1987), pp. 1–36.

Story, G. M., ed.: *Early European Settlement and Exploitation in Atlantic Canada* (St. John's: Memorial University of Newfoundland, 1982).

Trigger, B. G., ed.: *Handbook of North American Indians*, 20 vols, vol. 15, *Northeast* (Washington: Smithsonian Institution, 1978).

Tuck, J. A. and Grenier, R.: *Red Bay, Labrador: World Whaling Capital A.D. 1550–1600* (St. John's: Atlantic Archaeology, 1989).

Turgeon, L.: "Le temps des pêches lointaines: permanences et transformations (vers 1500 – vers 1850)" ["The Time of the Distant Fisheries: Permanence and Transformation (*c.* 1500–1850)"]. In M. Mollat, ed., *Histoire de pêches maritimes en France* [*History of the Sea Fisheries in France*] (Toulouse: Privat, 1987), pp. 134–81.

Turgeon, L.: "Bordeaux and the Newfoundland Trade during the Sixteenth Century." *International Journal of Maritime History* 9 (2) (1997), pp. 1–28.

Turgeon, L.: "French Fishers, Fur Traders, and Amerindians during the Sixteenth Century: History and Archaeology." *William and Mary Quarterly* 3rd ser., 55 (1998), pp. 585–610.

Upton, L. F. S.: *Micmacs and Colonists, Indian–White Relations in the Maritimes, 1713–1867* (Vancouver: University of British Columbia Press, 1979).

Wade, M.: "After the *grand dérangement*: the Acadians' return to the Gulf of St. Lawrence and to Nova Scotia." *American Review of Canadian Studies* 5 (1975), pp. 42–65.

Wallace, B. L.: "The L'Anse aux Meadows site." In G. Jones, ed., *The Norse Atlantic Saga* (London: Oxford University Press, 1986), pp. 285–304.

Wallace, B. L.: "The Vikings in North America: Myth and Reality." In R. Samson, ed., *Social Approaches to Viking Studies* (Glasgow: Cruithne Press, 1991), pp. 207–19.

Williams, A. F.: *Father Baudoin's War: D'Iberville's Campaigns in Acadia and Newfoundland 1696, 1697* (St. John's: Memorial University of Newfoundland, 1987).

CHAPTER TWENTY-TWO

Causes of the American Revolutions

SYLVIA FREY

The American Revolution is one of the central events in the history of the modern world. At once progressive and regressive, splendid and tragic, it was the outcome of a concurrence of causes, some psychological, some structural. Interpretations of that event have varied considerably over time and according to geographical and national perspectives. Nineteenth-century historians blamed George III and his Tory advisors for losing the thirteen colonies. Imperial historians writing in the early twentieth century set the parameters for a new generation of scholarship by placing colonial and revolutionary history within the larger context of the British empire. No historian is better known for taking a broad Atlantic approach to the subject than Lawrence Henry Gipson. Gipson's magisterial multi-volume study, *The British Empire Before the American Revolution* (1936–70), dismissed the notion that the Revolution was the result of political blunders, or poor leadership, or bureaucratic imperatives, or westward expansion, and stressed instead American nationalism and self-sufficiency, the result of Britain's acquisition of Canada in the Great or Seven Years' War. The "new British history," brilliantly represented by Linda Colley's *Britons* (1992), has in a sense come full circle. A study of the formation of British national identity, it argues for the essential composite character of the British empire while stressing the complex interactions within and between British and American nationalisms.

Some of the most important new scholarship on race and gender, values and cultures has opened up provocative new ways to reconfigure the controversy over causes. Among the defining features of this emerging and still provisional narrative is a conscious effort to develop a more pluralist account of the Revolution. For many Americans of the revolutionary generation the Revolution was a war for independence from British "tyranny," from restrictive mercantilist policies that limited markets, from the constraining ties of labor discipline based on patriarchal relations. For others it was a struggle in defense of constitutional rights. For enslaved people it was a war for liberty from the shackles of slavery. For Native Americans it was an anti-colonial war of liberation. For some, if not all women, it was an opportunity to loosen the fetters of patriarchy. For some of the ruling elite it was an attempt to re-establish their authority over the politicizing middling and lower orders. Neither in origins or consequences can it be explained as a single linear process. In terms of origins, it must be seen as the product of a slow accumulation of several closely linked but distinct processes – political, economic, cultural – that began at different times and spread through society at different rates before converging finally in the 1760s to produce the cataclysm of revolution. Ultimately, however, interpretations of politics, ideology, and culture must be tied together with the varied findings of social and economic historians to reunite the divided worlds of social and intellectual history.

In 1818, looking back on the American Revolution in which he had played so vital a role, John Adams mused that the Revolution had occurred in American hearts long before it developed in American minds. The feelings and sensibilities that lay in human hearts took seed in the quarter-century or so before the Revolution as a series of disparate but interrelated forces began to transform the cultural landscape. The momentous shifts that occurred in England and in the colonies between the 1720s and the 1750s created the cultural substructure of change. A scene described by Benjamin Franklin achieves a remarkable condensation of the larger political, economic, and cultural geography of the half-century of change before the Revolution. The year was 1739. The event was a stop on a tour of the American colonies by George Whitefield to raise money for an orphanage in Georgia. One evening Whitefield preached from the top step of the court house located in the middle of Market Street, before a crowd estimated at 6,000 to 8,000 people, representing perhaps three- to four-fifths of the total population of the city.

The opening act in the transformation of both the civic and the sacred landscapes, the scene pre-dated and pre-visioned the powerful intersection of ideas with demographic and economic developments in the transatlantic world. Philadelphia, the social and political center and pre-eminent colonial mercantile capital of British North America, was home to Philadelphia's rapidly growing merchant community. A complex and increasingly urbanized area, Philadelphia was the focal point for the rapidly growing regional, interregional, and international trade that was a vital part of the Atlantic economy. Franklin himself personifies a wider urban culture distinguished increasingly by its commercial wealth and the proliferation of knowledge. Editor of what was for a time the colony's only newspaper, Franklin had helped found presses in Charleston, South Carolina, New York City, Lancaster, Pennsylvania, New Haven, Connecticut, Dominica, and Antigua. He had printed eight different instalments of Whitefield's journals and travels in Europe and America plus nine books and pamphlets containing Whitefield's sermons or writings. The flow of information through an increasingly complex print network represented by Franklin thus linked together the secular and the sacred and played a major role in the creation of a critical community.

A visual spectacle, the scene also announced the onset of several constituent elements of an international and pan-Protestant phenomenon: a series of evangelical awakenings that swept the Atlantic from London to Boston, from South Wales to Philadelphia, from Lowland Scotland to Charleston, South Carolina. The cultural turning was represented in the figure of Whitefield, the leader of the new international movement. A revolution in religious thought, the movement fundamentally challenged religious establishments and questioned the cultural authority of educated elites through its emphasis on vernacular preaching and emotional persuasion. Its powerful message of the spiritual equality of all believers engaged for the first time people on the margins of American society in moral discussion of politics, religion, and ideology – women, the poor, enslaved and dependent people, and Native Americans.

Every revolution in worldview, Harry Stout has reminded us (1977), requires a new rhetoric as well as a change in the form of communication. Whitefield's new preaching style marked by freedom of rhetorical expression both symbolized and shaped the anarchic impulse implicit in spiritual egalitarianism. The "rhetoric of sensation," Perry Miller once called it, also conflated the spiritual and secular worlds. Fresh from his urban preaching experiments in London, where he discovered "how to ply a religious trade in the open air of the marketplace," Whitefield capitalized on the techniques of the incipient consumer revolution to make revival a consumer product. This he accomplished by articulating the Christian message of the brotherhood of man in mercantile terms, urging his listeners to "buy the truth," or invest in "the bank of heaven." His extensive use of newspaper publicity created a transatlantic community of faith and at the same time entwined his religious ministry in the spreading Atlantic market (Lambert, 1994, pp. 46–94).

The "cult of commerce" implicit in Whitefield's rhetoric was an increasingly important part of British identity. The commercial dynamism of imperial trade, particularly the colonial import and export trade, had by mid-century produced an extraordinary proliferation of goods so vast that scholars have labeled it a consumer revolution. Part of an ideological process that continued over several decades, consumerism was a powerful shaping influence on the construction of distinct national identities. In Britain it took the form of economic and cultural nationalism. Linda Colley, among others, has argued persuasively that eighteenth-century economic, social, and cultural transformations spawned a "mood of national awakening" that found expression in national art, in a succession of patriotic societies and voluntary associations, and in a brand of economic and cultural nationalism that became more strident with the outbreak of war in 1756. The most extreme expression of this "cult of England" was the Wilkite movement, that fed on a "noisy Scottophobia" that conflated the Scottish and the foreign and spoke to popular fears that Scottish growth and prosperity posed a serious threat to England's cultural hegemony (Colley, 1992, pp. 56, 68–9, 86–8, 108–17). For most Britons colonial Americans were a "mysterious and paradoxical people, physically distant but culturally close, engagingly similar yet irritatingly different" (Colley, 1992, p. 134). The vague, somewhat troubling perception of distinct American departures from British norms derived from the geographical distance and massive size of British North America, from the marked peculiarities of different regional societies, from differences in social structures, in particular a relatively large and enfranchised middle class and the generalized existence of chattel slavery. These differences were for the most part papered over until the "great war for empire" of 1763 ripped away the covering and exposed and magnified "a critical divergence in political perspectives" (Meinig, 1986, p. 302–7).

Up to the very eve of the American Revolution colonial consciousness remained "intensely British." Throughout their histories the thirteen British mainland colonies had existed as separate corporate entities, each with its own distinctive local history, peculiar constitution, legal system, economy, religion, and culture. Jealous and suspicious of one another, they were bound together principally by language and their common pride in being part of "an expanding British nation and empire" (Greene, 1986, p. 164; Murrin, 1987, p. 339). Contrary to what the metropolitan government feared and expected, loyalty to a political abstraction called "America" did not yet exist in the American imagination. Over the course of the eighteenth century Americans were becoming if anything more English. The Anglicization of legal culture and the enforcement of orderly pleadings by professional lawyers, imported cultural practices diligently copied by colonial elites and an emerging middle class, the rapid development of a commercial press that depicted England as "the most polite and progressive society the world had ever seen," the mass consumption of consumer goods that flowed in ever-growing quantities from scores of small manufacturing centers in England into American households, and the influx of a host of "celebrity itinerants" (Breen, 1997, pp. 22–3), outriders of a militant Protestant culture that was destined to reshape the colonial religious world, turned Americans into "imperial patriots" (Murrin, 1987, p. 338), albeit "upon an equal footing with Englishmen at home" (Greene, 1986, p. 163). Below the surface current of colonial habits of loyalty was an undertow of nagging anxieties about their pervasive dependence on British goods that was moving colonial attitudes toward Britain in the opposite direction.

Mutual mistrust was not then the product of traditional antipathy between two peoples but the ironic consequence of Britain's phenomenal success in the Seven Years' War. Victory over France and Spain "transformed Britain's position in the world" by consolidating its control of the plantation colonies in North America and the West Indies and extending its imperial embrace to Africa and India. It transformed as well the pre-war trading empire into a worldwide mercantile empire whose fastest-growing markets were the colonies in North America and the West Indies and its trading outposts in India. For all the benefits in prestige and power it brought, the unprecedented spoils of victory created new political problems that few of the inexperienced ministers responsible for shaping policies properly understood. It necessitated a vast reordering of the empire involving the accommodation of disparate peoples and cultures and different and often contradictory interests within the framework of the British empire. It required new expenditures for maintaining a navy sufficiently powerful to defend trade routes, colonies, and monopolies. Most of all it doubled the national debt and forced the London government to search for new sources of revenue, which necessarily implied new taxes and an increase in centralized authority.

If, as Linda Colley has put it, "one were rash enough to plump for only one underlying cause" of the American Revolution, it would perhaps be the failure of the metropolitan government to establish strong institutions of imperial control such as Spain was able to build in Latin America. Distracted by wars and dynastic change, the metropolitan government had failed to establish effective structures of royal authority in British North America. During two centuries of "benign neglect" the mainland colonies labored happily under the illusion that they were allies and equal partners in an expanding and inclusive empire (Colley, 1992, pp. 102, 135–6). Britain's belated efforts to bring the vigorous American colonies to heel and thereby delay what some foresaw as the inevitable loss of imperial dominion over the "jewels in Britain's commercial crown" precipitated a cultural and constitutional crisis that forced British North Americans to re-examine the nature and boundaries of their loyalty of Britain (Colley, 1992, p. 137).

The American Revolution has been variously described as the opening act in a conflict between democracy and imperialism and as a search for economic independence. Economic interpreters, among them Louis Hacker (1940), Carl Becker (1922), and Arthur M. Schlesinger (1918, rev. ed., 1968), saw the Revolution as a clash of economic interests, both in England and in America, but they by no means agreed on how precisely to order the hierarchy of economic causes. Other historians depicted the Revolution as a conflict between democracy and imperialism but neither could they arrive at an identical explanation. For Robert E. Brown (1955) the Revolution in

Massachusetts, and by implication elsewhere in the colonies, was a struggle of an essentially democratic society against British tyranny. Merrill Jensen (1957) revised Brown's argument by insisting that the Revolution was democratic not in its origins but rather in its results. In fact none of these themes are totally separate and distinct. Rather their interrelatedness demonstrates the complexity of the question. No neat line divides economic and political matters from cultural and moral concerns or separates the revolution of the heart from the revolution of the mind. A range of complex issues involving multiple actors and interests with varying agendas converged to create a sense of common identity and common cause that were at the very heart of the revolutionary movement. But regionally distinct priorities, the ordering of which reflected different conditions and locational experiences, and disparate values and commitments among socioeconomic groups, created complex patterns of causes.

At the very center of the American Revolution was the problem of indebtedness: Britain's national debt, which led to the rise in taxation; colonial indebtedness to British merchants, which created the underpinning for "American" identity as separate and distinct from Britain; and indebtedness of farming families to merchants, speculators, and lawyers, which gave rise to the largest rural insurgency in pre-revolutionary America. In the quarter-century before the Revolution personal indebtedness, particularly in the tobacco colonies, rose sharply. Older studies of colonial indebtedness as a causative factor stressed debt repudiation as a primary motive in influencing planters' decision for rebellion (Beard, 1915; Harrell, 1926). That somewhat oversimplified interpretation has been replaced by a more complex analysis that recasts the debt question in economic, social, and political terms and links it with the issue of slavery.

The changing patterns of interpretation present economic factors as more richly varied in character. The restructuring of the tobacco trade by Scottish syndicates during the forty years before the Revolution transformed economic life in Virginia and supported the rise of the great planters. It also led to the massive expansion of mercantile credit after 1740. In the quarter-century before the Revolution Virginia and Maryland accumulated a per capita debt that was triple the average for all the other British North American colonies. The sweeping Currency Act of 1764, which prohibited the further issue of paper notes, contracted the money supply and increased the burden of taxation, for gentry and cash-strapped farmers alike. A rising debt level, stagnant profits, falling land values, and declining personal fortunes were perceived by many as a serious threat to social stability, personal independence, and to the influence and authority of local elites. Although the staple trade depended upon slavery, it also perpetuated economic dependency on Britain by draining the colony of specie and restricting the growth of a diversified economy. Caught in a complex web of debt obligation and dependency, Virginians came increasingly to see credit and consumption as a moral issue, an attitude that crystallized in the1760s in a belief that excessive consumption was part of a conspiratorial design to preserve the ascendance of British merchants.

The grievances of the southern gentry over pervasive indebtedness, aggressive debt collection, a shrinking money supply, burdensome taxes, and economic dependency were in many ways analogous to those held by rural men and women and in certain ways linked the histories of those two disparate social groups. During the 1760s, the Piedmont areas of North and South Carolina erupted in massive resistance movements

that were in large measure a response to rapid economic and cultural change consequent to the Piedmont's growing integration into the Atlantic market. Participation in
the world market created opportunities but it also created debts. In the case of North
Carolina, the problem of debt was exacerbated by the land sales of Lord Granville,
whose agents deeded over 2,000,000 acres between 1751 and 1762; by petty government officials, especially lawyers who charged extortionate fees, and officers of the
county courts who set the local taxes; by the mercantile activities of British trading
firms, who used the courts to collect money from their customers. "These cursed
hungry caterpillers," as Herman Husband called them in his 1770 account of the
grievances of the Regulators, "will eat out the very Bowells of our common-wealth, if
they are not pulled down from their Nests" (Boyd, ed., 1927, p. 256).

Older depictions of the Regulator movement as an expression of sectional conflict
have been largely discounted but the history of the movement continues to generate
debate among historians. Marvin L. Michael Kay's interpretation of the movement as a
reaction to class exploitation (1976) contrasts sharply with A. Roger Ekirch's emphasis
on the ideological dimensions of the Regulator struggle against the corruption of local
officials (1981), and Marjoleine Kars' location of the radical ferment of the Great Awakening at the center of the movement (1993). What seemingly incompatible interpretations suggest is the existence of a cluster of deep-seated anxieties. For Piedmont families
no less than for the great Tidewater gentry, chronic and pervasive debt was a moral as
much as an economic issue. Ensnared in debt to a small commercial elite, caught up in
lawsuits that rendered land tenure insecure, frustrated at every turn by the collusion of
court officials and speculators, yeoman and artisan families turned to political activism
and ultimately to violent action. Taking their inspiration from the Stamp Act protests,
Piedmont families launched a mass movement and assumed the name Regulators. In
rallying the populace to their cause, Husband, the chief spokesman for the movement,
drew on radical Protestant moral precepts which stressed community, personal discipline, and frugality in consumption, but his call to arms resonated with Whig political
language: "as these practices are contrary to Law, it is our Duty to put a Stop to them
before they can quite ruin our County, or that we become willing Slaves to these law-
less Wretches, and hug our Chains of Bondage" (Boyd, 1927, p. 256).

Backcountry settlers in South Carolina shared certain grievances with their North
Carolina neighbors. Both were seeking to secure private property, and both were concerned with the issue of debt and excessive legal fees. But the South Carolina Regulation was a vigilante movement that arose in response to a rash of violent robberies
perpetrated by landless hunters who eked out a living by foraging, and by land-
holding bandits whose incorporation of women and blacks threatened the household
order and gender hierarchy. Whereas the North Carolina Regulators protested *against*
local government and the stringent credit policies of Scottish merchants, the middling
farmers who made up the bulk of the South Carolina Regulation were agitating *for*
local courts because the centralized court system made it difficult for them to bring
suit for debts.

However disparate their political goals, as aspiring participants in commercial agriculture many backcountry settlers were turning to slavery, "this destructive canker"
Herman Husband called it. Convinced that the spread of slavery "threat[e]ned ruin
and destruction to all my hopes" for the establishment of western North Carolina as a
"new government of liberty" for hard-working white farmers, Husband broke with his

followers and attacked the institution in a scathing "A New Government for Liberty" (Ekirch, 1977, pp. 641, 643). By contrast, Charles Woodmason, Anglican minister and leading spokesman for the South Carolina Regulation, demanded in the name of backcountry farmers that slavery be made secure from the bandits who stole slaves or offered them refuge. When Woodmason reproached the Lowcountry planters who were leading the resistance to the Stamp Act for making "such Noise about Liberty! Liberty! Freedom! Property! Rights! Privileges! & what not; and at the same time keep half their fellow Subjects in a State of Slavery," he had in mind the backcountry's under-representation in the colonial assembly. Like most of his contemporaries, Woodmason chose not to dwell on the obvious connection between liberty and chattel slavery (Klein, 1990, pp. 63, 67, 81).

For bondmen and women, however, slavery and liberty were intrinsically connected. An incident in Charleston, one of the principal centers for black slavery, sketches out the contours of a different war, this one about slavery if not over slavery. During the Stamp Act controversy bondmen and women watched with keen interest the same white crowds that Woodmason described as they demonstrated around the homes of suspected stamp officers shouting, "Liberty! Liberty and stamp'd paper." In a calculated reference to the transparent hypocrisy of the white protesters they staged their own demonstration, raising the same cry, "Liberty." The panic that ensued in Charleston and environs exposed what would become the pivot on which southern loyalty would swing. However divided the frontier, whatever their differences with the coastal plantation classes, when the Revolution came the majority of backcountry settlers became patriots, their differences with coastal elites over local political issues dissolved, their interests bound with the imperial question.

The rather different but equally complex interplay of economic and moral imperatives operated to create the psychological propensity for revolution in the urban Northeast. The "first scene of the first Act of Opposition," as John Adams described it, occurred in the aftermath of the Seven Years' War and was a product of new imperial policies intertwined with internal politics. The setting was the Council Chamber of the Massachusetts Superior Court. The protagonists were Chief Justice Thomas Hutchinson presiding over a panel of five judges, "all in their new fresh Robes of Scarlet English Cloth in their Broad Bands, and immense judicial Wiggs." Solemnly attired in "Gowns, Bands, and Tye Wiggs" were James Otis, Jr. and a team of Boston barristers representing merchants seeking immunity from prosecution for customs violations. There also sat the short, fat, twenty-five-year-old apprentice John Adams, hastily scribbling notes on what is generally accepted as one of the first assertions of colonial resistance to parliamentary regulation. At issue were three acts of Parliament passed in the late seventeenth century which collectively authorized the use of general standing search warrants, or writs of assistance, by colonial customs officials to search houses, shops, warehouses, and ships and to seize prohibited imported or exported goods for which duties were payable under the Acts of Trade and Navigation enacted in the seventeenth century. The Court ultimately decided in favor of the writ, but the arguments made for the merchants by Otis "in a rapid Torrent of impetuous Eloquence" articulated what most ordinary Americans only vaguely felt: resentment of the use of the writs to tighten customs controls; fear of the threat posed to individual liberties by the broad powers granted under general warrants; concerns that parliamentary restrictions on colonial manufacturing were inhibiting the growth of a diversified economy; and looming political and constitutional questions about the theory of absolute parliamentary sovereignty ([1761] Wroth and Zobel, 1965, pp. 106–47).

The "child independence" may not, as Adams later claimed, have been born in the Council Chamber, but the controversy over the writs of assistance did cause the two large entrepreneurial classes of merchants and artisans to reassess the restrictive and revenue measures passed by Parliament beginning in the late seventeenth century. Historians are in general agreement that the Navigation Acts had little direct impact on most colonies; nevertheless, as a recent work by Larry Sawyers has argued (1992), many long-sighted merchants were aware of future burdens the acts implied. Although the acts protected colonial merchants from Dutch and French competition, they forced competition with British merchants, who sold directly to colonial shopkeepers on liberal credit terms and low mark-ups. Adams' cryptic note on "Iron manufactures, Noble Lord's Proposal, that we should send our Horses to England to be shod," presumably refers to the 1750 British Iron Act prohibiting iron manufacturing in the colonies ([1761] Wroth and Zobel, 1965, pp. 107, 127–28, n. 74). Although the act encouraged colonial production of crude iron, it stirred a growing radicalism among artisans and mechanics whose primary business was manufacturing and was a significant factor in drawing them into the revolutionary movement.

Actor, manager, playwright all in one, Otis also put into play two of the deep issues that came to define ideological politics in the next decade. In explicitly challenging the constitutionality of the writs he implicitly questioned the prevailing orthodoxy of parliamentary sovereignty, an idea that others would carry to its logical conclusion. A short time later Otis, whose own father had been passed over for appointment to the high bench, began to articulate a moral case against Britain that aimed at transforming the social distribution of public power as well as the theory on which it rested. Although Hutchinson had not sought the chief judgeship and had even questioned his own professional qualifications for it, Otis denounced him for holding office simultaneously in the executive, legislative, and judicial branches of government. His crude misrepresentation of Hutchinson as a politically ambitious man who advanced his own family and friends to high office helped bring into sharp focus smoldering popular resentment of privilege, especially inherited privilege, and thereby called into question the very legitimacy of the ruling elite whose power and status derived from their imperial connections.

The controversy over the Stamp Act marked the birth of the revolutionary movement. The act constituted not merely a policy division but an epochal divide, both as the culmination of a new consciousness and the beginning of a rebellion. As long as they felt secure in their rights, colonial British Americans had remained excessively loyal to Britain. In a single act Britain "raised and spread, thro the whole Continent, a Spirit that will be recorded to our Honour, with all future generations," John Adams wrote later in his *Diary*. "Such an Union was never before known in America. In the Wars that have been with the French and Indians, a Union could never be effected" ([1777, 1778] Adams, 1962, pp. 263, 285). An essential moment in the history of the entire revolutionary movement, the Stamp Act controversy has been the subject of intense scrutiny by historians seeking to find in it the root causes of the Revolution.

The importance of economic factors in precipitating resistance in the northern commercial provinces was first noted by Arthur Schlesinger in his seminal work *The Colonial Merchants and the American Revolution* (1918, rev. ed., 1968). In it Schlesinger explained the extraordinary colonial response to the act in terms of the economic burden it placed on New England's commercial classes, although he conceded that colonial opposition was based on constitutional grounds and further that popular resistance and growing egalitarian sentiment were prominent factors. In their popular and polemical work, *The Stamp Act Crisis* (1953, rev. ed., 1963), Helen and Edmund Morgan insisted that colonial objections were based on fundamental principles, which Edmund Morgan later linked to Puritanism. This essentially conservative analysis of the Revolution was contested by Bernard Bailyn, the foremost representative of the intellectual interpretation of the Revolution. In *The Ideological Origins of the American Revolution* (1976) Bailyn stressed the importance of radical ideas derived from the writings of opposition politicians in seventeenth- and eighteenth-century England. Despite their disagreements both Morgan and Bailyn recognized the importance of crowd action, and Bailyn conceded the significance of popular grievances while the disciplined destruction of property led Morgan to the conclusion that colonial crowds were manipulated by the likes of James Otis and Sam Adams. A number of historians, among them Gary Nash, have reacted to what they considered an overemphasis on ideas by placing popular behavior at the heart of the revolutionary movement (Young, 1976 [Kay, 1976], 1993). Nash, for example, has traced the violent colonial reaction to the Stamp Act to the animosity of the common people toward Thomas Hutchinson and his clique and read into it a rejection of their elitist conception of politics. Nash's analysis is consistent with the notion of a "dual revolution" first suggested by Carl Becker to convey the argument that the Revolution in New York was both an internal struggle between social classes and an external revolution against Britain (Becker, 1922; Nash, 1979).

It was not one of these things alone but all of them together that best explains what brought the mercantile elite and the plebeian public together in shifting coalitions composed originally of master artisans, whose economic well-being was linked to the development of home manufacturing and merchants. When their economic interests clashed over non-importation, the coalition collapsed and the artisans went into coalition with the lower-class political movement. That the entrepreneurial classes of northern urban America were demonstrating against post-war inflation, economic stagnation, the tightening of trade regulations, and new revenue measures, and *for* freedom from government regulations, has been amply established. But recent histories of revolutionary crowd actions have demonstrated that a coalescence of artisans and workers came into their own on the field of revolutionary politics. Women lent the weight of their numbers to the revolutionary movement only to be displaced as actors and transformed into audience as part of a new role and a new identity defined by men. Playwright though he might have been, Otis did not command their agenda, nor did he lead the coalition of masters, petty entrepreneurs, and lower artisans who made up the bulk of the Stamp Act crowds. A cordwainer named Ebenezer MacIntosh did.

Like the entrepreneurial classes, the lower social orders were demonstrating against the hard times and undue economic burdens that wars and commercialization placed on the poor and middling classes. But it was not freedom *from* regulation they sought but a return *to* the traditional regulation of the market and to traditional patterns of local production and exchange and an end to the monopolization of wealth, power, and privilege by the prerogative elite. Their resentment of the developing capitalist ethos had a moral component as well. It involved a restructuring of social relations and the restoration of traditional marketplace ethics so as to prevent exploitation by merchants and public officials. These concerns took on new significance during the Stamp Act controversy when they became more and more central to the identity of "Americans" as a distinct group and to the development of an incipient nationalist sentiment.

The shock precipitated by the Stamp Act was the catalyst for an intense period of self-examination that occupied the decade of the 1760s and culminated in the Declaration of Independence. The notion that they were somehow different and even perhaps superior in virtue to Britain was intuitively felt by colonial Americans during the late colonial period. The radical transformation of colonial identity from "English" to variants of "American" was actively forged in colonial ambivalence about consumption. As the "western world's fastest growing market" most colonial peoples were acutely conscious of the reciprocal benefits of commercial prosperity. (Colley, 1992, p. 70). They were also aware that for all the benefits the market exchange economy brought, consumerism was creating a process of cultural as well as economic dependency. During the Stamp Act controversy Americans began constructing a republican mythos at the heart of which was the notion of their own unique political character. A cultural as well as a political creation, it involved the construction of a myth of British "corruption" and American "virtue" that was as necessary as it was inaccurate. The myth of unique moral strength and character evolved over several years, crystallizing finally in the Association drawn up by the First Continental Congress in 1774. The Association agreed to support economic boycotts and a program of moral proscriptions aimed at the identification and destruction of "enemies" of the people and the simultaneous creation of a virtuous citizenry by cleansing American iniquities through repentance and spiritual rejuvenation. In this sense, the American Revolution was, as Edmund Morgan noted nearly a quarter of a century ago, "an ethical movement" (Morgan, 1976, pp. 88–138).

The manifestly moral component present in colonial resistance to the Stamp Act crisis was rationalized in ideological rhetoric which drew on ideas and discourses derived from a variety of sources at once disparate and overlapping, making it very difficult for scholars to disentangle the multiple strands of ideological thought and tie them neatly to the Revolution. There is no need to review in tiresome detail the scholarly debate that has endured for half a century over the origins and role of ideology as a causative factor. In broad outline the scholarly discussion has evolved through several major constructions, beginning with the Lockean consensus of the 1950s (Morgan, 1953, rev. edn, 1963; Hartz, 1955). The republican synthesis that emerged in the 1960s and 1970s in the writings of Bernard Bailyn (1976) and Gordon Wood (1972) de-emphasized the importance of possessive individualism and gave primary place to the republican ideas associated with seventeenth-century English Commonwealthmen and with the Levellers. J. G. A. Pocock (1975) took republican revisionism a step further by stressing the centrality of the concept of civic humanism; put another way, the civic concept of individual virtue. Challenged on the grounds that it subordinated social and economic factors to political and constitutional ideology, the republican synthesis was succeeded by a rediscovery of Lockean liberalism in the 1980s most often associated with the work of Joyce Appleby (1984, 1978). Recent revisions of revisionism such as that advanced by James T. Kloppenberg (1987) point to the coexistence of ideas and discourses, a position that partisans of all traditions are increasingly willing to accept.

In fact revolutionaries drew power from divergent ideological perspectives and deployed particular concepts for different purposes. The obsession of classical republicanism with public corruption and popular degeneracy and its preoccupation with virtue as the lifeblood of the republic and the only secure antidote to private and public depravity functioned as a way to exorcise the deep feelings of inferiority Americans of the revolutionary generation felt in the face of British military might and cultural pre-eminence. It simultaneously provided the moral structure to justify resistance and the associated notion of a just war. The burgeoning middle group of Americans with access to mercantile enterprise and, in the South, to slaves were not always eager to play out the role of self-sacrificing, public-spirited citizenry demanded by Republicanism. Liberal ideology, with its emphasis on industry and merit, property rights, and a national policy of economic freedom, better suited their needs and the requirements of a market-driven economy. As property-holders, Piedmont inhabitants were drawn to liberal ideology, although they framed their objections to the new capitalist ethos in a rhetoric that drew simultaneously on radical Whig principles and evangelical religion. Urban crowds who led the Stamp Act protests derived their political ideas from a variety of sources and experiences, including participation in local networks of exchange and "the forms and values of Anglo-American plebeian politics" (Smith, 1994).

One core assumption around which diverse grievances coalesced, and one recognized by classical and modern analysts of revolutions, is the concept of sovereignty of the people – a "political fiction," Edmund Morgan calls it, whose roots extend to the English Civil War (1988, pp. 55–77). Although revolutionaries disagreed over the precise meaning of concepts like virtue, liberty, and equality, they united on the notion of individual and ultimately national autonomy. The "most important doctrine of eighteenth-century political science," Gordon Wood says of it (1972, p.372), the "fiction" of popular sovereignty "represent[ed] at once the fulfilment of the Puritan concept of the covenant, the republican idea of a public-spirited citizenry, and the liberal idea of responsibly self-interested individuals exercising their right to self-government" (Kloppenberg, 1987, p. 25). The denigration of the legislative authority of Parliament during the imperial crises of the 1760s upset the old understanding of how people should participate in government and led to a new and radical rendering of the theory.

The transforming power of ideas has long been a given among historians of the American Revolution. Ideas themselves, however, were transformed by economic and social conditions peculiar to time, place, and circumstance. Revenue issues, which were of paramount concern to seaboard patriots, paled before the long-lasting and deep-rooted conflicts over land in the Piedmont and the transmontane West. Indeed it can be argued that the conflict over territorial expansion was the precipitating cause of the Revolutionary War, anticipating by a full year events in the Boston area in the spring of 1775. There was, however, a dynamic connection between on the one hand the revenue laws passed to pay for the defense system in the West that precipitated the revolutionary movement in the urban East and on the other hand the issue of territorial expansion that provoked squatters and promoters in the backcountry and in the Ohio Valley. In each case resistance was justified by reference to ideas drawn from the same general body of ideas, although the meaning of those ideas was understood differently. Those ideas in their various constructions provided the ideological justification for the sequence of violent events that run in an upward spiral from the Stamp Act riots in 1765 through Pontiac's Rebellion in 1763 and Lord Dunmore's war against the Shawnees in 1774, through the Indian wars of the Revolutionary War and the violent suppression of slave revolts in the South.

Conflict between Native American and Europeans over land was one of the most resonant themes in the history of the British American mainland colonies from 1622 onward. European and African diseases, intertribal and European warfare had, by the eve of the American Revolution, decimated the original coastal Indian population. Only about 300 Indians still lived east of the mountains in Virginia; another 1,000 were divided almost equally between North and South Carolina. Indians made up barely 2 percent of the total population of Massachusetts, most of them clustered in small enclaves such as Martha's Vineyard and Nantucket. They survived by adapting to an Anglo-American lifestyle of individual landownership and material consumption. Those who declined to accommodate incorporated themselves as subjects of one of the main Indian confederacies of the interior: the Iroquois, western Delawares, and Shawnees in the Northeast, and the Cherokees, Creeks, and Choctaws in the Southeast. There they became part of a mixed world of rugged French *coureurs de bois*, sturdy English traders, and consummate hunter-warriors from distinct tribal groups, all bound together in complex entanglements created by a thriving trade in furs and skins for iron and steel implements, textiles, weaponry, and rum. Shared economic activities necessitated intercultural cooperation and blurred national and ethnic differences. But that mixed world of shared economic activities did not last.

The American Revolution in Indian country west of the Allegheny Mountains had its immediate origins in the involvement of culturally different people with market capitalism and in the extraordinary demographic and geographic expansion that preceded and followed the Revolution. The Native American population was neither large nor cohesive enough to withstand the pressures of immigration and rapid territorial expansion. During the 1760s and 1770s, waves of migrants from Pennsylvania, Virginia, and North Carolina began pouring through the Shenandoah Valley into the western Piedmont of South Carolina and across the Alleghenies into the Ohio Valley. The surging white population inevitably collided with the Indian nations whose hunting grounds were being nibbled away by the illicit settlements of opportunistic squatters and the raw ambitions of aggressive land speculators from Virginia and New York. The demeaning prospect of economic and cultural dependency and displacement from their ancestral lands propelled Native Americans to seek relief from the chains of credit, inequality, and exploitation through cultural renaissance and revolution.

The behaviour of Native Americans has typically been seen as merely reflexive to colonial aggression. It would be foolish to deny that Native Americans saw themselves as exploited by colonial governments and people, or that they were not often duped and defrauded in their dealings with both. Recent scholarship offers an alternative explanation (Dowd, 1991; Braund, 1993; Calloway, 1995). No mere passive victims of the system or of land-hungry settlers and developers, Native Americans initiated action and did not merely respond to events imposed on them. Alienated by colonial land encroachments, by their own crippling dependency on European trade, by the debilitating effects of guns, rum, and goods on traditional values and authority, Native Americans launched a movement of spiritual revitalization and cultural resistance, the origins of which coincided with the Great Awakening. A simultaneous but separate insurgent movement, it absorbed some Christian ideas but radically transformed them into new forms peculiarly its own. Led by mystical prophets preaching a blend of

Christian notions of spiritual equality and monotheism with traditional beliefs and rituals, the Nativist Great Awakening rested on the central idea of God-given distinctions between black, white, and red peoples, which found expression in a demand for spiritual reformation through ritual purification of white ways and implied a rejection of dependence on British trade and the eventual abandonment of European-made trade goods. Despite its seeming atavism, separation theology had radical implications for the development of pan-Indianism. It involved the construction of a non-traditional but nativistic Indian identity based on the exchange of religious ideas and the mutual recognition of cultural similarities. It reached beyond localism of past times as Indian nations and remnants of conquered and dispossessed southern and northern tribes realigned themselves with one another and with Europeans.

The dynamics of this process are inextricably linked to the paradox of British imperial expansion. Between 1675 and 1740, the population of British America quintupled, the fastest rate of growth in any European empire. The extraordinary growth of the population of British America was in large measure based on migration from Scotland and from Ulster and the north of Ireland. Attracted by expanding opportunities in the world's fastest-growing market, talented and ambitious merchants and traders, skilled artisans, craftsmen, and clerks set out from Scotland for the mainland colonies. Many of them found employment in the Chesapeake tobacco trade as warehousemen and shopkeepers or as factors in the employ of one of the Scottish syndicates that organized the marketing of Chesapeake tobacco. Before the Revolution, a quarter of a million Scots-Irish immigrated to the American colonies. Part of a large folk migration, they were steered toward the frontier by colonial officials to settle on lands expropriated from Indians. By the 1760s their farms were scattered within and beyond the Appalachian region between western New York and eastern Tennessee. To the Ohio Indians on whose lands the Scots-Irish trespassed as well as to the Virginia gentry whose social authority and economic independence the Scottish traders challenged, the Scots personified the advance of commercial capitalism that threatened to engulf them all.

Tensions were exacerbated by the Seven Years' War. The most "dramatically successful war the British ever fought," the Seven Years' War was also the most problematic (Colley, 1992, p. 101). Older studies of the war's effects follow the lead of the imperial school of history. Jack Sosin, for example (1961, repr. ed., 1980), views British policy from the vantage point of Whitehall and therefore stresses the ministry's desire to maintain peace and order in the colonies. Recent studies have not entirely abandoned this perspective but they have expanded it dramatically, both by turning their attention to the colonial perspective and alternatively to the perspective of Native Americans. The integration of Native American history into the paradigm changes the explanatory framework for the development of the revolutionary movement in the West. The ending of the Seven Years' War triggered a series of events that opened up Indian lands and unleashed a flood of settlers from Virginia and Pennsylvania. It ignited new Indian hostilities that culminated in Pontiac's turbulent campaign to establish territorial integrity and affirm cultural power. It accelerated the trend toward intertribal unity and created new problems for frontier defense. It doubled the national debt and forced the London government to search for new sources of revenue, which necessarily implied an increase in centralized authority. And it had a crystallizing effect on American attitudes toward race and laid the foundations for two centuries of racial conflict.

This "vast, disconnected, infinitely diversified empire," as Edmund Burke called it, demanded fiscal and administrative innovations. But Britain's erratic and inconsistent shift toward greater authority in the seaboard colonies in the aftermath of the Seven Years' War had a fatal parallel in its inability to evolve a coherent and consistent land policy in the western territories. A succession of ministries, all of them composed of men without political experience or history of public office, struggled and failed to devise policies acceptable to the various political factions in the House of Commons or to the colonies. Their failure to do so had decisive consequences for colonial politics. The post-war demographic and geographic expansion was viewed with ambivalence by the metropolitan government. On the one hand, colonial abundance provided a rich storehouse of raw products and a flourishing market for British manufactures. On the other hand, colonial expansion conflicted with British Indian policy and potentially with mercantilist policies. Two interconnected issues were of pressing concern to the ministry: the depopulation of the British Isles through transatlantic emigration and the incitement of western nations caused by trans-American emigration. In Britain there was growing anxiety that emigration was robbing the country of thousands of young men and women in their most productive years. This was particularly true of the agricultural tenant population of Protestant Irish, which had declined by 2 percent in a single decade.

The Proclamation of 1763 embodies what Bernard Bailyn has called "the dilemma of British policy" (1986, p. 29). When Pontiac, leader of the northern Ottawas, launched a coordinated attack on British outposts in the western Great Lakes region, the metropolitan government hastily devised a new Indian policy that placed the Indian nations of the trans-Appalachian region under British "protection" and effectively closed the region to future expansion. A vain effort to halt the exodus of British farmers and workers to the colonies and to regulate the settling of inland colonies, it prohibited royal governors from granting warrants of survey or passing patents for land in the region west and north of the headwaters of eastward flowing rivers; ordered the removal of settlements in lands reserved by treaty for the Indians; prohibited the private purchase of Indian reserved lands; and opened up Indian trade to all persons who obtained a license from royal governors. Staggering under an immense national debt incurred during a century of dynastic and colonial wars, Britain had neither the will nor the resources to enforce the provisions of the proclamation. No policy for managing the western lands could halt, in Bailyn's words, the "frantic peopling of half a continent" or arrest the rapid growth of the colonial economy that was a counterpart of it (1986, p. 173).

The attempt to forge a unified Indian policy for the British empire in America failed because of Britain's inability to enforce the Proclamation Line, or to properly control the thousands of small landholders who occupied land beyond it in defiance of metropolitan authority, or to quash the grandiose plans of colonial land developers, or contain the naked opportunism of Crown officials in the colonies. John Murray, the Earl of Dunmore, personifies all of these failings. A key figure linking the history of the Ohio country to the Chesapeake, his activities in both regions bring into a single focus the issue of race as – if not the essential core of the Revolution – an important part of it. His activities broadly reflected and stimulated the paradoxical changes that were slowly overtaking American politics: the efflorescence of popular aspirations for a better, more open world, in which individuals could engage their creative energies free of restraining authority and the concurrent emergence of an incipient racialist ideology as a counterpart to it.

Pressured by various speculative interests, the metropolitan government reluctantly agreed to a westward adjustment of the Proclamation Line that was in accord with the desires of western settlers. The Fort Stanwix agreement, which extended the western boundary of the Line to take in millions of acres of prime lands on the upper Ohio, became a point of major controversy because of overlapping and conflicting claims made by the governments of Virginia, Pennsylvania, and the ancient claims of the Shawnees and the Cherokees. The British decision to close the western posts of Fort Pitt and Fort Chartres as an economy measure created a power vacuum and opened the door to unrestrained Virginia expansion into central Kentucky in direct contradiction of England's policy of rational and controlled expansion. Dunmore, the recently appointed governor of Virginia, abetted and even stimulated migration by encouraging surveyors and settlers to stake out claims in the Kentucky and Salt River basins. When border violence inevitably erupted, Dunmore raised a militia company and without Crown approval led it against the Shawnees. The defeat of the Shawnees at the Battle of Point Pleasant in the summer of 1774 led to a mad land rush as squatter parties, small landowners, and militia veterans moved in with astonishing speed, scattering makeshift forts and a patchwork of towns and homesteads along the Ohio River and through the Clinch, Holston, Powell, and Watauga Valleys. These squatters soon found their dreams of unrestrained freedom to pursue economic expansion threatened by the Transylvania Company's dubious purchase of upwards of seventeen million acres of Cherokee lands in the very heart of Kentucky.

Eric Hinderaker (1997) has pointed out that Lord Dunmore's war against the Shawnees in the summer of 1774 simultaneously released the creative energies of thousands of ordinary Americans and turned the Revolution in the Ohio Valley into a "race-based struggle over land." In defending the legitimacy of their frontier communities against the Transylvania land developers, residents of the Harrodsburg settlement drafted a series of petitions to the Virginia assembly, calling into service the notion of popular sovereignty. In theoretical terms, the Harrodsburg settlers sought to reconcile the violent, opportunistic removal of Indian peoples from their ancestral lands with the political idealism of the revolutionary movement by a complex mixture of democratic idealism and rough equality intertwined with the notion of race and an attachment to violent solutions. The first line of approach called for a basic transformation of the social structure. The attempts of land developers to establish in Kentucky a proprietary system complete with quitrents was "inimical to American Liberty," and contrary to the principle of equality. The preservation of civil liberty required government to "discourage all monopolies of those lands" by granting them "in small or modest quantities." The farmers meant not only to do away with social distinctions based on inequality of property but also to advance a radical redefinition of the concept of popular sovereignty. Their claim that the Proclamation Line "is not founded upon Law, it cannot have any Force . . ." and their refusal to " . . . acknowledge any power or prerogative which is not derived from the Convention of Virginia whose subjects we desire to be considered," uprooted the orthodox concept of legislative sovereignty and planted in its place the notion of the hegemony of the people (Hinderaker, 1997, pp. 161–2, 170–4, 176–97).

The new popular sovereignty expounded by the Harrodsburg farmers made another

radical extension, the implications of which were as important for the institutionalization of popular violence and racial hatred as for representative government- and constitution-making. The historical connection that Hinderaker finds between the
theoretical concept of popular sovereignty and the violent actions of the revolutionary
generation was noted earlier by Gordon Wood in *The Creation of the American Republic* (1972) and by Richard Maxwell Brown, whose seminal essay on "Violence and
the Revolution" (1973) underscored the fact that popular violence was endemic in
Anglo-American history. What Hinderaker does is to extend that argument to race.

The Harrodsburg settlers' demand that Virginia extend its jurisdiction westward
before the Revolution had actually begun rested on the right of conquest. Virginia,
the petitions proclaimed, can "claim this country with the greatest justification and
propriety" because Virginians had "Fought and bled for it." Had it not been for the
"memorable Battle at the Great Kanaway [Point Pleasant], the vast Regions had yet
continued inaccessible" ([1769–1792] Robertson, 1914, pp. 35–40). The Harrodsburg
petitions thus lent to violence "an ideological and philosophical justification and an
awesome dignity." By acceding to the settlers' demands Virginia's revolutionary government gave implicit sanction to the unregulated occupation of western lands, and
implicitly identified the conflict between Indians and Euro-Americans over claims to
land as the central issue to be contested in the West. Thereafter, Euro-American settlers launched a "fierce and indiscriminate war against the Indian population of the
valley." In the ensuing struggle race became a defining category of the Revolutionary
War in the Ohio Valley and laid the foundations for Indian removal and for decades of
racial conflict (Hinderaker, 1997, pp. 212, 215).

This is a profoundly important insight, but there is more to it than that. Dunmore's
war in the Ohio Valley was merely the opening act in the transformation of the revolutionary movement in the South and the West into a war about race. The withdrawal of
Dunmore's forces from the Ohio country is, in fact, connected to another "race" war,
this one in Virginia. Together, these two events, symbolically joined in the person of
Dunmore, made race a central theme of the Revolution. Although he is generally
credited, or blamed, for "inciting" the black liberation movement, black resistance
emerged simultaneously with white resistance and ran parallel to it. Although there
had been parliamentary discussions about recruiting slaves as a disruptive tactic, no
action was taken because of the dangers inherent in such a plan. The path toward the
engagement of enslaved people was cut by the enslaved themselves when in April
1775, "some Negroes (by one of [Dunmore's] servants had offered to join him and
take up arms." Dunmore ordered them "to go about their business," and "threatened
them with his severest resentment, should they presume to renew their application"
([1775] Frey, 1991, p. 55). Six months later, Dunmore issued his famous proclamation offering freedom to indentured servants and slaves who defected to the British.
The purpose of the proclamation was practical rather than moral, to intimidate whites
rather than to emancipate blacks, but no single act was more important in propelling
the South to independence. Like a galvanic current, the black struggle to construct
their own movement for liberation from slavery spread through the country. Finding
in the chaos of the Revolution and in the promise of British support a chance to strike
a blow for freedom, tens of thousands of enslaved men and women joined the British
army or struck out on their own.

As in the white resistance movement and in the Nativist struggle for independence, this act of political defiance by enslaved people had its antecedents in the development of a distinct identity predicated on "race." Several historians, following Benjamin Quarles' important insight about the emergence of a "race-conscious" identity by 1774, have given us a much more complex understanding of the importance of "reidentification," from an African ethnically based identity to a African American racial identity, as the genesis of black responses to the revolutionary crises. Blackness as a "principal of unity" began to emerge out of the shared suffering and profound humiliation captive peoples experienced in the barracoons of Africa and on the Middle Passage. The recreation of a common language, an Africanized version of English, was crucial to that process (Gomez, 1998, pp. 165–77; Sidbury, 1997).

The Revolutionary War itself was a driving force in the social construction of racial identity. Dunmore's war in Virginia did more psychological than material damage, but it did produce a decisive shift in white southern political allegiance and a changing meaning attached to race. It was against the radical "otherness" of Dunmore's black regiment that white southerners increasingly defined their own identity and projected a racial identity to the men and women they held in bondage. Dunmore's organization of a segregated Ethiopian Regiment had a quite different meaning to enslaved people. It changed the way in which they imagined race. Being active participants in a struggle to realize "Liberty to Slaves" that was emblazoned on their regimental banner "expanded their sense of identity ideologically," and, as James Sidbury's sensitive reading has suggested, "offered a pathway to freedom" (1997, pp. 33–4).

In seeking to explain motivating forces this essay leans heavily on recent literature of the American revolutionary era. That literature suggests the difficulty, indeed the impossibility, of trying to explain the Revolution as an intellectual movement, or a democratic movement, or a war for economic independence. To the extent that there was a hierarchy of causes the ordering varied considerably according to region, race, and class. But there is more to it than that. One of the great lessons to be learned from recent literature is the need to think in terms not of a single revolution but of parallel revolutions, each fought for some of the same reasons though with very different objectives, each influencing in profoundly important ways the course and outcome of the others.

As casualties of economic change Native Americans waged a war for national sovereignty that lasted until the mid-1790s. Although as a movement it incorporated Christian rhetoric and certain Christian ideas, it was inspired mainly by Indian notions of equality and sovereignty. The Indian war, often fought in alliance with the British, was the climax of a long struggle, in part to protect ancestral lands from encroaching colonial settlers and speculators, in part to achieve moral reform through radical separation from the European world of trade and culture. The profoundly disillusioning denouement to their long struggle for national sovereignty was to be reduced to the status of a conquered people, their vast lands ultimately passing into the hands of land speculators and backcountry farmers to fulfill *their* revolutionary dreams of independence and sovereignty.

The African American experience was distinctive, although it too must be considered as part of revolutionary history. The outbreak of war created extraordinary historical conditions, particularly in the South, where the near-total collapse of the apparatus of control opened up seemingly realistic possibilities for freedom. Inspired by revolutionary rhetoric that apparently repudiated slavery and in many cases by evangelical

Christian ideas of liberty and equality, enslaved people were able, perhaps for the first time, to imagine a day when they would be free and their masters punished for enslaving them. Their struggles did not bring about an immediate end to slavery anywhere except in Vermont. What they did do was to challenge the moral foundations of slavery and in that way hasten its ultimate demise.

Colonial unity depended heavily on the presence of "internal" enemies as well as the "external" enemy. Expansion into Indian lands supplied the glue that bound Pennsylvania and Virginia speculators together. That same thirst for land fired poor whites and aspiring sons of eastern planters. The desire for property was as much an objective of poor white squatters as of great planters and large eastern speculators. All this is to say that ideas and experiences of all Americans – political, economic, and cultural – were interwoven strands of the same fabric. Precipitating factors in the East – revenue laws, economic restrictions, the idea of popular sovereignty – proceeded from and were connected to events in the West. All of the constituent elements of the war in the South – race, revenue, debt – were present, to one degree or another, in the West and the East. Britain's inability to establish imperial authority in the West was ironically connected to a belated shift toward greater authority in the seaboard colonies in the aftermath of the Seven Years' War.

This is not to say that there was consensus. There was not. Different groups of Americans subscribed to different sets of beliefs or in some cases to the same set of beliefs which, however, they understood and interpreted differently according to group interests and class values. Despite such differences, most men and women who supported the Revolution did so because they shared certain common objectives and certain fundamental beliefs. Class antagonism clearly existed but gentry anxiety over mounting debts, over the maldistribution of wealth and power, over elite control of the political and economic systems, grievances against the tax system and corruption in the handling of public money, coincided with the concerns of many backcountry farmers. At the center of this interlocking set of causes was the consuming concern for property as a crucial component in the creation of independence and the primary attribute of personal sovereignty. The powerful ideological drive to acquire, protect, and sanctify property that was a hallmark of the American Revolution represented both material concerns and a system of values, central to which were the Lockean principle of personal freedom, the classical republican ideal of civic virtue, and the evangelical vision of a moral community. Together they composed a millennial vision of an earthly paradise of free and equal citizens joined together as one moral community.

BIBLIOGRAPHY

Adams, John: *Diary and Autobiography of John Adams*, 3 vols, ed. L. H. Butterfield (Cambridge, Massachusetts: Belknap Press, 1962).
Appleby, Joyce: "The Social Origins of American Revolutionary Ideology." *Journal of American History* 64 (1978), pp. 939–58.
Appleby, Joyce: *Capitalism and a New Social Order: The Republican Vision of the 1790s* (New York: New York University Press, 1984).
Bailyn, Bernard: *The Ideological Origins of the American Revolution* (Cambridge, MA: Harvard University Press, 1976).

Bailyn, Bernard: *Voyages to the West: A Passage in the Peopling of America on the Eve of the Revolution* (New York: Knopf, 1986).

Becker, Carl: *The Declaration of Independence: A Study in the History of Political Ideas* (New York: Vintage Books, 1922).

Bermingham, Ann and Brewer, John, eds.: *The Consumption of Culture, 1600–1800: Image, Object, Text* (London: Routledge, 1995).

Bonomi, Patricia U.: *Under the Cope of Heaven: Religion, Society, and Politics in Colonial America* (Oxford, England: Oxford University Press, 1986).

Boyd, William K., ed.: *Some Eighteenth Century Tracts concerning North Carolina* (Raleigh, NC: Edwards and Broughton, Co., 1927).

Braund, Kathryn E. Holland: *Deerskins and Duffels: The Creek Indian Trade with Anglo-America, 1685–1815* (Lincoln, NE: University of Nebraska Press, 1993).

Breen, T. H.: *Tobacco Culture: The Mentality of the Great Tidewater Planters on the Eve of the Revolution* (Princeton, NJ: Princeton University Press, 1985).

Breen, T. H.: "Narrative of Commercial Life: Consumption, Ideology, and Community on the Eve of the American Revolution." *William and Mary Quarterly* 3rd ser., 50 (1993), pp. 471–501.

Breen, T. H.: "Ideology and Nationalism on the Eve of the American Revolution: Revisions *Once More* in Need of Revising." *The Journal of American History* 84 (1997), pp. 13–39.

Brown, Richard D.: *Knowledge Is Power: The Diffusion of Information in Early America, 1700–1865* (New York: Oxford University Press, 1989).

Brown, Richard Maxwell: *The South Carolina Regulators* (Cambridge, MA: The Belknap Press, 1963).

Brown, Richard Maxwell: "Violence and the American Revolution." In Stephen G. Kurtz and James H. Hutson, eds., *Essays on the American Revolution* (Chapel Hill, NC: University of North Carolina Press, 1973), pp. 81–120.

Brown, Robert E.: *Middle-Class Democracy and The Revolution in Massachusetts, 1691–1780* (Ithaca, NY: Cornell University Press, 1955).

Bushman, Richard L.: *The Refinement of America: Persons, Houses, Cities* (New York: Knopf, 1992).

Butler, Jon: *Awash in a Sea of Faith: Christianizing the American People* (Cambridge, MA: Harvard University Press, 1990).

Calloway, Colin G.: *The American Revolution in Indian Country: Crisis and Diversity in Native American Communities* (Cambridge, England: University of Cambridge Press, 1995).

Carson, Cary et al., eds.: *Of Consuming Interest: The Style of Life in the Eighteenth Century* (Charlottesville, VA: University Press of Virginia, 1994).

Clemens, Paul G. E.: *The Atlantic Economy and Colonial Maryland's Eastern Shore: From Tobacco to Grain* (Ithaca, NY: Cornell University Press, 1980).

Colley, Linda: *Britons: Forging the Nation, 1707–1837* (New Haven, CT: Yale University Press, 1992).

Dayton, Cornelia Hughes: *Women Before the Bar: Gender, Law, and Society in Connecticut, 1639–1789* (Chapel Hill, NC: University of North Carolina Press, 1995).

Dickerson, Oliver M.: *The Navigation Acts and the American Revolution* (Philadelphia: University of Pennsylvania Press, 1951).

Dowd, Gregory E.: *A Spirited Resistance: The North American Indian Struggle for Unity, 1745–1815* (Baltimore, MD: Johns Hopkins University Press, 1991).

Dunn, John: *Locke* (New York: Oxford University Press, 1984).

Egnal, Marc: "'A New Government of Liberty': Hermon Husband's Vision of Backcountry North Carolina, 1755." *William and Mary Quarterly* 3rd ser., 34 (1977), 632–46.

Egnal, Marc: *A Mighty Empire: The Origins of the American Revolution* (Ithaca, NY: Cornell University Press, 1988).

Ekirch, A. Roger: "The North Carolina Regulators on Liberty & Corruption, 1766–1771." *Perspectives in American History* 6 (1977–8), pp. 199–256.

Ekirch, A. Roger: *"Poor Carolina": Politics and Society in Colonial North Carolina, 1729–1776* (Chapel Hill, North Carolina: University of North Carolina Press, 1981).

Frey, Sylvia R.: *Water From the Rock: Black Resistance in a Revolutionary Age* (Princeton, NJ: Princeton University Press, 1991).

Frey, Sylvia R. and Wood, Betty: *Come Shouting to Zion: African American Protestantism in the American South and British Caribbean to 1830* (Chapel Hill, North Carolina: University of North Carolina Press, 1998).

Gipson, Lawrence H.: *The British Empire Before the American Revolution*, 15 vols (Caldwell, ID: The Caxton Printers, 1936–70).

Gipson, Lawrence H.: "The American Revolution as Aftermath of the Great War for Empire, 1754–1763." *Political Science Quarterly* 65 (1950), pp. 86–104.

Gipson, Lawrence H.: *The Coming of the Revolution, 1763–1775* (New York: Harper and Row, 1954).

Gomez, Michael A.: *Exchanging Our Country Marks: The Transformation of African Identities in the Colonial & Antebellum South* (Chapel Hill, NC: University of North Carolina Press, 1998).

Greene, Jack P.: "Political Mimesis: A Consideration of the Historical and Cultural Roots of Legislative Behavior in the British Colonies in the Eighteenth Century." *American Historical Review* 75 (1969), pp. 337–60.

Greene, Jack P.: *Peripheries and Center: Constitutional Development in the Extended Polities of the British Empire and the United States, 1607–1788* (Athens, GA: University of Georgia Press, 1986).

Hacker, Louis M.: *The Triumph of American Capitalism* (New York: Simon and Schuster, Inc., 1940).

Harrell, Isaac S.: *Loyalism in Virginia: Chapters in the Economic History of the Revolution* (Durham, NC: Durham University Press, 1926).

Hartz, Louis: *The Liberal Tradition in America* (New York: Harcourt Brace, 1955).

Hatch, Nathan O.: *The Democratization of American Christianity* (New Haven, CT: Yale University Press, 1989).

Hatley, Tom: *The Dividing Paths: Cherokees and South Carolinians through the Revolutionary Era* (New York: Oxford University Press, 1995).

Hinderaker, Eric: *Elusive Empires: Constructing Colonialism in the Ohio Valley, 1673–1800* (Cambridge, England: Cambridge University Press, 1997).

Jensen, Merrill: "Democracy and the American Revolution." *Huntingdon Library Quarterly* 20 (1957), pp. 321–41.

Kars, Marjoleine: *Breaking Loose Together: The Regulator Rebellion in Pre-Revolutionary North Carolina* (Chapel Hill, NC: University of North Carolina Press, 2002).

Kay, Marvin L. Michael, "The North Carolina Regulation, 1766–1776: A Class Conflict." In Alfred F. Young, ed., *The American Revolution: Explorations in the History of American Radicalism* (De Kalb, Illinois: University of Illinois Press, 1976), pp. 71–123.

Klein, Rachel: *Unification of a Slave State: The Rise of the Planter Class in the South Carolina Backcountry, 1760–1808* (Chapel Hill, NC: University of North Carolina Press, 1990).

Kloppenberg, James T.: "The Virtues of Liberalism: Christianity, Republicanism, and Ethics in Early American Political Discourse." *Journal of American History* 74 (1987), pp. 9–33.

Krammick, Isaac: "Republican Revisionism Revisited." *American Historical Review* 87 (1982), pp. 629–64.

Lambert, Frank: *Pedlar in Divinity: George Whitefield and the Transatlantic Revivals, 1737–1770* (Princeton, NJ: Princeton University Press, 1994).

Laslett, Peter: "Introduction." In John Locke, *Two Treatises of Government*, ed. Peter Laslett

(Cambridge, England: University of Cambridge Press, 1960), pp. 15–135.

Meinig, D. W.: *The Shaping of America: A Geographical Perspective of 500 Years of History*. 2 vols (New Haven, CT: Yale University Press, 1986).

Morgan, Edmund S. and Helen M.: *The Stamp Act Crisis* (New York: Collier Books, rev. ed., 1963).

Morgan, Edmund S. and Helen M.: "The Puritan Ethic and the American Revolution." In Edmund Morgan, ed., *The Challenge of the American Revolution* (New York: Norton, 1976), pp. 88–138.

Morgan, Edmund S. and Helen M.: *Inventing the People: The Rise of Popular Sovereignty in England and America* (New York: Norton, 1988).

Murrin, John M.: "'A Roof Without Walls': The Dilemma of American National Identity." In Richard Beeman et al., eds., *Beyond Confederation: Origins of the Constitution and American National Identity* (Chapel Hill, NC: University of North Carolina Press, 1987), pp. 333–48.

Nash, Gary B.: *The Urban Crucible: Social Change, Political Consciousness, and the Origins of the American Revolution* (Cambridge, MA: Harvard University Press, 1979).

Olton, Charles S.: *Artisans for Independence: Philadelphia Mechanics and the American Revolution* (Syracuse, NY: Syracuse University Press, 1975).

Pocock, J. G. A.: *The Machiavellian Moment: Florentine Political Thought and the Atlantic Republican Tradition* (Princeton, NJ: Princeton University Press, 1975).

Price, Jacob M.: *Capital and Credit in Britain's Overseas Trade: The View from the Chesapeake, 1700–1776* (Cambridge, MA: Harvard University Press, 1980).

Ragsdale, Bruce A.: *A Planters' Republic. The Search for Economic Independence in Revolutionary Virginia* (Madison, WI: Madison House, 1996).

Rahe, Paul A.: *Republics Ancient and Modern: Classical Republicanism and the American Revolution* (Chapel Hill, NC: University of North Carolina Press, 1991).

Richter, Daniel K.: *The Ordeal of the Longhouse: The Peoples of the Iroquois League in the Era of European Colonization* (Chapel Hill, NC: University of North Carolina Press, 1992).

Robertson, James Rood, ed.: *Petitions of the Early Inhabitants of Kentucky to the General Assembly of Virginia, 1769 to 1792* (Louisville, Kentucky, 1914; reprint ed., New York: Arno Press, 1971).

Rock, Howard B.: *Artisans of the New Republic: The Tradesmen of New York City in the Age of Jefferson* (New York: New York University Press, 1975).

Rosswurm, Steven: *Arms, Country, and Class: The Philadelphia Militia and "Lower Sort" During the American Revolution, 1775–1783* (New Brunswick, NJ: Rutgers University Press, 1987).

Salinger, Sharon V.: *"To Serve Well and Faithfully": Labor and Indentured Servants in Pennsylvania, 1682–1800* (Cambridge, England: Cambridge University Press, 1987).

Sandoz, Ellis: *A Government of Laws: Political Theory, Religion and the American Founding* (Baton Rouge, LA: Louisiana State University Press, 1990).

Sawyers, Larry: "The Navigation Acts Revisited." *Economic History Review* 45 (1992), pp. 262–84.

Schlesinger, Arthur M.: "Political Mobs and the American Revolution, 1765–1776." In American Philosophical Society, *Proceedings* 99 (1955), pp. 244–50.

Schlesinger, Arthur M.: *The Colonial Merchants and the American Revolution* (New York, 1918; rev. ed., New York: Atheneum, 1968).

Sidbury, James: *Ploughshares into Swords: Race, Rebellion, and Identity in Gabriel's Virginia 1730–1810* (Cambridge, England: Cambridge University Press, 1997).

Smith, Barbara Clark: "Food Rioters and the American Revolution." *William and Mary Quarterly* 3rd ser., 51 (1994), pp. 3–38.

Sosin, Jack M.: *Whitehall and the Wilderness: The Middle West in British Colonial Policy, 1760 to 1775* (Lincoln, NE, 1961; repr. ed., Westport, CT: Greenwood Press, 1980).

Stout, Harry S.: "Religion, Community, and the Ideological Origins of the American Revolution." *William and Mary Quarterly* 3rd ser., 34 (1977), pp. 519–41.

Wood, Gordon S.: *The Creation of the American Republic, 1776–1787* (Chapel Hill, NC: University of North Carolina Press, 1972).

Wood, Gordon S.: *The Radicalism of the American Revolution* (New York: Knopf, 1992).

Wroth, L. Kinvin and Zobel, Hiller B., eds.: *Legal Papers of John Adams*, 3 vols (Cambridge, Massachusetts: Harvard University Press, 1965).

Yolton, John W., ed.: *John Locke: Problems and Perspectives* (Cambridge, England: Cambridge University Press, 1969).

Young, Alfred F., ed.: *Beyond the American Revolution: Explorations in the History of American Radicalism* (De Kalb, IL: Northern Illinois University Press, 1993).

CHAPTER TWENTY-THREE

Postscript: Large Questions in a Very Large Place

EDWARD COUNTRYMAN

Supposedly, at least, Woodrow Wilson once made a trenchant comment about the history of colonial America. Recalling his doctoral examination at Johns Hopkins, he reflected on learning ten thousand useless facts on the subject, and immediately forgetting them when the exam was done. Or so the story goes. Whatever its veracity, it has a poetic truth. Colonial America can be profoundly confusing and the confusion can seem to lead nowhere.

Unlike the American Revolution or the Civil War, there is no single tale to be told. Even the old Virginia-and-New-England format requires narratives that had little in common beyond the bare facts of English people arriving on the American shore and staying. Another theme might be to see "the colonies" in terms of an eventual revolution that nobody wanted and very few even faintly predicted. But that is to lapse into teleology. Arguing that one place or another was most prototypically "American" amounts to arguing for one or another version of local patriotism. For all those reasons, I always have resisted using single-volume accounts in class, preferring to make students meet the confusion head on.

Even accepting the confusion has its perils. The changing contents of successive editions of the widely used reader *Colonial America* (Katz, 1971; Katz, Murrin, and Greenberg, 1993, 2001) suggest how that confusion has waxed and waxed again. I began using the catch phrase "pattern of patterns" to help students who wanted to make sense of the whole thing. That did conjure up the image of a crazy quilt, and quilting, like its musical analog jazz, is an American art. Still, moving on to the revolutionary period always has seemed a relief. Historians might argue about actors, motivations, events, and consequences. But the large story of the British empire coming to its end and the American republic taking shape could remain coherent.

About the time I moved from England to Texas in 1991 a new problem appeared. Even the fifth edition of *Colonial America* remains east-coast oriented. But it became apparent that many of the most interesting monographs were exploring places and problems well away from the Atlantic littoral. I found myself anchoring my courses on books like *The Indians' New World* (Merrell, 1989), *Powhatan's Mantle* (Wood, Waselkov, and Hatley, 1989), *The Middle Ground* (White, 1991), *Sugar and Slaves* (Dunn, 1972), and even *When Jesus Came, the Corn Mothers Went Away* (Gutiérrez, 1991).

One advantage of these is that though they stick to one place, they all cover very long periods, providing a chronological "spine" on which other topics could be hung. Among east-coast books only *American Slavery, American Freedom* (Morgan, 1975) and *A New England Town: The First One Hundred Years* (Lockridge, 1970) seemed to do the same in a way that undergraduates could handle. When I returned most recently to the east coast for a *longue durée* account, it was to use *Good Wives, Nasty Wenches, and Anxious Patriarchs* (Brown, 1996), which by no means is traditional.

But I turned out to be neither out of step nor hopelessly attempting to be trendy. In 1994 the Institute of Early American History and Culture (now the Omohundro Institute) sponsored a remarkable conference in New Orleans that brought "colonial" and "western" historians together to talk across their traditional boundaries. That meeting led to an equally remarkable volume (Cayton and Teute, 1998). Post-doctoral fellows in the Clements Center for Southwestern Studies at Southern Methodist University began getting "colonial" tenure-track jobs at major institutions. One, who had written on Texas, has spoken of being asked whether she could teach Virginia-and-New-England and responding that of course she could, but she wouldn't.

The essays collected here reflect that widening of the colonial American field, in both conceptual and geographical terms. Other than reviewers, very few people are likely to sit down and read this book straight through. It is a "companion," not a narrative. But anybody who did read it all would perceive a neat fit between the overall impact of these essays and *American Colonies*, Alan Taylor's recent attempt to bring the whole field together in one account (2001). Aiming for "general readership," Taylor avoids merely professional debate and citation-mongering. The state of such debate is precisely the subject here, and discussion of what different historians have said is appropriate.

The two books complement each other well. Both rest on the assumption that "colonial America" (my usage, although Taylor means the same thing by *American Colonies*) was vastly larger than the east-coast provinces that eventually rebelled against Britain. The subject of both books amounts to every place in North America and its neighboring islands that participated in the exchange which began when Europeans and Africans started traveling the great oceans in large numbers. That exchange was epidemiological, botanical, zoological, material, demographic, political, economic, cultural, and military. Taylor understands the colonial process as reaching all the way from the Bahamas and Cuba in 1492 to Hawaii and Alaska early in the nineteenth century. This collection is only slightly less ambitious in spatial terms and is equally ambitious in its time span. Like Taylor's book, the scope of these essays shows how large a field "colonial America" has become.

If the field is enormous in terms of space and time, the bibliographies in the separate essays are vast in a way that symbolizes their subjects. The time when one scholar really could claim to be able to master both the colonial and revolutionary periods is long past. Several of the sub-fields represented here by long, dense essays with huge reading lists did not exist even when my own doctoral mentor assembled an influential and highly useful collection on *Seventeenth-Century America* (Smith, 1958). They only were beginning to exist when Richard Hofstadter attempted to pull the field together slightly more than a decade later (Hofstadter, 1971). That point of the sub-fields themselves being new applies most notably to the essays by John Brooke on ecology, James Merrell on Indians, Philip Morgan on African Americans, and Carol Karlsen on women and gender. But turn from those to the essays on traditional subjects, such as Alan Tully on east-coast provincial politics, Marilyn Westerkamp on religion, Ned Landsman on migration, Margaret Newell on economics, and Gregory Nobles on social class. All of them (and the other essays whose authors I have not named) show that even topics which supposedly were familiar and very well worked have seen extensive recent or near-recent debate. Perhaps the most painful consequence of being privileged to read these before publication is to realize how many important studies I missed in a recent updating of my synthesis *The American Revolution* (Countryman, 2002).

If the spatial frame has been broadened, the temporal frame has as well. At one end, it no longer is enough to pay mere lip service to Native America's complexities prior to 1492. Smith and Anderson show otherwise. The problems and sources they discuss might be familiar to anthropologists and archaeologists. But historians need to know these matters and incorporate them, particularly at a time when the subject of what there was before Columbus is spilling over to high-end general readership (Mann, 2002).

The essay by Carole Shammas demonstrates that the meeting of European and Native American histories was far more complex than the notion of "discovery" normally connotes. Rather than a few great-name explorers encountering totally pristine Natives, we now must see the sixteenth century as a time of constant mutual probing, even in North America. Well before Henry Hudson and possibly before Giovanni da Verrazzano, fishing vessels probed offshore American waters and their crews established temporary camps. When a big ship did appear, Native people had good reason to know what sort of people were aboard, what goods they were likely to have, and what they wanted. They knew the visitors probably brought disease as well. By the middle of the sixteenth century, coastal Indians probably had a much better sense about Europeans than the Europeans who "saw" humanoid monsters in 1492 and who continued to see Indians for the "first time" had about Indians (Mann, 2002; Cohen, 1992).

Colonial America was a time as well as a place. That time used to end with the Treaty of Paris of 1763. Thereafter the subject became the American Revolution. That old formula still has its merits. The Revolution did emerge from the problems that attended the conquest of New France by the British, so 1763 marks a transition point (Anderson, 2000; Draper, 1996). The Revolution did take place within the enormous space stretching from the Atlantic coast to the Mississippi River and from the Florida boundary to the St. Lawrence Valley. The entirety of that space was defined as "British" by the 1763 agreement. The Revolution did lead to that same space being defined as "American" two decades later, again at a treaty made in Paris. The British subjects who turned themselves into American citizens were not rising against foreign mastery in the name of outraged ethnic identity. But they did bring their own colonial situation to an end.

Now, however, we see colonial America as comprehending much more than just the places that became the early United States. What happened as Europeans and often Africans approached and settled and spread their influence covered maritime Canada, New France, the upper Mississippi/Great Lakes *pays d'en haut*, the Great Plains, the Spanish Borderlands, New Spain, the Caribbean, and the west coast. These too saw the creation of colonial societies or colonial situations. The Comanche attack on the

Spanish outpost at San Saba, Texas, in 1758 was not a matter of Indians raiding be-cause raiding was what Indians naturally did. The Comanches had made themselves part of the large colonial world. They were participants in that world, not victims. They raided with firearms of French origin. They were acting within a field of forces that emanated from New Mexico, New France, the English colonies, and Louisiana. They generated considerable force themselves (Nathan, 2000 [1959]; Hamalainen, 2001; Barr, 1999). They were linked directly by trade and diplomacy both eastward to colonial Arkansas and westward to colonial New Mexico (Arnold, 1991).

East-coast independence created a powerful and permanent new force within that field. That force embarked almost immediately on a very successful and very rapid imperial venture. But outside its zone, the colonial situation of being beholden to a far-distant center of power persisted. Along the Pacific coast, from San Diego to Sitka, and in Hawaii, the colonial situation was just beginning.

That situation and these essays which consider its different aspects force a reconsid-eration of our explanatory terms. "The Colonies" still may connote Virginia planta-tion houses and New England villages (even if we understand that both the great houses and the picture-postcard villages are latter-day innovations, not artifacts of the origin). But that way of understanding "early America" will not do any more. Nor will any notion of a Turnerian frontier, however slowly it "moved" prior to the great leap westward that began when the young United States began to acquire its own empire. Europeans and often Africans were entering too many places from too many directions for any notion to stand that transformation emerged only from the east. In 1763 Indians east of the Mississippi were not yet defeated, let alone expelled by the nine-teenth-century policies that now would be called ethnic cleansing. But already they were virtually surrounded.

How, then, to make sense of it? We no longer can understand colonial America simply as a neo-Europe, however anxiously settlers and their progeny tried to re-create European ways. The notion of a syncretic and quasi-permanent borderland between Indian and European-dominated societies works well for the Southwest (Weber, 1993). But that concept does not define every place in the colonial world where Native people and colonizers met and where the Indians did not simply retreat. The metaphor of a Middle Ground provides a powerful understanding for a Euro-Native way of life that lasted close to two centuries (White, 1991). That way of life, with its emphasis on mutuality and creative mutual misunderstanding, stood off challenges from the French, the British, and initially the United States. It only really ended when settlers started to transform the *pays d'en haut* into the Great West. Historians studying other places where there was an extended Native/European encounter do not find that the Middle Ground image helps much at all (Merrell, 1999).

If no single image explains what we used to call "the frontier," fitting the whole of colonial America into one picture is even more difficult. As Newell suggests here, Bernard Bailyn's notion of colonial America as marchlands, rough, backward places where the normal rules – anybody's normal rules – did not hold for anybody at all does help (Bailyn, 1986). But that hardly explains urban development in Boston or Phila-delphia or Baltimore (Price, 1974; Earle and Hoffman, 1976). These became com-mercial market towns and provincial capitals, with all the economic and cultural complexity of town life on the Atlantic rim, akin to Bristol or Bordeaux. Still other places became at least seigneurial, if not quasi-feudal in European terms, whether we refer to New France, the Hudson Valley, the great barony called Pennsylvania, or New Spain's *Marquesado del Valle* (Greer and Ferry in this volume; Berthoff and Murrin, 1973). Perhaps the great French historian Fernand Braudel got it best when he called colonial America a "mosaic" that displayed "a hundred different colours: modern, archaic, primitive, or curious mixtures of all these" (Braudel, 1985).

It is tempting to invoke the Marxist notion of a social formation, in which one dominant mode of producing, exchanging, and living coexists with others. But it is difficult to see any dominant mode among the widespread people whom we encounter in this book. Protestant Europeans believed in private property, but whether that meant that capitalism came in the first ships, even the first English ships, seems entirely open to debate (Degler, 1959). Everybody within the colonial sphere felt the power of the profit-driven Atlantic market, but that does not mean they participated in the market with profit alone in mind. Slaves participated because they were forced to. Indian miners in New Spain also participated as forced labor, although their sojourn was temporary if they survived. Missionized Indians under Spanish dominion lived in communal situations that retained many pre-contact ways, despite the friars' attempts to dominate every aspect of their lives. Tribal Indians participated in terms of gift-giving, not buying and selling.

Some small farmers participated in order to become not-so-small, but others participated to meet their families' and communities' continuing needs. Virginia tobacco growers were entirely caught up in the consequences of transatlantic commerce, but they conceived their relations with merchants in terms of mutuality. In both town and country the eighteenth-century east coast saw both consumerism and refinement. Consumer and luxury goods had to be bought (Breen, 1993; Bushman, 1992). But the corporatist "moral economy of the crowd" that E. P. Thompson saw in eighteenth-century England had its American counterpart, and that counterpart proved powerful during the American Revolution (Thompson, 1971, 1991; Smith, 1994; Countryman, 2002). Material goods which had a way of becoming necessities and the market exchanges needed to obtain those goods were a major part of the power radiating into America from Europe. Beyond that bare realization, it seems impossible really to understand the larger colonial situation in terms of a single economic mode.

But as Newell notes, the marchlands concept does help us to understand how in America actions took place and situations emerged that would have been unthinkable among Europeans at home, however great their enmity. The old "No Peace Beyond the Line" formula points in the same direction, at least as far as outright war among Europeans is concerned (Bridenbaugh, 1972). But the massive dispossession of Indians wherever the thinning of their numbers by disease and shock made it possible to take their land was another matter. So was the creation of the Western Hemisphere's unique combination of the social condition of slavery, the economic situation of plantation production, and the ideological justification of both by the developing but not fully formed concept of "race."

Philip Morgan demonstrates here both the power and the complexity of the problems that slavery and the plantation system pose. The two were not completely the same. Slavery appeared as an institution from the St. Lawrence to the Rio de la Plata, and it flourished in many places where plantation production of staple crops was out of the question. New York provides the most powerful example. In their early stages neither enslavement nor plantation production necessarily required African people and their progeny. Early Spaniards enslaved Indians until the Crown forbade it. Puritans enslaved conquered Indians after King Philip's War, shipping them to Carolina and the West Indies. Carolinians themselves sent slaving parties beyond the Mississippi for captives. The tobacco economy began in both Virginia and Barbados with white indentured labor rather than slaves.

But in broad terms enslavement, plantation labor, and African descent became fused. The gains in our knowledge of each have been simply enormous since Edmund S. Morgan announced in his Organization of American Historians presidential address that we no longer can regard slavery as an "exception" to a general story of the development of American freedom from European origins (Morgan, 1972). Africans far outnumbered Europeans among colonial-era people who crossed the Atlantic. They did not come stripped of their identities and their heritage, whatever planters said about renaming them on arrival and however much enslavement brought dishonor and the cutting of all previous ties of belonging. Thomas Coram's widely reprinted painting of the eighteenth-century South Carolina plantation house called Mulberry illustrates the reality that developed. Seen from the front, the house is an eclectic and expensive tribute to its original owners' wealth, power, and intention to stay. Seen from the back, as Coram painted it, the house is deep in the frame, jostling for control of the image with a village of huts topped by African-style grass roofs. The contest was uneven, but the people who dwelt in the huts were not hapless victims (Morgan, 1998).

A few appear in the frame. Since the image is of lowland South Carolina in about 1800 these particular people almost certainly were rice-growing slaves who were creating Gullah culture. Almost certainly there were African-born women and men among them. After the reopening of the Atlantic slave trade in 1804 there probably would be more. Rather than just describing them as slaves, or Negroes, or black people, or Africans, we can come close to identifying the specific part of Africa from which they came, and the culture they brought. We have a very good idea of what they endured between capture in Africa and arrival in America (Wood, 1989; Littlefield, 1981; Morgan, 1998; McMillin, 1999; Miller, 1988).

The same is true of African people elsewhere in colonial America. Just as much as the French vis-à-vis the English, or different kinds of English people vis-à-vis one another, Africans brought as many distinctive folkways as they brought identities and languages. We can see as much complexity among them as there was among those English (Fischer, 1989). Their first task for survival was not to meld a broad African culture with the ways of their captors but to meld with one another. But that did not lead immediately to a uniform way of being African American. As many variations developed on that theme as there were ways of being an Indian or being a white colonist. In all cases, the ways of different peoples rubbed off on those of other peoples. Stressing this is not a matter of celebratory "contribution" history. It requires exploring how entirely different people with entirely different cultures collided as virtual strangers, how they forged new identities as well as retained old ones, and how all became transformed from whatever they had been before. The "new world" became new for everybody involved.

One of the striking qualities of this collection is that only New France, Atlantic Canada, the Caribbean, New Spain, and the Borderlands have their own chapters. All of these places were part of "colonial America." None were in the zone that eventually "became" the United States, and each does have a historiography that raises themes outside the ones that "American" historians usually consider. James Hijiya suggested some time ago that if early Americanists were to push beyond what they already knew, the study of, say, Connecticut would have to be abandoned. From the essays that do deal with places that eventually entered the United States it would seem that every other province between New Hampshire and Georgia needs to be abandoned too, at least as a discrete subject in its own right. Specific-province studies abound in the chapter bibliographies, but almost all are of interest because they address one of the themes that the writers here pull together. That is true whether we seek to understand empire (Richard Johnson), regionalism (Michael Zuckerman), consumption (Cary Carson), secular culture (Darren Staloff), or the origins of the east-coast revolutions (Sylvia Frey).

In almost all the essays themes pop up that have their own chapters elsewhere in the book. Religion used to mean Puritanism, Anglicanism, Quakers, and the Great Awakening. Now some historians are not sure that the Great Awakening ever happened, at least in the conventional sense. Puritanism is no longer a monolithic orthodoxy. Virginia Anglicanism is one distinct variant; northern-colonies Anglicanism is another. How women (of all sorts) experienced what was sacred is not necessarily how men did so. How African, Native, and European ways of believing and worshiping intermingled is a more compelling subject than the different schools of Protestant Christian theology and ecclesiology. How religions of all sorts dealt with such issues as marketplace relationships counts heavily. The same is true of gender, which involved both women and men of all sorts, in all the aspects of their lives.

If thirteen separate colonies, all British but differing from one another, have ceased to be an organizing principle for understanding colonial America, it would seem from these essays that intertwined themes that played differently in different places have replaced them. A really accurate map of colonial America at any point between first contact or first permanent arrival and the end of the whole colonial situation would not show sharp boundaries that separated Indian groups, European powers, or separate provinces. At all levels it would recognize the enormous contest that was under way to put authoritative lines on official maps. That contest was conducted by squatting, trade, land sales, diplomacy, fraud, and war. The map would show that people were in constant motion across those lines, and across whole oceans and continents. Yet the successful if unintended intertwining of most of these essays suggests that the English east-coast colonies and their hinterland were on their way to becoming a coherent entity, even if that entity would be tangled and self-contradictory in the way that Walt Whitman perceived. These essays go beyond the answer that Crèvecoeur gave to his own famous question: "What then, is this American, this new man?" To him, Americanness stemmed from the mixing of different kinds of European people. Now we have to think about "these Americans, these new women and men." We need to consider three groups that were only beginning to think of themselves as "race." In truth, those groups defined by their skins as red, white, black were only beginning to exist in terms of lived experience. Within them we need to be aware of many identities that sprang from ethnicity, religion, social class, and places.

None of the writers of these essays is triumphalist. Yet (as with the separate-colonies chapters in Part II of Alan Taylor's book), we still end up with more weight on the east coast. Perhaps that cannot be avoided completely, since the United States did colonize a large proportion of the whole continent as its first step toward becoming what it is now. One effect of taking these essays together is to abandon any notion that a given English colony was really "American" in a prototypical way. Another is to see the sector of colonial America that became the United States as very different, if not radically different, from what it would become. Taylor minimizes the American Revolution in his continent-spanning treatment, treating it under the general category of "Imperial Wars and Crisis" (2001). Writing here, Frey suggests good reason to see the events of United States independence as revolutionary for more people than rebellious white colonials.

But that still leaves the problem of comparison. Some topics lend themselves to comparison explicitly. One is European/Native encounters, whatever the languages that were spoken, the diseases that were spread, the goods that were exchanged, the version of Christianity that was preached, and the ways that Native people incorporated some of what was new to them. Overt searching for explicit events that seem the same might be futile, but not always so. Within the space of four years both Algonquians in New England and Pueblo Indians in New Mexico set out to drive the colonizers back. In both cases they had decades of experience with their foes. In both they understood their foes well enough to realize what was sacred to them. So in Protestant New England they desecrated the printed Word and in Catholic New Mexico they desecrated the altar and vessels of the Mass.

The pan-American experience of enslaved African people is another zone that is full of not only of comparative possibility but of comparative achievement. For as long as the study of North American slavery meant the nineteenth-century Old South the problem was virtually bound to remain at the level of whether slavery was fundamentally oppressive or fundamentally benign (Phillips, 1918; Stampp, 1956). That problem persisted in the early stages of comparative work (Tannenbaum, 1947; Elkins, 1959). But the remarkable trio of early-slavery, place-specific studies that appeared in the early 1970s demonstrated a different way's utility. The same combination of cheap land, readily available and highly exploitable labor, and a high return on profit, all combined with a strange disease environment, led to demographic disaster for the people doing the hard work as plantation society formed in Virginia, South Carolina, and the British West Indies. In Virginia it happened to white servants, and both the scale and the duration differed enormously from South Carolina and the sugar islands. But the fundamental process seems the same (Morgan, 1975; Wood, 1974; Dunn, 1972). None of those studies sets out to "compare." Each seeks only to illuminate its own subject fully. But taken together they have led to a major gain in slavery studies.

The ways that different quasi-European civil societies took shape seems another matter. New Spain was highly centralized and highly organized and incorporated *Indios* and *Mestizos*. The mainland British provinces supposedly flourished under loose, so-called "salutary neglect." They pushed Indians ever backward, and regarded black slaves as "in" society but not "of" it. New France saw the combination of *dirigisme* in the lightly settled St. Lawrence Valley, total freedom for *coureurs de bois*, and Jesuit missionary policies that did not try to extirpate Indian culture. But how Spaniards, Britons, and the French alike looked from "Indian Country" may show more similarities than differences. Lord Montcalm and Sir Jeffrey Amherst had the same project of moving Indians from partnership to subjection.

More to the point, however, is the imagined continent-spanning historical geography that underpins this book, as opposed to earlier approaches. That sense of enormous colonial space became possible because one way or another many facets of living in an invaded and colonized continent have attracted scholars' attention. Once upon a time "colonialists" tended to come from a white Anglo-Saxon Protestant culture that saw itself under greater and greater threat and that looked to its own origins for reassurance. One major scholar gained notoriety when he made that point explicit and criticized the takeover of the historical profession by former ethnic outsiders (Bridenbaugh, 1963). Now we accept that "America" did not begin just at Jamestown and Plymouth. Nor did it begin just with English people. "Colonial" incorporates everybody who became involved, however different their separate ways, and however far from one another they dwelt. "Development" did not mean either a declension from original high standards or the submerging of intense small communities into a larger impersonal society. What emerges here is none of those, but rather the understanding that colonial America was a very large space in which very many people had to confront very basic human questions. European, African, or Native, they differed from each other and among themselves to enormous degrees, and they faced one another on unequal terms. But all of them had to deal with the fact that they lived their lives amid pressures and forces that emanated from very far away.

BIBLIOGRAPHY

Anderson, Fred: *Crucible of War: The Seven Years' War and the Fate of Empire in British North America, 1754–1766* (New York: Alfred A. Knopf, 2000).

Arnold, Morris S.: *Colonial Arkansas, 1686–1804: A Social and Cultural History* (Fayetteville, AR: University of Arkansas Press, 1991).

Bailyn, Bernard: *Voyagers to the West: A Passage in the Peopling of America on the Eve of the Revolution* (New York: Alfred A. Knopf, 1986).

Barr, Juliana: "The Seductions of Texas: The Political Language of Gender in the Conquests of Texas, 1690–1821" (Ph.D. dissertation, University of Wisconsin, Madison, 1999).

Berthoff, Rowland and Murrin, John M.: "Freedom, Communalism and the Yeoman Freeholder: The American Revolution Considered as a Social Accident." In Stephen G. Kurtz and James H. Hutson, eds., *Essays on the American Revolution* (Chapel Hill, NC: University of North Carolina Press, 1973), pp. 256–88.

Brandel, Fernand: *Civilization and Capitalism, 15th–18th Century: III, The Perspective of the World*, trans. Sian Reynolds (London: Fontana, 1985, orig. pub. 1984).

Breen, T. H.: "Narrative of Commercial Life: Consumption, Ideology, and Community on the Eve of the Revolution." *William and Mary Quarterly* 3rd ser., 50 (1993), pp. 471–501.

Bridenbaugh, Carl: "The Great Mutation." *American Historical Review* 68 (1963), pp. 315–31.

Bridenbaugh, Carl and Bridenbaugh, Roberta: *No Peace beyond the Line: The English in the Caribbean, 1624–1690* (New York: Oxford University Press, 1972).

Brown, Kathleen M.: *Good Wives, Nasty Wenches, and Anxious Patriarchs: Gender, Race, and Power in Colonial Virginia* (Chapel Hill, NC: University of North Carolina Press, 1996).

Bushman, Richard L.: *The Refinement of America: Persons, Houses, Cities* (New York: Alfred A. Knopf, 1992).

Cayton, Andrew R. L. and Teute, Fredrika J.: *Contact Points: American Frontiers from the Mohawk Valley to the Mississippi, 1750–1830* (Chapel Hill, NC: University of North Carolina Press,

1998).

Cohen, I. Bernard: "What Columbus 'Saw' in 1492." *Scientific American* 276, no. 6 (December 1992), p. 100.

Countryman, Edward: *The American Revolution* (rev. ed., New York: Hill & Wang, 2002).

Draper, Theodore: *A Struggle for Power: The American Revolution* (New York: Times Books, 1996).

Dunn, Richard S.: *Sugar and Slaves: The Rise of the Planter Class in the English West Indies, 1624–1713* (Chapel Hill, NC: University of North Carolina Press, 1972).

Earle, Carville and Hoffman, Ronald: "Staple Crops and Urban Development in the Eighteenth-Century South." *Perspectives in American History* 10 (1976), pp. 7–79.

Elkins, Stanley M.: *Slavery: A Problem in American Institutional and Intellectual Life* (Chicago: University of Chicago Press, 1959).

Fischer, David Hackett: *In English Ways: Four British Folkways in America* (New York: Oxford University Press, 1989).

Gutiérrez, Ramón: *When Jesus Came, the Corn Mothers Went Away: Marriage, Sexuality, and Power in New Mexico, 1500–1846* (Stanford, CA: Stanford University Press, 1991).

Hamaleinen, Pekka: "The Comanche Empire: A Study of Indigenous Power, 1700–1875" (Ph.D. dissertation, University of Helsinki, 2001).

Hijiya, James: "Why the West is Lost." *William and Mary Quarterly* 3rd ser., 51 (1994), pp. 750–4.

Hofstadter, Richard: *America at 1750: A Social Portrait* (New York: Alfred A. Knopf, 1971).

Katz, Stanley Nider: *Colonial America: Essays in Politics and Social Development* (New York: Alfred A. Knopf, 1971).

Katz, Stanley Nider, Murrin, John M., and Greenberg, Douglas: *Colonial America: Essays in Politics and Social Development* (New York: Alfred A. Knopf, 1993).

Katz, Stanley Nider, Murrin, John M., and Greenberg, Douglas: *Colonial America: Essays in Politics and Social Development* (New York: Alfred A. Knopf, 2001).

Littlefield, Daniel C.: *Rice and Slaves: Ethnicity and the Slave Trade in Colonial South Carolina* (Baton Rouge, LA: Louisiana State University Press, 1981).

Lockridge, Kenneth: *A New England Town: The First Hundred Years, Dedham, Massachusetts, 1636–1736* (New York: W. W. Norton, 1970).

Mann, Charles C.: "1491." *The Atlantic* 289, no. 3 (March, 2002), pp. 41–53.

McMillin, James (1999): "The Final Victims: The Demography, Atlantic Origins, Merchants, and Nature of the Post-Revolutionary Foreign Slave Trade to North America, 1783–1810" (Ph.D. dissertation, Duke University, 1999).

Merrell, James H.: *The Indians' New World: Catawbas and their Neighbors from European Contact through the Era of Removal* (Chapel Hill, NC: University of North Carolina Press, 1989).

Merrell, James H.: *Into the American Woods: Negotiators on the Pennsylvania Frontier* (New York: W. W. Norton, 1999).

Miller, Joseph C.: *Way of Death: Merchant Capitalism and the Angolan Slave Trade, 1730–1830* (Madison: University of Wisconsin Press, 1988).

Morgan, Edmund S.: "Slavery and Freedom: The American Paradox." *Journal of American History* 59 (1972), pp. 5–29.

Morgan, Edmund S.: *American Slavery, American Freedom: The Ordeal of Colonial Virginia* (New York: W. W. Norton, 1975).

Morgan, Philip: *Slave Counterpoint: Black Culture in the Eighteenth Century Chesapeake and Low Country* (Chapel Hill, NC: University of North Carolina Press, 1998).

Nathan, Paul D., trans.: *The San Sabá Papers: A Documentary Account of the Founding and Destruction of San Sabá* (Dallas: Southern Methodist University, 2000 [orig. pub. 1959]).

Phillips, Ulrich B.: *American Negro Slavery: A Survey of the Supply, Employment and Control of Negro Labor as Determined by the Plantation Régime* (New York: D. Appleton, 1918).

Price, Jacob: "Economic Function and the Growth of Port Towns in the Eighteenth Century." *Perspectives in American History* 8 (1974), pp. 123–86.

Smith, Barbara Clark: "Food Rioters and the American Revolution." *William and Mary Quarterly* 3rd ser., 51 (1994), pp. 3–38.

Smith, James Morton, ed.: *Seventeenth-Century America: Essays in Colonial History* (Chapel Hill: University of North Carolina Press, 1958).

Stampp, Kenneth M.: *The Peculiar Institution: Slavery in the Ante-Bellum South* (New York: Alfred A. Knopf, 1956).

Tannenbaum, Frank: *Slave and Citizen: The Negro in the Americas* (New York: Alfred A. Knopf, 1947).

Taylor, Alan: *American Colonies* (New York: Viking Press, 2001).

Thompson, E. P.: "The Moral Economy of the English Crowd in the Eighteenth Century." *Past & Present* 50 (1971), pp. 76–136.

Thompson, E. P.: *Customs in Common* (New York: New Press, 1991).

Weber, David J.: *The Spanish Frontier in North America* (New Haven, CT: Yale University Press, 1993).

White, Richard: *The Middle Ground: Indians, Empires, and Republics in the Great Lakes Region, 1650–1815* (Cambridge, England: Cambridge University Press, 1991).

Wood, Peter H.: *Black Majority: Negroes in Colonial South Carolina from 1670 Through the Stono Rebellion* (New York: Alfred A. Knopf, 1974).

Wood, Peter H., Waselkov, Gregory A., and Hatley, M. Thomas: *Powhatan's Mantle: Indians in the Colonial Southeast* (Lincoln, NE: University of Nebraska Press, 1989).

Index

CPSIA information can be obtained at www.ICGtesting.com
Printed in the USA

266389BV00006B/1/P